"How do students learn? How can educational practices best suppo
Mitchell J. Nathan addresses these enduring questions and deftly bui
Embodied Learning as a new paradigm for education. He synthesizes
on the role of the body in learning, and he draws practical implicaʊʊʊ ʊ ʊʊʊ ʊʊʊ, ʊʊʊʊʊ
environment design, and assessment. This is an essential reading that will spark new insights and
approaches, both for researchers and for educators."
—Martha Wagner Alibali, Vilas Distinguished Achievement Professor in the
Department of Psychology at University of Wisconsin–Madison, USA

"Mitchell J. Nathan's book provides a superb review and analysis of work in the field of embodied cognition and makes a compelling case for the educational significance of this research program—a must-
read for educators and education researchers."
—John T. Bruer, President Emeritus of The James S. McDonnell Foundation

"*Foundations of Embodied Learning* is a heady achievement. Using his encyclopedic command of
literatures in cognitive psychology, embodiment, and education, mixing in cognitive neuroscience and
philosophy, Mitchell J. Nathan develops an account of learning processes that spans milliseconds to
years. By deriving principles that guide both learners and instructors, the text moves from a theoretical exposition of how things are to a practical guide for how things should be. This book is a must-
read for learning scientists, psychologists, teacher educators and teachers, instructional designers, and
everyone interested in all aspects of human learning."
—Arthur Glenberg, Emeritus Professor at Arizona State University, USA,
Emeritus Professor at the University of Wisconsin–Madison, USA,
and a member of INCO at the University of Salamanca, Spain

"This book convincingly argues that the best way—in fact, the only way—for people to really master
difficult topics is to ground them in bodily, perceptual, participatory, and encultured experiences.
Masterfully integrating a breathtaking gamut of evidence from neuroscience, psychology, education,
and social interactions, this book provides the antidote to modern educational practice, which has too
often tried to reduce understanding to mere symbol manipulation. The exciting alternative presented
here is to harness the millions of years that Mother Nature has spent honing our systems for perceiving, acting, and interacting to learn about things that haven't been around long enough to become
biological endowments: reading, writing, mathematics, logic, and science. The book erects a lasting
edifice from cognitive science theory to educational practice in curriculum, instruction, assessment,
and technology—one that offers real progress in constructing learning on top of concrete, robust
foundations."
—Robert L. Goldstone, Distinguished Professor and Chancellor's
Professor in the Department of Psychological and Brain
Sciences at Indiana University Bloomington, USA

"Mitchell J. Nathan takes us on an epic journey into the world of Grounded and Embodied Learning—
from its manifestations at the scale of neurons to the scale of social communities—and shows us a
powerful and synthetic way to understand how people learn. Along this journey, he clearly presents
both classic and recent studies from cognitive psychology and the learning sciences that make a con-
vincing case for why we need widespread adoption of a GEL paradigm in education and educational
research. This book is a must-read for anyone curious about embodiment and for anyone ready for a
fresh new perspective on the wonders of human learning."
—Victor R. Lee, Associate Professor of Learning Sciences and
Technology Design at Stanford University, USA

"Psychologists know a lot about the mechanisms of learning, and teachers know a lot about the practice of instruction, but, for too long, these two groups have had little contact with each other. This book should, and I hope will, change all that. It provides a masterful synthesis of a wealth of empirical research—much of which comes from Dr. Nathan's own lab—that reveals the importance of bodily processes in learning all manner of academic subjects: geometry, algebra, reading, second-language acquisition, to name just a few. If there is one book that belongs on the shelves of anyone interested in bringing the latest advances in educational psychology and embodied cognition into their classrooms, or in the evidence that supports a more body-centric form of pedagogy, this is it."

—Lawrence Shapiro, Professor of Philosophy at the
University of Wisconsin–Madison, USA

Foundations of Embodied Learning

Foundations of Embodied Learning advances learning, instruction, and the design of educational technologies by rethinking the learner as an integrated system of mind, body, and environment. Body-based processes—direct physical, social, and environmental interactions—are constantly mediating intellectual performance, sensory stimulation, communication abilities, and other conditions of learning. This book's coherent, evidence-based framework articulates principles of grounded and embodied learning for design and its implications for curriculum, classroom instruction, and student formative and summative assessment for scholars and graduate students of educational psychology, instructional design and technology, cognitive science, the learning sciences, and beyond.

Mitchell J. Nathan is Vilas Distinguished Achievement Professor of Learning Sciences in the Educational Psychology Department, Director of the MAGIC Lab, and a Fellow of the Teaching Academy at the University of Wisconsin–Madison, USA. Professor Nathan is a Fellow of the International Society of the Learning Sciences, where he was a founding officer, and is one of the founding members of EMIC, a consortium of scholars, designers, and educators interested in embodied mathematical imagination and cognition. He lives in Madison, WI with his two daughters, who keep him embodied and quite grounded.

Foundations of Embodied Learning

A Paradigm for Education

Mitchell J. Nathan

Routledge
Taylor & Francis Group

NEW YORK AND LONDON

First published 2022
by Routledge
605 Third Avenue, New York, NY 10158

and by Routledge
2 Park Square, Milton Park, Abingdon, Oxon OX14 4RN

Routledge is an imprint of the Taylor & Francis Group, an informa business

Library of Congress Cataloging-in-Publication Data
A catalog record for this title has been requested

ISBN: 978-0-367-34975-2 (hbk)
ISBN: 978-0-367-34976-9 (pbk)
ISBN: 978-0-429-32909-8 (ebk)

DOI: 10.4324/9780429329098

Typeset in Minion
by Newgen Publishing UK

We all need teachers to make it through this world. Yet few truly have the gift to pass teaching on to others. This book is dedicated to the memory of my mother, Sandra Alpert Nathan, an extraordinary educator and my first teacher and teacher-educator. You illuminated the paths for me and for so many—and did this so wholeheartedly—that even with your passing the radiance remains.

Contents

Preface

The goal of formal education is to *ground learning* of academic and scientific ideas and representations to things that are meaningful to learners. This is because otherwise these ideas and representations are so abstract and disconnected from students' lived experiences they are often inaccessible, incomprehensible, and easily misapplied or forgotten. **Grounded and Embodied Learning** (GEL) is the process of connecting unfamiliar and abstract ideas and representations to one's lived and felt experiences, including body-based interactions and perceptions. Based on philosophical reasons, I argue that it is only by designing educational experiences with GEL in mind that educational systems can provide students the opportunities to learn to their fullest potential. I provide selective reviews of the research illustrating how embodied learning processes operate in principle. I also show how, in practice, embodied learning is carried out in the authentic learning settings of K–12 classrooms and educational technologies in order to achieve educational goals with respect to instruction, learning, and assessment.

My goal for the book is to provide the reader with a coherent, evidence-based framework for understanding the ways that brain, mind, body, and environment together constitute an integrated system for learning, communication, and intellectual performance. I describe the implications of this framework for education by articulating principles of grounded and embodied learning. I illustrate the application of these principles to educational practices across academic content areas, including topics such as language and reading, mathematics, science, engineering, and teacher education and professional development. These practices include ways to support student thinking and learning, enhance classroom instruction, inform the design of learning technologies and curricula, and improve formative and summative assessments.

This book provides empirical and theoretical support for the **Grounded and Embodied Learning Thesis:** Thinking and instruction rely on body-based processes for learning to be meaningful. This thesis offers entirely new opportunities for redesigning educational experiences.

From a GEL perspective, the mind is shown to be extremely plastic and expansive—perhaps far more so than is typical in scientific volumes on education—while still fundamentally anchored to a form of epistemology that links ideas to actions and the material world. Consider, by analogy, how a kite, in the hands of an expert, can achieve such freedom of movement and expression over and over again, while untethered, it simply drifts away. Indeed, it may be *because* of this tethering to the materiality of the body that it is possible for the human mind and for communities of learners to achieve so much.

True to its roots of grounded learning, this book gives readers access to a variety of multimedia resources, and experiential activities and observations that help make the ideas presented here personally meaningful, concrete, and relevant, while cultivating a principled understanding of GEL that extends beyond my chosen exemplars.

MAIN THEMES AND OBJECTIVES

This book has two main objectives: (1) To provide a coherent, evidence-based framework for understanding the embodied nature of thinking and learning; and (2) to articulate principles that adhere to this framework and that can be used to inform the design of future educational practices and learning environments.

This book offers a curated, interdisciplinary review of the relevant theoretical and empirical literature on GEL, drawing from: Learning Sciences, Social Anthropology, Curriculum and Instruction, Educational Psychology, Cognitive and Social Psychology, Child Development, Cognitive Neuroscience, Philosophy of Mind, Robotics, Artificial Intelligence, Complex Systems Theory, and Human–Computer interaction.[1]

Much of how we think and what we know about the world emerges from an embodied nervous system that is organized to predict our future physical, social, and environmental interactions. Because this is what we know, we naturally relate novel and abstract ideas and representations to these interactions. This embodied foundation provides the basis of a grounded understanding of academic and scientific knowledge. This is a commonly held view among scholars of embodied cognition. **The unique contribution of this book is to describe how this framing of learning can be used to inform educational practices.**

I need to point out that this embodied view is at odds with many long-standing and widespread educational practices derived from classical Cognitive Science and its epistemological commitment to the mind as primarily a computational entity and the brain as the central processor for computation. Consequently, embodied approaches intended to promote conceptual understanding are often absent from traditional, formal scholastic settings. For these reasons, GEL offers a new paradigm for education.

Consider something as commonplace as administering a written test as a primary measure of a student's skilled performance. This assessment practice is consistent with traditional views of the mind as a disembodied information processor. It is ubiquitous in education. Traditional notions of cognitive development and disciplinary knowledge make the inclusion of embodied learning even rarer in later grade levels as mature learners encounter more abstract and technical content that is even more disembodied. However, this assessment practice stands in contrast to GEL. Still, this practice literally decides the economic and social futures of millions of students each year. The result is an inadequate educational system based on an impoverished framework that promotes ungrounded learning. Such a system is devoid of how people actually construct meaning and exhibit what they can do and how they can reason and learn. As such, it deprives many people of opportunities to perform to their fullest potential.

In terms of **learning theory,** the perspective presented in this book provides the reader with an integrative understanding of how thinking, teaching, and learning are mediated by our embodied nature. The GEL framework relies on a variety of processes that operate across a range of timescales, including biological, cognitive, knowledge-based, and sociocultural processes. GEL draws important distinctions between our conscious and unconscious learning processes, and the role of language for bringing unconscious processes into conscious awareness. GEL strives to explain why some learning is difficult or results in understanding that is narrow and brittle. GEL also seeks to explain why certain methods of classroom teaching and forms of instructional support, such as manipulatives and digital technologies, are more or less effective in promoting learning and cognitive development.

In terms of contributions for **educational practice**, this book provides an evidence-based, theoretically derived set of **principles of embodied learning** shown to improve education in four central areas: curriculum, instruction, assessment, and educational technology design. Demonstrations and structured activities invite readers to experience, reflect on, and apply the principles to learning and teaching situations they will personally encounter.

This book delves into some of the **obstacles** that impede the adoption of promising principles of GEL for informing educational practices and policies and for taking these principles to scale. These include obstacles rooted in philosophy of mind, scientific method, and historical inequities and oppression. Using a design-based framework for implementation, the book offers strategies and methods for addressing and overcoming these obstacles of adoption and for taking new educational innovations to scale.

The book also points the way toward a highly promising **program of basic and translational education research** that rejects dualist notions of a mind separate from body, recasting learning, teaching, and assessment in more holistic terms.

My selections of examples and evidence are chosen to inform and inspire educational researchers, leaders, designers, and teachers—as well as interested parents—so they may tap into, direct, and further investigate learning as an embodied phenomenon.

WHAT ABOUT THIS BOOK IS INNOVATIVE?

There are several prominent volumes on embodied cognition, such as:

de Freitas, E., & Sinclair, N. (2014). *Mathematics and the body: Material entanglements in the classroom*. Cambridge University Press.

De Vega, M., Glenberg, A., & Graesser, A. (2012). *Symbols and embodiment: Debates on meaning and cognition*. Oxford University Press.

Edwards, L. D., Moore-Russo, D., & Ferrara, F. (Eds.). (2014). *Emerging perspectives on gesture and embodiment in mathematics*. IAP.

Goldin-Meadow, S. (2005). *Hearing gesture: How our hands help us think*. Harvard University Press.

Lee, V. R. (Ed.) (2015). *Learning technologies and the body: Integration and implementation in formal and informal learning environments*. Routledge.

Newen, A., De Bruin, L., & Gallagher, S. (Eds.). (2018). *The Oxford handbook of 4E cognition*. Oxford University Press.

Shapiro, L. (Ed.). (2014). *The Routledge handbook of embodied cognition*. Routledge.

Shapiro, L. (2019). *Embodied cognition* (2nd ed.). Routledge.

Tversky, B. (2019). *Mind in motion: How action shapes thought*. Hachette UK.

Varela, F., Thompson, E., & Rosch, E. (1991). *The embodied mind: Cognitive Science and human experience*. MIT Press.

These scholarly works offer a perspective that is primarily philosophical and psychological. Among them, only Lee (2015) is primarily oriented toward the goals and challenges of educating children from an embodied perspective.

One **innovation** of this book is to build upon foundational works to put forth a view of GEL that has **relevance to educational concerns**. One objective is to derive **principles of grounded and embodied learning** to enhance student performance by improving teachers' classroom instruction, the design of educational technology, and assessments of student knowledge. As examples:

- Directing students to move in certain ways can improve students' reasoning and learning in areas such as early reading and beginning and advanced mathematics education.
- Teachers delve deeply into the curricular content when they express their thinking with their bodies and when they are in the company of others also using their bodies to explore and express these ideas.
- Teachers naturally gesture during instruction and can learn to make their instructional gestures effective for improving student learning.
- Some knowledge of students is uniquely presented through their body movements, and analyses or assessments limited only to what students can say or write underestimates their reasoning and depth of understanding.
- Intentionally imagining, or mentally simulating, movements can confer some of the same benefits for learning as carrying out the movements.
- Noticing how learners' body movements relate to their cognitive states leads to formative assessment methods that can inform teachers' instructional decision making.
- Summative assessments that inhibit students' gestures, by means such as typing, can impair test performance, an issue of growing importance as high-stakes tests are increasingly offered online.
- The emergence of motion capture sensors is fueling growth of a new genre of embodied learning technologies that track players' movements in real time, and guide their movements toward educationally relevant actions that help ground the meaning of novel ideas and representations.

A second innovation of this book is to **organize the research on embodied learning within an integrative framework that looks across the timescales of human learning processes.** This framework was adapted from Newell's 1994 *Unified Theories of Cognition*, and informed by other scholars (e.g., Lemke, 2000; West, 2017). The framework acknowledges that what educators often call "learning" is in actuality a highly dynamic, multi-level set of processes that enjoy both scale-specific qualities as well as rich interactions among these different levels of analysis.

This organizational framework also explicitly distinguishes those learning processes that operate within our conscious awareness (i.e., what I refer to as the *conscious spectrum*) and those that operate outside of conscious awareness. Educational practices often neglect these unconscious learning processes, even though they are highly impactful. In this book I explore the importance of unconscious processes and their interplay with conscious processes for the betterment of education.

By providing a unified framework with explicit attention to the **translation of research and theory to classroom instruction and assessment practices**, this book offers a uniquely educational perspective on embodied learning and design.

PURPOSES FOR THIS BOOK

This book can serve as a supplementary textbook for classes in educational psychology and teacher education. This book may serve as a graduate level text or supplementary text on embodied learning.

Sample courses for which this book is suitable include (but are not limited to): Teaching, Learning, and Teacher Education; Psychological Foundations of Teacher Education; Education and Psychology; Learning Technologies; Mathematics Education; Science Education; STEM Education; Methods in Mathematics Education; Methods in Science Education; Literacy, Language, and Culture; Embodied Cognition; Introduction to Learning Sciences; Introduction to Embodied Cognitive Sciences; Cognitive Psychology; Cognitive Science; Philosophical Foundations of the Cognitive and Information Sciences; Advanced Theories of Learning; Mind, Body, and Education; Perception, Action and Cognition; Brain and Cognition; Cognitive Neuroscience; Behavior-Based Robotics.

WHO SHOULD READ THIS BOOK?

Grounded and Embodied Learning offers educators, policy makers, designers, and students a scientific and phenomenological understanding of learning, teaching, and assessment. This book would serve as a supplementary textbook for classes in educational psychology and teacher education courses at the undergraduate level, as well as for a growing number of related fields interested in the science and engineering of learning, including (but not limited to): cognitive science, human–computer interaction, design of educational technology and video games for learning, workforce training, policy studies related to education and the achievement gap. Embodied learning is being studied in language and literacy, mathematics, science, engineering, computer science, the arts, and vocational and technical education.

This is an internationally appealing topic. The Gesture Studies community is already a vibrant international community of scholars and practitioners, as are the AI-ED and Learning Sciences communities. These are natural connections for the research audiences. Embodied approaches to education have also had a long tradition in European, Latin American, and Asian/Pacific Rim schools. Educational practitioners in these countries may be especially welcoming to a volume that addresses the theoretical and empirical bases for existing curricular activities and instructional practices, which offers principles for generating new designs and practices.

HOW THE BOOK IS ORGANIZED

I have organized this book into three parts. Part 1 encompasses Chapters 1 through 4 and addresses the fundamental problem for education and a proposed solution. In Chapter 3 I introduce the Grounded and Embodied Learning (GEL) timescale. This timescale then serves as the organizing structure for Part 2, Chapters 5 through 10. In Part 2, the chapters are paired, with Chapters 5 and 6 addressing learning in the conscious spectrum, Chapters 7 and 8 addressing learning as biological phenomena, and Chapters 9 and 10 addressing learning as sociocultural phenomena. Part 3 encompasses Chapters 11 and 12, and addresses the implications of GEL for education practice and research. In particular, Chapter 11 examines trans-scale aspects of learning and learning methodology. Chapter 12 addresses learning in and beyond the classroom, including future needs for GEL research and development, impact of the replication crisis in psychology, how oppression and racism inhibit learning, and approaches for providing educational opportunities for all learners. In all, this volume provides a broad and integrated view for educating the embodied mind.

A NOTE ABOUT READER ACTIVITIES, ONLINE RESOURCES, AND ORIGINAL ARTWORK

As noted above, I envision this book benefiting tremendously from a variety of online multimedia resources and activities for readers to engage with the ideas and phenomena under investigation. Many chapters close with some activities for the reader to further ground some of the major ideas that are introduced. The online materials provided throughout these pages include several formats of videos (documentary, YouTube type, authentic classrooms), links to learning systems, printed activity materials, and supplementary readings. Images with students are necessarily digitally processed to maintain their confidentiality.

Author-generated artwork, including figures and tables, is licensed under a Creative Commons Attribution-NonCommercial-NoDerivatives 4.0 International License, CC BY-NC-ND 4.0, to Mitchell J. Nathan. Artwork used in accordance with this license can be accessed at https://osf.io/aetb4/

—Mitchell J. Nathan, Madison, WI

NOTE

1   The interested reader can consult these references: Learning Sciences (Abrahamson & Lindgren, 2014; Goldstone, Landy, & Son, 2008), Social Anthropology (Lave, 1988; Lave & Wenger, 1991) Curriculum and Instruction (Pouw, Van Gog, & Paas, 2014; Smith, King, & Hoyte, 2014), Educational Psychology (Glenberg et al., 2004; Nathan, 2012), Cognitive (Barsalou, 2008; Casasanto & Henetz, 2012; Hostetter & Alibali, 2019) and Social Psychology (Schnall et al., 2008), Child Development (Church & Goldin-Meadow, 1986), Cognitive Neuroscience (Dehaene, 2009; Gallese & Sinigaglia 2011; Pulvermüller, 2005), Philosophy of Mind (Searle, 1990; Shapiro, 2019, Robotics (Brooks, 1991), Dynamic and Complex systems (Jacobson et al., 2016; Thelen & Smith, 1996), Artificial Intelligence (Wolpert, Doya, & Kawato, 2003), and Human–Computer Interaction (Norman, 1999).

REFERENCES

Abrahamson, D., & Lindgren, R. (2014). Embodiment and embodied design. In R. K. Sawyer (Ed.), *The Cambridge handbook of the learning sciences* (2nd ed.) (pp. 358–376). Cambridge University Press.

Barsalou, L. W. (2008). Grounded cognition. *Annual Review of Psychology, 59*, 617–645.

Brooks, R. A. (1991). Intelligence without representation. *Artificial Intelligence, 47*(1–3), 139–159.

Casasanto, D., & Henetz, T. (2012). Handedness shapes children's abstract concepts. *Cognitive Science, 36*(2), 359–372.

Church, R. B., & Goldin-Meadow, S. (1986). The mismatch between gesture and speech as an index of transitional knowledge. *Cognition, 23*(1), 43–71.

Dehaene, S. (2009). *Reading in the brain: The new science of how we read.* Penguin.

Gallese, V., & Sinigaglia, C. (2011). What is so special about embodied simulation? *Trends in Cognitive Sciences, 15*(11), 512–519.

Glenberg, A. M., Gutierrez, T., Levin, J. R., Japuntich, S., & Kaschak, M. P. (2004). Activity and imagined activity can enhance young children's reading comprehension. *Journal of Educational Psychology, 96*(3), 424.

Goldstone, R. L., Landy, D., & Son, J. Y. (2008). A well grounded education: The role of perception in science and mathematics. *Symbols, embodiment, and meaning*, 327–355.

Hostetter, A. B., & Alibali, M. W. (2019). Gesture as simulated action: Revisiting the framework. *Psychonomic Bulletin & Review, 26*(3), 721–752.

Jacobson, M. J., Kapur, M., & Reimann, P. (2016). Conceptualizing debates in learning and educational research: Toward a complex systems conceptual framework of learning. *Educational Psychologist, 51*(2), 210–218.

Lave, J. (1988). *Cognition in practice: Mind, mathematics and culture in everyday life.* Cambridge University Press.

Lave, J., & Wenger, E. (1991). Legitimate peripheral participation in communities of practice. In R. Pea & J. S. Brown (Eds.), *Situated learning: Legitimate peripheral participation* (pp. 89–117). Cambridge University Press.

Lee, V. R. (Ed.) (2015). *Learning technologies and the body: Integration and implementation in formal and informal learning environments.* Routledge.

Lemke, J. L. (2000). Across the scales of time: Artifacts, activities, and meanings in ecosocial systems. *Mind Culture and Activity, 7*, 273–290.

Nathan, M. J. (2012). Rethinking formalisms in formal education. *Educational Psychologist, 47*(2), 125–148. doi:10.1080/00461520.2012.667063.

Newell, A. (1994). *Unified theories of cognition.* Harvard University Press.

Norman, D. A. (1999). Affordances, conventions, and design. *Interactions, 6*(3), 38–41.

Pouw, W. T., Van Gog, T., & Paas, F. (2014). An embedded and embodied cognition review of instructional manipulatives. *Educational Psychology Review, 26*(1), 51–72.

Pulvermüller, F. (2005). Brain mechanisms linking language and action. *Nature reviews neuroscience, 6*(7), 576–582.

Schnall, S., Haidt, J., Clore, G. L., & Jordan, A. H. (2008). Disgust as embodied moral judgment. *Personality and Social Psychology Bulletin, 34*(8), 1096–1109.

Searle, J. (1990). Is the brain's mind a computer program? *Scientific American, 262*, 26–31.

Shapiro, L. (2019). *Embodied cognition* (2nd ed.). Routledge.

Smith, C. P., King, B., & Hoyte, J. (2014). Learning angles through movement: Critical actions for developing understanding in an embodied activity. *The Journal of Mathematical Behavior, 36*, 95–108.

Thelen, E., & Smith, L. B. (1996). *A dynamic systems approach to the development of cognition and action.* MIT Press.

West, G. B. (2017). *Scale: The universal laws of growth, innovation, sustainability, and the pace of life in organisms, cities, economies, and companies.* Penguin.

Wolpert, D. M., Doya, K., & Kawato, M. (2003). A unifying computational framework for motor control and social interaction. *Philosophical Transactions of the Royal Society of London. Series B: Biological Sciences, 358*(1431), 593–602.

Acknowledgments

I am truly grateful to my valued collaborators on embodied learning, Martha Wagner Alibali and Candace Walkington. You have played a huge role in the development of my thinking, my research, and my writing voice. Thank you! I also have special appreciation to Michael Swart, who helped me carry this over the finish line with artistry, grace, and humor.

To my esteemed co-authors on topics of embodied learning: Kristen Bieda, Rebecca Boncoddo, Breckie Church, Susan Wagner Cook, Emily Fyfe, Rogers Hall, Oh Hoon Kwon, Kevin Leander, Ricardo Nemirovsky, Voicu Popescu, Avery Harrison, and Nicholas Vest.

To those who trusted me as a mentor, and who have, in turn, mentored me. Thanks you to the students: Cecil Robinson, Eric Eiteljorg, Eric Knuth, Tim Boester, Michelle Bass, Matthew Gaydos, Chelsea J. Martinez, David Havas, Suyeon Kim, Elizabeth Pier, Joseph Michaelis, Julia Rutledge, John McGinty, Kelsey Schenk, Fangli Xia, Hanall Sung, Doy Kim, Matthew Grondin, Ariel Fogel, and Icy (Yunyi) Zhang. And thank you to the postdoctoral fellows: Rebecca Boncoddo, Virginia Clinton, Jennifer Cooper, Emily Fyfe, José Francisco Gutiérrez, Elise Lockwood, Candace Walkington, and Matthew Wolfgram.

Special acknowledgments to the members of my communities of practice, those in the University of Wisconsin MAGIC Lab, past and present: Michael Swart, Oh Hoon Kwon, Chelsea Martinez, Suyeon Kim, Libby Pier, Joseph Michaelis, Kelsey Schenck, Hanall Sung, Fangli Xia, Ariel Fogel, Doy Kim, and Veena Kirankumar. You truly rock, and even a pandemic could not slow the tide of your creativity and productivity! And my enduring appreciation to the leadership and my co-conspirators in the EMIC consortium: Dor Abrahamson, Martha Wagner Alibali, David Landy, Erin Ottmar, Hortensia Soto, Candace Walkington, and Caro Williams-Pierce.

I am very grateful for the investment of time and efforts to read and comment on early drafts of these chapters by the doctoral students of *Current Topics in the Learning Sciences* during the Fall of 2020—that chaotic semester when the world turned on its head. Thank you to: Joel Beier, Xuesong Cang, Jaeyoon Choi, Ariel Fogel, Yating Hong, Doy Kim, Claudia Matta, John D. McGinty, Jihyun Rho, Kelsey Schenck, Hanall Sung, Yuanru Tan, Yeyu Wang, and Fangli Xia. I am also appreciative of the editorial comments from Steven Greenstein and the students in his doctoral seminar. Special thanks also to Pilar Gauthier, MS. LPC, for sharing your wisdom and guidance that contributed to my understanding of issues of cultural appropriation and decolonization for mindfulness practices for improving education. And deep thanks to my colleagues who shared their time and insights so that my writing might gain small steps closer to clarity and relevance: Martha Wagner Alibali, John Bruer, Art Glenberg, Rob Goldstone, Teruni Lamberg, Victor Lee, Anthony Petrosino, and Lawrence Shapiro.

Thank you to the leadership at the University of Wisconsin–Madison School of Education and the Wisconsin Center for Education Research. I could not have envisioned a more collegial or supportive environment in which to produce this volume. I am thankful to my own mentors, who generously lent me their time, freely shared their wisdom along with their trials, and most valuably, gave me the space and time to find my own way. To my original graduate advisor, the late K. Anders Ericsson, my thesis advisor Walter Kintsch, and to John D. Bransford, Micki Chi, Susan R. Goldman, Kris D. Gutiérrez, Kathy Hirsh-Pasek, David Klahr, Richard Lehrer, James Pellegrino, Lauren Resnick, and Leona Schauble. I am deeply indebted and remain in awe of your intellects.

I am grateful to the members of the editorial team at Routledge, Dan Schwartz and Katherine Tsamparlis, and for the valued assistance and technical skills of the production team, including Helen Strain of Taylor and Francis Books, and Suba Ramya Durairaj and Ishwarya Mathavan at NewGen KnowledgeWorks. I am most appreciative of the tireless efforts of my copyeditor, Rosemary Morlin. I am sure there are many others behind the scenes who were also vital in making this come to fruition. Thank you, all.

And finally, my deepest appreciation to my family, who has seen me through this process all the way from the creative sparks to the hours and weeks of reading, writing, editing, rinse, repeat. I thank you for your unqualified love, enduring support, and much needed distractions.

Part I

A Fundamental Problem for Education
and a Proposed Solution

We are Learning Creatures Who Struggle to Design Effective Education Systems Framing the Problem

Very young children exhibit their understanding of balance and space as they first learn to navigate and walk without being instructed (Adolph, et al., 1997). To illustrate the complexity of these learning achievements, by comparison, programming robots to navigate and walk has been enormously challenging and is only recently showing success after some 50 years and at a cost of many hundreds of billions of dollars in research and development. The iRobot Roomba alone has been the product of an estimated $100M of R&D by 2015.

(Castellanos, 2015)

Having taught AI systems to play chess, computer scientists were surprised to learn how much more difficult it was to teach computers to recognize speech (Norman, 2017). Infants, on the other hand, readily develop speech, and by their first birthday they will have learned to both understand and produce verbal utterances that they have never heard before.

(Bergelson & Swingley, 2013)

This is also the age by which infants start to produce spontaneous hand gestures and arm movements to accompany their spoken language (Goldin-Meadow, 2015). Newborn babies demonstrate facial recognition through preferential looking. However, this is a capability that still eludes computer scientists, who struggle with how to provide this general skill across a broad range of facial forms.

1.1 THE CENTRAL PROBLEM: NEED FOR A COHERENT, EVIDENCE-BASED THEORY OF LEARNING

Learning is basic to the human experience. Throughout one's lifetime, a vast and highly varied amount of knowledge and skill is learned. Education is basically about engineering learning experiences. Despite the enormous importance of effective educational systems for social mobility, individual opportunity and a healthy and secure nation, educational institutions are not guided by a coherent, evidence-based theory of learning (e.g., Korthagen & Kessels, 1999). Without this overarching framework to guide educational design and decision making, teachers are left to make choices based on their own ideas about how learning takes place, and how to collect evidence that their students are learning.

Professionally trained educators are, of course, equipped with general and content area-specific pedagogical methods, but the connections of these practices to theory is often thin

DOI: 10.4324/9780429329098-1

and insufficient to help customize learning experiences to the suit the range of learners, topics, and teachers. Without appropriate guidance, educational administrators cannot make sound strategic choices on how to allocate limited resources, such as maintaining the professional training of their staff. With no scientific base to direct them, students are left to participate in inefficient exercises; they don't know how to direct their own study efforts, engage in effective self-teaching, or help their peers. As a nation, we spend billions of dollars to maintain and reform our educational systems and practices, design classrooms, order curriculum materials and educational technologies, institute testing regimens, and implement teacher training programs. We regularly make educational choices and implement educational programs with a poor understanding of how people learn. Furthermore, poor designs from K-12 education make their way into higher education and workplace learning, leading to additional lost opportunities.

Box I What is Learning?

I define learning as lasting changes in our behavior. Whenever we can observe these systemic changes in behavior, we can ascribe some learning process.

This definition is intentionally broad because people are able to perform an enormous range of behaviors and educators must appreciate that there are many different kinds of learning that people experience. This is why an integrative framework is necessary. If educators acknowledge that people's behaviors operate across a wide range of time scales, they may realize educational systems must attend to learning processes across a wide range of time scales as well.

The central goal of this book is to describe a coherent, evidence-based framework for how people actually learn. This description highlights something rather remarkable: Our natural ways of thinking, teaching, and learning are embodied. By *embodied*, I mean that people necessarily use body-based resources to make meaning and to connect new ideas and representations to prior experiences. I also mean that when we create educational systems that restrict our access to these natural, embodied resources, we impede our abilities to think and learn, and we may significantly underestimate what people know and how deeply they are engaged with the ideas of interest.

Take for example, the trend in schools to move away from concrete, hands-on thinking about mathematics and reading. Although there is strong evidence that both early mathematical thinking and early reading benefit from a Piagetian approach that fosters the development of serial thinking through concrete operations (Hattie, 2009, p. 43; the effect size of this approach is typically $d = 1.28$), widespread educational practices rapidly move to minimize these overt concrete behaviors in classrooms and regularly restrict students' use of concrete resources during testing. Another example is to look at students' self-employed study skills. When left on their own, students regularly choose some of the most ineffective methods. As double damage, they greatly overestimate the effectiveness of the study methods they choose, and often avoid the most effective methods, such as self-testing, even when they are aware of them, because of the greater effort (actions) involved in carrying out these methods (Dunlosky et al., 2013).

Educators specifically design classrooms to restrict students' physical and social interactions. This practice only increases with students' age. The education community creates testing situations that restricts children's ability to move their bodies in ways that can help them think, interact with objects, and interact with other people. For many students, schools with traditional instruction are a unique setting where they are blocked off from access to some of the most useful and flexible cognitive resources they have, resources that people ordinarily use while thinking and learning in nearly any other setting (Resnick, 1987).

However, there are many circumstances where learning is demonstrably improved by engaging one's body. Throughout this book, the reader will encounter a curated set of findings from scientific research and instructional designs that show embodied learning to be an asset for education. The examples reach across developmental levels, from pre-K through K-12 and into college and professional learning. The topics span language, mathematics, social studies, science, and engineering. The reader may experience an over representation of examples involving language and mathematics. This is largely because there is significantly more research that has been done in these areas to date. It is my hope that the ideas presented in this book can encourage more research in other scholastic content areas. Across these various examples, a pattern is emerging among theorists, educators, and designers that embodied learning is a natural human activity, and it is possible to design for it and harness it in ways that can inform educational practices and policies in order to usher in a new era of educating the embodied mind.

1.1.1 Example: Early Algebra Education

As one extended example, students can demonstrate an intuitive understanding of algebra relationships, such as how unknown quantities (such as X) behave, and how to describe general quantitative relationships for a given situation. Some readers may be cringing right now at the thought of doing algebra. For many people, learning algebra was a traumatic experience. They may have "gotten by" without developing a solid understanding of what algebraic expressions really meant, or why one would ever need to know how to use them.

There are informative studies of children who were given the freedom to talk about numerical quantities with their classmates—before they had formal instruction about algebra—while they moved about freely. These studies showed that students actually have some very good intuitions about how to think about unknown quantities and generalized relationships between quantities (French & Nathan, 2006; Koedinger & Nathan, 2004). These students naturally used their bodies and movement-based scenarios to act out ways that they think quantities can be in relation to one another.

For example, students intuitively realize they can use their bodies to act like a balance scale in order to depict the two sides of an equation. When in balance, both physically and conceptually, students readily recognize that there is an innate relationship between two sets of quantities being equated, even though each side can be very different visually. Young students can faithfully act out skits that capture the important quantitative relationships. They can depict operations such as multiplication by having multiple students each do the same thing in unison. Subtraction can be acts of removal, division, sharing and splitting, and so on (Nathan, 2008).

When speaking about relationships between unknown and known quantities, children can intuitively think of mathematical expressions as describing the order of events. Events are familiar, dynamic, embodied experiences that are very different than the static string of symbols often placed in front of them. Events have sequence and direction. Thus, to "undo" an event—or undo a mathematical operation—students will, without prompting, reverse the relationships as they were given, subtracting quantities that were added, dividing quantities that were multiplied, and so on. They naturally carry out the essential acts of *inverting* arithmetic operations—children need no formal training for this—and they will quite often do all of this algebraic reasoning without violating the sacred rules of *order of operations* (Koedinger & Nathan, 2004).

At other times, to gain insights into different types of quantitative relations, students will frequently invent and correctly apply iterative *guess-and-test* methods to see which values satisfy a set of algebraic constraints. Again, prior to formal instruction, and often without prompting, children intuit how to proceed and how to adjust their behavior so that each successive guess brings them systematically closer to the correct numerical answer. Ironically, when asked to describe how they used these intuitive methods to solve algebra level problems, these students will customarily report "I cheated," having internalized the view that such sensible, action-based methods are not legitimate mathematics, and unacceptable in school (French & Nathan, 2006).

1.1.2 What Holds us Back: Misguided Educational Systems

There are two deeply entrenched obstacles for improvement. The first is misguided educational practices and policies. That is the subject of this current section. The second set of obstacles emerge from scientific fields that are purportedly best positioned to inform educational practices and policies. I discuss these in the next section.

An examination of schools and schooling shows that society does not value embodied forms of knowing. Several scholars (e.g., Gee, 2004; Laurillard, 2013; also see Crawford, 2009; Rose, 2005) have raised concerns that students' formal education is structured so as to create conceptual distance between themselves and the physical world. Schools—certainly those associated with "college prep" and a general "liberal education"—rarely organize intellectual activities around the everyday or *practical experiences* of students, what Laurillard refers to as *first-order experiences*. In its place, scholastic discourse and activities focus on *second-order* "*descriptions of experiences*," (Laurillard, 2013, p. 55) such as mathematical equations and graphs, formal theories and notations for grammatical structures, and many other forms.

Educators seldom encourage students to engage in any sort of physical activity that brings learners directly in touch with ideas that are central to the disciplines of mathematics, language arts, the sciences, or social studies. Rather, educators seem to prefer that students sit at their desks in front of computers and textbooks, and spend their hours reading and manipulating arbitrary symbols and abstract terminology to "acquire" and "show" their knowledge. Macedonia (2019) labels this "mentalistic education." This view can be traced back to the mind-body separation (or *dualism*) of Descartes (1637), and was further expressed by the philosophy of Rationalism, and the Information Processing paradigm within Cognitive Science (which will be discussed in the next section). The mentalistic education view is what is often promoted in curricula and online exercises, what is central to professional teacher preparations, and what is emphasized during instruction. Meaning and sense making through personally grounded ways of knowing are not the primary objectives of these scholastic experiences. It justly matches what students most often say when asked what they are doing in school: "I don't know." The response is honest and accurate because, by design, they surely don't, even when they successfully perform the skills.

Restricting students' movements and social engagement does more than merely impede their connection to what they are supposed to be learning. Relegating the body to the periphery (literally, by limiting it to the hallways, the playground, and after school activities), also interferes with assessing students' knowledge. A child might look like they are underperforming, but that performance is so often mediated by learned *descriptions* of the world, rather than the workings of the world itself. For example, prior to formal arithmetic instruction, kindergartners can perform addition of large sets of elements across sensory modalities and formats, as when combining a visual array of dots and a sequence of tones (Barth et al., 2008). The children were successful because they used sensory based methods that directly experienced the quantities. However, they later became unsuccessful at performing these same calculations using arithmetic operations or direct fact retrieval. Many tests are assessments of students' knowledge of the second-order descriptions of experiences, rather than of the practical experiences with which they naturally engage in everyday life outside of school.

The implications of this are quite significant. In the short-term, a child who underperforms will very likely be labelled as incapable of handling more advanced ideas. Subsequent opportunities for this child become even more limited. To stay on mathematics as an example domain, a child might do extremely well at thinking about arithmetic story problems in terms of quantities that *change* from one person to another; that is, in terms of explicit *actions* that a child can act out with their bodies, or simulate using their imagination. Children readily do this for Joining and Separating problems of the type, *I picked 8 apples and I give you 5. How many do I have left?* But the same child may not do well with a problem with similar numbers asks them to make *comparisons* between quantities. *I picked 8 apples and you picked 5. How many more apples do I have?* Children's intuitive arithmetic reasoning builds on their use of action schemas (Carpenter, Hiebert, & Moser, 1981). Setting it up as a static comparison, devoid of action, as in the second story problem, is more difficult for the child to understand and solve.

It is tempting to think a child who cannot solve a compare problem cannot do arithmetic, when in fact thinking about compare relationships is not the same as thinking about the mathematics of change. Adults only think of them as interchangeable because we recognize that the two different scenarios can be modeled by the same arithmetic sentences; that is, the same second-order descriptions. When educators create restrictive environments to assess what students know, there is a serious risk of holding the student back from participating in activities that may make sense to them when they engage embodied learning processes.

Encountering these difficulties in school can have serious long-term implications as well. The child may develop an identity as someone who is not a mathematical thinker, one who is not good at using numbers and operations to reason about quantities and solve problems (Boaler et al., 2000). The trap is subtle, but rather damaging: Educators may think it helps the child and spares them the humiliation of struggling with mathematical tasks that seem out of reach. Yet the child may be inadvertently shut off from career pathways in engineering, computer science, or any of a range of disciplines because the child internalizes early on a view as "not a math person."

1.1.3 What Holds us Back: Inadequate Scientific Research on Education

It may seem easy, given this rather stark analysis, to lay blame on the educational systems and practitioners. But the causes of this unfortunate state of affairs are far broader. This is because the very scientific disciplines charged with the study of learning—neuroscience and psychology stand out as pre-eminent—often have little to say to teachers and educational leaders. I should correct myself: members of these scholarly communities often do not convey what they have learned in ways that align with the practices and institutions they hope to advise.

The shortcomings can be framed broadly as **the objects of study in the behavioral and social sciences do not map onto the malleable factors of the educational system**, including—and most notably—classroom learning and instruction.

An important element to this argument has been well reasoned by John T. Bruer, in a 1997 essay, "Education and the Brain: A Bridge Too Far." Bruer first presents and then dispels the *neuroscience and education* argument by showing that some of today's best understood neural behaviors do nothing to inform educational practices. This is not to say that neuroscience has been a static field, devoid of demonstrable progress.

On the contrary! Neuroscience—*cognitive* neuroscience, to identify the relevant area of specialization that applies here—has been a successful field. It has made great advances in instrumentation, data analysis, and visualization, progress mapping out brain function and dysfunction, and large gains in theorizing. The progress is evident in its own field as well as to interdisciplinary fields, such as complex systems. Yet, as Bruer point out, there is at this point in time, a basic conceptual disconnect between the phenomena that are studied and modeled by neuroscientists and the aspects of education that matter for student learning. He specifically identifies three areas of neural development: Synaptogenesis, critical periods and the effects of complex and enriched environments on the brain.

Synaptogenesis is the notable period in child brain development when the neo-natal brain experiences enormous growth in the formation of connections (synapses) between neurons. It is through these connections, rather than simply at the level of the neuron in isolation, that brains support the extraordinary functions they do, such as memory and inference-making, motor coordination, and language. Developmental neuroscientists do see growth in a number of capacities during synaptogenesis. Thus, it is tempting to draw from this a prominent *neuro-myth* that more will be learned if it occurs during periods of synaptogenesis.

However, in most cases the growth that is observed continues well beyond the synaptogenesis period. In fact, an important learning mechanism at the neural level is *pruning*. Pruning involves the *reduction* of connections, which supports learning by contributing to more efficient brain function. The changes during synaptogenesis that are most apparent occur roughly at the same rate despite the environments, nations, and cultures in which children are reared.

Myths regarding **critical period** research posit that children's intellectual development will suffer if they do not receive rich stimulation during a narrow, early window of opportunity. The claim is easily falsified on several fronts. First, human brain development has evolved over many millennia and in environments with a vast range in level of stimulation. For much of evolution children have been raised in environs far less stimulating than those of modern civilizations. Whatever experiences children need for basic sensory-motor and language development seems to occur in nearly any environment.

Second, the neural system demonstrates enormous plasticity. For functions that are insufficiently stimulated early on, children generally "catch up" once those opportunities arise, with no long-term cognitive delays. That window, if one can call it that, appears to be rather large and not nearly as abrupt as the phrase "critical period" suggests. There is no evidence that missing the "window" results in lasting deficits in culturally transmitted knowledge, such as reading and symbolic mathematics, for example. This suggests that whatever its potential influence, the critical period is limited to neural function, and any substantial deficits can expect to be circumvented or eliminated.

Research on critical periods and neuroplasticity does highlight the importance of children's basic sensorimotor function. It underscores the public health responsibility society has to evaluate all children early in their development. Diagnosed impairments in areas such as vision, hearing, vestibular system regulation, and motor movement must be treated so as not to interfere with developing perception, social participation, mobility, and agency. These general capacities, however, do not lead to specific guidance for improving educational practice.

Research on the effects of **complex and enriched environments** on the brain provides some of the most direct links between brain plasticity, synaptic change, and learning. Importantly, the resilience due to neuroplasticity occurs throughout one's lifespan, and well into old age. The resilience is not specific to school-age years.

Overall, we need to be skeptical of the direct implications from the neuroscience and education argument. What we know of neurodevelopment offers very little actionable guidance for education policy or practice. Bruer (1997), who served for many years as the president of the James S. McDonnell Foundation, which funds cognitive neuroscience research, sums it up thusly (p. 10),

> We simply do not know enough about how the brain works to draw educational implications from changes in synaptic morphology. We do not know how synaptic change supports learning. There is a gaping chasm between our understanding of what happens to synapses as a result of experience and what happens or should happen in preschool or third grade. The neuroscience and education argument attempts to bridge this chasm by drawing educationally relevant conclusions from correlations between gross, unanalyzed behaviors-learning to read, learning math, learning languages-and poorly understood changes in brain structure at the synaptic level. This is the bridge too far.

Some scholars extend this idea by advocating for neuroscience literacy among educators. Anasari and Coch (2006) are both neuroscientists interested in the growing interdisciplinary field of Mind, Brain, and Education. Anasari and Coch even caution that the literature reviews emerging that are tailored to teachers are often replete with inaccuracies and seriously over-stated implications.

Instead, they advocate for "future educators to become effective readers and critical evaluators of research findings" in neuroscience, including research methods. This is so teachers "understand the unique constraints of laboratory research," "ask crucial questions, know how to find answers, make connections across different sources of evidence, and think about how that evidence might affect pedagogy." I call this the *educators-learn-neuroscience* argument.

It is a profound goal, and indeed, all professionals can benefit by elevating their scientific literacy. However, for myself, as an educator and teacher educator who is also a psychologist, I have to say this is not a practical goal for most teachers. In fact, I would argue this is endemic to what holds us back from effective, evidence-based education improvement. The gap between neuroscience and education is wide, and the space between them is full of weak and inaccurate digests of findings from a field that is complex and rapidly changing. Few teachers are in a position to bridge that gap for neuroscientists.

The educators-learn-neuroscience position also reinforces existing power structure differences among academic scientists and educational practitioners. The large majority of the time these two communities talk, it is the academic scientists asking educators to come over to their side of the divide. How generous it would be to hear about cognitive neuroscientists pledging to immerse themselves into the science and praxis of classroom learning and instruction!

Bruer (1997) offers a different path to building the bridge than that proposed by either the neuroscience and education argument or the educators-learn-neuroscience argument. Rather than one enormous span, Bruer advocates for two bridges, with cognitive psychology serving as an intermediary. Cognitive psychology—which is sometimes folded into the moniker "brain-based education"—is charged with the behavioral study of mental function, including attention, memory, language, problem solving, decision making, and learning. The problem of spanning the gap shifts to a more manageable set of two separate challenges. The issue now is to span from neuroscience to cognitive psychology, and from cognitive psychology to education.

As a cognitive psychologist-turned-educational psychologist, I appreciate the sentiment and optimism in favor of my previous field helping heal this potentially important divide

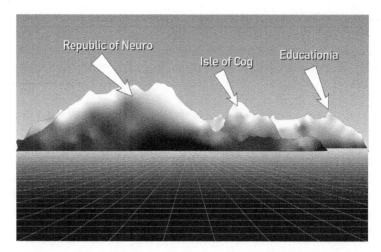

FIGURE 1.1 From one perspective the distance between cognitive neuroscience and education
policy and practice appears to be traversable.

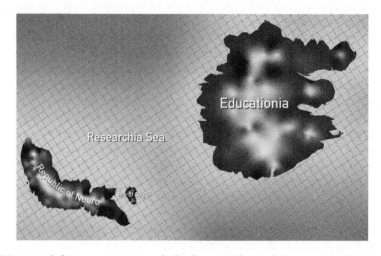

FIGURE 1.2 A shift in perspective reveals that here too, the gap between cognitive psychology
(the Isle of Cog) and education is still very far apart.

for the betterment of education. Indeed from the point of view of Figure 1.1, it is possible to
see a reason for optimism, since cognitive psychology seems like a close neighbor from the
perspective of neuroscience. Yet a shift in perspective, as shown in Figure 1.2, reveals that the
gap is still extremely wide.

I think the general argument of a bridge too far for brain science also applies, if less dramatically, to cognitive psychology. This is because here, too, the constructs that constitute the
object of study for cognitive psychologists do not map onto those of education. Cognitive
research generally studies different (though related) behaviors than those that actually take
place in educational settings. Also, cognitive research seldom addresses those aspects of the
learning environment that teachers and school leaders can control. This plays out in several
important ways that illustrate how the gap between cognitive psychology and education,
though smaller, is still formidable.

What stands between cognitive psychology and education? Having [...]
the space between the fields occupied by an ocean of methodology a[...]
next section addresses aspects of the epistemological chasm. That ch[...]
a framework that takes as its central defining premise that thought[...]
briefly, I first consider the methodological issues, which are significan[...]

A central methodological issue is that cognitive psychologists w[...]
thinking seldom study these behaviors in natural settings. Science has [...]
issue of *translational research*, that is, reproducing solid scientific findings from the laboratory into their natural settings. It goes beyond mere *methods*, or the procedures and tools
used to investigate learning in each setting. A *methodological* difference means that at the
outset the goals are different, the terms and ideas unaligned or even incommensurate, and
the metrics for evaluating success mismatched.

As a behavioral science, cognitive psychology seeks to employ theory and scientific method
to understand the nature of mental processes. It flows from a *science ethos*, and centrally asks
How are things? Cognitive psychology may attract psychologists looking to improve education. But, as a field of scholarship, it is primarily interested in producing generalizable theories that lead to predictive models that can be empirically and rigorously verified. It draws
inspiration from philosophical traditions such as Critical Rationalism (Popper, 2012). The
work, as such, is important for understanding the human experience.

However, developing effective interventions for fostering learning that works across a broad
range of settings and students is not a scientific pursuit, but one that flows from an *engineering ethos*. Education is, in Herb Simon's (1996) terminology, a "design science." Instead
of pursuing the science question, *How are things?* a design science is chiefly concerned with
How should things be? (Nathan & Swart, 2020).The primary objective is to develop and implement effective educational innovations (e.g., curricula, instructional practices, technology-
based learning environments) that are sensitive to the local constraints and goals of each
community. As such, educational design tracks more closely with the Pragmatism school of
thought (Dewey, 1899/2013).

It will help to illustrate the significant differences that need to be transcended to build
the proposed set of bridges into and out of cognitive psychology to connect neuroscience to
education. Consider, for example, how the fields each address the issue of *research criteria*.
Cognitive psychologists develop research designed primarily to ensure *construct validity*.
This means that the research activities, metrics, and analyses must, above all else, preserve
the close relationship between some actual measure (such as performance on a language
learning task), and a theoretical *construct* that is hypothesized to mediate task performance
(such as language comprehension).

Psychologists go to great lengths to ensure that construct validity is preserved during
a research study. The delivery is identical in each case. The environment is free from any
distractions or clues. Participants only interact with the assigned tasks and designated
researcher.

In order to fulfill all of these requirements (and many more), cognitive psychologists will
invent artificial tasks. This way the task demands can closely align with the theoretical construct under investigation. An artificial task can also help ensure that no one enters the study
with any special advantages that are not being explicitly investigated, such as prior exposure
of the task at hand. Researchers will often constrain the time on task to ensure this is comparable for each participant.

For example in studies of language learning, we may see children (Gomez & Gerken,
1999) or adults (Dienes et al., 1995) learn an artificial language (grammar) that is completely
novel and that never developed culturally. It is a language with no history, accent, food,
style of dress, music, country. It is a perfect way to isolate the cognitive processes that are

...nesized in learning a new grammar. These design constraints are important within a ...nce ethos, as the chief pursuit is a generalized theory of the specific mechanisms involved ...n language learning. It allows the psychologist to answer, *How are things?*

Education, in contrast, has many other influences. Chief among them, from a methodological point of view, is maintain the *ecological validity* of the learning environment, even when it is the subject of research. Here, the research classroom must be closely aligned with students' natural learning experiences as they occur when there is no research going on.

An important dissociation that reveals the wide division between the science and the design science is the description and implementation of *cognitive principles*. Cognitive psychologists will, as I mentioned, employ rigorous research methods to identify, isolate and test hypotheses about learning and instruction. A good selection of such principles can be found in the US Department of Education-Institute for Educational Sciences (IES) Practice Guide entitled "Organizing Instruction and Study to Improve Student Learning" (Pashler et al., 2007). The principles are summarized in Table 1.1. As the reader may recognize, these are very useful principles, and each, to make it into this report, had to demonstrate a wealth of empirical research supporting it across a range of task settings.

I have some first-hand experience working with these principles to improve classroom learning. I did this as a co-Principal Investigator for the National Math Center, sponsored by IES, which ran from 2010 to 2016 (Davenport et al., 2019). We surveyed and curated from among the principles listed in Table 1.1 to redesign an empirically based, and widely used middle school mathematics curriculum, *Connected Mathematics 2* (CMP2; Lappan et al., 2009). The specific principles we implemented (see Table 1.1) were # 1 (Spaced Learning), #2 & #7 (Worked examples with self-explanation), #3 Visual and Verbal integration, and #5 (formative assessment).

Our community was made up of scholars from cognitive psychology, developmental psychology, educational psychology, and mathematics education. We worked together for several years to implement the specific cognitive principles into the CMP2 curriculum. Our goal was to remain true to the original principles (remember that psychologists place a great deal of importance on construct validity!). At the same time, we had to remain faithful to the original curriculum (remember that educators place a great deal of importance on ecological validity!).

I can tell you this was hard. There were several major challenges. It was difficult to apply the principles to a novel curriculum beyond the circumstance in which the principles were initially studied and developed. It was complicated to apply them consistently across a range of curriculum materials and mathematics topics. The members of the team did not always agree on how to apply the principles. There was a great deal of iteration, discussion, and refinement.

TABLE 1.1

Several empirically well-established principles of learning and instruction, and those (*) implemented by the National Math Center

1*.	Space learning over time.
2*.	Interleave worked example solutions with problem-solving exercises.
3*.	Combine graphics with verbal descriptions.
4.	Connect and integrate abstract and concrete representations of concepts.
5*.	Use quizzing to promote learning.
6.	Help students allocate study time efficiently.
7*.	Ask deep explanatory questions.

I point this out because our team was uniquely trained in the theoretical and methodological foundations from which these principles arise. We knew the research literature, the mathematics content, and the specific curriculum. (I had personally worked for several years with this curriculum studying classroom-based learning and instruction; French & Nathan, 2006; Nathan & Kim, 2007; Nathan & Kim, 2009.) And, unlike most translational scholars, we even had access to the CMP2 authors (!) who graciously lent their time to make this project as success.

We kept things confined to math, and only to grades 6 through 8. We had a team of experts working on this for a few years. And it was still hard. I say this with an eye toward the prescriptive guidance offered by other behavioral scientists such as Anasari and Coch (2006) mentioned above. Studying the theory and method in order to implement fresh curricula that is closely aligned with scientific principles is a lot to ask of teachers. Simply put, **there is much to the "art" of applying the science!**

What's more, our task was to integrate all of our selected principles seamlessly into a single curriculum. But these principles were, for the most part, studied in isolation from the others, with work done by different research teams, on different content. Each principle provided valuable guidance to enlist the appropriate cognitive resources for learners when applied individually. But it was rare to investigate more than one or two in combination (most notably, worked examples with self-explanation methods; Booth et al., 2013). No one (to our knowledge) had ever implemented these all at once on a single set of classroom activities before, nor were they designed to be used in this way.

As it turned out, these principles sometimes conflicted with one another. That meant that judgment calls had to be made as to how to resolve the conflicts. There was no overarching set of *meta-principles* for how to select among competing principles, or, for example, to specify the order one should apply them. (We did, in fact, need to establish a set of meta-principles to determine that order as part of our work. See Davenport et al., 2019.) At other times, the principles signaled surprising redundancies that were not explicitly identified in the individual principles.

The larger point I wish to make is this: These were highly prized cognitive principles of learning that achieved their status as important advances in the field because of the rigorous studies of their isolated—and impressive—effects on learning. Even so, little was known about the combined effects of these principles on student performance and learning, or how to properly apply them for practical, prolonged use to enhance an existing curriculum.

In addition, even less was known about how teachers would use these principles during classroom instruction. That is, we went in with a theory of mathematical reasoning and learning, but with no explicit theory of action for how teachers would adopt these principles into a curriculum with which they had extensive experience.

This is another profound limitation that underscores the huge division I see between cognitive psychology and education (my colleagues and I have written more about this in Nathan, Rittle-Johnson, & Fyfe, 2016). Cognitive psychology has taken as its de facto scope of inquiry that the study of learning is chiefly about learners. This marginalizes or completely omits the influence of instruction, except as an intervention or "treatment." Any translational program of research that is poised to be successful and sustainable must—I argue—theorize much more deeply about teaching and teachers who will be the primary agents taking up these new practices and interacting directly with the learners.

This omission became quickly apparent in the work of the National Math Center. School districts partnered with us to implement the revised CMP2 curriculum, and we learned new things once they made their way into the classroom. One profound lesson for me was that the research team members and the teachers we partnered with demonstrated what I refer to as the "illusion of cognitive compliance" (Nathan, 2011). This is a very natural response, and there is a psychology literature on this (e.g., Festinger, 1957).

Essentially, when we introduced the curriculum in terms of the central cognitive principles of learning, teachers quite frequently reported that they were intimately familiar with the principles. They knew well the importance of such things as spaced learning, interleaving worked examples with problem solving, combining it with self-explanation prompts, and effectively combine visual and verbal information (and remove distracting visuals that compete for limited cognitive resources). They expressed confidence in their familiarity of the principles and how to implement them.

Yet, when they implemented them in the course of the complexities and buzzing confusion that is the middle school math classroom, it looked rather different than what we imagined in the calm confines of our research offices. This is to say, both the research teams and the teaching teams were operating under some form of illusion. Teachers and researchers shared terminology and understood why the principles were important, yet our respective visions of how to implement them were different. Shared terminology can mask important differences. The illusion of cognitive compliance recognizes that there is a great deal of work to forge common ground in teacher-researcher partnerships.

Education and cognitive psychology also have this common ground problem. Consider how each interprets the term "curriculum." Whereas a cognitive psychologist interested in reading comprehension might design a study to compare an experimental reading curriculum to the current one, education researchers recognize that the notion of a *curriculum* is a highly contested idea.

There is the idealized or intended curriculum and this differs—often substantially—from the enacted curriculum (Porter, 2004). The *intended curriculum* refers to the lesson or program content being studied. It typically means the printed course materials (textbook or online materials) and other closely connected resources (manipulatives, software, etc.). It often includes the mapping of the activities to the national and state curriculum standards, which articulate the grade- and topic-specific objectives expected of each student.

The *enacted curriculum*, in contrast, refers to the specific learning experiences of the students. This includes the content as it is taught by teachers and studied by students during learning and instruction. The enacted curriculum is far more dynamic and variable than the intended (or *idealized*) curriculum. It almost certainly differs across teachers. It even differs when the material is taught by the same instructor over the course of a single day, because the specific interactions will vary with different students.

In order to more fully appreciate the limitations of classical theories of cognitive psychology as a guiding framework for the future of education, it helps to better understand the nature of that field. Following that, I offer a more well-supported account of why embodied learning offers a better path forward.

1.2 THE VALUE AND LIMITATIONS OF CLASSICAL THEORIES OF COGNITION

There is a great difference between mind and body, inasmuch as body is by nature always divisible, and the mind is entirely indivisible… the mind or soul of man is entirely different from the body.

—René Descartes (1986)

To appreciate the challenges facing education it is important to first understand one of its most influential sources, the scientific research and principles of learning that come out of cognitive psychology and Information Processing Theory (Barab & Plucker, 2002).

1.2.1 Information Processing Theory

For over half a century, the dominant paradigm for thinking about learning in education has been shaped by Information Processing Theory (IPT; Anderson, 1996; Gardner, 1987; Miller, 1956; Newell & Simon, 1972).

The *mind*, in IPT, is a general-purpose computer that manipulates mental symbols and symbol structures to perform thinking and learning. These mental symbol structures are assumed to exist solely within the individual's mind. The *information processing* that is performed by the mind is the primary way people mentally represent and reason about the world and ideas. The idea of computing as emulating human thought has been a quest for many important scholars, and played a significant role in the rapid development of computer science as a field that converges on mathematics, electrical engineering, and psychology. Some prominent examples are shown in Figure 1.3.

Within IPT, the mind is disaffected from the world, and even from other minds. While the symbols and operations are intended to "model" the world and our actions in it, symbols in IPT remain unaffected by goings-on *in* the world or as a result of our actions. This is unless these external objects and events come to be represented by other symbols.

Manipulating these mental symbol structures provides a computational account about how people use intellect to reason about the world. An example is when people solve a problem or make an inference. One of the early computer programs devised to emulate human thought was The General Problem Solver (GPS), by Newell, Shaw, and Simon (1956; Newell & Simon, 1972). Despite the name, the program was not "general." The goal was to develop an artificial intelligence (AI) program specifically designed to solve a very large class of logic problems, including problems in logic, predicate calculus, and Euclidean geometry.

GPS built upon the central premises of IPT to represent all information as symbol structures and mathematical-logical operations on those symbols. However, GPS evolved past some earlier incarnations (such as the Logic Theorist; Newell, Simon, & Shaw, 1956) by incorporating an innovative set of pre-programmed problem-solving "shortcuts," of *heuristics*. GPS used heuristics such as "means-end analysis," that helped guide the program toward potentially fruitful paths, rather than blindly performing exhaustive (and very slow!) combinatorial search.

The significance of using heuristics, a class of problem-solving methods brilliantly articulated by scholars such as the mathematician George Polya (1945), was two-fold: First, many problems have systematic regularities to them that can be used to constrain the set of possible or likely solutions. Applying these regularities will often dramatically speed up the time and memory demands needed to reach an acceptable solution.

Means-ends analysis is a particularly clever heuristic. It is often discovered by older children, who realize it is usually quicker to move from both the start and end of a maze and try to meet in the middle, than to start only from the beginning.

The second significant aspect of heuristics is the psychological evidence that people use them frequently to minimize effort when solving problems. One widely used heuristic is that people will often settle for a problem solution that is *satisficing*. This means they find it acceptable to reach a solution that is *sufficient* to *satisfy* the constraints, even if it is not optimal, so long as it is less effortful (Simon, 1956). IPT-based computer systems continued to evolve as

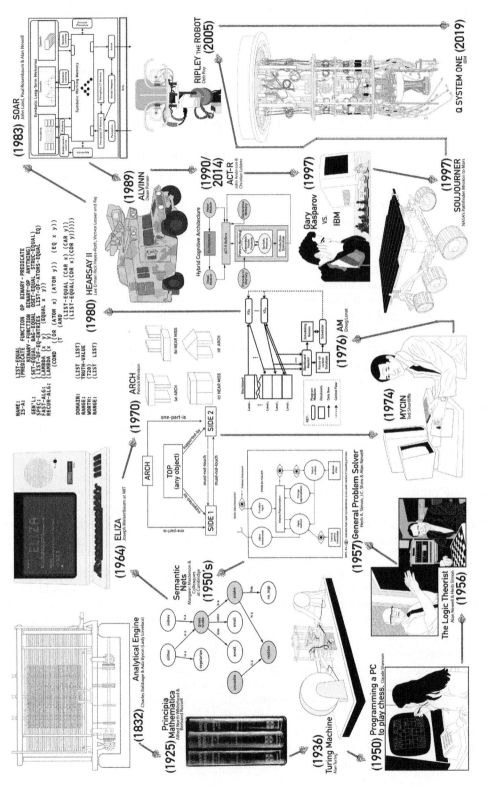

FIGURE 1.3 A brief visual history of artificial intelligence (AI).

FIGURE 1.3 Continued

Charles Babbage and Ada Byron (Lady Lovelace) designed the Analytical Engine (1832). Bertrand Russell and Alfred North Whitehead distributed *Principia Mathematica*, Alan Turing proposed the Turing machine (1936-37). Claude Shannon described programming a computer to play chess (1950). Logic Theorist composed by Allen Newell, J.C. Shaw and Herbert Simon (1956). The General Problem Solver (GPS) exhibited by Newell, Shaw, and Simon (1957). Margaret Masterman (1950s) and partners at Cambridge outline semantic nets for machine interpretation. Joseph Weizenbaum (MIT) created ELIZA to engage in human discourse. Patrick Winston's computer program could learned what an arch is (1970). Ted Shortliffe's MYCIN for medical diagnoses (1974). Doug Lenat's AM showed discovery learning (1976). Lee Erman, Rick Hayes-Roth, Victor Lesser and Raj Reddy's HEARSAY-II speech understanding framework (1980). John Laird Paul Rosenbloom, and Allen Newell's SOAR architecture to exhibit general intelligence (1983). Dean A. Pomerleau at CMU makes ALVINN (An Autonomous Land Vehicle in a Neural Network) (1989). ACT-R (short for "Adaptive Control of Thought—Rational"), an empirically based cognitive architecture for general intelligence, mainly developed by John Robert Anderson and Christian Lebiere (1990/2014). Deep Blue chess program beats world chess champion, Garry Kasparov, May 11, 1997. NASA's Pathfinder mission independent robot, Sojourner, explored the surface of Mars. (July 4, 1997). Deb Roy, Ripley the Robot (2005) learns to talk and think by interacting with objects and people in the world. IBM unveils the System Q quantum computer (2019).

```
;; If the child determines that the two sides are equally
;; weighted, then the conclusion is the beam will balance.

(p equal-weight-balance
    =goal>
            isa balance-beam--problem
            object ebeam
            prediction nil   ; must be unspecified
    =beam>
            isa bbeam
            sides (=lever1 =lever2)
    =lever1>
            isa lever
            posts =posts1
            total-weight =weight1
    =lever2>
            isa lever
            posts =posts2
        total-weight =weight1 ; constrained to have same weight as lever1
        - (=lever1>
            total-weight nil) ; the equal weight must not be nil
    =>
        !output! ("[PI] The weights are EQUAL so it will BALANCE ~%~%")
                ;; prevent matching by storing the prediction (replace nil)
        =goal>
            prediction BALANCE    ; Now a prediction is specified
```

FIGURE 1.4 ACT-R code depicting how a computer program can model the mental reasoning of children of different levels of intellectual development about the weights of a balance scale. It offers a symbol-manipulation based information processing theory account of how the mind can represent and reason about the world. © Mitchell J Nathan.

they incorporated more complex rule structures, allowed for probabilistic matching (as in the ACT-R system developed by Anderson & Lebiere, 1990/2014; see Figure 1.4).

A simple example of how mental symbols can represent the world and our reasoning about the world is shown in Figure 1.4. This provides one rule (written by the author) that is used to model how young children reason about the balance scale (Inhelder and Piaget, 1958). The rule is inspired by the work of Robert Siegler (1976).

1.2.2 Formalizing the Mind-Body Dualism

IPT has its origins within the Mind-Body Dualism famously associated with René Descartes (ca. 1700s; though see Aizawa, 2007 as one revisionist account that suggests Descartes also harbored views of the mind as embedded and extended.). Dualism is the view that the mind and body are fundamentally made of difference substances. In this view, the mind, is an entity for thinking and feeling, lacking any physically observable attributes. In contrast, the body is a material entity that cannot exhibit the ethereal, logical, or moral qualities associated with the mind. Although a mind can affect the body, as when we direct a body to act, and a body can affect our mind, as when we fall and feel pain, they remain forever distinct.

The dualist view is carried forward through the Analytic Philosophy of Bertrand Russell (1921), and later by cognitive scientists (Fodor, 1987; Pylyshyn, 1984). They postulated that a person's beliefs and attitudes about the world are not direct experiences from the state of the world or the person's bodily state. Rather their attitudes and beliefs are always mediated by the person's internal mental representation of what the attitudes and beliefs are about (ter Hark, 1994).

The idea of internal representations came about naturally enough. When we think about a horse or a powerplant, we do not find a horse or powerplant in our brains. Rather, the theory hypothesizes, we have some internal "image" or symbolic description of the horse in our mind—sometimes called our "mind's eye."

In keeping with the view of Logical Positivism, to which Russell was a central adherent, the nature of the internal representation was broken down into its most primitive parts. Mental representations were theorized to be ultimately composed of propositions that could be formalized into logical symbols. Thus, we find a historically rich tradition that describes thoughts as distinct entities from actions and events in the world, though capable of *representing* any objects and events, through a totally formal system comprised of symbols and logically consistent symbol manipulation operations. Thought, in this framework was equated with mentally performed computational processes on these internal symbolic representations.

IPT became the philosophical heir to this view of the mind and thought. To understand the power and utility of IPT, as well as recognize its limitations as an account of human learning, it is important to understand what these symbols are and how they are hypothesized to operate.

Symbols, in IPT, have several defining properties: They are assumed to be arbitrary, amodal, and abstract. It might be surprising to think of our mind as a computer that processes symbols that are *arbitrary*—why would this be of value for a theory of thinking and learning, when the contents of our mind seem anything but arbitrary? Yet, from a computational standpoint, there are tremendous advantages for hypothesizing a system of arbitrary symbols.

For starters, the computational architecture for manipulating arbitrary symbols is greatly simplified. It allows that every computational operation that is performed on a symbol is done so faithfully and without regard to what the symbol means or stands for.

Consider the example of the written alphabet, which is also composed of arbitrary symbols. The English alphabet is comprised of approximately 54 symbols. (I am using 26 letters both lower and upper case (52), plus grammatical markings such as the apostrophe and hyphens that are parts of words.)

The identity of each alphabetic symbol is determined exclusively by the shape of the symbol (not, for example, its associated phonetic sound). The shape of these alphabetic symbols is formed with no direct connection to the sounds they make or the meaning they convey. Yet from these 54 characters, over 200,000 words can be formed![1]

It is because of the arbitrary—and meaningless—nature of these 50 or so symbols that we see such an expansion in our ability to express so many unique words. Now, if we add to our set of 54 characters a mere dozen or so punctuation marks, the ten numerals (0 through 9), a blank space, and a few more common logograms (such as "&, @, #") we have a set of approximately 80 characters. Here, as we now group words, numerals, and punctuation we get to really see the combinatorial explosion of language as grammatically legal sentences.

Given a finite number of characters and a finite number of words, it might seem like the number of grammatically legitimate English sentences is also finite. This is not so. The set of grammatical rules (also finite in number) will allow any level of recursive nesting of phrases and can therefore generate an infinite number of grammatical sentences.

Many insights about the combinatorial nature of language comes from Chomsky's (1957/ 2002) hierarchy of grammars. Chomsky identifies the grammars closest to our natural language as a "recursively enumerable" grammar (or Type-0 grammar). For example, a sentence can be made by placing a conjunction (and, but, or) in between two sentences (S). This can be written as **S —> S conj S.** A sentence can also be rewritten as a noun phrase (NP) and a verb phrase (VP), often in that order. This can be written as **S —> NP VP.**

NPs can be further rewritten as a NP with an (optional) determiner (DET) and (optional) adjectives (ADJ), followed by a noun (N). VPs are composed of a verb (V), optionally followed by a NP and a prepositional phrase (PP). The formal rewrite rules can be depicted as in Table 1.2.

This, by the way, is also important for understanding the tremendous intellectual and practical contributions made by Alan Turing, the founder of artificial intelligence and one of the founders of field of computer science. Recursively enumerable languages are also defined computationally as *Turing-recognizable* languages.

To gain a further appreciation of the awesomeness of the combinatorial nature of language composed of arbitrary symbols, it helps to see how malleable language actually is. This is beautifully illustrated by the author Jorge Louis Borges (1962/2007). He conceived of the *Library of Babel* as an imaginary institution that contained every book that is mathematically possible, regardless of whether it is accurate or even readable (Borges, 1962/2007, p. 54).

> These examples made it possible for a librarian of genius to discover the fundamental law of the Library. This thinker observed that all the books, no matter how diverse they might be, are made up of the same elements: the space, the period, the comma, the twenty-two letters of the alphabet. He also alleged a fact which travelers have confirmed: *In the vast Library there are no two identical books*. From these two incontrovertible premises he deduced that the Library is total and that its shelves register all the possible combinations of the twenty-odd orthographical symbols (a number which, though extremely vast, is not infinite): Everything: the minutely detailed history of the future, the archangels' autobiographies, the faithful catalogues of the Library, thousands and thousands of false catalogues, the demonstration of the fallacy of those catalogues, the demonstration of the fallacy of the true catalogue, the Gnostic gospel of Basilides, the commentary on that gospel, the commentary on the commentary on that gospel, the true story of your death, the translation of every book in all languages, the interpolations of every book in all books.

Thus, the arbitrary nature of mental symbols in IPT strips it of any preconceived meaning, and in doing so, imbues it with a quality of neutrality that allows for the vast computational power to operate equitably on all symbols.

The *mental* symbols envisioned in IPT are theorized as analogous to these physical symbols of written language. They are also *amodal*; which enables two important properties: (1) the capability of the symbols to represent or stand for things and ideas does not depend on how those things or ideas are referenced; and (2) neither does it depend on how the algorithms for reading, generating, and manipulating these symbols are implemented computationally. In the first case, the symbol, CHAIR, for example, will activate the mental idea of a chair regardless of whether one encounters a chair by hearing its name, seeing

TABLE 1.2
A small portion of the formal rewrite rules for English grammar, with examples

S —> S conj. S	Michelle was walking and she saw the sunset.
S —> NP VP	The swollen river broke the dam after midnight.
NP —> NP (poss.) NP	The bike of [the sister of [the town's mayor]]
NP —> (det.) (adj.) N	The large dog
VP —> V (NP) (PP)	was the popular kid at school
PP —> P (NP)	Only the lonely

one, touching one, or simply imagining one. Its sensorial history, as it were, is irrelevant to the activation of the CHAIR symbol, as far as the IPT account is concerned (Glenberg & Gutierrez et al., 2004).

This may seem at odds with our phenomenological experiences that seem to depend upon the modal qualities of objects that we encounter. However, from a computational standpoint, it enables greater generality for representing a vast array of things within an IPT-based cognitive system. Were it relevant to capture the modal form in which the chair was seen, that, too, (*ironically*) can be captured amodally. It can be a designated property of the object, as in the expression Modal-Encounter(CHAIR, Time-Code-000458961) = Visual.

To describe symbols as amodal is to declare that the specific way the symbol is realized is independent from any particular computational architecture (Harnad, 1990). This is important because cognitive theories about how symbols represent things are intended to hold regardless of whether it is a biological brain, semiconductor-based micro-processor, genetic material, or any other computational medium.

Along with being arbitrary and amodal, mental symbols in IPT are *abstract*—idealized— with the symbol CHAIR representing all members of the class of chairs. This greatly streamlines the computational demands of the IPT system. It supports greater generality, so one may, for example, make new inferences about a particular chair (its stability, for example) that can be readily applied to all chairs (all members of the class CHAIR).

With these three qualities of IPT symbols—arbitrary, amodal, and abstract—how do they provide meaning? Several scholars propose that symbols gain their meaning through *covariation*. In this context, *covariation* refers to how the occurrence of one set of symbols varies in accordance with another set, so that one can essentially predict the occurrence of a symbol from the appearance of the other. In this way, the particular symbols do not matter, rather they are linked together because of the shared, or covarying pattern of occurrence. Meaning comes by virtue of how the symbols are used across a broad corpus of linguistic sources (Glenberg & Mehta, 2008). Latent Semantic Analysis is one of the most prominent systems for automatically inferring meaning of words and sentences (Landauer & Dumais, 1997). In this approach, when words are observed to frequently co-occur with other words in their linguistic role, they evidence similar meanings. That is, words with similar meaning show high covariance of the contexts in which they occur. Words that never co-occur together likely share no meaning.

Similarly, connectionist systems discern meaning from verbal and visual features through the patterns of covariation of those features (Rogers & McClelland, 2004; Rogers et al., 2004). Simply put, symbols do not acquire meaning from any of the properties of the symbols themselves, but by virtue of how the symbols are used in relation to other symbols. This is to say that context of how words are used are perhaps more important than the actual symbols used for the words themselves, as Figure 1.5 illustrates.

The ability to read statements in Figure 1.5 can be explained by the "word superiority effect" (Baron & Thurston, 1973). McClelland and Rumelhart (1981) provided a connectionist model showing how the effect captures the influence of the relations between markings,

For emaxlpe, it deson't mttaer in waht oredr the ltteers in a wrod aepapr, the olny iprmoatnt tihng is taht the frist and lsat ltteer are in the rghit pcale. The rset can be a toatl mses and you can sitll raed it wouthit pobelrm.

S1M1L4RLY, Y0UR M1ND 15 R34D1NG 7H15 4U70M471C4LLY
W17H0U7 3V3N 7H1NK1NG 4B0U7 17.

FIGURE 1.5 How symbols gain meaning and interpretation because of their relation to other symbols

letters, and words. At the lowest level of visual analysis, letters are collections of markings. Words, of course, are collections of letters.

When a letter is perceived as part of a word, the letters that belong to that word receive additional activation. That is, people may "perceive" reading the letter even if they do not attend directly to it, simply because people perceive the word in which the letter is a member. As suggested by Figure 1.6, the influences can either go "top down," with context influencing word and letter perception, as well as "bottom up," so that markings determine which letters people perceive and which words people read. Note also that choices between entries at a given level inhibit one another, since the letter a reader decides on cannot be both *A* and *I*, for example, either *Trip* or *Trap*.

There are many computational benefits of a hypothesized system of symbols that are arbitrary, amodal, and abstract (so-called *AAA symbols*; Glenberg & Gutierrez et al., 2004). These can be summarized simply: AAA symbols can be used to stand for anything and be used in support of any computational operation, even ones that could not have be foreseen when they were created. With such potential, they seem ideal as resources for mentally representing the word and supporting one's thinking about how the world functions and how it might operate in the future. Why offer an alternative account and mess with perfection?

It turns out we are far from achieving perfection with IPT. There are several reasons to articulate alternative theories of cognition and learning. First of all, there are several serious limitations to IPT and related computational theories of cognition. But, as Shapiro (2019)

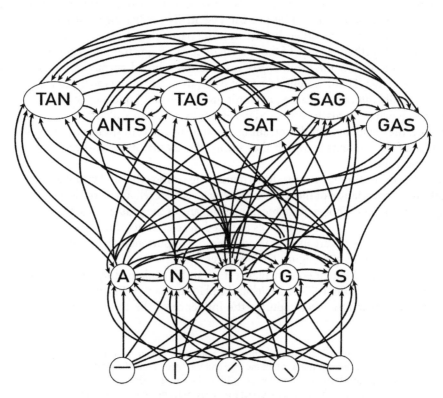

FIGURE 1.6 This depiction of a connectionist network models how top-down effects of context matters for reading and word recognition. The network can model effects seen among readers where letters within words gain additional activation, as do markings that are parts of letters (adapted from McClelland & Rumelhart, 1981).

notes, separate from the objections to symbolic accounts of cognition, there are beneficial reasons to build a case for an embodied account of learning and teaching in its own right. Here I first review some of the central objections with symbolist accounts of cognition, such as the one promoted by IPT. In the next section I discuss the benefits of an embodied account of cognition, and use that as the foundation for proposing a new way forward for the future of education.

1.3 CRITIQUES OF THE ROLE OF COGNITIVE PSYCHOLOGY IN EDUCATION

The reader may wonder why there is so much uncertainty and controversy for assessing the validity of any one theory of cognition. We have a whole field of neuroscience. Why not simply have a look at what the brain is actually doing when people think and learn?

It is worth pointing out that, unlike many other biological processes, there is no *direct* way to inspect thinking, or *directly* observe the products of learning. Even brain imaging reveals little about its role in specific thoughts. Where it does, neural data needs to be interpreted within a theoretical framework of cognition (Bruer, 1997). We cannot simply look and find concepts people have for color or triangles stored in our brains (Cummins, 1990). It is a bit like sorting through Borges' *Library*: The storage is vast and its structure is only very partially known (though it varies considerably), and the items people seek may be in there, but scientists cannot tell where they may be.

Furthermore, asking people to tell us what they are thinking is not always (or even usually) accurate. As I will discuss in later chapters, much thinking is performed outside of conscious awareness. People are terribly limited in the access to much of their thought processes. Infants, of course, cannot tell us what they are thinking. Yet, even for older people, their retrospective accounts can often be wrong, shaped, perhaps by what they think cognitive scientists want to hear (e.g., Wilson & Nisbett, 1977; Schooler & Engstler-Schooler, 1990).

Some methods, such as verbal reports and eye tracking, can be used to obtain more accurate accounts of thinking (e.g., Ericsson & Simon, 1984/1993; Just & Carpenter, 1976). But these are also limited to certain kinds of processes, during certain kinds of tasks. Because thinking is not available for direct inspection, scientists must use *inferential* methods for determining how people think and what people learn. The kinds of inferences people make, depends on the theoretical and methodological lens with which scientists observe behavior.

1.3.1 Empirical Critique of the Covariation Account of Meaning

There are several serious objections to IPT. Glenberg and colleagues (e.g., Glenberg & Robertson, 2000) empirically challenge the claim that covariation is sufficient to explain how AAA symbols come to reliably represent the world. Central to this challenge is the insight that words to human beings are not treated as arbitrary symbols, as they are for general-purpose computers. Rather the meaning of a word is derived from the affordances of the word for the context.

Affordances, in Gibson's (1977, 1979) theory of ecological psychology, addresses how people evaluate meaning and utility of things in terms of our own body, actions, and goals; and as such, are embodied ways to determine word meanings. As Norman (1999, p. 39) describes it, *affordances* "refer to the actionable properties between the world and an actor (a person or animal). To Gibson, affordances are relationships. They exist naturally: they do not have to be visible, known, or desirable."

Several computational models of human thinking treat words as AAA symbols. They align with disembodied computational accounts of how words gather meaning strictly through covariation with other words. To test whether affordances (embodied) or covariation (disembodied) tells a more accurate story of language comprehension, Glenberg and Robertson (2000) presented people with sentences like 1a and 1b, and asked them to judge each sentence's sensibility.

(1 a) After wading barefoot in the lake, Erik used his *shirt* to **dry** his feet.
(1 b) After wading barefoot in the lake, Erik used his *glasses* to **dry** his feet.

As proxies for the strong symbolist views, Glenberg and Robertson challenged computational methods, such as Latent Semantic Analysis (LSA; Landauer & Dumais, 1997) and Hyperspace Analogue to Language (HAL; Burgess & Lund, 1997), to accurately model meaning as covariational relations among words and events. The challenge was an appropriate theoretical comparison. This is because meaning in LSA and HAL is based on the covariation of frequencies of co-occurrence of the words, rather than on the affordances as a reflection of what the words actually mean in terms of body experiences. As Glenberg and Roberts (2000) explain, "Sentence (1 b) is grammatical," and the covariation association for "glasses" and "dry" is very similar to that of "shirt" and "dry." LSA makes little distinction between the appropriateness of the two sentences, or other similarly formed pairs. With meaning determined by covariation, these two words, which have similar covariation with *dry*, are basically interchangeable in LSA.

Not so for the typical reader! The reason readers decide that sentence (1 b) is not sensible, lies in the different affordances that glasses and shirts have for drying feet, not in the patterns of word co-occurrence. Glenberg and Robertson argue that the disconnection between the words and the world in computational systems such as LSA casts the words as *ungrounded symbols*. Further, these ungrounded symbols are poorly suited to represent the real meaning of novel events or support sensibility judgments involving these ungrounded words.

1.3.2 Philosophical Critique of IPT: The Symbol Grounding Problem

Another important objection is philosophical. It rests on a provocative thought experiment called *The Chinese Room*[2] posed by John Searle (1980, 1990). The Chinese Room is so named because, to those who cannot read Chinese (as Searle himself confesses), meaning is very difficult to discern from the forms that Chinese characters take. However, if one is given proper rules of manipulating symbols—rewrite rules that a speaker of Chinese would regard as grammatically acceptable and sensible—one can give an *appearance* of knowing the language to an outside observer (or so the thought experiment would have us believe).

Searle (1999, cited in Cole, 2004) illustrates the idea:

> Imagine a native English speaker who knows no Chinese locked in a room full of boxes of Chinese symbols (a data base) together with a book of instructions for manipulating the symbols (the program). Imagine that people outside the room send in other Chinese symbols, which, unknown to the person in the room, are questions in Chinese (the input). And imagine that by following the instructions in the program the man in the room is able to pass out Chinese symbols, which are correct answers to the questions (the output). The program enables the person in the room to pass ... for understanding Chinese but he does not understand a word of Chinese.

Searle, as the agent in the Chinese Room, may appear to converse with a proficient speaker, but Searle points out that he does not actually *know* Chinese.

When the meanings of symbols are established only by reference to other symbols, through formal rules and mappings (such as the book of instructions described by Searle), it necessarily results in an ungrounded understanding of those symbols. At a theoretical level, accounts that relate ungrounded symbols to ungrounded symbols lead to an inadequate account of how people actually form meaning and knowledge (Harnad, 1990; Searle, 1980). From an educational perspective, performance with words and formal systems of notations whose meaning is derived in this manner, leads to learning that is inevitably rote, shallow, and rigid (Whitehead, 1929/1967).

The idea illustrated by the Chinese Room is extended by recognizing it as an instance of *The Symbol Grounded Problem* (Harnad, 1990, p. 335), which (rather rhetorically) asks,

> How can the meanings of the meaningless symbol tokens, manipulated solely on the basis of their (arbitrary) shapes, be grounded in anything but other meaningless symbols? The problem is analogous to trying to learn Chinese from a Chinese/Chinese dictionary alone. ...
>
> How can you ever get off the symbol/symbol merry-go-round?

I consider these rhetorical questions because it is clear that the author—me as well— believes that one cannot derive meanings from within the symbol/symbol merry-go-round. Thus, it should be no surprise to hear that Harnad offers potential solutions to the Symbol Grounding Problem that involve—ta da!—*grounding*.

So what, exactly, does it mean to *ground* the meaning of something symbolic? How does an embodied perspective on thinking and learning offer solutions to the Symbol Grounding Problem and, in the words of Goldstone, Landy, and Son (2008, p. 327), the quest for a "well-grounded education?"

1.3.3 What is Grounding?

Grounding maps novel ideas and symbols to modality-specific experiences that are personally meaningful. In this way, grounding provides an account of how sensory-motor experience gives rise to conceptual understanding (Nathan, 2008; Pulvermüller, 2005). Grounding describes the mapping formed between an idea or symbol, and a more concrete referent, such as an object, movement or event in the world—as well as mental re-enactments of these experiences—in service of meaning making (Glenberg, De Vega, & Graesser, 2008).

Roy (2005, as cited by Glenberg et al., 2008) also suggests that *grounding* denotes the processes by which an agent (human or machine) relates mental structures to external objects. This notion is closely related to how grounding is used in instructional settings (Nathan, 2008). Grounding during instruction is often marked by *linking gestures*, hand movements that provide conceptual correspondences (or a *mapping*) between familiar and unfamiliar entities. This is particularly evident when the focus of instruction is on learning to understand and produce written symbols and formal (i.e., conventionalized) notations and representations that have an arbitrary mapping between a representational form and its meaning.

For example, a teacher may produce a gesture as a link between a mathematical symbol, such as X, and the length of a geometric shape by pointing to X and then tracing the longest side of a rectangle (Alibali & Nathan, 2005). The claim is that meaning of formal symbols comes ultimately through reference to grounded, non-symbolic entities such as perceptions, actions, objects, and experiences from the world (Barsalou, 2008; Glenberg, 1997; Harnad, 1990).

1.3.4 Educational Critique of IPT: Designing an Ungrounded Education

It is important to pursue the educational implications of IPT because it has been so influential, historically. The picture is a rich one, which illustrates many of the strengths that a long and well-researched area of psychological study has to offer. Pooling across multiple reviews of learning principles (Bransford, Brown, & Cocking, 2000; Dunlosky Rawson, Marsh, Nathan, & Willingham, 2013; Graesser, 2009; Pashler et al., 2007; which, by the way, were used by the National Math Center described earlier), the empirical research from an IPT perspective points to several overarching principles for facilitating learning: The importance of repetition and practice; managing the demands on cognitive and attentional resources; engaging the learner in the active construction of meaning and knowledge; and metacognitive awareness. Together, they offer constraints and design guidelines for the development of effective learning environments.

The vast majority of the evidence comes from laboratory and pull-out type studies in order to achieve methodological rigor for control of intervening variables. Rarely are these studies conducted in classrooms or other authentic learning settings. Regardless, these principles have had a valuable impact on school learning, primarily in early reading and mathematics education.

IPT principles tend to share an underlying commitment to AAA symbols. This commitment has been called the *Formalisms First* view of cognitive development (Nathan, 2012). In the *Formalisms First* (FF) view, the teaching and mastery of formalisms are often considered prerequisite to applied knowledge. Formalisms occupy this primary role because of deeply held beliefs in education and in society at large in a Formalisms First view. This view posits that learning and conceptual development proceeds first from knowledge and mastery of discipline-specific formalisms before learners can exhibit competency applying that knowledge to practical matters.

Formalisms are defined as "specialized representational forms that use heavily regulated notational systems with no inherent meaning except those that are established by convention to convey concepts and relations with a high degree of specificity" (Nathan, 2012, p. 125). If this sounds familiar, it should remind the reader of the concerns about AAA symbols. Table 1.3 shows an example of one formalism, an algebraic equation. It is compared to two grounded representations—a "word equation" and an algebra story problem. All three formats share the same underlying quantitative relationships, but elicit very different ways of thinking mathematically (Koedinger & Nathan, 2004).

TABLE 1.3

Example of the same quantitative relationships shown as (a) symbolic formalism, (b) word equation, and (c) story problem (adapted from Koedinger & Nathan, 2004)

Equation	Word equation	Story problem
Solve for X: $6X + 66 = 81.90$	*Starting with some number, if I multiply it by 6 and then add 66, I get 81.90. What number did I start with?*	*When Ted got home from his waiter job, he multiplied his hourly wage by the 6 hours he worked that day. Then he added the $66 he made in tips and found he earned $81.90. How much per hour does Ted make?*

I wish to note that formalisms are extremely valuable, and serve an important role in disciplinary discourses when properly used among those well-versed in their meaning and application. For example, the regulated notational systems used in algebra are meant to reduce ambiguity and increase the potential for processing them efficiently. Formalisms are often more concise than descriptive language. They use specialized terms and symbols to convey certain concepts with a precision that is difficult to obtain with everyday language and images. Formalisms also "scale" well in the face of increasing complexity (Koedinger, Alibali, & Nathan, 2008).

The term *formalisms* applies broadly to a wide array of written inscriptions (Latour, 1987; Latour & Woolgar, 1986) often found in the natural and information sciences, and include: mathematical expressions, stoichiometric equations and vector diagrams in the sciences; Boolean algebra, computer programs, formal grammars, and flow charts; various charts and diagrams, such as pie charts, coordinate system graphs (such as the *Cartesian coordinate system* attributed to Descartes); and many standardized tabular representations such as data tables, matrices, and balance sheets. These share the traits that they are all conventionalized and transcendent "forms" (hence the label *formalisms*) that are intended to describe attributes and relationships in abstract ways that remove them from any one material instantiation.

As the sociologist of science Bruno Latour describes them, formalisms are intended to document and to be "mobile, but also immutable, presentable, readable, and combinable with one another" (Latour, 1987, p. 7). In short, the educational practices that follow from IPT tend to reflect the theoretical commitment to AAA symbol processing, with the idea that these theoretical descriptions should also guide the design of learners' educational experiences.

In an article for the journal *Educational Psychologist* (Nathan, 2012), I describe the ubiquity of the Formalisms First perspective in education and the barriers it creates for learners. Algebra instruction serves as a valuable case study of how notions from IPT of how the mind represents knowledge influences the curricular designs and pedagogical practices that shape learners' educational experiences.

Unfortunately these influences take hold even when empirical evidence points in a different direction. Specifically, the commitment to AAA symbols underlies a Formalisms First approach to algebra instruction that places a premium on symbol manipulation rather than sense making of what algebraic expressions mean. Because these algebraic symbols are *ungrounded*, children as well as adults (see Koedinger et al., 2008) often make errors that show how *un*-meaningful these symbols truly are—and many of these errors persist even after students have successfully completed algebra instruction (e.g., Koedinger & Nathan, 2004; Koedinger et al., 2008). We see that when students are given opportunities to use approaches that are meaningful to them where they are able to ground the meaning of these formal symbols, their performance greatly improves (Nathan et al., 2002; Nathan, 2012). In sum (Nathan, 2012, p. 138),

> One explanation for students' poor understanding of formalisms across a range of fields is that students may not achieve a *grounded* understanding that allows them to construct meaning of these formalisms in terms of other things that they already understand, or things they can perceive and physically manipulate (Goldstone, Landy & Son, 2008; Martin, 2009). The computational properties of formalisms, such as equations, come about because of the syntactic, form-based (i.e., *form*-al) rules that govern the relations and transformations of these systems of notation. Yet, when formal representations are understood exclusively by reference to other formal representations in the form of rules and mappings, it can lead to an ungrounded form of understanding that appears to be rote, shallow, and rigid (Harnad, 1990; Searle, 1980).

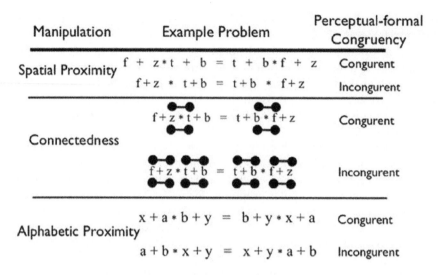

FIGURE 1.7 An illustration of how the perceptual properties of algebraic expressions can override the symbolic rules.

Goldstone, Landy, and Son (2008) build a case for the central importance of a "well-grounded education," which follows some of the emerging tenets of embodied cognition. The authors look at how formalisms are not processed in amodal ways by people. Rather, formalisms are very sensitive to the perceptual qualities they exhibit—despite their reputation! That is, even when people know formal rules for symbol manipulation, such as order of operations, must take precedent over visual cues, they still violate those rules when they conflict with perceptual cues, such as spatial proximity, connectedness, or alphabetic proximity (i.e., favoring grouping x with y and a with b; Figure 1.7).

In reviewing these findings across a range of experiments, the authors argued that "An embodied cognition perspective offers promise of scientifically-grounded educational reform" (Goldstone et al., 2008, p. 347). They continue, arguing that embodied approaches that draw on perceptual processes "can promote transfer where formalism centered strategies fail" (p. 347). For all of its many impressive qualities for advancing research about cognition, the theoretical commitments endemic to IPT foster educational designs that promote ungrounded learning. People may learn to mimic the rules, but like the agent in Searle's Chinese Room, they might not learn what the rules and symbols mean. Embodied learning draws on perceptual and movement-based processes to provide a grounded understanding of ideas, symbols, and rules, thereby promoting sense making.

1.3.5 Recap

I now want to return to an understanding of what is holding us back from having the educational systems we need and deserve. This, I claim, is the state of things: **Educational systems are left to operate without a valid account of how people learn and think, while the scientifically based theories of thinking and learning that are most widely held are not formed with educational concerns in mind.** Educational programs regularly provide ungrounded learning experiences without attending to the importance of meaningful learning and of the means to achieve it. Scientific recommendations for education are often absent of ecological validity or the realities of classroom teaching and learning, and they appear to neglect or avoid complex issues of educational and societal inequities that systematically follow along racial and economic lines. Recognizing this, it is no wonder that the American education system is currently in such dire circumstances. To this, I propose a way forward.

1.4 READER ACTIVITIES

1.4.1 Exploring Formal Systems

Searle's Chinese Room argument shines a light on the challenges humans face thinking in terms of pure formal systems. This activity lets one explore a simple formal system and deduce its meaning.

In the 1979 book *Gödel, Escher, Bach*, author and cognitive scientist Douglas Hofstadter introduced a formal system called the *pq-system* (pp. 49–53). The pq-system only has three allowable symbols, *p*, *q*, and the hyphen ("-"). The system also has one rule:

Let *x*, *y*, and *z* each be sequences of hyphens. If $xpyqz$ is a theorem, then $xpy-qz-$ is a theorem.

Here are the three shortest axioms of the pq-system.

```
1. -p-q--
2. --p-q---
3. ---p-q----
```

An interactive version is available from Wolfram that allows you to explore this formal system. https://demonstrations.wolfram.com/PqSystemExplorer/

Answer these questions.

a. Prove that the conjecture

```
--p----q------
```

is a theorem of the *pq-system*. That is, use the axioms and the system rule to derive this conjecture, thereby establishing it is indeed a theorem.

b. What does the *pq-system* actually do?

1.4.2 Ripley the Robot Learns Language

Ripley the Robot learns language by grounding its meaning in its interactions with the physical world.

www.npr.org/templates/story/story.php?storyId=5503683?storyId=5503683

NOTES

1 The Second Edition of the 20-volume *Oxford English Dictionary*, published in 1989, contains full entries for 171,476 words in current use, and 47,156 obsolete words. To this may be added around 9,500 derivative words included as subentries.

2 Historically, the Chinese Room metaphor was originally introduced to challenge the strong claims of artificial intelligence, the proposal that computer programs could think like human beings. In this case, the value of this thought experiment is to demonstrate the futility of deriving meaning from a symbol system (i.e., the room) that only admits formal symbol structures and rules for manipulating symbols (the program) to generate new symbol structures (the output).

REFERENCES

Adolph, K. E., Bertenthal, B. I., Boker, S. M., Goldfield, E. C., & Gibson, E. J. (1997). Learning in the development of infant locomotion. *Monographs of the Society for Research in Child Development, 62*, i–162.

Aizawa, K. (2007). Descartes and embodied cognition. *The Brains Blog.* Retrieved April 22, 2021, from http://philosophyofbrains.com/2007/03/04/descartes-and-embodied-cognition.aspx

Alibali, M. W., & Nathan, M. J. (2005, April). Teachers use gestures to link multiple representations of mathematical information. In "Gestures and Embodied Action in Teaching, Learning, and Professional Practice." Paper presented to the American Educational Research Association annual meeting. Montreal, Canada.

Anderson, J. R. (1996). ACT: A simple theory of complex cognition. *American Psychologist, 51*(4), 355.

Anderson, J. R., & Lebiere, C. J. (1996/2014). *The atomic components of thought.* Psychology Press.

Ansari, D., & Coch, D. (2006). Bridges over troubled waters: Education and cognitive neuroscience. *Trends in Cognitive Sciences, 10*(4), 146–151.

Ball, D. L. (1993). With an eye on the mathematical horizon: Dilemmas of teaching elementary school mathematics. *The Elementary School Journal, 93*(4), 373–397.

Barab, S., & Plucker, P. (2002). Smart people or smart contexts? Cognition, ability, and talent development in an age of situated approaches to knowing and learning, *Education Psychologist, 37*(3), 165–182.

Baron, J., & Thurston, I. (1973). An analysis of the word-superiority effect. *Cognitive Psychology, 4*(2), 207–228.

Barsalou, L. W. (2008). Grounded cognition. *Annual Review of Psychology, 59*, 617–645.

Barth, H., Beckmann, L., & Spelke, E. S. (2008). Nonsymbolic, approximate arithmetic in children: Abstract addition prior to instruction. *Developmental Psychology, 44*(5), 1466.

Bergelson, E., & Swingley, D. (2013). The acquisition of abstract words by young infants. *Cognition, 127*, 391–397.

Boaler, J., William, D., & Zevenbergen, R. (2000). *The construction of identity in secondary mathematics education.* ERIC Number: ED482654. Retrieved on April 22, 2021, from eric.ed.gov/?id=ED482654

Booth, J. L., Lange, K. E., Koedinger, K. R., & Newton, K. J. (2013). Using example problems to improve student learning in algebra: Differentiating between correct and incorrect examples. *Learning and Instruction, 25*, 24–34.

Borges, J. L. (1962/2007). *Labyrinths* (Trans. Donald A. Yates and James E. Irby). New Directions Publishing.

Bransford, J. D., Barclay, J. R., & Franks, J. J. (1972). Sentence memory: A constructive versus interpretive approach. *Cognitive Psychology, 3*(2), 193–209.

Bransford, J. D., Brown, A. L., & Cocking, R. R. (2000). *How people learn: Brain, mind, experience, and school: Expanded edition.* National Academy Press.

Brooks, R. A. (1991). Intelligence without representation. *Artificial Intelligence, 47*(1–3), 139–159.

Bruer, J. T. (1997). Education and the brain: A bridge too far. *Educational Researcher, 26*(8), 4–16.

Burgess, C., & Lund, K. (1997). Representing abstract words and emotional connotation in a high-dimensional memory space. In *Proceedings of the Cognitive Science Society* (pp. 61–66). Cognitive Science Society.

Carpenter, T. P., Hiebert, J., & Moser, J. M. (1981). Problem structure and first-grade children's initial solution processes for simple addition and subtraction problems. *Journal for Research in Mathematics Education, 12*, 27–39.

Castellanos, (2015). Retrieved April 22, 2021, from www.bizjournals.com/boston/blog/techflash/2015/09/irobots-smartest-robotic-vacuum-debuts-after-well.html

Chomsky, N. (1957/2002). *Syntactic structures.* Walter de Gruyter.

Cole, D. (2004, March 19). *The Chinese Room Argument.* Stanford Encyclopedia of Philosophy. Retrieved from https://plato.stanford.edu/entries/chinese-room/

Crawford, M. B. (2009). *Shop class as soulcraft: An inquiry into the value of work.* Penguin.

Cummins, R. (1990). *Meaning and mental representation.* MIT Press.

Davenport, J. L., Kao, Y. S., Matlen, B. J., & Schneider, S. A. (2019). Cognition research in practice: Engineering and evaluating a middle school math curriculum. *The Journal of Experimental Education, 88*, 1–20.

Dehaene, S., Spelke, E., Pinel, P., Stanescu, R., & Tsivkin, S. (1999). Sources of mathematical thinking: Behavioral and brain-imaging evidence. *Science, 284*(5416), 970–974.

Descartes, R., & Cottingham, J. (1986). *Meditations on first philosophy: With selections from the objections and replies.* Cambridge University Press.

Descartes, R., & Gröber, G. (1637/1905). *Discours de la méthode: 1637.* Heitz.

Dewey, J. (2013). *The school and society and the child and the curriculum.* University of Chicago Press.

Dienes, Z., Altmann, G., Kwan, L., & Goode, A. (1995). Unconscious knowledge of artificial grammars is applied strategically. *Journal of Experimental Psychology: Learning, Memory, and Cognition, 21*(5), 1322.

Duncker, K., & Lees, L. S. (1945). On problem-solving. *Psychological Monographs, 58*(5), i.

Dunlosky, J., Rawson, K. A., Marsh, E. J., Nathan, M. J., & Willingham, D. T. (2013). Improving students' learning with effective learning techniques: Promising directions from cognitive and educational psychology. *Psychological Science in the Public Interest, 14*(1), 4–58.

Ericsson, K. A., & Simon, H. A. (1993). *Protocol analysis: Verbal reports as data.* MIT Press.

Festinger, L. (1957). *A theory of cognitive dissonance.* Stanford University Press.

Fodor, J. A. (1987). *Psychosemantics: The problem of meaning in the philosophy of mind* (Vol. 2). MIT Press.

Fraser, S. (Ed.). (2008). *The bell curve wars: Race, intelligence, and the future of America.* Basic Books.

French, A., & Nathan, M. J. (2006). Under the microscope of research and into the classroom: Reflections on early algebra learning and instruction. In J. O. Masingila (Ed.), *Teachers engaged in research* (pp. 49–68). Information Age Publishing.

Gardner, H. (1987). *The mind's new science: A history of the cognitive revolution.* Basic Books.

Gee, J. P. (2004). *Situated language and learning: A critique of traditional schooling.* Psychology Press.

Gibson, J. J. (1977). The theory of affordances. In R. E. Shaw & J. Bransford (Eds.), *Perceiving, acting, and knowing.* Lawrence Erlbaum.

Gibson, J. J. (1979). *The Ecological Approach to Visual Perception.* Houghton Mifflin.

Glenberg, A. M. (1997). What memory is for. *Behavioral and Brain Sciences, 20*(1), 1–19.

Glenberg, A. M., De Vega, M., & Graesser, A. C. (2008). Framing the debate. In M. DeVega, A. M. Glenberg, & A. C. Graesser, (Eds.), *Symbols and embodiment:* Debates on meaning and cognition. Oxford University Press.

Glenberg, A. M., Gutierrez, T., Levin, J. R., Japuntich, S., & Kaschak, M. P. (2004). Activity and imagined activity can enhance young children's reading comprehension. *Journal of Educational Psychology, 96*(3), 424.

Glenberg, A., & Mehta, S. (2008). The limits of covariation. In de Vega, M., Glenberg, A. M., & Graesser, A. C. (Eds.), *Symbols and embodiment: Debates on meaning and cognition* (pp. 11–32). Oxford University Press.

Glenberg, A. M., & Robertson, D. A. (2000). Symbol grounding and meaning: A comparison of high-dimensional and embodied theories of meaning. *Journal of Memory and Language, 43*(3), 379–401.

Goldin-Meadow, S. (2015). Gesture as a window onto communicative abilities: Implications for diagnosis and intervention. *Perspectives on Language Learning and Education, 22*, 50–60.

Goldstone, R. L., Landy, D., & Son, J. Y. (2008). A well-grounded education: The role of perception in science and mathematics. In M. de Vega, A. M. Glenberg, & A. C. Graesser (Eds.), *Symbols and embodiment: Debates on meaning and cognition* (pp. 327–355). Oxford University Press.

Gould, S. J. (1996). *The mismeasure of man.* Norton.

Gomez, R. L., & Gerken, L. (1999). Artificial grammar learning by 1-year-olds leads to specific and abstract knowledge. *Cognition, 70*(2), 109–135.

Graesser, A. C. (2009). Inaugural editorial for Journal of Educational Psychology [Editorial]. *Journal of Educational Psychology, 101*(2), 259–261. https://doi.org/10.1037/a0014883

Harnad, S. (1990). The symbol grounding problem. *Physica D: Nonlinear Phenomena, 42*(1–3), 335–346.

Hattie, J. A. (2009). *Visible learning: A synthesis of over 800 meta-analyses relating to achievement.* Routledge.

Inhelder, B., & Piaget, J. (1958). *The growth of logical thinking from childhood to adolescence: An essay on the construction of formal operational structures* (Vol. 22). Psychology Press.

Just, M. A., & Carpenter, P. A. (1976). The role of eye-fixation research in cognitive psychology. *Behavior Research Methods & Instrumentation, 8*(2), 139–143.

Koedinger, K. R., Alibali, M. W., & Nathan, M. J. (2008). Trade-offs between grounded and abstract representations: Evidence from algebra problem solving. *Cognitive Science, 32*(2), 366–397.

Koedinger, K. R., & Nathan, M. J. (2004). The real story behind story problems: Effects of representations on quantitative reasoning. *The Journal of the Learning Sciences, 13*(2), 129–164.

Korthagen, F. A., & Kessels, J. P. (1999). Linking theory and practice: Changing the pedagogy of teacher education. *Educational Researcher, 28*(4), 4–17.

Landauer, T. K., & Dumais, S. T. (1997). A solution to Plato's problem: The latent semantic analysis theory of acquisition, induction, and representation of knowledge. *Psychological Review, 104*(2), 211.

Lappan, G., Friel, S., Fey, J., & Phillips, E. D. (2009). *Connected mathematics project 2: Grade 6.* Key Curriculum Press.

Latour, B. (1987). *Science in action: How to follow scientists and engineers through society.* Open University Press.

Laurillard, D. (2013). *Rethinking university teaching: A conversational framework for the effective use of learning technologies.* Routledge.

Macedonia, M. (2019). Embodied learning: Why at school the mind needs the body. *Frontiers in Psychology, 10*, 2098.

Martin, T. (2009). A theory of physically distributed learning: How external environments and internal states interact in mathematics learning. *Child Development Perspectives, 3*(3), 140–144.

MATHS DANCE (2018). www.mathsdance.com/ [Website].

McClelland, J. L., & Rumelhart, D. E. (1981). An interactive activation model of context effects in letter perception: I. An account of basic findings. *Psychological Review, 88*(5), 375.

Miller, G. A. (1956). The magical number seven, plus or minus two: Some limits on our capacity for processing information. *Psychological Review, 63*(2), 81.

Nathan, M. J. (2008). An embodied cognition perspective on symbols, grounding, and instructional gesture. In M. DeVega, A. M. Glenberg, & A. C. Graesser (Eds.) *Symbols, embodiment and meaning: Debates on meaning and cognition* (pp. 375–396). Oxford University Press.

Nathan, M. J. (2012). Rethinking formalisms in formal education. *Educational Psychologist, 47*(2), 125–148. doi:10.1080/00461520.2012.667063.

Nathan, M. J., & Kim, S. (2007). Pattern generalization with graphs and words: A cross-sectional and longitudinal analysis of middle school students' representational fluency. *Mathematical Thinking and Learning, 9*(3), 193–219.

Nathan, M. J., & Kim, S. (2009). Regulation of teacher elicitations in the mathematics classroom. *Cognition and Instruction, 27*(2), 91–120.

Nathan, M. J., Rittle-Johnson, B., & Fyfe, E. (2016). *Translational research at the intersection of cognitive science and education.* White paper written for the James S. McDonnell Foundation. Retrieved from www.jsmf.org/apply/teachers-as-learners/Executive_Summary_of_JSMF_Education_Panel.pdf

Nathan, M. J., Stephens, A. C., Masarik, D. K., Alibali, M. W., & Koedinger, K. R. (2002). Representational fluency in middle school: A classroom study. *Proceedings of the Twenty-Fourth Annual Meeting of the North American Chapter of the International Group for the Psychology of Mathematics Education* (Vol. 1, pp. 462–472). ERIC Clearinghouse for Science, Mathematics and Environmental Education.

Nathan, M. J., & Swart, M. I. (2020). Materialistic epistemology lends design wings: Educational design as an embodied process [Special issue]. *Educational Technology Research and Development*, 1–30. doi.org/10.1007/s11423-020-09856-4

Newell, A., Shaw, J. C., & Simon, H. A. (1956). *Problem solving in humans and computers* (No. P987). RAND Corp.

Newell, A., & Simon, H. A. (1972). *Human problem solving.* Prentice-Hall.

Nisbett, R. E., & Wilson, T. D. (1977). Telling more than we can know: Verbal reports on mental processes. *Psychological Review, 84*(3), 231.

Norman, D. A. (1999). Affordances, conventions, and design. *Interactions, 6*(3), 38–41.

Norman, K. L. (2017). *Cyberpsychology: An introduction to human-computer interaction.* Cambridge University Press.

Pashler, H., Bain, P. M., Bottge, B. A., Graesser, A., Koedinger, K., McDaniel, M., & Metcalfe, J. (2007). Organizing instruction and study to improve student learning. IES practice guide. NCER 2007–2004. National Center for Education Research.

Pica, P., Lemer, C., Izard, V., & Dehaene, S. (2004). Exact and approximate arithmetic in an Amazonian indigene group. *Science, 306*(5695), 499–503.

Polya, G. (1945/2004). *How to solve it: A new aspect of mathematical method.* Princeton University Press.

Popper, K. (1945/2012). *The open society and its enemies.* Routledge.

Porter, A. C. (2004). Curriculum assessment. In J. C. Green, G. Camill, & P. B. Elmore (Eds.), *Complementary methods for research in education* (3rd edition). American Educational Research Association.

Pulvermüller, F. (2005). Brain mechanisms linking language and action. *Nature Reviews Neuroscience, 6*(7), 576–582.

Pulvermüller, F. (2008). Grounding language in the brain. In M. DeVega, A, M. Glenberg, & A. C. Graesser (Eds.), *Symbols, embodiment and meaning: A debate* (pp. xx). Oxford University Press.

Pylyshyn, Z. W. (1984). *Computation and cognition.* MIT Press.

Resnick, L. B., & Science National Research Council (US). Committee on Research in Mathematics. (1987). *Education and learning to think* (Vol. 12). National Academy Press.

Rogers, T. T., Lambon Ralph, M. A., Garrard, P., Bozeat, S., McClelland, J. L., Hodges, J. R., & Patterson, K. (2004). Structure and deterioration of semantic memory: A neuropsychological and computational investigation. *Psychological Review, 111*(1), 205.

Rogers, T. T., & McClelland, J. L. (2004). *Semantic cognition: A parallel distributed processing approach.* MIT Press.

Rose, M. (2005). *The mind at work: Valuing the intelligence of the American worker.* Penguin.

Roy, D. (2005). Grounding words in perception and action: Computational insights. *Trends in Cognitive Sciences, 9*, 389–396.

Russell, B. (1921). *The analysis of mind.* Routledge.

Schooler, J. W., & Engstler-Schooler, T. Y. (1990). Verbal overshadowing of visual memories: Some things are better left unsaid. *Cognitive Psychology, 22*(1), 36–71.

Searle, J. R. (1980). Minds, brains, and programs. *Behavioral and Brain Sciences, 3*(3), 417–424.

Searle, J. R. (1990). Is the brain's mind a computer program? *Scientific American, 262*, 26–31.

Searle, J. (1999). The Chinese room. In R. A. Wilson & F. Keil (Eds.), *The MIT encyclopedia of the cognitive sciences* (pp. 115–116). MIT Press.

Shapiro, L. (2019). *Embodied cognition* (2nd ed.). Routledge.

Siegler, R. S. (1976). Three aspects of cognitive development. *Cognitive Psychology, 8*(4), 481–520.

Simon, H. A. (1956). Rational choice and the structure of the environment. *Psychological Review, 63*(2), 129.

Simon, H. A. (1996). The science of design: creating the artificial. In H. A. Simon (Ed.), *The Sciences of the Artificial* (pp. 111–138). MIT Press.

ter Hark, M. (1994). Cognitive science, propositional attitudes and the debate between Russell and Wittgenstein. In U. Wessels & G. Meggle (Eds.), Analyomen / analyomen. *Proceedings of the 1st Conference "Perspectives in Analytical Philosophy"* (pp. 612–617). De Gruyter.

Whitehead, A. N. (1967). *Aims of education.* Simon and Schuster.

Woolgar, S., & Latour, B. (1986). *Laboratory life: The construction of scientific facts.* Princeton University Press.

2

Why We Need Grounded and Embodied Learning to Improve Education

I noted reasons to challenge the ideas that cognition is computation on AAA symbols. Still, an important idea from this program of research must be carried forward. Through an ingenious set of analyses across a variety of studies of many different processing modes, the early Cognitive Psychologist George Miller (1956) identified a universal, if imprecise, limitation. **The cognitive processes of which we are most aware are serial processes with very limited channel capacity**.

Miller pegged the limit at *around seven* items that people can meaningfully attend to without completely breaking down. Bowing to the natural variability of both biological and psychological processes, he offered this imprecision as "the magical number seven, plus or minus two." Humans can reliably maintain a list of about seven items in memory, but cannot take on much else in the process. These can be seven or so grocery items, numbers of someone's phone, letters of an unfamiliar name. If people are interrupted with a pressing question, or need to suddenly make a detour in one's car, some of those seven (most often the middle ones in a list) will be lost.

This was accompanied by another important insight. What constituted an "item" was also variable. For a runner, a single "item" could be a string of numbers that make up a common running time (Chase & Ericsson, 1982). For a chess master, a single item might be a familiar opening that specifies the location of 32 pieces on the board. For an actor, one item might be a well-rehearsed soliloquy. All these groupings look quite different, but they have one important thing in common: The parts of each item belong together to the actor—**together, they *make sense*.**

With this boundless range of allowable choices, Miller realized these units of mental processing could not each be properly called an item, or a bit, and so he called each one a *chunk*. The prior knowledge of each person establishes what constitutes a chunk. However big or small the chunk seemed to the outside observer, they felt like one thing to the actor. Once a chunk was set by the person, the ability to attend to, processes, and report on the number of such chunks was brutally enforced.

The implications of this variable and highly limited cognitive capacity are enormous. People are easily overwhelmed and prone to making errors as a result of these limitations. People will also go to great pains to manage their resources when they are near (or past!) this limit, such as reaching for a pen, clearing a workspace, removing auditory and visual distractions. For example, driving on a straight highway during the day in pleasant weather, I can be easily conversing with a car passenger, music blaring, the vehicle hurtling at 60 miles per hour. As I approach a highway exit, however, when I must discern my destination among

DOI: 10.4324/9780429329098-2

the many signs and turn lanes, and make time-critical decisions, the conversation stops, the radio goes off, there is greater stress.

As I review a range of research findings and educational designs, the capacity limited nature of cognition should be front and center for the reader. That is, if you can keep all this in mind ☺.

2.1 THE PATH FORWARD

Earlier, I presented two major obstacles to achieving the type of educational systems that prioritize learning. Each of these obstacles is well entrenched, based on assumptions about the nature of knowledge, learning, and learning research that I will challenge in the coming pages. Here I want to show how learning and education is viewed matters. There is indeed a path forward to substantially improve the educational experiences for students and teachers, one that draws on the natural capabilities and resources of embodied learning that all people possess. To this end, I offer the **Grounded and Embodied Learning Thesis:** Thinking and instruction rely on body-based processes for learning to be meaningful. This thesis is a new paradigm for education because it focuses on aspects of learning and instruction that are often neglected. As the evidence emerges, I believe it shows the potential for an entirely new approach for designing educational experiences.

2.1.1 Design Educational Experiences with Meaning Making in Mind

The first obstacle to overcome shows some of the ways that education systems are misguided by outdated views that create an unnatural and unnecessary division between the body and the mind. This ancient idea falls apart under scrutiny, as will be shown with a vast array of empirical research. The form this division takes in education is characterized by a *Formalisms First* perspective, a view that students cannot successfully apply knowledge without first learning the formal, decontextualized ideas that experts use to describe that knowledge (Nathan, 2012; Sherman et al., 2016).

Education from an embodied learning perspective rejects this notion. It highlights the ways that direct experiences are meaningful to learners, while learners struggle to make meaning from formal descriptions of those experiences. Embodied learning offers an organized framework to replace *Formalisms First* views of learning and teaching by first demonstrating that it is usually the formalisms, rather than the ideas that those formalisms depict, that students most struggle with. This is needed because it is so difficult for learners, during their early stages of conceptual development, to derive meaning when formalisms are not inherently grounded in meaningful objects or actions.

In contrast, students can engage with many ideas through the movements and perceptions from which those ideas arise. When, for example, science ideas can be built through experiences, language can be used for personal expression, history used to tell one's stories, and mathematics to solve problems and model phenomena, then these ideas—however novel or complicated—are grounded for learners. When they are grounded, their meaning is well within reach, and learning follows in short order. The first step on this path to move forward from the system that people currently have is to reframe schooling as a process of meaning making through people's natural propensity to interact, experience, perceive, do, and imagine.

Learning to use and produce formalisms is a vitally important skill because of their value for representing ideas, patterns, and relationships that people already understand, and for participating in disciplinary discourse. The formalisms serve us. Graphs, for example, emerge in order to facilitate shared goals in collaborative projects and to communicate with one's collaborators. The axes, labels, points and trend lines are useful because they help visually depict measures and patterns that are meaningful. Here, I do not question the value of formalisms, or their utility, rather I am critical of when, developmentally—that is, where, along a learning trajectory—formalisms provide the greatest educational benefit.

Framing **education as the engineering of experiences for grounded and embodied learning** positions primary experiences ahead of secondary experiences. Following this literally inverts many educational practices. Susan Gerofsky (2011, 2018) has shown, for example, how students naturally perform the relations of a variety of mathematical functions that are graphically presented through finger, hand, and whole-body movements. Gerofsky observes how students' body engagements take on both the qualities of one "observing" the graph, and of depicting its shape, to "being" the graph, and embodying the functions.

Scientific theories are another type of formalism that can be a barrier to meaning and learning. Theories, it must be noted, are significant intellectual achievements of a community that allows scholars to descriptively summarize many findings and highlight underlying commonalities. This can lead to deeper explanation of phenomena, and emerging models that support predictions and experimental designs. Scientific theories achieve these lofty aims for students when the theories are themselves grounded for the learner by linking them to embodied experiences, and memories and simulations of past embodied experiences. When the theories remain ungrounded, they are empty phrases and relations, with meaning that only exists internal to itself.

Niebert and colleagues (2012) provide a careful analysis of how scientific theories are so often taught using examples, analogies, and conceptual metaphors. Conceptual metaphors are a powerful way to provide grounding for unfamiliar concepts and complicated theories. We will examine the scholarship on conceptual metaphor in greater detail later in this book. For now, Niebert and colleagues (2012) reviewed and re-analyzed findings across multiple studies that cumulatively identified 199 educational uses of conceptual metaphors and analogies as expressed in the science education literature. They looked at instances of using conceptual metaphors such as THE ATMOSPHERE IS A CONTAINER in lessons expressing relations on climate science, as in *The atmosphere is a greenhouse* and *Look at radiation coming in and going out of the atmosphere*.

Their analysis explores why these instructional approaches so often fall short and fail to achieve proper scientific understanding by students. In some of these failures, the metaphors do not conform to students' embodied experiences. For example, using a school dance may seem like an appropriate context to ground the concept of chemical equilibrium as a result of a dynamic process, rather than the naïve view of equilibrium as static. However, the metaphor failed to register when the source domain of the metaphor required that students attending the dance are blindfolded as they rapidly form couples and uncouple themselves. This, the authors suggest, is a metaphor that "is constructed and not embodied." As another example, a common metaphor used in biology, DNA AS A CODE, tends to be unsuccessful because students' grounded notion of CODE as a series of numbers hiding information is different than the notion of a program.

Now, it is worthwhile to step back and acknowledge that there is a great deal of artistry involved in making the appropriate conceptual metaphor selection and effectively applying the pedagogical tactics to establish for students the metaphorical mapping between source domain (e.g., container) and target domain (e.g., atmosphere). Ball (1993), for example, shares her own thinking as a teacher of early math, and in doing so, helps to reveal the complications involved in doing this well. Niebert and colleagues' (2012) review of science education practices underscores that how effective a metaphor proves to be for fostering meaning making and learning hinges on the degree to which it invokes an embodied grounding experience for the learner.

Mathematical notations are another common formalism used in schools, and rightly so. Mathematical notations, such as formulas, emerge to present ideas in forms that are concise, standardized for members of a discipline, and with reduced ambiguity among experienced mathematicians and scientists. Notation and mathematical equations can also expose shared relations that might not be obvious at first. In short, mathematical notations serve a very important role in education. However, they also serve as barriers to understanding for new learners. That is, students may actually be able to demonstrate their understanding of a concept, but fail to do so because of challenges of the notational systems that are being used to represent that concept. Examples abound (e.g., Koedinger & Nathan, 2004). An intriguing one is presented in McNeil et al. (2010).

> Cakes cost c dollars each and brownies cost b dollars each. Suppose I buy 4 cakes and 3 brownies. What does $4c + 3b$ stand for?

Students often misinterpret the expression in ways that seem to be fueled by their common understanding of what literal symbols *mean*. In this case, the confusion, as described initially by Küchemann (1978), is that students often interpret literal symbols (the b and c) in algebraic expressions incorrectly—stubbornly—as *labels* (i.e., as *a cake*, or *brownie*) rather than as quantities (*cost-of-each-cake, cost-of-each-brownie*). In such cases, the mathematical notation proves to be a formidable obstacle to students' mathematical reasoning. By raising these issues about learning mathematical notions I am in no way advocating that we rid ourselves of them. In fact, I am invested in students' success and facility with them as part of their path to successful education.

Like hammers and CAD/CAM systems, formalisms are vital tools. I believe that we will not be able to solve the major social, technological, and scientific problems of the world without them! My point is rather that to ensure success with using symbols, theories, graphs, and the myriad other formalisms infused throughout the disciplines, formalisms must be *meaningful*. Often, this entails a developmental process that supports grounding these formalisms in embodied and familiar experiences. Otherwise, the ungrounded notations and theories act not as gateways to understanding, but as gatekeepers (Ladson-Billings, 1997) that keep some students out and admit others based on their access to privileged knowledge rather than based on their conceptual understanding.

2.1.2 Employ Instructional Approaches for Grounded and Embodied Learning

Over the course of this book, I will introduce several approaches that share developmental approaches that favor starting with experiences and, only later, relating those ideas to formal systems of notation. One that has been around for a while, but is gaining prominence, is concreteness fading. *Concreteness fading* (Bruner, 1966; Fyfe et al., 2015; Fyfe & Nathan, 2019) is a theory of instruction that fosters understanding of powerful, abstract ideas. It does this by guiding learners through a progression in which the formalisms become grounded over time because they are linked explicitly to their concrete and meaningful referents.

For example, Fyfe and colleagues (2015) used sequences like those in Figure 2.1 to foster understanding of arithmetic equations. In that study, elementary grade students first experienced a physical form of the equivalency relations (on the far left of the figure) that were the focus of the learning episode. This concrete version of the equivalence relation was then related to an *iconic* form, which is somewhat *less concrete*; that is, the level of physicality

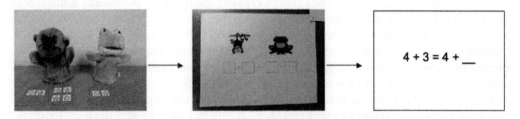

FIGURE 2.1 The ideal 3-part sequence used for concreteness fading.
Left frame shows the most concrete, physical form of the equivalency relations. Middle frame shows less concrete form that uses icons. Right frame shows the symbolic form. The ideal concreteness fading instruction approach presents the learner with the most concrete form, then the iconic form, and then the symbolic form.

and perceptual richness was faded as children were directed from the first physical version to the second iconic version (middle frame of Figure 2.1).

The explicit nature of the mapping from the physical instantiation to the iconic instantiation is a key feature of the instructional approach, because this helps to shift the meaning from the concrete and embodied form so that it carries over to the slightly more idealized form. The next step is to strip away much of the perceptual and physical properties and provide a fully *symbolic* instantiation—a formalism. This time, it is explicitly connected for the learner to the iconic version that preceded it. The hypothesis is that the final form, in all its formal glory, now stands as a *grounded formalism* imbued with all of the meaning that the learner experienced from the initial stage and throughout the progression. Indeed, empirical studies show that children (Butler et al., 2003; Fyfe et al., 2015; Miller & Hudson, 2007) and adults (Braithwaite & Goldstone, 2013; Goldstone & Son, 2005) showed greater learning gains of formalisms when the formalisms were grounded using some form of concreteness fading.

Other instructional principles have been put forth by teacher educators working in embodied cognition research. Several scholars (Abrahamson et al, 2020; Lindgren & Johnson-Glenberg, 2013; Johnson-Glenberg, 2019; Smith & Walkington, 2019) offer some general principles for embodied learning that are empirically supported. These have been used with students in classrooms and classroom-like research settings, so they meet some basic criteria of ecological validity.

One overarching principle is that the educational opportunities of embodied learning must be equitably available to all learners, regardless of their own or others' assessment of their learning preferences (Lindgren & Johnson-Glenberg, 2013). Unfortunately, learners often do not accurately predict the learning methods that are most effective for them (Dunlosky et al., 2013). Instructional accommodations will be necessary for those differently abled, just as teachers develop differentiated instruction for any heterogeneous group of learners. One principle states, the movement of learners should be meaningful and relevant to the learning objectives (Lindgren & Johnson-Glenberg, 2013; Smith & Walkington, 2019). This is commensurate with the importance of using task-relevant actions as described earlier.

Another principle prescribes that learners progressively move from the concrete to the abstract to build connections between a grounded form of a concept and increasingly formal ways of displaying that concept (Smith & Walkington, 2019). This, too, supports my earlier discussion of approaches such as concreteness fading that emphasize the early role of embodied experiences for grounding new ideas, and the progression to generalizations and abstractions that are vital for more advanced forms of modeling and analysis

The principle to make use of one's body's capacity for dynamic movement underscores that people's bodies do not just have a physical existence but also a dynamic one, with which people can readily experience change and interactions (Abrahamson et al., 2020; Smith & Walkington, 2019). The dynamics of change is important for thinking about time- and shape-varying phenomena and for exploring generalized truths, as when a relation is thought to apply to *all* of some class of objects, such as *all quadrilaterals*.

Embodied learning also demands that we rethink assessment practices, both formative and summative assessments (Abrahamson et al, 2020; Lindgren & Johnson-Glenberg, 2013). For example, students may convey knowledge through gestures that they cannot express in words. There are also ways that testing situations that interfere with students' motor movement will underestimate students' true knowledge. For example, in assessing science knowledge, the demands of typing during online testing inhibit gestures and impair test performance (Nathan & Martinez, 2015). Knowledge developed in action-based learning is particularly apt to be displayed through movement, raising concerns of the appropriateness of traditional testing. Once there is acknowledgment that knowledge is embodied and nonverbal, *as well as* verbally encoded, it should be apparent that students are being shortchanged if their nonverbal forms of understanding are neglected or interfered with.

Finally, scholars who study education in authentic settings acknowledge the importance for embodied learning opportunities to incorporate collaboration. Collaboration taps into people's natural drive to be social, to use gestures, representations, and metaphors to establish common ground with others, and to interact in ways that elicit meaningful, goal-directed movements that contribute to communication, comprehension, reasoning, and learning. Collaboration also invites people to explore multiple perspectives, which can increase their awareness and insights. Further, people often use interactions with others to extend their cognitive resources. Examples include behaviors such as incorporating others' bodies into depictions of complicated sequences of events or relations, and as external memory registers in order to carry out complicated action sequences.

An important part of carving a path forward is to recognize the central role of teachers in effective learning environments. Teachers may act in ways that are not aligned with research findings because of their pre-existing beliefs about learning. This provides an excellent opportunity for improvement, as these findings from research are shared with teachers. As noted, however, the ideas are going to be most impactful for education when they are packaged in actionable forms for teachers so they may use them during classroom instruction. Teachers operating with Formalisms First views of learning and teaching must have these views challenged. That is most formidable when Formalisms First is a result of the teacher's own expert blind spot (Nathan & Petrosino, 2003). This means that teacher education and professional development programs need to directly challenge and replace these views.

Although many teachers produce gestures, and do so often, teachers can also benefit from explicit training in the effective use of instructional gestures (Alibali & Nathan, 2012). One way is to alert teachers to the ways that pointing gestures enhance student learning by directing learners' attention, making connections, and grounding formalisms. Another way is to reveal how powerful representational gestures are for invoking simulations of movement and perception that are so important for imagery and language. Metaphorical gestures also enhance instruction because they invoke conceptual metaphors for important grounding domains such as space and time that allow learners to connect prior experiences to new and abstract ideas.

2.1.3 Bridging Research and Educational Practice: The View from the Other Side of the Divide

The second obstacle to overcome shows that the objects of study in the neuroscience and cognitive psychology often do not map onto the malleable factors of the educational system, such as classroom learning and instruction. Earlier, I offered my agreement with Bruer's (1997) argument that the steps from neuroscience to education is a bridge too far. I critiqued Bruer's proposal to span the neuroscience-education gap by building an intermediate bridge to cognitive psychology, because this, too, seems to me to still be a "bridge too far."

In proposing a way forward from the perspective of embodied learning, I suggest that these efforts fall short because they advocate building the bridges in the wrong direction. It seems to be Formalisms First applied to the level of science policy (Stokes, 2011). The premise seems to be that the science can drive the practices; that the application of general principles of learning derived from rigorous empirical investigations and modeling will inform the educational changes needed to promote learning. I am aware that the choice of which field one starts with—that is, which is *primary*—also sets up which behaviors are perceived as normative, and which are seen as deviant. The central translational goal of the study of learning behaviors is to improve *education* because of its tremendous social benefit. This makes it problematic if the observed educational behaviors are at risk of being subordinated to the theoretical constructs related to cognitive psychology.

I contend that **to achieve the translational goals, the bridge needs to be built starting from education and leading to—and then back from—the behavioral sciences.** This process is likely to be more fruitful for both education and for cognitive psychology and neuroscience. Building bridges in this way is the central concern of scale-down. *Scale-down methodology* (Nathan & Alibali, 2010; Nathan & Sawyer, 2014) focuses primarily on the authentic learning contexts in which learning takes place to identify rich practices as candidates for bringing educational innovation and improvement to scale.

Scale-down methodology is a broad framework that encompasses work on design-based systemic reform (e.g., McDonald, Keesler, Kauffman, & Schneider, 2006; Penuel et al., 2011). Scale-down is offered as an alternative to "scale-up" approaches that have traditionally been defined in terms of the breadth of dissemination and level of fidelity of an innovation (Glennan et al., 2004). In cognitive science, scale-up approaches tend to start with the successful study of learning phenomena investigated in contrived, carefully controlled settings. Broader interventions are then designed to reproduce the effects in their natural settings. Successful application of research-based interventions from laboratory to classrooms are rare, as many contextual intrusions that fall outside of the original investigations serve as barriers for successful translation to authentic learning settings (Penuel et al., 2011).

Research on systemic reform suggests that effective reform must conform to the constraints of the local learning environments. For example, the specific behaviors and knowledge of educational practitioners are critical for implementing any research-based innovations (Dede, 2006; McDonald et al., 2006; Rao & Sutton, 2014). To be responsive, scale-down methodology flips the traditional scale-up approach on its head. It begins by studying learning from a systemic perspective, examining the learning environment in the rich, cultural context in which it naturally occurs (e.g., a classroom). This is what I mean when I suggest that building the bridge starting at education recasts the entire enterprise.

Analysis of these system-level observations informs the generation of hypotheses for how to improve overall system performance by identifying potential subsystems that impact system performance. These subsystems are carefully described so that they capture the local cultural contexts present in the original learning environment, such as participant demographics and knowledge, environmental resources, teacher knowledge, beliefs and practices, and so on.

In the next phase of scale-down, analytic methods suitable for making causal inferences, such as those from cognitive psychology and neuroscience are applied to reveal malleable factors that affect contextually and culturally authentic learning and teaching performance. Here is where the bridge from education arrives to the behavioral sciences, delivering information about authentic learning experiences that can be further analyzed and redescribed in theoretical terms, and then designed as proposed innovations for scale-up. So we cross back over the bridge to education in order to see if the new designs benefit learners and teachers. A critical aspect of this process is that the new practices must be designed as to integrated back into the original learning environment. This, again, relies heavily on effective partnerships with teachers who, with their students, must take up these new practices. These practices are then observed in an expanded set of authentic learning settings.

Reciprocal Teaching appears to be a quintessential example of successful scale-down methodology (Palincsar & Brown, 1984). The behaviors of successful readers were observed *in situ* and isolated over the course of many studies. These practices were redescribed in terms of theoretical constructs of reading comprehension and metacognition, which were studied, again, in many research projects. With the assurances that these practices were causally beneficial for reading to learn, they were artfully repackaged as a scalable set of curricular activities involving students' roles in peer reading groups, and then studied in the authentic classroom settings (Rosenshine & Meister, 1994).

Embodied learning and instruction have tremendous potential to transform students' educational experiences and lead to experiences that are more deeply understood and better-connected to meaningful and familiar ideas. As ideas of grounded and embodied learning are embraced and appear more often in classrooms, in curricula, instruction, and assessments, the broad range of educational practices will need to adapt. Educational policies regarding inclusiveness, effective curriculum standards, teacher preparation, assessment, and even the nature of classroom design and class size are likely to come under scrutiny. This is because the central pillars of our educational system are still largely crafted out of views of learning and learners that treat students as disembodied minds. Next, I lay out the theoretical underpinnings of embodied learning.

2.1.4 Issues of Equity and Inclusion

Cognitive psychology, along with its close cousin, cognitive science, has one other glaring deficiency for informing educational practices and policies. Throughout its history, cognitive psychology has done little to theorize about social equity and inclusion. Yet, the education community identifies social inequities as a major obstacle to achieving the goals of education and economic prosperity (Apple, 2009; Ladson-Billings & Tate, 2006). Only a small number of cognitive psychology scholars have identified ways that cultural stereotypes have a negative effect on motivation, performance, and participation in some academic pursuits.

For example, there is acknowledgment that sex stereotypes favoring boys engaged in STEM activities has a negative and persistent effect on girls' low interests and negative attitudes towards STEM education, despite girls being equally competent at it (Hyde et al., 2008). Influences such as sociocultural stereotypes and different self-concepts around STEM-related activities are largely relegated to social and "nonacademic" factors (Cheryan et al., 2017; Master & Meltzoff, 2016). However, cognitive psychology studies that address systemic racial biases and inequities in academic settings are practically absent, framed largely as social psychology that falls outside of its individualist scope. This neglect of issues of race on cognition further limits the ways that cognitive psychology can meaningfully inform education.

One notable exception is the treatment of racial disparities in IQ testing. Authors Herrnstein and Murray (1994/2010) authored a sociological analysis of persistent disparities in intelligence test scores called *The Bell Curve: Intelligence and Class Structure in American Life*. They argued that there are measurable and reliable differences between the intelligence measurements (i.e., IQ) of different groups of people in America, and these differences largely determine a group's collective quality of life. For example, one's level of intelligence dictates someone's eventual class level, income, time frame of pregnancy, crime rate, etc. The authors argued that these differences are heritable, and they are widening. In framing this as heritable they are making an important—and intellectually suspect—argument; that the differences between low- and high-income Whites, and between Whites and Blacks, are permanent.

The title of the book comes from the bell-shaped data distribution commonly found among large populations who take the IQ test. As Figure 2.2 shows, IQ scores follow a smooth distribution with the largest number of people at the highest point of the curve (right around an IQ score of 100). The number of people trails off as we move away from the center in either direction. At the lowest end, we see those with IQ scores of 75 and below (about 5% of the population). At the highest end, with IQs above 125, we see the "brightest" 5%. By the way, the IQ test is actually *designed* to have a mean (average) of 100, and a standard deviation of 15 points, which explains why these numbers match the peak and drop-offs of the curve so precisely.

Herrnstein and Murray clearly see themselves as following the Classicist tradition of intelligence (along with Jensen, Spearman, Galton, and others). They regard intelligence

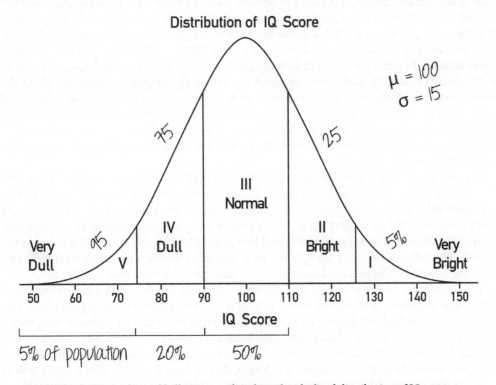

FIGURE 2.2 The traditional bell curve used to show the idealized distribution of IQ test scores on the general population. The vertical divisions show the percentages of the population that fall within each standard deviation from the mean score of 100.

as a unitary concept (psychologists refer to this concept as *G*), measurable through properly designed and administered IQ tests. They also see intelligence as a fixed entity, formed largely through inheritance, and relatively unchangeable over the course of one's lifespan. In their view intelligence (as measured in their data set by adults who took the Armed Forces Qualifications Test, which is essentially an IQ test similar to the WAIS and WISC) is determined by general knowledge and skill, rather than, say, domain-specific knowledge or metacognition. They show the statistical relationship between intelligence and a host of social measures, including social behavior, poverty, high school dropout rates, illness and injuries, illegitimacy, welfare, low birth weight, childrearing environment, and crime. Their point is that all of these social factors are worse for "low intelligence" people. And chief among these low intelligence people, they report, are Blacks.

Blacks in America, they note, typically exhibit IQ scores one full standard deviation (15 points) below those of White Americans, with a mean score of this subgroup falling at around 85. This difference between Black and White Americans persists across all levels of socioeconomic status (SES), and becomes even more pronounced at higher levels of SES.

Notably, we see that both Blacks and Whites have comparable numbers of people at the low end. This alone should dispel any notions that the social ills of society can be ascribed more to one race than another. But a larger point is that the differences at the high end are substantial. I offer only the briefest of critiques here, as there are many excellent volumes that treat this attempt to justify highly inflammatory writings about race in the name of scholarship (see Fraser, 2008; Gould, 1996).

My first critique is methodological. Herrnstein and Murray are often referenced as saying that "If you have to choose, is it better to be born smart or rich? The answer is unequivocally 'smart.'" (p. 127), with this applying to Blacks, who consistently had lower average scores than the average score for Whites. However, their investigation never showed this, because they only analyzed socioeconomic differences among Whites in their data. For example, they never showed the same pattern held among Blacks, or between Whites and Blacks. A second methodological issue is that their measures are extremely simplistic, especially given the much greater sophistication for parameters such as socioeconomic status and intellectual performance that existed at the time. They settled for a convenient and simple analysis to investigate complex social questions. When more sophisticated measures are used for SES, the results no longer support many of their main claims about intelligence superseding income (Fischer et al., 1996).

My second critique is developmental. Intellectual performance does change, and despite the authors' claims of the large role played by heritability, environment and family factors play large roles in how intelligence scores change. Even in their own data they demonstrate this by showing IQ gains that occur when people emigrate and when they are adopted, both circumstances that are not genetic and that generally raise the standard of living of the person. The authors also willfully ignore any effects of oppression on intellectual performance, including such factors as chronic stress, or educational conditions.

It is important to acknowledge that scientific methods can be applied for political and ideological purposes, and that there are scholarly ways to dispute these arguments. I also want to point out that intelligence and intelligence testing is a cognitive phenomenon, which sits squarely in the scope of cognitive psychology. However, the field has systematically skirted these politically and socially controversial issues regarding race and class in America, with only a few scholars (e.g., Bransford & Vye, n. d.; Gardner, 1995; Sternberg, 1995) willing to refute these claims. This abdication of responsibility leaves cognitive psychology unable or unwilling to address some of the central issues that educational institutions and practitioners face in its mission to educate all children.

2.2 IN DEFENSE OF A THEORY OF EMBODIED LEARNING
FOR EDUCATION

Embodied learning offers a framework for understanding thinking and learning as more than the manipulation of mental symbols. Embodied learning is an account of how people's intellectual processes necessarily rely on body-based processes and people's interactions with the material world, including how people perceive the world, move, and interact with the people and material objects within it.

2.2.1 The Philosophical Basis for a Theory of Embodied Cognition

Here I present the philosophical basis for a theory of embodied cognition as the foundation for effective educational systems. Chapters 5–10 provide the empirical basis for embodied cognition. The philosophical case for embodied cognition draws, in part, on Shapiro's (2019) three hypothetical justifications for embodied cognition: Conceptualization, Replacement, and Constitution. The three hypotheses are not intended to be mutually exclusive, so any or all of them may hold.

Conceptualization is the argument that the bodies, cultures, and languages with which people function determine the concepts people can intellectually sustain. Conceptualization has its closest parallels with linguistic determinism (Whorf, 1956). This is the position that one's image of the world is shared only by those who also share language; and, further, that one's language determines how people think and what people are able to think about.

Evidence in support of Conceptualization comes from several sectors. Members of the Pirahã tribe, who operate with a "one-two-many" system of enumeration, show degraded performance with calculations above 3 (Gordon, 2004). The *Mundurukú*, who have words for enumerating sets up to 5 (Pica et al., 2004) can accurately compare and estimate large quantities but apparently lack the ability to compute precise quantities larger than four. In industrialized societies, bilingual (Russian-English) Russian adults trained on exact sums in one language (either English or Russian) were less able to retrieve the number fact cued in the other language (DeHaene et al., 1999). Together, these studies show that Conceptualization is viable in adults as well as children, and in post-industrial cultures as it is in indigenous cultures.

Replacement holds that a system of material grounding can serve in place of some imputed mental representational system. Work by Brooks (1991) illustrates how much seemingly intelligent behavior can be accomplished without recourse to an overarching representational system that models the world and processes symbols to decide on worldly actions. Instead, Brooks's robots use a *subsumption architecture* that directly couples sensing and action, without an intervening representational model. Upon reflecting on the progress of a number of robots with this design ethos in mind, Brooks (1991) offers this conclusion to ponder:

> When we examine very simple level intelligence we find that explicit representations and models of the world simply get in the way. It turns out to be better to *use the world as its own model*.
>
> (p. 139, emphasis added)

There is also evidence that humans do this kind of thing as well. Evidence from ethnographies of the Oksapmin (Saxe, 1981, 1982), for example, demonstrate that locations on the body can serve as the basis of an ordered number system capable of supporting mathematical activity, but do not depend upon a symbol system of numerical representation. Furthermore, the body-based system can be appropriated to new systems of quantification, such as the

TABLE 2.1
Comparison of Shapiro's three hypotheses for embodied cognition

	Conceptualization	*Replacement*	*Constitution*
Description	People's bodies, cultures and languages determine the concepts that can be intellectually sustained	Material grounding can replace mental representations	The constituents of cognition include the body and environment
Example	Language for quantities affects exact numerical calculation	Robots that use the world as their own model	Gesture use can enhance self-directed learning and learning from instruction

huge cultural shift involved in adopting a monetary system, that does depend on symbolic representations.

The *Constitution* position is that the *constituents* of cognition extend beyond the brain to include the body and environment. *Constitution* posits that the body-based processes and resources for grounding cognition will both cause and actually *be* the cognitive behaviors. The Constitution Hypothesis holds that the qualities people take as cognition extend beyond the cranium and into people's bodies and the world with which people interact. For example, gestures provide such extended resources for thinking and learning. Children who were required to gesture while learning about mathematical equivalence produced solution strategies that they had not been taught and had not previously produced in either speech or gesture (Broaders, Cook, Mitchell, & Goldin-Meadow, 2007). These benefits persisted and improved their later learning during formal instruction.

Historically, cognitive science research has neglected those aspects of reasoning that are considered authentic *practices,* such as what plumbers, electricians, or chemists actually *do*, focusing instead on the mental operations involved in planning, problem solving, and decision making (e.g., Rose, 2005). Its strongest supporters are adherents of situated, extended, and distributed cognition (Brown, Collins, & Duguid, 1989; Clark & Chalmers, 1998; Cole & Engeström, 1993; Hutchins, 1995; Newen, De Bruin, & Gallagher, 2018).

Shapiro's three hypotheses—Conceptualization, Replacement, and Constitution—are briefly compared in Table 2.1. Each stands in contrast to the IPT view of cognition in several important respects. First, each proposes that cognition is not limited to the manipulation of formal symbols, but includes sensing and manipulating material things, including objects and one's own body. Second, each proposes that cognitive processes are not confined to the brain, but that thinking agents operate with an "extended mind" (Clark & Chalmers, 1998) that includes tools and cultural artifacts, external memory aids such as our smart phones, and even other people (Hutchins, 1995). Consequently, each of these conjectures offers new and exciting implications for how to design educational experiences that foster meaningful learning. Third, each involves situated interactions.

2.2.2 Educational Implications of a Theory of Embodied Cognition

Conceptualization implies that there is likely to be value in using movement and perception to achieve conceptual outcomes. This suggests we look to approaches that draw on perceptual learning (Goodwin, 1994; Kellman, Massey, & Son, 2010) and motor system engagement (Abrahamson & Sánchez-García, 2016; Nathan & Walkington, 2017) as prerequisite to conceptual learning, along with approaches that draw on the interplay between procedural and conceptual learning (Goldstone & Son, 2005; Koedinger, Corbett, & Perfetti, 2012; Rau, 2017; Rittle-Johnson & Siegler, 1998; Rittle-Johnson & Star, 2007, 2015)

The Replacement argument implies that educators can enhance one's thinking and learning by attending to the performance of the perception-action loop (Neisser, 1976). Replacement suggests a "mindful" approach of acting in the present rather than approaches that focus on linguistic labels that mediate between people's sensorimotor experiences and the phenomena of interest. The phenomenologist Martin Heidegger referred to this as the actions that are applied directly upon the world through one's state of being (*Dasein*; Dreyfus, 1991). In such circumstances, the instruments one uses seem to fade into the background and one is directly engaged, a phenomenon that Dreyfus (2002) refers to as "absorbed coping." I notice, for example, how well my writing flows when I lose track of the keyboard that is the medium of my writing, and my thoughts seem to flow through my hands directly onto the page; and they become labored once again when I fix a typo or other misstep.

The Constitution argument implies that what is included when describing *minds* can extend far beyond people's heads, and even beyond their bodies, so that one's cognitive processes are constituted by one's material and socially supported activities. Gesture production, for example, confers many educational benefits for both the speaker and the audience members (Goldin-Meadow, 2003). Constitution also highlights ways that people's understanding of cognition in many educational settings is stunted because of the historical focus on simple tasks that can be done by an individual thinking "in one's head." If education is truly to fulfill the goals of preparing children and adults to succeed on authentic tasks in a dynamic and uncertain world, then society needs to provide educational experiences in the situated activities that resemble the actual intellectual and physical behaviors that take place when performing applied and professional practices (Shaffer, 2004).

2.2.3 Does All Movement Lead to Learning? Why Evidence-Based Theory Matters

One important disclaimer needs to be stated early on: **Embodied learning does not claim that any and all movements will enhance learning**.

As I lay out arguments in support of embodied learning that call directly on the influential role that perceptual and motor systems have on cognition, I will portray a more nuanced basis for how the body supports learning and other intellectual processes. Here I wish to dispel an emerging myth that any and all movement aids learning. This is important because there is already a drive to commercialize movement-based curricula regardless of the evidence. As the adage goes, *caveat emptor*—"Let the buyer beware."

Several experimental studies offer empirical tests of the claim that all movement leads to learning. Thomas and Lleras (2007) tested the effect of performing task relevant versus task-irrelevant actions on insight problem solving. In a particularly elegant study, they engaged participants in eye movements to activate conceptual reasoning. Eye movement and foveal registration is often associated with attentional processes, such that the movement of the eye leads to a corresponding shift in attention. Participants were instructed to follow one of the five eye gaze patterns displayed in Figure 2.3. These were directed actions in that participants were instructed to look at the spot in the order that followed the number labels.

Afterwards, they were asked to solve a notoriously difficult problem-solving task, known as Duncker's (Duncker & Lees, 1945) "Radiation problem." Thomas and Lleras (2007, p. 663) posed this version:

> Given a human being with an inoperable stomach tumor, and lasers which destroy organic tissue at sufficient intensity, how can one cure the person with these lasers and, at the same time, avoid harming the healthy tissue that surrounds the tumor?

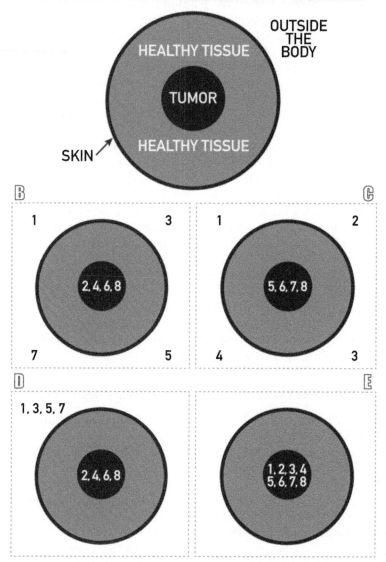

FIGURE 2.3 Participants were instructed to follow one of the five eye gaze patterns, as shown,
by following the numerical orders prior to solving Duncker's (1945) radiation problem.
Box A provides the legend for the experimental conditions B-E. Pattern B follows the embodied-
solution group by directing participants to cross a barrier line successively from multiple entry
points. Pattern C circles outside the skin, then the inside, near the tumor. Pattern D crosses
back and forth across the skin barrier without convergence. Patterns E continually gazes at
the tumor at the center.

In the preferred solution one avoids using high-intensity laser beams because it kills
healthy tissue and puts the patient at too much risk. Instead, one uses low-intensity laser
beams from multiple angles that converge at the tumor for a deadly cumulative effect
while having minimal impact on the surrounding tissue. Pattern B follows the embodied

solution by directing participants to experience visually crossing a barrier line successively from multiple entry points, enacting the convergence pattern. Group B was subsequently shown to be the most successful group at solving Duncker's radiation problem, both in terms of generating the most correct solutions and producing that correct solution in the fewest trials.

This study showed that even eye movements can help with complex cognitive processes. It also demonstrates the importance of the specificity of task-relevant actions for supporting the appropriate cognitive processes. Comparable task-irrelevant movements of the eyes, such as those shown in Patterns C and D in Figure 2.3 were not as effective in helping the solution process.

Nathan and colleagues (2014) illustrate another example of the importance of task-relevant movement for reasoning. They invited learners (N = 120) to perform directed arm motions prior to reasoning about mathematical statements. Some participants performed directed actions that were relevant to a geometry conjecture on triangles and a conjecture about gears. The conjectures are shown here:

Triangle Inequality Conjecture

Mary came up with the following conjecture: For any triangle, the sum of the lengths of any two sides must be greater than the length of the remaining side. Provide a justification as to why Mary's conjecture is true or false.

Gear Parity Conjecture

An unknown number of gears are connected in a chain. You know what direction the first gear turns, how could you figure out what direction the last gear turns? Provide a justification as to why your answer is true.

While one group performed a set of task-relevant directed actions for each conjecture, the other participants performed directed actions that were equated in the complexity of movements but that were conceptually irrelevant to the conjectures that were being evaluated. The relevant actions involved participants forming triangles with their arms (see Figure 2.4), or tapping back and forth with fingers to enact number parity of the gears. The researchers found that participants who made mathematically relevant directed actions were statistically more likely to show an understanding of key ideas behind each conjecture, compared to learners who performed physically comparable, but conceptually irrelevant actions.

Together, this and the Thomas and Lleras eye movement study provide a rather direct challenge to the claim that movement *in general* is responsible for the gains hypothesized for embodied learning interventions. Furthermore, results were obtained from both studies despite participants reporting that they were not consciously aware of the relevance of the eye gaze patterns and body movements they performed in the tasks.

Walkington and colleagues (2020) extended this idea to an experiment with players of an embodied video game, *The Hidden Village*, for teaching geometric reasoning. Participants were students (*N* = 85) from ethnically diverse, urban high schools in a major US metropolitan area. All the students were in a program specifically designed to support would-be first-generation college students. Consequently, this study also investigates how embodied learning may broaden participation and performance in an area of advanced mathematics that is important for future STEM studies and career pathways.

Digital avatars (Figure 2.5) were used in the game to direct players to perform directed actions. A Kinect™ sensor array tracked players' movements in real time and detected whether students successfully made the intended directed actions. These directed movements were

Triangle Actions	Gear Actions

Grounding (First Person): Participant places palms on pairs of dots. Dot locations are scaled so a participant cannot reach the last pair of dots.

Grounding (First Person): Participant alternates between tapping blue and yellow diamonds, placed anv arm span apart, with their palms.

Non-Grounding (First Person): Participant taps each dot with left palm moving left to right, then taps each dot with right palm moving right to left.

Non-Grounding (First Person): Participant repeatedly taps the blue diamond with palm

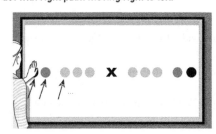

FIGURE 2.4 Directed actions performed for Triangle and Gear tasks in first-person perspective (from Nathan et al., 2014).
In the first column, participants in the Triangle Task performed either mathematically relevant directed actions (*top*) that had participants form various triangles with their bodies as they touched colored spots on an interactive white board; or make mathematically irrelevant directed actions (*bottom*) that touched all of the same spots, but in ways that never formed embodied triangles. In the second column, participants in the Gear Task performed either mathematically relevant directed actions (*top*) that had participants experience numerical parity with their bodies as they touched colored spots on an interactive white board; or make mathematically irrelevant directed actions (*bottom*) that touched all of the same spots, but in ways that never established numerical parity.

designed to be either mathematically relevant or irrelevant to the geometry conjectures students were later asked to evaluate (see Figure 2.5).

For example, a player might be asked to evaluate the conjecture "The diagonals of a rectangle always have the same length." Prior to seeing the conjecture, some of the students were directed to mimic avatars who were cuing the mathematically relevant actions shown of two congruent mirror-images of right triangles (see conjecture 6 in Figure 2.6). The right triangles' motions are intended to cue action-cognition transduction processes (Nathan, 2017; Nathan & Walkington, 2017) whereby actions would invoke in players the cognitive processes that might elicit a key insight related to evaluating the truth of the conjecture. In this case, a correct insight is that the diagonals of the rectangle must be congruent because they each are the hypotenuses of right triangles that have equal leg lengths.

FIGURE 2.5 Screen of *The Hidden Village*, an embodied video game, along with an inset showing how students move in response to game play.

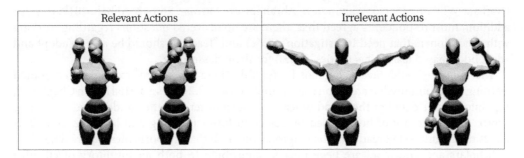

Relevant Actions	Irrelevant Actions

FIGURE 2.6 Mathematically relevant and mathematically irrelevant directed actions for the conjecture
The diagonals of a rectangle always have the same length.
These were used in *The Hidden Village,* an embodied video game, to test whether performing specific actions matter for enhancing high school students' (N = 85) cognitive processes for geometric reasoning.

The mathematically relevant directed actions cued by the avatars in the game were determined by previously examining the spontaneous gestures that successful problem-solvers tended to make when proving these conjectures, adjusted to meet the affordances and limitations of the motion detection technology. Mathematically irrelevant directed actions were then composed by scrambling poses from the relevant actions used for other conjectures throughout the game, so that they adhered to the same motion technology constraints and were plausible mathematical actions, albeit for multiple different conjectures than the one of current interest.

The study was a within-subjects design, such that each student performed relevant actions for half of the conjectures they evaluated, and irrelevant actions for the remaining half. The presentation of conjectures followed a Latin Square design to minimize order effects. The investigators found that performance on the proof and insight metrics was significantly higher for those in the relevant directed actions condition so long as students gestured as they gave their responses (thus activating the effects of action-cognition transduction). Here, as with the other studies reviewed, there is evidence that the specific types of movements do matter. Just moving for its own sake is not advised for enhancing reasoning since it is not likely to offer the advantages on reasoning conferred by task-relevant actions.

Despite the important qualifications on the fit of the movement to the concepts being learned, commercial programs such as *Action Based Learning™ Lab* (2018), *MATHS DANCE* (2018) and *Math in your Feet* (Rosenfeld, 2016) promise "optimal learning" using "brain research" to improve math teaching and learning. As inspiring as these body-based interventions may sound, there is an enormous difference between educational interventions and curricula that are founded on rigorous, empirical evidence of their effects on math education. Furthermore, even the best-designed embodied learning programs must also provide field-tested resources, including professional development for teachers, parents, self-use, whomever. These resources need to communicate effective strategies for adopting embodied learning approaches.

Survey findings from researchers and educators ($n = 49$) who attended a 2019 NSF Synthesis and Design Workshop on embodied mathematics for K-12 education showed overwhelming support (81%) for the statement that "teachers are professionals that should be deeply involved in developing, adopting, and adapting embodied learning activities" (Nathan, Williams-Pierce, Walkington, Abrahamson, Ottmar, Soto, & Alibali, 2019, p. 4). In addition, most respondents agreed that "there are unanswered questions regarding working with practitioners that need investigation" (75%) and "teachers should be able to adopt and adapt body-based learning activities" (75%) for their classrooms.

The *emptor* should *caveat*, but not be fearful. There are several exemplary embodied learning interventions that are empirically founded. Table 2.2 offers a partial list. In Chapter 12, I go into greater detail of these and other systems in order to better understand how these approaches make use of body-based processes to foster thinking and learning, as well as directing the interested reader to the empirical research that supports these approaches.

Scholars and educators are beginning to contribute to both an inventory of effective systems and methods, and the principles that can lead to effective instructional practices as well as the design of new systems. Thus, as recognition grows of the importance of embodied approaches for learning and teaching, there is a real and continued need for rigorous, empirical research that will provide evidence-based guidance for when and how to use these methods.

2.2.4 Summary

Embodied learning is a promising new paradigm for moving education forward. In this chapter, my focus has been to make a clear statement as to why we need grounded and embodied learning to improve education. For educational systems to deliver on their social promises depends on articulating a coherent, evidence-based framework for how people actually learn. Learning is defined as lasting changes in people's behavior.

TABLE 2.2
Examples of embodied learning systems that are based on empirical evidence in laboratory and real-world settings with age-appropriate users

Embodied approach or system	Content area(s): topic(s)	Contact info
EMBRACE	Early reading	www.movedbyreading.com/
BioSim	Elementary level Biology: Honeybees (BeeSim) or ants (AntSim)	www.joshuadanish.com/projects/ BioSim.html https://multiplex.videohall.com/ presentations/1217?search=eb77f 12cedd6b06f0a1223fdaa2ed2f376 2005d4
Amazon Adventure	Biology	www.embodied-games.com/
ELASTIC³S (Embodied Learning Augmented through Simulation Theaters for Interacting with Cross-Cutting Concepts in Science)	Secondary science: Earthquakes, acidity/basicity, and bacterial growth	https://emit.education.illinois.edu/ elastics
Kinemathics / Mathematics Imagery Trainer	Early math: Proportional reasoning	https://edrl.berkeley.edu/projects/ kinemathics/
From Here to There!	Secondary math: Algebra	https://sites.google.com/view/from-here-tothere/home
The Hidden Village	Secondary math: Geometry	https://multiplex.videohall.com/ presentations/1662
Walking Scale Geometry and Walking Scale Number Lines	Secondary Math: Geometry and Number and operations	https://steinhardt.nyu.edu/people/ jasmine-ma

As I note, there are several things that hold us back from achieving these important aims of education. One is misguided educational systems that do not prioritize learners' construction of meaning. Instructional designs and educational practices often assume it is best to adopt a Formalisms First approach that is not compatible with optimal cognitive development. Another is the observation that a great deal of scientific research on cognition does not align with educational concerns, and so the findings are not adopted by practitioners and designers. In order to achieve the translational goal of a well-designed, evidence-based education system, bridges need to be built starting from the education side of the divide to both constrain and inform the scientific fields that can be effectively recruited to investigate promising educational interventions. Scale-down methodology offers one such approach with this in mind. Both the educational obstacles and the scientific obstacles to realizing more effective educational experiences fall short because they operate from perspectives that separate mind and body and fail to prioritize grounding and engage natural body-based processes people have for meaningful learning.

In response to these shortcomings, I offer grounded and embodied learning (GEL) as an alternative paradigm for moving education forward. Some of the guiding principles are that embodied learning must be equitably provided to all learners; learning complex ideas must first be experienced as a concrete, primary experience, before it may develop into a fully abstract and generalizable concept or skill; noticing how learners express their thinking through movement such as gestures can inform better assessment practices; and collaborative embodiment offers many advantages for engagement and learning. Instructional approaches such as concreteness fading support the grounding of symbols into meaningful referents that can then support generalization and abstraction.

I also caution that this framework does not mean that all movement will improve learning. Rather, the types of actions and body-based resources that are used must be understood as task relevant. Education seen within this paradigm is reframed as the engineering of grounded and embodied learning experiences.

Grounded and embodied learning has a solid philosophical basis. Humans need to have a grounded understanding of the symbol systems and formalisms that are instrumental to participation in discipline-specific discourse, and this is achieved through sensorimotor interactions with the ideas represented by these formal, cultural tools. People's reasoning and capacity for learning is not confined to one's cranium, and operates as an "extended mind" that includes people's gestures and other movements, their interactions with tools and cultural artifacts, external memory aids, the environment, and other people.

Several powerful educational implications arise from this philosophical position that have been a source of innovation for a variety of scholars who have engaged grounding and embodied experiences for learning reading and language, mathematics, science, social studies, problem solving, and more. They share a commitment to the view that meaning making and learning will emerge through engagement of learners' sensorimotor systems. To change education requires a commitment to teacher education and professional learning. Embodied learning does not claim that any and all movements will enhance learning. Rigorous investigations have shown that task-relevant movements are most beneficial. A growing number of commercial endeavors that operate without a closely aligned research base fail to align with these theoretical considerations and as a result they are less likely to yield educational gains.

2.3 READER ACTIVITIES

This final section provides activities and demonstrations to experience and more deeply appreciate the types of embodied phenomena that contribute to effective learning.

2.3.1 Conceptual Metaphors Used in Science Education

Niebert and colleagues (2012) show how analogies and conceptual metaphors are so often used to develop students' understanding of scientific theories and abstract concepts. Consider the benefits and risks of each of these selected metaphors for science understanding.

- DNA Is a Ladder
- Eye Is a Camera
- Atmosphere Is a Container
- School dance Is a Chemical Reaction
- Gas Molecules Are Marbles
- Light Is a Wave
- Light Is a Particle

2.3.2 What Our Hands Can Tell Us about Our Minds: Dr. Susan Goldin-Meadow

This video from TEDxUChicago 2011 gives a valuable introduction to gesture for learning and teaching.

www.youtube.com/watch?v=tPPaJrhluS4

REFERENCES

Abrahamson, D., Nathan, M. J., Williams–Pierce, C., Walkington, C., Ottmar, E. R., Soto, H., & Alibali, M. W. (2020). The future of embodied design for mathematics teaching and learning. In S. Ramanathan & I. A. C. Mok (Eds.), *Future of STEM education: Multiple perspectives from researchers. Frontiers of Education.* doi: https://doi.org/10.3389/feduc.2020.00147

Abrahamson, D., & Sánchez-García, R. (2016). Learning is moving in new ways: The ecological dynamics of mathematics education. *Journal of the Learning Sciences, 25*(2), 203–239.

Action Based Learning™ Lab. (2018). Retrieved April 22, 2021, from www.youthfit.com/abl

Alibali, M. W., & Nathan, M. J. (2012). Embodiment in mathematics teaching and learning: Evidence from learners' and teachers' gestures. *Journal of the Learning Sciences, 21*(2), 247–286.

Apple, M. W. (Ed.). (2009). *Global crises, social justice, and education.* Routledge.

Ball, D. L. (1993). With an eye on the mathematical horizon: Dilemmas of teaching elementary school mathematics. *The Elementary School Journal, 93*(4), 373–397.

Braithwaite, D., & Goldstone, R. (2013). Integrating formal and grounded representations in combinatorics learning. *Journal of Educational Psychology, 105,* 666–682.

Bransford, J. D., & Vye, N. (n.d.). The concept of intelligence. Unpublished manuscript. Peabody College of Vanderbilt University.

Broaders, S. C., Cook, S. W., Mitchell, Z., & Goldin-Meadow, S. (2007). Making children gesture brings out implicit knowledge and leads to learning. *Journal of Experimental Psychology: General, 136*(4), 539.

Brooks, R. A. (1991). Intelligence without representation. *Artificial Intelligence, 47*(1–3), 139–159.

Brown, J. S., Collins, A., & Duguid, P. (1989). Situated cognition and the culture of learning. *Educational Researcher, 18*(1), 32–42.

Bruer, J. T. (1997). Education and the brain: A bridge too far. *Educational Researcher, 26*(8), 4–16.

Bruner, J. S. (1966). *Toward a theory of instruction.* Harvard University Press.

Butler, F. M., Miller, S. P., Crehan, K., Babbitt, B., & Pierce, T. (2003). Fraction instruction for students with mathematics disabilities: Comparing two teaching sequences. *Learning Disabilities Research & Practice, 18*(2), 99–111.

Chase, W. G., & Ericsson, K. A. (1982). Skill and working memory. In *Psychology of learning and motivation* (Vol. 16, pp. 1–58). Academic Press.

Cheryan, S., Ziegler, S. A., Montoya, A. K., & Jiang, L. (2017). Why are some STEM fields more gender balanced than others? *Psychological Bulletin, 143*(1), 1.

Clark, A., & Chalmers, D. (1998). The extended mind. *Analysis, 58*(1), 7–19.

Cole, M., & Engeström, Y. (1993). A cultural-historical approach to distributed cognition. In G. Salomon (Ed.), *Distributed cognitions: Psychological and educational considerations* (pp. 1–46). Cambridge University Press.

Dede, C. (Ed.). (2006). *Online professional development for teachers: Emerging models and methods.* Harvard Education Press.

Dehaene, S., Spelke, E., Pinel, P., Stanescu, R., & Tsivkin, S. (1999). Sources of mathematical thinking: Behavioral and brain-imaging evidence. *Science, 284*(5416), 970–974.

Dreyfus, H. L. (1991). *Being-in-the-world: A commentary on Heidegger's Being and Time, Division I.* MIT Press.

Dreyfus, H. L. (2002). Refocusing the question: Can there be skillful coping without propositional representations or brain representations? *Phenomenology and the Cognitive Sciences, I,* 413–425.

Duncker, K., & Lees, L. S. (1945). On problem-solving. *Psychological Monographs, 58*(5), i.

Dunlosky, J., Rawson, K. A., Marsh, E. J., Nathan, M. J., & Willingham, D. T. (2013). Improving students' learning with effective learning techniques: Promising directions from cognitive and educational psychology. *Psychological Science in the Public Interest, 14*(1), 4–58.

Fischer, C. S., Hout, M., Jankowski, M. S., Lucas, S. R., Swidler, A., & Voss, K. (1996). *Inequality by design: Cracking the bell curve myth.* Princeton University.

Fraser, S. (Ed.). (2008). *The bell curve wars: Race, intelligence, and the future of America.* Basic Books.

Fyfe, E. R., McNeil, N. M., & Borjas, S. (2015). Benefits of "concreteness fading" for children's mathematics understanding. *Learning and Instruction, 35,* 104–120.

Fyfe, E. R., & Nathan, M. J. (2019). Making "concreteness fading" more concrete as a theory of instruction for promoting transfer. *Educational Review, 71*(4), 403–422.

Gardner, H. (1995). Cracking open the IQ box. *American Prospect, 20,* 71–80.

Gerofsky, S. (2011). Seeing the graph vs. being the graph: Gesture, engagement and awareness in school mathematics. In G. Stam & M. Ishino (Eds.), *Integrating gestures: The interdisciplinary nature of gesture* (pp. 245–256). John Benjamins.

Gerofsky, S. (Ed.) (2018). *Contemporary environmental and mathematics education modelling using new geometric approaches: Geometries of liberation.* Palgrave Macmillan.

Glennan, T. K., Bodilly, S. J., Galegher, J. R., & Kerr, K. A. (2004). Expanding the reach of education reforms: Perspectives from leaders in the scale-up of educational intervention. RAND Education for the Ford Foundation. Retrieved April 22, 2021, from rand.org/content/dam/rand/pubs/monographs/2004/RAND_MG248.pdf

Goldin-Meadow, S. (2003). *Hearing gesture: How our hands help us think.* Harvard University Press.

Goldstone, R. L., & Son, J. Y. (2005). The transfer of scientific principles using concrete and idealized simulations. *The Journal of the Learning Sciences, 14*(1), 69–110.

Goodwin, C. (1994). Professional vision. *American Anthropologist, 96,* 606–633.

Gordon, P. (2004). Numerical cognition without words: Evidence from Amazonia. *Science, 306*(5695), 496–499.

Gould, S. J. (1996). *The mismeasure of man.* Norton.

Herrnstein, R. J., & Murray, C. (2010). *The bell curve: Intelligence and class structure in American life.* Simon and Schuster.

Hutchins, E. (1995). *Cognition in the wild.* MIT Press.

Hyde, J. S., Lindberg, S. M., Linn, M. C., Ellis, A. B., & Williams, C. C. (2008). Gender similarities characterize math performance. *Science, 321*(5888), 494–495.

Johnson-Glenberg, M. C. (2019). The necessary nine: Design principles for embodied VR and active STEM education (pp. 83–112). In P. Diaz, A. Ioannou, K. K. Bhagat, & J. M. Spector (Eds.), *Learning in a digital world: Perspective on interactive technologies for formal and informal education.* Springer.

Kellman, P. J., Massey, C. M., & Son, J. Y. (2010). Perceptual learning modules in mathematics: Enhancing students' pattern recognition, structure extraction, and fluency. *Topics in Cognitive Science, 2*(2), 285–305.

Koedinger, K. R., & Nathan, M. J. (2004). The real story behind story problems: Effects of representations on quantitative reasoning. *The Journal of the Learning Sciences, 13*(2), 129–164.

Koedinger, K. R., Corbett, A. T., & Perfetti, C. (2012). The knowledge-learning-instruction framework: Bridging the science-practice chasm to enhance robust student learning. *Cognitive Science, 36*(5), 757–798.

Küchemann, D. (1978). Children's understanding of numerical variables. *Mathematics in School, 7*(4), 23–26.

Ladson-Billings, G. (1997). It doesn't add up: African American students' mathematics achievement. *Journal for Research in Mathematics Education, 28*(6), 697–708.

Ladson-Billings, G., & Tate, W. F. (2006). Toward a critical race theory of education. In A. D. Dixson, C. K. Rousseau Anderson, & J. K. Donnor (Eds.) *Critical race theory in education: All God's children got a song* (pp. 11–32). Routledge.

Lindgren, R., & Johnson-Glenberg, M. (2013). Emboldened by embodiment: Six precepts for research on embodied learning and mixed reality. *Educational Researcher, 42*(8), 445–452.

Master, A., & Meltzoff, A. N. (2016). Building bridges between psychological science and education: Cultural stereotypes, STEM, and equity. *Prospects, 46*(2), 215–234.

Maths Dance. (2018). Retrieved April 22, 2021, from www.mathsdance.com/

McDonald, S. K., Keesler, V. A., Kauffman, N. J., & Schneider, B. (2006). Scaling-up exemplary interventions. *Educational Researcher, 35*(3), 15–24.

McNeil, N. M., Weinberg, A., Hattikudur, S., Stephens, A. C., Asquith, P., Knuth, E. J., & Alibali, M. W. (2010). A is for apple: Mnemonic symbols hinder the interpretation of algebraic expressions. *Journal of Educational Psychology, 102*(3), 625.

Miller, G. A. (1956). The magical number seven, plus or minus two: Some limits on our capacity for processing information. *Psychological Review, 63*(2), 81.

Miller, S. P., & Hudson, P. J. (2007). Using evidence-based practices to build mathematics competence related to conceptual, procedural, and declarative knowledge. *Learning Disabilities Research & Practice, 22*(1), 47–57.

Nathan, M. J. (2012). Rethinking formalisms in formal education. *Educational Psychologist, 47*(2), 125–148. doi:10.1080/00461520.2012.667063.

Nathan, M. J. (2017). One function of gesture is to make new ideas: Evidence for reciprocity between action and cognition. In R. B. Church, M. W. Alibali, & S. D. Kelly, (Eds.) *Why gesture? How the hands function in speaking, thinking and communicating* (pp. 175–196). John Benjamins. doi: 10.1075/gs.7.04der

Nathan, M. J., & Alibali, M. W. (2010). Learning sciences. *Wiley Interdisciplinary Reviews: Cognitive Science, 1*(3), 329–345.

Nathan, M. J., & Martinez, C. V. (2015). Gesture as model enactment: The role of gesture in mental model construction and inference making when learning from text. *Learning: Research and Practice, 1*(1), 4–37.

Nathan, M. J., & Petrosino, A. J. (2003). Expert blind spot among preservice teachers. *American Educational Research Journal. 40*(4), 905–928.

Nathan, M. J., & Sawyer, K. (2014). Foundations of learning sciences. In K. Sawyer (Ed.), *The Cambridge handbook of the learning sciences* (2nd ed.) (pp. 21–43). Cambridge University Press.

Nathan, M. J., & Walkington, C. (2017). Grounded and embodied mathematical cognition: Promoting mathematical insight and proof using action and language. *Cognitive Research: Principles and Implications, 2*(1), 9.

Nathan, M. J., Walkington, C., Boncoddo, R., Pier, E., Williams, C. C., & Alibali, M. W. (2014). Actions speak louder with words: The roles of action and pedagogical language for grounding mathematical proof. *Learning and Instruction, 33,* 182–193.

Nathan, M. J., Williams-Pierce, C., Walkington, C., Abrahamson, D., Ottmar, E., Soto, H., & Alibali, M. W. (2019). *Embodied design for mathematical imagination and cognition.* Retrieved April 22, 2021, from repository.isls.org//handle/1/6852

Neisser, U. (1976). *Cognition and reality: Principles and implications of cognitive psychology.* Freeman.

Newen, A., De Bruin, L., & Gallagher, S. (Eds.). (2018). *The Oxford handbook of 4E cognition*. Oxford University Press.

Palincsar, A. S., & Brown, A. L. (1984). Reciprocal teaching of comprehension-fostering and comprehension-monitoring activities. *Cognition and Instruction, 1*(2), 117–175.

Penuel, W. R., Fishman, B. J., Cheng, B. H., & Sabelli, N. (2011). Organizing research and development at the intersection of learning, implementation, and design. *Educational Researcher, 40*(7), 331–337.

Pica, P., Lemer, C., Izard, V., & Dehaene, S. (2004). Exact and approximate arithmetic in an Amazonian indigene group. *Science, 306*(5695), 499–503.

Rao, H., & Sutton, R. I. (2014). *Scaling up excellence*. Random House.

Rau, M. A. (2017). Conditions for the effectiveness of multiple visual representations in enhancing STEM learning. *Educational Psychology Review, 29*(4), 717–761.

Rittle-Johnson, B., Schneider, M., & Star, J. R. (2015). Not a one-way street: Bidirectional relations between procedural and conceptual knowledge of mathematics. *Educational Psychology Review, 27*(4), 587–597.

Rittle-Johnson, B., & Siegler, R. S. (1998). The relation between conceptual and procedural knowledge in learning mathematics: A review. In C. Donlan (Ed.), *Studies in developmental psychology. The development of mathematical skills* (pp. 75–110). Psychology Press.

Rittle-Johnson, B., & Star, J. R. (2007). Does comparing solution methods facilitate conceptual and procedural knowledge? An experimental study on learning to solve equations. *Journal of Educational Psychology, 99*(3), 561.

Rose, M. (2005). *The mind at work: Valuing the intelligence of the American worker*. Penguin.

Rosenfeld, M. (2016). *Math on the move: Engaging students in whole body learning*. Heinemann.

Rosenshine, B., & Meister, C. (1994). Reciprocal teaching: A review of the research. *Review of Educational Research, 64*(4), 479–530.

Shaffer, D. W. (2004). Pedagogical praxis: The professions as models for postindustrial education. *Teachers College Record, 106*(7), 1401–1421.

Shapiro, L. (2019). *Embodied cognition*. Routledge.

Sherman, M. F., Walkington, C., & Howell, E. (2016). A comparison of symbol-precedence view in investigative and conventional textbooks used in algebra courses. *Journal for Research in Mathematics Education, 47*(2), 134–146.

Smith, C., & Walkington, C. (2019). Four principles for designing embodied mathematics activities. *Australian Mathematics Education Journal, 1*(4), 16.

Sternberg, R. J. (1995). For whom the bell curve tolls: A review of The Bell Curve. *Psychological Science, 6*(5), 257–261.

Stokes, D. E. (2011). *Pasteur's quadrant: Basic science and technological innovation*. Brookings Institution Press.

Thomas, L. E., & Lleras, A. (2007). Moving eyes and moving thought: On the spatial compatibility between eye movements and cognition. *Psychonomic Bulletin & Review, 14*(4), 663–668.

Walkington, C. A., Nathan, M. J., & Wang, M. (2020, April). The effect of relevant directed arm motions on gesture usage and proving of geometry conjectures. Paper presented at the 2020 Annual Meeting of the American Educational Research Association, San Francisco, CA.

Whorf, B. L. (1956). Science and linguistics. In J. B. Carroll. (Ed.). *Language, thought, and reality: Selected writings of Benjamin Lee Whorf* (pp. 212–217). MIT Press.

3

Understanding Grounded and Embodied Learning

Early readers who manipulate a set of toys that are indexed to the story they are reading show large gains in reading comprehension compared to those in the same group who engage in re-reading. Children's reading gains persist when the children are simply asked to imagine manipulating the toys.

(Glenberg et al., 2004, 2011)

People's judgements about where they would rather place positive (versus negative) ideas, preferred (versus less desirable) toys, kinder (versus meaner) stuffed animals and more (versus less) intelligent cartoon creatures are shaped by their hand dominance. In accordance with the *body-specificity hypothesis*, children who are left-handed are much more likely to place preferred objects to their left, whereas right handers will do the opposite. Temporarily turning right-handed adults into lefties reverses these judgements.

(Casasanto & Chrysikou, 2011; Casasanto & Henetz, 2012)

Teacher use of gestures is beneficial for students' learning in areas such as second language acquisition (Tellier, 2005), and mathematics instruction on equations (Cook, Mitchell, & Goldin-Meadow, 2008) and symmetry (Valenzeno, Alibali & Klatzky, 2003), especially when students reproduce these instructional gestures.

Embodied learning is natural learning. *Embodied learning* occurs when the meaning of what is learned is grounded in body movement and perception. For example, infants learning the sounds of speech not only tune their hearing, but they also engage their lips and tongue in order to anticipate the mouth movements that will need to make to produce the sounds (Bruderer et al., 2015). Teething toys that interfere with infants' tongue and lip movements impair their auditory speech perception. Similarly, when science students have their gestures restricted while they read about the circulatory system, they develop impoverished mental models of the pathways of blood flow through the body (Martinez & Nathan, 2015).

When embodied learning is an explicit part of educational design, students often experience greater and more far-reaching gains in performance. The chapters that follow present an array of findings based on laboratory and classroom-based research that explores the extent of these advantages, the conditions under which they thrive, its limitations, and the likely reasons why embodied approaches to education bring about the observed results. I share a

DOI: 10.4324/9780429329098-3

broad selection of findings showing that engaging the body in performance and learning can lead to observable benefits in areas such as language, science, math, and social studies education. In this current chapter I lay a foundation for understanding the nature of learning and why grounding and embodied learning offer a promising approach for improving the effectiveness of educational experiences.

3.1 HOW SYMBOLS AND IDEAS ARE GROUNDED: EXAMPLES FROM READING AND MATHEMATICS

Grounding is a central idea for embodied learning and for the development of a framework of embodied education. In Chapter 1, I signaled the importance of grounding symbols and words in order that they have meaning for speakers and writers, and their listeners and readers. I also cautioned about the perils of trying to learn and use concepts and symbolic representations and procedure in the absence of grounding. Searle's (1980) Chinese Room metaphor (discussed in Chapter 1) illustrates the pitfalls of trying to function when symbols remain ungrounded, showing that a person in the room may be able to respond, but will likely feel like a *poseur*, merely acting the part of a native speaker. Now I want to dive a bit deeper into the idea of grounding, its relevance to learning and education, and its relation to embodiment.

Grounding describes the way people connect an idea or symbol with a more familiar or concrete referent, such as an object or event in the world that facilitates meaning making (Barsalou, 2008). Fincher-Kiefer (2019) *equates* grounding with embodiment.

> I will use the terms *embodied* and *grounded* as essentially synonymous terms; grounded does not mean that the concepts are simply and loosely connected to sensory or motor information (as suggested by Mahon, 2015), but instead that the body plays a constitutive role in conceptual knowledge.
>
> (Fincher-Kiefer, 2019, p. 1, emphasis in original)

I agree that grounding is central to embodied learning. But I don't see grounding and embodiment as synonymous. Grounding appears to be broader than either learning or embodiment. Grounding occurs with other cognitive processes that may not involve learning, such as reading and language comprehension, planning, problem solving, and performing intended actions. For example, children who use algebra word problems to invert the arithmetic operations implied by the words are grounding their understanding of numbers and operations in the sequential structure of language in ways that are not afforded by symbolic expressions (Koedinger & Nathan, 2004). Performing grounding in this manner may help students later to learn about algebraic modeling and symbol manipulation more readily when this is addressed through explicit instruction.

As the algebra example suggests, grounding does not always depend on a *direct* connection to body-based processes. Indeed, many forms of cognition proceed without direct engagement of the body (Barsalou, 2008). For it to be meaningful, however, the object of thought must be grounded in something familiar to the person. When it is grounded in body structure or body-based actions and perceptions, then calling it embodied cognition is warranted. Cognitive processes can also be grounded in simulations and language systems, which are less directly connected to the body, though they may be ultimately embodied. As Barsalou (2008, p. 623) writes, research on grounding processes and grounded cognition "increasingly suggest that simulations, situations, and bodily states play central roles in cognition." By

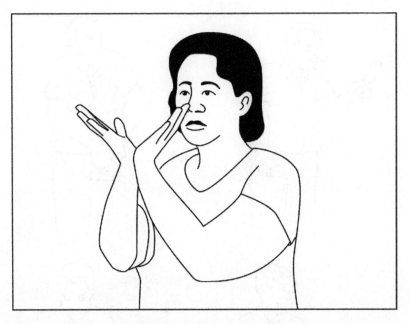

FIGURE 3.1 A mathematics teacher makes a gesture with her hands to ground the concept of a "right angle" during a lesson.

simulations, I mean "the reenactment of perceptual, motor, and introspective states acquired during experience with the world, body, and mind" (Barsalou, 2008, p. 618).

Thus grounding and embodied learning *together* cover a wide array of intellectual behaviors that are of educational relevance. Understanding each of them and how they function individually and in concert is part of the path I am advocating for improving the educational experiences of learners and teachers. In this chapter I offer additional ways of describing both grounded and embodied learning and exploring the educational implications.

Grounding is commonplace. A simple example is the actions performed by a mathematics teacher to ground the concept of a "right angle" by using her hands to form the corner of a piece of paper (see Figure 3.1; Alibali & Nathan, 2012). The act is fleeting. But acts of this sort are rapidly apprehended by students and are effective at providing the referents needed for achieving a clear interpretation.

I also like this more elaborate example from Curtis Lebaron and Jurgen Streeck (2000). Their excerpt from a house repair class illustrates how action can ground the name of a tool and its use. The instructor is demonstrating the types of tools used for scraping sheetrock (aka drywall) and applying compound, such as putty to the sheetrock. Images from the instructor's scraper tool demonstration are presented in Figure 3.2. The top row of the figure shows the initial demonstration that grounds the term "scraper" to several tools. The demonstration includes the up-down actions required to use the tools effectively for house repair. The demonstration is initially performed with a scraper tool in hand. Then the up-down movements are made in the air (not against a wall) while the instructor is facing the students.

At this point, the instructor provided the grounding for the idea of the scraper into a gesture that iconically mimics the up-down movements made when actually using the tool. When referencing the scraper and its use for students, the instructor subsequently invokes the up-down gesture without holding the tool, as shown in the bottom row of Figure 3.2.

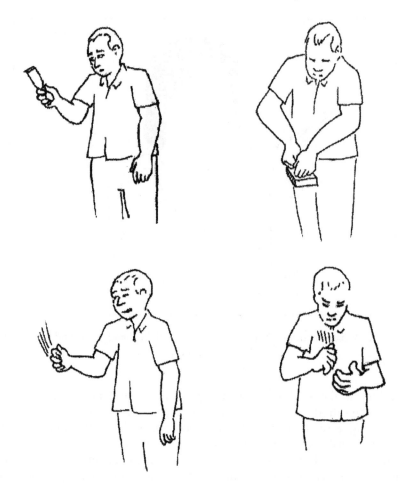

FIGURE 3.2 Top row shows the initial demonstration that grounds the term "scraper" to several scraper tools and the actions required to use the tools effectively during home repair. Bottom row, idea of the scraper is grounded by a gesture that iconically mimics movement of the tool.

These examples illustrate how new and unfamiliar ideas (right angle, scraper tool) gain meaning by virtue of being explicitly connected to body positions and actions in the world. Once grounded for learners, the terms become meaningful (Nathan, 2008). Grounding is necessary for making sense of symbols, language, and abstract ideas, be they derived from art, science, or craft (e.g., Glenberg and Robertson, 1999; Gombrich, 1960; Harnad, 1990; Lakoff and Johnson, 1999; Lakoff and Núñez, 2000).

Goldstone, Landy, and Son (2008) proposed grounding as the basis for a theory of learning and knowledge transfer. People may be somewhat oblivious to it. Regardless, they are highly influenced by spatial properties even for seemingly non-spatial things like the symbolic terms in mathematical equations. Despite their rapid and automatic nature, the perceptual processes that pick up on these spatial properties can be trained to apply to new tasks, and exhibit gains in learning. Thus, grounding is regarded as an aspect of cognition that is sensitive to the perceptual qualities of one's immediate environment, but capable of transcending the particulars by extending the set of things to which these perceptual processes apply.

Overall, grounding offers an account of how people's sensorimotor experiences give rise to concepts. Consider for example, work by Linda Smith (2005) showing that children rely on action, not only visual form, to establish shape categories. Shape categories seem rather basic and invariant. Still, the actions a child performs with an object (e.g., moving it vertically) alters children's shape categories in ways consistent with the movements. Notably, the influence on shape category only occurred when children acted on the objects versus when they merely watched the experimenter perform the same actions. In this way we can see how the actions children perform ground the shape categories.

Grounding a new concept based on sensorimotor processes also depends on one's cultural histories, since it matters what things are concrete and familiar, and what those familiar things mean to us. For example, whether people could correctly interpret and follow a simple *conditional* of the form "if *P* then *Q*" (e.g., postage rules) depended on their cultural experiences, if they grew up with the rule. Chang and Holyoak (1985) called these *pragmatic reasoning schemas*. They found that people who lacked the relevant cultural experiences, lacked the appropriate pragmatic reasoning schemas, and so tended to make common logical fallacies when testing the conditional. Thus, grounding abstractions to familiar experiences so that they are meaningful relies on both perceptual and cultural processes. Box 3A provides an extended example. As this example suggests, people can solve a reasoning task far more readily in its grounded form, but this likely will not lead directly to learning and transfer for symbolic versions, unless there is a clear connection made that helps learners invoke the pragmatic reasoning schema in other contexts.

Box 3A Pragmatic Reasoning Schemas as Culturally Grounded Forms of Logical Reasoning

This is the 4-Card Selection task in its classic form (Wason, 1966):
You are given a rule about the four cards: *If a card has a vowel on one side, then it has an even number on the other side. Which card(s) do you <u>need</u> to turn over in order to determine if the rule is true or false?*

Take a moment to decide the fewest number of cards you will need to turn over to determine whether or not the rule is being followed.

The task is one of the logical implications of a simple conditional, which can be written in formal logical symbols as *If P Then Q*. People are very poor at following the logical conclusions of a rule such as this. So psychologists such as Wason, Johnson-Laird, Cheng, and Holyoak and others have explored these alternative forms.

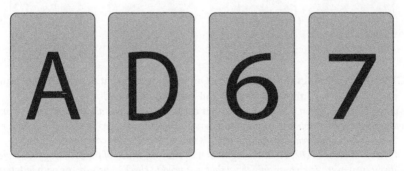

FIGURE 3A.1 You are given a rule about the four cards: *If a card has a vowel on one side, then it has an even number on the other side. Which card(s) do you <u>need</u> to turn over in order to determine if the rule is true or false?*

Most people given the four cards will naturally select the A card to turn over, since it's a vowel. If it exposes an odd number the rule fails, and if even, it is supported. People rule out needing to turn over the D, since the rule is silent about consonants. They overwhelmingly turn over the 6 but this provides no additional information. They seldom choose the 7. Yet it is necessary to turn over the non-even number. If this exposes a vowel, the rule has been violated! This essentially conforms to the logical reasoning that

If P Then Q,	If one side shows *Vowel*, Then the other must show *Even*
P	One side is *Vowel* (this is the A card) => The other side must be *Even*
NOT(Q)	One side is not *Even* (the 7 card) => The other side cannot be *Vowel*

Variants have emerged over the years. One of the most intriguing is from Cheng and Holyoak, Experiment 1.

*You are a postal clerk working in some foreign country. Part of your job is to go through letters to check the postage. The country's postal regulation requires that **if a letter is sealed, then it must carry a 20-cent stamp.** In order to check that the regulation is followed, which of the following four envelopes would you turn over? Turn over only those that you need to check to be sure.*

The above paragraph was followed by drawings of four envelopes: one sporting a 20-cent stamp, a 10-cent stamp, the word "sealed," and the word "unsealed."

As with letters and vowels in Wason's original version the correct response to this simple conditional is: *P (Sealed)* and *Not(Q) (10-cent stamp)*.

The task was given to college students in the United States, who were unfamiliar with this rule, and college students from Hong Kong, who lived with this rule up till about six months prior to the experiment. Despite the same logical structure, Hong Kong students who grew up with the postage rule learned a culturally grounded form of the

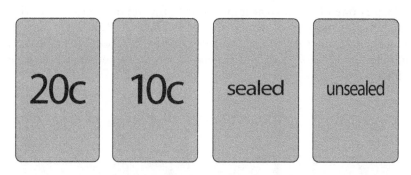

FIGURE 3A.2 Drawings of four envelopes: One sporting a 20-cent stamp, a 10-cent stamp, the word "sealed," and the word "unsealed."

Study participants are given a rule about the four cards: *You are a postal clerk working in some foreign country. Part of your job is to go through letters to check the postage. The country's postal regulation requires that if a letter is sealed, then it must carry a 20-cent stamp. In order to check that the regulation is followed, which of the following four envelopes would you turn over? Turn over only those that you need to check to be sure.* As with letters and vowels in Wason's original version, the correct response to this simple conditional is: P (Sealed) and Not-Q (10-cent stamp).

simple conditional and they made the correct selection at nearly 90%. US students were closer to 50% (Cheng & Holyoak, 1985).

As another interesting aspect of the experiment, half of the participants from the United States and half of the Hong Kong participants were given the following rationale for the rule (with the task and envelopes otherwise identical to the no-rationale condition).

The rationale for this regulation is to increase profit from personal mail, which is nearly always sealed. Sealed letters are defined as personal and must therefore carry more postage than unsealed letters.

In lieu of the lived experience, the simple conditional rule was grounded through a clear explanation. When students from either country were told the rationale, they all performed at nearly 90%. From this we recognize that grounding is most naturally achieved by lived cultural experiences, yet can also be achieved through meaningful instruction.

3.1.1 Grounding the Meaning of Words for Early Readers Through Actions and Imagination

Reading is an essential skill. Yet one of the most challenging things to learn is what words mean when presented on a page or screen. This may appear to be an odd statement, because language is easily mastered by nearly everyone. But speaking and reading are very different skills. Speaking and mastery of oral language is a biologically primary ability, for which people have vast neural and cultural supports (Geary, 1995). Neurally, people have specific areas of the brain dedicated to language (e.g., Dehaene, 2009). Culturally, verbal skills start from birth in the home (Golinkoff & Hirsch-Pasek, 2000).

In contrast, reading is not natural. Learning to read involves "decoding" arbitrary visual symbols into units of sound and meaning that are strung together to tell stories and convey information (Sanchez, 2018; Seidenberg, 2017). It is also a highly time-pressured task, because if a reader takes a long time to sound out each phoneme, memory for the previous sounds and words quickly fades. It is estimated that 250 million out of 650 million primary school age children worldwide cannot read (EdWeek, 2014). In the United States, only a third of schoolchildren read at grade level (NAEP, 2015).

Glenberg and colleagues (Glenberg et al., 2004) investigated how to improve early reading from an embodied perspective. First- and second-grade students were given access to toys that were used to imitate the actions in a story about "Breakfast on the Farm." The children all could see toys of a farm scene such as a barn, tractor, hay bales, and a variety of animals. An example is shown in Figure 3.3. Children directed to use the toys to imitate specific actions described in the story showed far better comprehension and better story recall than those directed to re-read the story but not actually manipulate the toys. Mapping objects and actions to the words was critical for helping early readers. This is significant in and of itself.

The impact of grounding and embodied learning for improving reading gets better, still. In a subsequent experiment (Glenberg et al., 2004), children were directed to *imagine* they were manipulating the toys, after they had used the toys to imitate actions in the story. If they could use imagined actions this would greatly extend the power of the intervention by showing that young readers may not need to touch and move the actual objects if they can *simulate* these same actions in their minds. Recall that Barsalou (2008) argues that simulations that engage modal processes such as perception and movement are some of the *strongest* evidence for grounded and embodied cognition.

FIGURE 3.3 An image from the *Moved By Reading* program that helps early readers to index words to objects.

The evidence showed that children's reading comprehension benefited almost as much from imagining the actions as they did when performing the actual actions! What's more, children could use this imagining strategy days later with a different toy scene, showing transfer of learning to new texts. Glenberg has replicated and extended these findings of the advantages of manipulating and imagining manipulating story-relevant objects to children from low-income families reading in small groups, as they often do in classrooms (Glenberg et al., 2007), and for monolingual Spanish-speaking children (Adams, Glenberg, & Restrepo, 2019). Glenberg has used this research to create the *Moved By Reading* program.

3.1.2 Grounding the Meaning of Algebraic Symbols Using Gestures and Role Play

As with early reading, students struggle to make meaning of mathematical symbols and the language of mathematical story problems (Koedinger & Nathan, 2004). The folklore is that algebra story problems are often regarded as particularly distressing. When the meaning of mathematical stories and symbols are grounded, however, students exhibit successful mathematical reasoning. This is demonstrated by the events in a middle school classroom (Nathan, 2008). The individual symbols such as the numbers, arithmetic operators, and letters, are familiar to students, but at sixth grade they have not yet used them to describe events or make future predictions. In this lesson, the teacher's goal is for these early algebra students to learn how mathematical symbols can be used to represent events of a story. The teacher presents them with the following:

The basketball problem

Mr. Robinson and his four daughters want to buy a special, autographed basketball. Mr. Robinson's daughters will each pay the same amount. Mr. Robinson will contribute $18 himself. If the ball costs $42, how much will each daughter pay?

The students, collaborating as a whole class, generated two mathematical descriptions of the information from the basketball problem that are shown in Figure 3.4. The "solution equation," was generated first as a way to summarize students' solution strategy, called "unwinding" (Nathan & Koedinger, 2000). During unwinding, the student reverses the events of the problem situation, "unwinding" them in each case by performing the inverse arithmetic operation. What one may recognize as a two-step algebra problem involving multiplication (the unknown amount each daughter paid times the four daughters) and addition ($18 contributed by Mr. Robinson) is reconceived as two separate arithmetic equations, one involving subtraction (take away Mr. Robinson's contribution) and the other, division (the amount given by each daughter).

Students also use mathematical expressions to describe the story as it was written, that is, write the Situation Equation. Figure 3.4 shows the parallel structure of the two equations. In the bottom panel, the teacher gestures with a flat hand underneath "+ 18" to ground a student reference to the amount the father contributes. She later repeats this same gesture for the corresponding element of the Solution Equation as with the Situation Equation to visually establish their connection across the two equations. This grounds the idea that the father's contribution is added in at the end for the Situation Equation, but subtracted at the beginning of the Solution Equation.

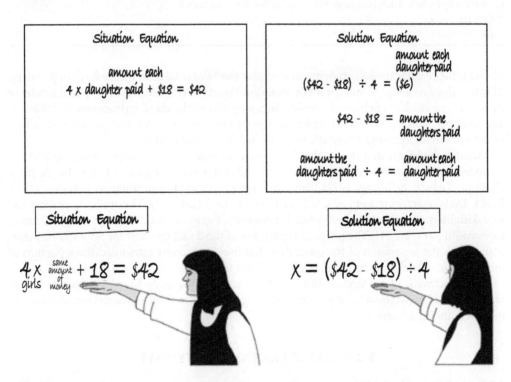

FIGURE 3.4 *Top row.* A recreation of the classroom whiteboard showing the parallel structure of the solution equation (right-hand side) and the situation equation of the Basketball Problem. *Bottom row.* The teacher gestures to a quantity in the Situation Equation and again in the Solution Equation to visually ground their connections across the two equations.

TABLE 3.1

Transcript from the sixth-grade classroom presentation of the Basketball Skit.

Teacher: Okay? Let's see it.

T: You got to talk really loudly; you're on stage now. I need everybody, I need the audience T: This is a performance, please!

Daughters: Wow look at this basketball!

D: Cool! It's $42 altogether, wow that's a lot! Can you help pay for it?

T: (To actors:) Nope, now nice and loud now.

Father: Um, I'll give eighteen dollars and you girls give the rest.

D: We need more dollars!

T: (To actors:) Okay, freeze!

T: (To class:) Have they described the situation so far if you have the numbers on the board?

T: Yep, they have, right? They mentioned $42; they asked Dad to help; Dad said he'd kick in $18; and they figured out how much left, left they'd have to pay.

T: (To actors:) OK. I'm going to let you finish off the problem even though we haven't done it on the board yet. Go ahead and just act out the situation; now what are you going to do?

D: (Unintelligible).

T: Okay you gotta gotta be really loud.

D: How much are we each going to have to pay?

D: (The four daughters in unison:) Well 24 divided by 4 is 6.

D: (To other actors:) So we … (unintelligible). So all of us have to … (giggling)

T: Talk it over with Dad, maybe finish it off here …

D: (All four in unison:) We're each gonna pay six dollars.

F: (Unintelligible).

T: Okay can you say that really loud again Matt, cos that was really good. (Unintelligible) listen over there.

F: Altogether plus the $18 dollars that'd be $42, so we can buy the … basketball

T: Give 'em a hand.

Class: (Applause)

Later, the teacher invited students to role play the interactions in the basketball problem. This was done as a way to interpret the Situation Equation (Figure 3.4) as a formal model of the story. The students delivered a highly engaging skit to the class, reproduced in Table 3.1. The students' words and actions explicitly depicted the additive and multiplicative structure of the underlying quantitative relations described in the story problem.

I want to highlight that the teacher built upon students' reading comprehension abilities to understand the relations between known and unknown quantities in this simple story (Nathan, Kintsch, & Young, 1992). The acting gave meaning to the Situation Equation (lines 5–10). Even operations were enacted, such as addition (Line 10). The students playing the four daughters grounded the multiplicative relation (4×) by announcing *in unison* how much each would pay (line 24)! The physical separation of the daughters and the father is also consistent with the separation of the quantities that they each contribute to additive portion of the algebraic model, thus bringing both quantities together.

This enactment of an algebra story problem shows how body-based structures, spatial relations, and language-based story structures together ground mathematical representations into meaningful actions.

3.2 WHAT IS LEARNING, ANYWAY?

3.2.1 Varieties of Learning

Learning encompasses a wide variety of behaviors. One may, for example, learn the sound of a person's voice, a new dance step, or the conceptual basis for a mathematical formula. We know people can learn new skills, as can animals. We associate learning with brain function and are aware that neural circuits go through changes as a consequence of repeated exposure and practice. Individuals, groups, and whole cities can learn to adopt behaviors to meet radical changes of the environment.

Consider how entire cities are learning to deal with changes in population growth, global climate patterns, and reducing the spread of disease during a pandemic. As Constable (2020) notes cities used to be some of the least attractive place to live, full of exposure to human waste and disease, and wasteful energy consumption. As they aspired to be the centers for commerce, culture, and political activity, they *learned* to become environments with planful waste and disease management. Modern cities are now far more efficient in terms of energy use because of a multitude of interdependent changes, including centralized energy distribution, economies of scale of power networks, political pressure to attract economic growth, and advances in innovation and engineering, and laws and policies regarding energy storage and transmission. As the physicist and systems scientist Geoffrey West (2017) observes, the data are strikingly clear, if you want to live "green" and make a smaller carbon footprint on this Earth, you should choose to live in a major city. "New York," West notes, "is the greenest city in the United States, whereas Santa Fe, where I live, is one of the more profligate ones."

With learning phenomena spanning neurons, individuals, groups, and whole cities, it seems daunting to seek out a single, unified account. Yet, just because it is intellectually challenging, does not mean scholars get a "pass" on *describing* learning and articulating what behaviors learning refers to. As the above examples illustrate, learning is commonplace, often desirable, and most certainly necessary for survival of the individual and one's community. As well, learning is personally satisfying, and greatly expands one's adaptability and resilience.

Indeed, learning is so ubiquitous and important to the human situation that an entire field has emerged to celebrate its study. The field of *Learning Sciences* (Box 3B) is a relatively young and highly INTERDISCIPLINARY field of study.

Box 3B What is the field of Learning Sciences?

Janet Kolodner's (1991a) editorial from the inaugural issue of *The Journal of the Learning Sciences* sets an agenda for the newly emerging field of Learning Sciences as inquiry into "new ways of thinking about learning and teaching that will allow the cognitive sciences to have an impact on the practice of education" (p. 1). This orients the field to the object of study as the design of learning environments and practices (p. 4) using multidisciplinary approaches and technology-based platform in a wide range settings (Nathan, Rummel, & Hay, 2016).

Elsewhere, Kolodner (1991b) affirms the commitment to rigorous investigations of learning in terms of all of the social, cultural, psychological, and physical influences found in authentic situations. As Klahr (2019) notes, in so doing, Learning Sciences is mutually inspired by basic and applied research, as well as its intersection, "use-inspired basic research" (Stokes, 1997).

The field of Learning Sciences is home to the International Society of the Learning Sciences (ISLS), which hosts an annual international conference, two scholarly journals, the Network of Academic Programs in the Learning Sciences (NAPLeS), and a growing list of handbooks; all of which are compiled on ISLS.org.

Those in education and the Learning Sciences will be familiar with many forms of learning, especially the types of learning we expect to happen in schools. Graduate students in the Learning Sciences and educational and developmental psychology, for example, will likely know of the work by Ann L. Brown and Joe Campione and colleagues showing the superior learning of high-needs, inner city students engaged in Fostering Communities of Learners experiences in their schools (Brown, 1997), which affects outcomes in reading comprehension (Brown, Campione, Reeve, Ferrara, & Palincsar, 1991), biological reasoning (Brown et al., 1997), production of deep analogies (Brown, 1992), and internalization of reflective thinking (Brown et al., 1993). Graduate students in cognitive psychology will have studied theories of memory, learning, and transfer. Researchers will have studied theories of memory, learning, and transfer, and designed investigations that allow them to observe learning taking place or show learner outcomes, such as measurable gains in performance or new forms of talk and participatory practices. Social anthropologists will know of the cross-cultural scholarship of Jean Lave and her student Étienne Wenger (Lave, 1988; Lave & Wenger, 1991) that has documented how learning in community is productively framed in terms of changing one's form of participation.

Teachers and other educational practitioners will be familiar with curriculum standards for learning in the content areas, such as those produced by the National Council of Teachers of Mathematics (NCTM; 2000) *Principles and Standards for School Mathematics*, National Council of Teachers of English/International Reading Association (NCTE/IRA) *Standards for the English Language Arts* (2009), and the Next Generation Science Standards (NGSS Lead States, 2013). Teachers will also have employed methods for assessing learning among their students. Educational leaders will recognize generational changes of students and teachers taking to new communication and learning technologies. Parents know well the emergence of their children's first steps, first words, first ride on a two-wheeled bike, and first time driving a car. Across these many perspectives, there is recognition of a common process that illustrates how smart and adaptable humans truly are, with *learning* as a powerful interconnecting theme running through all of these remarkable behaviors.

3.2.2 Learning Defined

Broadly speaking, **learning is defined as an enduring change in behavior.** Critical in this definition is that the changes are sustained. Also notable is that I am talking about changes that are observable, so that it is possible to show in some manner, quite possibly indirectly, that a change has taken place. Changes that take place may not be observable, however, if educators and researchers do not know where and how to look for them. We need the right type of instruments to make these observations, and the appropriate theories to drive this instrumentation and to interpret their results. Formation of these theoretical accounts come out of careful observation, thoughtful inquiry, and rigorous analysis of behaviors.

Box 3C provides some examples of learning to help to flesh out this broad concept.

Box 3C Learning Across Timescales: The Nevada Mathematics Project

1. **Organizational / Institutional Learning:** A school district or state Department of Education can operate as a learning organization to develop new capabilities to support integrated STEM education. Specifically, organization-level processes and structures are realigned to support new capabilities and outcome goals. Organizations at the state level, or even across states form a learning team. The State of Nevada, for example, has learned how to set professional goals around participation and to form networks that make it possible to allocate curriculum and

communication resources. This makes it possible to reach low-population density areas of the State and high-population areas in order to provide all teachers with what they need to be successful.

2. **Sociocultural Learning:** Teachers form a professional community of practice for integrated STEM education, including strategic use of curriculum, grounded instruction, and formative assessment (Lamberg, 2017). Members of the teacher education community at the university help to curate, create, train, and disseminate content and pedagogical content knowledge for the science of nanotechnology and the mathematics of measurement and proportional reasoning. Formal, face-to-face and online professional development experiences are provided to help teachers to effectively use content and pedagogical practices. This serves dual purposes of promoting effective integrated STEM instructional practices, and providing a self-sustaining professional learning community to further the objectives of the professional development events.

3. **Knowledge-based Learning:** Describe ways one's prior knowledge and understanding influences how people learn and perform intellectual tasks. Examples include metaphorical reasoning, including thinking of arithmetic in terms of its four grounding metaphors: Object collection, object construction, measuring stick, motion along a path (Lakoff & Núñez, 2000). Through metaphor a novel domain is made more concrete and familiar, which supports sense making, recall, and inference making.

4. **Cognitive Learning:** Teachers develop knowledge of the specific content area concepts of integrating mathematics and science through conceptual integration; and instructional practices that rely on gestures to make those connections across STEM topics explicit for their students. Students recognize mathematics as grounded in scientific inquiry and engineering design. They also see science and engineering ideas as generalizable in mathematical representations. This lessens learners' cognitive load and helps them to recognize patterns (e.g., linear behavior). It also helps generalize common ideas through shared formal vocabulary, diagrams, and symbolic notation.

5. **Biological Learning:** Students' neural circuits change with new perceptual learning and new motor learning that is involved in perceiving and making new connections. Teachers also form new connections through practice and rewards of effective instruction.

In each of these cases, I have some confidence that educators and scholars can describe particular kinds of learning, or show evidence it likely occurred because of a clear change in behaviors over time. Note, however, that behavioral changes may be evident in any or all of the organizational levels, including institutional, social group, individual, and neural functioning. This illustrates **an important principle of learning—it involves changes in behaviors across a wide range of scales**. The changes may be observable when scholars know at which scale to look, but may be hard to observe when their attention (and instrumentation) is aimed at other scales of behavior.

3.2.3 Timescales of Learning Processes

Allen Newell, whom we came across in Chapter 1, is one of the founders of both the fields of Cognitive Science and Computer Science. Newell shared an important insight about the broad nature of human behavior in his 1987 *William James Lectures* (Newell, 1994). Newell used a logarithmic timescale to illustrate the multitude of human actions, which I adapted for Figure 3.5. Newell's profound insight is masked by the simplicity of the timeline: As we sweep across, we encounter an enormous range of behaviors, so varied they may seem unrelated—indeed, entire scholarly fields, journals, conferences, and vocabularies arise and fade away as we shift across the timescale. Yet, Newell pointed out, this large set of behaviors are indeed related, and we only need to zoom in and out along one parameter—*time*—to reveal them all and illustrate the nature of their interconnections.

Newell was also wise to think of these in logarithmic terms because we would rapidly lose track of the relations between the different processes to one another with a linear scale. One such experience of this linear scale is found in many biking and hiking trails in the United States that mark the distances between the planets of our solar system. (Here is a link to one in my city of Madison, WI. www.spaceplace.wisc.edu/PTDCbrochure.pdf). Box 3D provides more context for thinking logarithmically.

Box 3D Understanding Logarithmic Scale

Most of us will not have much familiarity with using log scales (shorthand for logarithmic), but they are immensely valuable ways of illustrating how small and how large things actually get. Linear scales move along uniformly, and a depiction of the relative scale in linear terms of events that have a very wide scale range can be quite tedious.

To give a sense of how the log scale distorts our normal, linear sense of space, look at this log base 10 number line. On a linear scale we expect to see each incremental digit spaced equally apart. In a log scale, the lower numbers have more distance between them; the larger numbers are more compressed. Notice that 5 (and 50) are no longer at the halfway point, respectively, between 1 and 10, or 1 and 100.

As another example, here are the same data plotted on both linear and log base 10 scales (from Robbins, 2012).

What phenomena are most appropriate for using log scale? Cell growth is a good example of the intuitive need for a logarithmic scale, since cells divide in half, and then the doubled number of cells each grow and continue to divide and grow. Here, we use doubling, or log base of 2 (written $\log_2$) to describe how a population of cells grow.

Differences in loudness are also best described in logarithmic sales. Because of the properties of the human auditory system, people don't really perceive incremental changes the same way when the same increase is added to a soft sound versus a loud sound. In the case of sound, scientists use a factor of ten, or log base 10 (written as $\log_{10}$). They also use $\log_{10}$ scale to describe their sensations of the intensity of earthquakes: A difference in the Richter Scale measurement of a whole number, going from 3.0 to 4.0, is in actuality a ten-fold increase in intensity. Interestingly, as it increases by one whole number, the *frequency* at which that level of earthquake occurs also decreases by approximately one-tenth. That suggests the planet may, on average, experience earthquakes of Richter Scale 2.0 about 1 million times each year; RS 3.0 around 100,000 times per year; RS 4.0 about 10,000 times per year, and so on, reaching RS 8.0 about once per year, and RS 9.0 only about every decade.

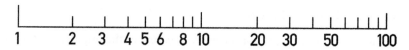

FIGURE 3D.1 An example of how numbers are distributed along the log base 10 ($\log_{10}$) scale.

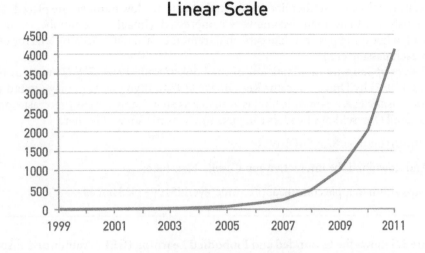

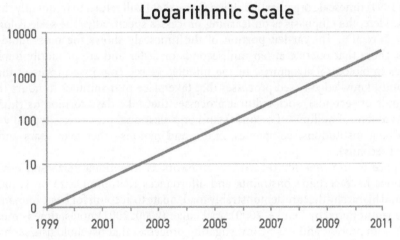

FIGURE 3D.2 The same data plotted on both linear and $\log_{10}$ scales.

The film, *Powers of Ten: A Film Dealing with the Relative Size of Things in the Universe and the Effect of Adding Another Zero*, was designed by the husband-and-wife design team, Charles and Ray Eames. The approximately nine-minute film can be seen here:

https://youtu.be/0fKBhvDjuy0

This 1977 film starts with the image of a man resting near the lakeside in Chicago, viewed from one meter away. The frame of the camera then uniformly zooms out until it reaches the edge of the known universe. Then, at a rate of 10^{10} meters per second (100 times faster than light itself can travel!), the film zooms back into the lakeside scene back on Earth, and continues to zoom in to the cellular and molecular structure of a patch of skin on the resting man's hand until viewers reach the subatomic structure of a single carbon atom. Thus, through the power of logarithmic scales we experience the entire universe from its largest expanse to some of the smallest known entities in the span of a few minutes.

Several things are notable. One is how things start to change gradually at first, and then ever more rapidly. This is akin to the spatial arrangement of the numbers on the log scale graphs and number line above. In that case, the low numbers are placed rather spaciously apart and then become very compressed. (Imagine the numbers with this spacing whooshing past you like cars on a train, increasing its speed by a factor of ten with each passing car.)

Powers of Ten was an adaptation of the book *Cosmic View: The Universe in Forty Jumps,* (1957) by Dutch educator Kees Boeke (1973). If you want to play around with scales, ***Cosmic Eye***, a 3-minute film, is available as an iOS app, developed by astrophysicist Danail Obreschkow. Readers can view the "Cosmic View" film here:

https://youtu.be/8Are9dDbW24

And download the interactive app *Cosmic View* here:

https://itunes.apple.com/us/app/cosmic-eye/id519994935?mt=8

Figure 3.5 shows the **Grounded and Embodied Learning (GEL) Framework**. Inspired by Newell's (1994) timescale organization, it is a figure that I will return to frequently throughout this book. Here, the emphasis is on learning processes specifically. The scale is logarithmic ($\log_{10}$; see Box 3D). The far-left portion of the timescale shows the most rapid learning processes, those that operate at ten milliseconds or faster and are primarily implemented as changes in biological structures. In the middle, we see cognitive processes that unfold over seconds, knowledge-based processes that take place over minutes to hours (hundreds to thousands of seconds), sociocultural processes that take days to months (hundreds of thousands to tens of millions of seconds), and organizational processes—typically observed at educational institutions, companies, cities, and nations—that take years and beyond (billions of seconds).

The choice to use *time* for the GEL Framework is intentional. Size and other spatial organizations have certain constraints and affordances that emphasize proximity, reductionism, and hierarchy that are demonstrably inadequate to account for basic human behavior (see arguments offered by Lemke, 2000). As Lemke (2000, 2001) notes, time is most closely associated with *process*, and it is by investigating processes that psychologists such as myself can theorize most directly about behavior.

Time also preserves the systemic nature of organization at each scale. That is, to properly describe the nature of learning at a biological scale, as an example, still allows me to identify the *complex systems* that are unfolding here at the level of neural structures. Time offers

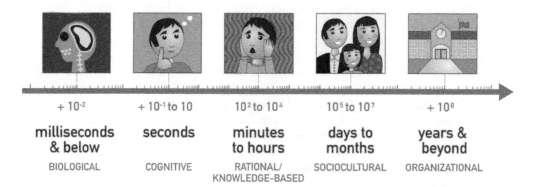

FIGURE 3.5 The Grounded and Embodied Learning (GEL) Framework depicting the timescales in which many learning processes operate. Figure uses a $\log_{10}$ scale.

an easy way to "zoom in" and still maintain a sense of the complexity involved. One quality I appreciate is that time offers a way to temporarily focus on a portion of human behavior that reduces some of the complexities in understanding learning as a whole, while still preserving much of the complexity that shapes those behaviors.

3.2.4 Conscious and Unconscious Learning Processes

Some, but not all, learning processes operate within people's conscious awareness. I will refer to those as falling within the *spectrum of consciousness*. In Chapters 5 and 6, I will spend a great deal more attention on this. For now, I want to make a few general remarks about conscious and unconscious learning processes.

As a species, human beings are capable of both explicit and implicit memory and learning. *Explicit learning* seems obvious—people are consciously aware of the learning experience taking place and its effects on us. They are given the goals explicitly, directed to learn a specific skill or pattern, shown its structure, and then engage in the learning activity. This kind of learning happens all the time. When I was learning to use a stand-up paddle board, there was overt discussion of body positioning to ensure proper weight distribution as I moved from kneeling to standing. Conscious learning processes are generally well remembered, subject to explicit monitoring and control, and can often be accurately described with words. The spectrum of consciousness largely encompasses the knowledge-based processes, and includes more coarse-grained cognitive processes, and finer-grained sociocultural processes.

So what is *implicit learning*? There are many learning processes—very likely the vast majority—that operate outside of conscious awareness. They, too, occur frequently, and—because they are *implicit*—people often do not notice. A striking example is how people learn spoken language. Native speakers develop the proper mental structures and processes to both understand and generate culturally appropriate statements in one's native languages. They do this without having to be told, without pointing out the structures, and without exerting much effort.

Implicit learning is common and important across a wide range of behaviors, from motor skills, language, cultural norms, and organizational practices. They often have no way of monitoring these processes, so it is very difficult to exert control over them (though it can be trained, as in cased of biofeedback). People often cannot recall the execution of these processes. We usually cannot provide accurate verbal descriptions of these processes (Ericsson & Simon, 1993; Nisbett & Wilson, 1977; Schooler, Ohlsson, & Brooks, 1993).

Interestingly, unconscious processes such as implicit learning can take place either because they unfold very rapidly (those on the left-hand side of the timescale) or, as with organizational and slower sociocultural processes on the right-hand side, because changes are so gradual they escape notice. In a fashion somewhat analogous to light (the spectrum of electromagnetic radiation), people only perceive a relatively small band of "visible light" across the entire range. And, much like light, even though most of it escapes people's direct awareness, "invisible" light affects us nonetheless, through sensations of warmth (infrared) and cellular degeneration in the skin and eyes (ultraviolet).

Humans have also created instruments that enable us to observe and measure those frequencies of electromagnetic radiation that extend beyond our vision. With this, people are able to bring the invisible into conscious awareness, to mathematically model the phenomena, and engineer devices that use them, such as higher frequency gamma rays (used to treat cancerous tumors) and X-rays, and, at lower frequencies, microwaves and radio waves.

As a learning theorist, my job is to find ways to measure the "invisible," describe these unconscious processes using words and mathematical models, and engineer educational experiences that use them to our benefit. I also want to better understand the benefits and costs for learning and academic performance when unconscious and conscious processes are brought together.

3.2.5 How the Timescale Structure Features Embodied Processes

The GEL Framework is a powerful organizational structure for understanding behavior. So much so, that I use this to structure Part 2 of the book. My choice is to start with the middle of the timescale, that is, those processes we find in the spectrum of consciousness. I made this choice because these are the processes of which people are most aware. They are the easiest to observe and discuss. They are also the most susceptible to learners' monitoring and control, which has important implications for many educational phenomena such as self-directed learning and instruction, as well as formative and summative assessment. I use the timescale structure to visit, in turn, the cognitive/knowledge-based learning processes (Chapters 5 & 6), biological processes (Chapters 7 & 8), and sociocultural, and organizational processes (Chapters 9 & 10). I then discuss the importance of trans-scale processes that collectively contribute to learning and instruction across the GEL framework (Chapter 11).

The timescale for organizing the varieties of learning is apt because this structure applies equally well to action systems. As I have expressed earlier, a central tenet of GEL is that "meaning ... is grounded in the action and the expected outcome of the action" (Gallese & Glenberg, 2011, p. 906). Theories of motor control (e.g., Haruno et al., 2003) explicitly model the multilevel structure that organizes finer-grained and coarser-grained systems.

An example is when a person reaches to grasp something. The body will orient; head position and eye gaze are coordinated so the most sensitive part of the visual system, the fovea, will register to that precise location of contact. One or both arms extend with joints expanding and contracting in concert with the overall movement. The hand moves into the proper position and shape for the object to be grasped well before contact is made. Then a proper amount of force of finger and hand enclosure is applied as the movement and gaze directed to capture the intended object is retracted. All of this is marvelously orchestrated to take place in synchronized fashion with little or no conscious awareness of the many systems that are involved.

Specific motor programs governing movement and nervous system control operate in this integrated, coordinated manner to fulfill specific goals and intentions. As a testament to the system's hierarchical structure and resiliency, those intentions often can be fulfilled through any of a variety of motor acts.

Gallese and Glenberg (2011) lay out their theory of action-based language. They explicate the multilevel structure of action systems along levels that can be applied to the current GEL Framework. They describe how the system coordinates levels to act, by meeting a high-level intention (such as grasping-to-eat), fulfilling goals related actions (such as approaching and grasping), and executing the finer-grained motor acts (motor movements of the body, arm, and hand) in order to carry out the actions.

Gallese and Glenberg (2011) note that the mirror neuron system demonstrates this quality of multilevel organization. Mirror neurons are specialized cells found generally in primates that appear to be central for managing highly social behaviors, such as imitation, cooperation and empathy (Rizzolatti, Fogassi, & Gallese, 2006). As an example, when I observe reaching actions of another person that correspond to reaching actions previously performed by my motor system, the mirror neuron system "fires" (that is, becomes activated). It offers a way for me to apprehend what the other person is doing—and *why* the other person is doing it—by triggering those same intentions, goals, and actions in me. I understand the actions by also *experiencing* them as internal motoric events, even though I might not be overtly performing them. Interestingly, mirror neurons will not only fire when my same actions are observed, but also when actions that match the same intentions that I have experienced, even if I observe another agent performing different specific motor acts to achieve those same, shared intentions.

Nearly all fields are faced with challenges to understand how processes that unfold at one band of time can be reconciled with those processes occurring at different bands of time for those same behaviors. How, for example can phenomena in the physical world be reconciled by models from the perspective of physics, chemistry, biology, Earth science, space science, and so on. This general question also applies to educational interests. To foster a literate society, there are learning processes taking place at the biological, cognitive, knowledge-based, cultural, and organizational levels—often simultaneously. One way we can talk about the interactions among processes *across* scales in a system is in terms of the *supervenience relation*. Supervenience describes how cognitive processes also connect to faster neurological processes, on one hand, and to slower social and cultural processes, on the other. In this terminology, it is appropriate to say that cognitive processes *supervene on* biological processes, while sociocultural processes are supervenient to cognitive processes. In this way, processes that occur at faster timescales contribute to emergent behaviors at slower timescales, while changes in processes at slower timescales result in a corresponding changes in, and impose certain constraints on more rapid processes (Sawyer, 2005).

I will also explore in Chapter 11 why systems of this sort often achieve organizational structure along these various levels of scale in the first place. Simon (2019) explores this question as applied to public administration and business organizations. Simon argues that systems with these organizational structures have greater stability in response to disruptions and perturbations. West (2017) grapples with a comparable question in understanding how patterns of growth and energy management seem to reoccur when one examines biological systems spanning sub-cellular processes, single and multi-cellular organisms, communities, corporations, all the way up to cities.

West offers that at each level there is allometric scaling. As things grow in size and complexity, each individual part does not necessarily grow in equal proportion. As a simple example, the size of one adult's head is not twice the size of another adult's head who weighs half as much. As a result of allometric scaling, the person who is twice the size need not consume twice the calories to maintain metabolic homeostasis, as would be predicted if the proportion of calories per gram was a constant. Instead it is about 25% *less* than would be expected.

West notes that a critical resource for any system (such as the blood delivering fuel and removing waste throughout the body) must be managed along networks. Fundamentally it is the growth and optimization of these networks that determine overall system behaviors such as energy consumption and longevity. This also applies to the various scales of learning I am interested in. In the case of learning, these are networks of neurons, blood vessels, memories, social connections, wires, and roadways, which serve the behaviors of systems at different scales and shape how learning processes at various scales interact with one another.

3.3 UNDERLYING ASSUMPTIONS FOR A GROUNDED AND EMBODIED LEARNING FRAMEWORK

As I have shown (Figure 3.5), action systems and learning processes operate at multiple timescales that align approximately with processes at the biological (ca. 10^{-2} s and below), cognitive (ca. 10^{-1} s to 10^1 s), knowledge-based (ca. 10^2 s to 10^4 s), sociocultural (ca. 10^5 s to

10^7 s), and organizational (ca. 10^8 s to 10^{10} s) levels. In addition several organizing concepts are introduced here that establish the GEL Framework.

3.3.1 The Mind Operates as a Predictive Architecture

First is the assumption that **the mind operates as a *predictive architecture*** so one's mental processes are tuned, not so much to perceive and store information, but to support us as active, embodied agents by anticipating what in the world will come next in order to achieve one's goals with minimal effort and maximal security (Clark, 2015; Glenberg, 1997). People continually anticipate what is to come in the stream of sensory input, and people are literally poised to respond. Furthermore, humans do not wait passively for input before they act.

Even with a predisposition toward predicting the future, if one were to only pick one most favorable prediction, the person might frequently be wrong and caught unaware. All of this person's wonderful cognitive power could be quickly snuffed out when someone failed to identify a predator, a poisonous plant, or misinterpret an enemy's social cues. Thus, a healthy cognitive system utilizes **parallel processes** to predict *all* of the plausible next-state of things. This is supported by some of the massively parallel processing power of our sensory systems.

For brief periods of time, *all* of the possible future motor states and perceptual recognitions are activated. Then, as more input comes in, the system prunes out those predictions that become less plausible. This extends well beyond the biological. There is evidence people even do this when they encounter words. Consider the word "bank" in the sentence, *Doris ran to the bank until she arrived at the water*. For a brief period of time (several hundred milliseconds), reading the word *bank* activates for readers many ideas, such as financial institution, pitched slope, and so on. Researchers can see evidence of this because the other related ideas (money, river, tilt) are briefly primed and activated. It is only after more processing occurs that the implausible associations become deactivated, leaving the most plausible meaning to be active.

These types of phenomena illustrate that people are always in prediction mode. They are processing the incoming stream of sensations about the world in ways that help with their readiness so they are most useful for queueing up future actions that will benefit their wellness.

3.3.2 Sensory Experiences Are Distortions of Reality

Sensory inputs are not all treated equally. Humans greatly favor sensory inputs that signal change. People even operate with specialized sensory systems to accentuate changes (Hubel & Weisel, 1962), because these differences provide the greatest amount of new information to inform one's readiness. Input that shows nothing new is of relatively low value. People notice the fan noise *after* it stops, and the smell of cooking onions when someone new enters the house.

Because of sensory adaptation, unchanging stimuli—be they sounds, smells, touch, and so on—are likely to become invisible to us. What's more, people mask their own ignorance. In response to "no input," the perceptual system will make up input, based on one's expectations, and treat it as a faithful record and a basis upon which to act. A startling example is the retinal blind spots (people have one such area, called a *scotoma*, in each eye!). People should rightly see a black splotch as part of their visual field whenever they look. This is because there is a moderately large area of the visual field in the back of each eye (the optical disc) that lacks any of the photoreceptor cells where the bundle of fibers that make up the optic nerve passes through the retina and onto the nervous system. People are largely unaware of this blind spot because processes downstream of the retina fill in this missing information based on the visual sensations immediately surrounding this area. They also use visual imagery from the second eye (the two scotomas typically do not overlap or register across the two visual fields). People are not only partially blind, but they are literally blind to their blindness!

3.3.3 Sensory Experiences are a Product of One's Actions, Perceptions, and Past Experiences

I take as a basic assumption that **people do not produce a verbatim, sensorial record of their environment. Rather, perceptions are constructed**, shaped by a variety of social, cognitive, and sensorimotor influences, in what Neisser (1976) referred to as a "perceptual cycle" (also called the *perception-action loop*; Spivey & Huette, 2014). People are driven to make sense of their sensory experiences, and often use context, prior experiences, and pending goals, in that process.

The phenomenologist Merleau-Ponty (from Varela et al., 2016, pp. 173–174) weighs in:

> Since all the movements of the organism are always conditioned by external influences, one can, if one wishes, readily treat behavior as an effect of the milieu. But in the same way, since all the stimulations which the organism receives have in turn been possible only by its preceding movements which have culminated in exposing the receptor organ to external influences, one could also say that behavior is the first cause of all the stimulations.

I liken this to how movement is used to enhance one's perceptual experiences: people move their eyes in order that a visual stimulus will register on the most sensitive sensory organs (in fact, human eyes move all on their own three times a second!); people actively inhale (sniff) for the olfactory organ to register smell, and people rub to feel touch. Without action, there is no sensation. In this way action and perception together constitute the experience. Figure 3.6 illustrates this fundamental interplay.

3.3.4 Sensory Experiences Are Also a Product of One's Environment

It is not just that action and perception are bound together; **the organism (us!) and the environment are also bound together**. People use environmental cues and context as much as the sensations themselves to perceive the world (Varela et al., 1993/2016). Consider the examples in Figure 3.7. In the first set, the identical stimulus is interpreted as either the letter *B* or the number *13*. In the second set, the handwritten word "is" in the first line of the phrase is identical to the digits "15" in the phone number. In each case, readers allow context to determine their interpretation, and they have almost no difficult shifting that interpretation.

As people look at a letter sequence, phrase, or phone number, they anticipate what they will see. Once the sensory stream confirms this expectation, they move on. When there is no contradictory experience, they keep on parsing the next phrase with no notice of the shift in interpretation of the same pen strokes that form letters in one case and numbers in the other.

3.3.5 Memories are Constructed and Easily Altered

It is not only perceptual processes that are constructed shaped by past experiences, context, and future goals, but **memory is constructed** as well. For example, when reading, Kintsch

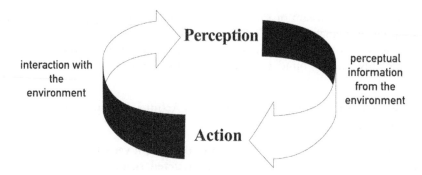

FIGURE 3.6 The perception-action loop depicting how the agent (person) experiences a perception event of an object by interacting with the environment.

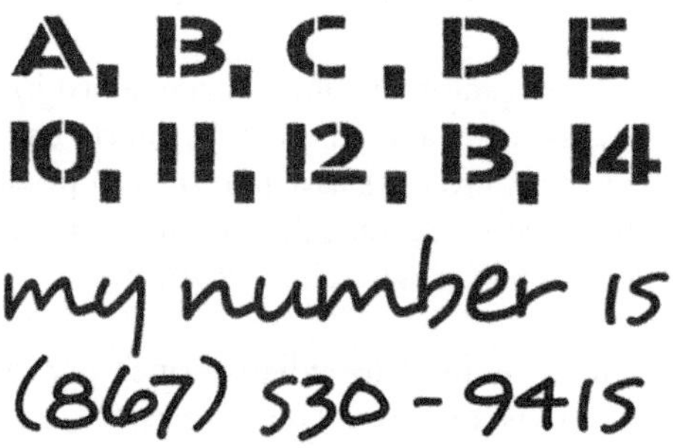

A, B, C, D, E
10, 11, 12, 13, 14

my number is
(867) 530 - 9415

FIGURE 3.7 Ambiguous symbols that changes with context.
Upper section. A symbol is seen as the letter "B" when part of a letter sequence and read as "13" when seen as part of a number sequence. *Lower section.* The "is" in the sentence becomes the number "15" when read in the context of a phone number.

(1998) provides evidence that readers automatically make many inferences that are cued by the reader's prior knowledge (called a *Situation Model*), current goals, and the context established by the prior sentences that have been read. Readers literally recall information that was never presented in a text if that information has been strongly cued by the context and the reader's prior knowledge and goals.

What's more, past memories of people's own lived experiences can be altered based on how they are retrieved. The wording of memory retrieval cues can have a large effect on what people actually recall, and on their future recollections of events that are already in their past. This can lead to the "retrieval" of "false memories." For example, in one study, children between 7 and 9 years old were presented with a false narrative, one that the research team confirmed with parents never happened. Children were asked:

> Your mother told me, that when you were 4 years old, you visited a burns center. Could you tell me everything you can remember about this event?

The theory posited that creating these believed false memories depended on three conditions being met: (1) Participants must consider the planted false event as something that is plausible. (2) They must construct contextual information for that event, such as an image or a feeling. (3) Source misattribution should be made in which they regard the false event as a genuinely experienced event.

In the analysis of the findings, it is important to note that the research team set a very high bar to cross for coding for a child's reporting of a false memory. They only coded for a false memory when a child reported remembering the false event and specifically recalled details that were not stated in the narrative, but that were related to the false event. In addition, a false memory was only coded when a child *elaborated* about the event and presented additional event-related details. It should also be noted that children in the study were also asked to recall their memory of a true event of their first day at school. On this, as a check, children showed near perfect agreement with parents' statements. And, as predicted, the majority of children did report having false memories of visiting a burns unit, often with embellishments that solidified their constructed memories.

With these basic ideas and assumptions in place, I am ready to go further into the nature of embodied learning and its relevance and role in education. That is the focus of the next chapter.

3.4 SUMMARY

In this chapter, I expounded on the nature of grounding and embodied learning. *Grounding* describes the way people connect an idea or symbol with a more familiar or concrete referent, such as an object or event in the world that facilitates meaning making. *Embodied learning* occurs when the meaning of what is learned is grounded specifically in body movement and perception. New ideas can also be grounded in language and simulations of prior experiences, where the embodied nature of the grounding is not direct. Examples from reading and mathematics education show how previously ungrounded symbols can become meaningful. Gestures and situated action are ways to foster embodied learning. Once grounding is established, people can use their imagination to expand their meaning making to new symbols and ideas.

In this chapter, I introduce the Grounded and Embodied Learning (GEL) Framework. I show that learning is a wide-ranging phenomenon, spanning some 12 orders of magnitude, and is best portrayed on a logarithmic timescale (Figure 3.5). Across these various processes, *learning* is defined as an enduring change in behavior. Still, the various learning processes exhibit different qualities at different timescales, as they move from biological, to cognitive, knowledge-based, sociocultural, and organizational levels. In the middle of this timescale, people are more apt to be consciously aware of these learning processes as they unfold. Thus, I refer to the portion of the timescale that enacts these processes as the *spectrum of consciousness*. Faster and much slower processes generally proceed outside of people's conscious awareness, though even these unconscious processes still exert tremendous influence on one's current and future behavior.

Several organizing concepts are introduced to further establish the theoretical foundations of the GEL Framework. The mind-body system operates as a *predictive architecture* and much of learning can be explained in terms of this overarching anticipatory orientation to events in the world. From a GEL perspective, it is useful to conceptualize people's experiences in terms of a perception-action loop. From this perspective, one's sensory systems do not provide an objective record of reality. Perception of reality is constructed using sensory information as influenced by one's current actions in context, along with one's goals and prior experiences. Memory, too, does not provide a veridical record of one's experiences, but accounts altered by one's context, goals and prior learning.

3.5 READER ACTIVITIES

3.5.1 Grounded Cognition

Pragmatic Reasoning Schemas for postage described above illustrates a way that people can perform a type of contextualized reasoning that is difficult when it is ungrounded.

a) Identify something you have learned that has been reframed in pragmatic terms that helped you to learn it.
b) Now I want you to identify something that you are having difficulty learning or using because it is presented as ungrounded symbols. How can you reframe this learning task in terms of a pragmatic reasoning schema that is meaningful to you?

3.5.2 Unconscious and Conscious Learning

a) Interview people about two types of conscious learning and two types of unconscious learning that they have engaged in.
b) Observe how they talk and gesture about each experience.
c) What differences do you notice?

3.5.3 The Unwind Strategy for Algebra Problems

Story-1 After hearing that Mom won a lottery prize, Bill took the amount she won and subtracted the $64.00 that Mom kept for herself. Then he divided the remaining money among her 3 sons giving each $20.50. How much did Mom win?

Word-Equation-1 Starting with some number, if I subtract 64 and then divide by 3, I get a 20.50. What number did I start with?

Story-2 After buying donuts at Wholey Donuts, Laura multiplies the number of donuts she bought by their price of $0.37 per donut. Then she adds the $0.22 charge for the box they came in and gets the total amount she paid, $2.81. How many donuts did she buy?

Word-Equation-2 Starting with some number, if I multiply it by 0.37 and then add 0.22, I get 2.81. What number did I start with?

Word-Equation-3 Starting with some number, if I multiply it by 6 and then add 66, I get 81.9. What number did I start with?

Symbol-Equation-3. $6X + 66 = 81.90$. Solve for X.

a) Solve these problems on your own.
b) Observe another person who has never been taught algebra applying the strategy. How does Unwind help ground the mathematical symbols and operations to the actions of the problems?
c) Interview a person who has a strong math background. Ask them to rank order the problems based on which they predict students will find most difficult and easiest to solve. Ask them to explain their ranking. How does their theory of student problem solving relate to grounded and ungrounded learning?

REFERENCES

Adams, A. M., Glenberg, A. M., & Restrepo, M. A. (2019). Embodied reading in a transparent orthography. *Learning and Instruction, 62*, 27–36.

Alibali, M. W., & Nathan, M. J. (2012). Embodiment in mathematics teaching and learning: Evidence from learners' and teachers' gestures. *Journal of the Learning Sciences, 21*(2), 247–286.

Barsalou, L. W. (2008). Grounded cognition. *Annual Review of Psychology, 59*, 617–645.

Boeke, K. (1957/1973). *Cosmic view: The universe in forty jumps.* John Day.

Brown, A. L. (1992). Design experiments: Theoretical and methodological challenges in creating complex interventions in classroom settings. *The Journal of the Learning Sciences, 2*(2), 141–178.

Brown, A. L. (1997). Transforming schools into communities of thinking and learning about serious matters. *American Psychologist, 52*(4), 399.

Brown, A. L., Ash, D., Rutherford, M., Nakagawa, K., Gordon, A., & Campione, J. C. (1993). Distributed expertise in the classroom. In G. Salomon (Ed.), *Distributed cognitions: Psychological and educational considerations* (pp. 188–228). Cambridge University Press.

Brown, A. L., Campione, J. C., Metz, K. E., & Ash, D. B. (1997). The development of science learning abilities in children. In A. Burgen & K. Hirnquist (Eds.), *Growing up with science: Developing early understanding of science.* Jessica Kingsley Publishers.

Brown, A. L., Campione, J. C., Reeve, R. A., Ferrara, R. A., & Palincsar, A. S. (1991). Interactive learning and individual understanding: The case of reading and mathematics. In L. T. Landsmann (Ed.), *Culture, schooling and psychological development* (pp. 136–170). Ablex.

Bruderer, A. G., Danielson, D. K., Kandhadai, P., & Werker, J. F. (2015). Sensorimotor influences on speech perception in infancy. *Proceedings of the National Academy of Sciences, 112*(44), 13531–13536.

Casasanto, D., & Chrysikou, E. G. (2011). When left is "right" motor fluency shapes abstract concepts. *Psychological Science, 22*(4), 419–422.

Casasanto, D., & Henetz, T. (2012). Handedness shapes children's abstract concepts. *Cognitive Science, 36*(2), 359–372.

Cheng, P. W., & Holyoak, K. J. (1985). Pragmatic reasoning schemas. *Cognitive Psychology, 17*(4), 391–416.

Clark, A. (2015). *Surfing uncertainty: Prediction, action, and the embodied mind.* Oxford University Press.

Constable, H. (2020). How do you build a city for a pandemic? *BBC Future,* 26 April 2020. Retrieved from www.bbc.com/future/article/20200424-how-do-you-build-a-city-for-a-pandemic

Cook, S. W., Mitchell, Z., & Goldin-Meadow, S. (2008). Gesturing makes learning last. *Cognition, 106*(2), 1047–1058.

de Vega, M., Glenberg, A. M & Graesser A. C. (Eds.). (2008). *Symbols and embodiment: Debates on meaning and cognition.* Oxford University Press.

Dehaene, S. (2009). *Reading in the brain: The new science of how we read.* Penguin.

EdWeek, (2014). 250 million children worldwide can't read. February 4, 2014. Retrieved from www.edweek.org/ew/articles/2014/02/05/20brief-1.h33.html

Ericsson, K. A., & Simon, H. A. (1993). *Protocol analysis: Verbal reports as data* (rev. ed.). MIT Press.

Fincher-Kiefer, R. (2019). *How the body shapes knowledge: Empirical support for embodied cognition.* American Psychological Association.

Geary, D. C. (1995). Reflections of evolution and culture in children's cognition: Implications for mathematical development and instruction. *American Psychologist, 50*(1), 24.

Glenberg, A. M. (1997). What memory is for. *Behavioral and Brain Sciences, 20*(1), 1–19.

Glenberg, A. M., Brown, M., & Levin, J. R. (2007). Enhancing comprehension in small reading groups using a manipulation strategy. *Contemporary Educational Psychology, 32*(3), 389–399.

Glenberg, A. M., & Gallese, V. (2011). Action-based language: A theory of language acquisition production and comprehension. *Cortex,* 48(7), 905–922.

Glenberg, A. M., Goldberg, A. B., & Zhu, X. (2011). Improving early reading comprehension using embodied CAI. *Instructional Science, 39*(1), 27–39.

Glenberg, A. M., Gutierrez, T., Levin, J. R., Japuntich, S., & Kaschak, M. P. (2004). Activity and imagined activity can enhance young children's reading comprehension. *Journal of Educational Psychology, 96*, 424–436.

Glenberg, A. M., & Robertson, D. A. (1999). Indexical understanding of instructions. *Discourse Processes, 28*(1), 1–26.

Goldstone, R. L., Landy, D., & Son, J. Y. (2008). A well-grounded education: The role of perception in science and mathematics. In M. de Vega, M. C. Glenberg, & M. A. Graesser (Eds.), *Symbols and embodiment: Debates on meaning and cognition* (pp. 327–355). Oxford University Press.

Golinkoff, R. M., & Hirsh-Pasek, K. (2000). *How babies talk: The magic and mystery of language in the first three years of life.* Penguin.

Gombrich, H. (1960). *Art and illusion: A study in the psychology of pictorial representation.* Phaidon.

Harnad, S. (1990). The symbol grounding problem. *Physica D, 42*, 335–346.

Haruno, M., Wolpert, D. M., & Kawato, M. (2003, October). Hierarchical MOSAIC for movement generation. *International congress series* (Vol. 1250, pp. 575–590). Elsevier.

Hubel, D. H., & Wiesel, T. N. (1962). Receptive fields, binocular interaction and functional architecture in the cat's visual cortex. *The Journal of Physiology, 160*(1), 106.

Kirsh, D., & Maglio, P. (1994). On distinguishing epistemic from pragmatic action. *Cognitive Science, 18*(4), 513–549.

Klahr, D. (2019). Learning sciences research and Pasteur's quadrant. *Journal of the Learning Sciences, 28*(2), 153–159.

Koedinger, K. R., & Nathan, M. J. (2004). The real story behind story problems: Effects of representations on quantitative reasoning. *The Journal of the Learning Sciences, 13*(2), 129–164.

Kolodner, J. L. (1991a). Effecting changes in education. *Journal of the Learning Sciences, 1*, 1–6.

Kolodner, J. L. (1991b). Improving human decision making through case-based decision aiding. *AI Magazine*, 12(2), 52–68.

Lakoff, G., & Johnson, M. (1999). *Philosophy in the flesh: The embodied mind and its challenge to western thought* (Vol. 640). Basic Books.

Lakoff, G., & Núñez, R. (2000). *Where mathematics comes from: How the embodied mind brings mathematics into being.* Basic Books.

Lamberg, T. (2017). A framework for integrating STEM and supporting teacher learning: Lessons learned from a professional development project on integrating nanotechnology and mathematics. Oxford University Symposium.

Lave, J. (1988). *Cognition in practice: Mind, mathematics and culture in everyday life.* Cambridge University Press.

Lave, J., & Wenger, E. (1991). *Situated learning: Legitimate peripheral participation.* Cambridge University Press.

Lebaron, C. & Streeck, J. (2000). Gestures, knowledge, and the world. In D. McNeill (ed.), *Language and gesture* (pp. 118–140). Cambridge University Press.

Lemke, J. L. (2000) Across the scales of time: Artifacts, activities, and meanings in ecosocial systems. *Mind, Culture, and Activity 7*, 273–290.

Lemke, J. L. (2001). The long and the short of it: Comments on multiple time-scale studies of human activity. *The Journal of the Learning Sciences, 10*, 17–26.

[NAEP] National Assessment of Educational Progress (2015). 2015 Mathematics & Reading Assessments. Retrieved from www.nationsreportcard.gov/reading_math_2015/#?grade=4

Nathan, M. J. (2008). An embodied cognition perspective on symbols, grounding, and instructional gesture. In M. de Vega, A. M. Glenberg, & A. C. Graesser (Eds.), *Symbols and embodiment: Debates on meaning and cognition* (pp. 375–396). Oxford University Press.

Nathan, M. J., Kintsch, W., & Young, E. (1992). A theory of algebra-word-problem comprehension and its implications for the design of learning environments. *Cognition and Instruction, 9*(4), 329–389.

Nathan, M. J., & Koedinger, K. R. (2000). Teachers' and researchers' beliefs about the development of algebraic reasoning. *Journal for Research in Mathematics Education, 31*, 168–190.

Nathan, M. J., & Martinez, C. V. (2015). Gesture as model enactment: The role of gesture in mental model construction and inference making when learning from text. *Learning: Research and Practice, 1*(1), 4–37.

Nathan, M. J., Rummel, N., & Hay, K. E. (2016). Growing the learning sciences: Brand or big tent? Implications for graduate education. In M. A. Evans, M. J. Packer, & R. K. Sawyer (Eds.) *Reflections on the learning sciences* (pp. 191–209). Cambridge University Press.

National Council of Teachers of English/ International Reading Association (NCTE/IRA) *Standards for the English Language Arts* (2009). Washington, DC: NCTE/IRA.

National Council of Teachers of Mathematics (NCTM; 2000) *Principles and Standards for School Mathematics.* Reston, VA; NCTM.

Neisser, U. (1976). *Cognition and reality: Principles and implications of cognitive psychology.* Freeman.

Newell, A. (1994). *Unified theories of cognition.* Harvard University Press.

NGSS Lead States. 2013. *Next generation science standards: For states, by states.* The National Academies Press.

Nisbett, R. E., & Wilson, T. D. (1977). Telling more than we can know: Verbal reports on mental processes. *Psychological Review, 84*(3), 231.

Rizzolatti, G., Fogassi, L., & Gallese, V. (2006). Mirrors in the mind. *Scientific American, 295*(5), 54–61.

Robbins, N. (2012). When should I use logarithmic scales in my charts and graphs? *Forbes Magazine, X.* January 19. Retrieved from www.forbes.com/sites/naomirobbins/2012/01/19/when-should-i-use-logarithmic-scales-in-my-charts-and-graphs/#59769f1d5e67

Sanchez, C. (2018). The gap between the science on kids and reading, and how it is taught. NPR Ed How Learning Happens. Retrieved from www.npr.org/sections/ed/2018/02/12/582465905/the-gap-between-the-science-on-kids-and-reading-and-how-it-is-taught

Sawyer, R. K. (2005). *Social emergence: Societies as complex systems.* Cambridge University Press.

Saxe, G. B. (1981). Body parts as numerals: A developmental analysis of numeration among the Oksapmin in Papua New Guinea. *Child Development*, 306–316.

Saxe, G. B. (1982). Developing forms of arithmetical thought among the Oksapmin of Papua New Guinea. *Developmental Psychology, 18*(4), 583.

Schooler, J. W., Ohlsson, S., & Brooks, K. (1993). Thoughts beyond words: When language overshadows insight. *Journal of Experimental Psychology: General, 122*(2), 166.

Searle, J. R. (1980). Minds, brains, and programs. *Behavioral and Brain Sciences, 3*(3), 417–424.

Seidenberg, M. (2017). *Language at the speed of sight: How we read, why so many can't, and what can be done about it.* Basic Books.

Simon, H. A. (2019). *The sciences of the artificial* (3rd ed.). MIT Press.

Smith, L. B. (2005). Action alters shape categories. *Cognitive Science, 29*(4), 665–679.

Spivey, M. J., & Huette, S. (2014). The embodiment of attention in the perception-action loop. In L. Shapiro (Ed.), *Routledge handbooks in philosophy. The Routledge handbook of embodied cognition* (p. 306–314). Routledge.

Stokes, D. (1997). *Pasteur's quadrant: Basic science and technological innovation.* Brookings Institution Press.

Tellier, M. (2005). How do teacher's gestures help young children in second language acquisition? Presentation to the International Society of Gesture Studies, ISGS, Lyon, France.

Valenzeno, L., Alibali, M. W., & Klatzky, R. (2003). Teachers' gestures facilitate students' learning: A lesson in symmetry. *Contemporary Educational Psychology, 28*(2), 187–204.

Varela, F. J., Thompson, E., & Rosch, E. (2016). *The embodied mind: Cognitive science and human experience.* MIT Press.

Wason, P. C. (1966). Reasoning. In B. Foss (Ed.), *New horizons in psychology* (pp. 135–151). Penguin Books.

West, G. B. (2017). *Scale: the universal laws of growth, innovation, sustainability, and the pace of life in organisms, cities, economies, and companies.* Penguin.

4

Forms of Embodiment and Embodied Learning

4.1 TYPES OF EMBODIMENT

I want to now identify the various processes I include under the umbrella term *grounded and embodied learning* (GEL). Moving forward, I will use the terms *body-based resources, embodiment, embodied cognition, embodied learning, embodied processes,* and *grounded education* to encompass the range of phenomena of interest.

In general, there are a variety of types of embodiment that highlight different qualities, but there is no single theoretical framework (though see proposals by Barsalou, 2008; Newen et al., 2018; Wilson, 2002). In thinking about education, I find it useful to distinguish between four types of embodiment. Embodied processes include body form and movement, to be sure, and this makes up my first type. A closely related type of embodiment with a strong literature of its own is gesture. Two other general classes of embodiment, simulation and materiality, have a rich and growing body of research on their role in learning. In one of the final chapters, I talk about emotion as another potential form. However, despite its importance, its connection to education is not well researched at this point in time. Together, these capture many, perhaps all, of the types of embodiment that are covered in this book. Note that these *types* of embodiment are different from how they *functionally* contribute to learning processes. That is addressed in the subsequent section.

4.1.1 Body Form, Movement, and Perception

A good place to start, as Diana Laurillard (2001/2013) might advise, is with our primary experiences. Our most primary experiences are of our body form, movement, and perception. This sense of embodiment comes about from our experiences with a body that has form and movement as well as specific perceptual capacities. From form comes axes of symmetry (e.g., left-right), alignment (e.g., up-down), and mass. From movement comes direction (front, back), speed and acceleration (and notions of linearity and nonlinearity), pathway, dynamics, and so on. Perception from the senses offers the experiences of depth, balance, contrast, sweet and bitter, smoothness, harmony, and so on.

As noted, movement, body form, and perception are tightly integrated processes, with fuzzy boundaries between them. Our perceptions rely on our body form and movement to experience contrast in the world, and we rely on our perceptual processes to move (Neisser, 1976). As embodied beings, we depend on an active and engaged perception-action cycle to live, pursue goals, and make sense of our experiences.

DOI: 10.4324/9780429329098-4

At the core of this seems to be what scholars from a variety of fields refer to as a *body schema*, a unified sense of the whole of the body and its abilities. As the phenomenologist Merleau-Ponty (2012, pp. 100–101) describes it, his body is not experienced as "an assemblage of organs juxtaposed in space," rather "as an indivisible possession." Body schema is especially notable in cases of "phantom limbs" (Ramachandran & Rogers-Ramachandran, 1996) and body integrity identity disorder (BIID; Blom, Hennekam, & Denys, 2012).

The body we have is also the basis of such concepts as distance. For example, people consider that which is within reach to be "close" and otherwise, "distant." Monkeys, for example, have "reachability neurons," located in the in the intraparietal sulcus. These neurons are active when there is something desirable like food that is within their reach and do not fire if the object is beyond their grasp. This creates a sense of close and far. Monkeys were trained to use a rake to get desirable objects, which extended their reach. The reachability neurons responded accordingly, firing when things were in reach of the rake (Iriki, Tanaka, & Iwamura, 1996).

Interestingly, the neurons did not fire when the monkeys merely held the rake, only when they intended to reach the object. This suggests that goals, environment, and body all interact in the formation of the bounds and expectations in forming our body schemas.

As another example, finger discrimination (e.g., digital gnosia) is an important skill for counting and early mathematics. One task (Reeve & Humberstone, 2011) is to see how quickly and accurately children can match a finger that it touched by an experimenter with the finger shown in a drawing (Figure 4.1).

Finger gnosia among 5- and 6-year olds is a strong predictor of later math performance (Fayol, Barouilette, & Marinthe, 1998). Adults retain their symbol-finger association for digital counting. They show left hand muscle activity for small numbers (1 through 4) and of the right hand for larger numbers (6 through 9).

Cognition in this view depends on *embodied action* (Varela et al., 2016). They are the experiences people have that are influenced by one's body form and sensorimotor capabilities. It is from form and movement that people develop the *basic concepts* that serve as the foundation of more complex conceptual structures (Lakoff & Johnson, 1980).

Consider how orientation such as *up* forms the basis of so many concepts (also see Shapiro, 2019): *More* is up, as is *control* ("She is on top of it."), *goodness,* and *morality* ("take the high road"), and so on. *Up* is basic to us because of our sensorimotor experiences. We live in a world with a gravitational field, so that it requires effort to get things to go up. Many things

FIGURE 4.1 Assessing finger discrimination (e.g., digital gnosia).
In the left panel, the child selects the proper finger on a diagram. In the right panel,
the child reports which finger is touched when hands are not visible. Reproduced from
(Reeve & Humberstone, 2011).

move upward as they grow—including people. When we stand, we go up. We avoid falling down because it is both painful and shameful.

Eleanor Rosch and colleagues (Rosch et al., 1976; Rosch & Lloyd, 1978) showed that *basic categories* organize much of our conceptual structure for ordinary, cultural things we encounter in our world, such as furniture, plants, and the like. In some sense, all of our memories and knowledge can be organized taxonomically, rather like the Plant Kingdom. In principle, different levels of a taxonomy are most apt for some specific purpose. For example, we may decide we want to buy a "plant" for the office, and then later decide to select a type of *Sansevieria trifasciata* (also known as the "snake plant") because it can thrive in low light and occasional neglect. We then purchase a specific instance of this category and bring it home. At each point, a different level of the taxonomy was most relevant.

Rosch found that people had preferences for certain taxonomic levels over others, which she called *basic levels* of a category. These were the levels in which category members were most frequently interacted. The interactions among members at that same level tended to use similar motor actions and they are usually the levels for which children learned the labels early in development. For example, cars were a basic category of vehicle, even though it, too, is still a category label (there are many types of cars). Chairs were basic to furniture, despite this too, being still a general class of object.

Metaphors allow us to extend these basic concepts to more complex ideas. Metaphors simulate the meaning of abstract and complex concepts in terms of familiar and concrete (source) concepts. Thus, embodied actions and percept, and their metaphor extensions ground the meaning of many of the concepts used to reason about and describe the world.

Body axis also provides the foundation for basic concepts. Casasanto and colleagues (Casasanto & Chrysikou, 2011; Casasanto & Henetz, 2012) explored this in terms of right-left relations to judgments. They show how our asymmetries regarding handedness influence a variety of cognitive processes. There is a strong preference to place things to the right that people regard as positive (rather than negative), kinder, more favorable. However, this preference is exactly reversed for left-handed people! The effect is so reliable that it holds even when the researchers temporarily turned right-handed adults into lefties—reversing their orientation of the judgments. It is as though our general *symmetry* that sensitizes us to a left/right axis, also uses the *a*symmetry within that structure to make preferences.

Nisbett and Wilson (1977) report that people unconsciously have these preferences. They showed a reliable effect on people's evaluation of commonplace consumer goods, such as nightgowns and stockings, depending on whether the items were to the left or the right of the midline axis of people's bodies. The effect is so pronounced that stockings in the right-most position were favored four time more than those in the left-most position—even though they were identical! When asked to explain their preferences, participants never mentioned position, and denied it was a factor—stridently so—in their selections.

Spatial systems also belong to this sense of embodiment (Tversky, 2019). Small-scale spatial movements, such as rotations, and large, whole-body spatial reasoning, such as navigation, contribute basic concepts that are readily available from a lifetime of manipulating objects and traversing past objects and other people through space. As is clear in the next section, people often use spatial concepts metaphorically to extend cognition beyond the basic concepts, in order to better apprehend novel and abstract concepts, such as infinity.

4.1.2 Gesture

Gestures are a special type of action that occur during communication, learning, and instruction. *Gestures* are movements of our hands and arms, as well as other body parts, that we make spontaneously as we talk with others and think to ourselves, including pointing and tracing actions. Instead of practical functions that initiate changes in the world, gestural actions serve cognitive and social functions (Goldin-Meadow & Beilock, 2010). Gestures are common-place, pan-cultural hand and arm movements that naturally occur during speech (Kendon, 2004). They are an integral part of communication, providing co-expressive meaning in ways imagistic, holistic ways that complement the sequential, syntactic nature of spoken language.

Gestures serve a communicative role that contribute to the listener's experience. They also reveal as well as influence the thought processes of the speaker. For example, gestures made by children when they are reasoning about conservation of the volume of liquid can reveal which children are most ready to make the developmental progression to understanding conservation more deeply (Church & Goldin-Meadow, 1986). Gesture production also can facilitate a speaker's access to words, especially spatial words, including for speakers diagnosed with aphasia (Krauss, 1998).

Teachers' gestures can enhance student learning (Cook & Goldin-Meadow, 2006; Valenzeno, Alibali, & Klatzky, 2003). A number of recent studies of classroom teaching have shown that gestures are frequent during instruction. Teachers seem to most often make instructional gestures when they are introducing new material to students, discussing abstract ideas, and when addressing a student area of difficulty or "trouble spot" (Alibali & Nathan, 2007; Alibali et al., 2013, 2014). Analyses suggest that teachers often employ gestures to direct students' attention, make connections between disparate ideas and to ground formal representations, and to help establish and maintain cohesion across lessons and foster common ground with learners (Alibali & Nathan, 2012; Nathan et al., 2013; Walkington et al., 2011)

Gesture scholars (e.g., McNeill, 1992) generally identify four main classes of gestures: index-ical, iconic, metaphoric, and beats. *Indexical gestures*, such as pointing, allow one to de-reference demonstratives (e.g., this, that, these) and add location information. Vygotsky (1988) hypothesized that pointing gestures develop from infants' attempts at reaching, where the action develops from pragmatic to indexical. *Iconic gestures* convey semantic information by using hand shape and the hand motion trajectory. *Metaphoric gestures* use iconic actions in a metaphorical manner. An example is when a teacher metaphorically acts out two adja-cent spaces when discussing the two sides of an argument. *Beat gestures* are rhythmic actions during speech that keep time. Whereas iconic and metaphoric gestures often resemble (either literally or metaphorically) the things mentioned during speech, beats capture aspects of the prosody and the discourse itself, such as enumeration of a list.

In all, body-based forms, movements and perceptions, including epistemic actions and gestures, constitute an important type of embodiment. This provides a source of grounding experiences and concepts, reduces cognitive demands, and reveal as well as influence cognition.

4.1.3 Embodied Simulation

The next type of embodiment I want to highlight is simulation. *Simulations* are those mental events that are conducted "offline," away from the place of their original intent. They are an aspect of our imagination that enable us to extend the cognitive processes we have for things that are present and familiar so that we can think about possible things and unfamiliar ideas (Nemirovsky & Ferrara, 2009). Our capacity for simulation has been the source of intri-guing narratives such as the film "The Matrix," and speculation that we may live in a dream (Zhuangzi, 2013) or other people's computer simulations (Bostrom, 2003); topics I will pursue further in the final chapter of the book.

Much of language comprehension, for example, uses simulations that we have already encountered in this book—*mental models* and *situation models* (Gentner & Stevens, 1983/ 2014; Kintsch, 1998; Gentner and Stevens, 1983). Glenberg, Meyer, & Lindem (1987) for example showed that readers automatically know that when a story character went on a jog so did the sweatshirt that he donned. One set of studies demonstrates that readers likely re-experience the orientation of objects depending on how the objects are presented in the story. Readers are faster to verify that an object such as a pencil was mentioned as being placed in a drawer or in a cup if their judgment was preceded by the matching image of the pencil as vertical or horizontal (Stanfield & Zwaan, 2001; Zwaan, Stanfield, & Yaxley, 2002).

How people perform mental rotation is another compelling example. When judging if an object is a match (but rotated) to a standard object, or its mirror image, people do something remarkable. We may feel as though we can perform the necessary rotation "all in our heads." However, the time it takes to respond is a direct function of the degrees we need to perform the rotation. It is as though we are physically rotating the object through all the intermediate angles in order to respond (Shepard & Cooper, 1986; Shepard & Metzler, 1971).

Scholars have realized human minds do more than run mental models like movies. They actually re-experience some of the sensorimotor processes of earlier experiences when imagining events, objects, and ideas. Neural imaging data using fMRI show that reading words with strong motor associations—such as *kick, lick,* and *pick*—activated, selectively, those motor areas of the brain that are activated when people moved their feet, tongue, and fingers, respectively (Pulvermüller, 2005, 2008; Hauk, Johnsrude, & Pulvermüller, 2004).

Barsalou (1999) proposed the theory of Perceptual Symbol Systems, in response to the Physical Symbol System Hypothesis I described in Chapter 1. In Barsalou's theory, modality-specific sensorimotor experiences are essential aspects of the memories people form for objects, events, and ideas. He describes how reinstating memory of the idea of CHAIR will also reinstate an amalgam of sensorimotor experiences of seeing, touching, sitting, and standing upon various chairs. Ideas for concepts such as CHAIR, Barsalou (1999, 2008) argues, will be *grounded* for the actor in these perceptual symbols that encapsulate these lived experiences. In contrast, models based on amodal symbol systems of meaning will remain ungrounded, like those of the Chinese Room.

Theories of meaning and learning that rely on grounding make some clear, testable predictions. For example, as Pulvermüller's studies demonstrate, we should expect to see sensorimotor activation when the ideas are activated. People engage the same neural systems when they encounter and use objects (see a red wagon, taste food, or strike a hammer down and up) as when they think about the objects or read words that label them (Martin, 2007).

Another testable hypothesis is that experiencing the sensations and motor movements of associated ideas and objects should activate the concepts. For example, educational researchers have shown movements can enhance mathematics learning. Crucially, it is not all movements but ones that are mathematically relevant to the concept.

Abrahamson and colleagues (Abrahamson & Sánchez-García, 2016; Howison et al., 2011) helped elementary grade children develop a deeper sense of proportion and multiplicative reasoning using the *Mathematics Imagery Trainer for Proportion* without explicit mathematics instruction. Instead, students were left to figure out for themselves how to make a screen go from red to green, and stay green, as they raised their two hands in front of a computer screen. In so doing, they realize that one hand must move at a rate in *proportion to* the other (e.g., a 2:1 or 3:2 ratio). In solving this motor control challenge, the inference is that they constructed new sensorimotor structures that formed the basis for grounded notions of proportion that served their development of more general multiplicative relationships.

Smith, King, and Hoyte (2014) engaged elementary grade students in making different types of angles with their bodies. They found that making conceptual connections between physical arm movements and the grounding metaphor "angles as space between sides" allowed students to demonstrate greater understanding of estimating and drawing angles.

Nathan and colleagues found evidence of actions influencing performance on advanced forms of mathematical reasoning—proof production. Across several studies, high school and college students were asked to assess and justify whether certain mathematical conjectures were either false or always true. An example conjecture is this:

> Mary came up with the following conjecture: "For any triangle, the sum of the length of any two sides must be greater than the length of the remaining side." Provide a justification as to *why* Mary's conjecture is true or false.

Those who produced more gestures, especially *dynamic gestures*, which demonstrated ways that participants were testing the generalizability of the geometric properties of the objects, performed better. They had more accurate intuitions, which were coded as their initial snap judgments of whether the conjecture was true or false. They showed superior insights about the core mathematical ideas associated with the conjecture. They were also significantly more likely to produce mathematically valid proofs, the most stringent of the outcome measures (Nathan et al., 2014; Nathan et al., 2020; Nathan & Walkington, 2017; Walkington et al., 2019). These results held when controlling for a variety of factors such as prior math education and spatial reasoning.

Scholars have also examined how interference with sensorimotor processes reduces one's reasoning. Goldstone, Landy, and Son (2010) varied the movement of visual patterns in the background of algebraic equations so that the pattern movements either were compatible or contradictory to the direction of expected symbol manipulation. Contradictory movements significantly reduced the accuracy of students' equation-solving performance. This effect held even though the symbols do not actually move—we just imagine that they do, and simulate that.

Yee and colleagues (2013) investigated how movements that interfered with people's hands (playing "patty cake," or "pat-a-cake") *selectively* interfere with thinking. The researchers hypothesized that if people use sensorimotor simulations to think about things, then movements that interfere would only hamper their ability to think about an object with which they had familiarity manipulating (e.g., a pencil). They predicted it should have little impact on objects for which they had no familiarity manipulating (e.g., a tiger). Yee and colleagues found that performing incompatible movements interfered with cognitive tasks with the primary object, such as judging whether it was abstract or concrete, or even naming the objects. Importantly, interference was greatest for objects that were frequently handled by participants.

One hypothesis regarding simulation-based processes is whether thinking incurs costs when switching between sensory modalities. It has long been known that when people perceive sensations there are delays (i.e., processing "costs") when shifting from hearing to tasting to seeing, etc. The question is whether there are comparable switching delays for making judgments about concepts when those judgments cross perceptual modalities. Keep in mind that the objects in question are not present and are not currently being perceived. Thus, the judgments being made are conceptual and based on people's memories.

In fact, people do exhibit such delays. When they are asked to verify a touch modality, for example, that peanut butter is sticky, people are slower if the preceding judgment involved sound or vision, then if it also involved touch. People do appear to rely on perceptual qualities when performing these conceptual tasks.

Together, this set of findings suggests that perceptual processes motor activation is a critical constituent of how we think about and represent in memory objects (pencils) and abstract symbols (algebra equations, angles). People do not seem to form a static *description* of the objects and ideas that we store in memory, like a notebook. Rather, the very way we think about both concrete and abstract things incorporates the ways we use them and experience them sensorially.

One final observation is how the body is conceptualized in virtual spaces. Gee (2008) uses video games as a microcosm for understanding human development and learning. In video games, as in real life, Gee notes that people often take on the role of "virtual characters" by "taking a projective stance" (p. 261). People first survey the world in terms of their own potential actions, and second, determine how those actions attain one's desires and goals. People then try to assume the identity of an actor for whom those desired goals are attainable and use that persona to participate in social spaces.

4.1.4 Materialist Epistemology

My next category of embodiment includes those ways we use physical objects and material in the world to perform epistemic operations normally thought to be exclusively intellectual. There are several examples of this phenomenon. One notable example is the discovery of DNA structure and replication by Watson & Crick. Many factors contributed to their discoveries in cellular biology. Still, there is evidence from their own accounts and notes that the use of physical cardboard cutouts and the famous ball-and-stick models were instrumental in discovering how DNA replication worked and created built-in checks that minimized copying errors (Watson, 1968).

I am of course talking about the realization that the purine nucleobase adenine (A) had to always pair with pyrimidine base thymine (T) on the complimentary strand, while the purine bases guanine (G) always matched with the pyrimidine base cytosine (C). In this way, veridical replication was aided when a strand of A and G would strip away, but could only join with a matched strand of T and C, respectively.

To give a sense of the complexities involved without such built-in checks, proteins typically are coded with about 1,000 base pairs, while human genes typically involve around 27,000 base pairs and can run up to 2 million! With such an enormous set of possible combinations, the physical models they built as they digested the many other scientific findings were key to making this discovery.

Michael Faraday's invention of the electromagnetic motor led to enormous breakthroughs on the nature of electromagnetic phenomena, including light, the fundamental relationship between electrical and magnetic fields, and the conservation energy as it is transferred between electrical and mechanical forms. Faraday's inventions were not a result of the application of scientific theories of energy—those advancements and the mathematical models known as *Maxwell's Equations* would not come until several years later. Rather, it was Faraday's mechanical skills that led to these discoveries. The theory was so subordinate to the material innovations that he did not provide a written account to prove its correctness. Instead, he shipped miniature, functioning motor assemblies to colleagues to prove his discovery in the same way scientists share academic papers.

Davis Baird (2004) coined the terms "materialistic conceptions of knowledge" and "materialistic epistemology" to describe these innovations. I find it helpful to think about how these and other physical developments remained distinct from the scientific theorizing in these same topics that often trailed and failed. Materialist epistemologies have several significant traits. One is that physical objects and material in the world are used to perform epistemic operations. The objects carry forward the creative theories, even when people are unable to describe the underlying theory in words or mathematical formalisms.

Another is that one does not need to believe something for the materiality of a device to exist and operate correctly. That is in contrast to scientific theory, which are usually formed as words or symbolic equations. The knowledge of a principle on display from a functioning device is not a property of *our* beliefs, but objectively the outcome of the device's mere existence and behavior.

One last trait is that materialistic science knowledge (often reified in the form of some technology) further distinguishes it from scientific theories. It has to work to be what is claimed of it. Relatedly, its functioning is not jeopardized by any flaws or omissions in foundational knowledge. This is aptly illustrated in the discoveries made by the Wright brothers of sustained, human-powered flight.

Orville and Wilber Wright made gains far ahead of efforts that were vastly better funded by sources such as the US Department of War, as compared to their personal resources as early Twentieth Century bicycle mechanics (McCullough, 2015). Their designs exemplified materialist epistemology. The incorrect theories of lift and drag that plagued the designs of Samuel Pierpont Langley and others were irrelevant. Instead they relied on brilliant engineering design cycles of important subcomponents, such as wing design, that focused on physical performance rather than theoretical consistency, which doomed other efforts (Bradshaw, 1992).

The philosophers Andy Clark and David Chalmers (1998) have explored this question in terms of individual cognition. They support the ideas, as articulated above, that our sensorimotor processes as we operate in the world contribute to cognition in important ways. Yet they are pitching something far more radical; that is, more fundamental. They argue that the interactions we have with objects in the world, such as notebooks and calculators, are often an inseparable part of thinking and knowing. Their position is that how people interact with objects in the world can—literally—*be* cognition. They call this *extended mind*. As part of the extended mind, they propose the following:

> If, as we confront some task, a part of the world functions as a process which, *were it done in the head*, we would have no hesitation in recognizing as part of the cognitive process, then that part of the world *is* (so we claim) part of the cognitive process. Cognitive processes ain't (all) in the head!
>
> (p. 10)

They call this the Parity Principle of cognition because it places external objects that figure into thought processes as being on equal footing with internal mental structures.

Scholars from sociocultural perspectives have long made a case that the proper unit of analysis of any complex behavior is socially organized human activity (Cole & Engeström, 1993, 2007; Engeström, 1987; Gauvain, 1993).

This general notion has appeared in learning theory under a variety of closely related labels, including *distributed intelligence* (Pea, 1993), *distributed cognition* (Hutchins, 1995), *situated cognition* (Brown, Collins, & Duguid, 1989; Resnick, 1987; Robbins & Aydede, 2008), *situativity* (Greeno, 1998), *communities-of-practice* (Brown & Duguid, 1991; Lave & Wenger, 1993; Wenger, 1999). At the core of all of these is the notion of an *Activity System* (sometimes referred to as *Scandinavian Activity Theory*; Engeström, 1987/2015; Leont'ev, 1981). Perceiving, acting, remembering, and reasoning, operate in concert to perform meaningful, goal-directed activity. This *systemic* view of learning and behavior rejects the *factoring assumption*, which posits that some components of the learning system, such as context, can be "factored out" and analyzed independently of one another (Greeno & Engeström, 2014).

Stepping back, it seems clear there is a rich and growing body of evidence that thinking and learning are embodied not only *in* and *by* our bodies, but they are embedded in and materially instantiated by the objects and environments in which we function (Pouw, van Gog, & Paas, 2014). Some ways of knowing and learning take place in an extended space beyond the body. Attention to materialist epistemology and extended mind reframes cognition as made up of our interactions with the world in a very material way. In so doing, extended mind posits that a more complete account of the loop between perception and action involves influences of the environment as well.

This materialist and extended form of embodied learning has important implications for education that I elaborate on in later chapters. As a preview, this type of embodied learning further underscores the value of Laurillard's (2001/2013) call for education to provide students with primary (i.e., direct) experiences for learning. It offers a scientific basis for why learning with manipulatives and physical models is important across the lifespan, from the most elementary level concepts, such as counting, to state-of-the-art scientific discovery (Pouw, van Gog, & Paas, 2014). Extended mind, distributed intelligence, and materialist epistemology invite designers to maintain a focus on the situated activity system, system resources, and interactions, rather than the learner's "internal" resources. It also gives a psychological and sociocultural basis for the role of materialist programs of learning through design (e.g., Penner, 1997, 1998) and making things (Blikstein, 2013). It also acknowledges the importance of documenting participation as a part of how learning is assessed.

4.1.5 Summary

In this section I reviewed four types of embodiment: body form, movement and perception, gesture, embodied simulation, and materialist epistemology. These types can overlap with one another but also have sufficiently distinct qualities as to warrant their own labels. For example, gestures are a kind of body movement but also have qualities of language that make them distinct. While these are each integral to understanding and designing for embodied learning, these forms of embodiment do not specify how learning happens. That is the topic of the next section. I then use the types of embodiment and ways of learning to organize a wide array of embodied learning behaviors, and identify where these learning behaviors fit along the timescale of Figure 3.5.

4.2 FOSTERING EMBODIED LEARNING: FOUR WAYS

There are several schemes for categorizing the ways embodiment fosters learning (e.g., Wilson, 2002). I prefer to organize these ways into four functions: learning by grounding, cognitive offloading, transduction and participation. I elaborate on each of these functions, and summarize their role in Table 4.3 at the end of this section. Briefly, grounding, the reader will recall, describes how ideas in our minds are made meaningful because of the ways they are connected to things we can sense and do. Cognitive offloading describes the various ways the external world reduces the demands on our limited cognitive resources and provides cognitive resources. Transduction describes how performing actions and experiencing sensations induces cognitive states, which can reinvoke past memories and generate new ways of thinking. Participation is the adoption of new practices to achieve group belonging.

4.2.1 Grounding

Grounding describes the connection between an idea, like *roundness*, and a more concrete referent, like a wheel (Glenberg, de Vega, & Graesser, 2008). In making connections of abstract ideas to things that are concrete or familiar, grounding facilitates meaning making (e.g., Glenberg & Robertson, 1999; Harnad, 1990; Lakoff & Johnson, 1999; Lakoff & Núñez, 2000).

I find the ethnographic account of the number system developed by the Oksapmin as particularly illustrative of the notion of grounding. Geoffrey Saxe (Saxe, 1981, 1982) lived among this cultural group in a remote area of Papua, New Guinea. Figure 4.2 shows how each number concept is grounded in one of 27 specific body parts. It traditionally served only ordinal (i.e., counting) and cardinal (e.g. total number) roles. As Saxe describes, the expression for "7th" is "the forearm," and for "14th" is "the nose."

Saxe found that although the system was not devised with money in mind, native Oksapmin could learn to reason about money by expanding this system. Saxe demonstrated this in a kind of teaching experiment. Figure 4.3 shows how they developed different strategies to accommodate the different arithmetic problems that would arise during trade. This shows that such grounded systems can still be flexible and support transfer of learning.

Importantly, grounding can also occur with language. Humans' capacity for processing natural language is a core system, much as perception and movement (e.g., Spelke, 2000). Language also may be unique in that it enables the extensions of other core capacities. This can happen, for example, when an idea that people can experience, such as "slope" in movement, such as walking up or down a hill, gains a label or symbol, as it does in algebra (e.g., m in $Y = \underline{m}X + b$). This symbolic labeling of a preexisting concept follows from the ideas of Charles Sanders Peirce, the polymath (Glenberg, de Vega, & Graesser, 2008, p. 1), who noted that for signs to have meaning–anything from words and phrases, notational symbols, and numerals—they need to be grounded in some type of experience, or connected to some other signs that are ultimately grounded. And once a sign has meaning, it can influence how people use and refer to the original grounding concept. Grounded signs connect the

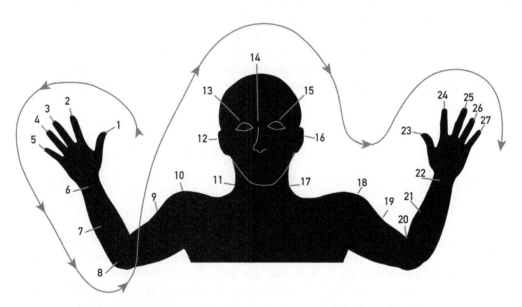

FIGURE 4.2 The counting system used by the Oksapmin. Numerals follow the order of occurrence of body parts used for counting and cardinality.

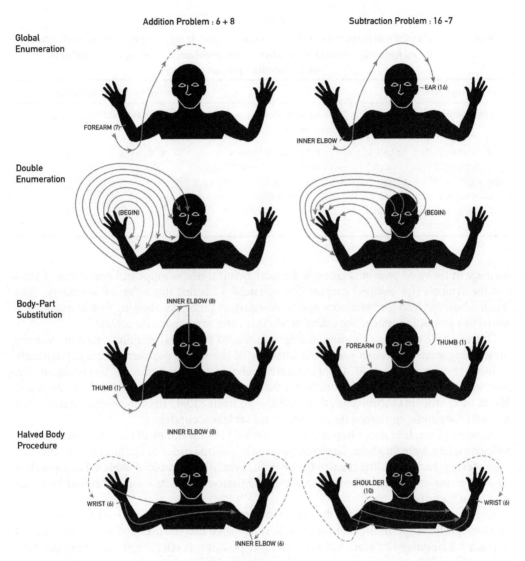

FIGURE 4.3 The counting system used by the Oksapmin as expanded in different ways to accommodate monetary arithmetic.

interpretant or idea referred to by the sign (e.g., the experience of traversing a slope on a hillside) to something tangible, such as an object (e.g., Mount Sanitas) or event (that time I ran down Mount Sanitas in a fluke summer snowstorm).

In a series of studies, Koedinger and colleagues showed the educational benefits incurred when mathematical ideas are grounded in language. They designed math problems with the same underlying quantitative relationships that were presented either symbolically or in one of two types of verbal presentations, story problems, or word-equations. As shown in Table 4.1, story problems had a simple narrative, while word-equation problems used words to describe the equation without a story narrative.

Koedinger and colleagues found that the same problems were better solved when they were presented in words than when they were presented as arithmetic and algebraic symbols (Koedinger & Nathan, 2004; Koedinger, Alibali, & Nathan, 2008). This is because the linguistic meaning of

TABLE 4.1

Materials used to show evidence of a verbal advantage. Example algebra problems with the same quantitative relationships presented as either a story problem, a word-equation problem, or a symbolic equation

Showed a verbal advantage		Showed a symbol disadvantage
Story Problem (most grounded)	Word-Equation Problem (words but no story context)	Symbolic Equation Problem (most symbolic)
As a waiter, Ted gets $6 per hour. One night he made $66 in tips and earned a total of $81.90. How many hours did Ted work?	Starting with some number, if I multiply it by 6 and then add 66, I get 81.90. What number did I start with?	$T \times 6 + 66 = 81.90$

language in the word problems grounds the mathematical relationships and operations in ways that the symbols (for novices) cannot. The researchers labelled this a "verbal advantage." The verbal advantage held for both story and word-equation problems, showing that language *itself* served as a grounding system, regardless of whether there was a narrative context.

One example of how grounding in language was so beneficial was illustrated in students "unwinding strategy." When presented with one of the verbal problems, students naturally deduced they could "unwind" the quantitative relationships by "running" the problems "in reverse" as a way to isolate the unknown values. When unwinding "add 66" or "he made $66 in tips," students intuitively subtracted the 66 from 81.90. The unwinding strategy was applied to symbolic equations far less often, and far less accurately.

Another example is how often students revealed how meaningless the ungrounded symbolic equations were for them. Students frequently violated order of operations or combined unlike terms (such as adding the 6 to the 66 in the symbolic example of Table 4.1), errors they rarely or never committed when those same quantitative elements were embedded in one of the verbal formats.

Grounding is commonly used during classroom learning and instruction (Nathan, 2008). Teachers perform grounding acts of several sorts. They use gestures and other movements to teach L2 languages to students. For example, pointing is effective for teaching deictics, such as *this* and *that*; while many imperative verbs are effectively taught using iconic gestures (Macedonia, 2019). As described above, math teachers will make indexical gestures to part of an equation or graph in order to ground a label or idea to an object or symbol (Alibali & Nathan, 2007). A teacher may form a corner with her hands—an iconic gesture—to give form to a novel idea, such as "right angle" (see Figure 3.1).

Metaphor also provides a powerful mechanism for grounding novel ideas. In social studies, for example, descriptions of systems of government are typically grounded in spatial referents, as when discussing the "higher and lower courts." Lakoff and Nunez (2000) argued that spatial-temporal metaphors are fundamental to how mathematics is understood by people, even professional mathematicians.

Teachers also structure grounded learning through material experiences. Students better understand principles of biomechanics when they have engaged in activities such as designing an elbow (Penner, 1997). Students also develop a better understanding of fractions when they can "physically distribute" their ideas with manipulatives (Martin & Schwartz, 2005) that reduce cognitive load (Pouw, et al., 2014). This understanding also supported improved transfer to novel problems.

Learning in school and many workplace settings also use collaborative projects that establish distributed intelligence around a topic, such as interdependencies among ecosystems. Cognition may also be extended to include common tools found in the workplace. Engineering students will learn to use CAD/CAM systems as part of a project to design new Lego™ pieces to expand the capabilities of robotic vehicles. Knowledge of inscribing a circle into a square is distributed to the CAD software that performs some of the calculations.

Metaphor and language also effectively ground ideas in ways that enhance meaning and learning. In these ways, grounding is closely related to Shapiro's (2019) Conceptualization hypothesis. This is because our body forms, types of movements, and perceptual abilities largely set the terms of what we can understand. Grounding is the means by which ideas and symbols are made meaningful. Indeed, it is through such qualities as the embodied basic concepts that are formed through our direct experiences that people naturally solve the Symbol Grounding Problem discussed in Chapter 1 (Harnad, 1990).

Shapiro (2019) regards grounding as aligned with his *Conceptualization Hypothesis*. He states (p. 80): "The kind of body an organism possesses constrains or determines the concepts it can acquire." Consistent with this, our types of bodies influence how we perceive things, for example, and the types of metaphors that are likely to be meaningful.

This claim has strong parallels with linguistic determinism (Whorf, 1956/2012). The Sapir-Whorf view, in its "strong" form, is that one's image of the world is shared only by those who also share linguistic, and presumably, cultural and physical backgrounds. It proposes that one's language actually determines how we think and what we are able to think about. Grounding, whether directly by the body, or via language, provides evidence in favor of the Conceptualization Hypothesis. Learners' bodies, embodied interactions with the material world, and systems of language *are* how people make meaning.

4.2.2 Cognitive Offloading

Cognitive offloading is a fancy way to describe why I reach for a pad of paper when I need to remember a phone number, or why someone else might grab an abacus. Offloading is the use of external resources to manage highly constrained cognitive and attentional resources. Offloading refers to ways to aid in *saving* information in response to one's limited *memory* capacity (the pad of paper) and also ways to aid in *manipulating* information in response to one's limited *processing* capacity (the abacus).

Kirsch and Maglio (1994) observed Tetris players offloading many of the cognitively and perceptually demanding processes onto the game environment. They distinguished between players' *pragmatic actions*, which were functional (such as dropping the shape down), and their *epistemic actions*, those that spared them cognitive and perceptual effort. Tetris is highly time limited, and the time demands can increase from further play.

An example of epistemic action was to manually rotate an object while it falls in order to increase a player's awareness of its exact shape so it may better interlock into the spaces below. Players could do this mentally, but it was faster and less effortful to use the rotation key to accomplish the same thing. Another offloading strategy was to reduce the perceptual demand of knowing of a piece would exactly fall into its intended place below. To better assess its precise position, a player may move the shape all the way to the left-hand side of the screen (rapidly with the left arrow key), then move it back, but this time knowing precisely how it lines up in order to make a match from very high up.

Offloading is a vital psychological function. It is not simply that cognitive processes would slow down, or be less exacting without offloading; rather, without it some cognitive processes could not operate at all.

As further examples, what of doing literacy? Or mathematics? Performing anything beyond the basics in these domains—and there are many others—may not be tractable without coordinating external resources for cognitive offloading.

Language developed along two general pathways: oral and written. Oral language developed many thousands of years before written language Christiansen & Kirby, 2003). As Geary (1995) and others have noted, while verbal language is a biologically primary capability for humans, the ability to read and write is not. Literacy requires that people be explicitly taught by those more knowledgeable to learn the "code" that standardizes written language.

Written literacy become important with the development of printing press (invented by Choe Yun-ui in Korea, ca. 1250 AD; and by Gutenberg in Europe, ca. 1440 AD; Newman, 2019). The shift to recording written language was an enormous change for human culture! With it, cultural knowledge can be recorded almost permanently. Ideas can be transported across great distances as well as through time. Donald (1993) posits that the symbolization and subsequent automation of the production of external memory stores—first walls, scrolls, and books, and now computers—were critical to the development of modern civilization.

As with literacy, offloading of mathematical symbols and procedures expands one's cognition. Scholars in developmental psychology and cognitive neuroscience have shown that there is basic support for two systems of mathematics. Humans are seemingly endowed with "core" mathematics knowledge (Feigenson, Dehaene, & Spelke, 2004). Part of that core knowledge is the "approximate number system," which humans share with a variety of other species. The approximate number system supports qualitative processing of magnitudes based primarily on perceptual (sensorimotor) processes. It enables us to determine quantities of up to 4 or so items placed a table at a glance, or that there are about twice as much of somethings in one tray than in another. Though often measured with visual stimuli it works across sensory modalities. The approximate number system is present in infants for very small numbers yet persists throughout our lifespan.

We also have an *exact* system for mathematics that includes skills for such mathematical activities as counting and precise calculations. To perform these well, and with ever larger and more varied types of numbers, we depend on external symbols. Consider performing even a relatively easy multiplication problem such as 314×27 completely in your head.

Now use writing. Writing this same problem down in a form suitable for column arithmetic reveals a variety of cognitive benefits: (1) One can keep visually revisiting the original written numbers (i.e., the multiplicand and the multiplier) rather than rehearse them and thereby add load to working memory; (2) the overall calculation can be subdivided into a series of much easier, single digit computations, with intermediate results also recorded; and (3) one can start from the units and proceed to the tens, hundreds, and then thousands, and then read the final answer in the conventional order, starting with thousands, then hundreds, and so on.

In a provocative thought experiment, philosophers Clark and Chalmers (1998) introduce the reader to Otto and Inga, and compare the ways they navigate their city. Otto, who suffers from Alzheimer's disease, depends on information in his notebook to make his way through each day. He writes down everything he learns each day and uses that as the most reliable source of long-term memory. We meet Otto on a day that he wishes to go to the Museum of Modern Art. His notebook is essential in navigating his way there. Inga, has committed all of the same navigation information to memory and executes them the same way as Otto does. Clark and Chalmers conclude that Otto and Inga are both engaged in comparable cognitive processes, albeit that Ott's "memory" is externalized, or extended.

It is, of course, no large stretch to replace a notebook for a smart phone. In this updated scenario, we are all Otto. I was recently reminded with the failure of my phone, how much information I need to get through my day that I have relegated to my phone—not as *backup* memory, but as my *primary* memory store. I should also note that in this scenario *both* Otto and Inga experience the extended mind. When Inga encounters a step in her navigation memory to, say, "turn right when I reach 53rd Street," she is relying on landmarks in the environment, rather than a complete internal map, to perform her goal.

Gestures can provide offloading support through acts such as pointing. Consider how a teacher may gesture to a blank whiteboard during a lesson. The board might have contained a detailed mathematical derivation during an earlier lesson. The act of pointing to the whiteboard can reinstate for the learner the prior contents of the board without having to recreate it.

The notion of an "open book" examination fits with cognitive offloading. Ideally, open book tests do not assess students on factual information that is easily looked up. Rather, learners are assessed for how they *use* certain knowledge rather than what they have memorized.

Cognitive offloading provides a useful way to test Shapiro's (2019) Constitution Hypothesis. This is the view that "the body or world plays a constitutive rather than a merely causal role in cognitive processing" (p. 5). This view posits that the phenomena we consider as cognition extends beyond the cranium and includes our bodies as well as the environments with which we interact. The claim that the body and body-based interactions with the world may *be* rather than merely *cause* cognition might seem to be an unorthodox claim. It certainly would be for scholars of classical cognitive science. It is, however, consistent with a growing body of work in distributed and situated cognition, some of which will be revealed in the coming chapters.

4.2.3 Transduction

When people engage embodied resources during thinking and communicating, what are they actually engaging, and how does it facilitate learning and thinking? So far, I have described two of the four types of embodiment to provide an account for how this can work. In the first account, people can use embodied resources to ground a new idea to something familiar and concrete. This establishes a relation between the new idea or symbol to the familiar experience. The relation may be direct, but it can also be metaphorical.

A second account of embodiment that facilitates thinking and learning is by offloading cognitively demanding information and processes onto one's body or the environment. This can free up resources to allow for cognition to proceed, as with writing down arithmetic problems. It can also offload the operations directly onto the environment, so that actions, like rotating a Tetris shape, can be performed physically rather than mentally.

Neither grounding nor offloading reveals how model-based processes lead to new realizations, however. A third account describes how people use movement and perception to engage in generative thinking, and have new thoughts such as making inferences, forming creative insights, and generating discoveries. For example, children playing with easily managed manipulatives, such as jellybeans will show shifts back and forth between actions and thinking as they move closer to an acceptable solution, such as how to share a collection of candies among multiple people. Martin (2009) describes this as a process of *coevolution* of actions and ideas. This reciprocity between actions and ideas actually increases the chances of coming up with a novel, satisfactory solution. This is because when attempts at solving the problem through actions hits a dead end—they experience what Martin calls a "breakdown"—it leads them to rethink the entire situation and goals. This in turn can generate entirely new actions.

New ways of thinking can also arise from emergent properties, even when there is no breakdown. Scholars have observed that increased variability is often a precursor to the generation of novel concepts and strategies. Novel arithmetic strategies (such as the MIN strategy) emerge spontaneously and gradually following periods of heightened variability in children's actions (Siegler & Jenkins, 1989/2014).

In such cases, the variability inherent in one's movements and one's thought processes can generate new, satisfactory ideas. Methods for eliciting movements (fiddling around, for example) and eliciting thought (such as brainstorming) contributes to the variability and therefore helps with emergence. Emergence and breakdowns are each examples of how generative thinking arises from the close interplay of actions and ideas.

I have already shown that our intellectual processes and sensorimotor processes interact, and therefore exhibit some form of coupling. *Cognition-sensorimotor transduction* describes a reciprocal process that occurs because of that coupling. Transduction describes how sensorimotor states induce cognitive states, and vice versa. Transduction is a vitally important process for supporting cognition because it provides an explanation for why, when we think about things outside of our immediate environment, we engage many of the same mental and sensorimotor processes as when those things are actually present. Thus, it is implicated in processes such as simulation, gesture, and ways that actions with manipulatives alter thought.

I describe how transduction works only briefly here, and give this much more attention in Chapter 7 (Section 7.2.3). But first, I mean to distinguish my use of transduction from its use in other fields, specifically genetics and microbiology. These fields emphasize the transfer of genetic material form one organism to another. Here, I am using transduction to describe how a *transducer* (some system or device) converts *energy* from one form to another.

All systems and devices use energy, and convert energy from one form to another. This follows from a fundamental principle of physics, the First Law of Thermodynamics, also referred to as the Law of Conservation of Energy. This physical law states that energy can neither be created nor destroyed; that energy can only be transferred or changed from one form to another.

When we run a system of any kind, we transform some of the energy of that system into another form. Thus, a blender converts electrical energy from the outlet to mechanical energy that turns the blade; an electrical signal, properly modulated, will produce sound waves; and when using an LED, electricity (a form of light we cannot see) is converted to light in the visible spectrum. We may think of each of these example devices as running in their intended, or "forward" direction. These are shown in Table 4.2.

These same devices can be run in "reverse." If one were to reach in and spin the rotor of an (unplugged!) blender, the mechanical input from this motion would produce electricity. It is, in effect, a generator (even if an inefficient one!). If one were to sing directly into the

TABLE 4.2
How transduction relates common devices when run "forwards" and "reverse"

"Forward" mode			Energy	"Reverse" mode		
Device	Input energy		Output (forward) / input (reverse)		Output Energy	Device
Blender	Electrical	→	Mechanical	→	Electrical	Generator
Speaker	Electrical	→	Acoustic	→	Electrical	Microphone
LED	Electrical	→	Visible Light	→	Electrical	Optical sensor

cones of a speaker, the acoustic energy from our voices will be converted to an electrical form of energy, thus making it an ad hoc microphone. A light shone on an LED will generate a voltage difference. If properly arranged in a room meant to stay dark, the LED would detect the stray light from an opened door, making it suitable as an optical sensor. As Table 4.2 shows, the "forward" devices operate in reciprocal fashion to the "reverse" devices. They are, in actuality, the same devices.

The top row of Figure 4.4 shows a simple LED with a voltage meter attached. When it is in shadow, cast by a nearby hand, the LED shows negligible voltage output. However, when a light shines on the resting bulb, it produces a current that registers as a detectible voltage difference, and—VOILÀ!—acts as a light sensor.

Note that I employ "scare-quotes" around *forward* and *reverse* when describing direction. As should be clear by now, this is because there is no single direction of functioning. Reverse is only relative to another perspective being forward. In a transduction model of cognition and action, neither the mind nor the action system occupies a central processing role, or, more aptly, *they both do*, as each serves a role shaping the state of the other.

This harkens to an insight offered by Eisenberg (2002, p. 1) regarding what does it mean to be *central* in an information processing system that includes a digital computer as well as a device like a printer that is used to perform physical actions in the world.

> As I write this sentence, I am glancing over at the color printer sitting beside my screen. In the popular jargon of the computer industry, that printer is called a "peripheral"—which, upon reflection, is a rather odd way to describe it. What, precisely, is it peripheral to? If the ultimate goal of my activity is to produce a physical artifact, then one would have to conclude that the printer is a central—maybe the central—technological device in sight.

Transduction as an embodied learning fundamentally shifts the ontology of thinking and doing because it decentralizes the intellectual processes by placing them in a reciprocal relationship with perceptuomotor processes.

Transduction holds not only for physical devices and systems, but for biological systems as well. One example of this reciprocity was demonstrated among patients receiving injections of botulinum toxin-A (i.e., Botox), a common cosmetic treatment to reduce the signs of aging by temporarily paralyzing the facial *corrugator supercilli* muscle used in frowning (Havas et al., 2010). Botox injections selectively slowed readers' responses to sentences that described situations that normally invoke the affected muscle for expressing the emotions evoked by the sentences.

As the bottom row of Figure 4.4 shows, within-subjects reading times post-injection were significantly longer than pre-injection times for angry sentences (e.g., The pushy telemarketer won't let you return to your dinner.) and sad sentences (e.g., Your closest friend has just been hospitalized for a mental illness.), while times for happy sentences (e.g., You spring up the stairs to your lover's apartment.) were unaffected. The authors propose that the interruption of afferent feedback from facial muscle information necessary for monitoring one's emotional state degraded the ability of the neural systems used in simulating affective content, thus selectively impairing cognitive function for reading comprehension of angry and sad events.

Transduction is relevant to embodied cognition because it offers a possible mechanism for how thinking can be related to and shaped by sensations and actions. Barsalou (1999) refers to transduction when describing how AAA symbols may emerge from perceptual states. Several empirical studies investigate whether and how sensorimotor processes and cognitive processes operate in a bidirectional relationship (Fincher-Kiefer, 2019).

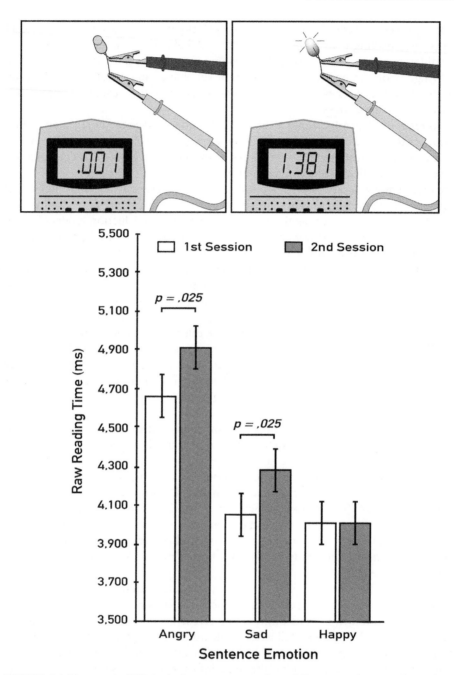

FIGURE 4.4 *Top row.* An LED in shade generates no voltage difference, and gains voltage when
light is shined on it, demonstrating it transduces light to electrical energy. *Bottom row.*
Havas et al., 2010 findings. Figure 2 showing how facial muscles transduce affective states.
Mean reading times for sentences describing angry, sad, and happy situations before (1st session) and
after (2nd session) botulinum toxin-A injection in the corrugator supercilia show increased reading times
(degraded performance) of some emotional content. Error bars indicate ± 1 SEM. Brackets indicate significant differences between sessions.

Earlier, I reviewed a set of experiments conducted by Yee and colleagues (2013). These provide important evidence in support of a specific type of cognition-sensorimotor transduction that I would call *action-cognition transduction*. Recall that Yee and colleagues found a "manual interference effect": performing a secondary task that was incompatible with the object interfered with cognitive tasks with the primary object, such as judging whether the primary object was abstract or concrete (Experiment 1), or even naming the objects (Experiment 2). In this case, the coupling of actions to cognition was the pathways for transduction.

Furthermore, interference from the incompatible secondary task was greatest when the objects were more frequently handled by participants. The ways people thought about the objects was coupled with how they handled them. The authors describe the reciprocity I expect in a transductive relationship between action and cognition: "In sum, our work shows that not only does thinking about manipulable objects influence activity in motor areas, but activity in motor areas influences people's ability to think about manipulable objects" (p. 918).

My colleagues and I have shown that action-cognition transduction can be incorporated in the design of effective learning interventions. I reported earlier that those who produced more dynamic gestures did better on geometry proofs. People also perform better when we engaged their actions beforehand in mathematically relevant ways. In one study, directed actions were cued by directing participants to touch highlighted spots on an interactive whiteboard (Nathan et al., 2014). In another, students played a motion-tracking video game that involved mimicking movements made by in-game characters. Across these studies, we found that students who performed mathematically relevant directed actions prior to assessing the truth of the conjecture had more accurate intuitions, better insights about the relevant mathematical ideas, and were significantly more likely to produce mathematically valid proofs (Nathan & Walkington, 2017; Walkington et al., 2019).

Cognitive-Sensorimotor transduction relates to Shapiro's (2019) Replaceability Hypothesis. This is a claim that there is no need for a specific system for a representational architecture for knowledge as these can be adequately *replaced* by dynamic sensorimotor interactions of the body with the world. Perceptions and actions work directly with intellectual processes to achieve goals and operate successfully in the world. As the claim goes, there is no need for maps of the world, for example, when we can directly use the world as a map. Or, as Dreyfus (2002, p. 373) writes, "The best representation of the world is thus the world itself."

This is evident among some of the most successful robotics work designed to operate in complex settings in the real world. Roboticists like Rodney Brooks (1991) have been developing adaptable robots that perform navigation in difficult environments. Brooks's robotic "creatures" effectively offload their navigation of the world onto the world itself and offer promising directions for the advancement of AI to address environmental complexity in order to meet real world needs. Shapiro acknowledges that this is not a resolved issue, but there are plenty of findings that suggest that a great deal of complex cognition can be achieved, enough to call into question the need for symbolic representation structures of the kind proposed by Information Processing theorists.

At the close of this final section, I want to address some of the critiques that have been leveled regarding transduction as an account of cognition. In so doing, I want to distinguish between my use of transduction and the way it is used by Bickhard and Terveen (1996). Bickhard and Terveen (1996, p. 31) consider only one direction of transduction.

> The basic idea is that system transducers—such as sensory receptors—receive energy from the environment that is in causal correspondence with things of importance in that environment.

They then "transduce" that energy into internal encodings of those things of importance in the environment.

They then critique that unidirectional process as an inadequate account of the emergence of representational contents,

> What is overlooked in such an approach is that the only thing an energy transduction produces is a causal correspondence with impinging energy—it does not produce any epistemic correspondence at all. Transduction may produce correspondences, but it does not produce any knowledge on the part of the agent of the existence of such correspondences, nor of what the correspondences are with. Transduction may be functionally useful, but it cannot be representationally constitutive. Again, it is the observer or user who knows of that discovered or designed transductive correspondence, and can therefore use the generated elements, or consider the generated elements, as encodings of whatever they are in correspondence with.

I address both issues here. First, I use transduction to describe the *reciprocal* relation of the corresponding sources of energy, as described in Box 3A. In specifying this dual relation, the different sources are brought into a much tighter correspondence that more strongly supports an emerging understanding for the learner of how one form instantiates and is instantiated by the other.

Second, while the correspondences are formed and can be "learned," I agree that the knowledge (or more aptly, meta-knowledge) of the correspondences are not inherent in the transduction process, but can be formed through self- and collaborative reflection, as well as being told. In my own work (Nathan et al., 2014) and that reported by others (Abrahamson & Trninic, 2015; Thomas & Lleras, 2007) we find that the correspondences learned via transduction can be formed without learners' conscious awareness, yet still benefit subsequent behavior. Thus, transduction provides a possible account of unconscious learning that can lead to other performance benefits—transfer of learning—in later tasks.

4.2.4 Participation

Participation describes a form of embodied learning that operates in communities of practice. Communities of practice are effective because they develop effective and efficient ways to collaborate, use cultural tools, and application-specific discourse practices, and instate the next generation of community members and leaders. Developing the skills and practices to be seen as a legitimate participant among experienced members is a hallmark of learning as participation.

Embodied learning as participation is common in apprenticeships (Sfard, 1998). The general form that learning takes has been outlined by Lave and Wenger (1991). They describe the developing participatory practices of midwives, tailors, sailors, and members of Alcohol Anonymous, among others. They identify how situated activity fosters learners' *legitimate peripheral participation*.

Initially, a "newcomer" entering a trade or group can only participate on the periphery, by observing, and with minimal interactions and contributions to the goals of the community. Apprentice tailors among the Vai in Liberia, for example, did benign tasks such as laying out cloth, measuring, and basic sewing—steps that could easily be undone and fixed—while cutting cloth was preserved until their skills developed (Lave & Wenger, 1991).

Across the many settings in which apprenticeship learning has been observed a pattern of learning as participation has emerged. Learning takes place through guided social interactions during primary experiences in the authentic contexts in which skilled perform-ance in needed. As newcomers develop facility with the cultural tools of the trade, perceptions of the appropriate patterns, and discourse practices of the discipline, they advance closer to the center of the community (Brown, Collins, & Duguid, 1989). Ultimately, the aim is that the person comes to take on the role of the master, or old-timer, and train the next generation of apprentices.

The situated nature of knowledge and skills that develop through this participation view are notably different than that of more formal knowledge. Scribner's (1984) ethnographic account of dairy workers illustrates this. Preloaders provide the cases for the delivery drivers. In solving their packing problems, preloaders develop a notation system that reflects the ecological reality of the objects they handle rather than decontextualized abstract arithmetic operations.

Often, preloaders' loading strategies reflected the least mental effort of calculating based on quick visual inspection. They also involved the least physical effort of actually filling the orders—traveling around the icebox, traversing slippery floors, lifting heavy containers filled with dairy products into or out of bins. In comparison, white collar workers with desk jobs generated solutions that minimized effort less than half the time. The strategies of students unfamiliar with the demands of actual milk delivery usually resulted in massive over-expenditure of physical effort in favor of performing the arith-metic in direct terms.

Young street vendors in Brazil (Nunes et al., 1993) provide another example. They could perform rapid mathematical operations in their heads for common types of finan-cial exchanges that occurred in the marketplace. The arithmetic performance of child street vendors was nearly 100% when the mathematical practices were conducted in the market-place. However, it dropped to below 50% when the identical quantitative relations used in the street were presented exclusively in symbolic form (Baranes, Perry, & Stigler, 1989).

Poor transfer across settings does not adequately reflect cognitive abilities because they solve problems with the same quantities when delivered in a different context. Rather, each setting elicits a fundamentally different form of participation. The varying contexts draw on different perceptual, motor, and cognitive resources in the different contexts. As Lobato (2012) notes, transfer from the perspective of participation depends on 1) the practices needed for the original learning context; 2) the participation of a learner with those practices; 3) the overlap between the new (transfer) context and the original learning context. When there is large overlap, then one can expect to see something akin to what psychologists often classify as transfer of learning. Moving between street market currency exchanges and scho-lastic worksheets exhibits poor transfer because the contexts share very little with regard to perceptuomotor processes.

Nasir (2002) examined a different community of practice and showed how participa-tion served transfer of complex skills. African American males participate in communities of practice of dominoes players. Nasir (2000, 2001) used ethnographic observation as well as mocking up boards with specific configurations so she could observe players' strategic reasoning. She examined cross-sectional differences between ages and levels of experience as well as longitudinal changes of individual players. She found that more sophisticated play emerged as players adopted new goals for themselves. Their level of game play was inex-tricably linked with changes in their identities as participants in the competitive commu-nity of players (Lave & Wenger, 1991; Nasir, 2002). Furthermore, their level of participation contributed to their mathematics performance.

Dominoes is played by two competing pairs of players who each take turns successively. Nasir observed the youngest players attempted to simply make legitimate moves using basic pattern matching. By middle school, players sought to optimize the number of points each move accrued by systematically comparing options based on the board configuration and the dominoes available to the player. By high school, players engaged in more sophisticated probabilistic thinking and counterfactual (if-then) reasoning to make reasonable judgments about their opponent's future moves. They would weigh options that blocked their opponent from making higher scoring moves, as well as optimizing one's own position.

Influences on players' identities were evident in the flexibility of their social (non-game) interactions during play. Neophytes generally maintained their roles within their relationships with school and neighborhood peers during the games. For older, more advanced players, their level of game play affected their social interactions, but this lasted only during a match. As players became more engaged in the game, they acquired new skills and knowledge that supported greater participation in their community that valued greater competence. In turn, this fostered more motivation to learn the mathematics involved in game play.

4.3 INTEGRATING FORMS OF EMBODIMENT AND WAYS OF EMBODIED LEARNING

Combining the four central types of embodiment and four ways that embodiment supports learning yields an array of effective forms of embodied thinking, learning and instruction. I have used Table 4.3 to show how these can be organized.

These various forms of embodied learning can be viewed along the timescales of learning processes shown in Figure 4.5. As an example, I want to illustrate this using Nasir's (2002) investigation of the community of domino players.

When examining domino play at the biological level (processes that operate in milliseconds, 10^{-2} s and below) and the cognitive level (where processes are operating on the order of fractions of a second to tens of seconds, 10^{-1} s to 10^1 s), Nasir provides insights about how turns are made during a game. She documents how pattern matching, tile placement, and score calculations are made by players both young novices and older, more experienced players.

Zooming out, knowledge-based processes (spanning minutes to hours; 10^2 s to 10^4 s) are evident as players develop their mathematics skills in the form of more sophisticated strategies such as assessing their options, blocking opponents from scoring, and assisting one's partner. For example, one's knowledge of multiples of five and addition fact retrieval inform choices of current placements. However, these choices can be influenced by a probabilistic assessment of the tiles held by one's opponent.

While cognitive and knowledge-based processes are in operation, players are learning to manage the interactions that navigate acceptable forms of participation, such as social norms

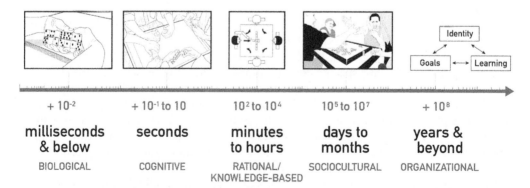

FIGURE 4.5 Images displayed along the GEL timescale of the various learning processes exhibited by communities of dominoes players, as described by Nasir (2000, 2001, 2002). The timescale is in $\log_{10}$.

TABLE 4.3

Instances illustrating how the major types of embodiment support learning

Forms of learning → Types of embodiment	Grounding	Offloading	Cognitive-sensorimotor transduction	Participation
Body form, movement and perception	Pragmatic actions Metaphors for abstract ideas in terms of spatial relations, perceptions and actions	Finger counting Epistemic actions (e.g., Tetris)	Performing certain actions interferes with thinking about familiar concepts Directed actions influence math reasoning, and relevant actions have relevant effects Botox and sentence processing Dominoes play helps foster math concepts	Social interactions are highly multimodal Communities of practice
Gesture	Pointing; Iconic gestures; metaphorical gestures	Pointing to neutral space Index to words and objects in the world; index to space in lieu of a name	Use gesture as lexical prime for word production Schematization Metaphors & simulation Gesture inhibition selectively impairs model-based reasoning such as inference making	Gestures for managing turn-taking and common ground Learn multimodal discourse practices
Simulation	Instance based instantiations	Right-hand rule Dynamic gestures enact transformations on objects	We activate motor system for kick, lick, pick Switching costs between sensory modalities shows up as costs for switching between perceptual representations of the same concept Switching costs across modalities	Participatory simulation
Materialist epistemology	Reification Direct representation (e.g., world represents itself)	Use objects to help with modeling Faraday's inductive motor Watson & Crick's DNA Number line, Cartesian graphs	Functional actions can induce cognitive states Makerspace Thought experiments	Robotics club FabLab makerspace Cottage cheese measurement Place-based history education

and manners of discourse. For example, the banter between partners and with opponents shifts the game to a whole other "level." These skills for interpreting and responding to verbal exchanges align with the timescale of socio-cultural processes (days to months 10^5 s to 10^7s).

As these social skills develop, players are reinventing themselves through participation practices. This occurs most notably through players' changing roles within the community of practice, while still rooted in their existing cultural identities.

At an even broader timescale, the availability of this set of activities for this community arises from cultural and historical processes (institutional processes that unfold over many years). As Nasir & Saxe (2003) note, dominoes is seen as a racially stereotyped activity by both in-group and out-group members. It also comprises a highly demanding and engaging set of activities that provide an effective locus for the development of mathematical knowledge for many young people. These activities—which promote lifelong skills—engage African American students in intellectually demanding practices while comparable school-based activities often do not (Ladson-Billings, 1995, 1997; Ogbu, 1992). This highlights the historical processes that are not simply about the emerging ethnic and academic identities of these youths, but of entire generations of citizens who seek to belong, to engage, and to develop into competent adults.

4.4 READER ACTIVITIES

Example top-down processes are that we expect to see a shadow cast over an object (The Dress); we predict we are seeing a corner of a wall (Müller-Lyer Illusion); we infer motion when there is merely change (marquis illusion).

4.4.1 Müller-Lyer Illusion

1. Interactive link https://michaelbach.de/ot/sze-muelue/index.html
2. Discussion of how the illusion varies by cultural setting http://cognitionandculture.net/blogs/simons-blog/culture-and-perception-part-ii-the-muller-lyer-illusion/

4.4.2 "The Dress"

From AsapSCIENCE. www.youtube.com/watch?v=AskAQwOBvhc

4.4.3 The Stroop Effect

We experience "interference" between naming the color of the ink and naming the word meaning (especially when it's a color name or a word with strong color associations)
www.psytoolkit.org/lessons/stroop.html
A variant of the Stroop Effect using numbers
https://en.wikipedia.org/wiki/Numerical_Stroop_effect
The fruit Stroop test (Okuzumi et al., 2015).
https://pdfs.semanticscholar.org/59a8/71283d481a3f278b47f3257256ad4cd348cc.pdf

4.4.4 Bottom-Up processes for Drawing

Upside-down drawing helps us to actually "see" rather than "interpret" what we are looking at. Here is an example activity using a drawing by Pablo Picasso of Igor Stravinsky.
https://1.cdn.edl.io/5RjFAhVPi9R1rvuycbK8YGE4EzxgAUhERftFcxeEFYdreghu.pdf

4.4.5 Auditory Illusions

Some "illusions" can be in auditory form.
This one is with sound, but it is like "The Dress." Do you hear "Yanny" or "Laurel?"
www.youtube.com/watch?v=_mPgnPHoiQk
from Ellen DeGeneres. There are audio illusions as well as visual illusions. An example is when you hear the correct pronunciation ahead of a highly distorted auditory signal.

https://y98.radio.com/blogs/listen-ellen-degeneres-tricks-audience-another-internet-debate

Examples of bottom-up processes includes our preference for contrast over constancy and making familiar things strange, so we see them more accurately.

4.4.6 Illusions Can also Be Tactile

The Phantom hand illusion is quite intriguing. But as the saying goes, "Don't try this at home!"

Tactile illusion: Is That My Real Hand? | Breakthrough | National Geographic. www.youtube.com/watch?v=DphlhmtGRqI

4.4.7 Another Interesting Type of Illusion: The McGurk Effect

The McGurk Effect combines multiple sensory modalities, in this case, visual and auditory. What we see influences how we hear.

www.youtube.com/watch?v=2k8fHR9jKVM

4.4.8 Beyond Sensory Modalities, the "Moses Illusion"

The "Moses Illusion" (Erickson & Mattson, 1981; Park & Reder, 2004) is an example of a **cognitive illusion**.

> Read the following sentence out loud and answer right away:
> "How many animals of each kind did Moses take on the Ark?"
> Most people respond "two." But is it?
> Not *two*, but *Moses*?

Even though most people who respond do know that it was Noah, not Moses, who built the ark in the Biblical story, they still fall prey to this illusion. We easily replace a term in a sentence with something that is semantically similar even when we might otherwise recognize that it is not the correct term to use. The top-down context of the meaning of the sentence makes it difficult to detect the incorrect replacement. The tendency to overlook semantic distortions in context is known as the Moses Illusion. Erickson and Mattson (1981) note this distortion can occur even when readers are warned beforehand about possible distortions. This effect is so robust that it does not require time pressure to elicit the illusion.

4.4.9 Making Illusions Still Will Fool the Senses

Even when *we* make the patterns and objects ourselves, we are still vulnerable to the illusions. Try making the impossible objects of mathematician Kokichi Sugihara using the paper templates below. Set them up in front of a mirror. Even when you know what the forms are you still experience the illusion!

- **Video**: Impossible objects www.youtube.com/watch?v=oWfFco7K9v8&list=PLLqU_7FllF5ewRp0EAsBf5NMn0px2cFZe&index=6&t=0s
- **Make** impossible objects designed by Kokichi Sugihara. www.isc.meiji.ac.jp/~kokichis/Welcomee.html

REFERENCES

Abrahamson, D., & Sánchez-García, R. (2016). Learning is moving in new ways: The ecological dynamics of mathematics education. *Journal of the Learning Sciences, 25*(2), 203–239.

Abrahamson, D., & Trninic, D. (2015). Bringing forth mathematical concepts: Signifying sensorimotor enactment in fields of promoted action. *ZDM, 47*(2), 295–306.

Alibali, M. W., & Nathan, M. J. (2007). Teachers' gestures as a means of scaffolding students' understanding: Evidence from an early algebra lesson. In Goldman, R., Pea, R., Barron, B. J., & Derry, S. (Eds.) *Video Research in the Learning Sciences* (pp. 349–365). Erlbaum.

Alibali, M. W., & Nathan, M. J. (2012). Embodiment in mathematics teaching and learning: Evidence from learners' and teachers' gestures. *Journal of the Learning Sciences, 21*(2), 247–286.

Alibali, M. W., Nathan, M. J., Church, R. B., Wolfgram, M. S., Kim, S., & Knuth, E. J. (2013). Teachers' gestures and speech in mathematics lessons: Forging common ground by resolving trouble spots. *ZDM, 45*(3), 425–440.

Alibali, M. W., Nathan, M. J., Wolfgram, M. S., Church, R. B., Jacobs, S. A., Johnson Martinez, C., & Knuth, E. J. (2014). How teachers link ideas in mathematics instruction using speech and gesture: A corpus analysis. *Cognition and Instruction, 32*(1), 65–100.

Baird, D. (2004). *Thing knowledge: A philosophy of scientific instruments.* University of California Press.

Baranes, R., Perry, M., & Stigler, J. W. (1989). Activation of real-world knowledge in the solution of word problems. *Cognition and Instruction, 6*(4), 287–318.

Barsalou, L. W. (1999). Perceptual symbol systems. *Behavioral and Brain Sciences, 22*(4), 577–660.

Barsalou, L. W. (2008). Grounded cognition. *Annual Review of Psychology, 59*, 617–645.

Bickhard, M. H., & Terveen, L. (1996). *Foundational issues in artificial intelligence and cognitive science: Impasse and solution.* Elsevier.

Blikstein, P. (2013). Digital fabrication and "making" in education: The democratization of invention. *FabLabs: Of Machines, Makers and Inventors, 4*(1), 1–21.

Blom, R. M., Hennekam, R. C., & Denys, D. (2012). Body integrity identity disorder. *PLoS One, 7*(4), e34702.

Bostrom, N. (2003). Are we living in a computer simulation? *The Philosophical Quarterly, 53*(211), 243–255.

Bradshaw, G. (1992). The airplane and the logic of invention. In R. Giere & H. Feigl (Eds.), *Cognitive models of science* (pp. 239–250). University of Minnesota Press.

Brooks, R. A. (1991). Intelligence without representation. *Artificial Intelligence, 47*(1–3), 139–159.

Brown, J. S., Collins, A., & Duguid, P. (1989). Situated cognition and the culture of learning. *Educational Researcher, 18*(1), 32–42.

Brown, J. S., & Duguid, P. (1991). Organizational learning and communities-of-practice: Toward a unified view of working, learning, and innovation. *Organization Science, 2*(1), 40–57.

Casasanto, D., & Chrysikou, E. G. (2011). When left is "right" motor fluency shapes abstract concepts. *Psychological Science, 22*(4), 419–422.

Casasanto, D., & Henetz, T. (2012). Handedness shapes children's abstract concepts. *Cognitive Science, 36*(2), 359–372.

Christiansen, M. H., & Kirby, S. (Eds.). (2003). *Studies in the evolution of language. Language evolution.* Oxford University Press.

Church, R. B., & Goldin-Meadow, S. (1986). The mismatch between gesture and speech as an index of transitional knowledge. *Cognition, 23*(1), 43–71.

Clark, A., & Chalmers, D. (1998). The extended mind. *Analysis, 58*(1), 7–19.

Cole, M., & Engeström, Y. (1993). A cultural-historical approach to distributed cognition. In G. Salomon (Ed.), *Distributed cognitions: Psychological and educational considerations* (pp. 1–46). Cambridge University Press.

Cole, M., & Engeström, Y. (2007). *Cultural-historical approaches to designing for development.* Cambridge University Press.

Cook, S. W., & Goldin-Meadow, S. (2006). The role of gesture in learning: Do children use their hands to change their minds?. *Journal of Cognition and Development, 7*(2), 211–232.

Donald, M. (1993). *Origins of the modern mind: Three stages in the evolution of culture and cognition.* Harvard University Press.

Dreyfus, H. L. (2002). Intelligence without representation–Merleau-Ponty's critique of mental representation: The relevance of phenomenology to scientific explanation. *Phenomenology and the Cognitive Sciences, 1*(4), 367–383.

Eisenberg, M. (2002). Output devices, computation, and the future of mathematical crafts. *International Journal of Computers for Mathematical Learning, 7*(1), 1–44.

Engeström, Y. (1987/2015). *Learning by expanding: An activity-theoretical approach to developmental research.* Cambridge University Press.

Erickson, T. D., & Mattson, M. E. (1981). From words to meaning: A semantic illusion. *Journal of Verbal Learning and Verbal Behavior, 20*(5), 540–551.

Feigenson, L., Dehaene, S., & Spelke, E. (2004). Core systems of number. *Trends in Cognitive Sciences, 8*(7), 307–314.

Fincher-Kiefer, R. (2019). *How the body shapes knowledge: Empirical support for embodied cognition*. American Psychological Association.

Gauvain, M. (1993). The development of spatial thinking in everyday activity. *Developmental Review, 13*(1), 92–121.

Geary, D. C. (1995). Reflections of evolution and culture in children's cognition: Implications for mathematical development and instruction. *American Psychologist, 50*(1), 24.

Gee, J. P. (2008). Video games and embodiment. *Games and Culture, 3*(3–4), 253–263.

Gentner, D., & Stevens, A. L. (Eds.). (1983/2014). *Mental models*. Psychology Press.

Glenberg, A., de Vega, M., & Graesser, A. C. (2008). Framing the debate. In M. de Vega, A. Glenberg, & A. C. Graesser (Eds.), *Symbols and embodiment: Debates on meaning and cognition* (pp. 1–10). Oxford University Press.

Glenberg, A. M., Meyer, M., & Lindem, K. (1987). Mental models contribute to foregrounding during text comprehension. *Journal of Memory and Language, 26*(1), 69–83.

Glenberg, A. M., & Robertson, D. A. (1999). Indexical understanding of instructions. *Discourse Processes, 28*(1), 1–26.

Goldin-Meadow, S., & Beilock, S. L. (2010). Action's influence on thought: The case of gesture. *Perspectives on Psychological Science, 5*(6), 664–674.

Goldstone, R. L., Landy, D. H., & Son, J. Y. (2010). The education of perception. *Topics in Cognitive Science, 2*, 265–284.

Greeno, J. G. (1998). The situativity of knowing, learning, and research. *American Psychologist, 53*(1), 5–26.

Greeno, J. G., & Engeström, Y. (2014). Learning in activity. In R. K. Sawyer (Ed.), *Cambridge handbook of the learning sciences* (pp. 128–147). Cambridge University Press.

Harnad, S. (1990). The symbol grounding problem. *Physica D, 42*, 335–346.

Hauk, O., Johnsrude, I., & Pulvermüller, F. (2004). Somatotopic representation of action words in human motor and premotor cortex. *Neuron, 41*(2), 301–307.

Havas, D. A., Glenberg, A. M., Gutowski, K. A., Lucarelli, M. J., & Davidson, R. J. (2010). Cosmetic use of botulinum toxin-A affects processing of emotional language. *Psychological Science, 21*(7), 895–900.

Howison, M., Trninic, D., Reinholz, D., & Abrahamson, D. (2011). The mathematical imagery trainer: From embodied interaction to conceptual learning. In G. Fitzpatrick, C. Gutwin, B. Begole, W. A. Kellogg, & D. Tan (Eds.), *Proceedings of the Annual Meeting of The Association for Computer Machinery Special Interest Group on Computer Human Interaction, 'Human Factors in Computing Systems.' (CHI 2011)*. ACM Press.

Hutchins, E. (1995). *Cognition in the Wild*. MIT press.

Iriki, A., Tanaka, M., & Iwamura, Y. (1996). Coding of modified body schema during tool use by macaque postcentral neurones. *Neuroreport, 7*(14), 2325–2330.

Kendon, A. (2004). *Gesture: Visible action as utterance*. Cambridge University Press.

Kintsch, W. (1998). *Comprehension: A paradigm for cognition*. Cambridge University Press.

Kirsh, D., & Maglio, P. (1994). On distinguishing epistemic from pragmatic action. *Cognitive Science, 18*(4), 513–549.

Koedinger, K. R., & Nathan, M. J. (2004). The real story behind story problems: Effects of representations on quantitative reasoning. *The Journal of the Learning Sciences, 13*(2), 129–164.

Krauss, R. M. (1998). Why do we gesture when we speak? *Current Directions in Psychological Science, 7*(2), 54–54.

Ladson-Billings, G. (1995). Toward a theory of culturally relevant pedagogy. *American Educational Research Journal, 32*(3), 465–491.

Ladson-Billing, G. (1997). It doesn't add up: African American students' mathematics achievement. *Journal for Research in Mathematics Education, 28*(6), 697–708.

Lakoff, G., & Johnson, M. (1980). The metaphorical structure of the human conceptual system. *Cognitive Science, 4*(2), 195–208.

Lakoff, G., & Johnson, M. (1999). *Philosophy in the flesh: The embodied mind and its challenge to western thought*. Basic Books.

Lakoff, G., & Núñez, R. (2000). *Where mathematics comes from* (Vol. 6). Basic Books.

Laurillard, D. (2001/2013). *Rethinking university teaching: A conversational framework for the effective use of learning technologies*. Routledge.

Lave, J., & Wenger, E. (1991). *Situated learning: Legitimate peripheral participation*. Cambridge University Press.

Leont'ev, A. N. (1981). *Problems in the development of mind*. Progress.

Lobato, J. (2012). The actor-oriented transfer perspective and its contributions to educational research and practice. *Educational Psychologist, 47*(3), 232–247.

Macedonia, M. (2019). Embodied learning: Why at school the mind needs the body. *Frontiers in Psychology, 10*, 2098.

Martin, A. (2007). The representation of object concepts in the brain. *Annual Review of Psychology, 58*, 25–45.

Martin, T. (2009). A theory of physically distributed learning: How external environments and internal states interact in mathematics learning. *Child Development Perspectives, 3*(3), 140–144.

Martin, T., & Schwartz, D. L. (2005). Physically distributed learning: Adapting and reinterpreting physical environments in the development of fraction concepts. *Cognitive Science, 29*(4), 587–625.

McCullough, D. (2015). *The Wright brothers*. Simon and Schuster.

McNeill, D. (1992). *Hand and mind: What gestures reveal about thought*. University of Chicago Press.

Merleau-Ponty, M. (2012). *Phenomenology of perception*. Trans. Donald Landes. Routledge.

Nasir, N. (2000). Points ain't everything: Emergent goals and average and percent understandings in the play of basketball among African-American students. *Anthropology & Education Quarterly, 31*, 283–305.

Nasir, N. (2001). Average and percent on the court: Statistics learning in basketball. Manuscript submitted for publication.

Nasir, N. (2002). Identity, goals, and learning: Mathematics in cultural practice. *Mathematical Thinking and Learning, 4*(2&3), 211–245.

Nasir, N. S., & Saxe, G. B. (2003). Ethnic and academic identities: A cultural practice perspective on emerging tensions and their management in the lives of minority students. *Educational Researcher, 32*, 14–18.

Nathan, M. J. (2008). An embodied cognition perspective on symbols, grounding, and instructional gesture. In M. DeVega, A. M. Glenberg, & A. C. Graesser, (Eds.) *Symbols, embodiment and meaning: A debate* (pp. 375–396). Oxford University Press.

Nathan, M. J., Schenck, K. E., Vinsonhaler, R., Michaelis, J. E, Swart, M. L, & Walkington, C. (2020). Embodied geometric reasoning: Dynamic gestures during intuition, insight, and proof. *Journal of Educational Psychology*. Advance online publication doi.org/10.1037/edu0000638

Nathan, M. J., Srisurichan, R., Walkington, C., Wolfgram, M., Williams, C., & Alibali, M. W. (2013). Building cohesion across representations: A mechanism for STEM integration. *Journal of Engineering Education, 102*(1), 77–116.

Nathan, M. J., & Walkington, C. (2017). Grounded and embodied mathematical cognition: Promoting mathematical insight and proof using action and language. *Cognitive Research: Principles and Implications, 2*(1), 9. doi.org/10.1186/s41235-016-0040-5

Nathan, M. J., Walkington, C., Boncoddo, R., Pier, E., Williams, C. C., & Alibali, M. W. (2014). Actions speak louder with words: The roles of action and pedagogical language for grounding mathematical proof. *Learning and Instruction, 33*, 182–193.

Neisser, U. (1976). *Cognition and reality: Principles and implications of cognitive psychology*. Freeman.

Nemirovsky, R., & Ferrara, F. (2009). Mathematical imagination and embodied cognition. *Educational Studies in Mathematics, 70*(2), 159–174.

Newen, A., De Bruin, L., & Gallagher, S. (Eds.). (2018). *The Oxford handbook of 4E cognition*. Oxford University Press.

Newman, M. S. (2019). So, Gutenberg didn't actually invent the printing press: On the unsung Chinese and Korean history of movable type. *Lit Hub*, June 19. Retrieved from https://lithub.com/so-gutenberg-didnt-actually-invent-the-printing-press/

Nisbett, R. E., & Wilson, T. D. (1977). Telling more than we can know: Verbal reports on mental processes. *Psychological Review, 84*(3), 231.

Nunes, T., Schliemann, A. D., & Carraher, D. W. (1993). *Street mathematics and school mathematics*. Cambridge University Press.

Ogbu, J. U. (1992). Understanding cultural diversity and learning. *Educational Researcher, 21*(8), 5–14.

Okuzumi, H., Ikeda, Y., Otsuka, N., Saito, R., Oi, Y., Hirata, S., … & Kokubun, M. (2015). Stroop-like interference in the fruit Stroop Test in typical development. *Psychology, 6*(05), 643.

Park, H., & Reder, L. M. (2004). Moses illusion: Implication for human cognition. In Pohl, R.F. (Ed). *Cognitive illusions* (pp. 275–291). Psychology Press.

Pea, R. (1993). Practices of distributed intelligence and designs for education. In G. Salomon (Ed.), *Distributed cognitions: Psychological and educational considerations* (pp. 47–87). Cambridge University Press.

Penner, D. E., Giles, N. D., Lehrer, R., & Schauble, L. (1997). Building functional models: Designing an elbow. *Journal of Research in Science Teaching, 34*(2), 125–143.

Penner, D. E., Lehrer, R., & Schauble, L. (1998). From physical models to biomechanics: A design-based modeling approach. *The Journal of the Learning Sciences, 7*(3/4), 429–449.

Pouw, W. T., Van Gog, T., & Paas, F. (2014). An embedded and embodied cognition review of instructional manipulatives. *Educational Psychology Review, 26*(1), 51–72.

Pulvermüller, F. (2005). Brain mechanisms linking language and action. *Nature Reviews Neuroscience, 6*(7), 576.

Pulvermüller, F. (2008). Grounding language in the brain. In M. de Vega, A. M. Glenberg, & A. C. Graesser (Eds.), *Symbols and Embodiment. Debates on meaning and cognition* (pp. 85–116). Oxford University Press.

Ramachandran, V. S., & Rogers-Ramachandran, D. (1996). Synaesthesia in phantom limbs induced with mirrors. *Proceedings of the Royal Society of London. Series B: Biological Sciences, 263*(1369), 377–386.

Reeve, R., & Humberstone, J. (2011). Five- to 7-year-olds' finger gnosia and calculation abilities. *Frontiers in Psychology, 2*, Article 359. https://doi.org/10.3389/fpsyg.2011.00359

Resnick, L. B. (1987). The 1987 presidential address learning in school and out. *Educational Researcher, 16*(9), 13–54.

Robbins, P., & Aydede, M. (Eds.). (2008). *The Cambridge handbook of situated cognition*. Cambridge University Press.

Rosch, E., & Lloyd, B. B. (Eds.). (1978). *Cognition and categorization*. Lawrence Erlbaum.

Rosch, E., Mervis, C. B., Gray, W. D., Johnson, D. M., & Boyes-Braem, P. (1976). Basic objects in natural categories. *Cognitive Psychology, 8*(3), 382–439.

Saxe, G. B. (1981). Body parts as numerals: A developmental analysis of numeration among the Oksapmin in Papua New Guinea. *Child Development, 52*, 306–316.

Saxe, G. B. (1982). Developing forms of arithmetical thought among the Oksapmin of Papua New Guinea. *Developmental Psychology, 18*(4), 583.

Scribner, S. (1984). Studying working intelligence. In B. Rogoff & J. Lave (Eds.), *Everyday cognition: Its development in social context* (pp. 9–40). Harvard University Press.

Sfard, A. (1998). On two metaphors for learning and the dangers of choosing just one. *Educational Researcher, 27*(2), 4–13.

Shapiro, L. (2019). *Embodied cognition* (2nd ed.). Routledge.

Shepard, R. N., & Cooper, L. A. (1986). *Mental images and their transformations.* The MIT Press.

Shepard, R. N., & Metzler, J. (1971). Mental rotation of three-dimensional objects. *Science, 171*(3972), 701–703.

Siegler, R., & Jenkins, E. A. (1989/2014). *How children discover new strategies.* Psychology Press.

Smith, C. P., King, B., & Hoyte, J. (2014). Learning angles through movement: Critical actions for developing understanding in an embodied activity. *The Journal of Mathematical Behavior, 36*, 95–108.

Spelke, E. S. (2000). Core knowledge. *American Psychologist, 55*(11), 1233.

Stanfield, R. A., & Zwaan, R. A. (2001). The effect of implied orientation derived from verbal context on picture recognition. *Psychological Science, 12*(2), 153–156.

Thomas, L. E., & Lleras, A. (2007). Moving eyes and moving thought: On the spatial compatibility between eye movements and cognition. *Psychonomic Bulletin & Review, 14*(4), 663–668.

Tversky, B. (2019). *Mind in motion: How action shapes thought.* Hachette UK.

Valenzeno, L., Alibali, M. W., & Klatzky, R. (2003). Teachers' gestures facilitate students' learning: A lesson in symmetry. *Contemporary Educational Psychology, 28*(2), 187–204.

Varela, F. J., Thompson, E., & Rosch, E. (2016). *The embodied mind: Cognitive science and human experience.* MIT Press.

Vygotsky, L. S. (1988). Development of the higher mental functions. In K. Richardson, S. Sheldon (Eds.), *Cognitive development in adolescence* (pp. 61–80), Lawrence Erlbaum.

Walkington, C., Chelule, G., Woods, D., & Nathan, M. J. (2019). Collaborative gesture as a case of extended mathematical cognition. *The Journal of Mathematical Behavior, 55*, 100683.

Walkington, C., Nathan, M., Wolfgram, M., Alibali, M., & Srisurichan, R. (2011). Bridges and barriers to constructing conceptual cohesion across modalities and temporalities: Challenges of STEM integration in the precollege engineering classroom. In Strobel, J., Purzer, S. & Cardella, M. (Eds.) *Engineering in Pre-College Settings: Research into Practice* (pp. 183–209). Purdue University Press.

Watson, J. D. (1968). *The double helix*: A personal account of the discovery of the structure *of DNA.* Atheneum Press.

Wenger, E. (1999). *Communities of practice: Learning, meaning, and identity.* Cambridge University Press.

Whorf, B. L. (2012). *Language, thought, and reality: Selected writings of Benjamin Lee Whorf.* MIT Press.

Wilson, M. (2002). Six views of embodied cognition. *Psychonomic Bulletin & Review, 9*(4), 625–636.

Zhuangzi. (2013). *The Complete Works of Zhuangzi* (Trans. B. Watson). Columbia University Press.

Zwaan, R. A., Stanfield, R. A., & Yaxley, R. H. (2002). Language comprehenders mentally represent the shapes of objects. *Psychological Science, 13*(2), 168–171.

Part II

The GEL Timescale

5

Embodiment in the Conscious Spectrum

People largely adhere to views that the mind functions quite well on its own, without much aid from the body, so long as our basic physical needs are met. Yet, as we will see in this book, how we think and what we think about is fundamentally linked to our physical make up and experiences in a sensory-rich, material world. We are far less *I think, therefore I am*, and far more *I am, therefore I think*, than we might recognize.

So it is with schools. The scholastic experience, for most of us, was framed as intellectual, to the near exclusion of our physical and perceptual processes. Our institutions cling to *Formalisms First* notions of instruction and cognitive development (Nathan, 2012), despite empirical evidence that they are not accurate models of learning and ill-suited for most learners. I believe we neglect the role of the body in education to our detriment. For our bodies provide a set of extremely valuable resources that often make learning and performance possible. In short: Our bodies and the ways we use them to perform actions in the material world determine what we can learn, how that learning takes place, and how we express what we know to others.

This chapter, and the next five, discuss grounded and embodied learning (GEL) processes as they are organized using the timescales of learning from Chapter 3 (Figure 3.5). In the current chapter I choose to start where our awareness starts, at the middle of the timescale—which I refer to as the "conscious spectrum"—and then move out to more fine-grained (faster) and coarse-grained (slower) processes in subsequent chapters. I chose to start here because the conscious spectrum is where learners and educators actually experience self-awareness of learning processes. It's also where schools primarily operate.

GEL in the conscious spectrum relates most closely to processes that span from around one second (coarse-grain cognitive processes) to about a day (finer-grain sociocultural processes). This is illustrated in Figure 5.1, a reproduction of Figure 3.5, where I highlight those portions that operate within the conscious spectrum. Throughout this chapter I will be showing empirical evidence that learning across the conscious spectrum is embodied. In the next chapter, I provide empirical evidence that is specifically drawn from a wide range of school subject areas such as language arts, science, and mathematics, to show the reality of the value of GEL for education.

DOI: 10.4324/9780429329098-5

FIGURE 5.1 You are here: Middle portion of the GEL timescale highlights the "Conscious Spectrum."
Figure uses a $\log_{10}$ scale.

5.1 GEL: THE UNCONSCIOUS, THE CONSCIOUS, AND THE COLLECTIVE

In order to appreciate which types of processing are most relevant to the conscious spectrum, I will situate this in the context of the processes that are faster and slower. Human behaviors are often characterized by psychologists and other behavioral scientists, such as economists, as drawing on rapid, automatic, unconscious Type 1 processing, or slower, more deliberate, conscious Type 2 processing (Evans & Stanovich, 2013). In addition, I introduce *Type 3 processing* as those that mediate and are activated by sociocultural interaction.

5.1.1 Type 1 Processes: Automatic, Unconscious Responses

Type 1 processing operates tacitly and rapidly, engaging largely unconscious processing triggered by heuristics and perceptual patterns. Type 1 processing functions automatically, without monitoring and control, and are relatively impervious to other demands on attention and memory. They generally occupy the faster portion of timescale. In his book, *Thinking Fast and Slow*, the Nobel prize-winning economist Daniel Kahneman (2011) offers this simple example of how Type 1 processing operates. Take a moment to answer.

> A bat and ball cost $1.10.
> The bat costs one dollar more than the ball.
> How much does the ball cost?

Effortless, right? And quick! One thing I like about this example is how confident people are that they get the answer correct and do so rapidly. This is the case even though you, readers should suspect I am likely setting them up to fail. That is the nature of Type 1 processing—rapidly process patterns and then shoot from the hip. For most people (over 80% of college-attending adults in one sample; Kahneman, 2011), the Type 1 response is that the ball costs one dime, and the bat one dollar. (I write these values out to prevent the reader's highly sensitive Type 1 pattern recognition from peeking!) But that is only a difference of 90 cents. Now take some time and work out this problem again. Note that I say much more about these rapid processes in Chapters 7 and 8.

A couple of points are worth highlighting: Type 1 processing generates results that people feel confident in, even when they may know they may be tricked, and even when they do have access to other, more deliberate problem-solving methods that are more reliable. Here is where Type 2 processing comes in.

5.1.2 Type 2 Processes: Conscious Rule Following

In contrast to Type 1 processing, *Type 2 processing* is a collection of structures and processes that carry out explicit, rule-based behaviors that are deliberately applied, monitored, and controllable by the person (Stanovich & West, 2000). Type 2 processing demands a great deal (at times, *all*) of one's attention. It demonstrably breaks down in the face of distractions and other demands that compete for attention and working memory.

Getting back to the bat-and-ball problem, What does Type 2 reasoning do? Why, deliberate, rule-based analysis, of course. The solution generation process is, admittedly, more involved when one writes it out as an algebraic equation. More involved, but more likely in this instance to be accurate.

$$\begin{aligned} \text{Cost}_{\text{Bat}} + \text{Cost}_{\text{Ball}} &= 110\,\text{cents} \\ + \ \text{Cost}_{\text{Bat}} - \text{Cost}_{\text{Ball}} &= 100\,\text{cents} \\ \hline 2 \times \text{Cost}_{\text{Bat}} + 0 \quad &= 210\,\text{cents} \end{aligned}$$

$$\therefore \text{Cost}_{\text{Bat}} = 210\,/\,2 = 105\,\text{cents, and}$$
$$\text{Cost}_{\text{Ball}} = \text{Cost}_{\text{Bat}} - 100 = 5\,\text{cents}$$

The bat costs 105 cents, and the ball 1 dollar less, for the proper total. Type 2 thinking produces an answer that satisfies all of the constraints.

Kahneman (2011, p. 21) sums up the interplay of Type 1 (fast processing) and Type 2 (slow processing) in shaping our behaviors in this way, using the older language of "systems," where System 1 performs Type 1 processing and System 1 performs Type 2 processing:

> When we think of ourselves, we identify with System 2, the conscious, reasoning self that has beliefs, makes choices, and decides what to think about and what to do. Although System 2 believes itself to be where the action is, the automatic System 1 is the hero of the book. I describe System 1 as effortlessly originating impressions and feelings that are the main sources of the explicit beliefs and deliberate choices of System 2. The automatic operations of System 1 generate surprisingly complex patterns of ideas, but only the slower System 2 can construct thoughts in an orderly series of steps. I also describe circumstances in which System 2 takes over, overruling the freewheeling impulses and associations of System 1.

I should point out that, while rapid and "unconscious," Type 1 processing can oftentimes be correct. For example, performance in one's area of expertise, such as experts reading x-rays or selecting chess moves, generally exhibits the best of all worlds—fast and accurate. How this is achieved, and what insights this offers education is an important topic that I will delve into in Chapter 7.

5.1.3 Type 3 Processes: Sociocultural Interaction

In addition to rapid pattern matching and deliberative rule following, people engage in collective social behaviors that have their own qualities. To capture these in a succinct way, I introduce the notion of Type 3 processing. Type 3 processing is primarily described in terms of social norms and social structures. Its reasoning unfolds through discourse patterns of group interaction. Type 3 processing operates on information and sensory input through a normative lens, influenced by what is socially permissible and afforded. Culture mediates Type 3 responses, as much as knowledge shapes Type 2 processing and perception Type 1 processing.

We saw an earlier example in Box 2.1 with the 4-card problem. Type 1 processing quickly selected one correct and one incorrect card to turn over, because it favored those cards (vowels and even numbers) named in the problem. If you, the reader, took the time, you would have experienced Type 2 processing that deliberatively evaluated each card and carefully matched it to the rule. This leads to the correct answer but it's painfully slow. In this task, we can also see some of the unique qualities of Type 3 processing that are not evident in the other types of processing. Note how Type 3 processing can succeed when the problem is reworded in terms of one's normative cultural practices, as with the postage stamp problem. When this logic problem was reworded in the context of a lived, cultural phenomenon for some, people who have these social norms rather quickly invoke the use of their pragmatic reasoning schemas (Cheng & Holyoak, 1985). Those for whom the cultural practice is familiar solve the simple conditional effortlessly.

What is the motivation for adding Type 3 processing to our discussion? It is because there are some intellectual behaviors that simply cannot be explained by either Type 1 or Type 2 processing. I want to illustrate an important contrast: Whereas Type 1 processing operates unconsciously, and Type 2 processing operates with conscious awareness, among Type 3 processing there can be a *hyper-self-consciousness* from normative expectations brought about through social interactions—just by the mere *social presence* of others. Even Type 1 processing that Type 2 processes cannot monitor or control, can be altered by social activity associated with Type 3 processing.

For this I want to examine performance on the Stroop task. (This task was introduced as a Reader Activity in Chapter 4.) The Stroop task (MacLeod, 1991; Stroop, 1935) nicely illustrates the interplay of Type 1 and Type 2 processing. I recommend doing this activity (see Figure 5.2). Ordinarily, a researcher would document how long it takes to read each word or number string presented individually. In this case, though, I think the effect will still be observed even without being timed.

In the Stroop task, readers are made aware of the automatic nature of Type 1 processing of symbols when they experience a conflict. In some versions of the task, the symbols are words such as color names (e.g., *red*) written in different colored fonts (green). In other version,

| 33 | 444 | 2 | 1111 | 3 | 44 | 222 | 4 |

| 11 | 2 | 3333 | 222 | 444 | 2 | 111 | 33 |

FIGURE 5.2 Stimuli used in the numerical version of the Stroop task. Try saying how many digits there are in each number string as rapidly and accurately as you can. Notice the sense of interference the numerals create.

such as shown in Figure 5.2, the symbols are numerals (e.g., 4) that are grouped in different size strings (e.g., length 3). The reader experiences a conflict (a delay in processing) when directed to report the length of the number string when the symbols used do not mismatch the string length.

One might think that counting the length of these strings of numerals is a more basic process than naming the numeral. Yet, as soon as the reader sees the familiar numerical symbol, Type 1 processing is already decoding the symbol and looking to say what is written, even as the string length is being processed. Since the instructions ask for the length and not the numeral, readers experience interference between these competing processes. This interference translates to a measurable increase in item response time, and increase in effort to inhibit the incorrect response. This is a variation of the well-documented Stroop Effect. The color word effect is even more pronounced, but does not work as well printed in grayscale.

When this task is performed in a social setting, the unique influences of Type 3 processing becomes evident. This leads to the surprising finding that even automated processes can be altered when social factors are at play. Scholars have observed that when people engage in the Stroop task in the presence of another attentive agent, even if that other agent is not visible or otherwise engaged (e.g., reading a book), word reading processes are enhanced (Huguet, Galvaing, Monteil, & Dumas, 1999). This *increases* the interference of the Stroop task, and leads to longer response times. However, in the social presence of a competing reader who is reported to be faster or at a similar level of performance as the participant, there is a significant *reduction* in interference. Readers are even faster at correctly naming the color than when doing the task alone or in the presence of a slower co-actor. These effects cannot be explained by Type 1 or Type 2 processing.

Since social presence can either improve or harm performance, depending on the type of perceived social pressure, this is called the *social facilitation-inhibition* effect (Zajonc, 1965, 1968). One explanation of the effect is that the readers respond to social pressures by focusing limited attentional resources and filtering out non-essential stimuli in service of the central goal. This attentional focus enhances performance on simple tasks—hence the social *facilitation* effect. Consistent with this, participants who benefited from social presence also exhibited worse recall for the words they had seen. Social presence narrowly focuses limited attentional resources for a primary task, but at the cost of poorer performance on secondary tasks (Huguet et al., 1999). When the task is more complex and broader attention is needed for success, narrowly focusing attention is detrimental to performance. Important elements can be overlooked or not adequately processed, leading to more errors. This then leads to the social *inhibition* effect. Both facilitation and inhibition effects due to social presence appear to be related to normative expectations people have for themselves when they believe their performance is being evaluated within a social context.

Descriptively, Type 3 processing seems to combine some of the traits of Type 1 and Type 2 processing, while also contributing unique qualities of its own. Whereas Type 1 processing is often experienced as effortless, and Type 2 processing as effortful, Type 3 experiences can be *energizing*, though they may also be experienced as effortful or effortless. For example, the back-and-forth of a conversation is an easy, enjoyable experience in many instances, despite the rapid processing demands that rely on recognizing deep semantic structure and sifting through the explosive combinatorics of linguistic options (Garrod & Pickering, 2004). Chi and Wylie (2014) show how greater levels of interactivity with others leads to greater levels of engagement, deeper processing, and superior learning. Indeed, there are many circumstances where group performances exceed individual performances on problem solving and decision making (e.g., Barron, 2003; Schwartz, 1995; Sigman & Ariely, 2017) even as they are more enjoyable (Olivera & Straus, 2004). I say much more about this type of processing in Chapters 9 and 10.

TABLE 5.1
A comparative summary of Type 1, 2, and 3 processing

	Type 1 processing	*Type 2 processing*	*Type 3 processing*
Timescale	ca. below 10^{-3} s to 10^{-1} s milliseconds	ca. 10^{0} s to 10^{4} seconds to hours	ca. 10^{5} s to 10^{8} s days to years
Energy	Effortless	Effortful	Energizing, effortless, effortful
Reasoning style	Impressions	Analytical	Discursive
Processing style	Automatic	Controlled, deliberate	Responsive to context
Awareness	Unconscious (unaware), unmonitored	Conscious (mostly), monitored	Can be collectively unconscious, conscious, or self-conscious
Pace	Fast	Medium	Slow
Processing dynamics	Associative & parallel	Linear & sequential	Networked
Method	Impulse following	Rule following	Norm following
Mode (primary) of thought	Perceptual recognition	Intellectual	Social
Cross-species	Innate skills shared with many species	Shared with very few species	Possibly uniquely human
Attention load	Few/no attention resources	Draw on attentional resources	Mixed
External control	Undisruptable	Executive control	Social pressure; guilt.
Response automaticity	Follows habits	Override habitual responses	Adopt group norms
Response mode	Anticipatory, predictive	Reactive, planful	Normative
Type of knowing	Knowing-how	Knowing-that	Knowing-with
	Overconfident, feeling of being right	Declarative facts and rules	A sociocultural lens on all one's experiences
Grounding processes	Perceptual fluency	Connection making	Common ground
Embodied learning	Transduction	Offloading	Participation internalized
Example: Reading	Stroop Effect	Sound out words	Social facilitation-inhibition (SFI)

5.1.4 Comparing Type 1, 2, and 3 Processing

Table 5.1 provides a summary of some of the comparative qualities across Type 1, 2, and 3 processing. In general, I will refer to their place on the timescale, as I find it more informative, but I will also make reference to their processing type in order to connect it to the pre-existing literature. Note these processes will often overlap and co-occur. In general—outside of carefully contrived laboratory experiments—processing at these different levels is all operating simultaneously. The actual behaviors we observe will often be the product of the *superposition*, or summation, of these various processes. This is a topic that gets revisited in Chapter 11.

5.2 EMBODIMENT IN THE CONSCIOUS SPECTRUM: TYPE 2 PROCESSING

In Chapter 2, I reviewed four broad types of GEL: grounding, off-loading, transduction, and participation. Grounding is basic to all embodied learning and is manifest in some form across the range of the GEL timescale. However, as the scale of the processes shifts, so does the form of grounding. In Type 1 processing, for example, grounding is often achieved via sensorimotor states such as perceptual fluency, which enables automatic response of the rapid pattern-matching system. Type 3 grounding primarily occurs by taking up social and cultural norms and practices through which participatory learning is achieved, such as the adoption of specific discourse practices. In Type 2 processing, the main means of grounding is via **connection making,** by which new ways of knowing are constructed in relation to prior knowledge and experiences.

In addition to grounding, ***off-loading*** is highly impactful to Type 2 processing. Tactics such as making a list or using math manipulatives, may be *helpful* for some cognitive tasks because they reduce cognitive load (Pouw, van Gog, & Paas, 2014). But off-loading is *necessary* for others, such as writing out complex mathematical procedures like long division, and the material supports that made possible the discovery of DNA structure. I elaborate on these processes as they relate to the conscious spectrum portion of the GEL timescale.

5.2.1 Type 2 Processing: Grounding and Off-Loading

Grounding via connection making
One of the most powerful ways that new and complex ideas are grounded and made meaningful for learners is through connection making. I have shown some prior examples where learning benefited because concepts and abstract objects, such as the number system, were grounded to body-based systems, such as that used by the Oksapmin (Saxe, 1982). Grounding often occurs when words and gestures connect concepts to spatial locations, like a whiteboard, or to spatial structures, such as the number line for ordering numbers. Type 2 grounding is also achieved by connecting quantities and relations to narrative structures, which helps children learn to invent effective algebraic strategies such as "unwinding" (Koedinger & Nathan, 2004).

Connection making is a fundamental process to support learning. One widely used method for making connections is analogy (Richland, Zur, & Holyoak, 2007). *Analogy,* much like metaphor, establishes a mapping between a familiar "source" domain, and a novel "target" domain. Children benefit from analogy when learning such basic abilities as how to spell and decode novel words by mapping them to similar looking and sounding words (Goswami, 1986). Students also demonstrate superior inference making for science concepts when analogies are provided when compared to literal descriptions of the concepts (Donnelly & McDaniel, 1993).

The research literature generally shows that connection making is an effective way to give meaning to new ideas and symbols. However, learners often fail to make these connections spontaneously, even when rich curricular materials are made available (Clement, 1993; Gick & Holyoak, 1983; Richland, Morrison, & Holyoak, 2006). Explicit connections are made most reliably by providing the proper visual materials, and through a caregiver's speech and gestures. This contributes to students' analogical reasoning and helps support meaning making, learning, and assessment of performance.

Grounding through connection making is important for teachers as well as learners. In an international comparison, Richland and colleagues (2007) observed classroom instruction among the 1999 TIMSS video corpus that US teachers and Asian teachers in Hong Kong and Japan. Students in these Asian countries consistently outperform American students in international mathematics assessments. It was discovered that teachers from all three countries offer comparable opportunities for their children to learn mathematics through connection making. However, Asian teachers were far more likely to use source material effectively to make connections, and to reduce the cognitive demands of their students through a variety of means to maximize efforts at making connections. For example, US teachers were much less likely to use gestures to connect grounding source information (such as an image of a balance scale) to novel target information (such as the equivalence relation in an algebra equation).

Gestures, the reader will recall from Chapter 2, are small, situated actions that can aid comprehension and learning by complementing and reinforcing information presented in speech or visually. Teachers often use gestures for grounding. This was revealed in an analysis of 18 classroom lessons—one of the largest such corpuses collected for the purpose of studying authentic gesture use (Alibali et al., 2014). Teachers were often observed pointing in order to ground ideas and formal representation for students to things in their learning environments. Teachers also used hand shape and movement to visually and metaphorically depict ideas. When metaphoric gestures were used in domains such as mathematics and science, teachers often provided a concrete source domain to help ground an abstract formalism.

Gestures have been shown to be effective ways to ground ideas in experimental contexts. For example, video lessons of symmetry were more effective when the teacher in the video included pointing and tracing gestures to ground the teacher's words by linking verbal utterances of abstract ideas to the concrete, physical environment (Valenzeno, Alibali, & Klatzky, 2003).

This role of instructional gestures is especially apparent when teachers introduced new ideas. In these instances, teachers' gesture production increased as if to anticipate the additional pedagogical needs of their students (Alibali et al., 2014). Similarly, teachers' gesture rates increased when students experienced trouble spots—moments of confusion, or incorrect understanding. When this occurred, teachers often—responsibly— increased their gesture rates so as to accommodate the real-time learning needs for their students.

As this suggests, teachers' gestures help learning by fostering and maintaining "common ground" during classroom instruction. Along with being necessary for effective communication, common ground serves a vital role for learning (Kelly, Byrne, & Holler, 2011; Nathan, Church, & Alibali, 2017; Singer, Radinsky, & Goldman, 2008). When teachers use gestures to effectively link ideas and formal representations, and provide common ground, students learn more (Alibali et al., 2013).

Off-loading and the Principle of Least Effort
One constraint above all seems to determine the nature of thinking and learning processes in the conscious spectrum: Type 2 processing is highly capacity limited, and performance degrades substantially when that capacity is reached. Because of this, humans avoid excessive intellectual work whenever possible. There is an overarching **Principle of Least Effort** that determines our intellectual behavior (Zipf, 1949/2016). Zipf illustrates this by showing that there are a small number of the most common words in a language. This minimizes the demands made on both speakers and listeners (i Cancho & Solé, 2003). Furthermore, these common words are often very short—think about *the, a, of,* and *and*. This, too, reduces energy expenditure for both production and processing. Kahneman (2011, p. 35) describes it so:

> A general "law of least effort" applies to cognitive as well as physical exertion. The law asserts that if there are several ways of achieving the same goal, people will eventually gravitate to the least demanding course of action. In the economy of action, effort is a cost, and the acquisition of skill is driven by the balance of benefits and costs. Laziness is built deep into our nature.

One way this plays out is that the effortless, automatic processes that are the hallmark of Type 1 processing are the default response and often prevail, regardless of its accuracy, even when someone can do better by applying analytic methods. For example, Kahneman (2011) notes that it is relatively easy to simply "check" that the answer to the bat-and-ball problem is correct by examining the proposed cost difference between the two items. However, in studies of this, less than 20% of college students in some samples ever bothered. More will be said about these tacit and impulsive behaviors in Chapter 4.

Another way that people manage the demands on Type 2 resources is by **off-loading** cognitive demands onto the environment. In Chapter 2, off-loading was shown to play out in several ways. I reviewed, for example, ways that a person like Otto, with extreme memory limitations, used a notebook to extend his cognition. As a metaphor, we should recognize that all people are a bit memory-challenged like Otto, and, similarly, all people benefit from using resources that extend people's cognitive processes.

Gestures are effective resources for supporting learning through off-loading. As mentioned earlier, gestures do this using situated pointing and tracing acts (Valenzeno et al., 2003). For example, children taught a grouping strategy only through gestures reproduced that strategy in over 90% of the post-test items. They were able to generalize the concept being modeled by the gestures to new items, even though it was not explicitly explained to them (Goldin-Meadow, Cook, & Mitchell, 2009). This can benefit learning even when the gestures are produced by a (life-like) computer-animated pedagogical avatar (Vest, Fyfe, Nathan, & Alibali, 2020). Students who watched a digital avatar present a lesson on polynomial multiplication sometimes produced gestures much like those produced by the avatar during their verbal explanations. Students whose gestures closely aligned with those of the avatar showed greater learning gains than their peers.

Gestures may seem to be for the benefit of the listener because they are expressive and performative. But gestures are involved for the speaker's benefit. This is evident because speakers will gesture in ways that are complementary and semantically co-expressive with speech (McNeill, 1992; Radford, 2003). This is the case even when the speakers cannot see one another because they are behind a screen (Alibali, Heath, & Myers, 2001) or speaking on the phone. This elevated pattern of gestures during social interactions is evident even when the speakers have congenital blindness, and may have never seen another person's gestures (Iverson & Goldin-Meadow, 1998). Both blind and sighted speakers will use similar forms and rates of gesture when talking about conservation of liquid, for example. Blind speakers will also produce gesture even when they are talking to other people they know to also be blindfolded (Iverson & Goldin-Meadow, 1997). These similarities in gesture production among blind and sighted speakers is evident across cultures, as well, as when comparing English and Turkish speakers (Özçalışkan, Lucero, & Goldin-Meadow, 2016).

Gestures also off-load complex relations by producing simulated actions. For example, a gesture can depict how a tool is to be used and provide a level of sensorimotor detail that may otherwise be very difficult to attain with words alone (Hostetter & Alibali, 2008, 2019).

The use of these off-loading supports—be they external memory aids, epistemic actions, gestures, or a host of other forms—frees up other cognitive resources, such as attention and working memory. It also frees up executive control, which is necessary for instituting the kind of monitoring that keeps Type 1 responses in check and subject to the deliberate, rule-based reasoning that Type 2 processing provides.

Off-loading recruits resources of the body and the environment to reduce the cognitive and attentional demands on Type 2 *processing*. These processes, in turn, help ensure there is greater likelihood of learning the intended *content*. The next section identifies that content. It describes *what* is actually learned in the conscious spectrum, and how that knowledge is structured and assessed.

5.2.2 Forms of Knowing and Learning in the Conscious Spectrum: Declarative Knowledge and "Knowing-That"

Humans know many kinds of things and in many different ways. Consequently, a scientific description of knowledge and knowing must also allow for multiple forms. These forms are often portrayed as knowing-how, knowing-with, and knowing-that (Figure 5.3; Broudy, 1977; Ryle, 1945). Each form captures assumptions about how these ways of knowing are instantiated by the mind, how it develops, and how it functions. In addition to informing theories of learning and cognitive development, the particularities of each form of knowing and learning have implications for instruction, assessment practices, and the design of technology-based learning experiences.

Knowing-how is primarily learned through doing and typically requires repetition with feedback. It is often associated with procedural knowledge and pattern recognition (Broudy, 1977; Ryle, 1945, 1949). As a largely unconscious process, I will discuss perceptual learning and knowing-how in Chapter 7.

Another form, *knowing-with*, characterizes the ways that our interactions with the world are affected by our cultural experiences and observing how skills and practices are performed. Knowing-with relies predominantly on our (often) implicit social and cultural perspectives that shape our perceptions and associations. Shaffer (2006) identifies knowing-with as central to the development of the epistemic frames that are central to the knowledge associated

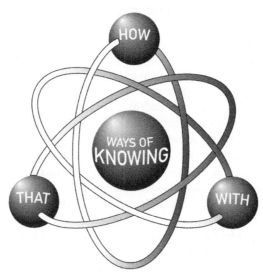

Type I	Type II	Type III
Knowing-how	Knowing-that	Knowing-with
Procedural knowledge	Declarative knowledge	Epistemic knowledge
Implicit learning of patterns of covariation in the environment through lived experience	Learn through reading, by being told in place; cognitive maps	Learn through participation, apprenticeship, social interaction
Unaware	Aware	Unaware and aware

FIGURE 5.3 The three ways of knowing are discussed in this book. This chapter focuses on *knowing-that*.

with communities of practice. Because of its critical role in sociocultural learning, knowing-with will be addressed in greater detail in Chapter 9.

The third form, **knowing-that,** is sometimes labeled ***declarative knowledge*** (Pirnay-Dummer, Ifenthaler, & Seel, 2012). *Knowing-that* includes fact knowledge—such as my immensely deep store of trivia about *Monty Python's Flying Circus*—and knowledge of events, categories, and concepts. It describes things we are generally aware of knowing, and we can readily talk about, deliberate on, mentally inspect, and exert considerable conscious control over. In this regard, knowing-that naturally resides in the conscious spectrum, and so, this form of knowing is the focus of this chapter.

In the cognitive psychology literature, declarative knowledge is often modeled as a network of richly interconnected nodes, sometimes called *semantic networks* (Anderson & Bower, 1973; Collins & Quillian, 1969; Rumelhart, Lindsay, & Norman, 1972) These networks relate language-like concepts to one another and are usually organized hierarchically. Declarative knowledge about dairy cows, for example, would be organized under knowledge of farm animals. Activation of the concept FARM would typically prime associated ideas of farm animals, the related information faster to access.

Some nodes in a declarative knowledge network are more complex than just category labels and are often modeled by more intricate structures, such as schemas. *Schemas* are hypothesized to be larger organizational structures that contain labeled and unlabeled *slots* that get *filled* with symbolic information. A restaurant-ordering schema, for example, is a common event that might include being seated, ordering from a menu by interacting with a food service worker, tabulating a gratuity, and then paying the final bill.

People's memory systems "chunk" all the elements commonplace for event sequences of this sort and conveniently treats it as a single element in our highly capacity-limited working memory system (Chase & Simon, 1973). Schema theory also allows for exceptions, such as payment in some contexts coming first (fast food or take-away), seating yourself, looking at a bulletin board for the food selections, and so on.

The pre-existing "slots" of objects (a menu) and events (payment) in schema theory are significant in that they organize the information in a structure that explicitly supports our expectations for that information, based on our prior experiences. This is an example of how *knowing-with* influences declarative knowledge while contributing to our predictive orientation for what actions are to come and how they are brought to bear in future contexts. Schema theory also helps explain memory *errors*, as when a person falsely recalls an exchange with a hostess because that element is highly activated in the generic schema structure even if it did not happen during the particular experience in question (e.g., Reyna & Brainerd, 1998).

To illustrate these different forms of knowing, let me offer a widely used decision-making task involving infectious disease, adapted from Tversky & Kahneman (1981), with slightly modified wording (Table 5.2). People's impressions (Knowing-How) are very different than that arrived at through a deliberative process (Knowing-That) and a response shaped by one's professional identity (Knowing-With). The solution process people use for this depends on framing it as lives saved or lives lost. This illustrates the differences between Type 1 and Type 2 processing.

The percentages listed in square brackets are the proportion of participants (university students) who made each selection. Two things should be observed. First is that regardless of the differences in Framing #1 and Framing #2, the certainty of saving (or losing) 200 people and the one-third probability of losing (or saving) 600 people has the same expected value. Based on Type 2 processing, there should not be reason to choose option A over option B, or option C over option D. Based on these calculations, the options should be chosen roughly 50%–50%, yet there are clearly unequal preferences. Specifically (Framing #2) certain death of 400 people is less acceptable than the two-in-three chance that 600 will die.

TABLE 5.2
TABLE 5.2
**Framing the infectious disease problem as lives saved or lost. The risks in both cases are
mathematically identical but the framing changes people's judgements**

The United States is preparing for the outbreak of an unusual disease, which is expected to kill 600 people. Two alternative programs to combat the disease have been proposed. Assume that the exact scientific estimates of the consequences of the programs are as follows:

Framing #1: Number of Lives Saved N = 152	Framing #2: Number of Lives Lost N = 155
A. If program A is adopted, 200 people will be saved. [72%, risk aversion]	C. If program C is adopted, 400 people will die. [22%]
B. If program B is adopted, there is a one-third probability that 600 people will be saved and a two-thirds probability that no people will be saved. [28%]	D. If program D is adopted, there is a one-third probability that nobody will die and a two-thirds probability that 600 people will die. [78%, risk taking]
Which of the programs would you favor?	Which of the programs would you favor?

Second, Framing #1 and Framing #2 describe essentially the same outcome probabilities. From the standpoint of Type 2 processing, it is surprising to see differences simply due to changes in the wording from saving to losing lives. Type 1 processing, however, treats the two framings very differently. Without much analysis, people strongly prefer the *risk aversion* option for choices involving lives gained (Framing #1), and, they strongly prefer *risk taking* for choices involving lives lost (Framing #2). However, conducting the analysis reveals that options A–D offer equivalent expected outcome probabilities. For the record, physicians are just as susceptible to the framing effect for making medical decisions when competing treatments are unidentified (McNeil, Pauker, Sox, & Tversky, 1982). But, in accordance with knowing-with, physicians make better decisions for treatment when the specific treatments are identified and allow for them to draw on their contextualized knowledge.

5.2.3 The Neural Basis of Embodied Declarative Memory: Maps for Facts

The memories we form to construct declarative knowledge are not simply disembodied nodes of information. Neuroscience evidence indicates that where and how learning experiences take place are integrated with what we know. Meaning, it seems, is about place and time as well as semantics.

The memories that make up declarative knowledge primarily reside in the hippocampus (American Association for Research into Nervous and Mental Diseases et al., 1997). The **hippocampus** is the small region of the brain located in the temporal lobe of the cerebral cortex. There are, in fact, two **hippocampi**, one in each of the two hemispheres of the cerebral cortex (see Figure 5.4).

Each hippocampus is centrally involved in several important cognitive functions: the formation of new, explicit memories of declarative information, a record of where things are located in space (Purves et al., 2018), and episodic memories of ordered events and when things were experienced in time (Tulving, 1972; Vargha-Khadem et al., 1997). That declarative knowledge of facts is co-located in the brain along with neural processing of temporal events and spatial locations might be a coincidence. After all, the human brain evolved over a very long period of time from vastly different functions and environments. During all this, its physical formation remains highly constrained by the available space provided by the cranium, and of pre-existing neural structures.

In this case, however, there is considerable behavioral and physiological evidence that the hippocampus does more than *independently* process semantic, spatial, and temporal

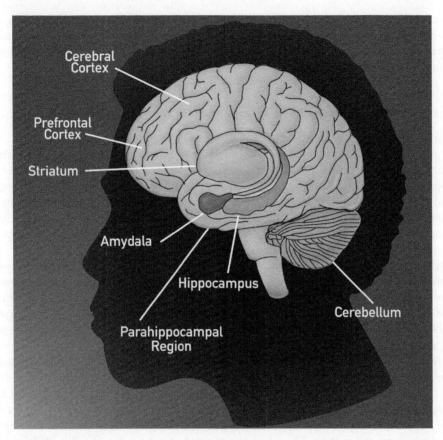

FIGURE 5.4 Hippocampus (left side of the brain) and neighboring brain regions involved in memory.

information. It is commonly believed that the co-location of these various brain functions allows us to process new memories into a kind of ***cognitive map,*** an organizational structure that integrates spatial and nonspatial information (Eichenbaum et al., 1999; O'Keefe & Nadel, 1978). As Tolman (1948) proposed, the cognitive map is analogous but not identical to a spatial map, and makes use of cognitive dimensionality much like a map uses the dimensions of physical space (Schiller et al., 2015).

This cognitive map provides a basic neural structure for registering where and when we encountered experiences and information that are worth remembering and retrieving. It also allows us to create allocentric memories that are formed with respect to landmarks rather than in relation our own ego-centric position. With this cognitive map, we appear to be able to flexibly use our ability to locate things and experiences in space and time to also "locate" nonspatial and non-temporal information, such as facts and concepts. We are auspiciously prepared to retrieve both spatial and nonspatial information when we revisit the locations and recall experiences in which they were previously useful—even when we only *imagine* revisiting a particular place and time (Lisman et al., 2017).

Cognitive maps as realized by hippocampal function offers the possibility for a neural basis for how the environment supports Type 2 processing through off-loading. One way to characterize this is by considering how the environment "scaffolds" cognition through off-loading (Sterelny, 2010). When the environment is recruited to perform some cognition it eases the process demands placed on the other processes. Cognitive maps perform this role by providing an organizational structure for both spatial and nonspatial information. Thus, as the next section reports, spatial experiences aid in the learning of declarative knowledge.

5.2.4 Declarative Knowledge Benefits from Spatial Experiences and Actions

Glenberg (1997), in a groundbreaking paper, poses a question to the cognitive psychology community, "What is memory for?" He argues against the conventional thinking of memory—or cognition, for that matter—as the capacity for pure symbol storage and processing, where the static information lies in wait to serve some future goal. He proposes instead "that memory evolved in service of perception and action in a three-dimensional environment, and that memory is embodied to facilitate interaction with the environment" (Glenberg, 1997, p. 2). This, Glenberg (1997, p. 3) notes, "is a call for an embodied approach to meaning."

If true, Glenberg's (1997) position implies that the ways we categorize the things we encounter in the world, and the very concepts that we form about those things, are a product of how we use them, rather than by some independent property. Evidence supporting the embodied view of memory and concept formation extends to how we form categories. In psychology, a *category* is a collection of instances that are all treated as if they were the same. A *concept* refers to all the knowledge one has about a category.

I previously mentioned research by Linda Smith (2005) showing that children's actions with objects determined the shape categories they assigned to these objects. That is, the actual outline of the object was not the sole determiner of how children categorized its shape at a later point. In the study, children between 2 and 3 years old were shown "a wug," a novel stuffed animal (see Figure 5.5). Children were directed to move their arm and the object in an up-down (vertical) motion. They then saw the two objects in Figure 5.5B side by side and were asked to select which was a wug.

Children overwhelmingly chose the vertically extended object over the horizontally extended one. The influence of children's actions on shape category was especially notable: the preference only held when children acted on the objects themselves, not when they watched an experimenter perform the same action. Here we see that even something as seemingly invariant and incontrovertible as shape category is influenced by one's actions. Actions ground the concept of a wug. By implication, the actions and use of many other objects and concepts may provide their grounded meaning.

5.2.5 Model-Based Reasoning as Embodied Thinking

People must have a capacity to reason beyond basic words and facts because people can make inferences and reason about complex processes. This suggests that people must be able to construct a richer view of things than how they might first appear and be literally described. *Mental models* (Gentner & Stevens, 1983/2014; Johnson-Laird, 1983; Kintsch & van Dijk, 1983) have been offered as a way to account for this rich way of thinking because they present ideas as fundamentally runnable simulations of events and relations rather than static objects and features. Mental models are implicated in a number of cognitive processes. Figure 5.6 presents a few tasks that all rely on simulation-based forms of thinking.

For the Gear Problem (from Hegarty et al., 2005), mental models are again implicated. Schwartz and Black (1996) initially found that problem solvers used their hands to manually simulate the gears and their direction of successive rotation. This suggested

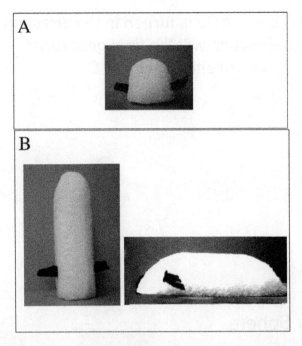

FIGURE 5.5 (A) Original "wug" example. (B) Children must decide which of the two objects
they categorize as a "wug" after moving it vertically or horizontally.

that the hand movements off-loaded the memory demands of the task, and may also provide the sensorimotor basis for carrying out the simulation. Over time, the simulation
of this simple alternating pattern gave way to an even more efficient rule of alternation
and parity.

Vosniadou and Brewer (1992) report on students' (inferred) mental models based on
interviews and drawings when they are told that the Earth is "round." As some of the model
illustrations show, it is possible to have a planet that is both round and flat (e.g., Disc Earth,
Dual Earth). They asked children questions about their models, such as "If you walked and
walked for many days in a straight line, where would you end up?" One child operating with
the sphere model of the Earth responded, "Back where you started." Another child operating
with the disc model, had this response, "Probably in another planet." So the investigators
pursued further:

Experimenter: Could you ever reach the end of the Earth?
Child: Yes, if you walked long enough.
Experimenter: Could you fall off that end?
Child: Yes, probably.

Mental models provide a way to describe how it is we can store and retrieve spatial and
causal relations that arise when we experience events and when we read and hear about events
(Kintsch, 1998). These all seem supported by a more general set of processes for performing
motor simulation. Mental rotation, for example, engages the motor cortex (Zacks, 2008).
Furthermore, engaging motor systems aids in mental rotation. For example, actually turning
one's body facilitates people's ability to mentally simulate turning. Similarly, rotating one's
hand helps people simulate mental rotation (Chu & Kita, 2008).

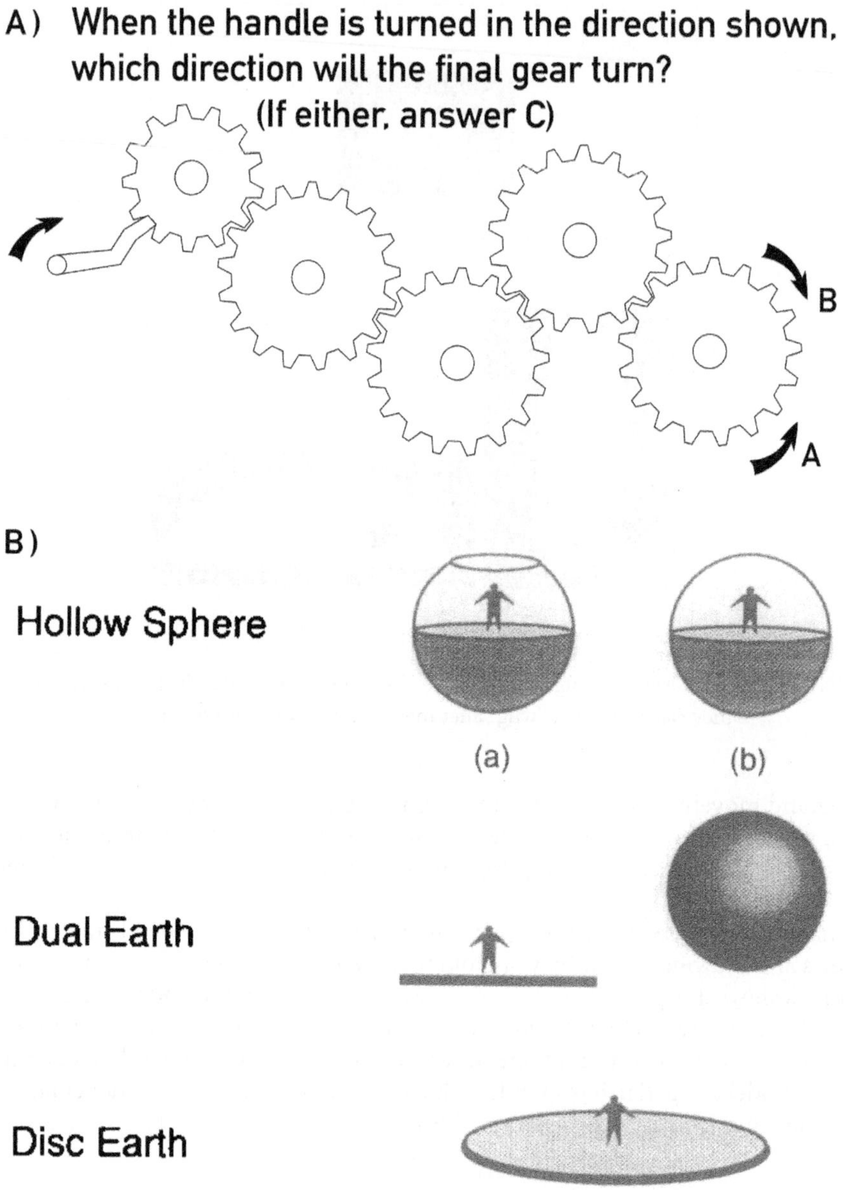

A) When the handle is turned in the direction shown, which direction will the final gear turn? (If either, answer C)

B)

Hollow Sphere

(a)   (b)

Dual Earth

Disc Earth

FIGURE 5.6 A. Gear Problem (from Hegarty et al., 2005). B. Children's mental models of the Earth (from Vosniadou & Brewer, 1992)

Hegarty and colleagues (2005) explored whether gestures and premotor processes were causally linked to people's reasoning. They concluded that gestures were functional for expressing one's mental models, but that there was insufficient evidence to conclude gestures helped produce the mental models.

5.2.6 The Neural Basis of Cognitive Simulations

Cognitive simulations are possible because there are neural systems that enable the integration of memories with time and space, decoupled from their *specific* points in time and space. Because of this, one can imagine new, future scenarios as more than pure abstractions. People can construct imaginations that are contextually rich in space and time, as well as recall prior knowledge and experiences that contextualize those memories (Lisman et al., 2017). As Nadel and Ranganath propose (in Lisman et al., 2017, p. 2),

> By separating the elements of past events from one's current time and place (e.g., by replaying in place A an event that occurred in place B), the hippocampus provides a form of representation that can be used in retrospective (i.e., episodic memory retrieval) or prospective (i.e., prediction or simulation) cognition.

What's more, the integration of declarative information with spatial-temporal information that is non-ego-centric, suggests that access of memories may reinvoke the prior histories. Thus, we can predict the activation of place-based associations when facts are retrieved. Likewise, we can predict recall of facts when places and events are cued, either by physically visiting them or imagining that we are visiting them. This is a powerful cognitive resource, made possible because—despite its rather static sounding label—declarative knowledge is an embodied experience.

Much of the research on the function of the hippocampus has been conducted in rats, yet is pertinent to inferences about human neural capabilities because of the high similarity in anatomical structure (Clark & Squire, 2013). Rats with damage to the hippocampus are able to recognize familiar objects, but only in their original spatial context (Eacott & Norman, 2004; Langston & Wood, 2010). Research has revealed the important role of "place cells" and "grid cells" (Moser, Kropff, & Moser, 2008). As a great oversimplification, *place cells* identify locations, and *grid cells* store information of where the locations are relative to one other. Together, place cells and grid cells contribute to an overall spatial sense. In rats, this spatial sense is principally used for navigation.

Hippocampal place cells and grid cells are also activated when cuing human spatial memory organization, for example, for information displayed on a computer screen (Eichenbaum & Cohen, 2014). In addition, the neural systems responsible for these spatial relations become appropriated to organize other mental contents for humans. Thus, these cells are implicated for their role in how people form concrete and abstract relations *as though* they were spatial (Tversky, 2019), such as placing a boss *above* employees in an organizational chart. In this way, the hippocampus provides a biological basis of both spatial and abstract thought using a common set of neural processes.

Another important source of information about the role of the hippocampus for storing and retrieving memory comes from the detailed analyses of the experiences of a couple of clinical patients. One is HM (later revealed to be Henry Molaison, following his death in 2008; Purves et al., 2018). During his late 20's, Mr. Molaison had surgery to treat severe epilepsy during which much of his hippocampus was removed or damaged. Although the surgery was effective in relieving Molaison of his seizures, he experienced a profound loss of the ability to form new explicit memories, especially memories that depended upon his conscious recollection of facts or prior experiences. Also notable was the selectivity of its impact on declarative memory since he retained his ability to recall new procedures as well as access older declarative memories.

Similarly, Clive Wearing, an accomplished musicologist, conductor, tenor, and keyboardist, suffered hippocampal damage from encephalitis. Clive Wearing still exhibits similar memory loss as Molaison in the form of chronic *anterograde* and *retrograde amnesia*. He can generally retain new information for only several seconds. As his wife, Deborah Wearing, revealed (Wearing, 2005), Clive Wearing literally loses his memories in the blink of an eye, noting that when he blinks "his eyelids parted to reveal a new scene. The view before the blink was utterly forgotten."

However, he is able to access non-declarative information. He has never forgotten his enduring affection for his loving wife, though each time he greets her—passionately—it is as though he has not seen her in years. He also retains the perceptual and muscle memories involved in sight reading musical scores and playing the piano with great skill. Significantly, Deborah Wearing reports that Clive Wearing's performance continues to improve with regular practice, though he has no recollection of having previously played a particular piece of music (Vennard, 2011).

5.2.7 Action Instills Cognitive Engagement

Engagement is an important aspect of cognition that is consciously regulated. As Chi and Wylie (2014) point out, *engagement* has several aspects. Motivational engagement acts as a precursor for whether one will interact with learning materials. Behavioral engagement focuses on level of participation, such as attendance. Emotional engagement tends to focus on one's positive or negative disposition toward something. In contrast, the focus for Chi and Wylie (2014, p. 219) is on *cognitive engagement*, which they describe as the "broad notions such as thoughtfulness and willingness to exert the necessary effort to succeed and master complex skills and ideas (Fredricks, Blumenfeld, & Paris, 2004)."

The ICAP hypothesis (Chi, 2009; Chi & Wylie, 2014) predicts that as students become more active, more "hands on" (constructive), and more social (interactive) with the materials, instruments, ideas, and collaborators—as they move from passive to active to constructive to interactive—they are more cognitively engaged, and so experience greater learning. In GEL terms (Table 5.1), I would say cognitive engagement increases as learners contribute more forms of grounded and embodied learning.

Passive forms of engagement, such as watching a video of how to build a digital voting machine, will elicit less cognitive engagement and therefore weaker forms of learning, than active, constructive, and interactive forms. An Active version could involve the learner manipulating components of a digital circuit (either the physical chips and wires, or a computer simulation). In the Constructive version, a learner participates in the design-and-test cycle that moves from a problem statement, through successive iterations toward a finalized product. Construction is more likely than Active and Passive modes, to draw on inference making, analogical reasoning, and generalization in support of knowledge transfer to novel situations. The Interactive version is a collaborative experience. Here learners engage in dialog, shared representations and explanations, co-inferencing and prediction processes as they co-create, test, and reflect upon new circuit designs.

A direct, empirical test of the theoretical claims was conducted (Menekse, Stump, Krause, & Chi, 2013) by looking at post-test gains in undergraduate engineering students' understanding material science concepts over a 5-day unit. The researchers found that student overall performance increased about 8–10% for each increase in the mode of engagement. Each modal shift from passive to active to constructive to interactive was statistically significant. For example, students in the Constructive treatment had hands-on experiences that directly helped them form a more coherent understanding of the relation between the micro- and macro-properties of a crystal under investigation than did students in the active and passive conditions. In turn, those in the Interactive condition engaged in much more critical thinking about the activities. Interactive treatment students showed the greatest gains in inference questions, compared to the other treatments. Interestingly, those in the Constructive condition outperformed all the other conditions in assessment items for integrating information. The ICAP framework reveals how the *forms* of learners' engagement with curriculum materials, rather than the choice of curriculum materials themselves, relate to the depth of understanding that can be achieved.

Each step of the way, greater learning emerges as students move closer to direct experiences of the phenomena of interest and interact with others. In doing so, students bring more perceptually enacted, socially and situationally embedded, cognitively extended, and physically embodied processes to the task (Newen, De Bruin, & Gallagher, 2018). Chi and Wylie provide an important perspective that bridges action-based views of learning that stem from the cognitive and developmental perspectives (e.g., Piaget) and participation-based views of learning that are more closely aligned with sociocultural perspectives (e.g., Vygotsky).

5.3 SUMMARY

This chapter focused on forms of reasoning and learning in the conscious spectrum. I introduced the three behavioral systems discussed in the literature. Type 1 processing functions automatically, without monitoring and control, and are relatively impervious to other demands on attention and memory. They generally occupy the faster portion of timescale. Type 2 processing, the focus of this chapter, is made up of a collection of structures and processes that carry out explicit, rule-based behaviors that are deliberately applied, monitored, and controllable by the person. Type 2 processing demands one's attention and greatly suffers when other demands compete for very limited attention and working memory.

Type 3 processing is primarily described in terms of social norms and social structures. Its forms of reasoning operate through discourse patterns of group interaction. Information and sensory input to Type 3 processing are managed through a pragmatic lens, based on what is socially permissible and afforded by the environment. Culture mediates Type 3 responses, as much as knowledge shapes Type 2 processing and perception Type 1 processing.

Declarative knowledge and model-based reasoning are the main ways people construct knowledge using Type 2 processing in the conscious spectrum. Both declarative knowledge and model-based reasoning are shown to manifest embodied ways of knowing. Declarative knowledge is grounded to the place and time when the memories were created. There is considerable neural support for this rich, sensorial experience for memory storage and retrieval. Model-based reasoning enables simulation and inference making by drawing on body-based and environmental resources. Cognitive engagement is also shown to be based in action, with the greatest learning benefits arising from those experiences where learners are most active and interactive with the environment and other learners.

5.4 READER ACTIVITIES

5.4.1 Model-Based Reasoning

Birthday Party Story
Billie had a birthday party. The house burned down.

a. Why did the house burn down?
b. Look carefully at the words of the story. How did you arrive at your conclusion?

Discussion. In the Birthday Party Story, readers naturally infer that the (unmentioned) candles from the (unmentioned) cake were involved in the house fire. As discussed earlier, schemas provide the memory organization for common, generic objects and events. A *birthday party schema* activates in memory a variety of things—presents, a cake, candles being lit, singing—even when these are not explicitly mentioned. From here, it is one's mental model that enables the causal chain of reasoning that led to the conclusion. In my own mental model for this, I actually saw a chaotic party with unruly children toppling the cake and precipitating the events.

5.4.2 Neural Basis of Spatial Memory and Visual Imagery

Here is an engaging talk about how your brain tells you where you are.
www.ted.com/talks/neil_burgess_how_your_brain_tells_you_where_you_are

REFERENCES

Alibali, M. W., Heath, D. C., & Myers, H. J. (2001). Effects of visibility between speaker and listener on gesture production: Some gestures are meant to be seen. *Journal of Memory and Language*, *44*(2), 169–188.

Alibali, M. W., Nathan, M. J., Church, R. B., Wolfgram, M. S., Kim, S., & Knuth, E. J. (2013). Teachers' gestures and speech in mathematics lessons: Forging common ground by resolving trouble spots. *ZDM*, *45*(3), 425–440.

Alibali, M. W., Nathan, M. J., Wolfgram, M. S., Church, R. B., Jacobs, S. A., Johnson Martinez, C., & Knuth, E. J. (2014). How teachers link ideas in mathematics instruction using speech and gesture: A corpus analysis. *Cognition and Instruction*, *32*(1), 65–100.

American Association for Research into Nervous and Mental Diseases, Squire, L. R., & Zola, S. M. (1997). Amnesia, memory and brain systems. *Philosophical Transactions of the Royal Society of London. Series B: Biological Sciences*, *352*(1362), 1663–1673.

Anderson, J. R., & Bower, G. H. (1973). *Human associative memory*. Winston.

Barron, B. (2003). When smart groups fail. *The Journal of the Learning Sciences*, *12*(3), 307–359.

Broudy, H. S. (1977). Types of knowledge and purposes of education. In R. C. Anderson, R. J. Spiro, & W. E. Montague (Eds.), *Schooling and the acquisition of knowledge* (pp. 1–17). Erlbaum.

Chase, W. G. & Simon, H. A. (1973). Perception in chess. *Cognitive Psychology, 4*, 55–81.

Cheng, P. W., & Holyoak, K. J. (1985). Pragmatic reasoning schemas. *Cognitive Psychology*, *17*(4), 391–416.

Chi, M. T. (2009). Active-constructive-interactive: A conceptual framework for differentiating learning activities. *Topics in Cognitive Science*, *1*(1), 73–105.

Chi, M. T., & Wylie, R. (2014). The ICAP framework: Linking cognitive engagement to active learning outcomes. *Educational Psychologist*, *49*(4), 219–243.

Chu, M., & Kita, S. (2008). Spontaneous gestures during mental rotation tasks: Insights into the microdevelopment of the motor strategy. *Journal of Experimental Psychology: General*, *137*(4), 706.

Clark, R. E., & Squire, L. R. (2013). Similarity in form and function of the hippocampus in rodents, monkeys, and humans. *Proceedings of the National Academy of Sciences*, *110*(Supplement 2), 10365–10370.

Clement, J. (1993). Using bridging analogies and anchoring intuitions to deal with students' preconceptions in physics. *Journal of Research in Science Teaching*, *30*(10), 1241–1257.

Collins, A. M., & Quillian, M. R. (1969). Retrieval time from semantic memory. *Journal of Verbal Learning and Verbal Behavior, 8*, 240–248.

Donnelly, C. M., & McDaniel, M. A. (1993). Use of analogy in learning scientific concepts. *Journal of Experimental Psychology: Learning, Memory, and Cognition, 19*(4), 975–987. Retrieved from https://doi.org/10.1037/0278-7393.19.4.975

Eacott, M. J., & Norman, G. (2004). Integrated memory for object, place, and context in rats: A possible model of episodic-like memory? *Journal of Neuroscience*, *24*(8), 1948–1953.

Eichenbaum, H., & Cohen, N. J. (2014). Can we reconcile the declarative memory and spatial navigation views on hippocampal function? *Neuron*, *83*(4), 764–770.

Eichenbaum, H., Dudchenko, P., Wood, E., Shapiro, M., & Tanila, H. (1999). The hippocampus, memory, and place cells: Is it spatial memory or a memory space? *Neuron*, *23*(2), 209–226.

Evans, J. S. B., & Stanovich, K. E. (2013). Dual-process theories of higher cognition: Advancing the debate. *Perspectives on Psychological Science*, *8*(3), 223–241.

Fredricks, J. A., Blumenfeld, P. C., & Paris, A. H. (2004). School engagement: Potential of the concept, state of the evidence. *Review of Educational Research*, *74*(1), 59–109.

Garrod, S., & Pickering, M. J. (2004). Why is conversation so easy?. *Trends in Cognitive Sciences*, *8*(1), 8–11.

Gentner, D., & Stevens, A. L. (Eds.). (2014). *Mental models*. Psychology Press.

Gick, M. L., & Holyoak, K. J. (1983). Schema induction and analogical transfer. *Cognitive Psychology, 15*, 1–38.

Glenberg, A. M. (1997). What memory is for. *Behavioral and Brain Sciences, 20*(1), 1–19.

Goldin-Meadow, S., Cook, S. W., & Mitchell, Z. A. (2009). Gesturing gives children new ideas about math. *Psychological Science, 20*(3), 267–272.

Goswami, U. (1986). Children's use of analogy in learning to read: A developmental study. *Journal of Experimental Child Psychology, 42*(1), 73–83.

Hegarty, M., Mayer, S., Kriz, S., & Keehner, M. (2005). The role of gestures in mental animation. *Spatial Cognition and Computation, 5*(4), 333–356.

Hostetter, A. B., & Alibali, M. W. (2008). Visible embodiment: Gestures as simulated action. *Psychonomic Bulletin & Review, 15*(3), 495–514.

Hostetter, A. B., & Alibali, M. W. (2019). Gesture as simulated action: Revisiting the framework. *Psychonomic Bulletin & Review, 26*(3), 721–752.

Huguet, P., Galvaing, M. P., Monteil, J. M., & Dumas, F. (1999). Social presence effects in the Stroop task: further evidence for an attentional view of social facilitation. *Journal of Personality and Social Psychology, 77*(5), 1011.

i Cancho, R. F., & Solé, R. V. (2003). Least effort and the origins of scaling in human language. *Proceedings of the National Academy of Sciences, 100*(3), 788–791.

Iverson, J. M., & Goldin-Meadow, S. (1997). What's communication got to do with it? Gesture in children blind from birth. *Developmental Psychology, 33*(3), 453–467.

Iverson, J. M., & Goldin-Meadow, S. (1998). Why people gesture when they speak. *Nature, 396*(6708), 228–228.

Johnson-Laird, P. N. (1983). *Mental models: Towards a cognitive science of language, inference, and consciousness* (No. 6). Harvard University Press.

Kahneman, D. (2011). *Thinking, fast and slow*. Macmillan.

Kelly, S., Byrne, K., & Holler, J. (2011). Raising the ante of communication: Evidence for enhanced gesture use in high stakes situations. *Information, 2*(4), 579–593.

Kintsch, W. (1998). *Comprehension: A paradigm for cognition*. Cambridge University Press.

Koedinger, K. R., & Nathan, M. J. (2004). The real story behind story problems: Effects of representations on quantitative reasoning. *The Journal of the Learning Sciences, 13*(2), 129–164.

Langston, R. F., & Wood, E. R. (2010). Associative recognition and the hippocampus: Differential effects of hippocampal lesions on object-place, object-context, and object-place-context memory. *Hippocampus, 20*(10), 1139–1153.

Lisman, J., Buzsáki, G., Eichenbaum, H., Nadel, L., Ranganath, C., & Redish, A. D. (2017). Viewpoints: How the hippocampus contributes to memory, navigation and cognition. *Nature Neuroscience, 20*(11), 1434–1447.

MacLeod, C. M. (1991). Half a century of research on the Stroop effect: an integrative review. *Psychological Bulletin, 109*(2), 163.

McNeil, B. J., Pauker, S. G., Sox, H. C., & Tversky, A. (1982). On the elicitation of preferences for alternative therapies. *New England Journal of Medicine, 306*, 1259–1262.

McNeill, D. (1992). *Hand and mind: What gestures reveal about thought*. University of Chicago Press.

Menekse, M., Stump, G. S., Krause, S., & Chi, M. T. (2013). Differentiated overt learning activities for effective instruction in engineering classrooms. *Journal of Engineering Education, 102*(3), 346–374.

Moser, E. I., Kropff, E., & Moser, M. B. (2008). Place cells, grid cells, and the brain's spatial representation system. *Annual Review of Neuroscience, 31*, 69–89.

Nathan, M. J. (2012). Rethinking formalisms in formal education. *Educational Psychologist, 47*(2), 125–148. doi:10.1080/00461520.2012.667063.

Nathan, M. J., Alibali, M. W., & Church, R. B. (2017). Making and breaking common ground: How teachers use gesture to foster learning in the classroom. In R. B. Church, M. W. Alibali, & S. D. Kelly (Eds.), *Why gesture? How the hands function in speaking, thinking and communicating* (pp. 285–316). John Benjamins.

Newen, A., De Bruin, L., & Gallagher, S. (Eds.). (2018). *The Oxford handbook of 4E cognition*. Oxford University Press.

O'Keefe, J., & Nadel, L. (1978). *The hippocampus as a cognitive map*. Clarendon Press.

Olivera, F., & Straus, S. G. (2004). Group-to-individual transfer of learning: Cognitive and social factors. *Small Group Research, 35*(4), 440–465.

Özçalışkan, Ş., Lucero, C., & Goldin-Meadow, S. (2016). Is seeing gesture necessary to gesture like a native speaker?. *Psychological Science, 27*(5), 737–747.

Pirnay-Dummer, P., Ifenthaler, D., & Seel, N. M. (2012). Semantic networks. In Norbert M. Seel (pp. 3025–3029) *Encyclopedia of the sciences of learning*. Springer.

Pouw, W. T., Van Gog, T., & Paas, F. (2014). An embedded and embodied cognition review of instructional manipulatives. *Educational Psychology Review, 26*(1), 51–72.

Purves, D., Augustine, G. J., Fitzpatrick, D., Hall, W. C., Lamantia, A. S., Mooney, R. D., Platt, M. L., & White, L. E. (Eds.). (2018) *Neuroscience* (6th ed.). Sinauer Associates. Retrieved from www.neuroscientificallychallenged.com/blog/2014/5/23/know-your-brain-hippocampus

Radford, L. (2003). Gestures, speech, and the sprouting of signs: A semiotic-cultural approach to students' types of generalization. *Mathematical Thinking and Learning, 5*(1), 37–70.

Reyna, V. F., & Brainerd, C. J. (1998). Fuzzy-trace theory and false memory: New frontiers. *Journal of Experimental Child Psychology, 71*(2), 194–209.

Richland, L. E., Morrison, R. G., & Holyoak, K. J. (2006). Children's development of analogical reasoning: Insights from scene analogy problems. *Journal of Experimental Child Psychology, 94*(3), 249–273.

Richland, L. E., Zur, O., & Holyoak, K. J. (2007). Cognitive supports for analogies in the mathematics classroom. *Science, 316*(5828), 1128.

Rumelhart, D. E., Lindsay, P. H., & Norman, D. A. (1972). A process model for long-term memory. In E. Tulving & W. Donaldson (Eds.), *Organization of memory* (pp. 197–246). Academic Press.

Ryle, G. (1945, January). Knowing how and knowing that: The presidential address. In *Proceedings of the Aristotelian society* (Vol. 46, pp. 1–16). Aristotelian Society, Wiley.

Ryle, G. (1949). *The concept of mind.* Barnes and Noble.

Saxe, G. B. (1982). Developing forms of arithmetical thought among the Oksapmin of Papua New Guinea. *Developmental Psychology, 18*(4), 583–594.

Schiller, D., Eichenbaum, H., Buffalo, E. A., Davachi, L., Foster, D. J., Leutgeb, S., & Ranganath, C. (2015). Memory and space: Towards an understanding of the cognitive map. *Journal of Neuroscience, 35*(41), 13904–13911.

Schwartz, D. L. (1995). The emergence of abstract representations in dyad problem solving. *The Journal of the Learning Sciences, 4*(3), 321–354.

Schwartz, D. L. & Black, J. B. (1996). Shuttling between depictive models and abstract rules: Induction and fall-back. *Cognitive Science 20*, 457–497.

Shaffer, D. W. (2006). Epistemic frames for epistemic games. *Computers & Education, 46*(3), 223–234.

Sigman, M. & Ariely, D. (2017). How can groups make good decisions. *TED Talk.* Retrieved from www.ted.com/talks/mariano_sigman_and_dan_ariely_how_can_groups_make_good_decisions/transcript?language=en

Singer, M., Radinsky, J., & Goldman, S. R. (2008). The role of gesture in meaning construction. *Discourse Processes, 45*(4–5), 365–386.

Smith, L. B. (2005). Action alters shape categories. *Cognitive Science, 29*(4), 665–679.

Stanovich, K. E., & West, R. F. (2000). Individual differences in reasoning: Implications for the rationality debate?. *Behavioral and Brain Sciences, 23*(5), 645–665.

Sterelny, K. (2010). Minds: extended or scaffolded. *Phenomenology and the Cognitive Sciences, 9*, 465–481.

Stroop, J. R. (1935). Studies of interference in serial verbal reactions. *Journal of Experimental Psychology, 18*(6), 643.

Tolman, E. C. (1948). Cognitive maps in rats and men. *Psychological Review, 55*, 189–208. doi:10.1037/h0061626.

Tulving, E. (1972). Episodic and semantic memory. *Organization of Memory, 1*, 381–403.

Tversky, B. (2019). *Mind in motion: How action shapes thought.* Hachette UK.

Tversky, A., & Kahneman, D. (1981). The framing of decisions and the psychology of choice. *Science, 211*, 453–458.

Valenzeno, L., Alibali, M. W., & Klatzky, R. (2003). Teachers' gestures facilitate students' learning: A lesson in symmetry. *Contemporary Educational Psychology, 28*(2), 187–204.

Vargha-Khadem, F., Gadian, D. G., Watkins, K. E., Connelly, A., Van Paesschen, W., & Mishkin, M. (1997). Differential effects of early hippocampal pathology on episodic and semantic memory. *Science, 277*(5324), 376–380.

Vennard, Martin. (2011, November 21). How can musicians keep playing despite amnesia? *BBC News.* Retrieved from www.bbc.com/news/magazine-15791973

Vest, N. A., Fyfe, E. R., Nathan, M. J., & Alibali, M. W. (2020). Learning from an avatar video instructor: The role of gesture mimicry. *Gesture, 19*(1), 128–155.

Vosniadou, S., & Brewer, W. F. (1992). Mental models of the earth: A study of conceptual change in childhood. *Cognitive Psychology, 24*(4), 535–585.

Wearing, D. (2005). *Forever today: A true story of lost memory and never-ending love.* Corgi.

Zacks, J. M. (2008). Neuroimaging studies of mental rotation: a meta-analysis and review. *Journal of Cognitive Neuroscience, 20*(1), 1–19.

Zajonc, R. B. (1965). Social facilitation. *Science, 149*(3681), 269–274.

Zajonc, R. B. (1968). Attitudinal effects of mere exposure. *Journal of Personality and Social Psychology, 9*(2p2), 1.

Zipf, G. K. (2016). *Human behavior and the principle of least effort: An introduction to human ecology.* Ravenio.

6

Grounding and Embodied Learning in the Conscious Spectrum

6.1 GEL OF ACADEMIC CONTENT AREAS IN THE CONSCIOUS SPECTRUM

Embodied learning in the conscious spectrum is often overlooked or misapplied in academic content areas. When learning experiences are designed with GEL principles at the fore, then there are powerful educational benefits to be had. I provide a select review of the research findings showing GEL for four major content areas: language arts, second-language learning, mathematics, and science. I show how embodied learning is realized by grounding the understanding of new ideas through connection making and by extending reasoning and knowledge to the environment through offloading. The other forms of GEL—transduction and participation—are reviewed in subsequent chapters.

6.1.1 Language Arts

Early Reading and the "Reading Wars"
Oral language, including speaking and listening, are biologically primary abilities (see Section 2.1.1). Their development is examined in Chapter 4. Reading written language is regarded as a biologically secondary skill because it draws upon those primary abilities and is of cultural relevance, rather than necessary for survival. As a biologically secondary ability it develops using very different GEL processes than oral language development.

Written words, the reader will recall, are arbitrary symbols that do not visually resemble what they mean or reference. *Small* is not small—it is certainly no smaller than *tall*—and neither is *large* particularly large. *Tiny* may sound small but *city* sounds similar. How are early readers able to learn and remember the meanings of the thousands of words they will encounter? The answer is that reading relies on solving the *symbol grounding problem* for arbitrary orthographic symbols. It therefore depends on connection making—forming a mapping between the image of a word and its meaning. The connections are typically provided through socially supported instruction and feedback.

In Chapter 2, I reviewed some of the important findings of the *Moved By Reading* program (Adams et al., 2018). That was based on a view of embodied learning derived from Glenberg's indexical hypothesis. In that program, early readers learned to explicitly connect words and sentences to toy objects (e.g., farm animals) and their relations and actions. Young readers also attained many of the same benefits by imagining performing the same type of indexing. That educational program focused on reading comprehension, and presumed these early

DOI: 10.4324/9780429329098-6

readers could already identify the shapes of written words—their *orthography*—and correctly utter the words *phonetically*. Substantial learning has to occur prior to this.

How written words attain meaning has been the focus of the "Reading Wars" for many years (Pearson, 2004). At its core, the reading wars address the following conflict: Do children learn best with phonics-based instruction that focuses on word decoding? Or is it best for children to have an immersive experience that treats language holistically through exposure and use without breaking language down into its phonetic structure?

While many philosophical and educational arguments have been offered, the issue has been settled empirically. In order to read, early readers must learn to make the appropriate connections between three components: letters, words, and sounds (Seidenberg, 2017). Explicit, phonetics-based instruction is necessary for early reading education. But the letters one sees are arbitrarily related to the phonetic sounds one must make when reading. The shape of the letter *A* does not convey the sounds that skilled readers make when they read the letter as part of a word. Because the mapping between shape and sound is arbitrary, children need to learn this mapping from those who already have this culturally developed knowledge. Word meaning (clusters of letters) is attained by grounding these arbitrary strings of symbols to early readers' perceptual processes and their prior experiences of familiar words. This happens when visual symbols such as letters and letter blends are grounded in the perceptual processes of seeing letters, retrieving their contextually appropriate sounds (phonemes) and associating the sounds and images to the words stored in the reader's long-term memory (lexicon).

Children can then build up their literacy skills by automating these associations and then using them when reading high quality materials. By "automating" I mean that what starts out as relatively slow, effortful steps that take great concentration, transforms into a rapid, unconscious process that takes only a few tenths of a second to effortlessly execute. This automatic process is necessary because it frees up the cognitive resources that are so important for building up meaning from multiple words in sequence.

Reading Comprehension
One the most widely adopted theories of reading comprehension, that of van Dijk and Kintsch (1983; Kintsch, 1998), posits that comprehension relies on constructing more than an understanding of the specific visual shapes of letters and words (the *verbatim representation*), and more than the explicit words, phrases, and organizational structure of a text (the *textbase*). Reading comprehension necessarily includes the construction of an elaborated account of the actions and interrelations that the words in the text describe. In a sense, we internalize the affordances cued by the objects and events in a text. This is called the *situation model*.

Consider the sentences in this example from Bransford, Barclay, and Franks (1972):

(1a). Three turtles rested on a floating log, and a fish swam beneath them.
(1b). Three turtles rested on a floating log, and a fish swam beneath it.
(2a). Three turtles rested beside a floating log, and a fish swam beneath them.
(2b). Three turtles rested beside a floating log, and a fish swam beneath it.

A strict interpretation of these sentences, one that might be performed by a computer program, would not confuse (1a) with (1b), because the words *them* and *it* do not perfectly match. However, when asked to recognize whether they saw a specific sentence, people are quite likely to confuse (1a) with (1b). This is because readers do not only do a verbatim recall of the isolated words and literal sentence structure. Rather, people naturally construct a situation model. Situation models are imagistic, holistic, and dynamic. As a result, these mental models support the automatic generation of relevant inferences (such as swimming under the log implies swimming under the turtles as well) (Kintsch, 1998). People "confuse" (1a) and (1b) because the words—although different—lead to the same situation model!

The contrast for the second pair of sentences (the *beside* relation) is striking. When people read (2a) they almost never confuse it with (2b). The verbatim words and the situation models clearly differ for each sentence.

Advanced Reading Comprehension for Problem Solving

The situation model is a powerful form of mental simulation. Along with imagination and inference making, it is also implicated in mental models of how people use information from text to solve problems and learn from reading (Kintsch, 1998). This is because people draw on prior knowledge and experiences in constructing the simulations.

Earlier, we encountered mental models as a way to describe children's observed behaviors when reasoning about mechanical systems and the Earth (Hegarty et al, 2005; Vosniadou & Brewer, 1992). The ANIMATE system draws on situation model construction as an intervention intended to improve students' reading comprehension during algebra story problem solving (Nathan, Kintsch, & Young, 1992). The hypothesis that drove this research was that students will naturally construct mental simulations of the algebra story problem narrative. However, they would struggle to connect the narrative to the formal symbols that make up the algebraic equations.

ANIMATE is a learning environment designed to enable students to build and run animations of the story problem scenarios. The unique feature is that the animations had to be constructed by writing algebraic equations—very much like the *situation equations* that students generated from their role playing. Using equations to drive the animation that students ran grounded the meaning of the variables and operators that made up the equation to the actions and interrelationships that appeared on the computer screen.

For example, students are presented with activities such as the "overtake" problem shown.

In a race to save the passenger train from possible destruction, a helicopter was sent out to warn the engineer of a bridge and radio tower that had been washed out only hours before. The train left Central City two hours before the helicopter operator had been notified of the incident. With the train traveling at an average speed of seventy-five miles per hour, the helicopter operator was ordered to fly at full speed—nearly three hundred miles per hour! If the train is 60 miles from the broken bridge, can the helicopter notify the engineer in time?

In prior research, students consistently made several errors in problems of this sort that indicated they were not adequately grounding the algebraic symbols to the situation (Nathan, 1998). One was that students typically did not know whether they should add or subtract the 2-hour delay from the equation that relates the times for each vehicle. Equation (3) in Figure 6.1 shows the *incorrect* relationship. When writing this equation, the animation shows that the (faster) helicopter leaves *before* the train has departed.

Students may not get the equations correct at first, but they naturally imagine the correct situation model. Students are aware when the animation does not match their imagined situation model. Because they have now used the computer animation system to connect the animation behavior (a form of situation model) to the equations, students realize the equations cannot be correct. "Debugging" an equation results in revising the animation so that it matches their imagined situation model. In so doing, it establishes the meaning of all of the symbols and operators. For example, students now understand the meaning of the "–"

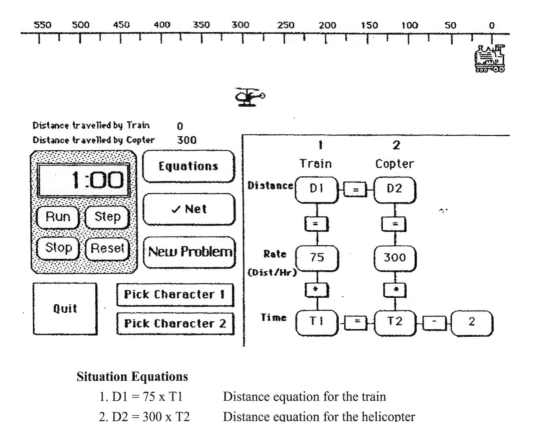

Situation Equations

1. D1 = 75 x T1   Distance equation for the train
2. D2 = 300 x T2   Distance equation for the helicopter
3. T1 = T2 – 2   Modeling the 2-hour delay incorrectly
4. D1 = D2   Distances are equal at the point of overtake

FIGURE 6.1 (a) A screen shot of the ANIMATE system showing a user-generated animation
for an overtake algebra story problem. (b) Situation equations used to model the story.
Note that Equation 3 *incorrectly* models the delay.

relation in Equation 3. (One way to think of it in situation model terms is that the faster, later-leaving vehicle can travel for 2 hours *less* than the first vehicle and still catch up.)

(*Funny anecdote: The members of my doctoral dissertation committee literally had an argument over how to correctly write this equation during my defense. That is, until they saw the animation! Needless to say, I passed.*)

Students were observed making two general types of errors: Errors of *omission* meant then inadvertently left out—or *omitted*—something that was necessary; while errors of *commission* meant they overtly *committed* and included something necessary but what was included was not mathematically correct. The time-delay equation is an example of a common error of *commission*. Students get it wrong because the equations initially have no meaning for them. They use heuristics like we saw with the 4-Card task, and write the equations to match the words, rather than as an accurate account of the situation model. Another common error is one of *omission*. Students often omit Equation (4) entirely. Mathematically, this leaves a student with an underspecified system of equations (i.e., 4 unknowns but only 3 equations) that cannot be solved for any specific value for the time till the helicopter reaches the train.

As expected by the GEL perspective, readers naturally simulate the actions and make the proper inference—students report visualizing that the train and helicopter have traveled the same distance from Central City at the moment the helicopter catches up. When left on their own, students typically fail to include this inference among the equations, which leads to lower performance. In ANIMATE, they observe that the animation never stops, even as the helicopter catches up. When students do realize they need to include Equation (4), the animation responds in a situationally appropriate way: The vehicles each travel as directed by the equation and the action stops when the distance traveled by the helicopter equals that of the train, revealing the exact distance and time they meet up.

The evidence in favor of this grounding approach to algebra story problem solving is very encouraging. Certainly, students correctly solve these problems far more frequently when they use the animation to "debug" the algebra. But the learning transcends the computer animation environment. Students start to identify and correct their own errors of commission even before they run the animation (Nathan, 1998). This suggests that the students are learning to simulate the meaning of the algebra equations they write in grounded, situational terms (Nathan & Resnick, 1994). Students also make fewer errors of omission by including their natural inferences in the equations. This happens even when they are tested without the animation to provide feedback. This indicates that students are learning to ground algebra symbols and equations to their own situation models. They also transfer that learning to problem-solving situations outside of the computer environment and become more autonomous algebraic thinkers.

Advanced Reading Comprehension for Reading to Learn
Nathan and Martinez (2015) investigated whether situation models could be theorized as embodied simulations that supported learning from text. In framing their study, they drew on the theory of Gesture as Simulated Action proposed by Hostetter and Alibali (2008, 2019). Methodologically, they extended the line of inquiry of Butcher (2006), who examined the role of images in forming inferences and learning from a scientific text about the human circulatory system. While the text involved spatial relations, such as the location of the four heart chambers, it also supported nonspatial inferences (i.e. "What would be the consequences of a large hole in the septum that separates the left and right sides of the heart?").

The new study explored whether readers' inference making was tied to their generation of embodied simulations. They reasoned that readers' simulations would elicit more gesture production (as predicted by Hostetter & Alibali, 2008). Gesture production was not expected to be strongly associated with learning general facts and vocabulary, because these two topics are not expected to depend on simulations so much as recall.

As predicted, Nathan and Martinez (2015) found that readers' gesture production was correlated with their spatial and nonspatial inference making. Readers' gesture production was associated with posttest inference-making performance, but not performance on tests of general knowledge (e.g., vocabulary) or of information explicitly stated in the texts. This relationship was replicated across four experiments and two different texts (Martinez, 2012; Nathan & Martinez, 2015).

To test the causal relation of gestures and inference making they conducted another experiment where gesture production during reading and testing was restricted by an overlapping spatial tapping task (similar to Hegarty et al., 2005). They found that restricting gesture production impaired spatial and nonspatial inference making, but left general knowledge and text-based knowledge unaffected. This provided evidence that gestures were functionally involved in inference making, and therefore implicated in running the simulations purported to mediate the inference-making process.

Martinez (2012) extended the original studies to a new science text (volcanoes and tectonic plates) and three forms of gesture impairment: passive restraint, tapping, and typing. The typing condition was chosen because it is a lot like spatial tapping and is commonplace in computer-based assessments. Martinez replicated the findings of Nathan and Martinez (2015). She found that typing one's answers had an insignificant effect on test performance of general knowledge and text-based knowledge. However, as expected, typing significantly reduced learners' inference making performance. She showed that typing one's answers interfered with gesture production and impaired inference making much like tapping and use of restraints! This provided further supporting evidence that the kind of reasoning while reading to learn relies on embodied simulations of the information presented in the text. Without access to movements that support simulation, readers are less likely to make important inferences.

This research raises serious concerns about the role of the body during assessment. The assumption seems to be that typing is a benign influence on test performance, but makes it easier to deliver and score tests accurately. Yet here (as with Nathan & Martinez, 2015) restrictions imposed on gesture production do significantly reduce intellectual performance. Typed testing may inadvertently be harming test performance by interfering with embodied learning processes. Furthermore, it is selectively degrading performance on inference making, which is one of the most complex forms of reasoning. While this is a small number of experiments, it is a troubling finding since it raises concerns about a widespread and growing assessment practice. At the very least, the findings suggest that the effects of impeding and allowing full gesture production deserves further investigation, especially as online assessments proliferate.

6.1.2 Second-Language Learning

Second-language learning is another important area for which there is empirical support for embodied learning. Second-language learners must solve the symbol grounding problem, but enjoy the additional support of connecting the new language to one's native language skills. Research has shown that gestures—specifically *iconic gestures* that depict the objects and ideas through handshape and movement—helps in students' connection making and offloading.

Preschool French children in one study benefit more from learning common second-language English words (e.g., scissors, swim) with gestures than with pictures (Tellier, 2008). Gestures also help adults learn new verbs in Japanese. In that study, the instructor combined verbal instruction with no gestures, semantically congruent gestures, or incongruent gestures (Kelly et al., 2009). The two gesture conditions allowed the team to see if gestures have a general effect of increasing attention and arousal, or if the particular alignment of the gestures with word meaning was critical. Semantically congruent gestures improved word learning best. Additionally, brain imaging (ERP) readings suggested that semantically congruent gestures helped learners with retrieval of the new words.

To help first-semester French students in college go beyond single words to learn common expressions, Quinn-Allen (1995) paired expressions with *emblematic gestures*. An example is *Si on s'en allait?* (Shall we go now?) paired with the touch of the left wrist with the right hand. Students in the treatment group who viewed videotaped lessons and copied the corresponding gestures showed improved recall and consistently higher performance over the five sessions of the unit. They did not show superior performance in the delayed final posttest, however. The study also showed the coding specificity effect (Tulving & Thompson, 1973) where the emblematic gestures needed to be present at both the original training and during testing to show the benefits.

Macedonia and colleagues also examined the role that performing gestures have on learning of an artificial second language, *Vimmi*, constructed to follow the grammatical structure of Italian (Macedonia et al., 2010; Macedonia & Knösche, 2011). German-speaking students showed greater recall for both short-term and long-term (60 days) retention intervals when they imitated the words aloud along with gestures shown in accompanying videos (Macedonia, Müller, and Friederici, 2011).

In studies of conversational speaking, Stam (2006) and several others (e.g., McNeill & Duncan, 2000) examined gesture production during more sustained interactions in students' newly emerging language. They concluded that second-language learners retained many of the gesture properties of their native language while speaking in a foreign tongue.

6.1.3 Mathematics Education

Mathematics is so obviously symbolic and abstract that it seems particularly distant from embodied accounts of learning and teaching. But we have already encountered examples of how counting, algebra, geometry, and various other topics in mathematics education benefit from offloading and connection making. A review of the research on the embodied nature of mathematics education was prepared by Nathan (2014). Some highlights and newer developments are featured here.

One program in particular has argued that mathematics is not abstract and disembodied at all, that mathematics ideas are fundamentally grounded in conceptual metaphors of embodiment of movement and space (see Section 2.5.1 for a reminder), and that this has guided the major advancements in mathematics. This position is described in the landmark book *Where Mathematics Comes From: How the Embodied Mind Brings Mathematics into Being* by George Lakoff and Rafael Núñez (2000). Although not an empirical account of actual mathematical discovery, the book proposes a theoretical account of an embodied mathematics, informed by psychology, history, linguistics, and neuroscience. Their analysis draws on many of the forms of embodied learning described in Section 2.6.

Lakoff and Núñez (2000) propose that mathematical ideas rely primarily on a small number of **grounding metaphors**. The reader may recall that a conceptual metaphor "is a *grounded, inference-preserving cross-domain mapping*—a cognitive mechanism that allows us to use the inferential structure of one conceptual domain (say, geometry) to reason about another (say, arithmetic)" (Lakoff & Núñez, 2000, p. 6, italics in the original). Of note here, is that grounding metaphors provide the basis for meaningful mathematics. What makes mathematics difficult for many people is not their inability to understand the ideas, but to learn the meaning of the formal notation and how it describes these basic ideas and their variants (Nathan, 2012).

One of the grounding metaphors relates quantities to collecting things. Humans develop the notion of TWO not primarily as some abstraction, but from our lived experiences of seeing collections that have two similar objects. To pick up two things the grasping action must be performed twice, once for each item. We would treat another set of two objects in much the same way. Similarly, when we hear two tones, the listening experience happens twice. We may "grasp" each sound; first one, and then the other. Collecting things is an authentic, grounded experience to think about quantity and can apply to many different objects.

The other grounding metaphors are similarly basic and flexibly applied. One relates object-construction operations—combining, removing, sharing, repeating—to arithmetic operations (addition, subtraction, division, and multiplication, respectively). Measurement, another fundamental idea, is grounded in the length of tangible things such as sticks. Objects that are of similar spatial extent to a common "measuring stick" are of equal length. Smaller objects can be positioned so their combined length may match the stick. Sticks can be combined, and they can also be divided. One can measure objects, and also motion along a path. Motion also grounds mathematical ideas of continuous quantities and direction. One can conceptualize the number system as discrete locations along such a path, with magnitude growing as one travels further, and the need for intervening numbers as falling between those discrete locations.

As should be clear, a system of quantification and analysis based on such fundamental ideas as collection, construction, length, and motion is powerful and flexible. Its generality then forms the basis of abstraction. For example, a FOOT is the measure shared by all such objects and motions that align to a foot-long stick. FEET emerges as a universal measure from multiples of a one-foot measure.

Grounding metaphors are limited, however. They work especially well for simple, foundational concepts. It gets more difficult to apply them as the phenomena people wish to explain grow in complexity and sophistication. Consider length as distance. The grounding metaphor assumes linear length. But many things travel along an arc, such as the Sun. One can extend the idea of (lineal) length to arc length, the amount of movement along a circular path. Similar to the FOOT, the RADIAN can measure this radial motion, and then apply to any other objects that travel in this way, such as wheels.

To extend beyond the small number of grounding metaphors to the enormous range of phenomena in the world and of our imagination, there is a need for **cognitive offloading** onto other things. **Linking metaphors** support this process. Linking metaphors allow people to offload the cognitive operations needed for a new domain, such as negative numbers, onto a previously grounded domain, such as counting numbers. Having done that, negatives now inherit the structure of counting numbers. Learners can then treat negative numbers like positives, though they also show some differences, such as how they carry "direction" away from zero.

The linking metaphor approach shows tremendous generativity for mathematics. Analytic geometry, for example, extends the grounding metaphor of measurement to apply to space and shape as well as its original application to numbers. Concepts such as INFINITY can be thought of as recurring processes, but ones that never end; and infinity can then be extended to the idea of cardinality (set size), with some infinities (e.g., for real numbers) greater than others (e.g., rational numbers). A vast portion of the mathematics canon can be explained by grounding and linking metaphors. Through it all is its basis in embodied experiences.

Numbers and Operations

While metaphors contribute to an account of how the field of mathematics may have grown, I think it is important to ask, How can these metaphors foster mathematics education? Take, for example, the conceptual metaphor of NUMBERS AS PLACES ALONG A PATH. It seems intuitive— schools assume children know it and so they don't actually teach it. But it is actually something that must be learned. It may get learned culturally, through participation opportunities in the home and community, much like playing dominoes or selling goods on the street. However, this can only happen when this idea is shared by others in one's culture. When it is not learned culturally, it must be taught explicitly. This is one of the traps for children from underserved communities.

Sharon Griffin, Robbie Case, and Robert Siegler (1994; Case & Okamoto, 1996) discovered this when they supported the education of recent Portuguese immigrants to Toronto. Primary grade teachers struggled with the poor progress some of these children who were learning basic arithmetic. To some, the children seemed "unteachable." Griffin and colleagues knew this could not be so. Rather, the team of educators and developmental psychologists realized they lacked the basic conceptual metaphors upon which arithmetic relied. These children never learned to see numbers along a number line, and they certainly never internalized a simulator that would allow them to imagine doing arithmetic by moving along a "mental number line."

To help construct the mental number line, the educational team devised a series of games, which they initially called **RightStart** and then named **Math Worlds** (Griffin, 2004). *Math Worlds* helped to ground the idea of a number line to children's actions and spatial experiences. Spinners and dice generated numbers. The children were taught to recite the counting numbers in a consistent order and move their game pieces that many steps as they counted. Moving down the number line—from higher to lower numbers—is just as important in mathematics as moving up (*N.B. Do you see my "down" and "up" spatial metaphors in use?*) A game like "blast off" taught the children how to count down from a number on the dice and then at the end—most excitedly—yell "Blast Off!"

If these games seem familiar, it is because many children in Western cultures learn these games at home and bring these concepts with them when they enter kindergarten. But many children do not have these opportunities—those living as refugees, for example. With practice, the legal game-playing moves ground the spatial layout of numbers. The actions, and their connections with number words and numeric symbols became internalized so that the children eventually could simulate the movements and anticipate where the game pieces should be placed whenever the numerals appeared. The games also supported student thinking by offloading their emerging construction of the number line onto the spatial layout of the game.

By providing explicit support through game-playing actions, these children came to be grade-ready in their mathematics education. The investigators found that the benefits for learning were still evident a year after the training ended (Griffin et al., 1994). In one of the earliest publications, the study team was able to report that (p. 64)

> Although children from different backgrounds may still need different sorts of programs to accommodate their needs as they progress formal schooling, the Rightstart program ensures that children from a diverse array of backgrounds will all start first grade with an understanding of quantities, numbers, and numerical terminology that builds on their existing insights and vocabulary, and that is well matched to the requirements of first grade.

Algebraic Equations

Grounding is critical for learning the meaning of algebraic terms and operators. For example, when students make the transition from arithmetic to algebraic reasoning, they need to learn to expand their notion of the *equal sign* to mean more than "produces a result" (Knuth et al., 2006). Early algebra students need to interpret the equal sign as a *relational* operator, meaning that the two sides of an equation are equal, even when they look different. Students understanding of the equal sign as a relational operator is associated with their equation solving performance.

An early algebra teacher will use pointing gestures to ground the equal-sign symbol to the idea of *balance*. One way to do this is by making connections between the equal-sign symbol and the fulcrum of a balance scale. Following this, the sides of the equation then map onto the corresponding sides of the balance (Nathan et al., 2017). Figure 6.2 shows three ways that teachers connected the symbolic structures of algebra equations to the grounded metaphor of EQUATION AS A BALANCE SCALE.

In the first instance, the teacher identifies the fulcrum of the balance scale as the point in which balance is established, and maps the balanced weight of the objects on the scale to a

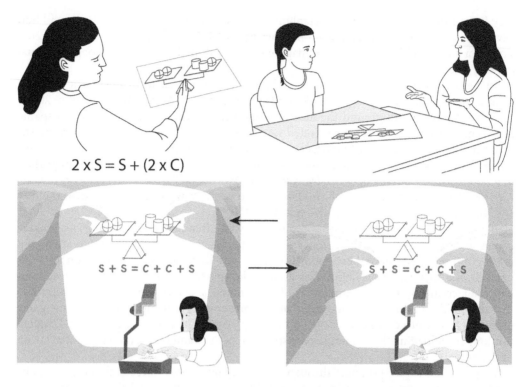

FIGURE 6.2 Three different ways teachers ground symbolic equations by using their bodies to connect algebraic structures to a balance scale.

balanced equation that equated the values of the variables on each side of the equation. The second example shows the teacher using her hands to iconically depict the behavior of the balance scale to a student. The third instance shows the symbolic equation lined up with the balance scale and then using gestures to show how simultaneously removing a sphere from each side maintains balance, just as removing the variable S from each side of the equation (Alibali, Nathan, & Fujimori, 2011). She says to her whole class:

> I am gonna take away a sphere from each side …
> Instead of taking it off the pans
> I am going to take it away from this equation

In these ways, symbols can be thought of as movable objects, subject to the constraints that the movements must maintain "balance." This is indicated by the newly understood equivalence relation, a revised interpretation of the equal sign.

GEOMETRY
Geometry is the scientific study of shapes and space. As part of this students learn how to measure properties of shapes and identify which properties are invariant under change. The interior angles of all triangles equal 180 degrees regardless of how small, tall or skewed they are. Geometry is important to many areas of mathematics and central to many other domains, such as materials science, architecture, mechanical engineering, and biochemistry, to name a few.

Students, however, do not easily apprehend the geometric nature of angular measure. They often incorrectly ascribe angle size to the lengths of the rays that meet to form the angle. They can mistakenly assume that the orientation of an angle is important in assessing its equivalence with other angles of equal measure.

Smith, King, and Hoyte (2014) helped third- and fourth-grade students learn angular measure by guiding them to form various angles with their arms. First, the members of the investigative team drew explicit connections of mathematical angles to physical angles as they arise in situations children typically experience in their daily lives, such as the angles made by scissors and the hands of a clock. They then helped students ground the meaning of various angular measures to the experience of the "space between sides" (p. 97).

They used the Kinect™ sensor array to track the movements and body shapes students made. As students moved, the angle of their arms changed the color of a screen projected in front of them. Acute angles turned the screen pink, right angles turned it yellow, obtuse angles turned it light blue, and straight angles turned the screen dark blue. To further connect this experience to standard angular measures, the researchers used the image of a protractor to match the angles students formed to benchmark angles measured in degrees, such as measures of 0°, 45°, 90°, 135°, and 180°.

The investigative team showed that students learned to connect their body shapes to the different color-coded categories of angles. Overall, they demonstrated statistically significant gains from pretest to posttest. Students' gains carried over to drawing activities on paper-and-pencil transfer tests.

In one case study analysis of a student, Ian, the team showed specifically how this learning was achieved through connection making. Ian improved from very poor pretest performance to 100% posttest performance. The gains came from Ian's emerging understanding based on making one-to-one connections between the angles he formed with the space between his arms to the angles depicted on the screen. He further learned to relate these general categories to specific angular measures. For example, in describing his understanding of obtuse angles, Ian reported "Light blue…it's from like 94 up to, like…oh yeah, it's 94 all the way up to about 178, and then dark blue starts." In this way, Ian described the range of angular measures, from slightly larger than a right angle ("94") to a supplementary angle ("about 178").

Summary
Grounded and embodied learning experiences are powerful ways to foster mathematical reasoning across a broad range of topics and developmental levels. Reasoning, problem solving and conceptual understanding in the conscious spectrum were supported by grounding-as-connection-making, and by offloading some cognitive resources and process onto the environment. Next, I review some of the work on this matter as it relates to science education for Type 2 processing.

6.1.4 Science and Engineering Education

Science and engineering are central to education as well as pivotal for maintaining economic health and national security. As the National Academies of Science, Engineering, and Medicine (2019, p. vii) state, "Students learn by doing. Science investigation and engineering design provide an opportunity for students to do." The introduction of *A Framework for K–12 Science Education* (NRC, 2012), the *Next Generation Science Standards* (NGSS, 2013), and the various state standards consistent with the *Framework* recognize that science and engineering combine to offer students the direct experiences necessary for learning how to empirically understand the world, predict its future behavior, and design for its betterment.

Students' science and engineering experiences in NGSS are organized into three interconnected types of experiences that are referred to as *three-dimensional learning*. (1) Core disciplinary ideas are those often associated with traditional science education in the various disciplines (chemistry, Earth and space science, life sciences, etc.) and include facts and theories such as heredity, atomic structure, and optimizing design solutions. (2) Cross-cutting concepts highlight the interconnecting ideas that run among all of the engineering and science disciplines. These include ideas such as conservation of energy, scale, cause and effect. (3) Engineering and scientific practices exemplify what practitioners actually do, such as engage in cycles of design or hypothesis testing, and communicate findings based on evidence.

It is worth mentioning that while science and engineering share a great deal in terms of "habits of mind," there are some important differences. Here is one central difference important for the epistemological considerations of what we expect of learners and teachers. Science is an inquiry discipline, and focuses on investigations with the intent of establishing evidence-based hypotheses of how things *are*. Engineering, in contrast, is a design discipline, with the intent of producing evidence-based innovations of how things *ought to be* (Nathan & Swart, 2020). Related to this, basic scientific inquiry is often positioned to be of higher intellectual status than engineering, which is often regarded in scientific communities as "merely applied." However this status difference is historically inaccurate. Each perspective contributes both basic and applied findings that improve our understanding and experiences in the world (Stokes, 1997/2011).

Science and engineering education rely, to various degrees, on each of the GEL processes. Here the focus on Type 2 processing addresses how GEL is supported by grounding the meaning of the various formalisms used throughout the sciences, including equations, graphs, visual models, technical specifications, and theories. Formalisms place substantial demands on people's limited cognition and attentional resources, and also benefit by providing offloading.

Grounding: Role of Direct Experiences
A common paradigm is for science teachers to present a lecture followed by a demonstration and hands-on laboratory experience of a phenomenon. Generally, transfer of learning to new settings is enhanced when students can ground these ideas with connection making across multiple contexts (Bransford and Schwartz, 1999).

Hands-on laboratory experiences are most effective for learning (NRC, 2006) when they (1) exhibit clear learning outcomes, (2) are aligned with students' other classroom activities, (3) consider both science content and process, and (4) incorporate learner reflection and discussion. These generally apply to computer-based representations and simulations of natural phenomena as well. *Chemistry That Applies* (WWC, 2012) is a highly recognized program that implements these four principles around a set of common chemical reactions: burning, rusting, the decomposition of water, and acid-base reactions. The program supports substantial learning as well as rich student discourse around scientific ideas and methods.

Offloading in Extended and Distributed Cognition
Learning and knowledge that is constituted in part by body-based resources, social actors, and resources in the material world is a significant source of complex cognition. As Wilson (2002, p. 626) describes, cognitive offloading is often helpful and can even be necessary:

Because of limits on our information-processing abilities (e.g., limits on attention and working memory), we exploit the environment to reduce the cognitive workload. We make the environment hold or even manipulate information for us, and we harvest that information only on a need-to know basis.

In this sense, offloading can serve as an external memory source, such as a scratch pad. But it can also be integral to the processing involved. In such cases, the cognitive processes might not take place at all, without these external resources in place.

For example, as described in Chapter 4, Watson (1968) reports depending on the critical role of the ball-and-stick models for carrying some of the understanding of DNA replication for Crick and Watson to correctly theorize the basic mechanisms for genetic replication. Einstein's discovery of General Relativity was rooted in the designs of new forms of technology as described in various patent designs he reviewed for solving the novel challenges of coordinated train travel. Many of the patent designs specifically aimed to work out systems of accounting for *relative time* as one traveled between cities (Galison, 2004). Cognitive ethnographies conducted by Hutchins (1995) revealed how sea navigation is offloaded onto the environment. In one account, Micronesian navigators use the motion of the landmark islands in relation to the arrangements of the stars to chart their path. Interesting, in this situated epistemology, they imagine the canoes to be stationary with respect to moving islands. Hutchins (1995) also described how Naval battleship navigation is distributed over multiple people, charts, and instruments, as no one person can perform the calculations rapidly enough to meet the time demands of the fix cycle. I say more about these various ways that cognitive processes are extended, distributed, and situated in Chapter 9.

As with science and engineering, offloading is important for engineering and science education. Project-based learning also provides the resources for extended cognition. Engineering teams often employ a "divide and conquer" approach, as a team member may dominate the Computer-Aided Design, while others are involved in mathematical analysis, schematic drawing, hands-on construction, and so forth (Nathan et al., 2010). Together the team members provide the knowledge of the engineering design. This means that learning engineering involves learning how to be part of a team, a topic that overlaps with participation learning (below).

Some scientific concepts are offloaded to the body. Chemistry education researchers have noted the important role of gestures, whole body movements, and manual actions on concrete manipulatives have for supporting the very complex spatial relations involved in reasoning about molecular structure (Flood et al., 2014; Ping et al., 2019; Stull et al., 2012). For example, Flood and colleagues (2014) document body-based offloading of first-semester general chemistry students. In one interaction, a student enacts the geometric structure of methane molecules with his entire body during a discussion with his partner. The first student cannot recall the term "tetrahedral" but the location of his feet and configuration of his legs and arms, along with the twisting motion he performs is sufficient for his partner, who then extends the enactment by inferring

"And that would make your torso like carbon?"
The first student pats his stomach and confirms, "Yes, yes. This is carbon."

People's bodies are extremely plastic resources for cognitive offloading of complex ideas. One common example in physics education is the "right-hand rule," which is used to understand how processes that operate in a two-dimensional plane lead to forces and fields

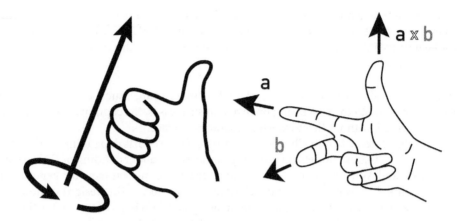

FIGURE 6.3 Using the Right-Hand Rule. (*Left*) Following the curl of fingers into the palm of one's right hand produces a force or field that follows in the direction of the thumb. (*Right*) A static display showing the three dimensions involved in the CURL operation. Using the right hand, Vector a (index finger) X Vector b (ring finger) produces a force or field in the direction of the thumb.

perpendicular to the plane. Many of us can relate to how this works when turning a screw-driver clockwise to drive a screw into a wall perpendicular to the plane in which the turning takes place. This is mathematically represented by the cross-product operation (denoted with a san serif X). An example is the CURL operation. This operation applies to numerous physical phenomena, such as electromagnetic fields and torque. Many physics and engineering students "know" how to resolve the forces involved in CURL by invoking the right hand to perform the right-hand rule (Figure 6.3).

Another form of offloading we have seen before is using the environment to extend cognition. Work by Tom Moher and colleagues (2005) employs the notion of *embedded phenomena* to foster scientific curiosity and inquiry. Students are immersed in experiences such as subterranean water transport, planetary motion, and ecosystems. One of the designed embedded phenomena teaches elementary students about earthquakes. *RoomQuake* creates a simulated earthquake in 5th grade students' classrooms by "randomly" creating seismic events that unfold over weeks. These events disrupt the class but enlist students to determine the epicenter and magnitude of the "quake," using techniques comparable to the trilateration of geologists.

6.2 EMERGING PRINCIPLES OF GEL IN THE CONSCIOUS SPECTRUM

The focus of this chapter has been on the grounded and embodied learning that occurs within the conscious spectrum, which is closely associated with Type 2 processing. Here I highlight some of the principles of GEL that can be extracted from among the various studies that were reported across learners' developmental stages and across a range of content areas. These principles are of theoretical and practical importance because they can be applied to foster learning, guide classroom instruction and the design of learning experiences, and inform educational assessment practices.

6.2.1 GEL Principles for Student Learning in the Conscious Spectrum

Grounding is a vital way to foster understanding and learning. Students encounter novel ideas and symbols that are unfamiliar and ambiguous throughout their education. One of the central ways that grounding supports students' meaning making is by making connections. In several studies student learning was seen benefiting when students could think of new ideas in terms of something already familiar to them. There were a few common ways this was experienced by learners.

The very experience of having a body is something always available to every learner at every moment. Often body-based resources are used spontaneously to understand commonly occurring ideas and events: Chairs are understood as furniture for sitting, for example. Learners form their categories based on how things are used. (e.g., Smith, 2005). Thus, a **principle of consistent action** will lead to favorable learning and semantic organization of new objects. This includes actions associated with perceptual acts, consistent with the perception-action loop (Neisser, 1976; Spivey & Huette, 2014). We can expect more rapid learning following consistent use and slower learning when the same objects, ideas, and symbols are used and perceived in multiple ways. For example, Uttal and colleagues (1997) found that when children were exposed to math manipulatives as objects to handle and play with *in addition* to their use as a symbol to represent mathematical ideas, students struggled to take up their representational functions.

This is related to another insight. There is a **principle of semantically congruent gestures** that explains how gestures used in ways that embody the ideas they are intended to convey (rather than, say, their visual similarity), will benefit learning. This is shown in a variety of studies reviewed here, including those in early reading, second-language learning, geometry learning, and science education (Adams & Glenberg et al., 2018; Lindgren & Johnson-Glenberg, 2013; Smith et al., 2014; Kelly et al., 2011). Gesture mimicry by students is an example of how gesture congruence fosters student learning (Goldin-Meadow, Cook, & Mitchell, 2009; Vest et al., in press).

The principle of grounding metaphors describes another powerful tenet for imbuing new ideas and unfamiliar symbols with meaning These are metaphors based on some of life's most familiar and basic experiences, such as movement, spatial extent, collections, and construction. People seem highly pre-disposed to think about connected ideas in terms of these grounding metaphors once the connections are made. It is easier to think of intangibles, such as one's *nation*, as family, and *numbers* as objects (Fischman & Haas, 2012). Conceptual metaphors must always be considered for their applicability as well as their divergence of the learning at hand (e.g., Ball, 1993). Still, they serve as important and reliable entry points for engaging learners' sense making processes.

We have developed specialized neural systems for memory that are highly spatialized. Memory storage and retrieval is bound up with the experiences of where something is learned and the episodic experience of when it was learned. From this follows a **spatial-temporal principle of situated memory retrieval**. Brain imaging data shows that retrieval is especially enhanced with spatial location and temporal ordering (Purves et al., 2018; Tulving, 1972; Vargha-Khadem et al., 1997).

Furthermore, people extend the applicability of the spatial-temporal principle of situated memory retrieval by *simulating* their location and contemporaneous experiences. This **principle of simulated situated memory** is achieved because neural systems that integrate memory with time and space can also be *decoupled* from their specific location and events (Lisman et al., 2017). This aids memory retrieval even when separated from the original context. It also fosters imaginative thinking, by projecting the thinker into these spatial-temporal contexts. For example, it is this capability that enables memory techniques such as the "memory palace," which uses our prior spatial-temporal associations of a familiar place to organize elaborate amounts of information, and even to recreate an entirely new "palace" for memory storage and retrieval (Roediger, 1980; Spence, 1985).

6.2.2 GEL Principles for the Design of Learning Experiences

Cognitive offloading as a design principle enhances student performance in two distinct ways. One way is by freeing up high capacity-limited cognitive resources, such as working memory, that are otherwise subject to physiological constraints. For example, Goldin-Meadow and colleagues (Goldin-Meadow, Nusbaum, Kelly, & Wagner, 2001) showed that children and adults experience lower demands on their limited cognitive capacity (as measured by performance on a secondary recall task) while they used gestures during their explanation of a mathematical problem-solving method. In this way, gesture production can "lighten" the load on cognitive resources during reasoning (Cook, Yip, & Goldin-Meadow, 2012).

A second way offloading helps performance is by extending cognitive systems, such as long-term declarative memory, onto structures and processes accessible in the environment (Choi, Van Merriënboer, & Paas, 2014; Wilson, 2002). For example, gesture production aids learning by bringing additional external resources into the cognitive system. Pointing includes relevant objects, while iconic movements can add spatial structures to the systems that effectively expand the available capacity to think and learn (e.g., Ping & Goldin-Meadow, 2010). This may be because gestures make demands on neural systems that are distinct from the verbal areas of the brain, that might already be highly loaded with reasoning and reporting demands (Paas & Sweller, 2012).

6.2.3 GEL Principles for Classroom Instruction

Teachers in language arts, science, and mathematics frequently use *linking gestures* as a means of grounding by connecting one idea to another idea, symbol, diagram, or objects and locations in learners' environment (Alibali et al., 2014). The **linking gestures principle** describes its function rather than its form, since linking gestures can be anything from simple points to iconic handshapes and arm movements.

On a more macrostructural level, making explicit connections of how a concept is instantiated, first in its most concrete form to its most idealized form is captured by the **principle of concreteness fading**. This principle was initially posed by Bruner (1966). It describes an instructional method that taps into students' authentic experiences with familiar objects and situations to support a grounded interpretation of formalisms for generalization and transfer. Concreteness fading incorporates qualities of both grounding and offloading. As Fyfe and Nathan (2019, p. 9) describe it,

> the goal of the fading process is not to explicate the similarities and differences across the varying representation, but rather to link the representations as mutual referents by aligning them on the continuum and presenting them in a specified order.

Grounding is achieved through the process that links successively more idealized forms of a concept, as when a teacher explicitly connects the physical behavior of a balance scale to its iconic depiction in the form of a drawing, and then relates that drawing to a symbolic equation. Offloading is supported because the fading process frees the learner from having to maintain the various forms in mind simultaneously and extract the relevant similarities from the differences.

One of the most poignant principles of GEL for design is for interactions to engage learners' body movements and perceptions in the construction of conceptual understanding. This **principle of embodied conceptual engagement** is evident in student learning with several interactive approaches, including the ANIMATE system for mathematics (Nathan et al., 1992, 1998), the *Moved By Reading* program (Adams et al., 2018), the materials science lessons (Menekse, Stump, Krause, & Chi, 2013), and the right-hand rule in science. Designing with this principle in mind requires that the interactions provide "grounded feedback," (Wiese & Koedinger, 2017, p. 449) of a form that enables the learner to ascertain the accuracy of their own performance. For example, the way students using the ANIMATE system identified errors by noticing mismatches between their situation model expectations and the animation behavior. Several systems have applied this principle with success in areas such as fractions (Wiese & Koedinger, 2017) and business mathematics (Mathan & Koedinger, 2005).

The **principle of concreteness fading** provides another important guide for the design of learning experiences (Bruner, 1966; Fyfe et al., 2015; Goldstone & Son, 2005). The struggle to understand ungrounded symbols so often leads to confusion, poor learning, and a lack of interest (Nathan, 2012). Concreteness fading offers a progressive path from the grounded, concrete experiences that have direct meaning for learners, to the symbolic formalisms that are important for transfer and disciplinary participation. Examples in mathematics include the introduction of board games to ground the idea of numerals and the number line (Griffin et al., 1994), and the explicit progression made in geometry from forming spaces between one's arms to the formalization of those arm shapes to benchmark angle measures (Smith et al., 2014).

6.2.4 GEL Principles for Assessment

The GEL framework offers some principles for summative assessment and formative assessment practices. *Summative assessment* is used to determine learning outcomes, as when teachers give an end-of-unit exam. GEL orients educators to look for ways to document students' verbal and nonverbal ways of knowing (Shapiro & Stolz, 2019). In interviews of students expressing their knowledge of geometry, Pier and colleagues (2019) found that students' gestures contained novel information about their knowledge of geometric relations that was not contained in their speech. To get a more complete account of what students knew, they showed that information from both student talk and gestures was necessary.

Assessment scoring, however, often privileges verbal forms of reporting and typically excludes nonverbal expressions of knowledge altogether (e.g., Ball, 1997; Kazemi & Franke, 2004; Walkoe, 2019). The **principle of nonverbal knowing** holds that educators will generally gain a far more accurate record of student learning when gestures are included in assessment rubrics. The practical implication of this principle is that educators create opportunities such as videotaped interviews that allow teachers to incorporate both verbal and nonverbal ways of knowing in their evaluations.

Summative assessments will also differentiate accounts of what one knows if they have access to resources that support cognitive offloading. The use of available tables, formulas, and calculators are commonly offered to students. These resources effectively expand students' access to fact knowledge. They can be a powerful aid for demonstrating students' reasoning and problem-solving skills, without getting bogged down on fact knowledge retrieval. The **principle of cognitive offloading** is also useful for designing assessments when educators are seeking to understand how students use basic information in service of higher-order forms of reasoning, such as problem solving, persuasive essay writing, and design activities.

Formative assessments are used to inform teacher instruction and curriculum planning, rather than to evaluate students' cumulative learning. Here, educators can exercise some of the techniques that learning scientists use to describe student reasoning. Church & Goldin-Meadow (1986) examined the speech and gestures produced by children while they thought about conservation of liquid as it was poured from a tall to a short, wide vessel. Children whose speech focused on one dimension (e.g., height) while their hands conveyed awareness of the other dimension (e.g., width) revealed that they were ready before their classmates to integrate two dimensions into their models for conservation. In this sense, gestures, along with speech, helps to convey learners' zones of proximal development (Goldin-Meadow, Alibali, & Church, 1993).

Gestures can also convey a student's reasoning process. For example, students may employ the right-hand rule while talking about phenomena in physics. Attending to how they use this, such as whether they are using the proper hand and making the conventional counter-clockwise rotation could indicate their level of understanding and inform subsequent learning activities. Similarly, students' use of finger counting may reveal of they are using different addition strategies that indicate their level of mathematical cognitive development.

Other grounded and embodied information by learners can provide insights into their ways of thinking. Students can also reveal their manner of thinking by the metaphors they use. Learners' metaphors can be elicited by using classroom discussion in small and large groups, class presentations, and writing assignments. For example, Groth & Bergner (2005) used writing prompts to capture the embodied metaphors for sampling produced by pre-service elementary teachers learning about statistics in order to identify some of their emerging misconceptions. The **principle of GEL formative assessment** serves as a reminder that students convey a great deal of their reasoning *process* using embodied forms of expression that can inform teacher planning and instruction.

6.2.5 Philosophy of Mind: Shapiro's Conceptualization Hypothesis and Constitution Hypothesis

Table 6.1 provides a list of the principles that have emerged from the research on GEL in the conscious spectrum. This is a table that I will continue to populate in the coming chapters. At this point, it is useful to relate the findings and these principles to two hypotheses that have been posed by Shapiro (2019) regarding the philosophical basis of embodied cognition.

TABLE 6.1

Principles for grounded and embodied learning, design, instruction, and assessment in the conscious spectrum of the GEL timescale

Educational concerns	*Principle*
Learning	The principle of grounding via consistent action and semantically congruent gestures,
	The principle of grounding with conceptual metaphors
	The principle of situated memory retrieval
	The principle of simulated situated memory
Design	The principle of cognitive offloading
Instruction	The principle of linking gestures. Concreteness fading
Assessment	The principle of summatively assessing nonverbal ways of knowing
	The principle of cognitive offloading for assessment
	The principle of GEL formative assessment

Conceptualization Hypothesis

Shapiro (2019, p. 80) posed the *Conceptualization Hypothesis* by stating "The kind of body an organism possesses constrains or determines the concepts it can acquire." Shapiro argues that the validity of this hypothesis hinges on whether "the properties of an organism's body are incorporated within, and perhaps indispensable to, the ordinary functioning of a cognitive system" (p. 140). As an example, he suggests that if facial muscles are incorporated within and indispensable to the concept SADNESS (mediated perhaps by the activation of the motor system), then the Conceptualization Hypothesis holds for SADNESS.

It seems, in terms of things most central to education, that this condition is satisfied. It directly relates to many of the principles proposed here, since the kinds of bodies and body-based processes that allow for movement and perception are incorporated within and indispensable to the metaphors that people consider to be grounded and meaningful, and the kinds of gestures and actions one can perform and notice from others. The **principles of semantically congruent gestures,** and **grounding metaphors** all affirm the *Conceptualization Hypothesis.* How people bind time and space to semantic content and declarative memory is also directly relevant to GEL and the **principles of situated memory retrieval, simulated situated memory** and some information from the **principle of GEL formative assessment.** The **principle of consistent action** is neutral regarding this, since what is central is the consistency rather than the particular form of the actions.

Fulfilling the Conceptualization Hypothesis affirms several GEL principles. On the surface, it is not clear that this affirmation informs these principles in ways that lead to new learning approaches or practices for instruction and assessment.

Constitution Hypothesis

Shapiro (2019) also posed the *Constitution Hypothesis*. This states that "the body or world plays a constitutive rather than merely causal role in cognitive processing" (p. 5). This establishes the idea that cognition extends beyond the skull and includes processes that involve movement and interactions with the environments and other people. The claim here is that the body and body-based interactions with the world *are* cognition, rather than *cause* cognition, as posited by work on extended cognition, distributed cognition, and situated cognition.

There are arguments for and against this hypothesis. In balance, the educational experience is pretty well accepting that we want to improve the cognitive *system* in which people operate. Support for the Constitution Hypothesis follows from the **principle of situated memory retrieval**, where we recognize that declarative memory is bound to the time and space when those ideas are formed. This includes the cultural tools they use for science and math, literary resources, search engines, and team collaboration, as often is revealed in during assessment by the **principle of cognitive offloading**. What's more, according to the **principle of simulated situated memory** people are able to naturally *simulate and recreate* these sensorimotor experiences even when they are removed from the original experiences.

The implications for education are also actionable. *Learning* means learning to use body-based resources such as gesture and manual manipulation skills, disciplinary and culturally appropriate resources and tools, and collaborative interactions in service of meaning making, problem solving, idea production, and design.

The most radical implications are for assessment. Once cognition is recognized as *extended*, the circumstances of assessment must allow for access to the resources that are encompassed within the cognitive system. Certainly, this underscores that the assessment experience should closely emulate the environments in which learning takes pace. Even when testing for transfer, the goal is usually to assess transfer of students' ways of knowing, rather than their performance in an impoverished environment. If the goal is to demonstrate performance in an impoverished environment, then students' learning experiences would ideally have some of the resources faded away so that other cognitive processes (such as memorization) are adequately developed.

6.3 AREAS NEEDING ADDITIONAL RESEARCH

Several important areas of learning, teaching, and assessment are underdeveloped and in need of further research.

6.3.1 Instruction

The embodied nature of instruction is certainly an area that is rapidly expanding and in need of more research as practitioners turn to research community for guidance. Consider instructional gesture as an example. There is a small but important set of studies showing some benefits for learning (Alibali et al., 2013; Perry et al., 1995; Roth & Welzel, 2001), but studies also show that the benefits are not evenly provided in all areas of instruction (e.g., Alibali, Nathan, Kim, Johnson, Wolfgram, Church, & Knuth, 2011). There are also looming questions about the locus of the effects of gesture on student learning. For example, we do not know whether gestures primarily help learners because gestures ground new ideas for students, whether they primarily aid teachers to be more articulate about their lessons, or some combination.

There is also a small body of evidence of how teachers learn to gesture during actual instructional interactions with students, with only a small number of empirical and controlled studies pointing the way to guide teacher education and professional development (Alibali et al., 2013; Hostetter et al., 2006). There is some early work on how teachers' beliefs about learning and attitudes about gestures influence when and how they use gestures during instruction (Nathan, Yeo, Boncoddo, Hoestetter, & Alibali, 2020), but not nearly enough to prescribe its application to the wide range of learning experiences that are offered by schools.

For example, there are large and persistent differences between US students and students from countries whose teachers effectively use gestures to make connections (Richland et al., 2007). We know these gestures help students from the **principle of linking gestures.** We do not know why US teachers are less likely to engage in these instructional acts. Identifying barriers to the uptake of these promising pedagogical practices could greatly improve student learning and scale up easily across teachers. We also need to understand how readily these effective instructional gestures apply to the rapidly growing area of virtual pedagogical agents.

6.3.2 Formative Assessment

For instruction to be most effective, teachers adjust their instructional practices in response to students' states of knowledge and developmental progression (Alibali et al., 2013; Nathan & Kim, 2009). Formative assessment (Black & Wiliam, 1998) of embodied learning depends on teachers' skills at "reading" the body states and gestures of their students. This follows from the **principle of nonverbal knowing** and **principle of GEL formative assessment**. There is some limited evidence that teachers can use student gestures diagnostically (Alibali & Goldin-Meadow, 1993; Goldin-Meadow et al., 1993). Still, much more needs to be investigated in order to understand how teachers notice students' gestures, and the types of knowledge that can be apprehended by teachers from students' movements.

6.3.3 Summative Assessment

I reported on evidence that interfering with students' gesture production can selectively impair students' inference making during assessment (Nathan & Martinez, 2015). These findings were replicated when typing was used as a condition to impose gesture restriction (Martinez, 2012). When typing, students cannot gesture freely, which violates the **principle of semantically congruent gestures**, since they can no longer embody the ideas they are intended to convey. Typing is rapidly becoming the norm for expressing one's knowledge as digital testing becomes the norm. The effects of typing on learning, problem solving, and other educationally relevant cognitive processes need to be better understood so inadvertent effects that impair performance can be documented and used to inform assessment design.

6.3.4 Embodiment in Academic Content Areas

In surveying major content areas, I found very few investigations and design studies on using embodiment for teaching and learning in the social sciences. In K–12, these include anthropology, ethnic studies, civics, history, geography, psychology, sociology, economics, law, political science, religious studies, and international affairs. There is tremendous value in understanding how the principles derived from language arts, science, and mathematics apply to these areas of study, and to identify new principles that may emerge from these disciplines.

6.4 SUMMARY

The chapter explored the embodied nature of learning, instruction, and assessment within the conscious spectrum, that portion of the timescale that we have the greatest awareness of and control over. Two GEL processes are primary: grounding by making connections, and offloading cognitive processes onto the body and the environment.

A survey of learning and instruction in academic content areas shows that GEL is well represented and provides an account of the circumstances where learning is most robust. From this emerges several actionable principles of learning, instruction, and assessment in the conscious spectrum (summarized in Table 6.1. These principles relate to and are affirmed by Shapiro's Conceptualization and Constitution Hypotheses. I also use the review to identify areas of future research that will benefit theory development and educational practice.

6.5 READER ACTIVITIES AND DEMONSTRATIONS

6.5.1 Mental Models in Reading: How Inference is Embodied

Try this with friends (it even works over Zoom!).

1. Read aloud this very short story.
2. After reading the story, ask your listeners the questions listed below.
3. Try to come up with stories and questions of your own.

Story: Turtles and Logs (from Bransford, Barclay, & Franks, 1972)
   Three turtles rested on a floating log, and a fish swam beneath them.

Questions:

a. Did the fish swim under the log?
b. Look carefully at the words of the story. How did you arrive at your conclusion?
c. As your reader expresses their reasoning, watch their gestures carefully!

6.5.2 Body Schema, Form, and Movement

- Body integrity identity disorder (BIID)
  www.youtube.com/watch?v=WNps5_ndHzY
- TED Talk: Curing phantom limb pain with mirrors.
  www.ted.com/talks/vs_ramachandran_3_clues_to_understanding_your_brain?
  language=en
  - How does this relate to Shapiro's Conceptualization Hypothesis?
- When imagining water pouring upside down (Schwartz & Black, 1999), the geometry
  is equivalent to conventional water pouring, but it is harder to imagine because it goes
  against our lived experiences in a gravitational field.
  - How does this relate to the Principle of Consistent Action?

6.5.3 Offloading

- Imagine balancing a 1-foot by 1-foot by 1-foot cube on one vertex so the longest body
  diagonal is vertical. Without using a real one, just using your imagination, point to all of
  the remaining corners (vertices) of the cube (Hinton, 1979)?
  - (Hint, after you or a friend try it: How many total vertices are there? How many had
    you located?)
  - In your mind, now position the cube flat on a table and locate all of the vertices.
  - What was different between the two tasks?
  - Cubes are pretty simple and familiar objects. Why do you think there are differences
    that favor doing this mental imagery task in one orientation or another?

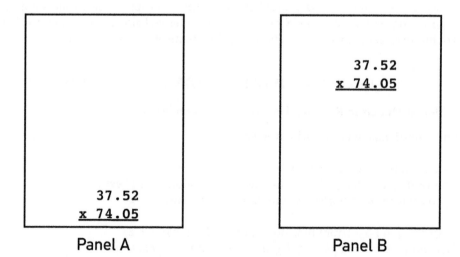

FIGURE 6.4 How do these experiences relate to the Principle of Offloading?

- Copy this math problem <u>just as written in Panel A</u> on a piece of paper or chalkboard and perform the calculation.
  - Which problem was more difficult? Why?
  - Now <u>copy the math problem just as written in Panel B</u>.
  - How do you describe the differences in your experience?
  - How do these experiences relate to the **principle of offloading?**

6.5.4 Simulation

- *Flatland* is an alternate reality, introduced in a novella by Edwin Abbott in 1884. Everything in Flatland is limited to a two-dimensional plane, including you and your friends! Its citizens can only perceive points (zero dimensional), lines (one dimensional), and polygons (two dimensional).
  - Imagine you are living in Flatland. Draw the following members of Flatland: Triangle, circle, a line from two different perspectives.
  - If you encounter a three-dimensional sphere from Sphereland visiting Flatland, how would this visitor appear to you? What would this visitor find difficult to understand about the citizens of Flatland?

REFERENCES

Abbott, E. (1884). *Flatland: A romance in multiple dimensions*. New American Library.

Adams, A. M., Glenberg, A. M., & Restrepo, M. A. (2018). Moved by reading in a Spanish-speaking, dual language learner population. *Language, Speech, and Hearing Services in Schools, 49*(3), 582–594.

Alibali, M. W., & Goldin-Meadow, S. (1993). Gesture-speech mismatch and mechanisms of learning: What the hands reveal about a child's state of mind. *Cognitive Psychology, 25*, 468–523.

Alibali, M. W., Nathan, M. J., & Fujimori, Y. (2011). Gestures in the classroom: What's the point? In N. L. Stein & S. W. Raudenbush (Eds.), *Developmental cognitive science goes to school* (pp. 219–234). Routledge.

Alibali, M. W., Nathan, M. J., Kim, S., Johnson, C., Wolfgram, M. S., Church, R. B., & Knuth, E. J. (2011, April). *Teachers' visual scaffolding and student learning: Effects of connecting representations via gesture*. Poster presented at the Annual meeting of the American Educational Research Association, New Orleans, LA.

Alibali, M. W., Nathan, M. J., Wolfgram, M. S., Church, R. B., Jacobs, S. A., Johnson Martinez, C., & Knuth, E. J. (2014). How teachers link ideas in mathematics instruction using speech and gesture: A corpus analysis. *Cognition and Instruction, 32*(1), 65–100.

Alibali, M. W., Young, A. G., Crooks, N. M., Yeo, A., Wolfgram, M. S., Ledesma, I. M., Nathan, M. J., Church, R. B., & Knuth, E. J. (2013). Students learn more when their teacher has learned to gesture effectively. *Gesture, 13*(2), 210–233.

Ball, D. L. (1993). With an eye on the mathematical horizon: Dilemmas of teaching elementary school mathematics. *The Elementary School Journal, 93*(4), 373–397.

Ball, D. L. (1997). From the general to the particular: Knowing our own students as learners of mathematics. *The Mathematics Teacher, 90*(9), 732.

Black, P., & Wiliam, D. (1998). Assessment and classroom learning. *Assessment in Education: Principles, Policy & Practice, 5*(1), 7–74.

Bransford, J. D., Barclay, J. R., & Franks, J. J. (1972). Sentence memory: A constructive versus interpretive approach. *Cognitive Psychology, 3*(2), 193–209.

Bransford, J. D., & Schwartz, D. L. (1999). Rethinking transfer: A simple proposal with multiple implications. *Review of Research in Education, 24*(1), 61–100.

Bruner, J. S. (1966). *Toward a theory of instruction*. Belknap Press.

Butcher, K. R. (2006). Learning from text with diagrams: Promoting mental model development and inference generation. *Journal of Educational Psychology, 98*(1), 182.

Case, R., & Okamoto, Y. (1996). The role of central conceptual structures in the development of children's thought. *Monographs of the Society for Research in Child Development, 61*(1/2).

Choi, H. H., Van Merriënboer, J. J., & Paas, F. (2014). Effects of the physical environment on cognitive load and learning: Towards a new model of cognitive load. *Educational Psychology Review, 26*(2), 225–244.

Church, R. B., & Goldin-Meadow, S. (1986). The mismatch between gesture and speech as an index of transitional knowledge. *Cognition, 23*(1), 43–71.

Cook, S. W., Yip, T. K., & Goldin-Meadow, S. (2012). Gestures, but not meaningless movements, lighten working memory load when explaining math. *Language and Cognitive Processes, 27*(4), 594–610.

Fischman, G. E., & Haas, E. (2012). Beyond idealized citizenship education: Embodied cognition, metaphors, and democracy. *Review of Research in Education, 36*(1), 169–196.

Flood, V. J., Amar, F. G., Nemirovsky, R., Harrer, B. W., Bruce, M. R., & Wittmann, M. C. (2014). Paying attention to gesture when students talk chemistry: Interactional resources for responsive teaching. *Journal of Chemical Education, 92*(1), 11–22.

Fyfe, E. R., & McNeil, N. M., & Borjas, S. (2015). Benefits of "concreteness fading" for children's mathematics understanding. *Learning and Instruction, 35*, 104–120.

Fyfe, E. R., & Nathan, M. J. (2019). Making "concreteness fading" more concrete as a theory of instruction for promoting transfer. *Educational Review, 71*(4), 403–422.

Galison, P. (2004). *Einstein's clocks, Poincaré's maps: Empires of time*. W. W. Norton & Company.

Goldin-Meadow, S., Alibali, M. W., & Church, R. B. (1993). Transitions in concept acquisition: Using the hand to read the mind. *Psychological Review, 100*, 279–297.

Goldin-Meadow, S., Cook, S. W., & Mitchell, Z. A. (2009). Gesturing gives children new ideas about math. *Psychological Science, 20*(3), 267–272.

Goldin-Meadow, S., Nusbaum, H., Kelly, S. D., & Wagner, S. (2001). Explaining math: Gesturing lightens the load. *Psychological Science, 12*, 516–522.

Goldstone, R. L., & Son, J. Y. (2005). The transfer of scientific principles using concrete and idealized simulations. *The Journal of the Learning Sciences, 14*, 69–110.

Griffin, S. (2004). Building number sense with number worlds. *Early Childhood Research Quarterly, 19*(1), 173–180.

Griffin, S., Case, R., & Siegler, R. S. (1994). Rightstart: Providing the central conceptual structures for children at risk of school failure. In K. McGilly (Ed.), *Classroom lessons: Integrating cognitive theory and classroom practice* (pp. 13–48). Mahwah, NJ: Erlbaum.

Groth, R. E., & Bergner, J. A. (2005). Pre-service elementary school teachers' metaphors for the concept of statistical sample. *Statistics Education Research Journal, 4*(2), 27–42.

Hegarty, M., Mayer, S., Kriz, S., & Keehner, M. (2005). The role of gestures in mental animation. *Spatial Cognition and Computation, 5*(4), 333–356.

Hinton, G. (1979). Some demonstrations of the effects of structural descriptions in mental imagery. *Cognitive Science, 3*(3), 231–250.

Hostetter, A. B., & Alibali, M. W. (2008). Visible embodiment: Gestures as simulated action. *Psychonomic Bulletin & Review, 15*(3), 495–514.

Hostetter, A. B., & Alibali, M. W. (2019). Gesture as simulated action: Revisiting the framework. *Psychonomic Bulletin & Review, 26*(3), 721–752.

Hostetter, A. B., Bieda, K., Alibali, M. W., Nathan, M. J., & Knuth, E. J. (2006). Don't just tell them, show them! Teachers can intentionally alter their instructional gestures. *Proceedings of the 28th Annual conference of the cognitive science society* (pp. 1523–1528). Erlbaum.

Hutchins, E. (1995). *Cognition in the Wild*. MIT Press.

Kazemi, E., & Franke, M. L. (2004). Teacher learning in mathematics: Using student work to promote collective inquiry. *Journal of Mathematics Teacher Education, 7*(3), 203–235.

Kelly, S., Byrne, K., & Holler, J. (2011). Raising the ante of communication: evidence for enhanced gesture use in high stakes situations. *Information, 2*(4), 579–593.

Kelly, S. D., McDevitt, T., Esch, M. (2009). Brief training with co-speech gesture lends a hand to word learning in a foreign language. *Language and Cognitive Processes, 24*, 313–334.

Kintsch, W. (1998). *Comprehension: A paradigm for cognition*. Cambridge University Press.

Knuth, E. J., Stephens, A. C., McNeil, N. M., & Alibali, M. W. (2006). Does understanding the equal sign matter? Evidence from solving equations. *Journal for Research in Mathematics Education, 37*(4), 297–312.

Lakoff, G., & Núñez, R. (2000). *Where mathematics comes from: How the embodied mind brings mathematics into being*. Basic Books.

Lindgren, R., & Johnson-Glenberg, M. (2013). Emboldened by embodiment: Six precepts for research on embodied learning and mixed reality. *Educational Researcher, 42*(8), 445–452.

Lisman, J., Buzsáki, G., Eichenbaum, H., Nadel, L., Ranganath, C., & Redish, A. D. (2017). Viewpoints: How the hippocampus contributes to memory, navigation and cognition. *Nature Neuroscience, 20*(11), 1434–1447.

Macedonia, M., & Knösche, T. R. (2011). Body in mind: How gestures empower foreign language learning. *Mind, Brain, and Education, 5*(4), 196–211.

Macedonia, M., Müller, K., & Friederici, A. D. (2010). Neural correlates of high performance in foreign language vocabulary learning. *Mind, Brain, and Education, 4*(3), 125–134.

Macedonia, M., Müller, K., & Friederici, A. D. (2011). The impact of iconic gestures on foreign language word learning and its neural substrate. *Human Brain Mapping, 32*(6), 982–998.

Martinez, C. V. (2012). *Manipulations of gesture production indicate the role of the body in situation model development: Implications for computer-based assessment* (Doctoral dissertation). University of Wisconsin–Madison.

Mathan, S., & Koedinger, K. R. (2005). Fostering the intelligent novice: Learning from errors with metacognitive tutoring. *Educational Psychologist, 40*(4), 257–265.

McNeill, D., & Duncan, S. (2000). Growth points in thinking-for-speaking. In D. McNeill, *Language and gesture* (pp. 141–161). Cambridge University Press.

Menekse, M., Stump, G. S., Krause, S., & Chi, M. T. (2013a). Differentiated overt learning activities for effective instruction in engineering classrooms. *Journal of Engineering Education, 102*(3), 346–374.

Moher, T., Hussain, S., Halter, T., & Kilb, D. (2005). Roomquake: Embedding dynamic phenomena within the physical space of an elementary school classroom. *Proceedings of ACM CHI 2005 Conference on Human Factors in Computing Systems* (Vol. 2, pp. 1665–1668). Association for Computing Machinery. doi:10.1145/1056808.1056992

Nathan, M. J. (1998). Knowledge and situational feedback in a learning environment for algebra story problem solving. *Interactive Learning Environments, 5*, 135–159.

Nathan, M. J. (2012). Rethinking formalisms in formal education. *Educational Psychologist, 47*(2), 125–148.

Nathan, M. J. (2014). Grounded mathematical reasoning. In L. Shapiro (Ed.). *The Routledge handbook of embodied cognition* (pp. 171–183). Routledge.

Nathan, M. J., Alibali, M. W., & Church, R. B. (2017). Making and breaking common ground: How teachers use gesture to foster learning in the classroom. In R. B. Church, M. W. Alibali, & S. D. Kelly (Eds.), *Why gesture? How the hands function in speaking, thinking and communicating* (pp. 285–316). John Benjamins.

Nathan, M. J., & Kim, S. (2009). Regulation of teacher elicitations in the mathematics classroom. *Cognition and Instruction, 27*(2), 91–120.

Nathan, M. J., Kintsch, W., & Young, E. (1992). A theory of algebra-word-problem comprehension and its implications for the design of learning environments. *Cognition and Instruction, 9*(4), 329–389.

Nathan, M. J., & Martinez, C. V. (2015). Gesture as model enactment: The role of gesture in mental model construction and inference making when learning from text. *Learning: Research and Practice, 1*(1), 4–37.

Nathan, M. J., & Resnick, L. B. (1994). Less can be more: Unintelligent tutoring based on psychological theories and experimentation. In S. Vosniadou, E. De Corte, & H. Mandl (Eds.), *Technology-based learning environments: psychological and educational foundations*, NATO ASI Series F, Computer and Systems Sciences (Vol. 137) (sub-series on Advanced Educational Technology) (pp. 183–192). Springer Verlag.

Nathan, M. J., & Swart, M. I. (2020). Materialistic epistemology lends design wings: Educational design as an embodied process. *Educational Technology Research and Development*, 1–30. doi.org/10.1037/edu0000638

Nathan, M. J., Tran, N. A., Atwood, A. K., Prevost, A., & Phelps, L. A. (2010). Beliefs and expectations about engineering preparation exhibited by high school STEM teachers. *Journal of Engineering Education, 99*(4), 409–426.

Nathan, M. J., Yeo, A., Boncoddo, R., Hostetter, A., & Alibali, M. W. (2020). Teachers' attitudes about gesture for learning and instruction. *Gesture, 18*(1), 31–56.

National Academies of Sciences, Engineering, and Medicine. (2019). *Science and engineering for grades 6–12: Investigation and design at the center*. National Academies Press.

National Research Council. (2006). *America's lab report: Investigations in high school science*. National Academies Press.

National Research Council. (2012). *A framework for K-12 science education: Practices, crosscutting concepts, and core ideas*. The National Academies Press.

Neisser, U. (1976). *Cognition and reality: Principles and implications of cognitive psychology*. W H Freeman.

NGSS Lead States. (2013). *Next generation science standards: For states, by states*. National Academies Press.

Paas, F., & Sweller, J. (2012). An evolutionary upgrade of cognitive load theory: Using the human motor system and collaboration to support the learning of complex cognitive tasks. *Educational Psychology Review, 24*(1), 27–45.

Pearson, P. D. (2004). The reading wars. *Educational Policy, 18*(1), 216–252.

Perry, M., Berch, D., & Singleton, J. L. (1995). Constructing shared understanding: The role of nonverbal input in learning contexts. *Journal of Contemporary Legal Issues, 6*, 213–236.

Pier, E. L., Walkington, C., Clinton, V., Boncoddo, R., Williams-Pierce, C., Alibali, M. W., & Nathan, M. J. (2019). Embodied truths: How dynamic gestures and speech contribute to mathematical proof practices. *Contemporary Educational Psychology, 58*, 44–57.

Ping, R., Church, R. B., Decatur, M. A., Larson, S., Zinchenko, E., & Goldin-Meadow, S. (2019). *Unpacking the gestures of chemistry learners: What the hands tell us about individuals' understanding of stereochemistry*. Retrieved from https://psyarxiv.com/qbzdg

Ping, R., & Goldin-Meadow, S. (2010). Gesturing saves cognitive resources when talking about non-present objects. *Cognitive Science, 34*, 602–619.

Purves, D., Augustine, G. J., Fitzpatrick, D., Hall, W. C., Lamantia, A. S., Mooney, R. D., Platt, M. L., & White, L. E. (Eds.) (2018). *Neuroscience* (6th ed.). Sinauer Associates. Retrieved from www.neuroscientificallychallenged.com/blog/2014/5/23/know-your-brain-hippocampus

Quinn-Allen, L. (1995). The effects of emblematic gestures on the development and access of mental representations of French expressions. *The Modern Language Journal, 79,* 521–529.

Richland, L. E., Zur, O., & Holyoak, K. J. (2007). Cognitive supports for analogies in the mathematics classroom. *Science, 316*(5828), 1128.

Roediger, H. L. (1980). The effectiveness of four mnemonics in ordering recall. *Journal of Experimental Psychology: Human Learning and Memory, 6*(5), 558.

Roth, W. M., & Welzel, M. (2001). From activity to gestures and scientific language. *Journal of Research in Science Teaching, 38,* 103–136.

Schwartz, D. L., & Black, T. (1999). Inferences through imagined actions: Knowing by simulated doing. *Journal of Experimental Psychology: Learning, Memory, and Cognition, 25*(1), 116–136.

Seidenberg, M. (2017). *Language at the speed of sight: How we read, why so many canot, and what can be done about it.* Basic Books.

Shapiro, L. (2019). *Embodied cognition* (2nd ed.). Routledge.

Shapiro, L., & Stolz, S. A. (2019). Embodied cognition and its significance for education. *Theory and Research in Education, 17*(1), 19–39.

Smith, L. B. (2005). Action alters shape categories. *Cognitive Science, 29*(4), 665–679.

Smith, C. P., King, B., & Hoyte, J. (2014). Learning angles through movement: Critical actions for developing understanding in an embodied activity. *The Journal of Mathematical Behavior, 36,* 95–108.

Spence, J. D. (1985). *The memory palace of Matteo Ricci.* Penguin Books.

Spivey, M. J., & Huette, S. (2014). The embodiment of attention in the perception-action loop. In L. Shapiro (Ed.), *The Routledge handbook of embodied cognition* (pp. 306–314). Routledge.

Stam, G. (2006). Thinking for speaking about motion: L1 and L2 speech and gesture. *International Review of Applied Linguistics in Language Teaching, 44*(2), 145–171.

Stokes, D. E. (1997/2011). *Pasteur's quadrant: Basic science and technological innovation.* Brookings Institution.

Stull, A. T., Hegarty, M., Dixon, B., & Stieff, M. (2012). Representational translation with concrete models in organic chemistry. *Cognition and Instruction, 30*(4), 404–434.

Tellier, M. (2008). The effect of gestures on second language memorisation by young children. *Gesture, 8,* 219–223.

Tulving, E. (1972). Episodic and semantic memory. *Organization of Memory, 1,* 381–403.

Tulving, E., & Thomson, D. M. (1973). Encoding specificity and retrieval processes in episodic memory. *Psychological Review, 80*(5), 352.

Uttal, D. H., Scudder, K. V., & DeLoache, J. S. (1997). Manipulatives as symbols: A new perspective on the use of concrete objects to teach mathematics. *Journal of Applied Developmental Psychology, 18*(1), 37–54.

van Dijk, T. A., & Kintsch, W. (1983). *Strategies of discourse comprehension.* Academic Press.

Vargha-Khadem, F., Gadian, D. G., Watkins, K. E., Connelly, A., Van Paesschen, W., & Mishkin, M. (1997). Differential effects of early hippocampal pathology on episodic and semantic memory. *Science, 277*(5324), 376–380.

Vest, N. A., Fyfe, E. R., Nathan, M. J., & Alibali, M. W. (in press). Learning from an avatar video instructor: The role of gesture mimicry. *Gesture.*

Vosniadou, S., & Brewer, W. F. (1992). Mental models of the earth: A study of conceptual change in childhood. *Cognitive Psychology, 24*(4), 535–585.

Walkoe, J. (2019, May). *Teacher noticing of student thinking as expressed through gesture and action.* Presentation to National Science Foundation Synthesis and Design Workshop: The Future of Embodied Design for Mathematical Imagination and Cognition (May 20–22, 2019). Madison, WI.

Watson, J. D. (1968). *The double helix: A personal account of the discovery of the structure of DNA.* Weidenfeld & Nicolson.

Wiese, E. S., & Koedinger, K. R. (2017). Designing grounded feedback: Criteria for using linked representations to support learning of abstract symbols. *International Journal of Artificial Intelligence in Education, 27*(3), 448–474.

Wilson, M. (2002). Six views of embodied cognition. *Psychonomic Bulletin & Review, 9*(4), 625–636.

7

Biological Basis of Learning

7.1 THE BIOLOGICAL LEVEL: EMERGENT, UNCONSCIOUS PROCESSES

As I have defined it, ***learning is an enduring change in behavior.*** In this chapter, I describe some of the ways these changes occur at the biological level in response to experiences, and how these changes influence how people think and learn. Following this definition, learning at the biological level involves lasting changes in the behavior and interconnections of nerve cells, also known as neurons. These are very rapid processes in the GEL timescale, taking place on the order of milliseconds (see Figure 7.1).

Neurons are like other cells in many ways: They have a nucleus, mitochondria, and organelles all contained in a cell membrane. They perform many of the same processes as other cells, including protein synthesis and energy production.

Neurons also have some unique properties. They do not change from experiences in the same ways that other cells do, which age, strengthen, weaken, etc. Neurons do not divide, and they rarely are replaced by fresh neurons if they die. They change in other ways, though. Most significantly, with regards to learning, neurons alter their collective behavior to reflect the statistical correlations of their environment (Churchland, 2004). They accomplish this using feedback and feedforward mechanisms. Feedback allows the system of interconnected neurons to self-regulate in response to changes in the environment. Feedforward mechanisms enhance the success of the neural system by giving it guidance in order to *predict* the world. I describe some of the basic properties of feedback and feedforward mechanisms in Box 7A.

It is by changing their interconnections in response to feedback and feedforward information that neural systems can operate successfully and learn. These networks of neurons operate as **dynamic systems** (see Box 7B) that give rise to **emergent behaviors**, that is, behaviors that are different than are to be expected from linearly combining the behaviors of the individual neurons. One of the most impressive examples is the emergence of consciousness from the interactions among many simple electro-biochemical objects. Some of the videos in Box 7A show very simple objects producing completely unexpected behaviors!

These dynamic neural networks use feedback and feedforward mechanism as a way to construct a bridge between system performance and conditions in the environment. Over time, the interactions give rise to an aggregate set of behaviors associated with **Type 1 processing**. Type 1 processing shapes our decision making, intuitions, automatic performance, and biases, even though they may completely escape our awareness. They enable forms of learning and intellectual performance that are distinct from those observed in the conscious spectrum dominated by Type 2 processing. Understanding neural behavior and its influences

DOI: 10.4324/9780429329098-7

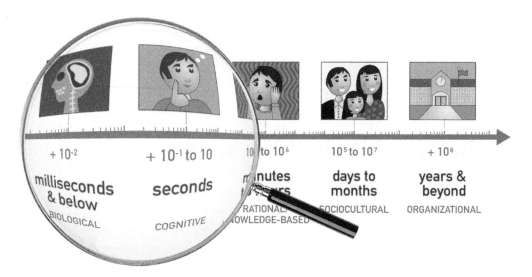

FIGURE 7.1 You are here: Biological portion of the GEL timescale. Figure uses a $\log_{10}$ scale.

on cognitive processes is the purview of the field of **cognitive neuroscience,** and the branch of Cognitive Science known as **connectionism** (described in the next section).

Box 7A Feedback and Feedforward

I want to describe two very important mechanisms for regulating mechanical and biological systems: Feedback and feedforward. I refer to *regulation* here in the sense of control. These systems are *self-regulating* so that they are able to change in response to changes in their environment. Most often, the self-regulation is designed to prevent the system from spiraling out of control, or completely stalling.

For this example, I want to use a rather common block diagram showing a very simple system. This might be the system description for a furnace such as the one that heats your home. In this diagram, there is INPUT to the system, which would typically be fuel, such as wood or natural gas, plus air. The PLANT is the heating component of the furnace. In the case of a furnace, the PLANT will generate more output—more heat—when there is an increase in the INPUT—more fuel is entered.

FIGURE 7A.1 Simple input-output system.

Such a system, however, will just keep producing more heat as more fuel is entered. When things get too hot, the occupants will need to stop the flow of fuel into the system. This is the case with a simple wood stove. When it gets too hot, simply no longer add anymore wood (fuel). When it gets cold again, someone has to get up and put more wood in the stove.

And so on, and so on, and so on. Sounds tiring, right? This is especially annoying if there is no one home to manage the flow of fuel; that is, to *regulate* the system. Here we can see the wisdom of feedback.

Feedback is the process of taking some of the output to tell the system when to add more fuel and when to stop. This is done be creating a *feedback loop*, of the kind shown in the next block diagram.

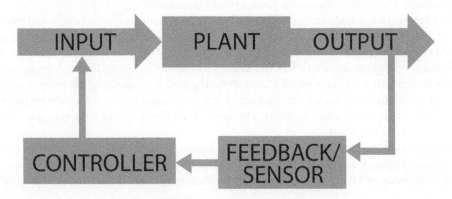

FIGURE 7A.2   Feedback system.

The feedback loop is achieved by adding two important components and some conduits (linked arrows) to connect them at the right places in the system. The FEEDBACK SENSOR takes information from one of the conduits and measures the OUTPUT to determine if this is still the desired output. If the SENSOR concludes the OUTPUT is too high, then there is a difference of what is desired and what is measured. This triggers the CONTROLLER to act and change the INPUT. If the furnace output is too hot, the CONTROLLER shuts down the flow of fuel into the system. If the SENSOR determines the OUTPUT is just right, then it doesn't do anything. That is, the whole feedback portion of the system is basically ignored, and the system performs like the simple linear diagram above.

This, incidentally, is an example of *negative feedback* because the difference between the OUTPUT and what is desired is used to *reduce* (*or* negate) the difference using the controller. In biological systems, an example of negative feedback is the regulation of blood sugar levels. As blood sugar rises (from eating), sensors in the pancreas sample glucose levels in the blood stream. If levels are deemed too high, the pancreas secretes insulin to reduce the levels of blood sugar.

The **control of blood sugar (glucose)** by insulin is a good **example** of a **negative feedback mechanism**. When **blood sugar** rises, receptors **in** the body sense a change. **In** turn, the **control** center (beta cells in the pancreas) secretes insulin into the **blood**, effectively lowering **blood sugar levels**. This regulatory control does not happen when the feedback mechanism is disrupted, as when the pancreas has been removed, or if an autoimmune response destroys the beta cells.

If you think about it, even the simple wood stove is actually in a feedback loop. It is just that the *occupants* are performing the feedback. They are the ones sampling the OUTPUT, providing the SENSOR information (is it too cold? Too hot? Just right?), and operating as the CONTROLLER (get up off the cozy couch, open the stove, and add more fuel). In the case of blood sugar regulation, the feedback loop is restored by manually measuring glucose levels and externally administering insulin through injections.

Feedback is a really smart innovation. But it does have one significant problem. The system will only regulate itself (i.e., add more fuel) *after* it is already getting too hot. Feedback is reactive. If you have lived in a home with this system, that is not very pleasant, and it is certainly not an efficient way to preserve precious fuel and minimize its impact on the environment. How can this problem be avoided? How can one *antici-pate* when the system will get too far ahead of itself, and slow or shut things down *before* this occurs? The answer is to use a feedforward mechanism.

Feedforward is proactive. A feedforward mechanism detects the trend of the system toward the conditions that will cause the feedback loop to reduce input. In a way, it predicts the future behavior of the system, and if the trend appears to be headed toward a shut down, it generates a CONTROL SIGNAL to slow the rate of input. A programmable thermostat is an example of a feedforward system for regulating the temperature in your home, since it uses information about trending information in the environment (such as the magnitude and valence of a temperature differential) to anticipate and initiate change in the system.

Feedforward mechanisms are common in biological systems. An example is the anticipatory upregulation of heartrate to muscles in preparation of physical exertion, such as running or lifting. The feedforward mechanism smooths out the continual on/

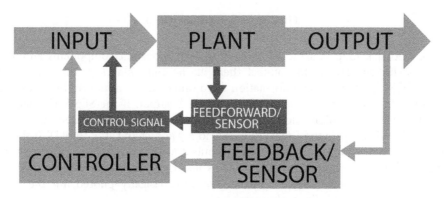

FIGURE 7A.3 Feedforward and feedback control system.

off behavior of the feedback system. This improves the performance of the system and enables it to handle even greater swings in its INPUT by reducing its impact on the OUTPUT.

7.1.1 Cognitive Neuroscience: Connectionism and Emergent Behavior

The field of cognitive neuroscience investigates and theorizes about the biological basis of cognition using evidence from neurobiology and brain imaging, behavioral research, and computational modeling. As the cognitive neuroscientist and pioneering connectionist scholar Jay McClelland (2001, p. 2133) reviews:

A starting point for cognitive neuroscience is the idea that a cognitive or mental state consists of a pattern of activity distributed over many neurons. For example, the experience an individual has when holding, sniffing, and viewing a rose is a complex pattern of neural activity, distributed over many brain regions, including the participation of neurons in visual, somatosensory, and olfactory, and possibly extending to language areas participating in representing the sound of the word "rose" and/or other areas where activity represents the content of an associated memory that may be evoked by the experience.

There are at least five points made here that are important to understanding the biological basis of learning and reasoning. One point is that knowledge is encoded by the nervous system as *patterns* of activity that are distributed across many neurons, rather than localized to a particular neuron or set of neurons. Readers may be familiar with the notion in popular media of a "grandmother cell" or "Halle Berry neuron," which *only* fires when a person sees, thinks or reads about the actor Halle Berry (Martindale, 2005). However, there is very little support for the view that people have individual neurons which are dedicated to recognizing complex stimuli such as an actor's photo, drawings, and name (Barwich, 2019; Khamsi, 2004). The proper unit of discussion for learning at this level is the patterns of neural activity via their interconnections.

A second point is that people's memories are *active*, not static, and so they are continually being recreated, and therefore are subject to modification. A focus on patterns of activation also supports a graded form of representation that need not be "all-or-none." We may, for example, access a memory that is sort of the rose that was encountered the day before, or perceive an image that is kind of a vase and kind of two faces. These are important considerations when considering the nature of memory and eye witness testimony, which is far less stable than was previously thought (Loftus, 2005).

A third point is that learning—forming new memories and modifying pre-existing knowledge—occurs primarily from changes to the *connections* among neurons. At the neural level, learning involves making new connections and removing useless ones (Bransford, Brown, & Cocking, 2000). Each is a type of learning since it follows my definition that **learning is an enduring change in behavior.** The central role of *connections* affords tremendous flexibility—often referred to as *neuroplasticity*—of the learning system. This is one reason why repeated practice and exposure is such a powerful method for learning, since it literally changes neural pathways and subsequent brain function. After all, even against estimates of approximately 100 billion brain cells, neuroscientists project there to be on the order of 100 *trillion* synaptic connections in the human brain (Zimmer, 2011). This means that a typical neuron is directly connected to—and affected by—1,000 other neurons.

A fourth point of McClelland's is that memories and learning experiences are naturally *multimodal*, with connections across sensory experiences part of forming meaning, while also useful for storage and later retrieval. Related to this, McClelland (2001, p. 2136) also points out a key "anatomical point" about the basic structure of the brain. Connectivity is not only rampant, "connectivity within and between brain areas is generally reciprocal: when there are connections from region A to region B, there are nearly always return connections." This is an important consideration as I review theories that explain how events "outside" of the brain, such as movement and perception, can be regarded as a constituent of cognition (Nathan, 2017; Shapiro, 2019).

Fifth, the behaviors that result from these active, multimodal patterns of interconnected neural systems are *emergent*, arising from nonlinear dynamic systems behavior (see Box 7B). These emergent behaviors can be modeled computationally in the aggregate, but they are not directly described by the behaviors of the constituent neurons involved.

Foundationalism: Empiricism and Nativism
Whenever discussing development, it is typically framed as managing tensions between two theoretical accounts: Empiricism and nativism (Newcombe, 2002). Also termed *nature versus nurture*, the dichotomy exists within the larger theoretical frame of *Foundationalism*,

since it fuels debates over the foundations of how knowledge and behavior are represented in the brain (Allen & Bickhard, 2013). Foundationalism has strong advocates in both camps. Simply put, nativism posits that people are born with innate knowledge and capabilities (some proponents are Chomsky, 1959; Fodor, 1983; Plato; Spelke & Newport, 1998). Empiricism holds that knowledge primarily develops from experience (these proponents include Dewey, 1905; Locke, in Nidditch, 1975; Newcombe, 2002; Skinner, 1938/2019). It certainly seems that human intellectual development draws on combined contributions of some innate processes early in life, along with a great deal of experiential learning.

Neurally, support for this comes from observing activity-independent processes (which are likely to be innate) and activity-dependent processes (which are experience-based; McClelland, 2001). An example activity-independent process observed at birth is one that connects neural activity in the retina to activity of other brain regions. Activity-dependent processes include connections formed through experience, such as spoken language production. Learning of this type is often modeled as Hebbian learning (Hebb, 1949), and described by the adage, "cells that fire together wire together," though Hebb did not himself propose that phrase.

Examples of this mix of activity-independent and activity-dependent processes are evident in research on early reading. Reading is a cultural invention that has formed relatively recently, in evolutionary terms, and is not likely to have exerted selection pressures on human evolution. There are innate visual, tactile, and language functions that have previously been identified within the brain. How they are used and integrated during the development of reading illustrates how in-born capacities and experiences contribute to learning as enduring changes in behavior.

Dehaene (2009) has shown that aspects of the brain become repurposed in early reading development—what he refers to as "neuronal recycling." Letter and word recognition processes utilize visual circuitry that might "ordinarily" be used for object recognition. Word recognition taps into neural circuitry in the left hemisphere (for right-handed participants) "typically" used during oral language recognition and production. With training, early readers develop a type of super-circuit called the *visual word form area* that shows coordinated activation of these distinct regions when words are observed. Interestingly, it also is activated for close pseudowords that are both visually similar and phonetically similar to authentic words in one's current lexicon. However, to show how it is "tuned" to predict the regularities in one's lexicon, the visual word form area does not respond to simply any and all letter combinations, and is not activated as strongly to randomly formed nonwords.

This phenomenon of neuronal recycling was also demonstrated in a series of studies on reading Braille. Hamilton and Pascual-Leone (1998) demonstrated using brain imaging that the occipital cortex—areas V1 and V2, normally associated with visual processing—is repurposed by proficient, blind Braille readers in service of touch-based reading that, while spatial, had no visual component. They also report findings (Cohen et al., 1997) that touch-perception that is so critical to Braille reading is temporarily disrupted when transcranial magnetic stimulation (TMS) is applied specifically to the occipital cortex (the primary visual region of the brain) of these blind participants. However, TMS to this brain region had no effect of the tactile perception of sighted participants.

Churchland (2004) reports that when sighted participants were taught to read Braille, it turned out to be vital that they were blindfolded at all times over the several days of training (not just when they were learning). While blindfolded, the occipital cortex underwent reorganization so long as the participants had no light exposure to their retinas. Progress was easily disrupted by any light exposure since this effectively reengaged areas V1 and V2 for visual rather than tactile processing and thus impeded this *touch-sight* skill development.

Reading has been identified as a biologically secondary skill (Geary. 1995). Here we see how reading skill development drives neural reorganization for sighted readers and for both sighted and unsighted readers using Braille. It shows that the nervous system enables learning by changing pre-existing neural function as well as incorporating new experiences (e.g., learning to recognize new letters and Braille patterns). The result is a system that becomes tuned to anticipate new cross-modal input in service of making meaning. Further, the skill generalizes: It applies to reading anything so long as it follows the proper constraints for clearly perceiving visual and tactile language.

Interactionism: Emergent Representation from Anticipatory Actions in the World
Perception and actions are integral to thinking and learning. This poses a serious challenge to Foundationalism, the prevailing epistemological framework for cognition and education. Foundationalism is rooted in a core epistemological "assumption that knowledge must be built up from a representational base, which is shared by both nativism and empiricism" (Allen & Bickhard, 2013, p. 114). Because of this commitment to a representational base that is distinct from the sensorimotor system, Foundationalism disallows the possibility that action could be part of cognition itself, except as output of an intellectual process such as fulfilling a goal.

There is an alternative framework for development and learning that rejects Foundationalism and the nativism-empiricism dichotomy altogether (Allen & Bickhard, 2013). This is the framework of *Interactionism*. Interactionism makes no such assumptions about a pre-existing representational base. It shares with Pragmatism the view of social behavior as unrestricted and emergent. The collective behavior of neural systems naturally forms "emergent representations," ways of mentally forming meaning using the patterns of interactions that make up collective neural activity. Allen and Bickhard show how the assumptions of Foundationalism prevent any possible account of a system of emergence of meaning. In Interactionism, emergent representations are far nimbler and fluid, forming and dissolving (ideally) to suit the impending environmental and cognitive needs.

Unlike symbols, patterns of neural activity do not *represent* or inscribe information, so much as they *construct responses* to their environments. When these responses are appropriate and generalizable to environmental variation, they can appear to be mediated by internal representations. Modeling of the **A-not-B error** provides a powerful example of how behavior that was thought to be described in Foundationalist terms of a representational base for object permanence is more accurately described using the non-representational (or "emergent representational") account offered by dynamic systems (Smith & Thelen, 2003; Thelen, Schöner, Scheier, & Smith, 2001; also see Munakata, 1998). The A-not-B error is described in greater detail in Box 7B.

As Smith and Thelen (2003, p. 346) summate,

> These results suggest that the relevant memories are in the language of the body and close to the sensory surface. In addition, they underscore the highly decentralized nature of error: the relevant causes include the covers on the table, the hiding event, the delay, the past activity of the infant and the feel of the body of the infant. This multicausality demands a rethinking of what is meant by knowledge and development.

Allen and Bickhard (2013) argue that Interactionism, as an action-based framework, is the only system that can account for representational emergence. As posed by other GEL scholars, the human cognitive architecture is oriented toward predicting the world. The basis of knowing and learning is anticipation, rather than knowledge for its own sake. This pragmatic account of cognition depends on one's abilities to process, predict, and respond to the world. When navigating and interacting in the world, it is the world itself that provides the best representation of what is being thought about. The use of some intricate representational machinery is unnecessary when cognition is viewed from this perspective. As Allen and Bickhard (2013, p. 126) propose:

> an action-based perspective places (inter)action at the core of what it means to know the world and representation is an emergent of functional interactive organizations that are appropriate for engaging with the environment. These interactive organizations cannot be impressed into a passive mind; but rather, they must be constructed "de novo" (Bickhard, 2001). That is, an action-based approach forces a constructivism, and because representation is emergent in the organization of (inter)action systems, it enables the possibility of an emergent constructivism.

In the Interactionism framework, action does not merely follow from one's mental processes, or signal it. Rather, it is part of its very constitution of cognition (cf. Shapiro, 2019).

Box 7B Dynamic Systems: Modeling the A-Not-B Error

Dynamic systems are mathematical models of real and imagined systems. The mathematics operates like an animation or simulation and in this way shows changes over time. Even though these models can be made of up relatively simple mathematical formulas that describe them, they can perform amazingly complex behaviors. For example they can be used to describe the behaviors of large crowds, storms on other planets, and disease transmission.

One of the central ideas behind the dynamic systems framework is that they are self-organizing. **The self-organization principle** proposes that "the system moves towards a characteristic orderly attractor state that is not prescribed or pre-coded by some external component" (Lichtwarck-Aschofff, Geert, 2004, p. 404).

A very simple system is the pendulum, shown in this video. We see it go through a very simple form of decaying harmonic motion, till it eventually settles to rest.

A simple variant is to have multiple pendula which all start swinging at the same moment. This example uses bowling balls. It is fascinating to see how they find various patterns or *modes* that show order. Equally interesting to me is the apparent chaos that takes place as one mode ends and the system moves (briefly) to another orderly mode.

VIDEO LINK: Multiple bowling ball pendula (3 mins) www.youtube.com/watch?v=YhMiuzyU1ag

Now rewatch the video of the original simple pendulum. Here is a really simple variation, attaching another freely swinging pendulum on the end of the first one. Try to predict the location of the free end of the second pendulum. This wild behavior, broken up by times of relative calm, is characteristic of *chaotic systems*, a special kind of dynamic system.

VIDEO LINK: Double Pendulum Displays Chaotic Motion
www.youtube.com/watch?v=AwT0k09w-jw

Dynamic systems have *attractors*, which are states that the system is striving to reach, such as a resting state where there would be no more motion. Many systems, however, have two or more attractors, so the system will start to settle towards one of them, and then—sometimes quite surprisingly—shift over toward the other. This back and forth can continue for quite a lot of cycles, and may even seem like it will never end.

A really interesting example of a *bistable dynamic system* is the model for the Necker Cube illusion (see Section 7.1.2). This is the visual illusion that makes the 2-dimensional line drawing of a 3-dimensional cube flip from one visual interpretation to the other, and then back. The dynamic system model does more than just depict that there are two states; it also shows what happens during the transitions, and what are the influences that lead up to a person flipping their visual interpretation. Another example is the spinning dancer. Both videos can be seen by following the links listed below.

VIDEO LINK: Bistable Systems:
(1) Necker Cube,
    https://studylib.net/doc/14456652/multi-stable-perception-necker-cube
(2) Spinning dancer
    www.verywellmind.com/optical-illusions-4020333#step-heading

Attractors are important properties of a dynamic system. This animation, created using MATLAB, illustrates two "chaotic" solutions to something called the Lorenz system of ordinary differential equations (ODEs).

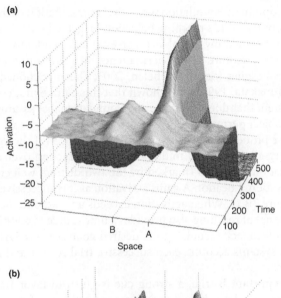

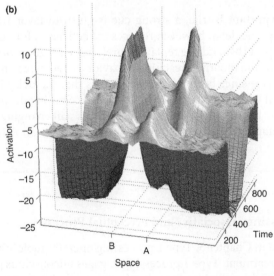

TRENDS in Cognitive Sciences

BOX FIGURE 7B.1 The time course of neural activation during planning when performing the A-not-B error reveals it to follow a dynamic system. (a) On the first trial, activation rises and is sustained as the object is hidden at location A. (b) There is greater activation at location A before the hiding event due to previous reaching behaviors. When the object is hidden at location B, activation increases for B, but still competes with activation for location A.

VIDEO LINK: Attractors
www.youtube.com/watch?v=8z_tSVeEFTA

An example of how dynamic systems can provide better explanations of cognitive development can be shown in a classic experiment involving infants. Infants (typically 8 to 10 months old) will successfully reach for a very desirable toy when they see it is repeatedly placed under a small well with a cover (Location A). When the infant observes the toy placed under a new cover (Location B), following a brief delay, the infant will continue to reach for it at Location A, the *old* location, often after a hesitation. Infants see the toy placed at Location B but continues to reach for it at Location A. Hence, it is called ***the A-not-B error.*** Babies at 12 months of age typically reach in the proper location.

From the standpoint of Foundationalism, the representation of the object is the central determinant of the child's reaching behavior. Piaget, who devised the original task, suggested infants do not know that objects can exist independently of their actions until they developmentally acquire "object permanence" at around 12 months of age. Thelen and Smith and colleagues (Smith & Thelen, 2003; Thelen, Schöner, Scheier, & Smith, 2001; also see Munakata, 1998) have shown that this can be modeled more effectively as a dynamic system that does not make any Foundationalist assumptions about when infants develop object permanence.

The alternative proposed by Thelen & Smith (2003, p. 345) shows that "the A-not-B error is the emergent product of multiple causes interacting over nested timescales." At baseline, Locations A and B (marked by the two distinct well covers) each receive comparable activation. Location A gains activation as it is successively chosen to house the toy (Box Figure 7B.1). When activation exceeds a threshold, the infant reaches for that location. The act of reaching also provides a new source of additional activation for Location A, with feedback (acquiring the desired goal; see Box 7A) further adding to it. As a dynamic systems account, each successive trial retains and replays the history of previous trials.

During the important B trial, a strong cue is given to favor Location B, the new location of the toy. The delay, however, reduces the activation for Location B over time (see Figure 7B.1, part (b)) and the replaying preference for A becomes dominant. This model accounts for the incorrect reaching behavior as described and also makes novel predictions that have since been confirmed. One is that the delay is crucial, and with no delay, the infant will correctly reach for Location B. Shifting the posture of the infant to standing for the B trials will eliminate the error, as will changing the salience of the B covers, and adding wrist weights to make the arms heavy on A trials but light on B trials.

7.1.2 Type 1 Processing: Associative and Perceptual Processes

As I briefly described in Chapter 3, Type 1 processing operates rapidly and tacitly. Here I give it a more thorough treatment. Type 1 processing engages unconscious processes that operate through association and perception. They dominate our thinking when we have limited capacity to do more effortful processes, as when we are fatigued, overwhelmed, or under time pressure. In Table 5.1, I previously showed how Type 1 processing relates to Types 2 and 3 processing.

Kahneman (2011) shares examples of how Type 1 processing operates in important settings such as the courts. In one example, the weighty decisions of parole board judges are unwittingly influenced by their blood sugar levels. The brain uses about 60% or the glucose of the entire body while in resting state, but is only 2% of the body weight. These judges reject the majority of parole requests over the course of each day. However, they reject much fewer immediately after they have caloric intake during meals and breaks! As the effects of a meal wear off, the rejections rates rise until they reach 100% right before their next meal. It is alarming to think that such consequential decisions are influenced by the vicissitudes of our physiological needs, but this is central to understanding the embodied nature of thinking and learning.

Type 1 processing is often responsible for the judgments we make by intuition, or "from our gut" (Kahneman, 2011). Thus, they are also likely responsible for heuristics— cognitive "shortcuts" we make when solving problems. This is not all *bad*. When people have insufficient information and may also be under pressure to make complex decisions, Type 1 processing cuts through the complexity and yields an outcome. What's more, people are confident in their Type 1 choices, even if they have overlooked important information (Reyna et al., 2014). In fact, empirically, people are more satisfied with their first choice than when they second guess themselves and revise their selection (Wilson & Schooler, 1991).

Because of the covert nature of Type 1 processing, people do not usually realize that these processes are exerting enormous influence on our reasoning and decision making. Furthermore, because these processes are predominantly nonverbal, they leave very little in the way of a memory trace, so we are unable to easily monitor them or direct them (Ericsson & Simon, 1993). People can learn to control them, but this often requires that these tacit processes be made overt in some way, as is done with biofeedback training.

Associative Processes
Type 1 processing relies on the predictive architecture upon which our cognitive system is built. Recall the propensity for our neural systems to extract the covariations in our environment and then align to them in order to be responsive. This means that strong associations that have been built up hold great sway in these rapid processes. By *associations*, I am referring to the interconnected web of ideas and sensations that are closely related to a current experience. A person may not be aware of them, but these associations are being activated and shaping the behaviors, judgments and decisions that are being made.

Quite a number of associative priming studies have shown how cuing associations leads to the activation of related ideas. For example (Lukatela & Turvey, 1994), the word TOAD is a strong associative priming for FROG. However, Frog is also briefly primed by the homophones TOWED (which has an alternative associative meaning) and TODE (a non-word with no prior associative meaning). This priming lasts for about 50 milliseconds (about the time it takes to read the word FROG). By 250 milliseconds, TOWED has dropped out as an associative prime, presumably because its competing meaning now inhibits the associative link. However, the links to TOAD and even TODE still persist.

Associative priming is also central to cuing stereotypes, prejudices, and biases (Devine, 1989). The biased judgments operate with autonomy. They do not depend upon the sequential chain of inference that is so characteristic of rational thought. And they are "inescapable," operating even when people intentionally try to prevent them, avoid them, or ignore them (Shiffrin & Dumais, 1981). Box 7C offers a glimpse into the power of biased thinking to commandeer reasoning and disrupt analytic problem solving.

One of the natural properties of associative systems is their reciprocity: The connections work both ways. Thus, it is that performing actions can also induce mental states. Students wearing a heavy backpack will judge a hill as steeper (Bhalla & Proffitt, 1999). Their judgments are particularly striking because they are not made verbally but by adjusting the tilt of a plate to match their perceptions. Others (e.g., Engelkamp & Zimmer, 2001) have reviewed findings that show a memory advantage for memory items (phrases) linked to self-performed actions than those who merely heard the phrases. Participants experience "involuntary memory" when performing the actions that trigger their recall. Findings by Thomas and Lleras (2007), which I reviewed in Chapter 1, showed that eliciting certain eye gaze patterns led participants to make the proper insight for a problem that people ordinarily struggle with, Duncker's (1945) Radiation Problem.

Together, these have been referred to as *ideomotor* processes (James, 1890) and relate our thoughts to our actions. Pfister and colleagues (2014, p. 164) state their motivations to study ideomotor links "How does our mind produce physical, goal-directed action of our body?" They demonstrate that this is possible because of neural circuits that anticipate the outcomes of actions.

Perceptual Processes

Type 1 processing makes use of perception in somewhat the same way that Type 2 processing uses cognition and knowledge-based processes. Perception produces sensations that serve as non-conscious judgments and intuitions to inform a predictive, embodied architecture.

Perceptions are the subjective experiences we have as we process sensory information, influenced, as I have described earlier, by our prior experiences, current goals, and contexts. Some of our perceptions reveal a great deal about how we experience the world, and how they influence what we may expect to otherwise be an objective portrayal of reality. Consider among my favorites, the Müller-Lyer Illusion, along with others (Figure 7.2)

The Müller-Lyer Illusion is that the lines appear to be of different lengths. Most people perceive the line segment with two arrow "tails" as longer than the line with two arrow "heads" (Figure 7.2(a)). It may seem odd to ask *Why?* since I just reported that we have little access to these processes—so we might not actually *know* why. In this case, we have strongly supported hypotheses, however. The segment with arrow *tails* is commonly experienced in walls and corners jutting out *to* the observer (Figure 7. 2(b)). Take a new look to see that. In contrast, the segment with arrow heads is commonly experienced in walls and corners receding *away* from the observer. Now consider (with your Type 2 processing hat on!) that if these two visual experiences appear to be the same, we will instantly judge the receding corner (arrow tails) as longer, since it is more likely to be further away from us. This reinforces how perception and action are so closely integrated, since we *care* how these images will affect us (approaching or receding corners), rather than as pure lines. It's especially odd to have this experience because it works even when we know it's an illusion. This is why I like it so much!

The Necker Cube Illusion (Figure 7.3) is an example of a bistable process.

Most observers can see this flip to one of two interpretations, the front wall as the lower-left face or as the upper-right face. Connectionist networks such as the one proposed by Rumelhart (1989) show how the bistability can be modeled.

Subjective contours (Figure 7.4) are delightful visual experiences because they show how much we fill in and try to predict what is there from very minimal visual information *Kanizsa's triangle* (Kanizsa, 1976) elicits in most viewers a second triangle (with the vertex pointing down). In keeping with the added impressions of that triangle perceived as being "on top of" the black triangle, its area appears to be much brighter than the surround. Obviously this is not the case—there is no triangle after all! But the added brightness is a result of our predictive architecture and our need to act on what we perceive. The added reflectance emerges

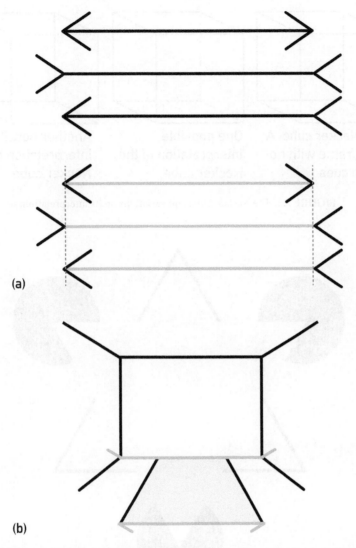

FIGURE 7.2 (a) Lines of equal length are perceived as unequal when arrow heads and tails are included. It is believed this is because they are interpreted as coming from (b) scenes where edges meet to corners that recede or protrude, and therefore are subject to rules of perspective.

when we do objectively see it as the same luminescence, if it *were* laying on top of the other objects, and therefore closer.

Just to mix it up, here is another illusion that combines the effects of subjective contours with the Necker Cube Illusion (Figure 7.5). You should still get the bistable effect of its interpretation flipping. This further exemplifies how the various processes combine hierarchically and interactively to produce the rich subjective experiences we often have (Marr, 1982).

Intuition
Scholars who study intuition hypothesize that it arises from rapid perceptual processes rather than any form of deliberate chain of reasoning. When people report making intuitive judgments, they have very little awareness of the process leading to the judgment ((Zander,

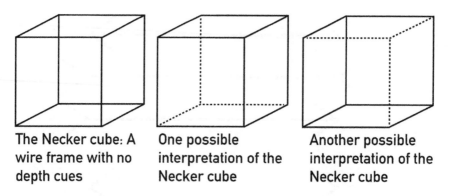

The Necker cube: A wire frame with no depth cues | One possible interpretation of the Necker cube | Another possible interpretation of the Necker cube

FIGURE 7.3 The Necker Cube and variations on its interpretation.

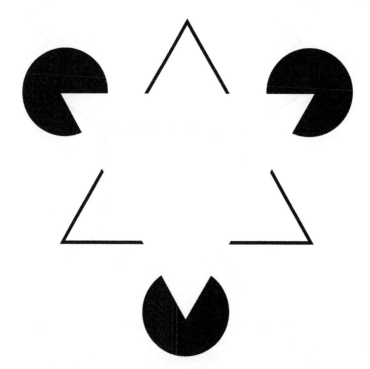

FIGURE 7.4 Subjective contours. A white triangle is implied and so shows up as brighter than its surround because it is perceived as being on top of the black outline.

Öllinger, & Volz, 2016). They also report that the process is not under conscious control. This distinguishes intuition from the closely related idea of insight (Zhang, Lei, & Li, 2016).

There have been some unusually introspective scholars to describe the intuitive process.

The great mathematician Henri Poincaré (1905) wrote "[T]here are many kinds of intuition. I have said how much the intuition of pure number, whence comes rigorous mathematical induction, differs from sensible intuition to which the imagination, properly so called, is the principal contributor." Albert Einstein, the Nobel prize-winning physicist whose work is often synonymous with creative thought, is reported to have said,

FIGURE 7.5 Subjective contours can exhibit the Necker Cube illusion.

Words and language, whether written or spoken, do not seem to play any part in my thought processes. The psychological entities that serve as building blocks for my thought are certain signs or images, more or less clear, that I can reproduce and recombine at will.

(Hadamard 1945, p. 142)

The tacit, rapid, and nonverbal nature of intuition makes its direct study difficult. To the Nobel Laureate, Herbert Simon, this also provides important clues as to its nature. Simon (1982, p. 155) has argued "Intuition is nothing more and nothing less than recognition." This puts intuition squarely among the realm of perceptual processes. A corpus analysis showed intuition as often (over 50% of entries) equated with "snap judgment" (Andow, 2015; the study used the British Academic Spoken English, or BASE, corpus). Some education scholars have also operationalized measures of intuition as the accuracy of participants' immediate true/false evaluation of each conjecture prior to any opportunity for sustained reasoning (Nathan et al., 2020; Nathan & Walkington, 2017).

Box 7C Associative Priming and Biases in Problem Solving and Decision Making

Associative priming and biases operate with impunity and can control one's reasoning and disrupt normally analytic problem solving. Kahan and colleagues (2013) illustrates this using a probabilistic reasoning task that is presented in a politically charged context. People have strong associations and biases about handguns and violence. Despite having skills for correctly solving the problem, people's responses are shaped by their political biases regarding gun control. Here is an adapted version of the problem they studied. For my purposes, I have provided it in the two conditions they used in the study (Figure 7.6; with the contrasted conditions circled). People were shown either the Crime Decreases version (on the left), or the Crime Increases version (on the right).

> You are instructed that a city government is trying
> to decide whether to pass a law banning private citizens
> from carrying concealed handguns in public.
> They then observed the number of cities that experienced
> "decreases in crime" and those that experienced "increases in crime" in the next
>   year. The data are below (Figure 7.6).
> Please indicate whether cities that enacted a ban on carrying concealed
> handguns were more likely to have a decrease in crime or instead were more likely
>   to have an increase in crime than cities without bans.

One or the other version of the chart (Crime Increases or Crime Decreases) was posed to a nationally representative sample of 1,111 US adults. The results may be surprising. First of all, this is definitely a complex task mathematically. It requires a good deal of careful analysis of the covariation of two factors and assess their relative ratios. But it is totally solvable. And respondents need only pick one option (an increase in crime) or the other (a decrease in crime), so there is a 50% of getting it correct simply by guessing.

(As a check on the underlying probabilistic reasoning involved, a completely different group from the same sample was given the same basic mathematical task but the problem was framed as whether a new skin cream improved people with rashes. Attesting to its difficulty, 59% of participants solving the skin cream version gave the incorrect response for their condition. Those who were categorized as higher in math performance did significantly better than those low in math, regardless of political affiliation.)

When the comparable problem was framed in terms of gun control—an area where people have strong biases—the story looks very different than for skin cream. Those participants strong in math with political views that favored banning guns did almost perfectly when the proper selection was that the weapons ban decreases crime. This presumable aligns the data shown in the problem with their pro-gun-ban biases. However, the pro-gun-ban people operated at chance when the correct answer conflicted with their political views. Participants strong in math with political views favoring gun ownership (against the gun ban) showed precisely the opposite pattern. They gave the correct response when the data aligned with their pro-gun rights views but were at chance when the data and their biases conflicted.

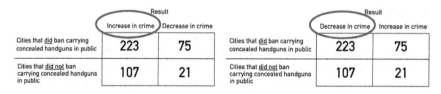

FIGURE 7.6 Bias in mathematics word problem solving.

To quote the title from one popular press account of this research, "Science Confirms: Politics Wrecks Your Ability to Do Math." I point out a seeming contradiction about what I have said about people's mental processing. I have gone to some lengths to show that humans are essentially "covariation machines." People have neural systems that are highly tuned to extract these deeply embedded patterns and use them to develop perception, language, emotional expression, and on and on. Yet those are *lived experiences* of the covariation in the world. Using covariation quantitatively to make decisions is in the realm of Type 2 processing, and therefore is subject to the proclivities of Type 1 processing. When one's biases align with the covariation information, people are in good shape. And, true to the nature of our lived covariation, this tends to happen more often than chance. It is, after all, through repeated exposure that people developed these associations. But people's biases can lead them astray when they are in conflict with thoughtful reasoning and decision making.

7.1.3 Implicit Memory

When people frequently and consistently perform a task, however laborious at first, it can, over time, become automated and effortless. It goes from taking up all one's attention, to taking (virtually) none of it. To Wilson (2002, p. 633), "Implicit memory is the means by which we learn skills, automatizing what was formerly effortful." In our recent verbiage, Type 2 thinking leads to Type 1 processing.

This automaticity process reveals several qualities about Type 1 processing. As described, *consistency* of the task performance is vital (Schneider & Shiffrin, 1977). There is also a coordination of multiple memory systems, with distinct memory systems for declarative knowledge and more effortless procedural knowledge (Cohen, Eichenbaum, Deacedo, & Corkin, 1985). This claim is also supported by neural data, including studies of amnesiac patients failing to retain declarative information but learning complex perceptuomotor skills (Cohen & Squire, 1980) and linguistic structures (Knowlton et al., 1992). In these instances, people often remain unaware of what was learned or that learning took place at all. Automaticity through consistent exposure and practice is a way that Type 2 reasoning becomes **grounded** in the perceptual pattern matching processes needed when correctly accessing that knowledge, and in the motor programs needed for performing that knowledge.

7.2 GEL AT THE BIOLOGICAL LEVEL: TYPE 1 LEARNING

7.2.1 Knowing-How

In his presidential address to the Aristotelian Society at the University of London, Gilbert Ryle (1945) made a case for notions of "intelligence" that went beyond thinking about the types of verbal, declarative knowledge that dominates Type 2 processing, as described in Chapters 5 and 6. Ryle pointed to "the distinction which is quite familiar to all of us between knowing *that* something is the case and knowing *how* to do things" (Ryle, 1945, p. 4; emphasis added). Ryle (1945) reasoned that knowing-how is legitimately on par with knowledge of facts, propositions, and maxims. One cannot, for example, be regarded as having the knowledge for riding a bicycle without actually riding it—knowing-how is critical for such skills. Ryle further argued "that knowledge-how is a concept logically prior to the concept of knowledge-that" (pp. 4–5). In defending this, he showed how one could not use knowing-that forms of knowledge to ever reason one's way to knowing-how. Rather, in practical terms, one needs knowing-how in order to apply much of knowing-that knowledge.

One of the unusual traits of knowing-how is that it is retained even among people with severe amnesia (Cohen & Squire, 1980). For example, those diagnosed with amnesia can demonstrate the same speed improvement of repeated memory tasks such as getting through a maze, even though they do not recall ever doing the maze. For a long time, it was thought that knowing-how memories remained intact because they were performed by the motor and perceptual systems (which were likely operating together, as perceptuo-motor processes) that used protected neural circuits exclusive of cognition. As the types of tasks with successful learning was studied more systematically, that view has evolved.

This view changed with data from a series of studies such as one of "mirror reading," reading words printed backwards. It is possible to teach mirror reading to patients diagnosed with severe amnesia who would ordinarily forget verbal information almost as quickly as they received it (e.g., from severe head injury or with Korsakoff syndrome). Surprisingly, these patients are able to learn to perform mirror reading at the same performance level as control participants with no such memory impairments. Those with amnesia showed the same level of speed up for words that were repeated over multiple days, even though they had no recollection of the words, or even participating in the activity at all. Furthermore, they also showed comparable gains with mirror reading skills for new words, demonstrating that the skill generalized to novel stimuli. In surveying the overall pattern of results, Cohen & Squire (1980) theorized that knowing-how knowledge extends beyond perceptuomotor processes to include general perceptual pattern learning, procedural learning, and rule-based learning more generally, a view that largely still stands today.

7.2.2 Perceptual Learning

As the discussion of knowing-how shows, perceptual processes are extremely flexible and influential for determining how we reason and learn. Because the processes are so rapid and out of awareness, it may be tempting to relegate perceptual learning to basic and low-level sensory processing and imagine that its effects are limited to enhanced processing of simple patterns. But as scholars are learning, perceptual learning can be very effective for enhancing people's sensitivity to complex relationships among abstract processes (Kellman & Massey, 2013; Rau, 2020).

For example, Rau, Michaelis, and Fay (2015; Study 4) found that perceptual fluency was associated with chemistry education, and important for establishing connection-making. The important role of perceptual learning has also been shown in surgery education, where attending surgeons provide nonverbal guidance, including gestures and directed gaze to residents-in-training (Cope et al., 2015).

Kellman and Massey (2013, p. 119) define *perceptual learning* as "experience-induced changes in the way perceivers pick up information." This fits my definition of learning as an enduring change in behavior. They elaborate that

> With practice in any domain, humans become attuned to the relevant features and structural relations that define important classifications, and over time, we come to extract these with increasing selectivity and fluency.

A broad slate of research has shown the effect of perceptual learning methods to complex domains involving formalisms for learning language, fractions, and proportional reasoning, algebra, and chemistry (Kellman et al., 2010; Landy & Goldstone, 2007; Silva & Kellman,

1999; Saffran, Aslin, & Newport, 1996). This body of work has led a number of scholars to theorize that perceptual processing is the basis for abstract reasoning (e.g., Barsalou, 1999; Goldstone, Landy, & Son, 2008). This is because abstractions highlight the generalizable *relations* among entities, which are the very types of associations that characterize perceptual learning.

The dynamic systems nature of these processes also suggests that some perceptual patterns will be more favorable than others. The Necker Cube Illusion, for example, must settle into one of the two states of the image, but not a blended form of the two. Similarly, people prefer certain ways of grouping objects, and even apply these preferred perceptual states to grouping algebra symbols (see Figure 1.7; Goldstone et al., 2017) even if the grouping violates Type 2 parsing rules.

Kellman and Massey (2013) have explicitly targeted the nonverbal processes endemic to perceptual learning and knowing-how, rather than the language-based nature of declarative knowledge, such as facts and definitions. Indeed, as they point out,

> It is not by accident that math teachers spend the first month of a new school year reviewing content from the prior year. Facts and procedures are subject to substantial forgetting over a period as long as a summer vacation from school. Although more research is needed, there are indications that the improved facility in picking up patterns and structure from [perceptual learning], like riding a bicycle, may be less subject to decay over time.

Another well-studied method for developing perceptual learning is the use of contrasting cases (Bransford & Schwartz, 1999; Schwartz & Bransford, 1998). Contrasting cases help develop learners' skills for noticing. Learners tune their abilities to distinguish between attributes, which allows them to actively refine how they think about and apply a concept. Thus, when subsequent instruction is offered, students are better able to learn from a teaching experience. Contrasting cases develop one's perceptual processes and so provide a basis for knowing-how that can enhance subsequent learning experiences.

7.2.3 Motor Control

Motor control involves the regulation and execution of goal-directed action in a changing environment. While there are several theoretical accounts of motor control, a prominent one is the HMOSAIC architecture (Haruno et al., 2003). Central to the HMOSAIC model is its predictive orientation toward control. Simply put, the approach is to assess the current state of things in order to anticipate (nominally) *all* of the next plausible actions and their influences on the body and the immediate surrounding. Feedforward is very valuable, but it is inadequate on its own. Being reactive is, in many cases, far too slow to respond to events and could make a person vulnerable or unprepared. An anticipatory response informed by **feedforward** networks working in concert with a **feedback** network enables a person to be better prepared for likely events as well as able to rapidly correct action errors (see Box 7A).

Consider the example of a person with the goal of picking up a tea kettle in order to fill a teacup with its contents. The body must be positioned to reach it and the muscles in the arm, hand, and the rest of the body engaged to properly grasp and lift it (Haruno et al., 2001; Wolpert & Kawato, 1998). In doing so, the person has some expectation of the weight and amount of resistance of the kettle, which is directed to the feedforward network. This can be estimated, but is not known with certainty until it is lifted, so a large number of plausible motor programs are generated and available at the ready as more proprioceptive feedback comes in.

Imagine now that the expectation is that the kettle is nearly full, but in fact it is empty. Many of us have had the surprise of giving too much force when lifting an object. In this case we would experience the kettle flying up. We even feel our arm fly up as though under its own power—which it *is*—and wonder how this is happening. Although our conscious Type 2 processing experiences are caught unaware, there are Type 1 processes already at work to correct the situation, though this is happening outside of our conscious awareness. In this event, more well-suited motor program modules are being selected to slow things down and get the system more accurately aligned.

This anticipatory response depends on the generation of multiple, paired predictor-controller modules—themselves small motor programs—that each anticipates a plausible next state of the motor system. These each provide feedforward and proprioceptive feedback signals to regulate muscle behavior toward the intended goal. There is continuous competition among the predictor-controller modules and the system favors those modules that are doing the best job following and guiding the body's behavior and interactions with the environment in real time. Since this is a dynamic system, there are also going to be preferred states ("attractors") for the motor system, just as we saw with perceptual pattern recognition like the Necker cube. For example, when people gesture, they tend toward certain forms of segmentation that show parallels with sign language and spoken language (Liddell, 2003). These constraints influence people's motor behavior and the types of simulations that can be induced by these behaviors.

There are several important advantages to this predictive motor architecture. One is that people achieve fairly accurate motor movement because they are continuously *simulating* their interactions with the world even as the world is constantly changing, often as a result of our interactions. Of course, the nervous system likes to re-purpose successful solutions to thorny problems that may put us at risk. For this reason, a number of scholars have used this architecture as the basis for supporting mental simulation more generally. HMOSAIC has been proposed as the basis for motor control in an uncertain environment (Wolpert, Doya, & Kawato, 2003), as a system to perceive and interpret other people's actions (Wilson & Knoblich, 2005), and as a general architecture for language comprehension (Glenberg & Gallese, 2012).

7.2.4 Affordances and Constraints

I have often referred to the perception-action loop (Chapter 2), and the tight interactions of the perception-action-world cycle (Neisser, 1976; Spivey & Huette, 2014). This tight set of interactions was most thoroughly articulated by J. J. Gibson (1979/2014), Eleanor J. Gibson (1969), and their colleagues and followers. As J. J. Gibson (1979/2014, p. 127) wrote in his culminating book:

> The affordances of the environment are what it offers the animal, what it provides or furnishes, either for good or ill. The verb to afford is found in the dictionary, the noun affordance is not. I have made it up. I mean by it something that refers to both the environment and the animal in a way that no existing term does. It implies the complementarity of the animal and the environment.

The notion of affordances captures the manner in which the world conveys its suitability to a body, and how the person with that body can perceive that suitability and act upon it. Thus, the theory of affordances integrates perceptual learning and motor control.

Famously, scholars have described the affordances of chairs, perhaps because they are ubiquitous, seemingly innocuous, and actually quite varied in their design. As Glenberg (1998) notes, we may encounter a standard adult-sized chair, and if the least tired or burdened immediately recognize its suitability for sitting. But not so the infant or toddler, who is far more likely (we may observe, because the child cannot tell us) that the same chair affords climbing under or pulling oneself up to, but certainly not sitting. A chair is simply a mismatch for the little person. What's more, there is no chain of reasoning needed to make these realizations. Rather, they are apprehended immediately and nonverbally, just as we may recognize that one object is occluding another. Affordances are fundamentally perceptual processes, as mediated by our physical form, ways of acting, and current needs.

This notion was appropriated and modified by Don Norman (1999) to focus designers on attending to people's "perceived affordances" (p. 39). Norman, you may know, is a prominent designer of computer interfaces and also a keen observer of how "everyday things" are designed, used and misused (e.g., Norman, 1988). He wants to address a couple of questions relevant to education. One is, "When you first see something you have never seen before, how do you know what to do?" Norman *detests* that doors, for example, may need to be labeled "Push" when there are perceived affordances that designers should exploit to take care of that instantly (such as a push plate). Norman also wants to use principles of design to avoid making errors and causing accidents. In broadening the notion of affordances in this way, Norman emphasizes that we may not readily grasp *any and all* possible acts with the things in our environment. Rather, we are more likely to interact in ways that match our current goals and past experiences. The designs such as the computer desktop and desktop trash cans are examples of this use of perceived affordances intended to elicit natural, helpful responses.

Greeno and colleagues (Greeno. 1998; Greeno, Smith, & Moore, 1993) extended the idea of affordances to theorizing about how and when students learn and transfer that learning to new situations. Because the situation in which interactions and cognition take place is central to theory, Greeno called it *situative theory*, or *situativity*. Previously I introduced the idea of *schemas* as highly regularized events, such as ordering food at a restaurant, that guides one's expectations for how to perform and predictive behaviors for what will likely come next.

In situative theory, the organization of expected events is described as one's *attunement* to the *constraints and affordances* common among regularized patterns of social interactions. In this view the environment offers affordances, as we described, and constraints, or ways that behaviors are limited. In shopping, for example, Lave (1988) showed that shoppers are operating with constraints such as the amount of money budgeted, needs on a shopping list, and so on. Affordances include the spatial layout of the store—which determines the sequence and may, if a budget limit is hit, limit later purchases.

Learning, in situative theory, is certainly rooted in enduring changes in social and organizational practices. *Situative learning* is also highly dependent upon becoming familiar with—that is, *attuned to*—the environmental constraints and affordances. Attunement to the constraints and affordances shaped the strategies and practices that shoppers would develop to optimize their food purchases for a given budget, within a specific grocery setting. *Transfer* of learning relies on developing attunement to constraints and affordances that are invariant across different settings, such as flexibly applying one's optimization strategies to a new grocery setting (Greeno et al., 1993).

7.2.5 Procedural Learning

Procedural learning is the development of lasting **action sequences** that, ideally are well-suited to the current conditions. This contrasts with the description I gave previously for declarative knowledge as changes in verbalizable rules and networks of facts. Indeed, procedural and declarative knowledge are often considered to point toward the opposing poles along a continuum of learning that emphasizes skill or concepts. But they are far from oppositional. In my view, the literature clearly shows that procedural and declarative knowledge are mutually beneficial for one another in a number of ways. One's prior conceptual knowledge greatly influences whether and how one learns and refines procedures, and *vice versa* (e.g., Rittle-Johnson & Alibali, 1999; Rittle-Johnson, & Siegler, 2001).

Procedural knowledge provides a form of **offloading** that facilitates learning of declarative knowledge and changes in conceptual reasoning. Chains of conceptual steps can become procedures under the proper learning conditions, as when there is adequate practice and helpful feedback. With further practice, a procedure can become *automated*, where it basically makes little or no demands on working memory on its own, and can therefore be performed alongside other processes without degrading its own performance or that of the multitasked process. Not all practices are equal, however. Experts, far more than even enthusiastic amateurs, engage in *deliberate practice* in their respective fields by structuring their sessions with feedback and refinement in mind (Ericsson, Krampe, & Tesch-Römer, 1993).

Procedural knowledge will be automated fastest when the conditions for applying it are consistent. When there is considerable variability, automaticity may take longer, but the learning is more robust when applied to changing conditions. Hatano and Inagaki (1986) offer the example of the farmer who must learn to apply procedures that must adapt to changing conditions. This illustrates how procedural learning supports development of forms of abstraction that are a central component of adaptive expertise.

Given the complementary qualities of procedural and declarative knowledge, it may surprise some readers (and be all-too-familiar to others) that a battle has been brewing in education between methods that favor procedural versus declarative learning. It has played out most prominently in early reading and math education. In its incarnation in mathematics, the "Math Wars" pit those favoring the early and consistent role of conceptual understanding as a basis for understanding procedures, versus those who champion the mastery of procedures as prerequisite to the investigation of generalizable and abstract concepts.

An example of the two positions can be seen in fraction learning. Specifically, I want to choose division of fractions because that is a topic that I believe most adults have mastered procedurally, but have a very poor understanding of its conceptual basis. Most adults can compute the following:

$$5/4 \div 3/4 = ?$$

Please take a minute and then respond to these prompts:

1. What answer do you get?
2. How did you determine that answer?
3. How confident are you that this is correct?
4. What is the basis of your confidence level?

As I mention, most people can accurately compute this to produce an answer of five-thirds. A smaller group perhaps determined it was one- and two-thirds. The second response is of course mathematically equivalent to the first but likely reveals that a very different method was used. This pertains to the second question, which most likely was the result of a well-known procedure: *flip-and-multiply*. Though well known, users may not have very high confidence, or if they do, it is based more on faith than understanding. Few people who correctly employ flip-and-multiply know how or why it works, and therefore appeal to authority, or perhaps some sense of induction over many trials, in explaining their basis for their level of certainty.

Some of you will also note some initial trepidation using flip-and-multiply even if you eventually prevailed. The label says what to do, but it is ambiguous which term gets flipped. Without a conceptual basis, there is a bit of guesswork involved. Some may have even tried each way before deciding, after applying some criteria, such as looking for an answer that had to be greater than 1.

Along with being (often) rote action sequences, this exposes another important aspect of procedural learning: To be effective, the application of learned actions sequences is predicated on the proper conditions. This was a huge inspiration to the Information Processing community in Cognitive Science (from Chapter 2). As a cornerstone of their computational theory, many explicitly modeled procedural knowledge as *IF-THEN rules* within a production system (e.g., Anderson & Lebiere, 2014; Laird, Newell, & Rosenbloom, 1987; Newell & Simon, 1972; VanLehn, 1990).

Knowledge of procedures is empirically distinguishable from other forms of knowledge. It shows a different forgetting function than declarative knowledge (Cohen, Eichenbaum, Deacedo, & Corkin, 1985). Furthermore, it is closely linked to different neural areas of the brain, predominantly the neostriatum (American Association for Research into Nervous and Mental Diseases, 1997) than declarative knowledge.

Procedural knowledge has several other unique characteristics (Star, 2005). Like perceptual knowledge, it is largely nonverbal. People may be able to retrospectively report on its execution, but those reports are often inaccurate, sometimes wildly so (Ericsson & Simon, 1993). As a self-check, consider quickly describing when you sit on a chair. It is difficult for the person performing the procedure to reflect on their knowledge, monitor their progress, and offer up ways to improve performance. Related to its nonverbal nature, it is generally best to assess procedural knowledge through performance rather than some form of verbal explanation.

Procedural knowledge is also highly driven by practice and feedback (Pashler et al., 2007). Scholars and coaches also understand the ways that a *practice schedule* can impact performance at a later time. In addition to practice, Rittle-Johnson & Star (2007) demonstrate that procedural learning is promoted by interventions that use contrasting cases that compare solution methods. As learned action sequences that are tied to perceptual processes for determining their conditions of use, procedural learning is well grounded in body-based processes.

7.2.6 Grounding: Perceptual Fluency, Affordances, and Automaticity

The GEL framework proposes that at each level along the timescale there will be processes that provide grounding of ideas, so they are meaningful to learners. As I have described, meaning of ideas can be grounded in the neural patterns of activities that emerge through three core mechanisms: perceptual fluency, affordances, and the automaticity that comes from procedural learning.

One form of grounding is achieved by the **perceptual fluency** that develops from learning. Through repeated exposure and practice, familiar patterns are immediately noticed and recognized. Perceptual processes are not confined to exact matches and in this way they attain a level of abstraction that allows people to recognize a broad class of instances all as members of the same general category. As scholars have noted, perceptually learned responses often substitute for reasoning and search. As noted in the research on implicit bias, these processes are powerful, and although they operate outside of consciousness, they wield enormous influence, even when contradictory to one's values.

Perceptual learning naturally supports the **affordances** that shape how people interact with the world. As people function, their perceived affordances shape what they will expect and how they act. The ideas of objects become grounded in the potential ways each person experiences these affordances. This, Greeno and colleagues (1993) point out, extends to conceptual "objects" as well. How people perceive and anticipate interacting with formal notations, or with ideas, can be described through the theory of affordances. Objects, symbols, and ideas come to mean for us those things we can do with them, and those potential actions are activated automatically through the lens of perceptually learned patterns.

Another form of grounding is achieved by **procedural learning and automaticity**. In this case, earlier steps involved in a skill or reasoning process become automated and operate much like perceptual processes. Once automated, they are no longer subject to the awareness and cognitive monitoring that is characteristic of the original effortful steps. Scholars often point out (e.g., Kellman & Massey, 2013) that the new, automated procedures do not replace the older, more deliberative processes. As far as it is known, the slow, deliberative steps coincide in memory with the fast, automated steps. Often, in competition to match and act, the faster automated procedural knowledge wins the race for selection. Following many of the lessons of cognitive neuroscience, as the automated process is repeatedly selected in favor, it gains further advantages of being selected in the future. Still, the slower steps can be chosen and revived under some circumstances.

7.2.7 Embodied Learning: Action-Cognition Transduction

The methods of grounding provide avenues for unfamiliar ideas, words, and experiences to gain meaning in terms of body-based responses. Where, though, do new ideas come from? Predictive processes that operate in accordance with motor control and perceptual simulation provide these opportunities for forming new thoughts. And these thoughts, emerging from our own perceptuomotor experiences, are naturally grounded for us.

We readily accept that our thoughts, such as goals, will generate actions and even guide the form those actions take. *Action-cognition transduction* acknowledges the coupling that is necessarily formed between our sensorimotor processing and our reasoning processing when fulfilling goal-directed actions. As described in Chapter 2, action-cognition transduction is the reciprocal exchange of energy and information from motoric processes to and from reasoning processes. Action-cognition transduction is closely related to perception-action loop. This is because, as I have shown, the GEL framework shows the interconnected nature of action, perception, and cognition. By acknowledging how these devices and systems can run either "forward" and "reverse" we come to appreciate that there is no real hierarchy between cognition and action; no one process that is primary or secondary.

Actions performed on either real or imagined entities generate **feedforward** (predictive) and **feedback** (responsive) signals that can activate cognitive states that are associated with important relationships, and behaviors of the entities (Nathan & Walkington, 2017). The earlier example of picking up the tea kettle illustrates how these mechanisms operate together during a motor control activity.

This can also be used to account for some learning phenomena. For example, people use dynamic gestures (Garcia & Infante, 2012) to successfully reason about the generalizable properties of geometric objects, such as triangles, even though the shapes of interest are completely imagined (Nathan & Schenck et al., in press). To explore the influence of expanding and shrinking a triangle, people actually physically experience that the angles remain invariant even as the triangles transform to be larger and smaller sizes, respectively. Following E. J. Gibson (1969), J. J. Gibson (1979), and Greeno and colleagues (1993, 1998), the motor programs that are generated to enact these movements are attuned to the triangle's affordances and constraints. This enables people to anticipate the outcomes of the transformations they simulate performing on the imagined objects. The actions themselves generate predictive expectations that naturally support inferences about the future states of the object, which forms the basis for embodied reasoning about generalized spatial properties (Nathan & Walkington, 2017).

As noted in the earlier discussion of motor control, the action system will (briefly) anticipate *all* of the future plausible outcomes of a motor operation, in order to track the motor behavior in real time and offer rapid, on-demand, corrections (Wolpert et al., 2003). These motor behaviors can induce inferences, even for complex concepts. For example, students who generated motor movements while reading about the circulatory system were significantly more likely to generate the appropriate inferences from what they read, compared to those whose movements were restricted (Nathan & Martinez, 2015). By connecting the anticipatory nature of the motor control system with reasoning processes, as mediated by perceptual processing of the affordances and constraints of the current environment, action-cognition transduction provides an account of embodied learning that supports generalization and transfer at the biological level.

7.3 SUMMARY

This chapter introduced the biological structures and processes that produce learning and intellectual behavior at the most rapid portion of the GEL timescale. The definition of learning as an enduring change in behavior is shown to apply at the neural level as changes in the interconnections of neurons and neural systems. Behavior at this level is best viewed within the framework of Interactionism. Behavior is regulated by feedback and feedforward mechanisms that allow these systems to succeed when they effectively react to as well as predict external events in their environment.

In the aggregate, emergent behaviors arise that manifest Type 1 processing, such as associative memory, pattern recognition, and procedural learning. These processes operate largely outside of conscious awareness, yet they have enormous influence on acting, intuitive reasoning, and decision making. These processes make little to no demands on working memory and can actually help to offload some of the cognitive demands that people experience when performing Type 2 processing. Because Type 1 processing defies monitoring and is difficult to consciously control, it can also produce biased behaviors that lead to erroneous judgments.

Learning processes that emerge at this portion of the timescale reveal ways of knowing-how, nonverbal forms of knowing best suited for perceptual fluency (recognizing faces) and procedural knowledge (such as riding a bicycle) that are difficult to accurately describe or introspect on. The boundaries between perception and action are difficult to discern, so many scholars favor characterizing these behaviors in terms of the perception-action loop, where actions are necessary for perceptual experiences, that in turn elicit and guide actions. These are active processes that are always perceiving the world in terms of its affordances, how one relates to and can interact with it. People use the affordances of their environment to support cognitive behaviors, such as how the layout of a grocery store influences how people make purchasing decisions.

The meaning of unfamiliar patterns and skills are grounded in these rapid biological processes used for perceptual fluency, procedural knowledge, and affordances. The creation of completely new ideas can also be described at the biological portion of the timescale through action-cognition transduction. Performing goal-directed actions, such as manipulating an object, activates predictive processes to model the state of the world and predict what the world will be like once the actions are completed. This induces a predictive model of their environment that supports a generalizable form of cognitive simulation. Transduction can be used when people are actually performing functional actions (online cognition), making inferences about the environment, and when they are imagining performing possible actions (offline cognition).

7.4 READER ACTIVITIES

7.4.1 Knowing-How: The Affordances of Doors

"Norman Doors" www.youtube.com/watch?v=q7CpRH2WbME

7.4.2 Feedback and Feedforward Mechanisms

Feedback and feedforward mechanisms are common to achieve self-regulation in physical and biological systems.

Shapiro (2019) uses Watt's governor as an example of self-regulation through feedback to show how it achieves near-constant engine speed under varying conditions.

A more contemporary example is found in the Atlas robot (by Boston Dynamics). See the robot here doing parkour.

www.youtube.com/watch?v=LikxFZZO2sk

You can read about the design of a digital model of the Atlas robot (Boston Dynamics; Jain, Kuo, & Sinkarenko, 2016).

7.4.3 Nonlinear Dynamic Systems and Emergent Behavior

Demonstrations of pendula as dynamic systems
   Video: Pendulum bowling balls (3 mins), www.youtube.com/watch?v=YhMiuzyU1ag
   Video: Double pendula (2 mins), www.youtube.com/watch?v=AwT0k09w-jw

7.4.4 Predictive Architecture: Sensory Illusions

i. Müller-Lyer Illusion.
    1. Interactive link https://michaelbach.de/ot/sze-muelue/index.html
    2. Discussion of how the illusion varies by cultural setting http://cognitionandculture.
        net/blogs/simons-blog/culture-and-perception-part-ii-the-muller-lyer-illusion/
ii. "The Dress." From AsapSCIENCE. www.youtube.com/watch?v=AskAQwOBvhc

7.4.5 Conceptual Understanding via Perceptual Processing

Here is an example of "doing" fraction arithmetic (following a rule that you know but might not understand) versus conceptualizing fraction arithmetic (from Thompson, 1995). You can do this yourself, and then try it with someone else.

Ask anyone in your family or circle of friends to perform this calculation <u>without</u> using quick methods like *flip-and-multiply*.

$$5/4 \div 3/4 = ?$$

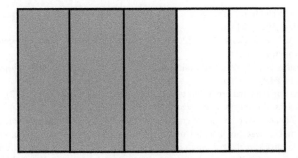

a) Can you see 3/5 of something?
b) Can you see 5/3 of something?
c) Can you see 5/3 of 3/5?
d) Can you see 2/3 of 3/5?
e) Can you see 1 ÷ 3/5?
f) Can you see 5/4 ÷ 3/4?

FIGURE 7.7 A display for conceptualizing arithmetic with fractions (adapted from Thompson, 1995).

Have someone try to explain how multiplication and division by fractions work. Most people, even accomplished in math and science, will struggle and often resort to shortcuts that actually mask the real mathematics.

1. Now draw the partially shaded image below. Go through each step (a) through (f) as a way to scaffold their understanding of fractions and fraction multiplication.
2. Notice how this diagram and line of questioning will activate mathematical intuition about fractions for some people.
3. Ask your participant to explain the shift in conceptualization. (You can also try it yourself.) Many will report this as a nonverbal experience. They may never look at fractions the same way again!

REFERENCES

Allen, J. W., & Bickhard, M. H. (2013). Stepping off the pendulum: Why only an action-based approach can transcend the nativist–empiricist debate. *Cognitive Development, 28*(2), 96–133.

American Association for Research into Nervous and Mental Diseases, Squire, L. R., & Zola, S. M. (1997). Amnesia, memory and brain systems. *Philosophical Transactions of the Royal Society of London. Series B: Biological Sciences, 352*(1362), 1663–1673.

Anderson, J. R., & Lebiere, C. J. (2014). *The atomic components of thought.* Psychology Press.

Andow, J. (2015). How distinctive is philosophers' intuition talk? *Metaphilosophy, 46*(4–5), 515–538.

Barsalou, L. W. (1999). Perceptual symbol systems. *Behavioral and Brain Sciences, 22*(4), 577–660.

Barwich, A. S. (2019). The value of failure in science: The story of grandmother cells in neuroscience. *Frontiers in Neuroscience, 13*, 1121.

Bhalla, M., Proffitt, D. (1999). Visual-motor recalibration in geographical slant perception. *Journal of Experimental Psychology: Human Perception and Performance, 25*, 1076–1096.

Bickhard, M. H. (2001). Why children don't have to solve the frame problems: Cognitive representations are not encodings. *Developmental Review, 21*(2), 224–262.

Bransford, J. D., Brown, A. L., & Cocking, R. R. (2000). *How people learn: Brain, mind, experience, and school: Expanded edition*. National Academy Press.

Bransford, J. D., & Schwartz, D. L. (1999). Rethinking transfer: A simple proposal with multiple implications. *Review of Research in Education, 24*(1), 61–100.

Chomsky, N. (1959). On certain formal properties of grammars. *Information and Control, 2*(2), 137–167.

Churchland, P. S. (2004). How do neurons know? *Daedalus, 133*(1), 42–50.

Cohen, L. G. et al. (1997) Functional relevance of cross-modal plasticity in blind humans. *Nature, 389*, 180–183.

Cohen, N. J., Eichenbaum, H., Deacedo, B. S., & Corkin, S. (1985). Different memory systems underlying acquisition of procedural and declarative knowledge. *Annals of the New York Academy of Sciences, 444*, 54–71.

Cohen, N. J., & Squire, L. R. (1980). Preserved learning and retention of pattern-analyzing skill in amnesia: Dissociation of knowing how and knowing that. *Science, 210*(4466), 207–210.

Cope, A. C., Bezemer, J., Kneebone, R., & Lingard, L. (2015). 'You see?' Teaching and learning how to interpret visual cues during surgery. *Medical Education, 49*(11), 1103–1116.

Dehaene, S. (2009). *Reading in the brain: The new science of how we read*. Penguin.

Devine, P. G. (1989). Stereotypes and prejudice: Their automatic and controlled components. *Journal of Personality and Social Psychology, 56*(1), 5–18.

Dewey, J. (1905). The postulate of immediate empiricism. *The Journal of Philosophy, Psychology and Scientific Methods, 2*(15), 393–399.

Duncker, K. (1945). On problem solving. *Psychological Monographs, 58*(5, Whole No. 270).

Engelkamp, J., & Zimmer, H. (2001). Categorical and order information in free recall of action phrases. *Psicologica, 22*(1), 71–96.

Ericsson, K. A., Krampe, R. T., & Tesch-Römer, C. (1993). The role of deliberate practice in the acquisition of expert performance. *Psychological Review, 100*(3), 363.

Ericsson, K. A., & Simon, H. A. (1993). *Protocol analysis: Verbal reports as data* (rev. ed.). MIT Press.

Fodor, J. A. (1983). *The modularity of mind*. MIT Press.

Garcia, N., & Infante, N. E. (2012). Gestures as facilitators to proficient mental modelers. In L. R. Van Zoest, J.-J. Lo, & J. L. Kratky (Eds.), Proceedings of the 34th Annual Meeting of the North American Chapter of the International Group for the Psychology of Mathematics Education (pp. 289–295). Western Michigan University.

Geary, D. C. (1995). Reflections of evolution and culture in children's cognition: Implications for mathematical development and instruction. *American Psychologist, 50*(1), 24.

Gibson, E. J. (1969). *Principles of perceptual learning and development*. Appleton-Century Crofts

Gibson, J. J. (1979/2014). *The ecological approach to visual perception: Classic edition*. Psychology Press.

Glenberg, A. M. (1998). Grounding meaning in affordances. AAAI technical report WS-98-06. Retrieved from www.aaai.org

Glenberg, A. M., & Gallese, V. (2012). Action-based language: A theory of language acquisition, comprehension, and production. *Cortex, 48*(7), 905–922.

Goldstone, R. L., Landy, D., & Son, J. Y. (2008). A well-grounded education: The role of perception in science and mathematics. In M. de Vega, M. C. Glenberg, & M. A. Graesser (Eds.), *Symbols and embodiment: Debates on meaning and cognition* (pp. 327–355). Oxford University Press.

Goldstone, R. L., Marghetis, T., Weitnauer, E., Ottmar, E. R., & Landy, D. (2017). Adapting perception, action, and technology for mathematical reasoning. *Current Directions in Psychological Science, 26*(5), 434–441.

Greeno, J. G. (1998). The situativity of knowing, learning, and research. *American Psychologist, 53*(1), 5.

Greeno, J. G., Moore, J. L., & Smith, D. R. (1993). *Transfer of situated learning*. In D. K. Detterman & R. J. Sternberg (Eds.), *Transfer on trial: Intelligence, cognition, and instruction* (pp. 99–167). Ablex.

Hadamard, J. (1945). *An essay on the psychology of invention in the mathematical field*. Princeton University Press.

Hamilton, R. H., & Pascual-Leone, A. (1998). Cortical plasticity associated with Braille learning. *Trends in Cognitive Sciences, 2*(5), 168–174.

Haruno, M., Wolpert, D. M., & Kawato, M. (2001). Mosaic model for sensorimotor learning and control. *Neural Computation, 13*(10), 2201–2220.

Haruno, M., Wolpert, D. M., & Kawato, M. (2003, October). Hierarchical MOSAIC for movement generation. *International Congress Series* (Vol. 1250, pp. 575–590). Elsevier.

Hatano, G., & Inagaki, K. (1986). Two courses of expertise. In H. A. H. Stevenson & K. Hakuta (Eds.), *Child development and education in Japan* (pp. 262–272). Freeman.

Hebb, D. O. (1949). *The organization of behavior: A neuropsychological theory*. Chapman & Hall.

Jain, A., Kuo, C., & Sinkarenko, I. (2016). Feedforward dynamics for the control of articulated multi-limb robots. *Multibody System Dynamics, 37*(1), 49–68.

James, W. (1890). *Principles of psychology*. Holt.

Kahan, D. M., Peters, E., Dawson, E., & Slovic, P. (2013). Motivated numeracy and enlightened self-government. *Behavioural Public Policy, 1*, 54–86.

Kahneman, D. (2011). *Thinking, fast and slow*. Macmillan.

Kanizsa, G. (1976). Subjective contours. *Scientific American, 234*(4), 48–53.

Kellman, P. J., & Massey, C. M. (2013). Perceptual learning, cognition, and expertise. *Psychology of learning and motivation* (Vol. 58, pp. 117–165). Academic Press.

Kellman, P. J., Massey, C. M., & Son, J. Y. (2010). Perceptual learning modules in mathematics: Enhancing students' pattern recognition, structure extraction, and fluency. *Topics in Cognitive Science, 2*(2), 285–305.

Khamsi, R. (2004). Jennifer Aniston strikes a nerve. *Brain*. Retrieved from www.nature.com/news/2005/050620/full/news050620-7.html

Knowlton, B. J., Ramus, S. J., & Squire, L. R. (1992). Intact artificial grammar learning in amnesia: Dissociation of classification learning and explicit memory for specific instances. *Psychological Science, 3*(3), 172–179.

Laird, J. E., Newell, A., & Rosenbloom, P. S. (1987). SOAR: An architecture for general intelligence. *Artificial Intelligence, 33*, 1–64.

Landy, D., & Goldstone, R. L. (2007). How abstract is symbolic thought? *Journal of Experimental Psychology: Learning, Memory, and Cognition, 33*(4), 720.

Lave, J. (1988). *Cognition in practice: Mind, mathematics and culture in everyday life*. Cambridge University Press.

Lichtwarck-Aschoff, A., & van Geert, P. (2004). A dynamic systems perspective on social cognition, problematic behaviour, and intervention in adolescence. *European Journal of Developmental Psychology, 1*(4), 399–411.

Liddell, S. K. (2003). *Grammar, gesture, and meaning in American Sign Language*. Cambridge University Press.

Loftus, E. F. (2005). Planting misinformation in the human mind: A 30-year investigation of the malleability of memory. *Learning & Memory, 12*(4), 361–366.

Lukatela, G., & Turvey, M. T. (1994). Visual lexical access is initially phonological: I. Evidence from associative priming by words, homophones, and pseudohomophones. *Journal of Experimental Psychology: General, 123*(2), 107.

Marr, D. (1982). *Vision*. Freeman.

Martindale, D. (2005). One face, one neuron. *Scientific American, 293*(4), 22–24. Retrieved from www.scientificamerican.com/article/one-face-one-neuron/

McClelland, J. L. (2001). Cognitive neuroscience. In N. J. Smelser & P. B. Baltes (Eds.), *International encyclopedia of the social and behavioral sciences*. Elsevier.

Munakata, Y. (1998). Infant perseveration and implications for object permanence theories: A PDP model of the AB task. *Developmental Science, 1*(2), 161–184. https://doi.org/10.1111/1467-7687.00021

Nathan, M. J. (2017). One function of gesture is to make new ideas: Evidence for reciprocity between action and cognition. In R. B. Church, M. W. Alibali, & S. D. Kelly, (Eds.), *Why gesture? How the hands function in speaking, thinking and communicating* (pp. 175–196). John Benjamins. doi.org/10.1075/gs.7.09nat

Nathan, M. J., & Martinez, C. V. (2015). Gesture as model enactment: The role of gesture in mental model construction and inference making when learning from text. *Learning: Research and Practice, 1*(1), 4–37.

Nathan, M. J., Schenck, K., Vinsonhaler, R., Michaelis, J., Swart, M., & Walkington, C. (2020). Embodied geometric reasoning: Dynamic gestures during intuition, insight, and proof. *Journal of Educational Psychology*. doi.org/10.1037/edu0000638

Nathan, M. J., & Walkington, C. (2017). Grounded and embodied mathematical cognition: Promoting mathematical insight and proof using action and language. *Cognitive Research: Principles and Implications, 2*(1), 1–20.

Neisser, U. (1976). *Cognition and reality: Principles and implications of cognitive psychology*. Freeman.

Newcombe, N. S. (2002). The nativist–empiricist controversy in the context of recent research on spatial and quantitative development. *Psychological Science, 13*, 395–401.

Newell, A., & Simon, H. A. (1972). *Human problem solving*. Prentice-Hall.

Nidditch, P. H. (1975). *John Locke: An essay concerning human understanding*. Oxford University Press.

Norman, D. A. (1988). *The psychology of everyday things*. Basic Books.

Norman, D. A. (1999). Affordance, conventions, and design. *Interactions, 6*(3), 38–43.

Pashler, H., Bain, P. M., Bottge, B. A., Graesser, A., Koedinger, K., McDaniel, M., & Metcalfe, J. (2007). *Organizing instruction and study to improve student learning. IES practice guide. NCER 2007-2004*. National Center for Education Research.

Pfister, R., Melcher, T., Kiesel, A., Dechent, P., & Gruber, O. (2014). Neural correlates of ideomotor effect anticipations. *Neuroscience, 259*, 164–171.

Poincaré, H. (1905). Intuition and logic in mathematics. In H. Poincaré (Ed.) *The value of science* (pp. 15–25). Dover Publications.

Rau, M. A. (2020). Comparing multiple theories about learning with physical and virtual representations: Conflicting or complementary effects? *Educational Psychology Review 32*, 297–325.

Rau, M. A., Michaelis, J. E., & Fay, N. (2015). Connection making between multiple graphical representations: A multimethods approach for domain-specific grounding of an intelligent tutoring system for chemistry. *Computers & Education, 82*, 460–485.

Reyna, V. F., Chick, C. F., Corbin, J. C., & Hsia, A. N. (2014). Developmental reversals in risky decision making: Intelligence agents show larger decision biases than college students. *Psychological Science, 25*(1), 76–84.

Rittle-Johnson, B., & Alibali, M. W. (1999). Conceptual and procedural knowledge of mathematics: Does one lead to the other? *Journal of Educational Psychology, 91*(1), 175.

Rittle-Johnson, B., Siegler, R. S., & Alibali, M. W. (2001). Developing conceptual understanding and procedural skill in mathematics: An iterative process. *Journal of Educational Psychology, 93*(2), 346.

Rittle-Johnson, B., & Star, J. R. (2007). Does comparing solution methods facilitate conceptual and procedural knowledge? An experimental study on learning to solve equations. *Journal of Educational Psychology, 99*(3), 561.

Rumelhart, D. E. (1989). The architecture of mind: A connectionist approach. In M. I. Posner (Ed.), *Foundations of cognitive science* (pp. 133–159). MIT Press.

Ryle, G. (1945, January). Knowing how and knowing that: The presidential address. In *Proceedings of the Aristotelian society* (Vol. 46, pp. 1–16). Aristotelian Society, Wiley.

Saffran, J. R., Aslin, R. N., & Newport, E. L. (1996). Statistical learning by 8-month-old infants. *Science, 274*(5294), 1926–1928.

Schneider, W., & Shiffrin, R. M. (1977). Controlled and automatic human information processing: I. Detection, search, and attention. *Psychological Review, 84*(1), 1.

Schwartz, D. L., & Bransford, J. D. (1998). A time for telling. *Cognition and Instruction, 16*(4), 475–5223.

Shapiro, L. (2019). *Embodied cognition* (2nd ed.). Routledge.

Shiffrin, R. M., & Dumais, S. T. (1981). The development of automatism. In J. R. Anderson (Ed.), *Cognitive skills and their acquisition* (pp. 111–140). Erlbaum.

Silva, A. B., & Kellman, P. J. (1999, August). Perceptual learning in mathematics: The algebra-geometry connection. *Proceedings of the Twenty-First Annual Conference of the Cognitive Science Society* (pp. 683–688). Erlbaum.

Simon, H. A. (1982). *Models of bounded rationality.* MIT Press.

Skinner, B. F. (1938/2019). *The behavior of organisms: An experimental analysis.* BF Skinner Foundation.

Smith, L. B., & Thelen, E. (2003). Development as a dynamic system. *Trends in Cognitive Sciences, 7*(8), 343–348.

Spelke, E. S., & Newport, E. L. (1998). *Nativism, empiricism, and the development of knowledge.* In W. Damon & R. M. Lerner (Eds.), *Handbook of child psychology: Theoretical models of human development* (p. 275–340). Wiley.

Spivey, M. J., & Huette, S. (2014). The embodiment of attention in the perception-action loop. In L. Shapiro (Ed.), *Routledge handbooks in philosophy. The Routledge handbook of embodied cognition* (pp. 306–314). Routledge.

Star, J. R. (2005). Reconceptualizing procedural knowledge. *Journal for Research in Mathematics Education, 36*(5), 404–411.

Thelen, E., Schöner, G., Scheier, C., & Smith, L. B. (2001). The dynamics of embodiment: A field theory of infant perseverative reaching. *Behavioral and Brain Sciences, 24*(1), 1–34.

Thomas, L. E., & Lleras, A. (2007). Moving eyes and moving thought: On the spatial compatibility between eye movements and cognition. *Psychonomic Bulletin & Review, 14*(4), 663–668.

Thompson, P. W. (1995). Notation, convention, and quantity in elementary mathematics. In J. T. Sowder & B. P. Schappelle (Eds.), *Providing a foundation for teaching mathematics in the middle grades* (pp. 199–221). State University of New York Press.

VanLehn, K. (1990). *Mind bugs: The origins of procedural misconceptions.* MIT Press.

Wilson, M. (2002). Six views of embodied cognition. *Psychonomic Bulletin & Review, 9*(4), 625–636.

Wilson, M., & Knoblich, G. (2005). The case for motor involvement in perceiving conspecifics. *Psychological Bulletin, 131*, 460–473.

Wilson, T. D., & Schooler, J. W. (1991). Thinking too much: Introspection can reduce the quality of preferences and decisions. *Journal of Personality and Social Psychology, 60*(2), 181.

Wolpert, D. M., Doya, K., & Kawato, M. (2003). A unifying computational framework for motor control and social interaction. *Philosophical Transactions of the Royal Society of London. Series B: Biological Sciences, 358*(1431), 593–602.

Wolpert, D. M., & Kawato, M. (1998). Multiple paired forward and inverse models for motor control. *Neural Networks, 11*(7–8), 1317–1329.

Zander, T., Öllinger, M., & Volz, K. G. (2016). Intuition and insight: Two processes that build on each other or fundamentally differ? *Frontiers in Psychology, 7*.

Zhang, Z., Lei, Y., & Li, H. (2016). Approaching the distinction between intuition and insight. *Frontiers in Psychology, 7*.

Zimmer, C. (2011). 100 trillion connections. *Scientific American, 304*(1), 58–61. Retrieved from www.scientificamerican.com/article/100-trillion-connections/

8

Grounding and Embodied Learning in the Biological Band

8.1 GEL OF ACADEMIC CONTENT AREAS IN THE BIOLOGICAL LEVEL

Although I have shown the importance and ubiquity of unconscious processes for thinking, unconscious processes are not very central to the curricular aims of formal education. It is a similar observation to the one made by Augusto (2010, p. 116) about psychology:

> The concept of unconscious knowledge is fundamental for an understanding of human thought processes and mentation in general; however, the psychological community at large is not familiar with it.

In this section, I show how unconscious processes are critical for understanding and cultivating learning in academic content areas of language arts, mathematics, and science education.

8.1.1 Language Development

The Cognitive Neuroscience of Reading
As Dehaene (2009) has argued, during early reading development, aspects of the brain become repurposed—what he refers to as "neuronal recycling." Letter and word recognition utilize visual circuitry that ordinarily are used for object recognition. Word recognition taps into circuitry in the left hemisphere that are used during language recognition and production. With training, early readers develop a type of super-circuit called the *visual word form area*. This neural system is activated when seeing actual words and also registers close pseudowords that are both visually similar and phonetically similar to words in one's current lexicon. However, it does not respond as strongly to letter combinations that occur as random nonwords.

Speech Perception is Embodied
Some of the basic processes involved in speech perception are learned when infants experience the feedforward and feedback from mouth and tongue movement characteristic of **transduction**. Pat Kuhl and colleagues (2014) showed that the both auditory and motor areas of infants' brains are active in response to speech, which suggests that part of speech perception involves using one's lips and tongue to anticipate the movements that will need

DOI: 10.4324/9780429329098-8

to be made to perceive and experience the sounds. Alison Bruderer and colleagues (2015) explored this hypothesis further. They studied the speech perception of preverbal infants. To reduce the effects of the infants' prior language exposure, they examined English-learning infants' ability to discriminate between unfamiliar speech sounds in their non-native language (Hindi). The investigators then used the placement of teething toys to see if impairing the movement of infants' tongue and lips, articulators that are critical for proper speech production, influenced infant speech perception.

They found that it did! Furthermore, hypotheses of the causal role of these movements for perceptual discrimination and learning was supported. Degradation of speech performance was specific to the oral movements that matched the specific speech sounds. Pacifiers, which restrict infants' mouths to make a round shape with their lips, had a different effect than did teethers, which spread out the lips. The investigators concluded that the ability to auditorily discriminate between unfamiliar speech sounds was not restricted to auditory processing of the speech that they heard, but depended on infants' ability to make speech-like oral actions consistent with the specific speech sounds. The fact that these infants never had experienced these particular sounds before implies that this is a basic mechanism for developing speech understanding.

The influence of motor movement on speech production is even evident in adults. When adult speakers gesture with their arms in ways that are compatible with their phonetic production, the quality of their vowel formation is enhanced. However, no such enhancement is observed when speakers move their arms in meaningless ways even when the same arm joints are used (Bernardis & Gentilucci, 2006).

Reading Comprehension

At a basic level, we have seen with the work on *lick, pick,* and *kick* that people relate simple, isolated, verbs to the actions associated with those verbs. At the heart of Pulvermüller's (2001) neural account of word meaning, a powerful mechanism in the brain is hypothesized in the form of perception/action circuits: As an **Interactionist** perspective would lead us to expect, we do not passively process words as they are perceived, but rather we engage in the actions with which these words are related.

As the above description for making sense of verbs suggests, there is neural evidence that we are sensitive to the *affordances* of objects as well as object names. We do not merely process nouns as static things or verbs as mere descriptions. Rather, we process written language in terms of actions we are highly likely to read about and imagine performing with them. This means that the meaning of nouns does not only emerge from the orthographic forms of the words or from simply the structural properties of the objects the nouns refer to (the shape, color, size, and so forth). Meaning is also formed by what our bodies are physically capable of doing with the things the words refer to.

According to Don Norman (1999, p. 39), *affordances* "refer to the actionable properties between the world and an actor (a person or animal)" and thus, at their core, describe the active relationships between an object, agent, and the agent's abilities and goals. Work by Pulvermüller and others provide neural evidence that we are highly sensitive to the *affordances* of objects, both when they are in our immediate environment (e.g., Graziano et al., 2002) and when they are referred to using words.

That bodily affordances are important for reading comprehension come from a number of studies. Comprehension is higher when, for example, readers are asked to first pretend to perform the actions described in a text, such as pinching one's fingers together when reading about throwing darts (Klatzky, Pellegrino, McCloskey, & Doherty, 1989). MacWhinney (1999) shows how cues in langue shift the perspectives that readers take on a scene and can lead to differences in what readers notice.

What about meaning of larger linguistic units such as phrases and stories? Glenberg and Gallese (2012) describe the *Action-Based Language* model, that integrates principles of motor control and simulation as an account of reading comprehension. In this model, the perception of words elicits predictive responses of the predictor-controller modules in order to anticipate what the reader may need to *do*, just as it would for directing motor movement. This anticipation includes a variety of potential actions in order to preemptively respond to the situation elicited by the words, along with a simulation of these potential actions.

Glenberg and Gallese (2012) offer the example of the sentence *The girl gives the horse an apple*. Parsing *The girl* activates mental imagery for the reader of a girl poised to do something, with a huge number of potential actions cued up, constrained by prior sentences that provide context. Reading the verb phrase starting with *gives* shuts down a host of other actions and then moves to activate forms of giving actions, recipients, objects to give, and so on.

Motor simulation processes will activate the hand and arm movements associated with giving. With sufficient activation and freedom from inhibitions (such as those that might be imposed by testing situations) the reader will likely gesture the simulated act of a giving suited for apples (Hostetter & Alibali, 2008). The reader will likely benefit if she does, since that act will further activate **transductive** processes for reaching, holding, giving and so forth that can support valuable inference making. For example, the reader's giving arm may reach way up, as is appropriate when a child feeds a much taller horse, even though this is nowhere mentioned in the story.

Pickering and Garrod (2007) have empirically shown how predictive processes facilitate language comprehension. For example, readers' comprehension is enhanced when pending words are highly predictable, either because of the context, or because of compatible syntactic cues (Wright & Garrett, 1984). The role of predictive processes for facilitating the development of reading comprehension among emerging readers has also long been known. Palinscar and Brown (1984) reported that spontaneous predicting of story actions (e.g., *what did the horse do next?*) was observed among strong readers. Palinscar and Brown then showed how its routine use in primary grade classrooms helped young readers to improve in their story understanding. Over time, these children internalized the predictive process, which aided their long-term reading development.

8.1.2 Mathematics Education

Mathematics learning presents many challenges for education. Many students struggle to make sense of the symbolic notations, diagrams, and procedures. Students and teachers—in the United States, at least—will, without any sense of irony, publicly proclaim, "I am not really a math person." Yet, from a neuroscience perspective, we are all "math people." We are literally wired for pattern recognition and relational thinking. Mathematics experiences, as with reading, uses neuronal recycling to repurpose regions of the brain that mediate spatial reasoning, visual processing, and basic quantification. Spatial reasoning predicts math performance, and improving spatial abilities contributes to gains in mathematics and science (Newcombe, 2010).

Transduction provides a means for mathematical quantities and operations to be meaningful. For example, when children's directed actions conceptually congruent the mathematical operations they were to perform, they showed superior performance than when performing actions that were not conceptually compatible (Segal, Tversky, & Black, 2014). Children did better on tasks involving discrete, one-to-one operations—as is characteristic with addition—when cued to perform discrete, one-to-one actions. Similarly, they performed better on continuous mathematics involved in number line estimation when they performed a continuous action.

Inverse operations intuitively undo operations, and undoing inverses gets you back where your started (usually). Composing operations offers a way to simulate how sequences of operation will come out, or to recognize that they cannot be performed (like division by zero).

The Cognitive Neuroscience of Mathematics

One of the prevailing hypotheses is that humans share with many species an innate form of mathematical cognition that enables us to represent and manipulate numerical quantities in a nonverbal format. This *approximate number system* (Feigenson, Dehaene, & Spelke, 2004; Wynn, 1998) forms the basis for very basic mathematical thinking, such as rapid number comparison and counting and arithmetic with small quantities of up to 5 or 6.

More recently, cognitive neuroscientists and educational psychologists have shown that this basic system forms the basis for more advanced mathematics, including exact arithmetic for all numerical quantities and even symbolic algebra. As with the emergence of reading from visual and language regions, high-level math recycles neural processes originally involved in space, time, and number (Amalric & Dehaene, 2016). Brain imaging studies using high-resolution whole-brain fMRI show that areas of the brain that the intraparietal sulcus and prefrontal cortex, are involved in the approximate number system, are engaged during more advanced mathematics. The neural system develops a "visual number form area" that selectively responds to written Arabic numerals over letter strings or other images. In general, this math network is not activated by comparable tasks for sentence comprehension and accessing general semantic knowledge.

One notable insight from this work is that there develops a highly specialized network for advanced mathematics that is only observed among professional mathematicians. The brain areas associated with numerical processing only experience sustained activation for "meaningful" mathematics. It is activated only briefly by "meaningless" mathematical statements and completely unaffected by nonmathematical statements matched on visual complexity. This held across topics of analysis, algebra, topology, and geometry. It is not even observed among highly educated non-mathematicians (in this case, humanities professors)!

Scholars have also recently identified the neural basis for a "ratio processing system" used for perceiving nonsymbolic visual ratios. There is evidence that this system is recruited for recognizing, comparing, and calculating with fractions and other forms of proportional reasoning (Lewis, Matthews, & Hubbard, 2016). Tapping into this system via repetitive ratio processing tasks such as card games and video games is proving to be a promising way to improve people's performance on symbolic fractions.

Fractions Education Using Perceptual Learning

Learners struggle with fractions, but they serve a critical role in the mathematical cognitive development of children and adults (National Mathematics Advisory Panel, 2008). Students can learn to interpret and use fractions when they have the appropriate educational experiences. Part of students' struggle is tied to their poor conceptual understanding of what fractions *mean*, and *how* that meaning is depicted by various representational forms, such as symbolic fractions, shaded pie chart, or point along a number line. But sensemaking alone is not sufficient. Students also need to develop their perceptual competencies for visual fraction representations (Koedinger et al. 2012).

Sensemaking competencies draw on some of the verbally mediated Type 2 processing I reviewed in Chapter 3 that address the conceptual aspects of fraction understanding. Rau and Matthews (2017) provide the example of students who are explicitly directed to verbally explain how the fraction showing a numerator over a denominator relates to the number of divisions of a unit-length number line (one that shows a segment extending only from 0 to 1.0).

To develop the visual competencies relevant for fraction understanding students must engage the rapid, nonverbal, implicit Type 1 processing that constitutes **perceptual fluency**. Well-developed perceptual fluency processes greatly aid learning by reducing the cognitive demands of interpreting the visual information and patterns, thus freeing up resources (Kellman & Massey, 2013). They also provide a source of **grounding** by mapping aspects of the fraction concepts to the perceptual chunks.

Perceptual fluency is attained inductively, by exposing students to many instances of visual representations that vary irrelevant features (e.g., the color) and apply them to a range of tasks, while maintaining the essential features for that visual representation (e.g., equal units in a number line).

Rau and colleagues (2015) designed an interactive cognitive tutoring system that implemented sensemaking and perceptual fluency support for fraction learning. The *Fractions Tutor* has reached several thousand students. Experimental studies using control groups show that the Fractions Tutor has helped students to achieve greater learning gains by incorporating sensemaking and perceptual-induction activities together.

Algebra Symbol Manipulation

Most often, the research evidence for GEL comes from early mathematics education that most commonly occurs in the primary grades. Important contributions have also been made in secondary mathematics where the concepts are more abstract and the procedures more complicated. Kellman and colleagues (2010) have shown how the principles of **perceptual learning** apply to learning algebraic symbol manipulation. They developed the *Algebraic Transformations* perceptual learning module to investigate its effects on learning and later problem solving. Participants were 8th and 9th graders currently taking Algebra I. As described earlier, their focus was to train students to made speeded judgments using a classification task for selecting the appropriate symbolic transformation among several false choices. Training took place in two 40-min learning sessions. Critically, students received immediate feedback. Incorrect answers were met with interactive feedback that directed students' attention to the relevant relations that would help them perceive the correct algebraic structure.

The intervention showed impressive results! Accuracy in perceptual classification performance went from about 57% on initial learning trials to about 85% at the end of the learning module. They not only got more items correct, but response time also dropped by about 55%, from nearly 12 s per problem to about 7 s, demonstrating that students had developed greater fluency in perceiving symbolic structure across a range of equations.

What's more, students demonstrated considerable gains in problem-solving performance, even though their training did not include problem-solving activities! This demonstrated that algebra problem solving was highly dependent upon perceptual processes, and these processes can greatly improve with a small but focused training experience. These benefits were also long-lasting. Advantages from perceptual learning were observed at a two-week delayed test, and students even continued to improve. This is consistent with the impact of this method on fraction learning that showed no loss of the perceptual learning gains when tested after a 4-to-5-month delay.

An exciting innovation in GEL that draws on learners' motor control systems to promote algebra symbol manipulation is ***Graspable Math*** (Ottmar et al., 2015). The theory of this approach lies in the realization that, despite its abstract and amodal appearance, people treat algebra symbols like any perceptual object (Landy & Goldstone, 2007). Graspable Math grounds the meaning of algebra symbolic expressions by highlighting its perceptual and structural properties. Students (typically grades 6–10) can use the affordances of a touch-sensitive tablet to highlight and physically move algebraic expressions. Users come to perceive the structure and understand the meaning of algebra manipulation moves through action and perception. There has been a strong evaluation component to this program, with over 10,000 US students experiencing the benefits of symbol grounding through direct action.

Mathematics Imagery Trainer: Ecological Dynamics
Abrahamson and colleagues (Abrahamson & Sánchez-García, 2016) developed the Mathematical Imagery Trainer for Proportion (see Figure 8.1) to explore how students' physical enactments of the covariation of two constant (but unequal) rates using hand motions detected by the Kinect platform fostered an understanding of proportional reasoning. This activity allowed students' unschooled, goal-directed sensorimotor activity to be structured through mediated activity to give rise to formal and generalizable mathematical ideas (Abrahamson, 2015).

Abrahamson and Sánchez-García (2016, p. 203) argue for an **ecological dynamics** account of mathematics education. This theory frames learning as moving in new ways. As such it draws on changes in motor performance as I have described above, as emergent, nonlinear, and self-adaptive processes. Here, mathematical reasoning is very clearly described in terms of nonsymbolic forms of reasoning and representation.

Action Geometry
The **Action Geometry program** is another set of innovations that illustrate the range of embodied learning processes: grounding, offloading, transduction, and participation. I have had the great opportunity to be part of this research and development project. The focus is on an advanced topic, the production of proof during secondary and post-secondary school geometry. The innovations have taken several forms: a relatively low-tech method of prompting movement, and a high-tech motion-capture video game used by individuals and groups.

The *Action Geometry* program draws on earlier work showing how movement benefits mathematics education. Smith and colleagues (Petrick & Martin, 2012; Smith, King, & Hoyte, 2014) demonstrated how primary and secondary grade students' understanding of angles improves when manipulating their body position and movement.

We investigated hypotheses that mathematical intuitions and proof performance are enhanced when producing mathematically relevant actions. An early test of this was investigated in the *action geometry study* (Nathan et al., 2014). We recruited people to generate informal proofs of mathematical conjectures after they engaged in mathematically

FIGURE 8.1 Mathematical Imagery Trainer for Proportion (MIT-P).
The display screen turns green when participants maintain the expected fixed interval as they move vertically with one hand in proportion to the other (in this case, 1:2 ratio).

relevant actions or carefully matched irrelevant actions. The comparison is important for testing whether relevant actions cause observed differences, or if benefits are because actions *generally* help—through elevated alertness, or by some other mechanism. I will focus on the *Triangle Inequality Conjecture*.

> Mary came up with the following conjecture: For any triangle, the sum of the lengths of any two sides must be greater than the length of the remaining side. Provide a justification as to why Mary's conjecture is true or false.

Prior to reading the conjecture, participants were directed to touch colored dots projected onto an interactive whiteboard. The dot positions were scaled with the participant's height and arm span. (We have also used paper versions of this task, tacked to walls.)

For the *mathematically relevant-actions* condition (Figure 8.2, right side), participants stood midway between each pair of dots and simultaneously touched dots of the same color with each hand. The dot pairs were positioned progressively farther apart, starting at the body midline and extending outward. The final dot pairs were positioned to be just out of reach, so the participant's chest came into contact with the whiteboard (i.e., the altitude was reduced to zero). These actions embody the idea that when one side of a triangle (in this case, the base) grows longer than the sum of the remaining two sides (participants' arms) the sides no longer form a triangle. In the irrelevant-action condition (Figure 8.2, left side), participants touched the dots in the same positions with each hand individually. Thus, they did not experience forming the series of triangles, including the final, degenerate triangle.

We found that making mathematically relevant actions benefited participants significantly more in generating appropriate mathematical insights and producing a mathematically valid proof. What's more, these beneficial effects of mathematically relevant actions appeared to be unconscious. Most participants reportedly had no sense that the actions they performed were related to the mathematics they were asked about. When they were alerted to the relevance of the actions in the form of a pedagogical hint, the benefits were even greater (!) and both valid insights and proof performance climbed.

We also learned that some of the relevant mathematical knowledge students expressed was simply not present in their verbal utterances but in their gestures. Analyses of student proof performance showed that students' speech and gestures *independently* contributed significantly to the statistical models of what students actually knew about the mathematics conjectures (Pier et al., 2019). In order to provide the most accurate account of how

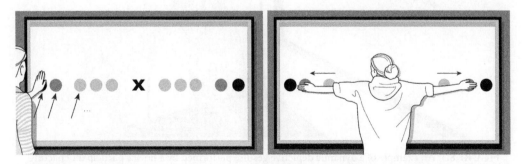

FIGURE 8.2 Participants touch dots to perform directed actions where (right panel) mathematically relevant actions form a set of possible and impossible triangles that enact the triangle inequality conjecture, or (left panel) mathematically irrelevant actions that serve as an experimental control.

students thought, both verbal and nonverbal channels of information were needed. This has implications for principles of assessment in a later section.

This study provided early support for the **action-cognition transduction hypothesis**, which proposes that task-relevant actions can induce cognitive states that enhance intellectual performance and learning. It showed that the benefits can arise via both unconscious and conscious processes.

This work, while successful, prompted a question: *How* does action influence the kind of generalized thinking that is so crucial for proof? The answer relies on the role of the body to support grounding and offloading, as well as transduction. It led to the appreciation of a special class of actions called *dynamic gestures*. *Dynamic gestures* go beyond the static properties of an object and strive to depict movement-based transformations. Examples of this include showing how a triangle might grow or shrink but keep its angles constant.

Garcia and Infante (2012) were among the first to distinguish dynamic and static gestures in mathematics. They observed dynamic gestures were most frequent when students engaged in conceptual reasoning. Figure 8.3 shows an example of a student's reasoning about the following conjecture.

The segment that joins the midpoints of two sides of any triangle is parallel to the third side.

It's a rather bold claim, since to be true, it must be so for *any and all* triangles. During her exploration, the student first makes a static (iconic) triangle shape with her hands and arms. As she does so, she reports

"this is … false" (1:09), because the statement won't hold for triangles "with varying lengths … at all three sides, the midsegment would therefore not be parallel to the third side."

FIGURE 8.3 An example of a dynamic depictive gesture performed by a novice participant enacting generalizable properties of a mathematical object (triangle) to reason through the midsegment conjecture: *The segment that joins the midpoints of two sides of any triangle is parallel to the third side.*

But then she starts to distort the triangle with dynamic gestures. She explores the conjecture by skewing a triangular shape using her forearm while maintaining a midsegment with her other flat hand. This reveals to her that the midsegment always stays parallel to its base no matter how flat or tall the triangle. She continues to report:

"(1:51) If you have a very, very long side going up, and a short siii …
    [She pauses, touches her hand to her mouth, then resumes speaking]
    … a shorter side, it would…"
    [at 1:58 she makes the dynamic gesture shown and pauses speaking]
    [She studies her dynamic gesture, and at 2:04 she resumes]
    "Actually, I'm gonna change it to true … because if you take the midsegments of a triangle it would, it would be parallel."

It's a striking example. By performing and observing her own dynamic gestures, she made a realization that reversed her initial intuition, and supported mathematically valid reasoning. This illustrates several forms of GEL: The initial object of interest was **grounded** using body-based resources; she **offloaded** visualization of skewing the triangle while also maintaining the location and angle of the midsegment. The movements, initially directed to fulfill cognitive goals, then fed back to those cognitive processes via **transduction** with a contradiction that caused her to update her mental model and change her mind.

Even when controlling for expertise, prior knowledge of geometry, and spatial reasoning ability, proof performance was statistically related to one's use of dynamic gestures (Nathan et al., 2020). Dynamic gestures allowed participants to physically experience generalized properties through enactment, as shown in Figure 8.3. Intuition, as predicted, was statistically associated with gesture production but not participants' speech.

By demonstrating the importance of gesture production on intuition and proof performance, the next logical questions were: Can we design learning experiences that elicit these gestures to assist their mathematical reasoning? My colleagues and I explored this next using a video game platform.

Players of *The Hidden Village* are invited into an embodied video game for promoting mathematical reasoning and proof practices. Players are first told they crash landed during a visit to the Planet Socatoah-3 that has left them isolated from their group and in unfamiliar lands. Players encounter various members of an alien community residing in The Hidden Village, who invite the players to perform everyday actions such as cooking, medical procedures, dancing, etc. By matching the movements of the characters in the game, players engage in *directed actions* that are designed to be (covertly) mathematically relevant for reasoning about various geometry conjectures that are presented later to the players.

The game uses the Kinect 2 sensor array to track players' movements in real time. This determines whether players matched movements of in-game characters, and earn glyphs that can be used to acquire the energy pods they need to return home. The basic set-up and flow of the game is shown in Figure 8.4. A video of the video game and how it is used in classrooms is available at this link: https://multiplex.videohall.com/presentations/1662. The game has been played by hundreds of middle and high school students in lab settings, summer programs, and in students' classrooms in urban and rural communities.

So what did we learn from these studies? The central finding is that game play helps students to produce mathematically valid proofs (Nathan & Walkington, 2017; Walkington et al., 2019).

During the game, players' mathematically relevant movements help to **ground** the mathematical ideas. As predicted by the action-cognition **transduction** hypothesis, these

FIGURE 8.4 Students playing the embodied video game, *The Hidden Village* (*Top panel*). (*Bottom panel*) Game Flow of *The Hidden Village* (starting from left to right): Meet a Villager; mimic *directed actions* by villagers for each conjecture; generate intuition, insight and proof; select a multiple-choice response; and finally receive a token of knowledge and expose more of the village map.

mathematically relevant movements elicit cognitive processes that support deep and meaningful mathematical reasoning. Mathematically irrelevant directed actions are not as beneficial (Walkington et al., 2020). Dynamic gestures were again the strongest predictors of mathematically valid proofs, elicited by following the in-game characters.

As Figure 8.5 shows, students performed better when they made gestures. The game playing experience proved highly beneficial for high school students who were in a program for first-time college-attending students (Walkington & Nathan et al., 2020). We also found that the emphasis on body movement as a way to ground and **offload** mathematical ideas onto actions was very helpful for English Language Learners/Limited English Proficiency students from a Title 1 high school (Nathan & Swart, 2020 ETR&D). Furthermore, as Figure 8.5 shows, the experience was especially helpful when students formed extended representations of mathematical objects and operations across the bodies of their classmates in the form of joint, collaborative gestures (Walkington & Nathan et al., 2019). This will be explored in greater detail when I discuss **learning as participation** in a later chapter.

8.1.3 Science Education

Sometimes the concrete grounding experiences that are taught must be linked to learners' conceptual understanding in order to generalize. For examples, science students can become fluent with visual representations in physics even when they have not developed the conceptual understanding of the phenomenon that is depicted (Airey & Linder, 2009). One early experiment demonstrating this was performed by Scholckow & Judd (described in Judd, 1908; and replicated and extended by Hendrickson & Schroeder, 1941). Children practiced throwing darts at a target underwater. One group of children received a scientific and

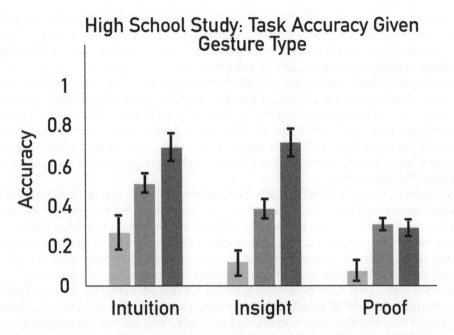

FIGURE 8.5 Performance differences for high school students proving geometric conjectures depending on whether and how each of the learners in a group gestured (from Walkington, Wang et al., 2020). Light Grey = No Gestures, Medium Grey = Individual Gestures, Dark Grey = Collaborative Gestures.

mathematical explanation of refraction of light which causes light to bend and the apparent location of the target under water to be deceptive. The other group only practiced, receiving no scientific instruction. Without the scientific explanation, the actions could be mastered but they were not deeply understood. Both groups did equally well on the practice task which involved a target 12 inches under water, but the group with a scientific explanation did much better when asked to transfer to a situation where the target was now under only 4 inches of water. Combining abstract instruction with concrete experiences is often better than either one alone.

The question of how to combine more concrete and more abstract experiences most effectively for science learning has been the subject of some inquiry of its own. Goldstone and Son (2005) provided learners with concrete and abstract learning experiences for teaching about the nonlinear dynamics of complex systems. They found the largest learning gains and best transfer to a new complex system when learning started with the perceptually rich (concrete) materials that subsequently "faded" to more idealized (abstract) presentation. In this approach, the core scientific ideas are grounded in students' perceptual experiences. Further studies of the various ways to combine concrete and abstract experiences have shown that *concreteness fading*, which starts with concrete and shifts to abstract, offers the best learning and transfer outcomes (Braithwaite & Goldstone, 2013; Fyfe et al., 2014)

Transduction and Simulation in Science Education
Transduction of motor system behaviors to cognitive processes are evident in science learning. The role of simulation environments that can elicit directed actions is also opening up new avenues for engineering and science education, just as in mathematics education.

One study (Kontra, Lyons, Fischer, & Beilock, 2015) showed that student learning of the concept of torque (see the prior discussion of using the right-hand rule, in Section 3.3.4) is enhanced when students experience forces associated with angular momentum. Participants read about angular momentum and its influences and then experienced one of a variety of resistive forces from holding the axle of spinning wheels, or they observed but did not experience the resistive force (control group). A spinning wheel produces an angular-momentum vector that points along the axle of the wheel. Torque is the rate of change of angular momentum. Thus, when the axle of a spinning wheel is tilted, say from vertical to horizontal, someone holding the axle experiences a resistive force. If a wheel is spinning faster, or a larger wheel is used, there is greater angular momentum and a greater resistive force from the larger torque.

The findings across both laboratory- and classroom-based interventions showed that the sensorimotor experience of torque (relative to observation) led to improved assessment performance as shown in pre-test/posttest differences, accuracy on delayed quizzes, and delayed homework completion. Neural data obtained from functional magnetic resonance imaging (fMRI) showed increased activation of sensorimotor systems used for dynamic physical concepts. This activation, in turn, enhances understanding of torque and angular momentum. Thus, physically experiencing torque for this phenomenon improved conceptual performance on tests of angular momentum and torque. This appeared to be mediated by activation of sensorimotor brain systems used to simulate past actions, but not past (passive) observations of those actions.

Mixed-reality environments provide ways to elicit enhanced scientific thinking through physical and sensory engagement. Lindgren (2015; Lindgren et al., 2016) describes interventions that uses a mixed-reality laser-scanning and floor-projected simulation to "cue" body movements, much like the directed actions in action geometry. He found that body cueing led to higher achievement in understanding how objects move in space and more positive attitudes towards science learning. Enyedy and Danish (2015) also used a mixed-reality environment to support students' understanding of Newtonian force using motion-tracking technology. They found that verbal and physical reflection on embodied activity and first-person embodied play allowed students to engage deeply with challenging concepts.

Mina Johnson-Glenberg's *SmallLab* provides a range of mixed-reality learning experiences that foster conceptual learning through body cueing and directed action. Students in one study who engaged in higher levels of embodiment showed gains in generative physics knowledge, whereas the low-embodied group decreased in their knowledge (Lindgren & Johnson-Glenberg, 2013). Johnson-Glenberg and her colleagues have shown across a range of immersive learning environments that *congruency* is a critical design consideration (Johnson-Glenberg, Birchfield, Tolentino, & Koziupa, 2014; Lindgren & Johnson-Glenberg, 2013). For example, centripetal force is best learned when the environment elicits movements involving circular motion rather than operating a linear slider bar (Johnson-Glenberg, Megowan-Romanowicz, Birchfield, & Savio-Ramos, 2016).

With the rise of virtual manipulatives and learning environments come important questions of whether they foster comparable learning to the experiences with physical materials. Triona and Klahr (2003) set up close comparisons for elementary science education learning about designing effective experiments using the control-of-variables paradigm. Fourth- and fifth-grade students were assigned to either the virtual or physical groups and trained to design unconfounded experiments using control of variables through direct instruction. Children designed four paired-comparison experiments to determine which properties of materials mattered for assessing which wooden ramps led to balls rolling farthest, and how far springs of various dimensions will stretch. Notably (as this *was* itself about control of variables!)

the physical materials and computer-based virtual interventions were otherwise identical in terms of the teacher, lesson plan, script for instruction, time on task, use of examples, pedagogical probes and, learners' choices of how to design and set up the experiments.

The results showed that the quality of experimental design changed significantly from pretraining to the testing. However, there were no differences between the physical and virtual conditions. They also found no differences in the degree to which children's explanations of their designs mentioned their intent to control of all the other variables. The results held both for the group averages and on an individual basis.

A subsequent study (Klahr, Triona, & Williams, 2007) involved middle school students designing simple cars propelled by mousetraps. This intervention used discovery learning rather than direct instruction. The results replicated the general findings that showed comparable learning and quality of experimental designs for isolating the relevant causal factors in car performance. These findings are important because they show that comparable cognitive processes are invoked in virtual and simulation environments. These educational environments are growing in areas of driving, navigation, and medical training (Checa & Bustillo, 2020). It seems that many of the same types of learning are possible when carefully designed virtual environments are available.

8.2 GEL PRINCIPLES

There are a number of general principles regarding learning at the biological level from the review of the scientific literature.

8.2.1 GEL Principles for Student Learning

Grounding of meaning in the biological portion of the GEL timescale is very different than in the conscious spectrum. For these faster processes, grounding is achieved by automating one's responses through the construction of procedural knowledge, and by forming patterns of recognition through perceptual learning. These contribute to creation of affordances where the environment is experienced in terms of how it suits the person's body, actions, and goals. True to the idea of knowing-how, these forms of grounding alter how the world is experienced, not just how it is seen or felt. They actually "grab" one's attention and mental resources, often completely without awareness of the person (Shiffrin & Schneider, 1977). When new knowledge is grounded in these ways, people *feel* as though they know, and are often quite confident in their self-assessment.

The **principle of grounding via perceptual learning, procedural automaticity, and affordances** captures all of these important ways of meaning making. Grounding via perceptual learning addresses the importance of perceptual competencies (Kellman & Massey, 2013) and perceptual fluencies (Rau et al., 2017) that substitute for reasoning. Earlier, I provided examples from chess, word learning, and ratio processing showing how people make important intellectual realizations by activating patterns of recognition rather than through deliberative processes such as search or logical reasoning. Lest perceptual competencies be thought of as an inferior form of thinking, it is good to point out some of the benefits (Kellman & Massey, 2013, pp. 156ff.): (1) learned patterns of perceptual competence generalize to novel instances that are perceived as similar, thus supporting transfer and abstraction; (2) fluency is achieved, which contributes to faster performance, less effort, and reduced load on attention and cognitive processing; (3) gains in implicit pattern recognition do not require accompanying changes in explicit, declarative knowledge; and (4) learning effects often last far longer than memory for facts and for steps in non-automated procedures.

The automating of one's well-practiced responses recognizes how procedures come to make ideas happen. These highly refined procedures offer a way of knowing-how that gives them meaning. Grounding though affordances complementary fashion to perceptual learning and procedural automaticity. Interactions with the world convey what things mean in reference to what one can naturally do with them.

In addition to grounding, an emergent principle of embodied learning is the **action-cognition transduction principle** that knowledge can be in nonverbal form, accessed and expressed through movement. For example, the transduction support in the action geometry project show that movement serves as an alternate channel of sorts for learning. Predictive motor programs enable learners to conduct simulations that naturally support inference making, which can otherwise be rare and effortful. This also has implications for instruction and learning environment designs, and for learning assessments.

8.2.2 GEL Principles for Learning Environment Design

An important design principle that comes from this body of research is to distinguish the processing demands that educators wish to develop in the learner from those they do not wish to develop. Learning environments should seek to reduce the cognitive demands for those parts of the learning experience that are not part of the learning objectives. This is part of the premise of Cognitive Load Theory (e.g., Sweller, 2010). In this work, the goal is to reduce *extraneous cognitive load*, such as use of technical jargon, while managing the demands intrinsic to the complexity of the information to be used and learned. An apt name for this then is the **principle of reduced cognitive load.**

The forms of grounding that operate at the biological band of the GEL time scale each provide support for reducing the cognitive load for those aspects of the task that would compete for limited learning resources. Perceptual learning offloads reasoning and search to pattern matching and perceptual fluency. Procedural automaticity reduces demands of performing sequential operations. Affordances develop that attune the sensorimotor system to the perceptual qualities of the environment that match one's abilities and goals.

The computer desktop is one of the classic modern examples that show the power of applying these design considerations to optimize one's intellectual efforts. Most computer users do not need to know about the details of directory structures, file extensions, removing files, and so on. The affordances of drag-and-drop icons let these important tasks be done so the primary tasks can be accomplished. The right-hand-rule is another such affordance to help engineers focus their limited efforts. Reading is a similar demand. For many students, being caught up in the enormous processing demands of letter and word recognition, meaning construction, inference making, and so on would make many other tasks, such as understanding a historical record or building a device from written directions nearly impossible. The educational community recognizes that reading needs to be automated. (So much so, we are susceptible to phenomena such as the Stroop Effect; see Reader Activities.) This frees up those precious resources for the intellectual demands that are needed for reasoning and learning.

8.2.3 GEL Principles for Instruction and the Design of Learning Experiences

Several principles emerge for instruction and the design of learning environments that can foster learning and successful performance. Learning experiences that draw on **transduction** rely on activating the two-way connections formed between cognitive processes and goal-directed sensorimotor processes. Transduction based interventions can cultivate conceptual understanding through nonverbal, action-based interventions. This is a valuable alternative channel in which to develop learners' intuitions as well as contribute to understanding complex knowledge structures. Examples from the action geometry project as well as those in science education show how emerging motion-capture technology and mixed reality (MR, including augmented reality and virtual reality) offer promising new learning experiences for eliciting directed actions that support advanced understanding of STEM concepts. For these to be effective, the directed actions must be *conceptually relevant* to the target concepts. In practice, videos of successful reasoning provide rich data sources of conceptually relevant motor behavior that can be mined for inclusion in these embodied learning environments.

Research on procedural and perceptual learning also offer promising principles for effective instruction and learning environment design. Recall that procedural learning involves the improvement of separate action steps, each of which may initially be slow, effortful, and error prone. For procedural learning to reach automaticity, it is vital that the training experiences offer consistent presentation (Schneider & Shiffrin, 1977). It is through these consistently mapped responses to a select set of training activities that the benefits of fast, accurate responses with little or no demands on attention and cognitive load arise. Distractions and other task-irrelevant demands on cognitive and attentional resources should be kept to a minimum. The training experiences should include very little verbal instruction, but offer immediate feedback. This is because the goal of procedural learning is to speed up performance of a fixed sequence of actions. Collectively, these can be articulated within the **principle of procedural learning.**

In contrast, perceptual learning seeks to extract invariant properties across a wide range of patterns through repeated exposure. As Rau and others (2017) have shown, perceptual fluency for visual representations can develop prior to forming a conceptual understanding of what those representations stand for. The learning experiences for this depends on presenting many *varied* (i.e., not consistent) examples in short trials focused on classification. Exposure to contrasting cases offers one such instructional method. The **principle of perceptual learning** states that by varying those features across cases that are not of central importance, learners come to identify the invariant visual features that are essential for accurate classification. While the objectives of procedural and perceptual learning are distinct and their instructional designs differ, the development of these nonverbal processes both operate most efficiently with minimal, verbal instruction.

8.2.4 GEL Principles for Assessment

The central principle for assessment to come out of studies in the biological portion of the GEL time scale is the **principle of assessing nonverbal ways of knowing.** Assessment methods that restrict students to verbal formats of expressing what they know often overlook implicit knowledge. Assessment methods that support showing what one can provide ways to document nonverbal knowledge. Analyses of video clips of students' gestures provide an example of how nonverbal reporting can enhance assessment practices, as I showed in the case of geometry proofs. The preparation for future learning approach to assessing transfer is an example described earlier in this chapter.

Other methods that assess perceptual competency and perceptual fluency examine the speed as well as the accuracy on classification tasks, and the strength and speed of the associations that people have among different images and concepts. Educators should be skeptical when using verbal language-intensive ways of assessing forms of knowing-how, such as perceptual and procedural knowledge. Students will meet those task demands but their verbal

TABLE 8.1

Principles for grounded and embodied learning, design, instruction, and assessment at the biological portion of the GEL timescale

Educational concerns	Principle
Learning	The principle of grounding via perceptual learning, procedural automaticity, and affordances
	Embodied learning via simulation and action-cognition transduction, where actions induce cognitive processes, and cognitive processes induce actions
Design	Principle of reduced cognitive load to minimize task-irrelevant demands by using all three forms of grounding in design
Instruction & learning Experiences	Principles of procedural and perceptual learning
Assessment	The principle of assessing nonverbal ways of knowing

accounts of these unconscious processes will often be quite inaccurate, and likely to better reflect what they think they know, rather than what they have actually learned.

The principles for learning, design, and assessment are summarized in Table 8.1.

8.2.5 Philosophy of Mind: Shapiro's Replacement Hypothesis

Shapiro's (2019) Replacement Hypothesis is highly relevant to this chapter's treatment of GEL. Recall that Foundationalism is based on a core tenet that knowledge is built up from a dedicated representational architecture in the mind. The nature-nurture debate is largely about where and when this representational architecture comes about, but both assume its central role in human behavior. The Replacement Hypothesis claims that there is no need for a dedicated representational architecture for knowledge in the mind since the representational needs can be adequately *replaced* by other systems during their normal operations.

Shapiro points to the dynamic sensorimotor interactions of the body with the world as offering such a replacement. In this proposal, perceptions and actions work directly with intellectual processes to achieve goals and operate successfully in the world. As the claim goes, there is no need to represent the world by some kind of internal *map* when *the world itself is the ideal map* (Brooks, 1991; Dreyfus, 2002). This analyses conjures for me the clever short story by Jorge Louis Borges (1946/1998, p. 325), *On Exactitude in Science*, in which he writes,

> In time, those Unconscionable Maps no longer satisfied, and the Cartographers Guilds struck a Map of the Empire whose size was that of the Empire, and which coincided point for point with it.

I appreciate the absurdity of the perfect map as representation, because, as Borges implies, in attaining representational perfection, it is not a representation at all!

The embodied learning processes of affordances and action-cognition transduction offer a plausible approach to satisfying the Replacement Hypothesis. Each draws on the framework of Interactionism, which allows that sensorimotor processes form emergent representations as they are needed (Allen & Bickhard, 2013). The predictive orientation of the human mind provides for the simulation of plausible scenarios that are either reinforced or culled as more sensorimotor information comes in. The feedforward and feedback mechanisms modulate behaviors at multiple levels creating the dynamic systems performance that has been used to model such things as navigation, object permanence, language learning and production, and visual (and other sensory) illusions. Shapiro concedes that the issue is unresolved. I agree with his instincts that embodied accounts of intellectual behavior offer promising alternatives for a system of learning that would seem imminently more flexible for accommodating the fluid nature of an ever-changing world.

8.3 SUMMARY

Knowledge and learning are conceptualized as the emergent effects from patterns of activation across many interacting neurons. These activations are largely made through associations that are built up over time and can become strengthened with repetition and feedback. These give rise to a way of knowing called *knowing-how*, which enables rapid ways of recognizing, interpreting, and evaluating the world around us through the lens of these patterns of activation. These patterns also are the basis for implicit bias (Devine, 1989), which can lead to people carrying our discriminatory practices even when they may contradict their values for equitable treatment.

Neuronal recycling (e.g., Dehaene, 2009) provides an account of how new capabilities arise as cultural demands change. Areas of the brain selected for basic processes such as auditory processing, object recognition, spatial reasoning, and approximate number processing get recruited into new societal roles that show adaptation to the changing environment and cognitive demands.

The macro-level behaviors of these aggregate neural circuits can be modeled as nonlinear dynamic systems. This model allows for the plasticity of the system that supports learning and development. This also provides an account of how graded representations are achieved that enables partial matching and bistable perceptual experiences such as those I showed for several optical illusions. These neural systems operate in a reactive (feedback) manner that helps the system to self-regulate and maintain functioning within a highly variable environment. They also operate in a predictive (feedforward) manner, offering resources as they are anticipated rather than waiting until they are needed. This has the benefits of improving readiness and survival, while also supporting inference making and simulation of the world as it might be once one's actions are carried out.

These insights about learning at the neural level, however, remain a long way from prescribing effective educational interventions. As Bruer (1997) has argued, this is still a bridge too far. These important insights do, however, provide the foundational evidence and theory of why a GEL approach to these educational concerns can, in principle, be achieved. As I argued earlier, part of the enduring chasm from neuroscience to education is also because the bridge, metaphorically speaking, is often designed and built starting from the neuroscience "side" of the divide. In this section, I compile principles starting from the educational side, connecting academic practice to emerging principles of GEL.

8.4 READER ACTIVITIES

8.4.1 Action-Cognition Transduction: Inducing Cognitive States Through Action

i.   This is a good activity to do with a partner or video record yourself.
ii.   Perform the following movements as fluidly as you can.
iii. Consider whether the following mathematical claim is ever false or always true.
iv.   Answer TRUE or FALSE as quickly as you can after reading it. What is your first impression?

```
The opposite angles formed by two lines that cross are
always equal.
```

FIGURE 8.6 Mathematically relevant directed actions.

v.   While standing, not holding anything in your hands, explain out loud why you believe
       your answer to be TRUE or FALSE.
vi.   Review the video or your partner's observations.
vii.   How did the movements affect their reasoning?
viii. Pose this task to someone else. However, this time don't have them do the movements
       until <u>after</u> they give their first impression (TRUE/FALSE) and explanation. Then have
       them explain again.
ix.   How did the movements affect their reasoning?

The conjecture is known as the vertical angles theorem and it is always true for lines in a
common plane (like drawn on a flat surface). It is possible to experience the relationship
between the angles that are opposite to one another when one's arms open and close like
scissors.

REFERENCES

Abrahamson, D. (2015). The monster in the machine, or why educational technology needs embodied design. In V. R. Lee
    (Ed.), *Learning Technologies and the Body: Integration and Implementation* (pp. 21–38). Routledge.
Abrahamson, D., & Sánchez-García, R. (2016). Learning is moving in new ways: The ecological dynamics of mathematics
    education. *Journal of the Learning Sciences, 25*(2), 203–239.
Airey, J., & Linder, C. (2009). A disciplinary discourse perspective on university science learning: Achieving fluency in a
    critical constellation of modes. *Journal of Research in Science Teaching: The Official Journal of the National Association
    for Research in Science Teaching, 46*(1), 27–49.
Allen, J. W., & Bickhard, M. H. (2013). Stepping off the pendulum: Why only an action-based approach can transcend the
    nativist–empiricist debate. *Cognitive Development, 28*(2), 96–133.
Amalric, M., & Dehaene, S. (2016). Origins of the brain networks for advanced mathematics in expert mathematicians.
    Proceedings of the National Academy of Sciences, 113(18), 4909–4917.
Augusto, L. M. (2010). Unconscious knowledge: A survey. *Advances in Cognitive Psychology, 6*, 116.
Bernardis, P., & Gentilucci, M. (2006). Speech and gesture share the same communication system. *Neuropsychologia,
    44*(2), 178–190.
Borges, J. L. (1998). *Collected fictions* (Trans. A. Hurley). Penguin.
Braithwaite, D. W., & Goldstone, R. L. (2013). Integrating formal and grounded representations in combinatorics learning.
    Journal of Educational Psychology, 105(3), 666.
Brooks, R. A. (1991). Intelligence without representation. *Artificial Intelligence, 47*(1–3), 139–159.
Bruderer, A. G., Danielson, D. K., Kandhadai, P., & Werker, J. F. (2015). Sensorimotor influences on speech perception in
    infancy. *Proceedings of the National Academy of Sciences, 112*(44), 13531–13536.
Bruer, J. T. (1997). Education and the brain: A bridge too far. *Educational Researcher, 26*(8), 4–16.
Checa, D., & Bustillo, A. (2020). A review of immersive virtual reality serious games to enhance learning and training.
    Multimedia Tools and Applications, 79(9), 5501–5527.
Dehaene, S. (2009). *Reading in the brain: The new science of how we read.* Penguin.
Devine, P. G. (1989). Stereotypes and prejudice: Their automatic and controlled components. *Journal of Personality and
    Social Psychology, 56*(1), 5–18.
Dreyfus, H. L. (2002). Intelligence without representation – Merleau-Ponty's critique of mental representation The rele-
    vance of phenomenology to scientific explanation. *Phenomenology and the Cognitive Sciences, 1*(4), 367–383.

Enyedy, N., & Danish, J. (2015). Learning physics through play and embodied reflection in a mixed reality learning environment. In *Learning Technologies and the Body* (pp. 109–123). Routledge.

Feigenson, L., Dehaene, S., & Spelke, E. (2004). Core systems of number. *Trends in Cognitive Sciences*, *8*(7), 307–314.

Fyfe, E. R., McNeil, N. M., Son, J. Y., & Goldstone, R. L. (2014). Concreteness fading in mathematics and science instruction: A systematic review. *Educational Psychology Review*, *26*(1), 9–25.

Garcia, N., & Infante, N. E. (2012). Gestures as facilitators to proficient mental modelers. In L. R. Van Zoest, J.-J. Lo, & J. L. Kratky (Eds.), Proceedings of the 34th Annual Meeting of the North American Chapter of the International Group for the Psychology of Mathematics Education (pp. 289–295). Western Michigan University.

Glenberg, A. M., & Gallese, V. (2012). Action-based language: A theory of language acquisition, comprehension, and production. *Cortex*, *48*(7), 905–922.

Goldstone, R. L., & Son, J. Y. (2005). The transfer of scientific principles using concrete and idealized simulations. *The Journal of the Learning Sciences*, *14*(1), 69–110.

Graziano, M. S., Taylor, C. S. & Moore, T. (2002). Complex movements evoked by microstimulation of precentral cortex. *Neuron*, *34*, 841–851.

Hendrickson, G., & Schroeder, W. H. (1941). Transfer of training in learning to hit a submerged target. *Journal of Educational Psychology*, *32*(3), 205.

Hostetter, A. B., & Alibali, M. W. (2008). Visible embodiment: Gestures as simulated action. *Psychonomic Bulletin & Review*, *15*(3), 495–514.

Johnson-Glenberg, M. C., Birchfield, D. A., Tolentino, L., & Koziupa, T. (2014). Collaborative embodied learning in mixed reality motion-capture environments: Two science studies. *Journal of Educational Psychology*, *106*(1), 86.

Johnson-Glenberg, M. C., Megowan-Romanowicz, C., Birchfield, D. A., & Savio-Ramos, C. (2016). Effects of embodied learning and digital platform on the retention of physics content: Centripetal force. *Frontiers in Psychology*, *7*, 1819.

Judd, C. H. (1908). The relation of special training and general intelligence. *Educational Review*, *36*, 28–42.

Kellman, P. J., & Massey, C. M. (2013). Perceptual learning, cognition, and expertise. *Psychology of learning and motivation* (Vol. 58, pp. 117–165). Academic Press.

Kellman, P. J., Massey, C. M., & Son, J. Y. (2010). Perceptual learning modules in mathematics: Enhancing students' pattern recognition, structure extraction, and fluency. *Topics in Cognitive Science*, *2*(2), 285–305.

Klahr, D., Triona, L. M., & Williams, C. (2007). Hands on what? The relative effectiveness of physical versus virtual materials in an engineering design project by middle school children. *Journal of Research in Science Teaching*, *44*(1), 183–203.

Klatzky, R. L., Pellegrino, J. W., McCloskey, B. P., & Doherty, S. (1989). Can you squeeze a tomato? The role of motor representations in semantic sensibility judgments. *Journal of Memory and Language*, *28*(1), 56–77.

Koedinger, K. R., Corbett, A. T., & Perfetti, C. (2012). The knowledge-learning-instruction framework: Bridging the science-practice chasm to enhance robust student learning. *Cognitive Science*, *36*(5), 757–798.

Kontra, C., Lyons, D. J., Fischer, S. M., & Beilock, S. L. (2015). Physical experience enhances science learning. *Psychological Science*, *26*(6), 737–749.

Kuhl, P. K., Ramírez, R. R., Bosseler, A., Lin, J. F. L., & Imada, T. (2014). Infants' brain responses to speech suggest analysis by synthesis. *Proceedings of the National Academy of Sciences*, *111*(31), 11238–11245.

Landy, D., & Goldstone, R. L. (2007). How abstract is symbolic thought? *Journal of Experimental Psychology: Learning, Memory, and Cognition*, *33*(4), 720.

Lewis, M. R., Matthews, P. G., & Hubbard, E. M. (2016). Neurocognitive architectures and the nonsymbolic foundations of fractions understanding. *Development of mathematical cognition* (pp. 141–164). Academic Press.

Lindgren, R. (2015). Getting into the cue: Embracing technology-facilitated body movements as a starting point for learning. In *Learning Technologies and the Body* (pp. 51–66). Routledge.

Lindgren, R., & Johnson-Glenberg, M. (2013). Emboldened by embodiment: Six precepts for research on embodied learning and mixed reality. *Educational Researcher*, *42*(8), 445–452.

Lindgren, R., Tscholl, M., Wang, S., & Johnson, E. (2016). Enhancing learning and engagement through embodied interaction within a mixed reality simulation. *Computers & Education*, *95*, 174–187.

MacWhinney, B. (1999). The emergence of language from embodiment. In B. MacWhinney (Ed.), *The Emergence of Language* (pp. 213–256). Lawrence Erlbaum Associates, Inc.

Nathan, M. J., Schenck, K. E., Vinsonhaler, R., Michaelis, J. E., Swart, M. I., & Walkington, C. (2020). Embodied geometric reasoning: Dynamic gestures during intuition, insight, and proof. *Journal of Educational Psychology*. doi.org/10.1037/edu0000638.

Nathan, M. J., & Swart, M. I. (2020). Materialist epistemology lends design wings: educational design as an embodied process. *Educational Technology Research and Development*, 1–30. doi.org/10.1007/s11423-020-09856-4.

Nathan, M. J., & Walkington, C. (2017). Grounded and embodied mathematical cognition: Promoting mathematical insight and proof using action and language. *Cognitive Research: Principles and Implications*, *2*(1), 1–20.

Nathan, M. J., Walkington, C., Boncoddo, R., Pier, E., Williams, C. C., & Alibali, M. W. (2014). Actions speak louder with words: The roles of action and pedagogical language for grounding mathematical proof. *Learning and Instruction*, *33*, 182–193.

National Mathematics Advisory Panel. (2008). *Foundations for success: The final report of the National Mathematics Advisory Panel.* U.S. Department of Education.

Newcombe, N. S. (2010). Picture this: Increasing math and science learning by improving spatial thinking. *American Educator, 34*(2), 29.

Norman, D. A. (1999). Affordance, conventions, and design. *Interactions, 6*(3), 38–43.

Ottmar, E., Landy, D., Weitnauer, E., & Goldstone, R. (2015). Graspable mathematics: Using perceptual learning technology to discover algebraic notation. *Integrating touch-enabled and mobile devices into contemporary mathematics education* (pp. 24–48). IGI Global.

Palinscar, A. S., & Brown, A. L. (1984). Reciprocal teaching of comprehension-fostering and comprehension-monitoring activities. *Cognition and Instruction, 1*(2), 117–175.

Petrick, C., & Martin, T. (2012). Mind your body: Learning mathematics through physical action. In *Annual meeting of the American Educational Research Association Vancouver, Canada.*

Pickering, M. J., & Garrod, S. (2007). Do people use language production to make predictions during comprehension? *Trends in Cognitive Sciences, 11*(3), 105–110.

Pier, E. L., Walkington, C., Clinton, V., Boncoddo, R., Williams-Pierce, C., Alibali, M. W., & Nathan, M. J. (2019). Embodied truths: How dynamic gestures and speech contribute to mathematical proof practices. *Contemporary Educational Psychology, 58*, 44–57.

Pulvermüller, F. (2001). Brain reflections of words and their meaning. *Trends in Cognitive Sciences, 5*(12), 517–524.

Rau, M. A., Aleven, V., & Rummel, N. (2015). Successful learning with multiple graphical representations and self-explanation prompts. *Journal of Educational Psychology, 107*(1), 30–46.

Rau, M. A., Aleven, V., & Rummel, N. (2017). Supporting students in making sense of connections and in becoming perceptually fluent in making connections among multiple graphical representations. *Journal of Educational Psychology, 109*(3), 355.

Rau, M. A., & Matthews, P. G. (2017). How to make "more" better? Principles for effective use of multiple representations to enhance students' learning about fractions. *ZDM, 49*(4), 531–544.

Schneider, W., & Shiffrin, R. M. (1977). Controlled and automatic human information processing: I. Detection, search, and attention. *Psychological Review, 84*(1), 1.

Segal, A., Tversky, B., & Black, J. (2014). Conceptually congruent actions can promote thought. *Journal of Applied Research in Memory and Cognition, 3*(3), 124–130.

Shapiro, L. (2019). *Embodied cognition* (2nd ed.). Routledge.

Smith, C. P., King, B., & Hoyte, J. (2014). Learning angles through movement: Critical actions for developing understanding in an embodied activity. *The Journal of Mathematical Behavior, 36*, 95–108.

Sweller, J. (2010). Element interactivity and intrinsic, extraneous, and germane cognitive load. *Educational Psychology Review, 22*(2), 123–138.

Triona, L. M., & Klahr, D. (2003). Point and click or grab and heft: Comparing the influence of physical and virtual instructional materials on elementary school students' ability to design experiments. *Cognition and Instruction, 21*(2), 149–173.

Walkington, C., Chelule, G., Woods, D., & Nathan, M. J. (2019). Collaborative gesture as a case of extended mathematical cognition. *The Journal of Mathematical Behavior, 55*, 100683.

Walkington, C., Nathan, M. J., & Wang, M. (2020, April). *The effect of relevant directed arm motions on gesture usage and proving of geometry conjectures.* Paper presented at the annual meeting of the American Educational Research Association, San Francisco, April 17–21.

Wright, B. & Garrett, M. F. (1984) Lexical decision in sentences: Effects of syntactic structure. *Memory & Cognition, 12*, 31–45.

Wynn, K. (1998). Psychological foundations of number: Numerical competence in human infants. *Trends in Cognitive Sciences, 2*, 296–303.

9

Sociocultural Basis of Learning

Middle school students will turn to a whiteboard as a source of external memory while solving a challenging problem involving three-dimensional reasoning. A drawing becomes *taken-as-shared* during the discourse, and the meaning of various lines that are drawn goes through periods of negotiation in order to establish the common ground needed to construct agreement among the members of a class.

Teachers in a video club form a community of learners for improving their instructional practices. To achieve these professional goals, teachers must also develop appropriate shared group norms of interaction. This contributes to creating a safe and informative environment that encourages analysis and reflection on one another's classroom videos, and supports professional learning.

Students who learned together are collaborating on a group assessment designed to document their collective intellect as they engage in real-world problem solving. These students apply their learning to new activities while demonstrating their distributed knowledge skills. The assessment rubric includes measures of productive group discourse and the cooperative use of tools and technology.

Learning processes at the sociocultural band of the GEL timescale involve developing new practices for engaged community participation. *Practices* are embodied behaviors that enact "socially patterned activities organized with reference to community norms and values" (Nasir & Saxe, 2003). In order to successfully engage, members of a community need to operate with shared understandings and expectations, or *common ground*.

Following a common metaphor for these sociocultural behaviors, new members of a community enter on the "periphery" (Lave & Wenger, 1991). Members who are central to the community anchor these practices, norms and values, which provides stability. New members learn by adopting these practices and norms, including community forms of talk and habits of mind. Newcomers may demonstrate changes in participatory practices, but initially they may act without the practices being meaningful. Over time, as they demonstrate they can participate in accord with shared norms and provide useful contributions for the community, newcomers "move toward the center." New members also bring in diverse views that can lead to questioning and renegotiating of norms and practices, which leads to enduring changes at the community level.

At this timescale of behavior, *change in engaged participation* **is the central means of learning**. For new practices to attain meaning, they must be **grounded** in shared ways of knowing for the learner, which is also referred to as **common ground**. In this way, newcomers

DOI: 10.4324/9780429329098-9

will have adopted the culturally established norms of the community, including what they value and how community members act, perceive, and think about phenomena. Thus, sociocultural processes are embodied in that they are rooted in changes in people's patterns of actions and grounded in their shared experiences and norms.

What also stands out at this level is the realization that our mental processes are deeply situated, highly contextualized, **culturally embedded,** and **physically extended**. The boundaries between our cultural, social, physical, and mental experiences are blurry, at best, and often nonexistent. This is evident, for example, in how people use various resources in the environment, as well as physical and cultural tools. As Lave (1988, p. 1) describes it, "'Cognition' observed in everyday practice is distributed—stretched over, not divided among—mind, body, activity and culturally organized settings (which include other actors)."

In this chapter, the focus is on processes for improving how people think and learn through socially and culturally embedded activity. They offer an important complement to considerations of the intellectual power of the human mind operating on its own. It also stems, in part, from the realization that some scholars may overestimate the contributions of individual cognition to cultural advancement (e.g., Pinker, 2010). The bedrock of culture is the seemingly natural desire and "ability to learn from others … This capacity enables humans to gradually accumulate information across generations and develop well-adapted tools, beliefs, and practices that no individual could invent on their own" (Boyd, Richerson, & Henrich, 2011, p. 10919).

The learning processes of interest in this chapter typically unfold over days, months, and years (see Figure 9.1). Meaningful learning of the kind we need to tackle the grand problems of a global society and to continue its forward progress depend on more than a focus on the development of smart individuals. These aims cannot be achieved through mere mimicry of others' behaviors. Rather, they are achieved when learners adopt new practices that are meaningful to them for interacting with people, objects, and shared representations. When learners do so, they also adopt corresponding new ways of seeing, believing, and knowing.

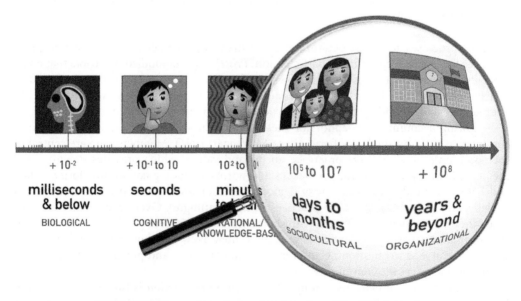

FIGURE 9.1 You are here: Sociocultural portion of the GEL timescale.
Figure uses a $\log_{10}$ scale.

Learning, the reader will recall, is based on enduring change. Social situations can make people hyper-aware of their surroundings and changes in manners. It is also the case that humans are rather "slow blind." Changes in very slow processes can be difficult to notice and operate outside of conscious awareness. As part of this description, I introduce *Type 3 processing* as a complement to Type 1 and Type 2 processing. I show that this distinct form of processing can be unconscious, conscious, and even hyper-conscious, affecting the performance of other processing types. After reviewing the evidence for Type 3 processing, I summarize the general theoretical and empirical support for the grounded and embodied nature of learning at the sociocultural timescale.

The interconnections between sociocultural processes and embodiment comes in two distinct and complementary forms. There is evidence of the sociocultural basis of embodiment. There is also evidence of the grounded and embodied nature of sociocultural processes. I review evidence for each of these forms.

9.1 FOUNDATIONS: THE SOCIOCULTURAL BASIS OF EMBODIMENT

9.1.1 Knowing-With and Epistemic Frames

Knowing-with serves as a complement to knowing-that and knowing-how. In Broudy's (1977) taxonomy, *knowing-with* describes the way a person "thinks, perceives and judges with everything that he has studied in school, even though he cannot recall these learnings on demand" (p. 12). As Broudy points out, this knowledge often remains tacit and unavailable for direct inspection. Still, it is extremely influential. Bransford & Schwartz (1999) identify knowing-with as the cornerstone of a model of transfer as the *preparation of future learning*. They show the merits of re-casting transfer in terms of one's progresses while being taught, rather than attending to common elements across different performance tasks.

Shaffer (2006) builds upon knowing-with in his theory of epistemic frames. *Epistemic frames* encapsulate the ways of knowing shared by a community of practice, "of deciding what is worth knowing, and of adding to the collective body of knowledge and understanding of the community" (p. 227). As Shaffer notes, citing Broudy (1977), such frames are central to providing the context—the *frame*—in which ways of knowing-that and knowing-how are exercised, how they are used, and why the knowledge that emerges from them matters at all.

Shaffer (2006) describes how high school students develop an epistemic frame of the profession of biomedical mediators. Practitioners in this field help families to make complex medical decisions and help communities determine policies around public health. The epistemic frame of the biomedical mediator incorporates content knowledge of immunobiology (knowing-that) and skills in mediation and negotiation (knowing-how), along with principles and values of bioethics. Combined, they form a frame for knowing-with that Shaffer shows can be adopted by students through extended, weeks-long role-play experiences.

Sociocultural processes emphasize the practices and forms of knowing-with that emerge from prolonged social interactions, such as being part of a sustained community, and adopting the collective values, norms, and ways of seeing, talking and reasoning. When individuals participate in these forms of collective, culturally-rich interactions, I contend that they generally activate Type 3 processes. Whereas Type 1 processing is primarily associative, and Type 2 sequential, Type 3 processing is networked, with behaviors focused on adopting and internalizing social and cultural norms. A comparison is provided in Table 9.1.

Type 3 processing exhibits several unique qualities. First, Type 3 processing reveals a fundamental predisposition for humans to develop shared intentions when they interact. Scholars who examine cross-species development observe that many species can cooperate. But non-human primates generally use others as a form of "social tool" (Tomasello, 2009a; Tomasello

TABLE 9.1
Comparative summary of processing Types 1, 2, & 3 processes. Type 3 is highlighted

	Type 1 processing	Type 2 processing	Type 3 processing
Timescale	ca. below 10^{-3} s to 10^{-1} s milliseconds	ca. 10^0 s to 10^4 seconds to hours	ca. 10^5 s to 10^8 s days to years
Energy	Effortless	Effortful	Energizing, effortless, effortful
Reasoning style	Impressions	Analytical	Discursive
Processing style	Automatic	Controlled, deliberate	Responsive to context
Awareness	Unconscious (unaware), unmonitored	Conscious (mostly), monitored	Can be collectively unconscious, conscious or self-conscious
Pace	Fast	Medium	Slow
Processing dynamics	Associative & parallel	Linear & sequential	Networked
Method	Impulse following	Rule following	Norm following
Mode (primary) of thought	Perceptual recognition	Intellectual	Social
Cross-species	Innate skills shared with many species	Shared with very few species	Possibly uniquely human
Attention load	Few/no attention resources	Draw on attentional resources	Mixed
External control	Undisruptable	Executive control	Social pressure; guilt.
Response automaticity	Follows habits	Override habitual responses	Adopt group norms
Response mode	Anticipatory, predictive	Reactive, planful	Normative
Type of knowing	Knowing-how	Knowing-that	Knowing-with
	Overconfident, feeling of being right	Declarative facts and rules	A sociocultural lens on all one's experiences
Grounding processes	Perceptual fluency	Connection making	Common ground
Embodied learning	Transduction	Offloading	Participation internalized
Example: Reading	Stroop Effect	Sound out words	Social facilitation–inhibition (SFI)

et al., 2005). They may engage in forms of cultural transmission, such as tool use, through imitation, but they are not really teaching (Whiten, Horner, & De Waal, 2005). Only humans appear to engage in shared intentionality, working with others (even strangers) toward a shared goal (e.g., Tomasello, 2009b; Tomasello & Rakoczy, 2003). Pre-requisite to this, people need to operate with **common ground**. They must establish shared cultural norms and social structures that prescribe appropriate forms of interaction within the community.

Newcomers learn to be accepted members largely by appropriating the practices of the community. This includes learning how a community uses language and cultural tools. Cultural norms mediate Type 3 responses, just as knowledge shapes Type 2 processing and perception Type 1 processing. For example, Jacobson and Lehrer (2000) observed second grade students learning about geometry through quilt making. The classrooms in which members established social norms around productive mathematical talk, students learned to engage in productive disciplinary discourse around the craft and mathematics. These students voiced conjectures about the patterns they observed and described their ideas in terms of geometric transformations of more basic patterns.

Second, Type 3 processing acknowledges the power of collective and **distributed knowledge**. Barron (2003) showed key ways that middle school students successfully worked in groups on hard problems. Groups were more successful when there was greater discussion among its members and the ideas of each were more thoughtfully considered and collectively evaluated within a "joint problem space." Less successful groups operated more like parallel individuals who did not engage in those collective interactions even though they had comparable prior achievement levels and generated acceptable proposals at similar frequencies.

Third, people can become *hyper-self-conscious* in social settings, which can affect how highly automated Type 1 processing unfolds. Earlier (Chapter 5), I described social effects on the Stroop task. Interactions such as competition, and even mere social presence of someone otherwise out of sight and unengaged, can lead to either **social facilitation** or **social inhibition** effects (Huguet et al., 1999). These effects appear to arise when people believe their performance is being evaluated against some internalized social norms of behavior (Zajonc, 1965, 1968).

Fourth, Type 3 processing can be **energizing**. Giving a lecture or even listening to one is far more cognitively demanding than engaging in a conversation with someone (e.g., Garrod & Pickering, 2004). This is because the back-and-forth interaction of a social exchange enables speakers to align their ways of interacting along multiple levels (e.g., word choice, syntax, body positioning), which reduces the cognitive demands for either speaker. Social relationships are another source of energizing interactions, and are generally viewed as one of the most important ways that people are motivated and flourish in their pursuits (Seligman, 2012). Coordination of people working toward mutually beneficial goals can also be highly energizing, which feeds back into the efforts and motivation to cooperate further (Quinn & Dutton, 2005).

9.1.2 Shared Intentionality and Common Ground

At a very young age, humans demonstrate an understanding of social norms and their significance in learning and communication. One hypothesis is that humans are motivated toward social interactions through a process of *shared intentionality*, a fundamental disposition toward having shared goals with others (Tomasello et al, 2005). Shared intentionality spans a wide range of social behaviors, from cooperation to collaboration and co-construction. By 2 months of age infants and mothers mutually regulate one another's feelings and attention through imitation of vocalizations, facial expressions, and gestures while intentionally looking and listening to one another.

Intersubjectivity, or common ground, is an important component of shared intentionality because it describes the state where all parties engaged in interaction have a shared understanding (Rommetveit, 1979). Intersubjectivity is so central to human interactions that sociocultural theorists such as Vygotsky (1986) and Lerman (1996) position it at the heart of learning and of consciousness itself. Intersubjectivity is basic to human interaction. For example, Trevarthen (1979) filmed the most basic interactions among mothers and their infants. Infants naturally engage in turn-taking with their mothers. This revealed that infants were engaged in primary intersubjectivity—they responded to the mother's touch and sounds, but also *communicated* they were engaged in the shared intentions with the mother by responding in similar ways during their turns.

Intersubjectivity is central to instructional scaffolding. *Scaffolding* is a socially embedded form of instruction that comes from interactions with teacher and other knowledgeable agents, including peers (Wood, Bruner, & Ross, 1976). Scaffolding is based on Vygotsky's (1978) notion of the *zone of proximal development*, which is defined as the

> distance between the child's actual developmental level as determined by independent problem solving and the higher level of potential development as determined through problem solving under adult guidance and in collaboration with more capable peers.
>
> (Vygotsky, 1978, p. 86)

Scaffolding provides these social supports within a structured form of pedagogical interactions. As Puntambekar and Hübscher (2005, p. 2) note in their review of the literature, scaffolding depends on a "shared understanding of the goal of an activity" and its collaborative restructuring that conform to the children's current capabilities and those that the children can attain.

Scholars have also observed that gestures produced during speech are effective as a means to manage common ground among learners. For example, speakers in one study were more likely to use gesture when referring to objects that were unfamiliar to listeners, but not when speaking to knowledgeable listeners (Holler & Stevens, 2007). Classroom teachers regularly engage their bodies in multimodal communication to create and maintain common ground with their students (Nathan, Alibali, & Church, 2017). Analyses also show that teachers are more likely to gesture when they perceive that they lack common ground with their students. Teachers will increase their gesture rates when their students encounter trouble spots (Alibali et al., 2013). Teachers will also produce more gestures when they are presenting new information, compared to reviewing prior information (Alibali & Nathan, 2007). For example, a teacher introducing algebra to her students for the first time will use her body to invoke the operation of the playground teeter totter as a way to relate to the need to balance two sides of an equation (Nathan et al., 2017).

9.1.3 Argumentation

Learning through social interaction is evident in many studies, with the greatest gains for conceptual tasks, rather than perceptual learning or basic fact retention (Cohen, 1994; Damon & Phelps, 1989; Dillenbourg, 1999; Johnson, Johnson, & Stanne, 2000; Rogoff, 1990). Socially-mediated learning also benefits most when members of a group do not share the same initial ideas about the concept in question (Schwartz, 1995; Williams & Tolmie, 2000). This suggests that the social exchanges are apt to elicit conflicting views. When group members engage in socially-mediated arguments, they often learn more about the topic. This is because the act of inspecting one's own rationale and justifying it to others increases one's clarity of thought.

During an argument, students exercise the process of retrieving and using new knowledge and relating new and familiar knowledge. To remain productive, the interactions also necessitate establishing common ground, which encourages reflection on what one knows in relation to others (Baker et al., 1999). Arguments also can trigger knowledge construction events in order to fill gaps or correct errors (Osborne, 2010; Schwarz, 2009). This may be part of the reason that groups learn more when their members express differing views.

Howe (2009) questioned some of the common assumptions about how collaborative group work promotes children's learning at the group and individual levels. Many scholars subscribe to one of two accounts. In the first account, children jointly construct a novel understanding. In the second account, an individual student proposes a novel concept that is taken up by the members of the group. This is the simpler form, since it only depends on students to listen and follow the suggestions of one other group member. While arguably less complex, this, too, is unlikely to cover the range of socially-mediated learning.

Howe (2009) provided evidence for a third alternative. Learning through group interactions can be due to the exchanges around unresolved contradictions among group members. In this hypothesis, knowledge continues to be sought out so long as contradictions among group members' views persist. Several types of evidence supported this claim. One is the correlations between occurrences of statements of unresolved contradictions among the group level discussions and student performance improvement. The second is that the learning gains do not show up immediately, but only after delays of several days or more.

Delayed knowledge growth is more likely when the changes in thinking need time to integrate conflicting positions.

This may seem like a contradiction: interactions where dissenting views might seem to counter the benefits of intersubjectivity and common ground. In fact, intersubjectivity is vital for constructive arguments just as it is necessary for collaboration (Nathan, Eilam, & Kim, 2007).

9.1.4 Activity Systems and Discourse Practices

As portrayed by situated and distributed views of cognition, sociocultural learning is primarily interested in the behavior of the *activity system* (Greeno & Engeström, 2014). This framing foregrounds the idea that what is most important in social learning is changes at a system level. This includes changes in the relations among the nature of the *activity* in which actors are engaged (such as problem solving or collaborative design), the *instruments and artifacts* they use, and the physical and historical *setting* in which these activities, or *practices*, occur. The number of participants in the activity system can vary greatly, from one person to entire organizations (Dillenbourg, 1999).

The theoretical nature of the interactions during learning are illustrated in Figure 9.2. At the top is the triad of *subjects* (i.e., the actors involved in the activity), *objects* (the focal work of the subjects), and *instruments* (resources and artifacts used by subjects to do the work on the objects in service of a set of outcome goals). Observations across many activities have revealed that this triad has yet other influences. *Community* describes those agents who are operating with the shared outcome goals and adhering to a common set of practices, though those practices may be assigned (implicitly or explicitly) through a *division of labor* and are governed by a set of socially accepted *rules* or norms within the system. This division of labor is one of the forms of distributed knowledge that supports effective group functioning.

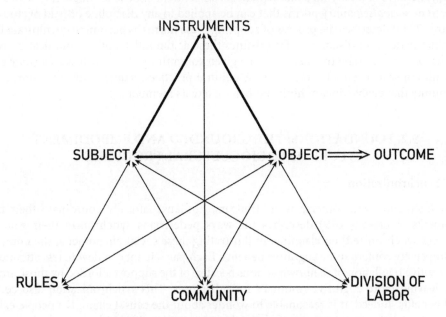

FIGURE 9.2 Illustration of a generic activity system.
The triad of subject-object-instruments is highlighted.

Activity systems can be used to describe any manner of events, but for our purposes, the activity system most relevant to understanding sociocultural learning is the *discourse environment*.

Discourse practices are closely related to the activity systems that describe sociocultural-level behaviors. This means that language plays a powerful role in the participation and learning that are observed within these social structures. *Language* is regarded here as *multimodal*, including verbal utterances, the use of physical and special metaphor, and gesture production and comprehension. I explore gestures in greater depth in the next section. In his penetrating writings about discourse, Gee (1999/2014) notes that in order to deeply understand language requires listeners to apprehend three things: What a person is saying, what that speaker is doing in speaking, and who the speaker is. Naïve students need to learn to appreciate the sociocultural and historical context of an utterance in order to grasp what is truly being said, and what is expected of them in response.

Gee makes an important distinction: The specifics of what is said is an act of discourse with a lowercase "*d*." This is an instance of the conventional manner in which a social group conducts its affairs. It includes all of the vocabulary and syntax, mannerisms and body language, historical references, and cultural metaphors that help constitute a community, efficiently convey rich meaning, and distinguishes itself from others. Big "*D*" Discourse focuses on the broader, cultural forms that people historically bring, including language, forms of interactions, cultural tools, world views and values. Children readily adopt the *primary Discourse* of their family community. Over time, people also adopt *secondary Discourses* (Gee, 2015) related to their educational institutions, places of worship, workplaces, and new habitats.

Professional communities organized around disciplines also develop Discourses that reflect the histories, values, and goals of scholarly fields of study. In their studies of the nature of discourse in mathematics classrooms, Yackel and Cobb (1996) describe these as "sociomathematical norms." These are agreed-upon rules of the field, such as what constitutes appropriate ways of justifying a mathematical conjecture. I choose to broaden this idea a bit more, to be *sociodisciplinary* norms that can be applied to any discipline or field of study.

Sfard (2000) describes the process of adopting these norms as becoming enculturated into particular patterns of discourse. Sfard defines these as the full set of communication activities that are practiced by the members of a given community. As we will see, *learning* at the sociocultural scale occurs by adopting the cultural practices, values, and social norms of a community that enable one to think and behave like its members.

9.2 FOUNDATIONS: THE GROUNDED AND EMBODIMENT NATURE OF SOCIOCULTURAL PROCESSES

9.2.1 Synchronization

When interacting with others, even strangers, humans naturally coordinate their body movements. Tversky (2019) describes the ways pedestrians synchronize their gait, and audiences synchronize their clapping. In illustrating these social phenomena, she notes that this propensity confers some cognitive benefits. Each participant can devote less attention to the executive regulation of their own actions because of the support afforded by those around them, leaving more cognitive resources for other uses. This synchronization also confers social benefits. Indeed, it is reasonable to wonder about the causal chain: Do people exhibit synchronized behaviors because of their shared intentionality and established common ground? Or, do people experience shared intentionality and common ground because they achieve synchronization? In all likelihood, they co-constitute one another. This interplay within Type 3 processing is quite like the perception-action loop that is so prominent in Type 1 processing.

Gallese and colleagues (2003a; Rizzolati, Fogassi, & Gallese, 2001) point to *mirror neurons* as basic neural mechanisms which allow people (and other primates) to understand the actions and the intentions of others. For example, Iacoboni and colleagues (2005) found that premotor mirror neuron areas that are active during the execution and the observation of an action are also involved in understanding others' intentions. In recognition of the powerful social impact that this creates among people interacting with one another, Gallese (2003a) theorizes that intersubjectivity arises by embodying this shared response, which then supports further coordination and mutual understanding (Gallese, 2003b).

9.2.2 Gestures During Social Learning

Earlier, I reviewed evidence of the importance of gestures for GEL learning in the conscious spectrum. In addition to their role in Type 2 processing, gestures are also observed in Type 3 processing, where, among other things, they provide an effective way to manage common ground among group members through overt communication. This is because in this role, gestures invoke long established past cultural experiences that were formed over months and years. Gestures constitute a flexible and well-developed system for multimodal communication and cognition that people naturally use during social interactions (McNeill, 1992).

Communication is *multimodal* in that it integrates multiple sensory and effector modalities, including auditory speech, gestural actions, body posture and movement, and so on. Gestures bring together many of the entailments of sociocultural learning. For one, gestures play an important role in establishing and maintaining common ground in the learning environment. As an example, people gesture more frequently when common ground is more important to the discourse. When speaking during a high-stakes scenario, sharing survival information for a wilderness scenario, Kelly, Byrne, and Holler (2011) found gesture frequency was triple that for a comparable, low-stakes scenario. Gesture rates are also higher when a speaker lacks common ground with listeners, and declines when common ground is established (Gerwing & Bavelas, 2004; Holler and Wilkin, 2009).

Classroom settings are high-stakes scenarios. For example, Alibali and colleagues (2013) find that teachers significantly increase their gesture production when students demonstrate that they lack common ground with their teachers, as when they are learning completely new curriculum material and when students exhibit trouble understanding the lesson (Alibali and Nathan, 2007; Alibali et al., 2013; Nathan & Alibali, 2011; Nathan, Alibali, & Church, 2017). In project-based learning units in high school engineering, teachers regularly employ gestures as a central instructional device to maintain common ground. For example, video analyses of these events show that teachers actively use gestures to help students track the continuity of a common concept over multiple days, across different physical settings (such as the classroom and machine shop), and among the various objects and formal representations (Nathan et al., 2013, 2017; Walkington et al., 2014).

Managing the participants during a discussion is also an important way to implement shared social norms. Gestures are commonly used to manage turn-taking in order to promote productive organization of discourse practices (Mondada, 2013).

Another important sociocultural role of gestures is to draw attention to relevant referents in the common visual field such as object features or scientific diagrams. Although all listeners may have access to a feature in principle, it does not necessarily follow that they know where to direct their gaze. For example, Figure 9.3 shows gestures by an engineering

FIGURE 9.3 Teaching about forces that act on a bridge.
Left panel. Gesturing how excessive tension and compression forces can affect a bridge span, with no model present. *Middle panel.* Gesturing how sheer forces are applied to the ends of a bridge, with a model present. *Right panel.* Gesturing how torsion forces are applied through twisting, with a model present.

instructor used to discuss the forces that can be applied to bridges under load—tension, compression, sheer and torsion. The teacher uses gesture to emphasize that each force has different properties and is applied to different locations along the members of a bridge span, and to different effect.

Previously (Chapter 5), I discussed how important gestures are for supporting one's embodied thought processes. Gesture studies has always provided special insights about the link between the individual and the activity system in which the individual operates. Gesture production has well-established cognitive benefits for the individual who is speaking and producing the gestures (e.g., Goldin-Meadow, 2003). At the same time, gesture production serves a social role as well (e.g., McNeill, 1992). People gesture more when they are speaking with others (e.g., Goodwin, 2000; Moll & Tomasello, 2007; Vygotsky, 1978).

9.2.3 Extended, Distributed, Situated, and Embedded Knowledge

While shared interactions with other people are vital to GEL at the sociocultural scale, learning also relies on interactions as they occur in context, in physical places, and with material objects and other social agents. A number of scholars have used various adjectives—*extended, distributed, situated,* and *embedded*—to describe how human intellectual behavior expands beyond the individual. All of these capture related but distinct qualities, which I sort through in Box 9.1.

Box 9.1 Comparing Extended, Distributed, Situated, Embedded Knowledge

Extended, distributed, situated, and embedded knowledge are all terms that capture some unique as well as overlapping aspects of how people interact with their environment while thinking and learning. I share some of the distinguishing aspects of these terms.

Extended cognition takes as the focal unit of analysis a central agent whose cognition is "extended." This agent operationalizes the environment in order to carry forth a set of intellectual processes that, if done by the agent in isolation using only mental processes, would be recognized as individual cognition (Clark & Chalmers, 1998). The earlier example of Otto's use of his notebooks illustrates this. The central figure in extended cognition is the individual operating within a malleable environment. I also appreciate the way Gregory Bateson (1972) describes the circumstances of the blind man and his walking stick, in his essay "Form, Substance and Difference."

> Suppose I am a blind man, and I use a stick. I go tap, tap, tap. Where do I start? Is my mental system bounded at the handle of the stick? Is it bounded by my skin? Does it start halfway of the tip of the stick? But these are nonsense questions. The stick is a pathway along which transforms of difference are being transmitted. The way to delineate the system is to draw the limiting line in such a way that you do not cut any of these pathways in ways which leave things inexplicable. If what you are trying to explain is a given piece of behavior, such as the locomotion of the blind man, then for this purpose, you will need the street, the stick, the man, the street, the stick, and so on, round and round.
>
> (Bateson, 1972, p. 459)

In this metaphor, Bateson shows that there are times when the elements of a unified system cannot be separated without destroying its performance. This highlights the *actor-centric* perspective (Lobato, 2003). There is empirical evidence favoring such a perspective when describing situated behavior.

For example, scholars of embodiment have found that the neural systems of closely related primates react to objects within one's personal space differently than objects beyond that boundary (Iriki, Tanaka, & Iwamura, 1996). When the monkeys were given a rake to extend their reach, some object locations previously regarded as "far," now registered as being "close." Adult humans also made different assessments of the relative distance of objects when they held a baton that increased their reach, but only when the agent intended to use the tool to reach the object (Witt, Proffitt, & Epstein, 2005). From an *actor-centric* perspective, one's sense of personal space and proximity is not only a function of the person's size, but also of their augmented reach and intentions.

Distributed cognition takes as the unit of analysis the system in operation within an environment populated by agents and assets. In this account, no one element is anymore central to the process than any other. Hutchins's (1995) analyses of sea navigation exemplifies this. In the naval ships, the process of determining the "fix cycle" is distributed over multiple people, charts, and instruments. No one agent is more responsible or critical than any of the others for its operation. As Hutchins (2014, p. 37) notes, "[s]ome systems have a clear center while other systems have multiple centers or no center at all" (Hutchins, 2014, p. 37).

Situated cognition is a term that has been adopted by philosophers, psychologists, and learning scientists to refer to closely related phenomena. To philosophers Robbins and Aydede (2008, p. 3), it refers to mental processes that are "dependent on the situation or context in which it occurs." In their view, situated cognition subsumes all other forms. "According to our usage, then, situated cognition is the genus, and embodied, enactive, embedded, and distributed cognition and their ilk are species." To those in education and the learning sciences, the rejection of the "factoring assumption" is the chief criterion of situated cognition, and the closely related notion of *situativity* (Greeno, 1994; Greeno & Moore, 1993).

In both senses, situated cognition is closely linked to the term **embedded cognition** and a newer term, ***cognitive ecology*** (Hutchins, 2010). As posited by Gibson's (1979/2014) theory of affordances and *ecological psychology*, cognitive, perceptual, and motoric processes are analyzed as *relations* between agents and other systems. The *relation* is the central unit of analysis. Any separation will disrupt the system into a collection of independent phenomena that behave differently than originally intended.

An illustrative example of situated cognition is the study of what some have called "street mathematics" (Carraher, Carraher, & Schliemann, 1985). The research combines experimental and ethnographic methods to document how children and adults make use of the regularities of the social and physical situations of human activity. An example of situated cognition is knowing how to do calculations based on how fruits are typically bundled and sold. This stands in contrast to developing calculation methods based on the properties of the number systems, such as the base-ten structure, regardless of what one is purchasing.

Gestures also contribute to extended and distributed representations. One form of distributed representation is when people use the space between them—so-called *neutral space* (Butcher, Mylander, & Goldin-Meadow, 1991)—to construct an idea. Another is when speakers in a collaborative group setting use one another's hands and arms to augment the physical limitations of their own bodies. For example, Walkington and colleagues observed teachers making *collaborative gestures*. Walkington and colleagues (2019) define collaborative gestures as "gestural exchanges that take place as learners discuss and explore mathematical ideas, using their bodies in concert to accomplish a shared goal." During one episode, teachers recruited one another's hands to complete a circle as a resource to explore its geometric properties, engaging in what the researchers called "collaborative co-construction" (Walkington et al., 2019). Gestures can influence group learning because they can be constructive and co-constructive. For example, students can also produce *joint gestures*, as shown in Figure 9.4 where multiple learners are seen coordinating their body positions in order to co-construct and co-manipulate geometric shapes that capture socially shared ideas.

9.2.4 Material Epistemology and Scientific Discovery

Our interactions with material *things*, much like our social interactions, shape our collective thinking. The philosopher of science Davis Baird (2004) notes that much of the scientific

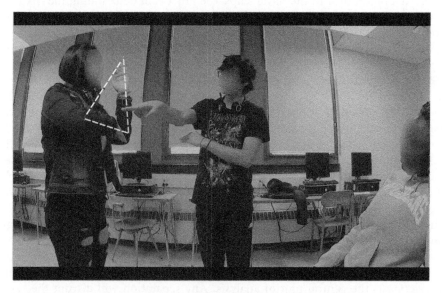

FIGURE 9.4 Example of two students (standing) engaged in a joint gesture during a classroom activity on geometry. Another participating student (seated) looks on.

knowledge produced by a community is first conceptualized in material form. Unfortunately, science historians often tell stories of how deep abstract thought of a single investigator, or occasionally a team of close collaborators, drives science and technological innovation. It may be more accurate to say that it is the group's material developments and their affordances for action and thinking that drive these innovations and lead to later theoretical advancements.

Baird identifies three forms of "materialistic conceptions of knowledge" that have enormous influence on scientific advancement (p. 17): devices, models, and instruments.

Devices exhibit a material mode of effective action. Devices have to work as expected, but they are essentially nonrepresentational. In this sense, devices reify practical knowledge. They also help people operate in the world, even when people lack an explanatory theory about why and how the world works this way. An example of how a device achieves this nonrepresentational stance is the electromagnetic motor invented by Michael Faraday. Farady showed how to control a magnetic field using electrical current. At the time, Faraday and his contemporaries lacked any of these theoretical notions that now explain electromagnetism. Yet his devices were groundbreaking, contributing to basic notions of light and conservation of energy. When asked by colleagues to share his research, instead of sending an academic paper or mathematical analysis, Faraday shipped prebuilt motor assemblies that demonstrated but did not explain the phenomenon. An important quality of devices is that they work regardless of whether the operator believes they will.

Models are material configurations that have representation as their primary function. Models serve an epistemic role in a way that is *similar* to symbol- and verbal-based theories. However, models are also fundamentally different from theories in that they describe the relations and outcomes using a materialist format. The ball-and-stick models of DNA developed by James Watson, Francis Crick, and Rosalind Franklin (Lloyd, 2010; Watson, 1968) illustrate this representational capacity. The model does not actually fulfill the functions of DNA, but it allowed these investigators to make testable inferences about biological structures that were conceptually out of reach without them.

Baird (2004) places these forms of object-based ways of knowing within a framework of "materialist epistemology" (p. 15:1), where veridical knowledge of the world exists through demonstration. Some have argued that material forms are flawed because they are imperfect, unlike the Platonic ideal of a scientific *theory*. Theory is an abstraction of the actual phenomenon that operates within the domain of *scientific epistemology*. It is privileged by virtue of "semantic ascent," the move away from the imperfectness of the material world, toward ideals such as perfection that only abstractions can provide. Scientific theory is knowledge composed of propositional content that describes one's mental state regarding claims (i.e. beliefs) about the world (Goldman, 1986). Thus, for a scientific theoretical claim to be true, one or more people have to believe that it is true, as well as provide a logical argument for its veracity.

Yet, materialist epistemology has something over the theories that derive from scientific epistemology. Objects from materialist epistemology establish universal truths through physical enactment that people may experience for themselves. From the perspective of a materialist epistemology, one does not need to first hold some set of beliefs about the truth of the claim. Truth is established, instead, through the material existence of something and its operation.

Instruments can be thought of as a hybrid of the nonrepresentational action of devices and the representational function of models. Instruments use action to produce representations. One example is the mercury thermometer, which uses the thermal reaction of mercury to expand and contract as a way to generate a numerical measure or representation of temperature. Consider that throughout history, technicians, such as the Wright brothers, made technological advancements in the instruments and devices they built and tested well ahead of a correct scientific theory. In fact, the prevailing theory of lift, which was so important for developing a functional aircraft, was based on incorrect estimates for the coefficient of air pressure (an incorrect number that was used faithfully by engineers for over 150 years!). It was only after their extensive practical development of their prototypes that they created instruments that directly measured lift and obtained a more accurate measure of this important physical constant (Bradshaw, 1992, 2005; McCullough, 2015).

Furthermore, working directly with the imperfect nature of materiality is actually a goal of the intellectual and practical efforts of innovation. This is in direct conflict with the Platonic ideals of semantic ascent. One reason for this goal is to find general solutions to practical problems that will still apply even under varying conditions. Often, the simplifying assumptions necessary to articulate a coherent scientific theory, also rest on highly restrictive, often implausible assumptions, such as frictionless surfaces and point (zero-dimensional) masses (Cartwright, 1999). Thus, despite their seemingly complementary nature, materialist epistemologies and science theory epistemologies are fundamentally incommensurate.

Materialist epistemology provides a basis for practical knowledge growth through practice that is attuned to the actual qualities of the world. By making new devices with epistemic function, developers can contribute to cultural knowledge growth. As society comes to rely on each successive generation of such material innovations, Tomasello (1999) posits that culture advances unabated. This is because the material contributions act as a form of cultural "ratchet" that present people in the society from slipping back simply because they themselves could not recreate the invention. Advancements such as furnaces, the written alphabet, the automobile, and smart phones all illustrate such dramatic cultural advancements.

9.2.5 Grounding at the Sociocultural Band

Grounding describes how cultural symbols and novel ideas are made meaningful by virtue of **how they are used in practice by participants** and perceived by them. At the sociocultural band of the GEL timescale, there may plausibly be several candidates for achieving grounding. Physical interactions with tangible materials is one such candidate. Another is the purposeful contributions made through participation within a distributed knowledge system. Synchronization of movement systems offers another plausible candidate for grounding. My take is that central to all of these is the realization of a shared participatory experience, the common ground which enables and supports these other processes. For this reason, I see common ground as the primary means of grounding in the sociocultural band.

9.3 GEL AT THE SOCIOCULTURAL LEVEL: TYPE 3 PROCESSING DURING LEARNING

GEL at the sociocultural level often emerges as the interplay between the sociocultural basis of embodiment and the embodied nature of sociocultural processes The sociocultural basis of embodiment is evident by the ways in which people's behaviors, forms of discourse, and manners of thought become "socialized" by the communities in which they participate. This form of knowing-with permeates one's reasoning and decision making. The embodied nature of sociocultural processes is evident in the ways behaviors among collaborators achieve shared intentionality and common ground, through automatic synchronization and overt orchestration using gesture. Sociocultural processes also rely on the epistemic role of the tangible realm, which support distributed ways of knowing. Type 3 processing encompasses both the sociocultural basis of embodiment and the grounded and embodied nature of socio-cultural processes.

Collectively, these contribute to the constitution of a coherent activity system (Engeström, 1999; Figure 9.2). When sociocultural scholars explore the developmental trajectories of learning (M. Simon, 1995) it is designed for the collective behavior of the classroom community, acknowledging that there will be considerable variability among the individual students (Cobb & Bowers, 1999). Sociocultural accounts document how students become "initiated into" culturally accepted practices, as guided by their teachers (Cobb, 1994, p. 26), which develop over weeks, months, even years. Throughout this process, students must actively construct their ways of knowing, through the adoption of discourse practices and use of cultural instruments and disciplinary formalisms.

9.3.1 Legitimate Peripheral Participation and Communities of Learners

Lave and Wenger (1991) use ACCEPTANCE AS MOVEMENT TOWARD THE CENTER as their chosen metaphor for describing the process that takes place as newcomers learn the cultural norms of interaction of communities of practice. At first, newcomers enter at the periphery. From this position, they observe strange norms of practice, unfamiliar patterns of discourse, and ungrounded formalisms. Over time these experiences start to fit together into a coherent whole. This awareness of the structure that was often hidden from view provides support for the growth in skill, vocabulary, and knowledge. The performance of the newcomer is now becoming *legitimate*, conforming to the norms of the community.

For example, among the Vai and Gola communities in Liberia, apprentice tailors start out doing tasks that seem at first to be trivial and unrelated to the "real" work. They lay out the materials and tools for the more accomplished tailors, run errands, deliver messages, and so on. In time, the apprentice starts to take on practices that have greater permanence, such as cutting fabric. Their role becomes more *central*. They attain *legitimate peripheral participation*.

The spatial metaphor is not merely evocative. It is intended to evoke a sense of space that places participants in context. Sociocultural learning processes are slow because they are not designed chiefly around transmission of information. It is not in the community's interest to simply *tell* newcomers what they know, and for old timers to gain status by virtue of their store of declarative and procedural knowledge. This is not in keeping with knowing-with. Rather, learning by participation is *transformative*, with the change coming about by transforming who a person is becoming, rather than merely what they know. For example, in the Alcoholics Anonymous community, one observes "a transformation of their identities, from drinking non-alcoholics to non-drinking alcoholics, and it affects how they view and act in the world" (Lave & Wenger, 1991, pp. 80–81).

Ethnographies of the apprenticeship process reveal that it is not accurate to say the knowledge flows from master to apprentice, or from old timer to newcomer. The process, rather, is described by another spatial metaphor, the "decentering" of the master from the learning process. As the authors describe it, "mastery resides not in the master but in the organization of the community of practice of which the master is part" (Lave & Wenger, 1991, p. 94).

Jordan (1989, p. 934) illustrates the embedded nature of training of Yucatec Mayan midwives in Mexico. Throughout the education, the young trainees (always girls, usually daughters or granddaughters of midwives)

> absorb the essence of midwifery practice as well as specific knowledge about many procedures, simply in the process of growing up. They know what the life of a midwife is like (for example, that she needs to go out at all hours of the day or night), what kinds of stories the women

and men who come to consult her tell, what kinds of herbs and other remedies need to be collected, and the like.

An example of legitimate peripheral participation in an educational context comes from the study of high school robotics teams by Joseph Michaelis (Michaelis & Nathan, 2016). Initially, Eli, a newcomer, is given rather peripheral assignments that provide a small aid to the project team as it readies their robotic systems for competitions. During the pre-competition season, one of the old timers (Walter) gives Eli a tour of the computer code used to control the robots. Walter's language is steeped in the discourse of the community of practice ("class," "child," "A-star"), whereas Eli's language is noticeably nontechnical. By the time competition season arrives, Eli's role is far more central. On the final day of competition season, Eli is now seated with the robot operators and Walter, the head programmer. Thus, Eli is now both organizationally and physically more central, where the "center" of community activity is determined by proximity to the robots as they compete with those built by other teams.

Participation is a powerful framing for understanding learning as development and socialization. With it comes the adoption of shared community practices (midwives, tailors), and the transformation of one's sense of self (Alcoholics Anonymous). Across these various communities of practice, the learning is gradual and often implicit to the learner. The education process, further, is unlike Type 2 processing, with its emphasis on explicit knowledge transmission, or Type 1 processing, with its emphasis on repeated practice. Rather, educating from the Type 3 processing perspective initiates learners into the social environment in which one works and lives.

9.3.2 Taken-As-Shared Forms of Knowing

A central element to investigations of socially-mediated learning is how students adopt taken-as-shared forms of knowing as they participate in the cultural practices of the classroom (Cobb, 1994). *Taken-as-shared* forms of knowing refers to the shared intentionality—common ground—among the members of a discourse community for how something is to be interpreted. A given term or symbolic formalism will not initially be "shared" or have a common interpretation among all the members of a discourse. Central to learning at this scale is the process of *negotiation* of taken-as-shared meanings. Negotiation in this context refers to a process of reaching a mutual agreement of how something will be interpreted or used (Bauersfeld, Krummheuer, & Voigt, 1988).

9.3.3 Project-Based Learning

Project-based learning offers students a socially-mediated learning experience (Barron et al., 1998; Blumenfeld et al., 1991; Hmelo-Silver, 2004; Krajcik & Blumenfeld, 2006). Typically, these are multi-day, collaborative tasks that seek to answer societally relevant questions or to design artifacts that can improve people's lives. Students in engineering classes, for example, may design voting booth security systems that check whether the adjoining voting booth is occupied before allowing entry (Nathan et al., 2013). Environmental sciences projects include collecting data to show the air quality that commuters who use subways may experience (Wen et al., 2020).

Structuring learning within a collaborative, social context offers the potential of many advantages over the individualized, short-term exercises that so commonly mark academic learning. In project-based settings, students get to tackle much larger tasks that are more societally relevant and personally meaningful. Increased personal and social relevance can enhance student motivation and cognitive engagement (Blumenfeld et al., 1991; Chi & Wylie, 2014). The collaborative group process elicits greater discussion and argumentation. For example, in the *Fostering Communities of Learners* program, Ann Brown and Joe Campione and their colleagues (Brown, 1997; 1993) showed how middle school students in under-resourced schools used their emerging interests in ecosystems to delve deeply into the biological principles of interdependency, biodiversity, adaptation, and natural selection.

Students exhibited knowledge building as well as metacognitive processes at work, as they structured their own learning opportunities to address knowledge gaps that they observed during classroom discussions. These rich communicative interactions can enhance the quality of students' projects, first by addressing constructive criticism and fixing errors, and also by instilling a reflective perspective on the work students are engaged in. These forms of sophisticated thinking did not just spontaneously arise, but came about by emulating scientists and other adults who modeled these forms of thinking for the students in their classes (Brown, 1997).

Participating in projects contextualizes the academic content. This contextualization **grounds** the procedures, facts, and formalisms that students are using to actual objects, relations, and events in the world. For example, students collaboratively solving "Boone's Meadow" in *The Adventures of Jasper Woodbury* series learned far more about distance-rate-time equations than students typically learn solving traditional algebra problems (CTGV, 1997). They designed a plan to rescue an injured eagle in a remote location. The solution space included thinking about multiple forms of transportation, constraints on the weight of payloads (both before and after the rescue), and speeds and fuel efficiencies for different aircraft. Digital simulation and video game resources allowed students to collectively explore multiple solutions and make selections based on a variety of criteria (Gresalfi & Barnes, 2016; Bell & Gresalfi, 2017).

As the Boone's Meadow example illustrates, project-based learning often takes a more integrative approach to using discipline-specific formalisms and tools. Rather than learning to manipulate symbolic equations or write computer code as tasks on their own, these cognitive tools are used in service of a greater objective, such as solving a problem or designing a device.

Students working with Wisconsin Fast Plants™, for example, integrate biology and math concepts as they devise systems for measuring plant growth and for organizing and presenting data (Lehrer & Schauble, 2000). For example, fourth grade students engaged in meaningful discussions about how the shapes of data distributions provided different explanations of plant growth. They considered quantitative criteria to decide if two distributions were "really different." They discussed how choices about sampling may have affected their findings. Topics of representing data and using descriptive and inferential statistics are often challenging for many adult students because they are learned using ungrounded formalisms, rather than the experiences afforded both by context and by participating in collaborative reasoning about the phenomena occurring in this real-life context.

As illustrated by interventions such as the Fast Plants unit and Fostering Communities of Learners, a central benefit of many of these activities is that project-based learning places an emphasis on the *construction* of shared knowledge rather than its storage and use (Chi & Wylie, 2014). Students in project-based learning who address problems in their communities about presenting information about water quality in their local watershed have to decide how the information they have accumulated will be represented and talked about (Marx Blumenfeld, Krajcik, & Soloway, 1997). They also need to decide how to select the most important findings from the array of outcomes they have amassed.

Project-based learning creates experiences that more closely emulate the ways that practitioners actually use and build knowledge in the disciplines. Students in these settings use many of the same tools and resources, work in collaborative teams with assigned roles, refine ambiguous or ill-formed objectives as they tackle authentic problems. Even when they have "solved" it, they find they need to make decisions regarding the information they will choose to share and how to display it to others who have not been immersed in the investigation to the same degree.

9.3.4 Social Constructionism

Manipulatives and constructionism (Harel & Papert, 1991) would seem to be natural allies to grounded and embodied learning. Manipulatives, such as algebra tiles, are educationally chosen and designed objects for promoting learning, typically in math and science. Learning is thought to arise from manipulative use by performing concrete actions that follow a formal system. Learners eventually internalize these formal relations into mental structures and sociocultural practices that are applied to similar situations in the future.

Constructionism, like its close sibling, Piaget's Construc*tiv*ism, provides a developmental framework for actively building knowledge through engaged interactions with people, objects, and the world. One important distinction of these two similar-sounding terms is that constructivism encapsulates many of Piaget's claims about *epistemology*, while constructionism advances claims about the ways people learn that inform the design of learning activities. Constructionist forms of learning "happens especially felicitously in a context where the learner is consciously engaged in constructing a public entity, whether it's a sand castle on the beach or a theory of the universe" (Papert, 1991, p. 1). Many learning environments have arisen since Papert's ideas have spread within the education world, including LOGO and LEGO/LOGO, Scratch, and the Maker Movement. Historically, the constructionist objects are typically digital objects that can be programmed to adapt their behavior to changing circumstances, such as robotic systems.

Far less controversial are the observed benefits of building artifacts and "things to think with" in sociocultural settings. These benefits arise in a couple of different ways. One way is through "guided instruction" and "guided learning." It is a common, but naïve, assumption that well-crafted manipulatives are sufficient to promote conceptual and procedural learning. A preponderance of empirical evidence, however, has shown that this is not the case (Kirschner, Sweller, & Clark, 2006; Mayer, 2004).

One study tested whether 11- and 12-year old children could learn programming in the LOGO environment through discovery. Though children engaged in rich social and physical interactions over many hours, they learned programming concepts to the same level as those who had no LOGO experiences (Kurland & Pea, 1984, 1985). Guided instruction showed consistent and far-reaching advantages over discovery-based learning of programming concepts using LOGO (Fay and Mayer, 1994; Lee and Thompson, 1997).

Guided learning promotes intellectual growth by helping manage limited attention and working memory (Arocha & Patel, 1995; Kirschner, Sweller, & Clark, 2006). It also models appropriate participation practices with the objects at hand. In this way, students of computer programming, medical clinical practices, science, and mathematics experience legitimate disciplinary practices. Over time they internalize and adopt the proper situated practices that have been developed and refined over generations.

Things to think with can ground abstract operations and relations to familiar concepts. This, by the way, is one reason perceptual saliency of the objects can interfere with learning. When using objects to think with, the objects act as *symbols* that externalize the concepts being represented. The ants moving about in Goldstone and Son's (2005) simulation are not only meant to be interpreted as ants foraging for food. In the lesson they are active computational elements enacting competitive specialization in a complex system. Seeing them as ants exclusive of their role as symbols representing a concept interferes with the benefits they provide for facilitating transfer of learning. The benefits of guided instruction are seen in science learning as well, including designing superior scientific experiments (Klahr & Nigam, 2004).

Another way constructionist activities benefit learning at a sociocultural level is through the *rachet effect*, by creating artifacts that are imbued with the knowledge of their creators. These artifacts follow some of the key principles of materialist epistemology discussed earlier in that they carry knowledge in their design and function (Baird, 2004). According to Tomasello (1999), each generation operates within its own "ontogenetic niche" that is made up of the unique cultural, technological, and sociopolitical forces occurring at that time. People learn the sociocultural norms of their ontogenetic niche, including how to effectively use the cultural tools and participation in the discourse practices. The rapid uptake of social media by students is a clear illustration example of an ontogenetic niche.

9.3.5 Grounded and Embodied Learning as Changes in Participation Practices

I have argued throughout this book that *meaning* is central to effective education. Meaning is also central to culture. This is because meaning creates the shared experiences and common ground necessary to interact socially and to thrive. In support of this idea, the anthropologist Clifford Geertz (1973, p. 89) defines culture as "an historically transmitted pattern of meanings embodied in symbols." As Wertsch (1991) notes, when discussing psychological processes at the level of the individual (such as our discussion of Type 2 processing) meaning is *owned* by the speaker. In contrast, at the sociocultural level, where Type 3 processing is dominant, meaning is *lent* among the members of a community, to be *shared* and used collectively. In this sense, meaning making that is supported by Type 3 processing are distributed ways of knowing. Developing meaning depends on participating in these distributed activity systems.

Of course, the meaning of symbols and representations are grounded in the shared social practices aligned to the specific cultural context. Type 3 processing supports learning through changes in participation that occur within the context of a community of practice. These practices involve the use of both cultural and psychological tools. Cultural tools, such as hammers and computers, influence how people interact with and influence the world. In turn, these tools also shape people's behaviors. In this sense the tools are *mediational*, inherent go-betweens between people and the world.

Psychological tools are a broad category that include such cultural creations as language, art, mathematical notations, maps, and diagrams. As Wertsch (2009) interprets, they too, are mediational, in that

> the psychological tool alters the entire flow and structure of mental functions. It does this by determining the structure of a new instrumental act, just as a technical tool alters the process of a natural adaptation by determining the form of labor operations.
>
> (Vygotsky, 1981, p. 137)

As Wertsch (2009) interprets, cultural resources such as language and science that mediate between one's mental life and one's cultural life do more than assist one's thinking. They enable physical and mental actions that would not otherwise occur. Learning at the sociocultural level is characterized by changes in the mediated actions of people as shaped by their interactions with the cultural and psychological tools that facilitate their participation in communities of practice. These changes are governed by the appropriation of cultural norms. *Norms* are social and institutionalized common ground. They are the social and cultural rules and expectations people follow to fit in and gain a sense of belonging. Norms provide grounding of sociocultural ideas because people understand them in terms of their own actions and shared cultural experiences of what is and is not culturally appropriate (Baker et al., 1999).

Type 3 processing can operate with either implicit or explicit awareness. A newcomer, attempting to adhere to cultural norms, will adopt practices and patterns of speech well before any type of explicit rule is offered to justify these norms. The tacit nature of norms and the high price for infractions makes this an effortful process that can make newcomers self-conscious of their own practices and assumptions. Ironically, these same norms may be implicit to old timers. Over time, with sufficient experience and feedback, newcomers move, metaphorically, from the periphery of the community toward the center. The tacit social practices become routine and internalized (Vygotsky, 1978). Once internalized, they, too, recede from awareness, even as they govern behavior.

Still, these learned social practices often remain highly situated—activated in certain contexts but not others (Greeno, Moore, & Smith, 1993). In the situative account, transfer is determined not by the reapplication of knowledge structures (as in Type 2 processing) nor by pattern recognition (as in Type 1 processing), but in the forms of participation across contexts. The sociocultural transfer of learning is recast as the degree to which one's participatory practices in a new activity are shaped by the development of these practices from a prior activity.

For example, in the Fostering Communities of Learners program in Oakland, California (Brown et al., 1993), students formed interdisciplinary teams where students specialized in the various aspects of understanding the topic at hand, such as ecosystems. Specialists in these student groups would confer across groups in jigsaw configurations and also converse with disciplinary experts. Students showed that they could take up the ways of talking and acting modeled by scientists and integrate them into classroom practices around their own scientific investigations. This did not mean that students would apply them outside of these scientific contexts, however.

In another example, students appropriated the practices of historians as they learned the discourse practices of historical argumentation as well as the facts that relate to the events in question (Schwarz, 2009). Yet, in one study (Goldberg, Schwarz, & Porat, 2008), perspectives of 12th-grade Israeli students of different ethnic backgrounds were much closer to that offered by historians for events that were "dormant" and not part of the current cultural zeitgeist. For events that were just as distant historically, but which still played a more vital part of the "living collective memory," students exhibited greater bias and were less inclined to change their views based on the historical evidence. This provides evidence that GEL is highly tied to one's cultural views and forms of knowing-with that shaped their historical reasoning. As these findings suggest, meaning making needs to be regarded as a culturally sensitive process.

9.4 SUMMARY

In this chapter I describe Type 3 processing which reveals both the sociocultural nature of embodiment, and the embodied nature of sociocultural processes. The sociocultural nature of embodiment is demonstrated by the influence of social presence, shared intentions, social norms, and epistemic frames. Type 3 processing also exposes the embodied nature of sociocultural processes, as evident by synchronization among people who interact, the role of gesture in fostering and maintaining common ground, and the important role of tools and materiality for supporting socially distributed knowledge and the reification of cultural knowledge. Notably, Type 3 processes are not to be confused with the emergent sociocultural behaviors exhibited by groups or "swarms" (Gee, 2020). In my view, Type 3 processes are those processes activated by individuals when they are engaged in sociocultural forms of activity, including social interactions as well as the interactions that can come about with culturally-rich resources. Evidence from these perspectives contribute a strong evidentiary basis for GEL and the sociocultural band.

Type 3 processing appears to have qualities distinct from those we encountered earlier. Social presence and social interactions can alter—positively and negatively—Type 1 processing that is ordinarily considered to be relatively impervious to many capacity constraints and external influences. An essential quality of sociocultural behavior is the establishment and maintenance of common ground, the shared forms of behaving and thinking that make productive social exchanges possible. Many scholars assert the need to investigate sociocultural behaviors within the frame of an activity system. This theoretical and methodological perspective attends to inviolable relations among the *activity* in which actors are engaged, the *instruments and artifacts* they use in that activity, and the physical and historical *setting* or *context* in which these activities, or *practices*, occur.

Multimodal discourse practices are important for describing Type 3 behavior. They address the nature of verbal and nonverbal interactions as well as the ways of thinking that are demonstrated when one interacts with other actors and culturally-laden material resources. Gestures are a particularly notable form of multimodal discourse for studies of learning and teaching. Gestures are a very flexible resource for bringing about many of the entailments of sociocultural interactions, such as maintaining common ground, managing social norms such as turn-taking, and constructing and using resources to support extended and distributed cognition, such as pointing and using the neutral space among speakers. Thus, gestures serve an important role in Type 2 as well as Type 3 processing. Material objects are also an important element of distributed knowledge and extended cognition. The epistemic role served by shared material devices and instruments has been important for scientific progress and for designing learning environments.

In addition to the foundations of sociocultural processes summarized, I described and illustrated several sociocultural-level learning processes. Meaning was shown to be grounded by relating new practices to previous ones via one's common ground, the shared understandings and expectations that support effective social interactions. Legitimate peripheral participation describes how newcomers develop into contributing members of a community through their changing practices, types of talk, and ways of thinking. Socially-mediated learning also hinges on the extent to which participants develop a shared understanding of the phenomena in question and reflect this with taken-as-shared representations and ways of knowing. Argumentation is shown to be a crucial way that these shared meanings are negotiated. Project-based learning integrates many of the benefits and challenges when striving towards engineering learning experiences suited to sociocultural processes. Overall, learning processes at the sociocultural band of the GEL timescale involves developing new practices for *engaged community participation* while operating with shared understandings and expectations, or *common ground*.

9.5 READER ACTIVITIES

9.5.1 Teaching as Breaking and Making Common Ground

1. Select a new skill or concept for this activity. For example, you can use the area model for multiplication of numbers or polynomials.

2. Find a willing person or small group and tell them you are going to teach them something new.
3. Be sure to video record this session, and be certain the camera can see you (the instructor) and your hands.
4. Be sure the lesson explains what is being taught, why it is helpful, and why it "works." Also give everyone who is learning a chance to practice and to receive feedback.
5. When reviewing the video, identify any ways common ground was broken, such as when people are being informed this is different than what they already do and think.
6. Also identify any ways common ground was constructed or repaired, as when people are being informed this is like something they already know and think.
7. How could this lesson have been done without breaking or making common ground?

9.5.2 Materialist Knowledge In Food Preparation

1. In this activity you get to follow a recipe of your choosing. If you don't have a preference, baking cookies or muffins is an idea. The key is to follow the recipe exactly. Except I want you to make twice as many servings as called for in the recipe.
2. I want to deconstruct the materialist epistemological roles of some of the artifacts used in this activity.
3. Measurement: What instruments were used for measurement (weight, volume, temperature, time)? How could these measurements be achieved without these instruments?
4. Models: Doubling the recipe, for most people did not mean doing the entire process twice. Rather, mathematical calculations and measuring instruments were probably used to double the recipe. In this regard, the cooks used a model that scaled the recipe by a factor of two. Yet not everything was doubled—such as the baking time.
5. Self-regulatory Devices: Here I want to home in on the oven and its built-in ability to maintain a relatively constant internal temperature. Consider these events:
   a. Pre-heating the oven. How was the goal temperature achieved and not exceeded?
   b. Opening the oven—either initially, or when checking on progress—will greatly reduce the internal temperature. Yet the cook did not have to do anything to bring it back to temperature.
6. Enjoy your treats with friends! Ask them about some of these materialist ideas. Are there any quirky things you do when you cook? Check out "Sylvia's recipe" by Gergely and Csibra, (2006).

9.5.3 Engaging with Communities of Practice

1. Identify a community of practice that you participate in.
2. If you are a "newcomer," reflect on some of the most unfamiliar aspects of this group? Consider things such as:
   a. new terms (especially acronyms), or terms that are being used in new ways
   b. Manners of dress
   c. Forms of greetings
   d. Implicit and explicit norms for social interaction. For example, are parts of gatherings structured by formal rules such as *Roberts Rules of Order*? If so, contrast the social interactions during these portions with times before and after these events.
3. If you are an "old timer," consider these things:
   a. What are some behaviors that are important for newcomers to adopt?

b. How have norms been renegotiated over time? Often these occur when groups become more diverse. What prompted these renegotiations? Was it their pushback, and if so, what was the rationale?

9.5.4 What Constitutes an Argument?

- A fun skit from the Monty Python troop. Was this an argument? www.youtube.com/watch?v=xpAvcGcEc0k

REFERENCES

Alibali, M. W. & Nathan, M. J. (2007). Teachers' gestures as a means of scaffolding students' understanding: Evidence from an early algebra lesson. In R. Goldman, R. Pea, B. J. Barron, & Derry, S. (Eds.) *Video Research in the Learning Sciences* (pp. 349–365). Erlbaum.

Alibali, M. W., Nathan, M. J., Church, R. B., Wolfgram, M. S., Kim, S., & Knuth, E. J. (2013). Teachers' gestures and speech in mathematics lessons: Forging common ground by resolving trouble spots. *ZDM: The International Journal on Mathematics Education, 45*(3), 425–440.

Arocha, J. F., & Patel, V. L. (1995). Novice diagnostic reasoning in medicine: Accounting for evidence. *The Journal of the Learning Sciences, 4*(4), 355–384.

Baird, D. (2004). *Thing knowledge: A philosophy of scientific instruments.* University of California Press.

Baker, M., Hansen, T., Joiner, R., & Traum, D. (1999). The role of grounding in collaborative learning tasks. In P. Dillenbourg (Ed.), *Collaborative learning: cognitive and computational approaches* (pp. 31–63; 223–225). Elsevier.

Barron, B. (2003). When smart groups fail. *The Journal of the Learning Sciences, 12*(3), 307–359.

Barron, B. J., Schwartz, D. L., Vye, N. J., Moore, A., Petrosino, A., Zech, L., & Bransford, J. D. (1998). Doing with understanding: Lessons from research on problem-and project-based learning. *Journal of the Learning Sciences, 7*(3–4), 271–311.

Bateson, G. (1972). *Steps to an ecology of mind.* Ballantine.

Bauersfeld, H., Krummheur, G., & Voigt, J. (1988). Interactional theory of learning and teaching mathematics and related microethnographical studies. In H.-G. Steiner & A. Vermandel (Eds.), *Foundations and methodology of the discipline of mathematics education* (pp. 174–188). Proceedings of the TME Conference.

Bell, A., & Gresalfi, M. (2017). Teaching with videogames: How experience impacts classroom integration. *Technology, Knowledge and Learning, 22*(3), 513–526.

Blumenfeld, P. C., Soloway, E., Marx, R. W., Krajcik, J. S., Guzdial, M., & Palincsar, A. (1991). Motivating project-based learning: Sustaining the doing, supporting the learning. *Educational Psychologist, 26*(3–4), 369–398.

Boyd, R., Richerson, P. J., & Henrich, J. (2011). The cultural niche: Why social learning is essential for human adaptation. *Proceedings of the National Academy of Sciences, 108*(Supplement 2), 10918–10925.

Bradshaw, G. (1992). The airplane and the logic of invention. In R. Giere & H. Feigl (Eds.), *Cognitive models of science* (pp. 239–250). University of Minnesota Press.

Bradshaw, G. (2005). What's so hard about rocket science? Secrets the rocket boys knew. In M. E. Gorman, R. D. Tweney, D. C. Gooding, & A. Kincannon (Eds.), *Scientific and technological thinking* (pp. 259–275). Erlbaum.

Bransford, J. D., & Schwartz, D. L. (1999). Rethinking transfer: A simple proposal with multiple implications. *Review of Research in Education, 24*(1), 61–100.

Broudy, H. S. (1977). Types of knowledge and purposes of education. In R. C. Anderson, R. J. Spiro, & W. E. Montague (Eds.), *Schooling and the acquisition of knowledge* (pp. 1–17). Erlbaum.

Brown, A. L. (1997). Transforming schools into communities of thinking and learning about serious matters. *American Psychologist, 52*(4), 399.

Brown, A. L., Ash, D., Rutherford, M., Nakagawa, K., Gordon, A., & Campione, J. C. (1993). Distributed expertise in the classroom. In G. Salomon (Ed.), *Distributed cognitions: Psychological and educational considerations* (pp. 188–228). Cambridge University Press.

Butcher, C., Mylander, C., & Goldin-Meadow, S. (1991). Displaced communication in a self-styled gesture system: Pointing at the nonpresent. *Cognitive Development, 6*(3), 315–342.

Carraher, T. N., Carraher, D. W., & Schliemann, A. D. (1985). Mathematics in the streets and in schools. *British Journal of Developmental Psychology, 3*(1), 21–29.

Cartwright, N. (1999). *The dappled world: A study of the boundaries of science.* Cambridge University Press.

Chi, M. T., & Wylie, R. (2014). The ICAP framework: Linking cognitive engagement to active learning outcomes. *Educational Psychologist, 49*(4), 219–243.

Clark, A., & Chalmers, D. (1998). The extended mind. *Analysis, 58*(1), 7–19.

Cobb, P. (1994). Where is the mind? Constructivist and sociocultural perspectives on mathematical development. *Educational Researcher, 23*(7), 13–20.

Cobb, P., & Bowers, J. (1999). Cognitive and situated learning perspectives in theory and practice. *Educational Researcher, 28*(2), 4–15.

Cohen, E. G. (1994). Restructuring the classroom: Conditions for productive small groups. *Review of Educational Research, 64*(1), 1–35.

CTGV [The Cognition and Technology Group at Vanderbilt]. (1997). *The Jasper Project: Lessons in curriculum, instruction, assessment, and professional development.* Erlbaum.

Damon, W., & Phelps, E. (1989). Critical distinctions among three approaches to peer education. *International Journal of Educational Research, 13*(1), 9–19.

Dillenbourg, P. (1999). What do you mean by collaborative learning? In P. Dillenbourg (Ed.) *Collaborative learning: Cognitive and computational approaches* (pp. 1–19). Elsevier.

Engeström, Y. (1999). Activity theory and individual and social transformation. In Y. Engeström, R. Miettinen, & R. Punamaki (Eds.), *Perspectives on activity theory* (pp. 19–38), Cambridge University Press.

Fay, A. L., & Mayer, R. E. (1994). Benefits of teaching design skills before teaching LOGO computer programming: Evidence for syntax-independent learning. *Journal of Educational Computing Research, 11* ,187–210.

Gallese, V. (2003a). The manifold nature of interpersonal relations: The quest for a common mechanism. *Philosophical Transactions of the Royal Society B: Biological Sciences, 358*, 517–528. Retrieved from www.journals.royalsoc.ac.uk/media/nntr48g0hl1yrjb14j4k/contributions/u/t/a/2/uta2fm7w4y0w51yb.pdf

Gallese, V. (2003b) The roots of empathy: The shared manifold hypothesis and the neural basis of intersubjectivity. *Psychopatology, 36*(4), 171–180.

Garrod, S., & Pickering, M. J. (2004). Why is conversation so easy? *Trends in Cognitive Sciences, 8*(1), 8–11.

Gee, J. P. (2014). *An introduction to discourse analysis: Theory and method.* Routledge.

Gee, J. P. (2015). *Social linguistics and literacies: Ideology in discourses* (5th ed.). Routledge.

Gee, J. P. (2020). *What is a human? Language, mind, and culture.* Springer Nature.

Geertz, C. (1973). *The interpretation of cultures.* Basic Books.

Gergely, G., & Csibra, G. (2006). Sylvia's recipe: The role of imitation, and pedagogy in the transmission of cultural knowledge. In N. J. Enfield & S. C. Levinson (Eds.), *Roots of human sociality: Culture, cognition, and interaction* (pp. 229–255). Berg.

Gerwing, J., & Bavelas, J. (2004). Linguistic influences on gesture's form. *Gesture, 4*(2), 157–195.

Gibson, J. J. (1979/2014). *The ecological approach to visual perception: Classic edition.* Psychology Press.

Goldberg, T., Schwarz, B. B., & Porat, D. (2008). Living and dormant collective memories as contexts of history learning. *Learning and Instruction, 18*(3), 223–237.

Goldin-Meadow, S. (2003). *Hearing gesture: How our hands help us think.* Harvard University Press.

Goldman, A. I. (1986). *Epistemology and cognition.* Harvard University Press.

Goldstone, R. L., & Son, J. Y. (2005). The transfer of scientific principles using concrete and idealized simulations. *The Journal of the Learning Sciences, 14*(1), 69–110.

Goodwin, C. (2000). Gesture, aphasia, and interaction. *Language and Gesture, 2*, 84–98.

Greeno, J. G. (1994). Gibson's affordances. *Psychological Review, 101*(2), 336–342.

Greeno, J. G., & Engeström, Y. (2014). Learning in activity. In R. K. Sawyer (Ed.), *The Cambridge handbook of the learning sciences* (2nd ed., pp. 128–147). Cambridge University Press.

Greeno, J. G., & Moore, J. L. (1993). Situativity and symbols: Response to Vera and Simon. *Cognitive Science, 17*(1), 49–59.

Greeno, J. G., Moore, J. L., & Smith, D. R. (1993). Transfer of situated learning. In D. K. Detterman & R. J. Sternberg (Eds.), *Transfer on trial: Intelligence, cognition, and instruction* (pp. 99–167). Ablex Publishing.

Gresalfi, M. S., & Barnes, J. (2016). Designing feedback in an immersive videogame: Supporting student mathematical engagement. *Educational Technology Research and Development, 64*(1), 65–86.

Hmelo-Silver, C. E. (2004). Problem-based learning: What and how do students learn? *Educational Psychology Review, 16*(3), 235–266.

Holler, J., & Stevens, R. (2007). The effect of common ground on how speakers use gesture and speech to represent size information. *Journal of Language and Social Psychology, 26*(1), 4–27.

Holler, J., & Wilkin, K. (2009). Communicating common ground: How mutually shared knowledge influences speech and gesture in a narrative task. *Language and Cognitive Processes, 24*(2), 267–289.

Howe, C. (2009). Collaborative group work in middle childhood. *Human Development, 52*(4), 215–239.

Huguet, P., Galvaing, M. P., Monteil, J. M., & Dumas, F. (1999). Social presence effects in the Stroop task: Further evidence for an attentional view of social facilitation. *Journal of Personality and Social Psychology, 77*(5), 1011.

Hutchins, E. (1995). *Cognition in the wild* (No. 1995). MIT Press.

Hutchins, E. (2010). Cognitive ecology. *Topics in Cognitive Science, 2*(4), 705–715.

Hutchins, E. (2014). The cultural ecosystem of human cognition. *Philosophical Psychology, 27*, 34–49. doi: 10.1080/09515089.2013.830548

Iacoboni, M., Molnar-Szakacs, I., Gallese, V., Buccino, G., Mazziotta, J. C., & Rizzolatti, G. (2005). Grasping the intentions of others with one's own mirror neuron system. *PLoS Biol, 3*(3), e79.

Iriki, A., Tanaka, M., & Iwamura, Y. (1996). Coding of modified body schema during tool use by macaque postcentral neurones. *Neuroreport, 7*(14), 2325–2330.

Jacobson, C., & Lehrer, R. (2000). Teacher appropriation and student learning of geometry through design. *Journal for Research in Mathematics Education, 31*(1), 71–88.

Johnson, D. W., Johnson, R. T., & Stanne, M. B. (2000). *Cooperative learning methods: A meta-analysis.* University of Minnesota.

Jordan, B. (1989). Cosmopolitical obstetrics: Some insights from the training of traditional midwives. *Social Science & Medicine, 28*(9), 925–937.

Kelly, S., Byrne, K., & Holler, J. (2011). Raising the ante of communication: evidence for enhanced gesture use in high stakes situations. *Information, 2*(4), 579–593.

Kirschner, P. A., Sweller, J., & Clark, R. E. (2006). Why minimal guidance during instruction does not work: An analysis of the failure of constructivist, discovery, problem-based, experiential, and inquiry-based teaching. *Educational Psychologist, 41*(2), 75–86.

Klahr, D., & Nigam, M. (2004). The equivalence of learning paths in early science instruction: Effects of direct instruction and discovery learning. *Psychological Science, 15*(10), 661–667.

Krajcik, J. S., & Blumenfeld, P. C. (2006). *Project-based learning* (pp. 317–34). In R. K. Sawyer (Ed)., *The Cambridge handbook of the learning sciences.* Cambridge University Press.

Kurland, D. M., & Pea, R. D. (1985). Children's mental models of recursive LOGO programs. *Journal of Educational Computing Research, 1,* 235–244.

Lave, J. (1988). *Cognition in practice: Mind, mathematics and culture in everyday life.* Cambridge University Press.

Lave, J., & Wenger, E. (1991). Legitimate peripheral participation in communities of practice. In R. Pea & J. S. Brown (Eds.), *Situated learning: Legitimate peripheral participation* (pp. 89–117). Cambridge University Press.

Lee, M., & Thompson, A. (1997). Guided instruction in LOGO programming and the development of cognitive monitoring strategies among college students. *Journal of Educational Computing Research, 16,*125–144.

Lehrer, R., & Schauble, L. (2000). Developing model-based reasoning in mathematics and science. *Journal of Applied Developmental Psychology, 21*(1), 39–48.

Lerman, S. (1996). Intersubjectivity in mathematics learning: A challenge to the radical constructivist paradigm? *Journal for Research in Mathematics Education, 27*(2), 133–150.

Lloyd, R. (2010). Rosalind Franklin and DNA: How wronged was she. *Scientific American, 3.* Retrieved from https://blogs.scientificamerican.com/observations/rosalind-franklin-and-dna-how-wronged-was-she/

Lobato, J. (2003). How design experiments can inform a rethinking of transfer and vice versa. *Educational Researcher, 32*(1), 17–20.

Marx, R. W., Blumenfeld, P. C., Krajcik, J. S., & Soloway, E. (1997). Enacting project-based science. *The Elementary School Journal, 97*(4), 341–358.

Mayer, R. E. (2004). Should there be a three-strikes rule against pure discovery learning? *American Psychologist, 59*(1), 14.

McCullough, D. (2015). *The Wright brothers.* Simon and Schuster.

McNeill, D. (1992). *Hand and mind: What gestures reveal about thought.* University of Chicago Press.

Michaelis, J. E., & Nathan, M. J. (2016). *Observing and measuring interest development among high school students in an out-of-school robotics competition* (ASEE Paper ID #16242). Paper presentation to the American Society of Engineering Education ASEE 2016, New Orleans, LA: ASEE.

Moll, H., & Tomasello, M. (2007). Cooperation and human cognition: The Vygotskian intelligence hypothesis. *Philosophical Transactions of the Royal Society B: Biological Sciences, 362*(1480), 639–648.

Mondada, L. (2013). Embodied and spatial resources for turn-taking in institutional multi-party interactions: Participatory democracy debates. *Journal of Pragmatics, 46*(1), 39–68.

Nasir, N. I. S., & Saxe, G. B. (2003). Ethnic and academic identities: A cultural practice perspective on emerging tensions and their management in the lives of minority students. *Educational Researcher, 32*(5), 14–18.

Nathan, M. J., & Alibali, M. W. (2011). How gesture use enables intersubjectivity in the classroom. In G. Stam & M. Ishino (Eds.), *Integrating gestures: The interdisciplinary nature of gesture* (pp. 257–266). John Benjamins.

Nathan, M. J., Alibali, M. W., & Church, R. B. (2017). Making and breaking common ground: How teachers use gesture to foster learning in the classroom. In R. B. Church, M. W. Alibali, & S. D. Kelly, (Eds.), *Why gesture? How the hands function in speaking, thinking and communicating.* (pp. 285–316). John Benjamins. doi 10.1075/gs.7.04der

Nathan, M. J., Eilam, B., & Kim, S. (2007). To disagree, we must also agree: How intersubjectivity structures and perpetuates discourse in a mathematics classroom. *The Journal of the Learning Sciences, 16*(4), 523–563.

Nathan, M. J., Srisurichan, R., Walkington, C., Wolfgram, M., Williams, C., & Alibali, M. W. (2013). Building cohesion across representations: A mechanism for STEM integration. *Journal of Engineering Education, 102*(1), 77–116. doi:10.1002/jee.20000

Nathan, M. J., Wolfgram, M., Srisurichan, R., Walkington, C., & Alibali, M. W. (2017). Threading mathematics through symbols, sketches, software, silicon and wood: Teachers produce and maintain cohesion to support STEM integration. *The Journal of Educational Research, 110*(3), 272–293. doi:10.1080/00220671.2017.1287046

Osborne, J. (2010). Arguing to learn in science: The role of collaborative, critical discourse. *Science, 328*(5977), 463–466.

Papert, S. (1980). *Mindstorms: Children, computers, and powerful ideas.* Basic Books.

Papert, S. (1991). Preface. In: I. Harel & S. Papert (Eds.), *Constructionism, research reports and essays,* 1985–1990 (p. 1). Ablex Publishing Corporation.

Pea, R. D., & Kurland, D. M. (1984). On the cognitive effects of learning computer programming. *New Ideas in Psychology, 2,* 137–168.

Pinker, S. (2010). The cognitive niche: Coevolution of intelligence, sociality, and language. *Proceedings of the National Academy of Sciences, 107*(Supplement 2), 8993–8999.

Puntambekar, S., & Hübscher, R. (2005). Tools for scaffolding students in a complex learning environment: What have we gained and what have we missed? *Educational Psychologist, 40*(1), 1–12.

Quinn, R. W., & Dutton, J. E. (2005). Coordination as energy-in-conversation: A process theory of organizing. *Academy of Management Review, 30,* 38–57.

Rizzolati, G., Fogassi, L., & Gallese, V. (2001). Neurophysiological mechanisms underlying the understanding and imitation of action. *Nature Reviews Neuroscience, 2,* 661–670.

Robbins, P., & Aydede, M. (Eds.). (2008). *The Cambridge handbook of situated cognition.* Cambridge University Press.

Rogoff, B. (1990). *Apprenticeship in thinking: Cognitive development in social context.* Oxford University Press.

Rommetveit, R. (1979). On negative rationalism in scholarly studies of verbal communication and dynamic residuals in the construction of human intersubjectivity. In R. Rommetveit & R. M. Blakar (Eds.), *Studies of language, thought, and verbal communication.* (pp. 147–162). Academic.

Schwarz, B. B. (2009). Argumentation and learning. In N. M. Mirza & A.-N. Perret-Clermont (Eds.) *Argumentation and education* (pp. 91–126). Springer.

Schwartz, D. L. (1995). The emergence of abstract representations in dyad problem solving. *The Journal of the Learning Sciences, 4*(3), 321–354.

Seligman, M. E. (2012). *Flourish: A visionary new understanding of happiness and well-being.* Simon & Schuster.

Sfard, A. (2000). On reform movement and the limits of mathematical discourse. *Mathematical Thinking and Learning, 2*(3), 157–189.

Shaffer, D. W. (2006). Epistemic frames for epistemic games. *Computers & Education, 46*(3), 223–234.

Simon, M. A. (1995). Reconstructing mathematics pedagogy from a constructivist perspective. *Journal for Research in Mathematics Education, 26,* 114–145.

Tomasello, M. (1999). The human adaptation for culture. *Annual Review of Anthropology, 28*(1), 509–529.

Tomasello, M. (2009a). *The cultural origins of human cognition.* Harvard University Press.

Tomasello, M. (2009b). *Why we cooperate.* MIT Press.

Tomasello, M., Carpenter, M., Call, J., Behne, T., & Moll, H. (2005). Understanding and sharing intentions: The origins of cultural cognition. *Behavioral and Brain Sciences, 28*(5), 675–691.

Tomasello, M., & Rakoczy, H. (2003). What makes human cognition unique? From individual to shared to collective intentionality. *Mind & Language, 18*(2), 121–147.

Trevarthen, C. (1979). Communication and cooperation in early infancy. A description of primary intersubjectivity. In M. Bullowa (Ed.), *Before speech: The beginning of human communication* (pp. 321–347). Cambridge University Press.

Tversky, B. (2019). *Mind in motion: How action shapes thought.* Hachette UK.

Vygotsky, L. S. (1978). *Mind in society: The development of higher mental processes.* (Trans. M. Cole, V. John-Steiner, S. Scribner, & E. Souberman) Harvard University Press.

Vygotsky, L. (1986). *Thought and language* (Ed. and Trans. A. Kozulin). MIT Press.

Vygotsky, L. S. (1981). The instrumental method in psychology. In J. V. Wertsch (Ed. and Trans.), *The concept of activity in Soviet psychology* (pp. 137–143). Sharpe. (Original work published 1930)

Walkington, C., Chelule, G., Woods, D., & Nathan, M. J. (2019). Collaborative gesture as a case of extended mathematical cognition. *The Journal of Mathematical Behavior, 55,* 100683. doi.org/10.1016/j.jmathb.2018.12.002

Walkington, C. A., Nathan, M. J., Wolfgram, M., Alibali, M. W., & Srisurichan, R. (2014). Bridges and barriers to constructing conceptual cohesion across modalities and temporalities: Challenges of STEM integration in the precollege engineering classroom. In J. Strobel, S. Purzer, & M. Cardella (Eds.) *Engineering in pre-college settings: Research into practice* (pp. 183–209). Purdue University Press.

Watson, J. D. (1968). *The double helix: A personal account of the discovery of the structure of DNA.* Atheneum.

Wen, Y., Leng, J., Shen, X., Han, G., Sun, L., & Yu, F. (2020). Environmental and health effects of ventilation in subway stations: A literature review. *International Journal of Environmental Research and Public Health, 17*(3), 1084.

Wertsch, J. V. (1991). The problem of meaning in a sociocultural approach to mind. In A. McKeough & J. L. Lupart (Eds.), *Toward the practice of theory-based instruction* (pp. 31–49). Routledge.

Wertsch, J. V. (2009). *Voices of the mind: Sociocultural approach to mediated action.* Harvard University Press.

Whiten, A., Horner, V., & De Waal, F. B. (2005). Conformity to cultural norms of tool use in chimpanzees. *Nature, 437*(7059), 737–740.

Williams, J. M., & Tolmie, A. (2000). Conceptual change in biology: Group interaction and the understanding of inheritance. *British Journal of Developmental Psychology, 18*(4), 625–649.

Witt, J. K., Proffitt, D. R., & Epstein, W. (2005). Tool use affects perceived distance, but only when you intend to use it. *Journal of Experimental Psychology: Human Perception and Performance, 31*(5), 880.

Wood, D., Bruner, J. S., & Ross, G. (1976). The role of tutoring in problem solving. *Journal of Child Psychology and Psychiatry, 17*(2), 89–100.

Yackel, E., & Cobb, P. (1996). Sociomathematical norms, argumentation, and autonomy in mathematics. *Journal for Research in Mathematics Education, 27*(4), 458–477.

Zajonc, R. B. (1965). Social facilitation. *Science, 149,* 269–274.

Zajonc, R. B. (1968). Attitudinal effects of mere exposure. *Journal of Personality and Social Psychology, 9*(22), 1.

Grounded and Embodied Learning in the Sociocultural Band

10.1 GEL OF ACADEMIC CONTENT AREAS IN THE SOCIOCULTURAL LEVEL

Sociocultural learning processes center around changing practices for engaged community participation by following norms of accepted forms of discourse. Learners develop manners for knowing-with that shape how they talk and act, use tools and representation, and how they think. I have described them loosely as exhibiting Type 3 processing that complements those I described for Type 1 and 2 processing. I identified several GEL processes that operate on the sociocultural time scale.

As I established in Chapter 9, participation, and learning by adopting one's practices and use of tools, as well as manner of talk and ways of thinking are central at this scale. These changing practices are possible by participants establishing and maintaining common ground, which is necessary in order to have productive interactions with others. While interacting, people develop and use taken-as-shared ways of knowing, including shared tools, formalisms, and other forms of representation. Taken-as-shared ways of knowing include material as well as symbolic entities, and each can serve epistemic roles, with materialist epistemology adding to cultural advancements through social construction. These taken-as-shared entities join social interactions to make distributed knowledge possible. The social dynamics naturally lead to argumentation and negotiated forms of meaning as people adopt, broach, and challenge group norms and taken-as-shared objects. This underscores the interplay of GEL behaviors across levels: individuals conform to join communities of practice and also change those communities by their involvement.

My main objective in this chapter is to show how these sociocultural level GEL processes contribute to educational aims in a variety of content areas: Literacy, history, mathematics, science and engineering, computing, making, and learning to teach. I draw on these examples and others from Chapter 9 to compile a set of GEL principles for improving education by enhancing student learning, classroom instruction, ways of designing educational innovations, and carrying out assessment practices. By increasing awareness of these learning processes I hope to show how they can be cultivated in order to contribute more effectively to successes in education.

DOI: 10.4324/9780429329098-10

10.1.1 Literacy

Notions of literacy are generational and cultural. At various times and among various groups, there have been dominant periods of oral, written, digital, and multimedia forms of literacy. diSessa (2001) notes how computers and digital media have transformed classic notions of literacy to include images, spreadsheets, hyperlinked text, and more; and to which one could add the rapid, networked image-based qualities of social media that have emerged since. Gee (2012, p. 418) acknowledges the economic and social power of achieving "premium quality digital literacy" and to "use specialist/technical language connected to digital tools" in this digital age. Each of these scholars frames literacies quite broadly, and consistent with Barton and colleagues (2000, p. 39) contends that "literacy is best understood as a set of social practices."

For example, with the increased availability and relevance of geospatial positioning technologies, "locative literacies" (Taylor, 2017) have recently come to prominence, and with these, educational approaches to support its development (Hall, Ma, & Nemirovsky, 2014). *Locative literacies* are a way people can share their documented accounts of digital, place-based representations of their neighborhoods. Talk about common ground! These are the places they walk and ride every day, passing by their neighbors, shops, and parks. For example, the "mobile mapping" activity uses GPS drawings created by tracing the path of someone walking. The written products are situated records of movements through the neighborhood. They are a form of literacy because they are used to inscribe ideas that can be shared with others in ways. By sharing these *passages*—in both a literal and literary sense— can help them understand people's lives in terms of places and movement. Locative literacies provide access to embedded representations that are distributed across space, digital devices, and the participating agents in an activity.

Taylor (2017) investigated the behaviors and interactions of a group of six 12- to 15-year-old teenagers to document how young people engaged in "learning along lines" formed by their movements, and how they planned their pathways to create intentional literary products in their community. (As the reader will see below, thinking about the movements has many of the same qualities as the body syntonic reasoning with the Logo turtle.) Taylor analyzed video records of students' speech and activity over the various phases of GPS drawing. Several forms of literacy were observed. Students developed a way to "read" the GPS records of movement. This motivated them to inscribe messages at the scale of their city by walking, and to read and interpret the messages provided by others. Composition skills were engaged through planning and revising the messages, which could then be narrated to others. An example is shown in Figure 10.1.

The passages made people think and change their views. These inscribed messages were shared with urban planners, cartographers, and other stakeholders at community meetings. Initially, the adults found the information incommensurate with their existing community plans that were established by their prior ways of knowing-with. This is because urban planning is traditionally done with static plans and maps of the city. Now there is growing realization of the potential to improve city planning to respond to the ways spaces are actually navigated and used. These new forms of geospatial literacy create new ways of knowing-with that invite greater citizen involvement. As Taylor (2017, pp. 539–540) describes it, "The analysis shows that learning along lines foregrounds humans not merely as consumers or generators of texts but as being part of that text, literacy agents of a text they populate."

10.1.2 History and Social Studies

History is an area of social studies education that addresses many aspects of individual and collective behavior, such as culture, continuity and change, and power, authority, and

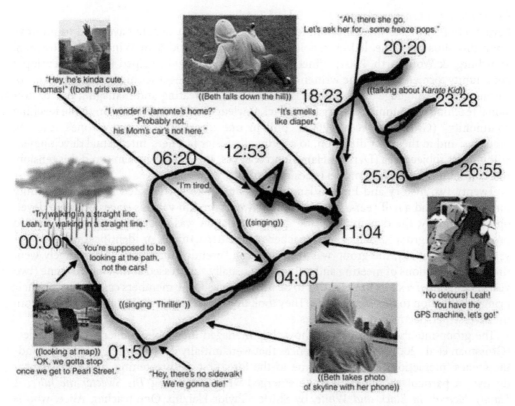

FIGURE 10.1 Students use global positioning system to inscribe "LOVE" by tracking their movement over several blocks in their neighborhood.

governance. Students at the middle and high school levels are expected to exhibit certain "purposes, knowledge, and intellectual processes" for social studies (National Curriculum Standards for Social Studies, 2018). These include a wide range of social and civic skills, such as: assessing historical sources and appreciating the influences and values of different perspectives; building interpretations of past events, and evaluating the interpretations of others; developing a historical perspective, such as understanding how the world has changed and its relevance for what is to come; evaluate and use methods of historical inquiry; and so on. Themes of meaning making and interpretation, which are central to GEL, are clearly also paramount for social studies education. Social studies also contributes to GEL the importance of developing a sense of perspective, and of locating one's self and one's generation within historical and cultural contexts.

Two lines of intervention offer promising approaches to these broad curricular expectations. One is to form ongoing learning communities that support teachers in their daily teaching and long-term planning. Another is to immerse students in the practices of using computational media to simulate complex historical events and social patterns of activity.

History education explores questions beyond dates and simple causes of major events. For students to understand history they must also grapple with the complexities of the events, the different perspectives of those who leave behind the historical records, and the relevance of past events to current and future social movements. At the high school level, teachers bring tremendous expertise to this content. However they need regular support from colleagues to achieve the kind of ongoing professional learning that can keep their teaching relevant and their own viewpoints fresh.

Communities of Learners Among High School Teachers
Several efforts of fostering communities of learners among teachers have tried to improve
upon this situation. One, led by scholars Pam Grossman and Sam Wineburg (Grossman,
Wineburg, & Woolworth, 2001; Wineburg & Grossman, 1998), helped teachers develop a
community formed around the written word. They brought together high school teachers of
socials studies, language arts, and special education. In creating and managing this professional teaching community, the organizers acknowledge an "essential tension in the teaching
community" (Grossman, et al., 2001): pull in one direction to improve one's teaching
practices, and in the other direction, to continually foster teachers' intellectual development
within their subject area (Darling-Hammond & Sykes, 1999). Rather than avoid this tension,
this community of learners model is designed for it.

Twenty-two history and English/language arts teachers participated in this community
for about two and a half years. The community went through various stages of group development. Initially, the dynamics during group formation was structured primarily around
pre-existing subgroups, such as each teacher's home department, or identification as a first-
year teacher. Initially, the group was regarded as a "pseudocommunity." They largely went
through the motions of meeting and talking and usually suppressed conflict. Over time (two
years is still rather a short time for this to be fully achieved) the members came to assign their
primary affiliation to this community. They took up shared responsibility and benefited from
the diverse perspectives of its members.

The group members also grew in how they managed inevitable intellectual "fault lines"
(Grossman et al., 2001, p. 988). Differences that were initially denied or relegated to behind-
the-scenes interactions eventually came to the fore, first as threatening, and then as productive. A particularly illustrative one emerged when discussing *The Sweeter the Juice: A
Family Memoir in Black and White,* by Shirlee Taylor Haizlip. One teacher, Alice, who is
coming to more deeply understand the form and impact of systemic racism, identifies the
accidental drowning of Black children as the result of institutionalized racism, because
they had fewer opportunities than white children to learn to swim. (For example, the local
YMCA was segregated.) Alice relates this to policies in her own school, such as tardiness,
that unfairly penalize Black students. Not all the others agree, and there are some breaches
of social norms during this discussion that reveal how fragile that can be early in the life of
a group. Yet they also illustrate how such discussions ultimately can strengthen the group, as
members striving to meet the ideals of the nascent community take more risks, explore more
tricky topics, and seek clarity for themselves as they understand the social structures in place
to create a safe space.

The experiment with community had many objectives. One of the most central, though,
is that to teach the ideals and complexities of human history to young minds necessitates
understanding the power of each individual's voice. By participating in this group, many
of these teachers were able to experience what it was like to speak with uncertainty as they
strove to understand the complexities of the human situation. This realization had grown
stale for some teachers. It also gave them empathy for what their students may experience as
they make sense of contested interpretations of events that might otherwise be considered
as "settled." As Wineburg and Grossman (1998, p. x) assert, "At the heart of our work is this
simple but indisputable principle: Schools cannot become exciting places for children until
they first become exciting places for adults." Teachers' involvement in this project also had a
positive effect on the students and the school climate (Wineburg & Grossman, 1998).

Simulating Social Phenomena
WorkingShops was another school-wide professional learning project (Nathan & Kalmon,
2000). This one was initiated by the teachers, who then then sought out partnerships with

educational technology developers and learning scientists. One of the initiatives, led by history teacher John Zola, looked at how students could understand the role of protest in achieving social change (Repenning et al., 2000). For these students, the actual events were rather abstract in that the students' lives were remote from the sociopolitical upheavals that were often taking place, and they occurred in the distant past (for them!). The phenomena were somewhat outside of the students' ways of knowing-with, and they regarded simply as facts to memorize. Zola reasoned that students could develop a deeper understanding of the social impacts of protest if the students themselves could develop computer simulations of the events in terms of the interactions of different participants.

Students worked together in groups, using AgentSheets, a visually based computer programming environment, like Scratch, which allows users to quickly build simulations and computer games (Ioannidou et al., 2003; Repenning, Webb, & Ioannidou, 2010). In one of the earliest group projects, three girls developed a website that organized information about the United Farmers Grape Boycott. In it, they embedded a simulation in order to depict how things unfolded among the different participants: farmers, workers, consumers, and organizers. Initially, their simulation predicted no grapes were picked when the Mexican and Filipino workers who were terribly underpaid and overworked became angry enough to organize under the leadership of César Chávez and form a strike. However, this contradicted information they read that the grapes went to market even while the workers were on strike. This led to the awareness that farmers and factories hired workers illegally to maintain their productivity, which was then added to the simulation and website.

Teacher Zola described the initial process as a general success, even with many lessons to learn from them. In an interview (Nathan, 2000), he reported

> It worked really well. … I think the learning kids did was really significant …
>
> Kids got very independent in their learning, was another thing. In the learning of social studies.
>
> Once we got things conceptualized they really took off. … Pretty remarkable to watch how hard they worked on stuff.
>
> Also neat in terms of a product that is up on the Web, something that moves and grooves and does that sort of stuff. … Where the learning came was in the building [of the simulations].

The students also offered insights about their process and learning.

Student Claire:	I didn't know anything about the boycott before. Having to apply it to the technology made me get into it more and understand it fully so that I could have it come out correct.
Teacher Mr. Zola:	More so or differently so than if you had created a poster board?
Student Susana:	You had to know more because you couldn't leave out things. So if you didn't know everything you couldn't do it.
Student Steph:	It's not like you can copy it out of an encyclopedia and put it on the poster board.
Student Mara:	It wasn't just boring writing stuff down; we got to interact with what we were doing.
Student Steph:	[making the protest simulation] totally made you apply what you know towards like what you're doing!
Student Susana:	I took this class just for history; I didn't know it was gonna be anything with computers, but now that I did the whole computer thing, it's changing my daily life cause I used to hate computers and now I don't.

In subsequent years, Zola used simulations created by students to teach those concepts about protest and prompt new simulations. Students in subsequent years used these tools to simulate events such as: The United Autoworkers (UAW) sit-down strike of Flint, Michigan in 1936; Rosa Parks and the Montgomery Bus Boycott of 1955; and the protests at the 1968 Democratic Presidential Convention in Chicago.

Site-Based History Education

Much of history inquiry and education centers around the study, evaluation, and interpretation of historical documents (e.g., Rouet, Favart, Britt, & Perfetti, 1997; Wineburg, 1991, 1998). As Baron (2012) notes, however, most people will engage in history through historic places (Rosenzweig and Thelen, 1998). *Site-based history education* uses location-based experiences such as exploration of historical buildings, homesteads and battlefields, to engage the multisensory nature of learning. However, in practice, little learning happens for most students during "field trips" to historical sites. This is because students are seldom guided for how to engage with these rich experiences (Baron, 2012).

As a primary starting point, Baron selects the physical structure of the building as the common ground for improving the educational influences of these experiences. From a materialist epistemology, buildings offer a grounded resource for historical events. The very nature of their existence is the product of the time, place, and social events. Baron sought to understand how to guide educational experiences by investigating the processes used by professional historians when they visit a historic building.

As an example, Baron chose the Old North Church in Boston, Massachusetts, which was the site where lanterns were hung to initiate Paul Revere's famous ride in 1775. Baron offers these heuristics for facilitating historical thinking at historical sites: discerning the origin of the building and how it came to reside in this place; relating this to other buildings of this place or of this time period; its role through various eras; and, empathetically, how the assortment of people touched by this building have responded to this space at various points in time.

10.1.3 Mathematics Education

Participation in a community motivates the need for its members to formalize shared experiences. This allows them to be recorded and used for analysis and prediction. Mathematics was developed, in part, to provide this formal system of symbolic representation and analysis. To participate in communities, such as those in the natural and social sciences—also in art and design—one must learn the discourse of mathematics.

Situating formalisms in a social context enables students to ground these formalisms. The symbols become meaningful in relation to events the students themselves experienced. For example, children engaged in a socially interactive, embodied learning environment came to enact and then internalize ideas of numerical magnitude into a mental number line (Fischer, Link, Cress, Nuerk, & Moeller, 2015). Grounding also helps students to understand the *purpose* of using formalisms to concisely summarize and persuade others. This provides guidelines for generating their own representations and interpret the representations made by others.

Mathematics of Democracy and Civic Engagement

Robert Moses's "Algebra Project" (Moses & Cobb, 2001) provides a rich illustration of using situated representations to their experiences. The project started with Moses observing attitudes toward math achievement among his daughter's classmates "skewing along racial and class lines" (p. 96). He set out to devise an experiential mathematics education program with goals and supports for educating historically marginalized students. Moses thought about the Algebra Project in terms of "community organizing" and integrated input from parents, teachers, and students to address community needs.

Moses developed the "math of trips." These were learning experiences that drew on students' familiarity with navigating the subway system in Boston. For example, he would take a group of sixth graders from Cambridge to Boston and return to a different station back in Cambridge. Students were then guided to work out a progressive formalization from the lived experience to an algebraic representation. This approach should remind the reader of some of the qualities of concreteness fading that I reviewed earlier.

Units in the Algebra Project directed students to address five important steps. First, students would start with a shared experience, like the subway ride. Second, from this common ground, they would co-create pictorial representations to model the events. Third, students used intuitive language (regular "people talk") to describe the events. Students would have to collectively negotiate the meaning of these pictorial and verbal representations. In this step, students were learning to adopt the sociomathematical norms that made for a proper representation of their travels. Fourth, they would then move to more carefully structured language, including "feature talk." For example, students would need to identify four fundamental mathematical features common among all trips: the start, finish, direction, and distance traveled. From this, the fifth and final stage would be to put this in terms of an algebraic representation.

As one example shared by Dubinsky and Moses (2011, pp. 304–306), students would determine the starting point, and then set x_1 for the first location, x_2 for the location of Harvard, and DELTA-x for the displacement. Then the first feature-talk sentence is mathematized into the equation,

$$x_1 + \Delta x = x_2$$

and the second is mathematized into the equation

$$x_2 - x_1 = \Delta x$$

Students would then create a "trip line." This is a form of number line marked with locations along the trip. The positive and negative displacements (distance from the baseline starting point) were represented as positive and negative integers. This helped to capture the events as movements using a cultural tool, and then reify the movements into mathematical objects for symbolizing. In this way, the meaning of these symbols is grounded in the students' shared experiences. These grounded formalisms provided an abstract representation of the experiences that encouraged generalization to other trips. The Algebra Project showed how embodied, socially constructed learning can provide a path from shared experiences to conventionalized mathematical abstractions.

William Tate (1995) described mathematics learning from another set of shared experiences. Tate documented how one teacher, Sandra Mason, engaged students in a predominantly African American school in the practices of epidemiologists by prompting them to explore questions about the safety of their neighborhood. The children identified the preponderance of liquor stores near their schools as a root cause of the negative environment in their community. Mason encouraged her students to research the causes and solutions. They examined zoning laws and maps. They learned their city created fiscal incentives for liquor stores to open in their neighborhood, which led the students to propose a different incentive system to the city to protect their school community from the liquor stores. They used measurement, ratios and percentages, methods of data visualization, and statistics to advance their arguments for public purposes. They brought this all to the state senate and shared it with the local newspaper, which got picked up by the Associated Press and shared worldwide. This led to citations to offending citizens and liquor store owners, shutting down some of the stores and relocating others. The city council created a 600-foot liquor buffer zone around their school.

Taken-As-Shared Representations
Earlier, I reviewed aspects of the social perceptive on mathematics education and the central role that taken-as-shared representations play in the classroom (Cobb, Stephan, McClain, & Gravemeijer, 2001). *Taken-as-shared* is a form of knowing that draws on the shared intentionality among members of a discourse community (Cobb and Bowers, 1999). Its role is to provide a common interpretation. In one example, an entire sixth-grade classroom negotiated taken-as-shared meaning of the drawings and operations proposed by their peers while reasoning about a spatial reasoning task posed by one of the students (Nathan, Eilam, & Kim, 2007). The student asked: *How do you cut a pie into eight equal-sized pieces making only three cuts?* Over the next hour, students offered ideas through diagrams, gestures, object manipulation and verbal utterances in order to publicly present and then critique one another's proposals for solving the pie problem.

A significant proportion of these interactions centered around a two-dimensional drawing intended to convey time-varying operations in three dimensions. It is notoriously difficult to depict 3D information in two dimensions. People adopt certain cultural conventions of perspective when viewing these images. It is a whole other matter for young people to *create* depictions that convey this information in unambiguous ways (e.g., Smith, diSessa, & Roschelle, 1994). This was further complicated in that some of the "cuts" referred to in the problem were performed in three dimensions.

Figure 10.2 shows one frame from this interaction. Notably, the teacher had spent several weeks preceding this on fostering a respectful climate for how to engage with one another, even when confused or offering conflicting ideas (French & Nathan, 2006). They had experiences with commenting on and judging one another's solutions. Their exchanges were always respectful, though at times very energetic, with students jumping up from their seats, grabbing pens from one another, and occasions when a student's drawing was repeatedly erased and redrawn by several students.

As a clear display of extended cognition, a student struggling with words and gestures to convey how the eight pieces of the pie get produced used the whiteboard to work out his ideas. This immediately became a taken-as-shared representation that was pointed to, discussed, and altered by many of the other students in the classroom. A second student (Figure 10.2) appropriated the representation generated by the first, yet viewed it through an alternative interpretive frame. In so doing, the student proposing the new interpretation actually found it necessary to assume the physical place where the first student had been standing when initiating the drawing. These kind of physical instantiations of negotiation "common ground" provide a rich illustration of the powerful sociocultural interactions that happen in a classroom that is based on solid norms of classroom discourse.

Sociomathematical Norms
Meaning at the sociocultural level emerges through *negotiation* of taken-as-shared interpretations until mutual agreement is reached. For example, in the candy bar factory unit, students

FIGURE 10.2 Student negotiations of taken-as-shared meaning of a 2D drawing intended to convey a time-varying operation on a 3D object during a whole class discussion of solutions to the Pie Problem.

participated in mathematical discourse with the goal of solving problems of counting, packaging, and distributing the proper number of bars. In so doing, they internalized practices that aligned with decimal place-value norms of mathematical practice.

In order to have these productive interactions, class participants must accept and adhere to social norms of the discourse community. Cobb et al (2001) and Sfard (2007) distinguish between the classroom social norms and the sociomathematical norms accepted by the field. Classroom social norms can include such negotiated guidelines as respecting the value of every student's ideas, an appreciation of alternative perspectives, and the importance of justifying one's ideas (French & Nathan, 2006; Nathan & Kim, 2009). Establishing these classroom norms requires that students feel ownership of them and are willing to practice them and respectfully enforce them. Generally, classroom social norms are not specific to the content area but apply more broadly (Cobb & Hodge, 2002).

In order that students engage in appropriate practices for the professional field, students' interactions must also conform to the sociomathematical norms accepted by the field. Sociomathematical norms (Yackel & Cobb, 1996) and metalevel norms (Sfard, 2007) are those that adhere to accepted practices of the specific professional community of mathematical practitioners. Students have opportunities to inquire about their rationale, but they generally have no hand in creating them. These can include such norms as standards for what counts as an acceptable mathematical solution or proof, what counts as a unique solution, and criteria for comparing and evaluating solutions, such as elegance and efficiency.

It is by leaning on these norms that Type 3 processing can take place. Participation is the act of behaving in ways that conform to the norms of the community. As Cobb and colleagues (Bowers et al., 1999; Cobb and Bowers, 1999) describe, practices are not merely patterns of action, they are also (or come to be) patterns of speech and thought as well. Through these practices, the individual student and the learning community in which each student is situated enjoy a reflexive relationship. Students contribute to the development of practices within the classroom community through their individual practices. These community practices then shape the environment in which norms are internalized and later reproduced.

For example, one sociomathematical norm in the candy factory class was that explanations had to be provided in terms of the actions one performed on the contextual objects (candy, boxes, etc.) rather than decontextualized operations on numbers (Bowers, Cobb, & McClain, 1999). That is, the mathematical operations and relations discussed had to be *grounded*. This social norm fostered a climate of careful meaning making that helped students' mathematical development.

10.1.4 Science and Engineering Education

Scientific Inquiry
Inquiry is central to science and to science education. For the disciplinary practice of science, *inquiry* describes one of the core ways that science advances, through the investigation of the workings of the natural world (Anderson, 2002). Inquiry-based science education is a broad term that encompasses a range of active learning experiences for students. Scientific inquiry is often portrayed in textbooks, movies, and popular culture as an individual activity. However, science and engineering advancement is predominantly collaborative (Latour, 1987). As Furtak and colleagues (2012, p. 301) note, it generally "includes students drawing upon their scientific knowledge to ask scientifically oriented questions, collect and analyze evidence from scientific investigations, develop explanations of scientific phenomena, and communicate those explanations with their teacher and peers (NRC, 1996)." To learn science is to take up the practices and habits of mind that are used by scientists (NRC, 2012).

Duschl (2003, 2008) framed inquiry-based science education in terms of three dimensions—conceptual, epistemic, and social aspects. The first is used to describe the conceptual structures and cognitive processes used for scientific reasoning. The second is the epistemic framework for understanding how scientific knowledge is formed. It recognizes that students themselves can engage in this process, and that scientific knowledge and methods constantly change in the face of new findings. The third addresses the social interactions by which knowledge is constructed, such as collaboration and argumentation. Social aspects also include how scientific phenomena are communicated and represented to the scientific community and to the public, including the use of appropriate disciplinary norms of discourse. To this list of three, Furtak and colleagues (2012) add a fourth, that they call procedural knowledge. Similar to how I used it earlier, procedural knowledge in inquiry-based science is knowledge for performing the methods and practices for doing "hands-on activities where students manipulate materials and collect their own data" (p. 306). This can also include creating an experimental design and executing scientific procedures.

Furtak and colleagues performed a meta-analysis of ten years of research literature during which the notions of inquiry-based science education emerged and rose as a major focus. They used the four domains above to guide their analysis. In all, they looked at 37 studies (published in 22 papers) that were conducted in ten countries across the K–12 grade levels. These fell within multiple content areas of science, including biology, Earth and space science, physics, chemistry, and general science. Overall they found strong support in favor of inquiry-based science in comparison to more traditional forms of classroom learning. Among the sample of 37 studies, 30 of them had positive effects, and 7 had negative effects. The average effect size was 0.5, favoring inquiry-based approaches. Digging a bit further, the inquiry-based approaches that showed the greatest benefits incorporated procedural, epistemic, and social aspects of inquiry, especially when these were used together.

One example of the effective integration of procedural, epistemic, and social aspects of inquiry-based learning is a study of astronomy education at the middle school (Alexander, Fives, Buehl, & Mulhern, 2002). The astronomy lessons were framed around Galileo, the person, and his discoveries. The lessons addressed the social, cultural, and personal upheaval caused by these scientific discoveries. Students were asked to address the question "Should scientific evidence be kept from the public if it will cause confusion or unrest?" They were to consider this in terms of both the historical events of Galileo's time and current debates in the sciences.

At a procedural level, students engaged in understanding the steps scientists use to collect evidence for making persuasive arguments. At an epistemic level, students were engaged in critical evaluation of the sources and nature of scientific knowledge. At a social level, persuasion played a central role in the activities, as students evaluated arguments for and against public acceptance of Galileo's proposed paradigm shift. This illustrates ways that attending to procedural, epistemic, and social aspects of scientific inquiry can provide the basis for understanding science. This investigation also contrasted teacher- and student-led inquiry. The evidence showed that teacher-led inquiry led to greater gains in students' knowledge than student-led gains, which were more effective in changing students' beliefs.

Participation in Scientific Communities
Participation is central to learning as well as doing science and engineering. Consequently, the Next Generation Science Standards (NGSS Lead States, 2013; see also NRC, 2012) places substantial emphasis than sciences standards of the past on the importance of creating learning experiences that model and promote the adoption of proper scientific practices through participation. Participation is a broad form of learning.

In the Kids as Global Scientists project, Songer (1996) showed the intellectual impact when students' classrooms are networked to other classrooms around the world. Students were provided with access to atmospheric science mentors and the same data and other resources available to professional meteorologists. Participation in this vast learning community fueled the level of student-driven inquiry and scientific discourse, as documented in students' written assessments, interviews, and portfolios. Students who participated in the Kids as Global Scientists community demonstrated that they could explain atmospheric phenomenon (e.g., winds, precipitation, clouds and humidity, the environment, and severe weather) in general terms. Many were able to elaborate further by providing appropriate examples of these concepts.

Participation in learning communities structured around big ideas allow children to engage in sophisticated scientific reasoning and practices around the construction, evaluation, and revision of scientific models. Lehrer and Schauble (2000, 2007) designed several of these participatory learning experiences. One was designed around the cultivation of Wisconsin Fast Plants®. Plants will sprout in a day and will produce harvestable seeds about 40 days after planting. This educational resource affords observation of growth, data collection, data visualization, modeling and prediction all within a relatively short amount of time. This type of approach supports STEM (science, technology engineering, and mathematics) education more generally since these activities naturally bridge across science and mathematics via mutually reinforcing conceptual connections for each content area.

In designing these model-based learning experiences, teachers rely on a "tool kit" of five common elements: tasks (instructional activities), tools (usually mathematical, and scientific instruments such as microscopes and rulers, as well as computational resources), inscriptions (graphs, maps, and symbolic equations), methods of argumentation (such as reasoning from evidence), and activity structures (such as laboratory investigations and class discussions).

Elementary grade students used their observations of the plants over time to measure and chart their growth. They came to realize, for example, that the graphs of plant growth did not have to retain actual features of the plants, such as the leaves. They came to realize through their interactions that what became important for their discussions was representing the *measures* of plant properties, such as height. These interactions also led to students' assessment gains in math topics of number sense (especially proportional reasoning), measurement (including origin of concepts related to using a scale), space (shape), data and variability, and probability (sampling). By situating these scientific modeling practices, students showed performance gains across STEM content areas.

Participation in Hobbyist Communities

A second form of participation that is more likely to occur outside of the classroom is joining sustained communities around common activities and interests. The world needs and has depended upon the contributions of these so-called "amateur scientists" for centuries, including: the discovery of the planet Uranus by William Herschel in 1781; discovery of the Shoemaker-Levy 9 comet by Carolyn and Gene Shoemaker and David Levy in 1993 (Chapman, 2002), which struck Jupiter about one year later; and John Dobson's invention of "The Dobsonian telescope," a highly robust and affordable instrument in the 1950s, which fueled the proliferation of amateur astronomy. Observations of hobbyist communities of practice provide a rich source of information about learning through participation.

Azevedo (2013, 2015) has examined the scientific practices that arise from interactions around model rockets and amateur astronomy. Azevedo and Mann (2018) offer a particularly useful lens regarding the embodied nature of scientific knowledge, representation, and communication as exhibited by amateur astronomers. Their ethnographic analyses showed how the community propagated embodied scientific practices regarding perception and representation of celestial objects and events. Thus, *practice*, rather than knowledge, was central to learning in this out-of-school science education contexts.

For example, a year-long ethnography of the Club Astronomers of Central Texas documented various practices to ensure good celestial observing and of sharing the wonder of astronomy with members of the greater public. This investigation documented the routines employed by members of the community and revealed how the routines were reproduced during the club's activities. The researchers documented frequent use of physical tools for measuring and instruments (e.g., telescopes) for observing phenomena of interest. Gesture use among participants was also common and critical for conveying meaning and guiding practices.

Success also depends on refine a number or embodied practices. Hands and body size were often used as highly accessible and well-grounded forms of linear and angular measurement. Club members also worked on developing *averted vision*. The conditions of astronomy remind us that this is a situated practice. It has to occur in the dark, usually on clear nights. *Averted vision* is a form of disciplined perception (Stevens & Hall, 1998) that uses the heightened light sensitivity of one's peripheral vision as the primary point of fixation. This is truly an abnormal behavior and requires considerable practice. Training the eye to direct one's visual attention with one's peripheral vision is unnatural, but it is highly advantageous for many key routines of astronomy.

Science education has long grappled with how to span the symbolic and experiential realms that science straddles. Works of this kind that employ highly careful analyses of situated, socially mediated science activity and science talk show that the symbols and phenomena are observable as embodied practices. These practices connect rich body-based behaviors to deep forms of reasoning and help ground scientific ideas and abstract formalisms.

Participatory Simulation

In addition to inquiry and participation in scientific and hobbyist communities, people engage in scientific ideas through participatory simulation experiences. Learners gain understanding by taking on the role of the phenomenon of interest. These may combine play with video or computer tagging, and often these are then accompanied by opportunities for reflection and redescription of these highly interactive learning experiences. For example, Colella (2000), used participatory simulation with high school students to support their embodied understanding of viral transmission. Student discourse showed how readily they suspended disbeliefs and took on the characteristics of the agents of the simulation. The participatory experience allowed students to explore concepts in virology such as latency and immunity that are otherwise very difficult for students to grasp.

In another intervention, children in kindergarten and 1st grade role-played the behavior of bees (Danish, 2014). The activity initially elicited children's impressions of the behaviors. Later, students created scripts for more structured activity, such as collecting nectar. Peers and the teacher commented on drafts of the script so that it iteratively became more scientifically accurate. The unit included modeling software that enabled the students to see the connections between the behavior of individual bees, such as "dances" to communicate the location of a nectar source, and the collective behavior of the hive as a whole. In this way, students learned about system-level behavior and how to relate structure (e.g., proboscis shape), behavior (nectar gathering), and function (hive survival).

Johnson-Glenberg and colleagues have conducted a variety of studies of multi-day, high school science education using mixed reality environments. These are highly interactive experiences that engage body movement, gesture use, physical object manipulation, and a sensation of immersion, along with classroom discussions to foster disciplinary based discourse practices. Some of these allow up to four students to be in these immersion environments at the same time, with additional collaboration taking place with the other students positioned on the periphery of the active, mixed reality space. Students in these embodied settings learned more about Earth science (Johnson-Glenberg, Birchfield, Savvides, & Megowan-Romanowicz, 2011), chemistry, and disease transmission than students in traditional science lessons (Johnson-Glenberg, Birchfield, Tolentino, & Koziupa, 2014). Johnson-Glenberg and colleagues (2014) identified several embodied behaviors as important for explaining the educational effectiveness of these mixed reality learning environments: level of motoric engagement, with full body movement and locomotion being the highest; degree of gestural congruency, as an assessment of how closely the mixed reality movements map to the physical or conceptual content being learned; and the perception of an immersion experience, or sense of "being there."

Participation is a powerful method of learning science through first-order experiences. The experiences can be manifest with participants being the phenomena themselves, emulating scientists in their classrooms, or adopting the practices of a sustained, out-of-school community of amateur scientists with whom they wish to engage. Discussion, interaction, and reflection support the learning of concepts such as complex systems behavior, the relation of individual behavior to population parameters, or connecting structure and function. These important cross-cutting science concepts are grounded through learners' participatory experiences.

Engineering

High school engineering offers an example of an educational activity system (Greeno & Engeström, 2014). Students work in teams to design, build, and test devices that serve a social need. In so doing, they engage in integrated STEM activities that can support learning through participation. In Figure 10.3, students can be seen co-designing the logic circuit for a voting booth that uses sensors to ensure privacy when casting a ballot (Nathan, Srisurichan, Walkington, Wolfgram, Williams, & Alibali, 2013). Students have to design the sensors to detect the presence of another voter in an adjoining booth, and then work out the logic mathematically and then electronically so it will correctly alert a voter when to grant or deny entry to a secure booth. Students then have to collaboratively build a working version and present their final circuit, including the budget, to a planning board, so they may determine which design is most practical and feasible to fund.

An important outcome is to learn an important norm in engineering: Project design is an iterative process; one that goes through cycles of innovation, testing, and redesign; and to solve real world design problems, engineers must bring to bear many skills and ideas from algebra, geometry, accounting, computer science, physics, technical drawing, language arts, and social-emotional learning that have heretofore been taught in relative isolation. Here we can see the interactions of the numerous components of the activity system (Figure 10.3): Subjects (students), objects (booth design), and instruments (digital electronics, booth materials, sensors) interact with division of labor (designers, analysts, artists, presenters, team leaders), community (the classroom and the elections board), and rules (norms of effective collaboration, policies for safeguarding voter privacy). The important skills necessary for success of the engineering project arise out of the various engagements with tools, materials, and other people, as well as with algorithms and inscriptions (Johri & Olds, 2011).

To ask whether a student "learned" in such a setting is an ill-fitting question. To assess the learning of an individual student based on the performance of many agents and resources is complicated. For example, those entrusted with the presentation or the budgeting did not engage with all the same concepts and formalisms as those who were debugging sensors and logic boards. The knowledge of any one member did not match that of the others, but the knowledge of the *team* produced effective designs. This kind of **distributed knowledge** is highly characteristic of sociocultural level learning and of the engineering field.

Also, not all teams had the same experience, which is also true-to-life. One of the groups in the later class periods found that certain logical chips necessary for their design were used up by other teams, and the remaining ones were defective. The students had to redesign the logic of their digital circuit to achieve the same outcome with different chips. At the level of the mathematics of Boolean Logic, they had to transform the logical relations of the original design to accommodate the relations and operators that were available (e.g., changing out OR for AND operations). Practically, this also meant delving into the catalog of logic chips offered by different vendors to understand the different layouts and electrical parameters. Furthermore, all of these caused considerable delays. This complication might be regarded

FIGURE 10.3 High school students working on the design of a digital voting booth.
Left panel. Collaborative group work using simulation software. *Middle panel.* Collaboratively wiring the logic circuit. *Right panel.* Analyzing the circuit design diagram.

as lesser performance along some standard criteria, such as meeting the initial deadline, or creating a design with the fewest chips. As a result, though, greater learning took place for other criteria, such as navigating practical problems and finding out how different designs could yield the same control logic.

10.1.5 Computing and Making

Since its earliest days, computer programmers have sought to bridge the symbolic-physical divide. As early as 1967, computer scientists and educators Wally Feurzeig, Seymour Papert, and Cynthia Solomon created Logo, a programming language meant for teaching concepts in computing. It was designed to allow programming students to realize the program behaviors physically and visually, as enacted by a physical or graphical turtle. Logo also inspired a new area of mathematics, Turtle Graphics and Turtle Geometry (Abelson and diSessa, 1986), where motion was characterized in terms of the point of view of the turtle. This meant that the student could adopt the embodied state of the turtle and simulate the behaviors provided in the computer program. Papert referred to this as "body syntonic" reasoning. It provided a way for the student to enact, predict, and debug a program using body movement, and further ground the programming constructs into meaningful movement-based experiences. In addition to engaging people in mathematical and computational thinking, the "mobile mapping" activity reported earlier (Taylor, 2017) reveals how this can also engage locative literacies.

Logo has since developed along multiple paths, but maintained its educational commitment. One that has grown immensely popular in recent years is the Scratch programming language (Resnick et al., 2009). One 18-month study of the members of an after-school center for computer programming examined 536 Scratch projects by participants aged 8 to 18. The rich interactions of the group supported learning of a range of important programming concepts and forms of computational thinking.

Another of Logo's descendants, NetLogo, was developed by Uri Wilensky (1999; Wilensky & Reisman, 2006) to allow for entry-level programmers as well as experts to explore emergent phenomena, such as the behavior of atoms to make materials, and prey-predator (sheep-wolves) relationships. For example, in "MaterialSim" (Blikstein & Wilensky, 2009), students design materials at the atomic level and test for their predicted macroscopic (material level) behaviors. Materials science enjoys many formal equations that are used to describe and predict their behavior. However, the science involves many different levels of reasoning about macrostructure and microstructure, and includes many nonlinear relationships operating in three dimensions. Consequently, the formalisms for materials science are rather opaque to students, and therefore meaningless and ungrounded.

The researcher team recruited second-year undergraduates as learners because of the complexity of the topic. Students initially had difficulty expressing their understanding of some of the core phenomena in words. MaterialSim in the NetLogo environment gave them new ways to express their understanding more accurately and to observe and explore emergent relationships. The role the students played as model builders at the atomic level gave them a greater appreciation of the design of materials with intended properties. It empowered students to see themselves as material scientists. The grounding experience also helped students to apprehend how general principles, such as "lowering free energy," were useful for explaining many different phenomena.

The educational role of model building and simulation has been even further extended to support participatory simulation of human actors as agents in emergent phenomena, such as the factors that influence traffic patterns (e.g., HubNet; Wilensky & Stroup, 1999; also see a special issue edited by Barab & Dede, 2007). I have already described some of the learning that is fostered through participatory simulations. Several studies have shown the value of participatory simulation and virtual simulations for understanding transmission of infectious diseases (e.g., Klopfer, Yoon, & Perry, 2005; Neulight, et al., 2007). In one simulation, students experience how social distancing affects viral transmission among a population (Maharaj, McCaldin, & Kleczkowski, 2011). Klopfer and colleagues (2005) investigated how mobile technology (in this case Palm Pilots) also enable participatory simulations.

The process of modeling phenomena naturally extends to building things. The connection of computing to constructing physical artifacts, crafts, and devices is central to the Maker Movement (Halverson & Sheridan, 2014). The Maker Movement is distinguished from earlier movements that have attracted builders and tinkerers (e.g., Watson, 2002) by connecting it to digital design tools that support *shared* artifact construction (Anderson, 2012). At its core is the idea of the democratization of new designs, brought about by using inexpensive parts, increased access to digital fabrication (e.g., 3D printers), and a culture of sharing software tools and designs. The Movement has a broad reach and includes fabrics and e-textiles (Buechley & Eisenberg, 2008; Peppler, 2016), prostheses and exoskeletons (Eisenberg, 2017), as well as a range of hardware creations (e.g., Peppler, Halverson, & Kafai, 2016a, 2016b; Vossoughi & Bevan, 2014).

Halverson and Sheridan (2014) theorize that the Movement is framed in terms of three interconnected themes: "*making* as learning activities, *makerspaces* as communities of practice and designed learning environments, and *makers* as identities of participation that afford new forms of interaction between self and learning" (p. 502–503, italics in original). By integrating engaged participation with activities to produce and share working products (Constructionism), the Movement exhibits the many facets that constitute Type 3 processing for grounded and embodied learning.

10.1.6 Teaching and Learning to Teach

In addition to reviewing some of the ways that Type 3 processing supports student learning, I want to illustrate ways that these sociocultural processes contribute to effective approaches for teaching and learning how to teach. The first way explicitly addresses the role teachers play in managing common ground in support of student learning. The second way focuses on how teachers, themselves, gain professional skills and knowledge through their participation in communities of practice.

Making Common Ground
As I discussed earlier, *common ground* is central to all of our social interactions. Its foundational role in discourse is well established (Clark, 1996; Schegloff, 1992; Vygotsky, 1986). It is less commonly identified in discussions of successful learning and effective instruction. This is a serious oversight. At its core, teaching is a never-ending set of cycles of *breaking* and then *making* common ground (Nathan, Alibali & Church, 2017). This is because learning involves doing things that were previously not familiar, such as being introduced to novel patterns, procedures, concepts, and practices.

One exception to this is instructional scaffolding (Puntambekar & Hübscher, 2005; Wood, Bruner, & Ross, 1976). As noted, scaffolding is built upon a foundation of the shared understanding with the learners and their teachers. Learning is supported by extending the capabilities learners through distributed supports of tools, peers, and teachers, who then grow into these new levels of performance as supports are faded. An important way to provide and maintain common ground is by embedding the learning in an authentic task for learners.

Some breaks to common ground during learning with students are inevitable. Alibali and colleagues (2013) examined a corpus of six mathematics classroom teaching episodes. They found that students frequently encountered difficulties in their understanding during the lessons—over ten per episode —which the investigators labelled "trouble spots." Trouble spots were identified as those episodes during classroom discourse when students exhibited difficulty or uncertainty with the instructional material. These are breaks with common ground. Examples include students giving an incorrect response to a question, showing uncertainty, asking questions about the lesson, or producing responses that were dysfluent.

In response to trouble spots, teachers in the sample were very responsive. They increased the multimodal discourse resources at their disposal as soon as they detected them. This meant that teachers produced significantly more gestures in the turn-of-talk immediately *following* a trouble spot compared to the turns immediately *preceding* the trouble spot. This pattern was consistent across all six teachers.

Part of the art of teaching—the sophistication of one's *pedagogical content knowledge*— is selecting the appropriate common ground-breaking experiences for learners so that repairing the break supports valuable ways of making meaning of the world. An example of such a break is illustrated with a case of teaching high school students polynomial multiplication (Nathan, Church, & Alibali, 2017). Many students have learned the FOIL method, a shorthand for "first, outer, inner, last." Like many shorthand procedures of this sort in mathematics (long-division comes to mind), students can rather faithfully execute it, even though it is not meaningful for them. Students, for example, do not know why FOIL works, whether or not it matters if one changes the order of the four steps (it does not), that it is only applicable to multiplying binomials (expressions of the sort $a + x$), or how to extend it to other polynomials more generally. For these reasons, it is useful to introduce a better conceptual foundation for polynomial multiplication.

The "area model" of multiplication provides such a foundation (Lischka & Stephens, 2020). The area of a rectangle is a useful *taken-as-shared* object that students will recognize as familiar and meaningful. My colleagues and I explored video recordings of teachers' mathematics lessons using the area model to teach polynomial multiplication. The first thing we observed is a break in common ground shared between students and the teacher. The teacher alerts students that they will be doing something unfamiliar, and possibly even intimidating.

Teacher: We'll be looking at more complex [polynomials by polynomials] now.

The teacher then works to quickly restore common ground, in order that students are able to relate the concepts and procedures to something that is already meaningful to them. He relates this more complex scenario to the simple multiplication examples students have already seen in class.

Teacher: So think about [the ideas] that we've had in the cou-, last couple of days, and, let's kinda extend that.

As shown in Figure 10.4, the model builds on something familiar to high school students— the notion that any product can be thought of as the area of some hypothetical rectangle with sides that are represented by the two multipliers, the *multiplier* and the *multiplicand*. In

FIGURE 10.4 Teaching the "area model" for polynomial multiplication. *Top*. For $(a + b + c + d) \times (x + y + z)$. *Middle*. The teacher using a gesture to identify the area for the term dx. *Bottom*. The final product in symbolic form.

this case, the two "sides" are $a + b + c + d$ and $x + y + z$, respectively. It also brings to mind another fact about area: The *total area* can be written as either the *product* of the two sides, *or* as the *sum* of all the little areas (i.e., the boxes shown in the top portion of Figure 10.4). In the middle panel of Figure 10.4, the teacher uses speech and gesture to identify the partial product of one of the squares in the area model as dx.

Using these principles of common ground to students, one can now multiply polynomials of arbitrary length, whereas FOIL can only accommodate polynomials of length 2. This is shown in the bottom portion of Figure 10.4. The new method relates to familiar ideas of multiplication that now encompass a broader range of mathematical objects. In this way, common ground, once broken, is now repaired, with grounded learning supported.

Teachers intentionally break common ground when introducing new ideas, and following these breaks, they work to re-establish and maintain common ground in ways that expand students' knowledge. Furthermore, the maintenance of common ground is largely rooted in embodied forms of instruction. Teachers regularly use gestures as a means to repair common ground. Researchers observe this role of gesture in cases when trouble spots arise spontaneously, as well as when the teacher has intentionally chosen to break common ground as a way to foster new ways of understanding.

Communities of Teachers as Learners

As I previously reviewed, the communities of learners model (e.g., Grossman et al., 2001; Wineburg & Grossman, 1998) offers a sustained and effective way for teachers to engage in new forms of participation that can positively influence their instructional practices and their students' learning. Another model for bringing teachers together to improve their practices is the use of video clubs (Sherin, 2007; van Es, 2012). Classroom instruction is ordinarily a very individual process for teachers, from a professional point of view. There are, of course, students present. But there are rarely other colleagues who can observe and provide feedback on a teacher's instruction.

Video clubs are regular sessions where teachers get together and share videos of their own classroom instruction and discuss the events with their colleagues. It enables teachers to effectively revisit their classroom choices and consider their effects and alternatives. It is essential in these sessions that the members create a safe space in which to share these potentially vulnerable events. Sharing these videos among a team of like-minded practitioners can create a safe and effective community of learners all working to meet teachers' professional goals.

For example, Van Es (2012) initially observed a small number of mathematics teachers dominating these sessions. Over the course of a year together, the group dynamics shifted to be far more inclusive and mutually supportive of one another. As a community, participants learned how to better *participate in* their communities, and this improved the interpersonal interactions within the group (Russ, Sherin, & Sherin, 2016).

Sherin and colleagues (Sherin & van Es, 2009; Sherin et al., 2011; van Es & Sherin, 2010) documented the ways that participating teachers' "noticing" changed. Practitioners developed what they referred to as teachers' *professional vision*. Teachers became more attuned to identifying the mathematically relevant ideas that students were expressing when talking and in written form, which in turn helped to better orient teachers to effective institutional practices that could meet their students' learning needs. Similarly, in the Cognitively Guided Instruction (CGI) project, teachers were supported to use videos of their students performing mathematical reasoning (Fennema et al., 1996; Franke, Carpenter, Levi, & Fennema, 2001). Discussions over these videos enhanced teachers' awareness of the various ways that students engage in mathematical reasoning.

This general community of learning model has also been used to support efforts for systemic mathematics education reform involving teachers alongside school administrators and other district specialists. Cobb and his colleagues (Cobb & Jackson, 2011; Cobb et al., 2003; Cobb et al., 2009) noted that even the teacher practitioner communities still operate in isolation of the many other exogenous factors that influence classroom instruction and student learning and performance. Through these ongoing sessions, Cobb and colleagues observed that these educators could work together to negotiate appropriate norms around instructional practices, norms of mathematical reasoning, and norms of institutional behavior that would be more supportive of effective teaching and learning. For example, initially, teachers primarily discussed institutional constraints as sources of frustration. Over a two-year period, teachers came to view institutional constraints as subject to their influences. Constraints such as their time became something they found they had more control over. They came to use their control over their time to foster more collaborative planning in order to develop practices that supported students' mathematical reasoning (Cobb, Zhao, & Dean, 2009).

10.2 GEL PRINCIPLES

Type 3 processes show some common qualities across a range of educational settings and topics that we can use to inform and improve future practices. At this point, it is useful to

TABLE 10.1

Principles for grounded and embodied learning, design, instruction, and assessment at the sociocultural portion of the GEL timescale

Educational concerns	Principle
Learning	**Principle of managing common ground**, the idea that without this, learners cannot participate and cannot change to suit a community.
	Participation principle can be achieved by structuring learners' involvement in ways that motivate and support taking on the intended discourse practices, including one's speech, actions, use of tools and representations, and ways of thinking.
	The **principle of internalization** states that people will internalize the epistemic properties of tools and technologies and the ways they support distributed and extended systems of community knowledge.
Design	The **principle of collaborative engagement**, which favors active, constructive, and interactive modes over passive modes.
	Support **bidirectional** influences of individual (mental, affective state) and social (group norms, audience, disciplinary norms) processes.
	The **principle of social capital through making** acknowledges the benefits to the learning of generating products, especially those that are relevant and useful to others.
Instruction and Classroom learning experiences	The **principle of socio-disciplinary norms** recognizes that learning and participation are supported by adherence to routines that specify behaviors for group engagement and expectations for discipline-specific discourse.
	The **principle of instructional gestures** recognizes how gesture use brings together many of the entailments of sociocultural learning.
	The **expert blind spot principle** is intended to caution teachers that, as old timers, they do not see the world of norms and representations the same way as do newcomers.
Assessment	The **principle of situated formative assessment** states that teachers can obtain valuable information to adjust their instruction by observing students interacting in rich, collaborative activity systems.
	The **principle of situated summative assessment** acknowledges that applying summative assessment practices and instruments designed for Type 2 learning processes will often greatly under-represent the capabilities of the students whose learning and performance is bound up in the activity system.

summarize the emergent principles for learning, instruction, design, and assessment that follow from Type 3 processing. These are provided in Table 10.1.

10.2.1 Learning at the Sociocultural Level

The empirical evidence suggests that the Type 3 process that is effective for promoting learning are those that establish and maintain common ground, foster participation as an active process, and support the internalization of acceptable social practices, and uses of cultural tools.

I defined *learning* (in Section 3.2.2) "as an enduring change in behavior." At the sociocultural scale, *grounding* is accomplished when members of a discourse community recognize the importance of establishing and maintaining common ground. Common ground is an essential quality of any interpersonal interaction and is a necessary precursor for any other involvement, such as collaborative knowledge construction. Above, I reviewed examples of locative literacies, site-based history education, students' analysis of liquor store locations, and using algebra for trip planning using the Boston subway system.

This leads to the **principle of building on common ground**, the idea that relating what is familiar to people to new ways of acting and new forms of representation makes them meaningful. Further, without common ground, learners cannot participate and cannot change to suit a community. One form of common ground is establishing social norms. Norms contribute to the "meta-discourse" by specifying, explicitly or tacitly, what discourse practices are allowed (Sfard, 2007). Common ground is also fostered when collaborators operate with taken-as-shared forms of knowing.

Learning occurs when people change their ways of participating. Examples from earlier include students in problem-based learning classes such as the engineering voting book, social studies and language arts teachers forming a community of learners. In some cases, there were new practices taken up by group members to ensure community effectiveness, such as the averted vision of the astronomers and the improvements in teacher noticing among video club members. The **engaged participation principle** states that learning is supported when one participates in a community of practice. It can be achieved by structuring learners' involvement in ways that motivate and support taking on the intended discourse practices, including one's speech, actions, use of tools and representations, and ways of thinking. When coming to adopt the appropriate practices of a community, people engage in a developmental process of legitimate peripheral participation. At first, they enter as outsiders, then newcomers, and over time as accomplished central participants and experts.

Through these social interactions, new practices play a significant role in the social construction of the individual's identity, in part, as a member of various communities and their corresponding cultural practices. During this process people develop facility with the cultural tools—representations, methods, and technologies, for example—that distinguish a community or discipline. The **principle of internalization** states that people will internalize the epistemic properties of these tools and technologies and the ways they support distributed and extended systems of community knowledge. For example, students using the candy factory as a context came to think in terms of place value and recognize its properties and benefits for arithmetic, while those in the Kids as Global Scientists project and those who joined amateur astronomy groups internalized the discourse practices of science experts. Taken together, sociocultural GEL processes entail adopting and internalizing the shared cultural practices of an effective community.

10.2.2 Instruction and Classroom Learning Experiences at the Sociocultural Level

The **principle of socio-disciplinary norms** recognizes that learning and participation are supported by adherence to routines that specify behaviors for group engagement and expectations for discipline-specific discourse. The **scaffolding principle** acknowledges the central role of common ground in effectively supporting and extending learners' autonomous and socially supported capabilities when their contributions are situated within a system of distributed knowledge. For example, when teachers use gesture to foster common ground.

The **principle of instructional gestures** recognizes the multimodal nature of teaching. Of particular note is how gesture use brings together many of the entailments of sociocultural learning, such as: managing turn taking, establishing and maintaining common ground, modeling practices of discourse community; and directing attention to help in the enculturation of newcomers. An effective method for coordinating these instructional practices is the use of collaborative investigations via project-based learning (PBL). For example, students in math and engineering classes benefited from their teachers' uses of gestures to establish common ground and maintain coherence across the range of spaces, tools, and materials they used. Gestures also were important for enculturating new members of hobby groups, so they understood the normative practices of the community. During exchanges about the taken-as-shared representation for the pie problem, students also engaged in instructional gestures to explain their solution to the other members of the class.

Knowing-with also has a downside, for educators whose knowledge is very different than that of their students (Nathan & Petrosino, 2003). The **expert blind spot principle** is intended to caution teachers that, as old timers, they do not see the world of norms and representations the same way as do newcomers.

To be an effective teacher means being able to use Type 2 processing to step outside of one's own expert ways of knowing-with and tailoring instruction to the capabilities of one's students.

10.2.3 Design Principles at the Sociocultural Level

Several guiding principles for innovations support processes. Generally, GEL is supported by Type 3 processing when learners and their teachers adhere to the **principle of collaborative engagement**, which favors active, constructive, and interactive modes over passive modes. This provides another reason to implement PBL to promote GEL in schools. In out-of-school contexts, legitimate peripheral participation is common as learners enter sustained communities of practice, such as amateur science communities. I showed how participatory simulations in science and social studies also offer these embodied experiences of collaborative engagement. They allow learners to obtain first-person experiences of the ways complex (and often unintuitive) phenomena arise by following simple rules of physical and social interaction. Students also had these primary experiences when analyzing the locations of liquor stores near their schools and presenting their findings to their city council.

When possible, designs of Type 3 experiences are effective that allow for learners to appreciate the bidirectional nature of learning, as they reflect on influences of how individual (mental, affective) states shape behavior at the social level (group norms, audience, disciplinary norms), which in turn shape the individual (e.g., development of self-identity). This was evident in the teacher communities of practice and video clubs, where the individual behaviors and adherence to social norms affected the entire group experience.

Generating products, especially those that are relevant and useful to others, fosters greater motivation to engage, increased levels of participation, and facility with cultural tools. Examples of this include the simulations of historical protests, the voting book redesign, and the makerspace projects. The learning observed in these contexts support the **principle of social capital through making**, which states that opportunities for students to co-construct artifacts that intend to work and be used by others instills conceptual and procedural knowledge of how systems work. Constructivist activities also contribute to sociocultural learning through the rachet effect, creating artifacts imbued with the knowledge of their creators that are then used by others to innovate further.

10.2.4 Assessment Principles at the Sociocultural Level

Performance based on Type 3 processing is highly situated and dependent on contextual factors, access to cultural tools, division of labor across other people, and material resources. When students learn within a rich, distributed activity system such as a PBL environment and a makerspace, their developing knowledge and skills are bound up with these distributed resources. The **principle of situated formative assessment** states that teachers can obtain valuable information to adjust their instruction by observing students interacting in rich, collaborative activity systems. Video clubs offer a supportive way for teachers to sharpen their skills of noticing and interpreting their students' multimodal interactions. This includes recognizing how behaviors such as students' gestures and uses of metaphors offer insights into their ways of thinking about the topics of interest.

The **principle of situated summative assessment** acknowledges that applying summative assessment practices and instruments designed for learning based on Type 2 processing will often greatly under-represent the capabilities of the students whose learning and perform- ance is bound up in the activity system. This is because the knowledge that is constructed is integrated with the context, resources, and social interactions that are disrupted by the assessment design. For example, the students in the Algebra Project developed their alge- braic reasoning in the context of collaboratively experiencing and then representing traveling through their local cities. Reproducing these same mathematical skills during a test item using a story problem is a poor match that may underestimate their actual level of algebraic reasoning. Those using GPS sensors and cartography software to exhibit their location liter- acies would ideally have access to the same resources during assessments.

It can also be the case with project-based learning that students are not all having the same learning experience, but that they are collectively meeting the design objectives. Alternative assessment methods such as group projects and portfolios provide a better record of what each learner is capable of. Interviews that elicit reflection on the collaborative learning pro- cess, including the role of tools and collaborators, can help both teachers and learners to appreciate the bidirectionality of their individual role in a group process, as well as inform educators.

10.2.5 Philosophy of Mind: Shapiro's Constitution Hypothesis

In Chapter 6 I described Shapiro's (2019) *Constitution Hypothesis* and its relation to GEL principles in the conscious spectrum. The Constitution Hypothesis is also relevant to some of the principles provided here. As a review, Shapiro's Constitution Hypothesis states that "the body or world plays a constitutive rather than merely causal role in cognitive processing" (p. 5). This proposes a form of situated, distributed cognition. The focus is on the cognitive *system*, where intellectual processes extend beyond traditional bounds of the individual to include environments, its artifacts, and other people.

Support for the Constitution Hypothesis follows from the **participation principle**, which describes learning as changes in discourse practices, broadly conceived. By framing learning as a sociocultural process of conforming to cultural and social norms, this recognizes how learners achieve some of their most profound forms of cognitive development, as noted by scholars such as Vygotsky (1978).

The implications of this hypothesis are highly relevant to education. As noted, it makes the case for creating participatory experiences for learners, emulating some of the examples such as communities of learners and hobbyists groups, recruiting professional role models, such as scientists and historians, to engage with students around disciplinary discourse and tool use, and seeking out immersive and participatory technological experiences. As I noted earlier, some of the most radical implications address assessment practices. By describing learning knowledge in situated and distributed terms naturally calls for assessments that are suited to these resource-rich, interactive, social contexts. This is consistent with both the **prin- ciple of situated formative assessment** and **principle of situated summative assessment**, listed above.

Bransford and Schwartz (1999) argue for this approach as well, casting assessment practices in terms of how one's emerging ways of knowing-with prepare one for future learning.

Once cognition is recognized as *extended*, the circumstances of assessment must allow for access to the resources that are encompassed within the cognitive system. Certainly, this underscores that the assessment experience should closely emulate the environments in which learning takes pace. Even when testing for transfer, the goal is usually to assess transfer of students' ways of knowing, rather than their performance in an impoverished environment. If the goal is to demonstrate performance in an impoverished environment, then students' learning experiences would ideally have some of the resources faded away so that other cognitive processes (such as memorization) are adequately developed.

10.3 SUMMARY

This chapter reviewed the nature of GEL among sociocultural processes, often over weeks, months, and years. As observed across a variety of educational content areas, learning often occurs as people adopt new forms of participation and internalize the ways of knowing-with that characterize the social norms and practices of a community. This includes participation in the distributed forms of intelligent behaviors that emerge from interactions with others, and with the epistemic contributions of material devices as well as cultural and disciplinary tools. Examples are provided from educational experiences in literacy, history, mathematics, science, engineering, computing, and teacher professional learning. Several principles are identified that provide broad insights into ways educational change can support successful learning with greater attention to the embodied nature of thinking, teaching, and learning.

10.4 READER ACTIVITIES

10.4.1 Constructing With HyperGami

Mike Eisenberg and Ann Nishioka Eisenberg created a rich repository of aesthetic origami projects as part of the HyperGami project. You can download some pre-existing patterns and learn more about using JavaGami to make patterns of your own.

https://hypergami.org/

You can find more crafts and automata in the Sheppard Craft Tech Lab at the University of Colorado at Boulder. https://cucraftlab.org/

10.4.2 Body Syntonic Reasoning

Taking the perspective of the Logo turtle gives a first-person perspective on movement through the world (Papert, 1980, 1991). In this task, I invite the reader to spell out a word through motion.

1. I suggest using the word MIND, though you may pick another. Plan out how you would walk this. In the parlance of the Logo turtle, you will need to specifically say DOWN PEN when you want to leave a mark, and UP PEN when you don't. Perform the actions while doing a "think aloud" so you have a record of the movements, turns, and pen placement.
2. Write this out as a pseudo-code program for directing another agent (a person or Logo turtle) to copy this. What would you need to do to make it twice as big in every direction? What would you need to do to make it the same as the original but write it upside down?

3. Consider how this could be done at the scale of your neighborhood, using GPS technology. Using a map of your town, identify where you would start and finish.
4. List any new insights you have about the physical layout of your neighborhood. What might these imply for the future development of your neighborhood? Consider issues such as universal physical access.

REFERENCES

Abelson, H., & DiSessa, A. A. (1986). *Turtle geometry: The computer as a medium for exploring mathematics*. MIT Press.

Alexander, P. A., Fives, H., Buehl, M. M., & Mulhern, J. (2002). Teaching as persuasion. *Teaching and Teacher Education, 18*, 795–813.

Alibali, M. W., Nathan, M. J., Church, R. B., Wolfgram, M. S., Kim, S., & Knuth, E. J. (2013). Teachers' gestures and speech in mathematics lessons: Forging common ground by resolving trouble spots. *ZDM, 45*(3), 425–440.

Anderson, C. (2012). *Makers: The new industrial revolution*. Crown.

Anderson, R. D. (2002). Reforming science teaching: What research says about inquiry. *Journal of Science Teacher Education, 13*(1), 1–12.

Azevedo, F. S. (2013). The tailored practice of hobbies and its implication for the design of interest-driven learning environments. *Journal of the Learning Sciences, 22*(3), 462–510.

Azevedo, F. S. (2015) Sustaining Interest-Based Participation in Science. In K. A. Renninger, M. Nieswandt, & S. Hidi (Eds.), *Interest in mathematics and science learning* (pp. 281–296). American *Educational* Research Association.

Azevedo, F. S., & Mann, M. J. (2018). Seeing in the dark: Embodied cognition in amateur astronomy practice. *Journal of the Learning Sciences, 27*(1), 89–136.

Barab, S., & Dede, C. (2007). Games and immersive participatory simulations for science education: An emerging type of curricula. *Journal of Science Education and Technology, 16*(1), 1–3.

Baron, C. (2012). Understanding historical thinking at historic sites. *Journal of Educational Psychology, 104*(3), 833–847.

Barton, D., Hamilton, M., & Ivanic, R. (2000). *Situated literacies: Reading and writing in context*. Routledge.

Blikstein, P., & Wilensky, U. (2009). An atom is known by the company it keeps: A constructionist learning environment for materials science using agent-based modeling (CCL). *International Journal of Computers for Mathematical Learning, 14* (2): 81–119.

Bowers, J., Cobb, P., & McClain, K. (1999). The evolution of mathematical practices: A case study. *Cognition and Instruction, 17*(1), 25–66.

Bransford, J. D., & Schwartz, D. L. (1999). Rethinking transfer: A simple proposal with multiple implications. *Review of Research in Education, 24*(1), 61–100.

Buechley, L., & Eisenberg, M. (2008). The LilyPad Arduino: Toward wearable engineering for everyone. *IEEE Pervasive Computing, 7*(2), 12–15.

Chapman, M. G. (2002). Carolyn Shoemaker. Astropedia. Retrieved from astrogeology.usgs.gov/people/carolyn-shoemaker

Clark, H. H. (1996). *Using language*. Cambridge University Press.

Cobb, P., & Bowers, J. (1999). Cognitive and situated learning perspectives in theory and practice. *Educational Researcher, 28*(2), 4–15.

Cobb, P., & Hodge, L. L. (2002). A relational perspective on issues of cultural diversity and equity as they play out in the mathematics classroom. *Mathematical Thinking and Learning, 4*(2–3), 249–284.

Cobb, P., & Jackson, K. (2011). Towards an empirically grounded theory of action for improving the quality of mathematics teaching at scale. *Mathematics Teacher Education and Development, 13*(1), 6–33.

Cobb, P., McClain, K., de Silva Lamberg, T., & Dean, C. (2003). Situating teachers' instructional practices in the institutional setting of the school and district. *Educational Researcher, 32*(6), 13–24.

Cobb, P., Stephan, M., McClain, K., & Gravemeijer, K. (2001). Participating in classroom mathematical practices. *Journal of the Learning Sciences, 10*(1–2), 113–163.

Cobb, P., Zhao, Q., & Dean, C. (2009). Conducting design experiments to support teachers' learning: A reflection from the field. *Journal of the Learning Sciences, 18*(2), 165–199.

Colella, V. (2000). Participatory simulations: Building collaborative understanding through immersive dynamic modeling. *Journal of the Learning Sciences, 9*, 471–500.

Danish, J. A. (2014). Applying an activity theory lens to designing instruction for learning about the structure, behavior, and function of a honeybee system. *Journal of the Learning Sciences, 23*(2), 100–148.

Darling-Hammond, L., & Sykes, G. (1999). *Teaching as the learning profession: Handbook of policy and practice. Jossey-Bass education series*. Jossey-Bass.

diSessa, A. A. (2001). *Changing minds: Computers, learning, and literacy*. MIT Press.

Dubinsky, E., & Moses, R. P. (2011). Philosophy, math research, math ed research, K-16 education, and the civil rights movement: a synthesis. *Notices of the American Mathematical Society, 58*(3), 401–409.

Duschl, R. A. (2003). Assessment of inquiry. In J. M. Atkin and J. E. Coffey (Eds.), *Everyday assessment in the science classroom* (pp. 41–59). NSTA Press.

Duschl, R. (2008). Science education in three-part harmony: Balancing conceptual, epistemic, and social learning goals. *Review of Research in Education, 32*(1), 268–291.

Eisenberg, M. (2017, October). Self-made: The body as frontier for the maker movement in education. *Proceedings of the 7th Annual Conference on creativity and fabrication in education* (pp. 1–4). Association for Computing Machinery.

Fennema, E., Carpenter, T., Franke, M. L., Levi, L., Jacobs, V. R., & Empson, S. B. (1996). Mathematics instruction and teachers' beliefs: A longitudinal study of using children's thinking. *Journal for Research in Mathematics Education, 27*, 403–434.

Fischer, U., Link, T., Cress, U., Nuerk, H.-C., & Moeller, K. (2015). Math with the dance mat: On the benefits of embodied numerical training approaches. In V. Lee (Ed.). *Learning technologies and the body: Integration and implementation in formal and informal learning environments* (pp. 149–163). Routledge.

Franke, M. L., Carpenter, T. P., Levi, L., & Fennema, E. (2001). Capturing teachers' generative change: A follow-up study of professional development in mathematics. *American Educational Research Journal, 38*(3), 653–689.

French, A., & Nathan, M. J. (2006). Under the microscope of research and into the classroom: Reflections on early algebra learning and instruction. In J. O. Masingila (Ed.), *Teachers engaged in research* (pp. 49–68). Information Age Publishing.

Furtak, E. M., Seidel, T., Iverson, H., & Briggs, D. C. (2012). Experimental and quasi-experimental studies of inquiry-based science teaching: A meta-analysis. *Review of Educational Research, 82*(3), 300–329.

Gee, J. P. (2012, October). The old and the new in the new digital literacies. *The Educational Forum, 76*(4), 418–420).

Greeno, J. G., & Engeström, Y. (2014). Learning in activity. In R. K. Sawyer (Ed.), *The Cambridge handbook of the learning sciences.* (2nd ed.) (pp. 128–150). Cambridge University Press.

Grossman, P., Wineburg, S., & Woolworth, S. (2001). Toward a theory of teacher community. *The Teachers College Record, 103*, 942–1012.

Hall, R., Ma, J. Y., & Nemirovsky, R. (2014). Rescaling bodies in/as representational instruments in GPS drawing. *Learning technologies and the body* (pp. 124–143). Routledge.

Halverson, E. R., & Sheridan, K. (2014). The maker movement in education. *Harvard Educational Review, 84*(4), 495–504.

Ioannidou, A., Repenning, A., Lewis, C., Cherry, G., & Rader, C. (2003). Making constructionism work in the classroom. *International Journal of Computers for Mathematical Learning, 8*(1), 63–108.

Johnson-Glenberg, M. C., Birchfield, D., Savvides, P., & Megowan-Romanowicz, C. (2011). Semi-virtual embodied learning-real world stem assessment. *Serious educational game assessment* (pp. 241–257). Brill Sense.

Johnson-Glenberg, M. C., Birchfield, D. A., Tolentino, L., & Koziupa, T. (2014). Collaborative embodied learning in mixed reality motion-capture environments: Two science studies. *Journal of Educational Psychology, 106*(1), 86.

Johri, A., & Olds, B. M. (2011). Situated engineering learning: Bridging engineering education research and the learning sciences. *Journal of Engineering Education, 100*(1), 151–185.

Klopfer, E., Yoon, S., & Perry, J. (2005). Using palm technology in participatory simulations of complex systems: A new take on ubiquitous and accessible mobile computing. *Journal of Science Education and Technology, 14*(3), 285–297.

Latour, B. (1987). *Science in action: How to follow scientists and engineers through society.* Harvard University Press.

Lehrer, R., & Schauble, L. (2000). Modeling in mathematics and science. In R. Glaser (Ed.), *Advances in instructional psychology* (Vol. 5) (pp. 101–159). Lawrence Erlbaum Associates.

Lehrer, R., & Schauble, L. (2007). Scientific thinking and science literacy. *Handbook of child psychology, 4*. Wiley.

Lischka, A. E., & Stephens, D. C. (2020). The area model: Building mathematical connections. *Mathematics teacher: Learning and teaching PK-12, 113*(3), 186–195.

Maharaj, S., McCaldin, T., & Kleczkowski, A. (2011, June). A participatory simulation model for studying attitudes to infection risk. *Proceedings of the 2011 Summer Computer Simulation Conference* (pp. 8–13). Association for Computing Machinery.

Moses, R. P., & Cobb, C. E. (2001). *Radical equations.* Beacon.

Nathan, M. J. (2000, October), Teachers crafting their own professional development: the working shops model. Presentation to the CILT Group.

Nathan, M. J., Alibali, M. W., & Church, R. B. (2017). Making and breaking common ground: How teachers use gesture to foster learning in the classroom. In R. B. Church, M. W. Alibali, & S. D. Kelly (Eds.), *Why gesture? How the hands function in speaking, thinking and communicating* (pp. 285–316). John Benjamins. doi 10.1075/gs.7.04der

Nathan, M. J., Eilam, B., & Kim, S. (2007). To disagree, we must also agree: How intersubjectivity structures and perpetuates discourse in a mathematics classroom. *Journal of the Learning Sciences, 16*(4), 523–563.

Nathan, M. J., & Kalmon, S. (2000). Teachers crafting their own professional development for educational technology: The working shops model. Paper presented to the annual meeting of the American Educational Research Association. AERA.

Nathan, M. J., & Kim, S. (2009). Regulation of teacher elicitations in the mathematics classroom. *Cognition and Instruction, 27*(2), 91–120.

Nathan, M. J., & Petrosino, A. (2003). Expert blind spot among preservice teachers. *American Educational Research Journal, 40*(4), 905–928.

Nathan, M. J., Srisurichan, R., Walkington, C., Wolfgram, M., Williams, C. & Alibali, M. W. (2013). Building cohesion across representations: A mechanism for STEM integration [Special issue]. *Journal of Engineering Education, 102*(1), 77–116.

National Curriculum Standards for Social Studies (2018). A framework for teaching, learning, and assessment. National Council for the Social Studies. Retrieved from www.socialstudies.org/national-curriculum-standards-social-studies-chapter-2-themes-social-studies

Neulight, N., Kafai, Y. B., Kao, L., Foley, B., & Galas, C. (2007). Children's participation in a virtual epidemic in the science classroom: Making connections to natural infectious diseases. *Journal of Science Education and Technology, 16*(1), 47.

NGSS Lead States. (2013). *Next generation science standards: For states, by states.* The National Academies Press.

NRC (National Research Council). (1996). *National science* education standards. National Academies Press.

NRC (National Research Council). (2012). *A framework for K-12 science education: Practices, crosscutting concepts, and core ideas.* National Academies Press. https://doi.org/10.17226/13165.

Papert, S. (1980). *Mindstorms: Children, computers, and powerful ideas.* Basic Books.

Papert, S. (1991). Preface. In: I. Harel & S. Papert (Eds.), Constructionism, research reports and essays, 1985–1990 (p. 1). Ablex Publishing Corporation.

Peppler, K. (2016). A review of e-textiles in education and society. *Handbook of research on the societal impact of digital media* (pp. 268–290). IGI Global.

Peppler, K., Halverson, E., & Kafai, Y. B. (Eds.). (2016a). *Makeology: Makerspaces as learning environments* (Vol. 1). Routledge.

Peppler, K., Halverson, E. R., & Kafai, Y. B. (Eds.). (2016b). *Makeology: Makers as learners* (Vol. 2). Routledge.

Puntambekar, S., & Hubscher, R. (2005). Tools for scaffolding students in a complex learning environment: What have we gained and what have we missed? *Educational Psychologist, 40*(1), 1–12.

Repenning, A., Ioannidou, A., & Zola, J. (2000). AgentSheets: End-user programmable simulations. *Journal of Artificial Societies and Social Simulation, 3*(3), 351–358.

Repenning, A., Webb, D., & Ioannidou, A. (2010, March). Scalable game design and the development of a checklist for getting computational thinking into public schools. *Proceedings of the 41st ACM Technical Symposium on Computer Science Education* (pp. 265–269). Association for Computing Machinery.

Resnick, M., Maloney, J., Monroy-Hernández, A., Rusk, N., Eastmond, E., Brennan, K., ... & Kafai, Y. (2009). Scratch: programming for all. *Communications of the ACM, 52*(11), 60–67.

Rosenzweig, R., & Thelen, D. P. (1998). *The presence of the past: Popular uses of history in American life* (Vol. 2). Columbia University Press.

Rouet, J. F., Favart, M., Britt, M. A., & Perfetti, C. A. (1997). Studying and using multiple documents in history: Effects of discipline expertise. *Cognition and Instruction, 15*(1), 85–106.

Russ, R. S., Sherin, B. L., & Sherin, M. G. (2016). What constitutes teacher learning. In D. H. Gitomer & C. A. Bell (Eds.), *Handbook of research on teaching* (pp. 391–438). American Educational Research Association.

Schegloff, E. A. (1992). Repair after next turn: The last structurally provided defense of intersubjectivity in conversation. *American Journal of Sociology, 97*, 1295–1345.

Sfard, A. (2007). When the rules of discourse change, but nobody tells you: Making sense of mathematics learning from a common standpoint. *Journal of the Learning Sciences, 16*(4), 565–613.

Shapiro, L. (2019). *Embodied cognition* (2nd ed.). Routledge.

Sherin, M. G. (2007). The development of teachers' professional vision in video clubs. In R. Goldman, R. Pea, B. Barron, & S. Derry (Eds.), *Video research in the learning sciences* (pp. 383–395). Erlbaum.

Sherin, M., Jacobs, V., & Philipp, R. (Eds.). (2011). *Mathematics teacher noticing: Seeing through teachers' eyes.* Routledge.

Sherin, M. G., & van Es, E. A. (2009). Effects of video club participation on teachers' professional vision. *Journal of Teacher Education, 60*(1), 20–37.

Smith III, J. P., Disessa, A. A., & Roschelle, J. (1994). Misconceptions reconceived: A constructivist analysis of knowledge in transition. *Journal of the Learning Sciences, 3*(2), 115–163.

Songer, N. B. (1996). Exploring learning opportunities in coordinated network-enhanced classrooms: A case of kids as global scientists. *Journal of the Learning Sciences, 5*(4), 297–327.

Stevens, R., & Hall, R. (1998). Disciplined perception: Learning to see in technoscience. In M. Lampert & M. Blunk (Eds.), *Talking mathematics in school: Studies of teaching and learning* (pp. 107–149). Cambridge University Press.

Tate, W. F. (1995). Returning to the root: A culturally relevant approach to mathematics pedagogy. *Theory into Practice, 34*(3), 166–173.

Taylor, K. H. (2017). Learning along lines: Locative literacies for reading and writing the city. *Journal of the Learning Sciences, 26*(4), 533–574.

van Es, E. A. (2012). Examining the development of a teacher learning community: The case of a video club. *Teaching and Teacher Education, 28*(2), 182–192.

van Es, E. A., & Sherin, M. G. (2008). Mathematics teachers' "learning to notice" in the context of a video club. *Teaching and Teacher Education, 24*, 244–276.

van Es, E. A., & Sherin, M. G. (2010). The influence of video clubs on teachers' thinking and practice. *Journal of Mathematics Teacher Education, 13*, 155–176.

Vossoughi, S., & Bevan, B. (2014). Making and tinkering: A review of the literature. *National Research Council Committee on Out of School Time. STEM*, 1–55. National Research Council.

Vygotsky, L. S. (1978). *Mind in society: The development of higher psychological processes*. (Trans. M. Cole, V. John-Steiner, S. Scribner, & E. Souberman). Harvard University Press.

Vygotsky, L. S. (1986). *Thought and language* (Trans. A. Kozulin). MIT Press.

Watson, B. (2002). *The man who changed how boys and toys were made: The life and times of A. C. Gilbert*. Viking Press.

Wilensky, U. (1999). NetLogo. Center for connected learning and computer-based modeling, Northwestern University.

Wilensky, U., & Reisman, K. (2006). Thinking like a wolf, a sheep, or a firefly: Learning biology through constructing and testing computational theories – an embodied modeling approach. *Cognition and Instruction, 24*(2), 171–209.

Wilensky, U., & Stroup, W. (1999). Learning through participatory simulations: Network-Based design for systems learning in classrooms. Computer supported collaborative learning (CSCL '99). A participatory simulation model for studying attitudes to infection risk. Retrieved from www.researchgate.net/publication/231614880_A_Participatory_Simulation_Model_for_Studying_Attitudes_to_Infection_Risk

Wineburg, S. S. (1991). On the reading of historical texts: Notes on the breach between school and academy. *American Educational Research Journal, 28*(3), 495–519.

Wineburg, S. S. (1998). Reading Abraham Lincoln: An expert/expert study in the interpretation of historical texts. *Cognitive Science, 22*(3), 319–346.

Wineburg, S. S., & Grossman, P. (1998). Creating a community of learners among high school teachers. *Phi Delta Kappan, 79*(5), 350.

Wood, D., Bruner, J. S., & Ross, G. (1976). The role of tutoring in problem solving. *Journal of Child Psychology and Psychiatry, 17*(2), 89–100.

Yackel, E., & Cobb, P. (1996). Sociomathematical norms, argumentation, and autonomy in mathematics. *Journal for Research in Mathematics Education, 27*, 458–477.

Part III

Implications of GEL for Education Practice and Research

11

Trans-Scale Considerations

11.1 UNDERSTANDING AND CULTIVATING GEL ACROSS TIMESCALES

In this chapter, I explore interconnections of learning processes across the range of timescales. In describing the problems facing education and the obstacles for improvement, I stated that students are seldom viewed by those in the education system as embodied learners, especially in later grades. Educational designs rarely incorporate learners' body-based resources or grounding of new ideas to their direct lived experiences. In contrast, I have shared how successful learning is rich with grounded and embodied experiences. In my view, the evidence suggests that society has a great deal to gain by adopting the paradigm of grounded and embodied learning as the basis for designing learning experiences within its educational systems.

As we have seen, embodied learning takes place across a broad range of scales. It covers at least ten orders of magnitude (see Figure 3.5), from the rapid biological processes that unfold on the order of 10^{-2} sec to far more gradual processes observed in communities that take place on the order of years, or 10^8 sec (Nathan & Alibali, 2010). As with phenomena in the natural sciences—think about comparisons of physical sciences, biological sciences, and social sciences, for example—processes operating at each scale have their own set of structures and behaviors.

For simplicity, it has been helpful to isolate aspects of learning at each of these timescales to identify their properties. Learning, of course, can occur at any of these timescales simultaneously. These different processes combine in important ways that must also be taken into consideration. My central objective in this chapter is to show that by looking across as well as within the various timescales, the GEL framework portrays new views of learners and learning, one that can inform an alternative path for effective education. Before starting that, I wish to review what I have compiled about embodied learning up to this point.

11.1.1 GEL Across the Timescales: A Review

The fields primarily focused on learning and cognition have often recognized the many scales in which intellectual behaviors unfold. There is considerable interest in investigating questions of how to relate processes operating at different levels and to understand how theoretical accounts of behavior at one level of abstraction influence those accounts at other levels (Colombo & Knauff, 2020; Marr, 1982; Lemke, 2001; Nathan & Sawyer, in press; Newell, 1994). Examples abound. For one, the study of so-called "designer drugs" reveals

DOI: 10.4324/9780429329098-11

how malleable factors at the molecular level can induce predicable mental behavior (Bickle, 2019). As another example, Bender (2020) describes the interplay of sociocultural processes on people's gene expression, which, in turn, affects neural development of cognition, that then, in turn, influences cultural evolution.

To remind the reader, *learning* **is defined as an enduring change in behavior.** Consider the variety of learning behaviors. Forming and strengthening activation of synaptic connections that contribute to the retrieval of an associative memory is quite different than adopting norms and discourse practices among members of an enduring community of practice. At each time band, different structures, resources, and processes are recruited to initiate and preserve these changes and facilitate their appropriate retrieval (reinstatement) at the appropriate time, in the proper context. These comparisons are summarized in Table 11.1.

At the cognitive and knowledge-based scales (Chapters 5 & 6), where learning operates in the conscious spectrum, changes in knowing-that arise by making meaningful connections that are often language- and rule-based. New facts become learned by relating them to prior declarative knowledge. To gain meaning, new concepts are grounded by conceptual metaphors. In this timescale band, learning, and knowledge are predominantly conscious and deliberate, following overt, verbally stated rules and methods that are carried out sequentially and with oversight. They often leave behind a verbalizable trace in working memory. The

TABLE 11.1
A comparative summary of GEL processes

	Type 1 processing	*Type 2 processing*	*Type 3 processing*
Timescale	ca. below 10^{-3} s to 10^{-1} s milliseconds	ca. 10^0 s to 10^4 seconds to hours	ca. 10^5 s to 10^8 s days to years
Energy	Effortless	Effortful	Energizing, effortless, effortful
Reasoning style	Impressions	Analytical	Discursive
Processing style	Automatic	Controlled, deliberate	Responsive to context
Awareness	Unconscious (unaware), unmonitored	Conscious (mostly), monitored	Can be collectively unconscious, conscious, or self-conscious
Pace	Fast	Medium	Slow
Processing dynamics	Associative & parallel	Linear & sequential	Networked
Method	Impulse following	Rule following	Norm following
Mode (primary) of thought	Perceptual recognition	Intellectual	Social
Cross-species	Innate skills shared with many species	Shared with very few species	Possibly uniquely human
Attention load	Few/no attention resources	Draw on attentional resources	Mixed
External control	Undisruptable Executive control	Social pressure; guilt.	
Response automaticity	Follows habits	Override habitual responses	Adopt group norms
Response mode	Anticipatory, predictive	Reactive, planful	Normative
Type of knowing	Knowing-how	Knowing-that	Knowing-with
	Overconfident, feeling of being right	Declarative facts and rules	Sociocultural lens on all one's experiences
Grounding processes	Perceptual fluency	Connection making	Common ground
Embodied learning	Transduction	Offloading	Participation internalized
Example: reading	Stroop Effect	Sound out words	Social facilitation–inhibition (SFI)

large attentional demands to perform Type 2 processing leads people to seek out opportunities for cognitive offloading, whenever possible. This includes short-circuiting effortful Type 2 processes using effortless Type 1 processes, such as using pattern matching and heuristics. When they do proceed, the attention-demanding Type 2 processes in the conscious spectrum can be evaluated, redirected, or paused altogether. For example, many forms of verbal problem solving have this effortful quality and leave behind a trace that enables solvers to give a fairly accurate verbal report of the steps they took (Ericsson & Simon, 1993).

At the biological scale (Chapters 7 & 8), changes in knowing-how take place among interconnections between groups of neurons. These changes predominantly lead to enhanced pattern recognition and procedural knowledge. The associations that form are driven by a need to predict and anticipate events in the world, rather than merely react to these events. Many optical illusions of shape and color are experienced because of this predictive orientation. I have also mentioned how people's handshape anticipates the shape and functionality of knobs and push plates as people approach doors. These associations reflect the regularities of one's environment and experiences in the face of tremendous variability and noise.

Type 1 processing operates largely outside of one's conscious awareness. It takes up little if any of one's very limited attentional resources, and often proceeds without oversight or control. Recall how people performing directed eye gazes to solve the tumor-radiation problem (Figure 2.4) showed superior performance but without explicit awareness they were learning about convergence. Similarly, students matching the directed actions in *The Hidden Village* motion-based video game showed improved mathematical intuitions and proof practices, also without awareness of these influences on their thinking. When people are aware of these at all, they experience them as impulsive behaviors and flashes of insight.

Learning at sociocultural scale (Chapters 9 & 10) occurs as people change the ways they participate in groups as well as how people interact with other agents and with the resources in their environment. The participatory practices necessarily operate with a foundation of common ground that affords ways for unfamiliar behaviors to be grounded in familiar ones. These changes in knowing-with alter people's interpretive frame, as they adopt the social norms of their communities. Learning is often observed as changes in people's discourse practices, including how they talk, perceive, use tools, and reason. For example, students engaged in communities of learners about biodiversity, weather, and historical events appropriated the ways that scientists and historians talked and reasoned about evidence. Teachers also showed how their practices and ways of thinking about and perceiving their students can change with their participation in communities of practice. These changes can be experienced as energizing by learners, because they are situated within familiar and very dynamic social exchanges.

11.1.2 GEL Principles: A Synthesis

In the earlier chapters, I reviewed ways GEL processes at these various scales play out in academic content areas. From these, I derived scale-specific principles that describe ways educational experiences can be made more successful than in traditional classrooms so that they lead to more meaningful learning, more effective instruction, better designs of learning technology and learning environments, and improved assessment practices. Rather than review them all again here, I summarize the principles from each of the major bands of the GEL timescale in Table 11.2. The reader is invited to review them in their respective chapters. As I have discussed, learning processes operating at different scales exhibit remarkably different traits. Here I offer a synthesis that takes these principles across the timescales of learning to inform a set of trans-scale themes for GEL.

TABLE 11.2
Summary of GEL principles and trans-scale themes

Educational concerns	Biological principles (Chapt. 8)	Cognitive principles (Chapt. 6)	Sociocultural principles (Chapt. 10)	Trans-scale themes (Chapt. 11)
Grounding	Grounding via perceptual learning, procedural automaticity, and environmental affordances	Grounding via consistent action and semantically congruent gestures Grounding metaphors	Common ground supported by shared body states, as well as by social norms and taken-as-shared objects and representations	**Grounded meaning** is achieved by • Connecting concepts and disciplinary formalisms to perceptual and motor processes, along with physical and spatial metaphors of those perceptual and motor processes • Semantically congruent gestures; and the • Common ground as supported by shared body states, as well as by social norms and taken-as-shared objects and representations
Learning	Simulation / sensorimotor transduction	Situated memory retrieval Simulated memory retrieval Inference-preserving metaphors	Participation in discourse practices, Internalization of epistemic properties of cultural and scientific tools and technologies	**Learning** is advanced by • Sensorimotor & place-based simulation processes and linking metaphors that support model-based reasoning and inference making • Internalization of social practices and epistemic properties of cultural and scientific tools
Design	Reduced cognitive load using all forms of grounding eliciting action-cognition transduction	Cognitive offloading	Collaborative engagement Bidirectional influences of individual on social processes Social capital through making	**Design** effective learning environments by • Managing cognitive load via offloading, and extended and distributed cognition • Promoting cognitive engagement, through action, participation, and social construction
Instruction	Procedural learning via practice Perceptual learning via exposure and contrasting cases	Linking gestures Concreteness fading	Socio-disciplinary norms Scaffolding Sociocultural entailments of instructional gestures Expert blind spot	**Instruction** effectiveness is enhanced • Using gestures to direct attention, forge links to new ideas and representations, and manage common ground of learners by establishing and maintaining social and socio-disciplinary norms • Guiding learners through trajectories of concreteness fading • Operating with conscious awareness of one's expert blind spots
Assessment	Assessing nonverbal ways of knowing	Summative assessment of nonverbal ways of knowing Grounded and embodied formative assessment	Situated formative assessment Situated summative assessment	**Assessments** in formative (diagnostic) and summative (evaluative) forms must • Document multimodal, nonverbal, situated, and distributed ways of knowing

Looking across the scales reveals trans-scale GEL themes for **grounded meaning.** Grounded meaning is achieved, in part, by connecting novel concepts and symbolic formalisms to perceptual and motor processes, as well as to metaphors derived from those perceptual and motor processes. Semantically congruent gestures that enact the concepts during communication also ground new ideas and formalisms. Grounding is also established by common ground. One way this manifests is as empathetically shared body states activated by mirror neurons, which allows one to literally experience the body states of others. Common ground is also supported by taken-as-shared objects and representations and by adopting social norms of a community. For example, consider how an abstract set of concepts for arithmetic are grounded. As one component, pattern recognition of small collections of objects are rapidly enumerated via subitizing. This neural process forms the basis for the conceptual metaphor of ARITHMETIC AS OBJECT COLLECTION. Thus, basic cognitive principles of enumerating object collection supervene on neural processes of subitizing. This conceptualization of basic arithmetic expands to a general set of definitions and properties of the rules of arithmetic for all natural numbers that are represented by conventionalized symbol system (e.g., the numbers 0 through 9, equal sign, and the arithmetic operators) adopted by a disciplinary community, and then by society at large. In this way, social conventions of arithmetic and the formal properties of numeric computation supervene on conceptual metaphors of enumerating and combining objects.

Learning across scales reveals several overarching trans-scale GEL themes. For one, people use multiple means for achieving understanding. Learning is far better supported and more robust when learning engages a variety of systems and is experienced over different contexts. People have both unconscious and conscious processes that contribute to meaningful learning. Their respective trade-offs provide a complementarity that help people to be effective and adaptive learners. Socially organized learning experiences often provide contexts for this integration to occur naturally. Unconscious and conscious processes also interact. People internalize overt social practices of the communities in which they participate, and the epistemic properties of cultural and scientific tools that community members use. Inter-personal interactions invite people to re-voice and re-present implicit norms and knowledge to others for discussion and negotiation. Bringing unconscious knowledge into awareness contributes to reflection, refinement, and reification for its preservation for others.

Another is that model-based reasoning and inference making are enacted through sensorimotor and place-based simulation processes, such as action-cognition transduction, and the role of inference-preserving linking metaphors. For example, grasping comes to mean an act of making reference to a desired object. This act leads to the generation of a pointing gesture. Pointing then transcends location and can come to refer to any form of deixis to reference things. In turn, this gets signified as iconic references (such as an arrow), linguistic references (e.g., *this* and *that*), and formal, symbol references, such as the use of formal symbols by practitioners of rhetoric and science.

Three trans-scale themes for the **design of effective learning environments** emerge from the GEL principles. One design theme is the benefits that are exhibited when promoting cognitive engagement through action, participation, and social co-construction. A second design theme recognizes the benefits of eliciting action-cognition transduction by directing learners to perform semantically relevant movements—a form of knowing-how—as a way to facilitate generation of corresponding conceptual knowledge—ways of knowing-that.

A third trans-scale theme for **design** is attending to the management of cognitive load by providing offloading, and supporting extended and distributed cognition. GEL processes benefit from reduced cognitive load by minimizing task-irrelevant demands when forming perceptual patterns and procedures and constructing schemas and models. However, the enormous parallel processing capacity provided by associative memory and perceptual processes have to funnel through a very restrictive channel of limited attention and working memory for the primarily sequential processes at the cognitive and knowledge-based scales. People will offload cognitive processes onto environmental resources that perform epistemic functions, and onto social networks of agents that enable distributed cognition. The large changes necessary to accommodate these shifting resources while maintaining the essential qualities of the processes illustrates the kind of disproportionate *scaling* that is managed by the entire GEL system.

The effectiveness of **instruction** is enhanced using gestures to direct learners' attention, forge links to new ideas and representations, and manage common ground of learners by establishing and maintaining social and socio-disciplinary norms. Instruction planning also considers the common ground of the learners. It is informed by the developmental implications of curricular sequencing that supported grounding and embodied learning by guiding learners through trajectories of concreteness fading interventions, from material manifestations to visually iconic depictions, and then to symbolic abstractions. Teachers who are content experts must also maintain awareness of their expert blind spots, owing to the unique ways they experience their own affordances of the world, where they may not share common ground with their students. This illustrates *superposition* (see Box 11.A) of principles of instructional gestures operating simultaneously at different scales to produce an overall experience intended to support learning.

Assessments, in both their formative (diagnostic) and summative (evaluative) roles must be sensitive to the underlying multimodal, nonverbal, situated, and distributed ways of knowing exhibited by learners in the GEL framework. Good assessment practices should follow good instructional practices (Bransford, Brown, & Cocking, 2000). In practice, to account for students' nonverbal ways of knowing and thinking, teachers across the range of content areas will need to provide some assessment opportunities for students to freely gesture while they describe their reasoning in response to test items. Students working in collaborative, resource-rich settings also should expect that assessment experiences are closely matched to the learning experiences, and are designed to document the distributed nature of their thinking and learning.

A sample rubric (Table 11.3) for assessing students' multimodal and distributed geometry knowledge illustrates how to conduct this in practice (cf., Nathan, Schenck et al., 2020; Walkington et al., 2020). In the example, I have offered three levels for the rubric, while in practice these are analytic choices made by teachers to suit their assessment goals. In this scheme, the assessor should not be using this to assess student understanding (for formative assessment) or performance (summative assessment) as *independent* expression as verbal, nonverbal, and distributed ways of knowing. Rather, assessors are looking to document the *highest level* across verbal, nonverbal, and distributed forms of expression for each outcome measure. Collaborative gestures such as those illustrated in Figures 9.4 (students; also see Nathan & Swart, 2020; Walkington et al. 2020) provide an account of how multiple agents and objects are naturally invoked to express distributed ways of knowing about geometric relationships.

Capturing these distributed, multimodal reports via video is especially helpful for assisting teachers in the application of stringent rubrics. Neglect of this trans-scale theme by restricting responses to written and verbal channels can be expected to significantly underestimate the knowledge and capabilities of the learner in many cases.

The summary of these trans-scale GEL themes is provided in the final column of Table 11.2. Together, these give a portrait of the nature of learning processes. While it may be tempting to highlight these themes on their own and treat them as "take-aways" of this long path through timescales, I think that would not give the whole—or even the most important

TABLE 11.3

A sample rubric for assessing students multimodal and distributed geometry knowledge

Truth value, insights and proof for each of the four mathematical conjectures.

Conjecture label	Conjecture text	Truth	Insight	Proof
Parallelogram area	The area of a parallelogram is the same as the area of a rectangle with the same length and height	True	(1) States a parallelogram is a rectangle tilted over or pushed over (2) States area of a parallelogram and a rectangle have the same formula	(1) Shows cutting off a triangle from the parallelogram, or rearranging the area makes them congruent. (2) State all rectangles are parallelograms and therefore the formula for area is the same
Midsegment triangle	The segment that joins the midpoints of two sides of any triangle is parallel to the third side	True	(1) True because the two triangles are similar (2) True because it is scaled	(1) Shows base sliding up and says similar triangles or scaled so angles are the same (2) Explicitly says SAS and that corresponding angles are congruent
AAA	Given that you know the measure of all three angles of a triangle, there is only one unique triangle that can be formed with these three angle measurements	False	States similar triangles or infinite/many triangles	(1) Gives specific counterexample (2) Visually shows scaling or discusses scaling and similar triangles
Circumscribed	A circle can be circumscribed about any triangle	True	(1) Any three points on a plane make a triangle. (2) The circumcircle always passes through all three vertices of a triangle	(1) Demonstrate with vertices as points along the circumcircle (2) Show with the perpendicular bisectors of each side of the triangle

part—of the story. In my view, the scale-specific principles are the more valuable lessons, tied, as they are, more directly to the actual GEL processes and to the empirical findings that lend them theoretical support.

11.2 SPANNING SCALES OF LEARNING: SUPERPOSITION, SUPERVENIENCE, SCALING, AND GENERATION

In addition to identifying GEL principles across timescales, this synthesis illustrates some of the key ways that processes at different scales function in relation to one another. A process operating at one scale often combines with processes operating at different scales. For example, biological processes of pattern recognition operate alongside sociocultural processes of community participation. *Superposition* provides one way to describe how these effects get combined. Processes also *supervene* on, or hierarchically depend upon, other processes. As processes use feedforward and feedback mechanisms to anticipate and react to changes occurring at other levels, such as available resources or incurred performance costs they go through change through disproportionate (i.e., allometric) *scaling* while still maintaining a through-line along the timescale spectrum. Finally, a process at one scale can lead to the *generation* of new processes that operate at different scales. In this section, I explore super-position, supervenience, scaling, and generation as exemplars of trans-scale relations and operations and their relevance for understanding and enhancing learning in educational settings.

11.2.1 Superposition: Combined Effects Across Scales

The GEL timescale provides a particular analytic view of learning processes. For educative purposes, I use the GEL timescale to artificially separate out the processes along different time bands in order to simplify my discussion while I expose their scale-specific qualities. In practice, these various processes operate at the same time. When people see actual behaviors—rather than *formalisms* such as models used to describe these behaviors—they witness the *cumulative* effect of multiple GEL processes operating at different timescales. As another simplification, I think it is helpful to think about their cumulative effects in a similar way to the arithmetic *sum* of these influences, although, of course it is much more complex than this simplification. This simplified way of combining effects of co-occurring processes is called *superposition*. I provide more information about how superposition works in Box 11.A.

Box 11.A A brief introduction to superposition

Superposition literally means to place one thing on top of another. For simplicity, I ask readers to think of these things as time-varying signals, like the waveform that is made when someone plucks a guitar string. When two identical processes are superposed—when both co-occur and the effects of one can be directly combined with the effects of the other—the combined effect doubles the amplitude (the vertical peaks and troughs), and leaves the frequency (the number of peaks and troughs in a given amount of time) intact, as shown in the top of Figure 11.1. This illustrates "constructive interference." When the same two processes are again superposed, but they are exactly out of sync, we can say that one of them is "180-degrees out of phase" with the other. Now the peaks of one match up with the troughs of the other—the two waves (if indeed they are identical) will exactly cancel each other out. This illustrates "destructive interference."

The reader may now imagine a variety of effects. Identical processes can be a small or a large amount out of phase. One may combine with processes of different frequencies and amplitudes. Superposition of signals with these various differences will produce all sorts of different combined effects. One example is using combinations of smooth sinusoidal waves to approximate a "square wave" (see bottom of Figure 11.1). With so many combinations, superposition of a large number of even simple processes can have a very complex combined effect, such as the signals from an EEG, with lots of wiggles and much less predictability.

In the GEL framework, actual behaviors are like this. They are the combination of simpler processes at various time scales, such as those at the biological, cognitive, knowledge-based, and sociocultural scales. When they combine at any one time in some particular context, superposition produces a complex looking, seemly highly

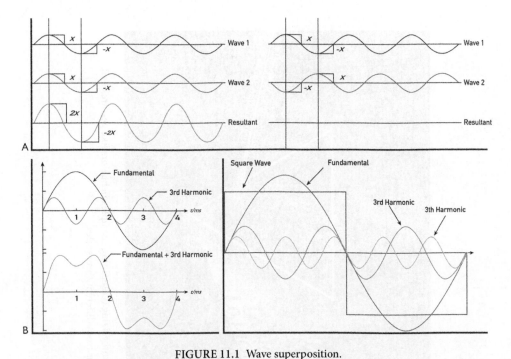

FIGURE 11.1 Wave superposition.
Top Left. Constructive interference. *Top Right.* Destructive interference. *Bottom Left and Right.* Sinusoidal components show how constructive and destructive interference combine to make a square wave.

unpredictable pattern of behavior. Some constituents constructively increase the output, while others are destructively reducing the output, or changing its phase. Furthermore, sometimes reducing output is beneficial, such as when the system successfully suppresses an inappropriate impulse. At other times, constructive interference is most desirable. Most often, the system prefers to operate within a modest range.

The superposition scheme works in the reverse, as well. When complex behaviors are observed, it is possible to imagine them as the combined effect of many simpler processes. It's rather like a prism, which takes light that is already composed of signals of many wavelengths (like that from the Sun) and separates out the constituent components. This is often referred to as a "frequency analysis," because it separates out the constituent frequencies in space. The GEL framework, with its attention to the distinct timescales, is a prism for analyzing complex learning into its components (Figure 11.2). It may seem unlikely that the superposition of, say, pattern recognition processes, sociocultural practices, gesture production, and cognitive simulation are responsible for producing some observed form of historical or scientific reasoning. But think of how surprising it is (every time!) to see all the colors of a rainbow coming from "white" light.

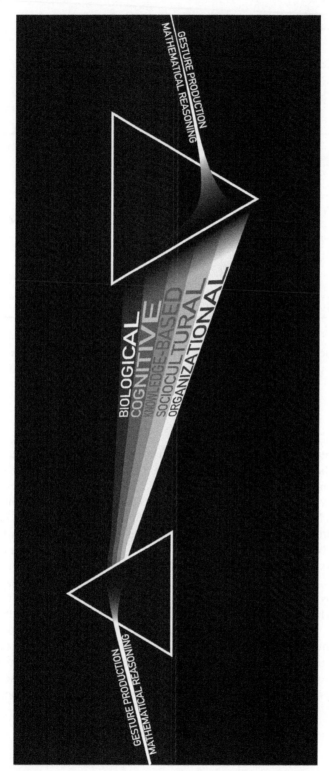

FIGURE 11.2 The GEL framework is a prism for analyzing (separating) and synthesizing (combining) complex behaviors like gestures and mathematical reasoning into learning processes from different time scales.

Classroom instruction is an illustrative example of how superposition of simpler, scale-specific processes combine to form a more complex whole. At rapid, biological levels of processing, teachers recognize patterns of behavior among their students, such as when students display cues, both subtle and overt, that they are no longer operating on common ground with the teacher. These cues trigger responses that modify a teacher's instructional practices. Observational studies reveal teachers frequently use gestures along with speech to manage common ground and regulate student participation in class discourse (Alibali et al., 2014; Nathan & Kim, 2009). Yet teachers report that they often have no conscious awareness of their use of gestures during classroom instruction (Nathan, Yeo, Boncoddo, Hostetter, & Alibali, 2019). At a cognitive level, teachers are conveying the declarative facts and rules of a domain, such as when to apply certain mathematical rules. Socioculturally, they are modeling healthy practices and habits of mind, such as respectful interactions with students. These are simple pedagogical acts when taken on their own. But observing teaching in actual classrooms is anything but simple (Russ, Sherin, & Sherin, 2016). Rather, what is observed is the cumulative result when all of these pedagogical processes operate simultaneously.

The GEL framework builds a case for appreciating the *holistic* nature of human behavior. Yet the framework also demonstrates the value in understanding how these complex, holistic behaviors arise. An analytic view of complex processes as the cumulative effects through superposition can offer new insights into how teaching and learning can be improved. Sometimes, the ideal method is to operate with the system in its entirety. This is consistent with the systemic methods I discussed earlier. Other times, benefits to instruction, learning, and performance can be achieved most effectively by addressing the contribution of constituent processes and their combined effect on the system as a whole.

11.2.2 Supervenience: Hierarchical Relations Across Scales

I showed some ways that superposition and frequency analysis allow people to see how to combine and separate out common effects of components. Another set of considerations takes place when the operation of a process depends on—*supervenes on*—processes operating at a different scale. Supervenience illustrates one of the most marvelous and enigmatic aspect of the behavior of complex systems: the *emergence* of properties that are not pre-specified by the components, but arise from their interactions. Emergence is the gift that complexity offers up to produce behaviors beyond what is clearly given at the outset.

As an example, Figure 11.3a (see Henriques, 2003) depicts how various fields of study emerge and supervene on the field positioned below it. As illustrated, culture supervenes on the behaviors of individual minds, while what emerges in the collective cultural interactions is not readily apparent from the individual properties of mind and behavior as revealed by psychological studies. The mind, in turn, emerges from cellular behavior, with surprises not readily apparent from biological models. Life emerges from the molecular interactions of matter, which in turn arise from sub-atomic interactions. Supervenience describes but does not explain how, in each case, the awesome gifts that arise as each system emerges (Davidson, 1970; Sawyer, 2005). Each is itself an area of wonderment that puzzles scientists, philosophers, and artists.

Figure 11.3b illustrates an important set of supervenient processes for one aspect of word learning called the "word superiority effect." This effect is shown as it can be modeled by a kind of connectionist network called a PDP system by McClelland & Rumelhart (1986; PDP stands for parallel distributed processing). The word superiority effect is an emergent effect from the repeated exposure of words and nonwords in a lexicon. Both bottom-up and top-down processes are conveyed by the network in Figure 11.3b. For bottom-up processes,

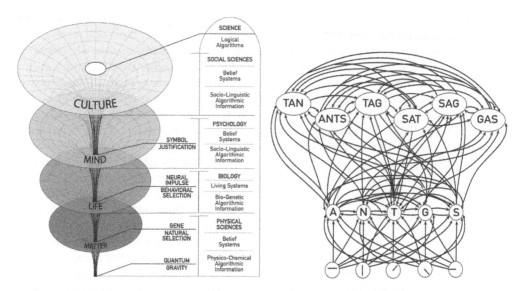

FIGURE 11.3 *Left.* Seeing how the various fields of study emerge and supervene on the one below it. *Right.* Word superiority effect as modeled by a connectionist network by McClelland & Rumelhart (1986).

individual pen strokes (bottom layer of the network) combine in regulated ways to form letters. Letters are then combined to form words. Words in this network, in turn, supervene on letters, while letters supervene on pen strokes. Behaviorally, reading researchers also document a top-down effect. Readers actually "lose" awareness of the letters when attending to familiar instances at the word level. That is, when common words are the object of focus of one's cognitive and perceptual processes, awareness of the individual letters recedes into the background.

Even though readers lose their awareness of the individual letters when they appear in familiar words during reading, another emergent property that is consistent with the research is that priming for the supervened-upon letters that make up the word is actually stronger than when the same letters appear in nonwords. This is rather remarkable and shows the interplay of top-down and bottom-up processes.

There are also inhibitory mechanisms at play for letters that do not belong to an activated word. Readers' priming for *excluded* letters (those that are similar to other letters but that are *not* in the current word) is *weaker*. This holds even for those letters that share line strokes with letters that are *included* in the activated word.

How does supervenience offer insights into trans-scale learning behaviors? It does so by proposing that the behaviors of a system are the product of both emergent/bottom-up behaviors, and top-down influences. For example, learning to read draws on GEL processes at different timescales that exhibit supervenience (Gee, 1992/2014; Graesser & McNamara, 2011). Reading is a mid-level process, using cognitive and knowledge-based processes of knowing-that. One's participation in the community of readers is contingent on one's knowing-with of the experience of reading. Reading provides a unique interpretive frame, one where an author's ideas are reinstated in new form in the mind of a reader, that can travel across time, distance, and cultures. The processes that support adoption of the practices of communities of readers supervene on one's cognitive processes of word decoding, lexical access, and meaning making. Those cognitive skills supervene on the procedural knowledge of knowing-how to physically read, along with pattern recognition processes for letter and word recognition.

In my synthesis across GEL principles (Table 11.2), I described ways that student learning of the meaning of concepts and of disciplinary formalisms supervene on their perceptual and motor processes, such as pattern recognition and action-cognition transduction, in a top-down fashion. It is also the case that bottom-up processes orient the student to a set of concepts upon processing the perceptual field of symbols and images.

As another example, teachers' instructional moves supervene on tacit beliefs about what their students know and how they learn. The beliefs of teachers who are also subject-matter experts on a given topic for their students exhibit emergent behaviors based on their highly refined perceptual and procedural processes that recognize and rapidly apprehend meaning of formalisms (such as symbolic algebra equations) that are as yet ungrounded to their students. This provides an account of how an expert blind spot emerges from teachers' perceptual and procedural processes to shape their instruction and expectations for their students.

Assessment practices offer another illustrative example. Students' ways of knowing-with supervene on the distributed system of tools and actors, as found in project-based learning contexts. When assessments are designed without these resources, students' ways of knowing-with are disrupted. There is no longer a way to activate the reasoning processes that successfully operated in the distributed knowledge system, with the result that students are likely to underperform compared to their earlier performance.

11.2.3 Scaling: Variability and Consistency Across Scales

Throughout the book I presented evidence that supports embodied learning as a way to enhance the effectiveness of students' educational experiences. By and large, the empirical studies do show that interventions that engage students' grounded and embodied learning processes are beneficial. In addition, they often show GEL interventions support better comprehension and learning than use of business as usual. In the earliest chapters I explained why GEL can foster learning through meaning making. In this section, I explore some of the reasons that GEL can support greater learning. The effects on how learning is affected by changes in scale help to reveal the material nature of the learning process itself. I propose that one reason GEL is more effective than many other types of educational experiences, is that it taps into *sublinear scaling efficiencies* while also gaining *superlinear learning benefits*. But I am getting ahead of myself.

First, I want to review how performance characteristics change with changes due to scaling. I explore how this relates to changes in learning performance across timescales. The answer appears to lie with allometric scaling. *Allometric scaling* is the account of how processes and functions in a system scale *disproportionately* as they change in size (Huxley, 1950). The contrast is with *isometric scaling*, where changes occur in equal proportion. If isometric scaling were the norm in biological and social systems, then puppies would look identical in shape to their mothers, only smaller. Saplings would be smaller versions of the trees they will become; ponds would be exactly like small oceans, super-metropolises as larger versions of small towns and villages. We know this not the case. More accurately, some facets of animals, plants, water sources, cities, and the like, change at different rates than others as they grow. Bogin (1997) proposes that this is why baby animals are so darn cute!

Geoffrey West (2017) built upon the realization of allometric scaling from developmental biology to show what happens when systems go through changes in scale. To account for a broad range of systems and processes, West uses logarithmic scales, just as I have done throughout the book (for a review, see Box 3D). When discussing logarithmic patterns, the exponents used to mathematically model growth are very important. When exponents describing logarithmic growth are equal to 1.0, there is isometric scaling. In that case, when there is a change in the size of one dimension, such as the mass of an animal, other measures of interest (e.g., heart rate, calories consumed, walking speed) would change proportionately. In mathematical terms, the relationship of the size of the animal to these other metrics of interest (heart rate, etc.) is **linear** when the slope of the line of system size plotted against the metrics of interest in a log-log graph is 1.0.

Sublinear Scaling

As it turns out, linear relationships in biological and social growth are not very common. Often, the slope of the growth line is *less* than 1.0, indicating *sublinear scaling*. In this case some metrics grow *more slowly* than one might expect from an increase in size (West, 2017). The practical effect of sublinear scaling is that as these entities grow, they become *more* efficient in some ways. As West notes, a 200-lb person does not need to consume twice the calories of a 100-lb person, but is comfortable with between 75% and 85% of the amount that a linear model would predict (West, 2017). This 15% to 25% *increase* in efficiency of caloric use applies to an enormous range of animals, including mammals from the tiny shrew to the great blue whale: as well as many fish, birds, crustacea, insects, plants, and so on.

The pattern is also evident at the subsystem level. For example, aortas are the main arteries for supplying oxygenated blood to the circulatory system for animals. The scaling of aortas operates with a savings of about 25%. Genomes also save 75%. Plants require only three-fourths of the linear amount of leaves to furnish food as they grow. Cities need only 85% of the expected amounts of roadways, lengths of pipes, electrical wiring, and other infrastructure investments. Across many types of systems, operating at various scales, West (2017) shows there is a tremendous regularity in the ways systems achieve an economy of scale, and become more efficient in distributing necessary resources, while consuming fewer resources and energy as they grow.

Superlinear Scaling

Things get even more interesting when one looks at *superlinear scaling*—how systems produce *more* with growth than a linear model would expect. These are log-log growth relationships with slopes greater than 1.0. Notably, brain growth exhibits superlinear scaling. For example, the growth in the amount of white matter (in log scale) as a function of grey matter (in log scale) is about 1.25 (West, 2017). *White matter,* the reader may know, contains high density of the myelinated (protected) axons, that form the vast network of connections in the brain. This interconnectivity is key to the processing power of the brain. This is because one's ideas and associations are not simply stored in the 86 billion (nearly 10^{11}) neurons in the human brain. Rather, it is through the 100 *trillion* neural connections (that is 10^{14}, which is 1,000 larger!) that humans achieve their vast mental capabilities. When white matter scales up faster than the growth of brain mass more generally, it shows how brain growth leads to even greater and faster mental capabilities for sensory, motor, autonomic, and cognitive processing.

What drives this unexpected benefit with scale? West (2017) posits that it has to do primarily with the *networks of connections* that make proper function happen. These networks are the physical conduits by which transportation of nutrients, energy, waste, information, and all manner of resources that enable the systems to function. The increased efficiencies from sublinear scaling (as with reduced metabolic demands) plus the enhanced growth of superlinear scaling (as with neuronal connectivity) emerge because of the growth of the complexity of the networks of interconnections that follow from the increases in size at biological scales. These gains in network efficiencies and intellectual power also emerge at the cognitive, sociocultural, and organizational scales.

Combined Effects of Sublinear and Superlinear Scaling
In my discussion of the cognitive/knowledge-based level, I reviewed how knowledge structures can be modeled as *networks*. Connectionists model the growth in knowledge using networks of sub-symbolic nodes. As "neurally-inspired" architectures for sensorimotor and cognitive behavior, the processes modeled by these systems are not encoded locally in the nodes, but through the interconnections between nodes (McClelland & Rumelhart, 1986; Rumelhart & McClelland, 1986). In addition, other models for cognition at a symbolic scale (e.g., Anderson et al., 2004) also rely on the interconnections among knowledge elements to depict intellectual behaviors. Both accounts—and many others—of reasoning and learning at the cognitive scale draw on network-based models of mental elements to describe cognitive behaviors. As these physical networks grow, these network models of cognition are all subject to the gains in processing capacity predicted by superlinear scaling as well as the cost efficiencies obtained with sublinear scaling.

At the sociocultural scale, superlinear scaling networking among group members reveals how groups often outsmart the same number of unorganized individuals (Barron, 2003; Navajas et al., 2018, 2019; Schwartz, 1995). These advantages with increased scale are also evident among organizations and cities. For example, tracking the number of new patent filings is one way to measure learning and innovation. West (2017) shows that the growth in patents as a function of growth in city size, as presented in a log-log graph, has a slope of approximately 1.15. This is a 15% increase in innovation as compared to that projected by linear growth. Here again, West argues that it is the networks—conduits for ideas such as cafes and college campuses—that provide rich exchanges of ideas, social interactions, cultural contributions, and material goods that underlie these superlinear growth rates that drive these added benefits to innovation. Here, too, as expansion of these networks incurs superlinear advantages in innovation and learning, they also receive sublinear cost efficiencies allowing them to use fewer resources than linear scaling would predict.

Learning is critical for the health and wellbeing of the individual and survival of the community. In terms of the GEL framework, the advantages for learning processes brought about through allometric scaling seem to arise from disproportionate increases in capacity and decreases in operating costs supported by the physical interconnections among system elements. Even in cases where processing is highly capacity limited, such as cognitive scale processes of sequential information through working memory, people develop ways to take advantage of highly networked parallel systems available in the form of long-term working memory (Ericsson & Kintsch, 1995), and from cognitive offloading and extended and distributed cognitive processing (Clark & Chalmers, 1998; Hollan, Hutchins, & Kirsh, 2000; Salomon, Perkins, & Globerson, 1991). In this sense, grounded and embodied processes experience overall **scaling advantages** brought about by the physical networks operating across the range of biological, cognitive, and sociocultural processes that enable them to function more efficiently as they expand, while also exhibiting disproportionate increases in intellectual processing capacity.

11.2.4 Generation: Producing Processes Across Scales

Generation: Cognitive to Procedural Through Practice
One of the interesting qualities of verbal reasoning at cognitive and knowledge-based scales is that they can contribute to the formation of highly automated procedural knowledge.

With appropriate practice and well-structured error feedback, the rather slow, deliberative reasoning and sequential pattern matching commonly associated with knowing-that, or declarative knowledge, can produce rapid procedural knowledge and perceptual fluency that uses parallel processing. The generation of Type 1 processing from Type 2 processing is called *automaticity* (Anderson, 1992). This is evident in many circumstances. The initial stages of motor skill learning are refined through automaticity. This is why it is better initially to execute these skills slowly, with precision, than it is to start out performing them quickly, but with frequent errors. The rate of automaticity is also improved when the skills are performed relatively consistently each time.

Reading is, of course, a skill with enormous consequences for learning throughout one's lifespan. Reading fluency and automatic word recognition are critical for developing basic literacy, reading comprehension, and using reading in support of learning (Logan, 1997; National Institute of Child Health and Human Development [NICHD], 2000; Rasinski, 2006). Several aspects signal automaticity in reading, most notably, its speed, effortlessness, autonomy, and lack of conscious awareness (Logan, 1997). Rather than actually *transforming* the deliberative processes *into* automated processes, it is thought that both the original and automated processes coexist, with the faster processes used whenever possible but the slower processes activated under circumstances that prevent more rapid processes from being performed (Gazzaniga, 2009).

The co-existence of deliberate, verbal processes and automated perceptual and motor processes leads me to wonder about their places of interaction. Action-cognition transduction is exactly such a place. Here, conscious goals that are often in verbal form direct motor behavior as a means to fulfill those goals. These established lines of interaction also support, in reciprocal fashion, pathways for motor and perceptual behavior to shape cognitive processing. When new forms of movement are enacted this can produce novel ideas (Nathan, 2017). In our terminology, perceptuo-motor processes that form of the basis of knowing-with can lead to the generation of forms of knowing-that. For example, students who follow the directed actions elicited by playing *The Hidden Village* motion-capture video game can formulate conceptual understanding of general properties of shape and space that enhance their geometry reasoning and proof performance.

This interplay also is evident in the interplay of conceptual and procedural knowledge. Rittle-Johnson and colleagues (Rittle-Johnson, Siegler, & Alibali, 2001; Rittle-Johnson & Star, 2007) have shown that gains in children's procedural knowledge for decimal fractions predict their gains in conceptual knowledge. Reciprocally, students' initial conceptual knowledge predicts later procedural knowledge gains.

Generation: Sociocultural to Psychological Through Internalization
A central idea for understanding the embodied nature of learning at the sociocultural band is Vygotsky's *general genetic law of cultural development*. Although it is much closer to a hypothesis than an established law, Vygotsky (1997) theorized that individuals acquire their psychological capacities for directed, abstract thought by first overtly performing them in social settings and later internalizing these social interactions. The premise is that *internal* (or "psychological") cognitive processes derive from *external* interactions. For example, social conversation internalizes into reflective inquiry; shared social objects form the basis for imagining mental objects; and so on. This was posed as a theoretical alternative to other accounts of intellectual development, such as abstraction arising from a spontaneous developmental process.

Following the GEL framework, common social experiences serve to *ground* abstract concepts such as enumeration. Hamilton & Ghatala (1994, p. 156) provide the example of an adult reading to a child while pointing at each object and counting out loud "one, two, three." Later, the child points on her own and tries to count, but may not remember all the number words. The parent may fill them in at first. Over time the child will internalize the practice of pointing and saying each number in order as counting, first to the parent, and then even when alone.

The example described three steps of grounding. First, the child is participating by *being read to* by the parent. Then the child is participating *by reading to* the parent. Lastly, the child participates by *autonomously reading* to an internalized image of the parent, while re-enacting the same actions of enumeration. It is by internalizing *inter-personal* (or *interpsychic*) processes that children develop their *intrapersonal* ways of thinking. Vygotsky (1934/1963, p. 31) summarized it so:

> All higher mental functions make their appearance in the course of child development twice: first, in collective activity, social activity, i.e. as *inter*psychic functions, second in individual activity, as internal properties of the child's thinking, i.e. as *intra*psychic functions.

(Emphasis added)

As Vygotsky's collaborator Luria described the theory (as quoted in Brown, Heath, & Pea, 2003, p. 350), "It is through the interiorization of historically determined and culturally organized ways of operating on information that the social nature of people comes to be their psychological [i.e., individual] nature as well." Vygotsky noted the ways in which people use *psychological tools* to expand their cognitive abilities, much like notions of *extended cognition* from earlier. He reasoned this was similar to the way cultural tools extend people's physical abilities.

Vygotsky applied this same interpretation to the development of entire cultural systems of symbolic representations. He reasoned that important early interactions take place around the physical and social use of tools—useful objects such as sticks to mark the location of a food source for the community. Vygotsky called these "cultural tools." He also theorized the use of cultural tools forms the basis of *psychological tools*—internalized mental processes, such as spatial reasoning and mathematics, that extend the social forms of symbolizing to mental symbolic structures. Indeed, Vygotsky theorized that the emergence of these psycho-logical tools—the symbols of written language as principal among them—was critical to the emergence and progression of civilization. For example, the nature of human memory was transformed by the written word, and with that the spread and growth of collective know-ledge, such as the emergence of such institutions as libraries and universities.

Vygotsky also used this to frame important educational objectives. He argued that children must learn to use psychological tools such as written language, counting systems, mathemat-ical notation, and art in order to engage in higher-order forms of thought and behavior. This point is echoed by contemporary scholars such as Gee (1992/2014). Children develop these psychological skills through early social activities, such as play, parent-child interactions, and schooling. As Hamilton and Ghatala (1994, p. 156) describe it, "[Cultural] tools are used to change objects or to gain mastery over the environment; psychological tools are used to organize or to control thought and behavior."

The reciprocal relation is also observed, where psychological processes of individuals influence the sociocultural processes of groups. Earlier, I described ways that people have negotiated the meaning and use of taken-as-shared objects. As communities diversify, and as majority members start to see things from the perspective of others, community members may question the appropriateness or meaning of norms and representations that are part of old timers' knowing-with. Science, for example, is replete with metaphors that imply hier-archy. One of the most striking metaphors is the use of "master/slave" terminology to denote electronic systems where one device controls others (Reuters, 2003). Its use dates back to the early 1900s, but its evocation of inhuman treatment has raised issues among many scholars and educators. As Eglash (2007, p. 2) reflects:

> Much of my work as a social scientist has been in the area of minority-student math and science education, working on pedagogies that help underrepresented students aspire to technical careers. Did that figure of speech add to the alienation these students often report? Just how was it that a morally criminal social practice became the metaphor of choice for a ubiquitous phenomenon in engineering?

Many businesses and government agencies now recognize this choice of terminology simply has no place in modern science and engineering. Many in industry now advocate replacing it with "primary/replica," or "primary/secondary" to describe these systems. The influence individuals can have on groups, even for well-entrenched practices, is a significant source of social change.

11.3 INTERPLAY OF UNCONSCIOUS AND CONSCIOUS LEARNING PROCESSES

A vital aspect for understanding learning is to recognize that attention and working memory are highly capacity limited. One consequence of this is that people are not able to monitor all of the things that affect their reasoning and decision making, such as pattern recognition. Much of how people think, decide, act, and learn is simply invisible to them. Rapid processes that operate at the biological scales are not encoded in forms that enter into one's awareness. These sub-cognitive processes leave no cognitive trail for people to monitor, reconstruct, or reflect upon. Some scholars (e.g., Kahneman, 2011; Lakoff & Nunez, 2000; Stanovich & West, 2000) have posited that *most* of one's intellectual processes are unconscious. This squares with the timescale framework, which depicts the conscious spectrum as occupying only a small slice of the span of all learning and thinking processes.

11.3.1 Integrating Unconscious and Conscious Processes for Greater Learning

The interplay of unconscious and conscious processes is important for illuminating the nature of GEL. Students engaged in the action geometry activities of making triangles with their bodies showed significant learning advantages over those who performed all the same movements but never experienced forming various triangles (Nathan, Walkington, Boncoddo, Pier, Williams, & Alibali, 2014). Notably, the majority of participants reported no awareness of the relevance of the movements to their mathematical reasoning. When students were subsequently informed that the movements *were* mathematically relevant, their performance as a group further improved. This illustrates how unconscious forms of knowing-with one's body can influence one's conscious knowing-that about mathematical properties and principles. It also reveals the additional benefits that can be incurred when those unconscious processes are explicitly brought into awareness.

Aleven and Koedinger (2002) provided one of the most thorough investigations of the empirical effects of bringing unconscious processes into conscious awareness to promote learning. This investigation drew on a well-developed program for high school geometry education. The program combined classroom instruction with targeted practice that included immediate feedback provided by a sophisticated computer-based cognitive tutoring system. The intervention was successful at promoting students' knowing-how for geometry through a "learning-by-doing" approach.

Their observations showed that some major topics were largely *unconscious* to learners. Students developed rapid heuristics, such as "if angles look the same in the diagram, they are the same." These proved highly effective for solving some of the visually based assessment problems. However, students succeeded without developing a deeper understanding of mathematical reasoning and argumentation, such as how to establish without any doubt whether two angular measures were equal. Aleven and Koedinger referred to this as *shallow learning*.

Aleven and Koedinger investigated the effects of combining their original learning-by-doing program, designed to foster unconscious learning, with prompts for students to verbally explain their reasons for their actions, an approach called *self-explanation* (Chi, Bassok, Lewis, Reimann, & Glaser, 1989; Chi, de Leeuw, Chiu, & Lavancher, 1994; VanLehn, Jones, & Chi, 1992). In contrast to learning-by-doing, self-explanations raise students' *conscious awareness* of what they are learning and why. This inquiry is an ideal way to investigate the potential benefits of combining unconscious and conscious processes in a common learning experience.

What Aleven and Koedinger (2002) found was remarkable. Students who only had support for learning patterns and procedures with learning-by-doing did learn a great deal. Many instructors and technology designers might have called it a clear success. But these researchers went deeper into what was actually learned. Those students with support only for patterns and procedural learning demonstrated more shallow learning, as exhibited by their errors and overgeneralization of visual cues to guide their responses. Students' over-reliance on visual cues cut short their need to do much reasoning. This led to frequent mistakes for problems designed as harder-to-guess problems (based on visual cues), even though students did well on easier-to-guess problems.

The big pay-off came for those students who were prompted to combine pattern recognition and procedural learning with self-explanation; that is, to develop both the unconscious, visual patterning skills that come from learning-by-doing, with the more conceptual, verbally encoded knowledge that comes from generating explanations of their visual pattern identification. This powerful combination, the authors argued, supported "more integrated visual and verbal declarative knowledge" (Aleven & Koedinger, 2002, p. 169). The combined understanding propelled those with support for both unconscious procedural learning and conscious explanation-based learning to show superior performance in the harder-to-guess items. They also transferred this heightened level of performance to paper and pencil assessments. The effects even went further, because those with training in explanations were also able to appropriately respond to a class of "not-enough-info" items that were mathematically under-constrained and so could not be solved for a single, correct, numerical answer.

There is tremendous educational value in understanding how to bring unconscious processes into consciousness, and thereby incur some of their combined advantages of rapid pattern recognition with sensemaking and deliberative reasoning. I believe that education can benefit from a deeper understanding the relative strengths and limitations of conscious and unconscious learning processes and of the considerations for instruction, design, and assessment that make explicit use of these trade-offs.

11.3.2 Integrating Unconscious and Conscious Processes for Enhanced Instruction

Instruction is another behavior consequential for learning that is mediated by both conscious and unconscious processes. Instruction is made up of a constellation of behaviors that includes planning, delivery (what people often emphasize as "instruction"), classroom management, and assessment. Operating in each of these behaviors are the teacher's procedural and declarative knowledge about how to teach and what to teach. Teachers have firm views about how to organize the learning experiences of their students, based to a large degree on content area-specific expectations—in the form of curriculum standards—and their own beliefs about cognitive development.

One of these sets of beliefs can be seen by the commitment teachers make for how to introduce students to a new content area. This is a developmental consideration because it is based on teachers' views of the ideal sequence that a student will follow in order to construct over time the appropriate knowledge and skills for grasping a set of concepts and procedures.

It turns out that one's expertise in a content area has a lot of influence on these beliefs about student learning that are not all beneficial for learners. This is because experts in a topic who become teachers operate with unconscious processes that are the result of their knowing-how and knowing-with, which are generally not shared by their students. Experts, as we have discussed, see the world differently than non-experts. As we have seen with other areas of procedural knowledge and perceptual learning, experts-turned-teachers lack access to some of their most highly trained knowledge. Over time and with practice, these skills become unavailable to monitoring and reflection.

One unfortunate consequence of this is that teachers with highly developed domain knowledge often have poor intuitions about how their students learn (Nathan & Koedinger, 2000a, 2000b). This phenomenon is aptly termed *expert blind spot* because it underscores ways that unconscious knowledge of teachers interferes with their professional goals (Hellman & Nuckles, 2013; Huang, 2018; Verity, 2011; Nathan, Koedinger, & Alibali, 2001; Nathan & Petrosino, 2003; Tofel-Grehl, & Feldon, 2013). Across a range of content areas—including reading, second-language learning, mathematics, science, engineering, surgery, law, and more—domain-expert teachers generally believe that students are most likely to succeed in learning a new domain if they must first learn it in the abstract. This directive leads domain-expert teachers to privilege the formal and theoretical properties of their content areas. Verity (2011, p. 154) even found that emerging TESOL instructors suffer "from 'expert blind spot' syndrome (being unable to see a body of knowledge from a novice's perspective) even before they are expert enough to have a blind spot." They appeared to be firmly committed to formal rules of grammar at the expense of practical knowledge and self-expression.

At the beginning of this book, I introduced the *Formalisms First* view of cognitive development as one of the pervasive shortcomings of the current education system (Nathan, 2012; Nathan & Koedinger, 2000b; Nathan & Petrosino, 2003; Petrosino & Gordon, 2011; Walkington, Sherman, & Petrosino, 2012). To recap, within the Formalism First approach to instruction, students must first master the formal ideas of the discipline. Only after demonstrating this knowledge, are students permitted to apply that knowledge productively to activities that resemble real world events and problems. For example, in learning high school language arts, domain-expert teachers held that the formal rules of grammar were necessary prerequisites to adolescents writing about their personal experiences (Grossman, 1990). Similarly, literature domain-expert teachers expected students to demonstrate mastery of formal literary techniques, such as mimesis and intertextuality, in order for them to understand and enjoy literature. Formalisms First learning is a "folk theory" of intellectual developmental that is widely held by domain-expert teachers in areas such as language arts, the social sciences (e.g., economics, psychology), and STEM fields (science, technology, engineering, and mathematics; Nathan, Tran, Atwood, Prevost, & Phelps, 2010; NRC, 2005; NAE/NRC, 2014).

As with learners, teachers can also be unaware of their highly automated forms of pattern recognition. It would seem equally likely that integrating teachers' unconscious processes used during instruction with conscious forms of pedagogical reasoning can yield significant benefits. Several approaches have been investigated to overcome teachers' propensities for expert blind spot (Foley & Donnellan, 2019; Goertz, 2013; Rau, Sen, & Zhu, 2019).

In one study (Nathan, 2003), instructors explicitly exposed to the perils that Formalisms First holds for their students learned to suppress those tendencies. In a professional development intervention with algebra teachers, I observed math teachers from urban schools who served a predominantly (80%) minority population in schools where the majority of students (75%) qualify for free/reduced-price lunch. During a professional learning experience, I gave them a task that elicited their expert blind spots, by asking them to predict which of several types of math problems students would find easiest and most difficult (see Nathan & Petrosino, 2003). After making their individual predictions they had to discuss and defend their predictions to other teachers. This was followed by a facilitated, whole-group discussion of the various rationales teachers expressed. These discussions brought teachers' folk theories into their conscious awareness. Changing implicit views is much more difficult than changing explicit views. I then showed them, quantitatively, how their views led to poor prediction of students' problem-solving performance (based on actual student data). This disequilibrium prompted a rich discussion of the source of these beliefs that were, for many, previously uninspected. It motivated teachers to want to transcend these views in order to be more in tune with their students' learning needs.

Teachers then participated in a guided activity where they engaged in conscious reasoning by deliberately applying a general rubric for evaluating students' reasoning as exhibited by their written work. The student examples were chosen with the goal of enhancing the development of teachers' "algebraic eyes and ears" (Kaput & Blanton, 2000). It focused teachers on students' actual problem-solving processes and the ways they could use that to infer students' algebraic reasoning.

Three weeks later, these teachers were sent a set of follow-up tasks designed to elicit their views of students' mathematical development along with teachers' personal written accounts of how they were thinking about their current students. These records showed how teachers' views of their students' developmental progressions from arithmetic to algebra changed. For example, teachers exhibited greater awareness of students' difficulties with formal notation. They remarked that students initially regard strategies with symbols as rather meaningless, and subject to the shallow learning of the kind observed by Aleven and Koedinger (2002). Teachers also were much more aware of the efficacy of students' invented solution methods. They also were more attuned to ways students' reasoning with verbally presented problems could serve as scaffolds for supporting the development of their reasoning with formal, symbolic representations.

As with student learning, the integration of conscious and unconscious ways of thinking can enhance educational practices. The strengths of each can be complementary, but care must be taken to raise the awareness of the unconscious. Two methods—self-explanation, and group discourse—each properly facilitated, reveal methods for supporting this integrated form of thinking and learning.

11.4 METHODOLOGICAL CONSIDERATIONS: ELEMENTAL AND SYSTEMIC PERSPECTIVES

In taking this wide view, it is important to also reflect on the ways methodological choices in research influence how scholars theorize about learning. I tend to shy away from the qualitative-quantitative dichotomy that has been prominent in education and the social sciences (e.g., Feuer et al., 2002; Eisenhart & Towne, 2003). I find it most productive to distinguish between elemental and systemic methods (Nathan & Sawyer, 2014; Salomon, 1991).

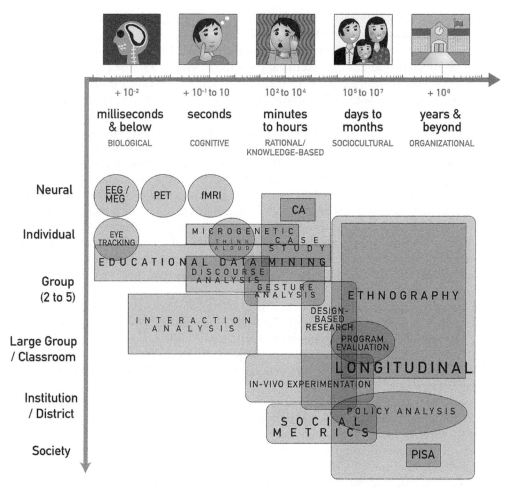

FIGURE 11.4 A sampling of elemental (ovals), systemic (rectangles) and hybrid (rounded rectangles) research methods for studying learning placed within the GEL timescale.

11.4.1 The Factoring Assumption

Recall that the distinction I made between elemental and systemic methods rests on the factoring assumption. The *factoring assumption* states that various components of the learning system, such as one's knowledge or environmental and cultural context, can be "factored out" and analyzed independently from its interactions with other processes (Barab & Kirshner, 2001; Greeno & Engeström, 2014). Elemental research methods adhere to the factoring assumption, while systemic methods do not. A sample of these research methods are shown in Figure 11.4, with their primary placements shown across the GEL timescale.

11.4.2 Elemental Research Methods

Elemental methods generate models of learning in their reductionist simplicity and potential for generality by focusing on universals that influence behavior. Common elemental methods are eye tracking, experimental design, and concurrent think aloud reports. Some forms of experimental design strive for causal claims about controlled interventions leading to predicted outcomes. Elemental methods generally conform to an acquisition metaphor of learning (Sfard, 1998). Analysis is a proposed way to reduce the complexities of learning by people and groups. Each line of interaction of the activity system of Figure 9.3 presents a challenge for controlling the variability of these influential factors in order to offer a clear, causal account of learning.

11.4.3 Systemic Research Methods

A *systemic perspective* on research rejects the factoring assumption. It accentuates the richness of the interrelationships among system components, from which learning processes emerge. Systemic approaches to learning research examine the ample interactions among behaviors and contexts in a holistic manner. Common systemic methods are case studies, ethnographies, teaching experiments, and network analyses. These generally conform to participation metaphors and knowledge-creation views of learning (Sfard, 1998).

Synthesis is a preferred way to describe the complexities of people and groups learning to participate in authentic practices. The research methods employed tend toward "thick descriptions" of learning (Geertz, 1973; Ryle, 1949), which also provide evidence that can support causal inference. Indeed, while some elemental methods try to control for the tangle of interactions, the rich and varied interactions are the *point* of systemic accounts, which expressly seek to understand the ways these many components interact to manifest the complex, emergent behaviors of interest. While systemic methods have traditionally aligned with qualitative methods drawn from ethnographic traditions, the growth of learning analytics methods and tools have made quantitative methods for obtaining thick descriptions more practical and useful (e.g., Shaffer, 2017).

Systemic research can be pragmatic in that these are the actual learning experiences of students and teachers, which are taking place in suitable places to study thinking, teaching, and learning. It is also theoretical in that the particular instance under investigation should serve as an exemplar from which methodological and theoretical generalizations can be derived, and new investigative questions generated (Cobb, Confrey, DiSessa, Lehrer, & Schauble, 2003).

Janet Bowers and Paul Cobb (Bowers, 1996; Cobb & Bowers, 1999; Bowers, Cobb, & McClain, 1999) showed how one teaching experiment enabled the establishment of classroom *microculture* for early mathematics education. Third-grade students pretending to be workers in a candy factory developed norms for talking about packaging candies in rolls of ten, and packaging rolls in boxes of ten. Over nine weeks, these sociocultural practices grounded for them the ideas of place value in the decimal (base 10) system for addition and subtraction. The students developed the practices as well as ways of symbolically recording and discussing the practices and products of their work.

11.4.4 Scale-Down: Integrating Elemental and Systemic Methods

Several scholars have argued that investigations of learning rely on an integrated approach of both elemental and systemic methods (Nathan & Alibali, 2010; Nathan & Sawyer, 2014; Salomon, 1991; Sfard, 1998). Such an approach draws on their complementary perspectives for analysis and synthesis of empirical observations. The proposal makes sense in principle, but in practice there is a need to specify how these methods are to be coordinated. For research to achieve far-reaching impact, there is also a need for effective interventions to be taken to scale. Because of this responsibility, I provide a methodological guide for scaling interventions that seems to be responsive to the multiple levels of processes at play in a complex educational intervention.

Scale-down methodology (Nathan & Alibali, 2010; Nathan & Sawyer, 2014) introduced in Chapter 2 provides one integrated approach. Scale-down methodology proceeds by identifying authentic contexts in which learning takes place. Systemic methods such as a teaching experiment or ethnography provide thick descriptions of contextualized learning. This ecological validity can be very important to document since it is these settings that the scale-down method ultimately seeks to change. Systemic methods are the source for stating testable hypotheses of the influences on learning and for predicting ways to implement learning improvements.

The next step is to exercise the factoring assumption to identify potential malleable factors that can be modified to foster learning for the intended student population. Here, the system begins to be examined as composed of subsystems (Simon, 1996/2019). Fully decomposable systems are composed of modules that function relatively independently, such that the overall system behavior is the superposition of the behavior of its constituents. Such simple systems are rare in real life. In social settings, complex systems that display emergent behaviors due to a high degree of inter-component interactions are far more common (Jacobson et al., 2019).

To gain purchase on complex systems of this sort, it is helpful to theorize that these are composed of a collection of *nearly decomposable systems*. These are constituents of a system where "the short-run behavior of each of the component subsystems is *approximately independent* of the short-run behavior of the other components" (Simon, 1996/2019, p. 474). Interactions are relatively strong within each subsystem, but relatively weak—though certainly non-negligible—between the subsystem and the rest of the system.

Nearly decomposable systems are subject to a process of functional decomposition. Historical discovery illustrates this. As Bradshaw (1992) described it, the key to the Wright brothers' success in human-powered flight over efforts that were far better funded (see Nathan & Swart, 2020) was how they approached the engineering design challenge through the lens of near decomposability. *Functional decomposition* "requires a complex invention (such as an airplane) to be divided into functional parts (wings that produce lift, propellers that produce thrust) that are refined in isolation from the whole." (p. 263). The Wright brothers made one other important methodological advancement—the use of the *wind tunnel*. They built miniature versions of wing subsystems, and tested a range of wing designs and behaviors in a custom-built wind tunnel where risk was low and information gathering was high. This allowed them to iterate on design modifications relatively quickly and cheaply, compared to competitors (such as the US Government), who often lost entire aircraft in crashes due to poor designs.

Scale-down calls for educational innovators to consider identifying investigative contexts that serve an analogous role to that of the Wrights' wind tunnel. Some scholars have done this by effectively using methods such as in vivo experimentation (Koedinger, Aleven, Roll, & Baker, 2009). In this approach, investigators use random assignment of instructional treatments (for high internal validity) as they occur in live classrooms (for high external validity). Teaching experiments (Cobb et al., 2003) offer another form of wind tunnel for exploring educational innovations within the rich contexts of the classroom. Still others (Alibali & Nathan, 2010) have brought together teachers and students in artificial classroom settings to provide the regularity of the intervention and control of factors such as distractions, while preserving the social interactions among students and between students and their teacher.

Elemental methods such as in vivo experimentation coupled with analysis of variance can be strategically employed to identify individual factors that are causally related to the intended outcomes. In making this turn toward analysis, it is vital that the learning interventions are constructed to be commensurate with the original authentic learning environment. At the same time, these analytic methods must enable the collection of high-quality data to inform modeling and future design decisions. With factors identified, the approach then relaxes the factoring assumption in order to reconstitute the authentic learning experience once again, with new appreciation of some of the ways it operates both analytically and synthetically.

Scale-down methodology has many commonalities with *design-based research* and *design experiments*, especially as articulated by Brown (1992). In the design experiment approach, Brown describes a powerful and inventive method for the iterative transformation of complex, situated learning interventions. As with scale-down, Brown (1992) also starts with an investigation of ecologically valid learning and offers ways to iteratively adjust the nature of the intervention as information comes in. The main difference between design experiments and scale-down is the explicit attention scale-down makes to the factoring assumption. Brown's design experiment approach remains at the systemic level, in my terminology. By choosing when to exercise the factoring assumption and enlist elemental methods, scale-down provides a sanctioned way for integrating elemental and systemic methods at appropriate places along the developmental trajectory of the methodology. A design benefit of this approach is the production of useful formative information to guide mid-course corrections (Dede, 2004). A theoretical benefit of the strategic use of elemental methods during functional decomposition is the potential for identifying causal influences that may generalize across implementations.

The scale-down method uses both science and engineering approaches to gain a basic understanding of learning, while seeking to improve the educational experiences for all students (Nathan & Alibali, 2010). Scale-down offers a systematic way to bring together the complimentary qualities of systemic and elemental research methods, while gaining purchase on complex learning phenomena.

11.5 SUMMARY

In this chapter, I explore interconnections of learning processes and principles across the range of timescales. A synthesis of the GEL principles I developed for specific scales of time identifies several trans-scale GEL themes for grounding, learning, design of learning environments, instructional practices, and formative (diagnostic) and summative (evaluative) assessments. The overarching themes reveal several though-lines that reach across scales. The synthesis across GEL processes and principles also reveals some of the interrelationships and interactions of processes across scales, including superposition, supervenience, scaling, and generation.

In this chapter, I also discuss the interplay of unconscious and conscious learning processes. While formal education often neglects explicit focus on unconscious learning processes, I have already demonstrated how they are vital for meaningful learning and intellectual performance. Here I have illustrated some of the advantages when educational experiences are designed to explicitly connect unconscious and conscious processes that operate in student learning. Instructional practices also operate with both unconscious and conscious processes. I illustrated this with expert blind spot, which are views teachers exhibit of student learning that function outside of teachers' awareness. These can be brought into awareness through thoughtful professional learning experiences. Here, too, the integration of unconscious and conscious processes can lead to more effective instructional practices.

As a way to honor the multi-scale structure of learning processes, there are several methodological considerations to account for when looking to take effective educational interventions to scale. Elemental research methods, such as experimental design, rely on the factoring assumption. This assumption treats various aspects of the social system, such cultural context, as separable factors that can be analyzed independently from their interactions with other processes. Systemic research methods, such as ethnographies, reject the factoring assumption in order that the interactions are preserved to inform a holistic account of behavior. Rather than fueling tensions between them, both elemental and systemic methods work together to support the translational objectives of scale-down methodology that can help bring evidence-based education practices to scale in authentic learning settings.

11.6 READER ACTIVITIES

11.6.1 Identify a "Wind Tunnel" for Education Research

1. This is an exercise in scale-down method.
2. Select a learning or teaching phenomenon in an authentic setting that is considered to be effective. I think of examples like the learning and teaching that happens in a recreational club or online gaming setting.
3. Generate one or more hypotheses about how learning is supported. You are trying to identify a factor or set of factors that appear to be responsible for the learning that leads to achieving acceptable performance, which, if removed, would thwart learning.
4. Recruit some of the people who would likely be learners in the authentic setting for this exercise. If you cannot find anyone who is not already participating, you can also do this as a thought experiment.
5. Now perform functional decomposition by isolating some part of the interaction that centers on the factors hypothesized for learning.
6. Next, create a microcosm (a "wind tunnel") that recreates some portions of the setting while enabling greater access and intervention to influence participants' behaviors. It is important to identify performance measures and other indicators you can use to evaluate your progress toward the intended level of performance.
7. Consider the changes you can now make to the wind-tunnel version of this alternate learning setting. Use this as an opportunity to iterate more freely that might otherwise be possible in the authentic setting. Be sure choices are informed by the performance measures.
8. Ideally, a new set of practices will be generated that achieves the performance objects, and does so more rapidly, more easily, or with a higher level of performance.
9. If such an advancement in learning design was achieved, consider how these new practices can be integrated back into the original setting.
10. Confer with the original instructor about ways these design improvements can be implemented.

11.6.2 Trans-scale Learning

For this activity, you are invited to pick an authentic learning or instruction behavior. Ideally, video record this behavior so you can review it carefully. Identify these elements:

• Identify what specifically is being learned or taught in the video recording.
• Categorize the observed behavior as one, or a combination, of these educational experiences. It is really interesting if you find any to be something outside of these!
  • Grounding
  • Learning

- Design of learning environments
- Instructional practices
- Formative (diagnostic) assessment
- Summative (evaluative) assessment
- What GEL principles do you see being employed? To answer this I recommend doing multiple passes through the video record to determine this for each of these:
  - Conscious spectrum (cognitive and knowledge-based processes)
  - Biological processes
  - Sociocultural processes
- See if you can ascertain which of these trans-scale processes describe how the scale-specific processes are interrelated. Perhaps you will find a trans-scale process that is not in this list.
  - Superposition
  - Supervenience
  - Scaling
  - Generation
- Can you identify contributions of unconscious and conscious processes? If so,
  - To what extent are unconscious and conscious processes operating independently, and in an integrated fashion?
  - What ways do you propose integration of unconscious and conscious processes could be further supported to enhance learning or instruction?

REFERENCES

Aleven, V. A., & Koedinger, K. R. (2002). An effective metacognitive strategy: Learning by doing and explaining with a computer-based cognitive tutor. *Cognitive Science, 26*(2), 147–179.

Alibali, M. W., Nathan, M. J., Wolfgram, M. S., Church, R. B., Jacobs, S. A., Johnson Martinez, C., & Knuth, E. J. (2014). How teachers link ideas in mathematics instruction using speech and gesture: A corpus analysis. *Cognition and Instruction, 32*(1), 65–100.

Anderson, J. R. (1992). Automaticity and the ACT theory. *The American Journal of Psychology, 105*(2), 165–180.

Anderson, J. R., Bothell, D., Byrne, M. D., Douglass, S., Lebiere, C., & Qin, Y. (2004). An integrated theory of the mind. *Psychological Review, 111*(4), 1036–1060.

Barab, S. A., & Kirshner, D. (2001). Guest editors' introduction: Rethinking methodology in the learning sciences. *The Journal of the Learning Sciences, 10*(1–2), 5–15.

Barron, B. (2003). When smart groups fail. *The Journal of the Learning Sciences, 12*(3), 307–359.

Bender, A. (2020). The role of culture and evolution for human cognition. *Topics in Cognitive Science, 12*(4), 1403–1420.

Bickle, J. (2019). Laser lights and designer drugs: New techniques for descending levels of mechanisms "in a single bound"? *Topics in Cognitive Science, 12*(4), 1241–1256.

Bogin, B. (1997). Evolutionary hypotheses for human childhood. *Yearbook of Physical Anthropology, 40*, 63–89.

Bowers, J. S. (1996). *Conducting developmental research in a technology-enhanced classroom* (Doctoral dissertation, Vanderbilt University, 1996). Dissertation Abstracts International, 57, 3433A.

Bowers, J., Cobb, P., & McClain, K. (1999). The evolution of mathematical practices: A case study. *Cognition and Instruction, 17*(1), 25–66.

Bradshaw, G. (1992). The airplane and the logic of invention. In R. Giere & H. Feigl (eds.), *Cognitive models of science* (pp. 239–250). University of Minnesota Press.

Bransford, J. D., Brown, A. L., & Cocking, R. R. (2000). *How people learn: Brain, mind, experience, and school: Expanded edition*. National Academy Press.

Brown, A. L. (1992). Design experiments: Theoretical and methodological challenges in creating complex interventions in classroom settings. *The Journal of the Learning Sciences, 2*(2), 141–178.

Brown, J. S., Heath, C., & Pea, R. (2003). *Vygotsky's educational theory in cultural context*. Cambridge University Press.

Chi, M. T. H., Bassok, M., Lewis, M. W., Reimann, P., & Glaser, R. (1989). Self-explanations: How students study and use examples in learning to solve problems. *Cognitive Science, 13*, 145–182.

Chi, M. T. H., de Leeuw, N., Chiu, M., & Lavancher, C. (1994). Eliciting self-explanations improves understanding. *Cognitive Science, 18*, 439–477.

Clark, A., & Chalmers, D. (1998). The extended mind. *Analysis, 58*(1), 7–19.

Cobb, P., & Bowers, J. (1999). Cognitive and situated learning perspectives in theory and practice. *Educational Researcher, 28*(2), 4–15.

Cobb, P., Confrey, J., DiSessa, A., Lehrer, R., & Schauble, L. (2003). Design experiments in educational research. *Educational Researcher, 32*(1), 9–13.

Colombo, M., & Knauff, M. (2020). Editors' review and introduction: Levels of explanation in cognitive science: from molecules to culture. *Topics in Cognitive Science, 12*(4), 1224–1240.

Davidson, D. (1970). Mental events. In L. Foster and J. W. Swanson (Eds.), *Experience and theory* (pp. 79–101). University of Massachusetts Press.

Dede, C. (2004). If design-based research is the answer, what is the question? A commentary on Collins, Joseph, and Bielaczyc; diSessa and Cobb; and Fishman, Marx, Blumenthal, Krajcik, and Soloway in the JLS special issue on design-based research. *The Journal of the Learning Sciences, 13*(1), 105–114.

Eglash, R. (2007). Broken metaphor: The master-slave analogy in technical literature. *Technology and Culture, 48*(2), 360–369.

Eisenhart, M., & Towne, L. (2003). Contestation and change in national policy on "scientifically based" education research. *Educational Researcher, 32*(7), 31–38.

Ericsson, K. A., & Kintsch, W. (1995). Long-term working memory. *Psychological Review, 102*(2), 211.

Ericsson, K. A., & Simon, H. A. (1993). *Protocol analysis: Verbal reports as data* (rev. ed.). MIT Press.

Feuer, M. J., Towne, L., & Shavelson, R. J. (2002). Scientific culture and educational research. *Educational Researcher, 31*(8), 4–14.

Foley, C. E., & Donnellan, N. M. (2019). Overcoming expert blind spot when teaching the novice surgeon. *Journal of Minimally Invasive Gynecology, 26*(7, Supplement), S20. doi: https://doi.org/10.1016/j.jmig.2019.09.509

Gazzaniga, M. S. (2009). *The cognitive neurosciences*. MIT Press.

Gee, J. P. (1992/2014). *The social mind: Language, ideology, and social practice*. JF Bergin & Garvey.

Geertz, C. (1973). *The interpretation of cultures*. Basic Books.

Goertz, P. W. (2013). *Seeing past the expert blind spot: developing a training module for in-service teachers* (Master's thesis). The University of Texas at Austin. https://repositories.lib.utexas.edu/bitstream/handle/2152/23989/GOERTZ-MASTERSREPORT-2013.pdf?sequence=1

Graesser, A. C., & McNamara, D. S. (2011). Computational analyses of multilevel discourse comprehension. *Topics in Cognitive Science, 3*, 371–398.

Greeno, J. G., & Engeström, Y. (2014). Learning in activity. In R. K. Sawyer (Ed.), *The Cambridge handbook of the learning sciences* (2nd ed., pp. 128–147). Cambridge University Press.

Grossman, P. (1990). *The making of a teacher*. Teacher's College Press.

Hamilton, R., & Ghatala, E. S. (1994). *Learning and instruction*. McGraw-Hill.

Hellman, K., & Nuckles, M. (2013). Expert blind spot in pre-service and in-service mathematics teachers: Task design moderates overestimation of novices' performance. *Proceedings of the Annual Meeting of the Cognitive Science Society* (Vol. 35). Cognitive Science Society.

Henriques, G. (2003). The tree of knowledge system and the theoretical unification of psychology. *Review of General Psychology, 7*(2), 150–182.

Hollan, J., Hutchins, E., & Kirsh, D. (2000). Distributed cognition: toward a new foundation for human-computer interaction research. *ACM Transactions on Computer-Human Interaction (TOCHI), 7*(2), 174–196.

Huang, E. (2018). Rearview mirrors for the "expert blind spot": Using design to access surgeons' tacit knowledge and create shared referents for teaching. In A. Bakker (Ed.), *Design research in education: A practical guide for early career researchers* (pp. 193–206). Routledge.

Huxley, J. S. (1950). Relative growth and form transformation. *Proceedings of the Royal Society of London. Series B-Biological Sciences, 137*(889), 465–469.

Jacobson, M. J., Levin, J. A., & Kapur, M. (2019). Education as a complex system: Conceptual and methodological implications. *Educational Researcher, 48*(2), 112–119.

Kahneman, D. (2011). *Thinking, fast and slow*. Macmillan.

Kaput, J. J., & Blanton, M. L. (2000). *Algebraic reasoning in the context of elementary mathematics: Making it implementable on a massive scale*. University of Massachusetts–Dartmouth.

Koedinger, K. R., Aleven, V., Roll, I., & Baker, R. (2009). In vivo experiments on whether supporting metacognition in intelligent tutoring systems yields robust learning. In D. J. Hacker, J. Dunlosky, A. C. Graesser (Eds.) *Handbook of metacognition in education* (pp. 897–964). Routledge.

Lakoff, G., & Núñez, R. (2000). *Where mathematics come from: How the embodied mind brings mathematics into being*. Basic Books.

Lemke, J. L. (2001). The long and the short of it: Comments on multiple time-scale studies of human activity. *The Journal of the Learning Sciences, 10*, 17–26.

Logan, G. D. (1997). Automaticity and reading: Perspectives from the instance theory of automatization. *Reading & Writing Quarterly, 13*(2), 123–146. doi:10.1080/1057356970130203

Marr, D. (1982). *Vision: A computational investigation into the human representation and processing of visual information.* Freeman.

McClelland, J. L., Rumelhart, D. E., & PDP Research Group. (1986). *Parallel distributed processing. Explorations in the microstructure of cognition (vol. II). Psychological and biological models.* MIT Press.

National Academy of Engineering and National Research Council (NAE/NRC). (2014). *STEM integration in k-12 education: Status, prospects, and an agenda for research.* National Academies Press. https://doi.org/10.17226/18612.

Nathan, M. J. (2003). Confronting teachers' beliefs about algebra development: Investigating an approach for professional development. Institute of Cognitive Science Technical Report no. 03-04. University of Colorado.

Nathan, M. J. (2012). Rethinking formalisms in formal education. *Educational Psychologist, 47*(2), 125–148.

Nathan, M. J. (2017). One function of gesture is to make new ideas: Evidence for reciprocity between action and cognition. In R. B. Church, M. W. Alibali, & S. D. Kelly, (Eds.) *Why gesture? How the hands function in speaking, thinking and communicating* (pp. 175–196). John Benjamins. doi.org/10.1075/gs.7.09nat

Nathan, M. J., & Alibali, M. W. (2010). Learning sciences. *Wiley Interdisciplinary Reviews: Cognitive Science, 1*(3), 329–345.

Nathan, M. J. & Kim, S. (2009). Regulation of teacher elicitations in the mathematics classroom. *Cognition and Instruction, 27*(2), 91–120.

Nathan, M. J., & Koedinger, K. R. (2000a). Teachers' and researchers' beliefs about the development of algebraic reasoning. *Journal for Research in Mathematics Education, 31*(2), 168–190.

Nathan, M. J., & Koedinger, K. R. (2000b). An investigation of teachers' beliefs of students' algebra development. *Cognition and Instruction, 18*(2), 209–237.

Nathan, M. J., Koedinger, K. R., & Alibali, M. W. (2001, April). Expert blind spot: When content knowledge eclipses pedagogical content knowledge. *Proceedings of the Third International Conference on Cognitive Science* (Vol. 644648). Cognitive Science Society.

Nathan, M. J., & Petrosino, A. (2003). Expert blind spot among preservice teachers. *American Educational Research Journal, 40*(4), 905–928.

Nathan, M. J., & Sawyer, K. (2014). Foundations of learning sciences. In K. Sawyer (Ed.), *The Cambridge Handbook of the Learning Sciences* (2nd Edition) (pp. 21–43). Cambridge University Press.

Nathan, M. J., & Sawyer, K. (in press). Foundations of learning sciences. In K. Sawyer (Ed.), *The Cambridge handbook of the learning sciences* (3rd Edition). Cambridge University Press.

Nathan, M. J., Schenck, K. E., Vinsonhaler, R., Michaelis, J. E., Swart, M. I., & Walkington, C. (2020). Embodied geometric reasoning: Dynamic gestures during intuition, insight, and proof. *Journal of Educational Psychology.* doi.org/10.1037/edu0000638

Nathan, M. J., & Swart, M. I. (2020). Materialist epistemology lends design wings: educational design as an embodied process. *Educational Technology Research and Development*, 1–30. doi.org/10.1007/s11423-020-09856-4

Nathan, M. J., Tran, N. A., Atwood, A. K., Prevost, A., & Phelps, L. A. (2010). Beliefs and expectations about engineering preparation exhibited by high school STEM teachers. *Journal of Engineering Education, 99*(4), 409–426.

Nathan, M. J., Walkington, C., Boncoddo, R., Pier, E., Williams, C. C., & Alibali, M. W. (2014). Actions speak louder with words: The roles of action and pedagogical language for grounding mathematical proof. *Learning and Instruction, 33*, 182–193.

Nathan, M. J., Yeo, A., Boncoddo, R., Hostetter, A. B., & Alibali, M. W. (2019). Teachers' attitudes about gesture for learning and instruction. *Gesture, 18*(1), 31–56.

National Institute of Child Health and Human Development. (2000). Report of the National Reading Panel. Teaching children to read: An evidence-based assessment of the scientific research literature on reading and its implications for reading instruction (NIH Publication No. 00-4769). U.S. Government Printing Office

Navajas, J., Heduan, F. Á., Garrido, J. M., Gonzalez, P. A., Garbulsky, G., Ariely, D., & Sigman, M. (2019). Reaching consensus in polarized moral debates. *Current Biology, 29*(23), 4124–4129.

Navajas, J., Niella, T., Garbulsky, G., Bahrami, B., & Sigman, M. (2018). Aggregated knowledge from a small number of debates outperforms the wisdom of large crowds. *Nature Human Behaviour, 2*(2), 126–132.

Newell, A. (1994). *Unified theories of cognition.* Harvard University Press.

National Research Council (NRC). (2005). *How students learn: History, mathematics, and science in the classroom.* The National Academies Press. https://doi.org/10.17226/10126.

Petrosino, A. J., & Gordon, J. (2011). Algebra expert blind spot: A comparison of in-service and pre-service teachers. In *Presentation at the annual meeting of the American Educational Research Association,* New Orleans, LA.

Rasinski, T. V. (2006). A brief history of reading fluency. In S. J. Samuels & A. E. Farstrup (Eds.), *What research has to say about fluency instruction* (pp. 4–23). International Reading Association.

Rau, M. A., Sen, A., & Zhu, X. (2019, June). Using machine learning to overcome the expert blind spot for perceptual fluency trainings. In *International Conference on Artificial Intelligence in Education* (pp. 406–418). Springer.

Reuters (2003). "Master" and "Slave" computer labels unacceptable, officials say. 26 November. Retrieved from www.cnn.com/2003/TECH/ptech/11/26/master.term.reut/index.html (accessed 3 November 2020).

Rittle-Johnson, B., Siegler, R. S., & Alibali, M. W. (2001). Developing conceptual understanding and procedural skill in mathematics: An iterative process. *Journal of Educational Psychology, 93*(2), 346.

Rittle-Johnson, B., & Star, J. R. (2007). Does comparing solution methods facilitate conceptual and procedural knowledge? An experimental study on learning to solve equations. *Journal of Educational Psychology, 99*(3), 561–574.

Rumelhart, D. E., & McClelland, J. L. (1986). *Parallel distributed processing: Explorations in the microstructure of cognition* (Vol. 1). *Foundations.* MIT Press.

Russ, R. S., Sherin, B. L., & Sherin, M. G. (2016). What constitutes teacher learning. *Handbook of research on teaching,* (pp. 391–438). American Educational Research Association.

Ryle, G. (1949). *The concept of mind.* Hutchinson.

Salomon, G., Perkins, D. N., & Globerson, T. (1991). Partners in cognition: Extending human intelligence with intelligent technologies. *Educational Researcher, 20*(3), 2–9.

Sawyer, R. K. (2005). *Social emergence: Societies as complex systems.* Cambridge.

Schwartz, D. L. (1995). The emergence of abstract representations in dyad problem solving. *The Journal of the Learning Sciences, 4*(3), 321–354.

Shaffer, D. W. (2017). *Quantitative ethnography.* Lulu.com.

Sfard, A. (1998). On two metaphors for learning and the dangers of choosing just one. *Educational Researcher, 27*(2), 4–13.

Simon, H. A. (1996/2019). *The sciences of the artificial.* MIT Press.

Stanovich, K. E., & West, R. F. (2000). Individual differences in reasoning: Implications for the rationality debate? *Behavioral and Brain Sciences, 23*(5), 645–665.

Tofel-Grehl, C., & Feldon, D. F. (2013). Cognitive task analysis–based training. *Journal of Cognitive Engineering and Decision Making, 7*(3), 293–304. doi:10.1177/1555343412474821

VanLehn, K., Jones, R. M., & Chi, M. T. H. (1992). A model of the self-explanation effect. *The Journal of the Learning Sciences, 2*(10), 1–59.

Verity, D. P. (2011). The reverse move: Enriching informal knowledge in the pedagogical grammar class. In K. E. Johnson & P. R. Golembek (Eds.), *Research on second language teacher education: A sociocultural perspective on teacher professional development* (pp. 153–167). Routledge.

Vygotsky, L. S. (1934/1963). *Thought and language.* MIT Press.

Vygotsky, L. S. (1997). The history of the development of higher mental functions. In R. W. Rieber (Ed.), *The collected works of L. S. Vygotsky Vol. 4: The history of the development of higher mental functions.* Plenum Press. (Originally published 1931.)

Walkington, C., Sherman, M., & Petrosino, A. (2012). "Playing the game" of story problems: Coordinating situation-based reasoning with algebraic representation. *The Journal of Mathematical Behavior, 31*(2), 174–195.

Walkington, C., Wang, M., & Nathan, M. J. (2020). Collaborative gestures among high school students conjointly proving geometric conjectures. In *Proceedings of the 14th International Congress on Mathematics Education (ICME-14).* Shanghai, China, International Congress on Mathematics Education.

West, G. B. (2017). *Scale: The universal laws of growth, innovation, sustainability, and the pace of life in organisms, cities, economies, and companies.* Penguin.

Grounded and Embodied Learning in the Classroom and Beyond

12.1 A VISION OF GROUNDED AND EMBODIED LEARNING IN SCHOOLS

In Chapter 2, I introduced the **Grounded and Embodied Learning Thesis**, which stated that it is necessary for learning experiences to engage body-based processes in order for learning and instruction to be meaningful. At its core, the GEL paradigm is a commitment to educating embodied learners. This thesis offers an entirely different epistemological basis for evaluating the current state of education and for redesigning educational experiences. In this chapter, I revisit the case for this thesis and present a vision it offers for school-based learning. This "big picture" view helps identify important growth areas for educational practices and policies, research, and development to realize the potential more fully for transforming school-based learning. For the reader's benefit, I summarize the benefits of the GEL framework in Box 12A.

Box 12A Summary of the Benefits of the GEL Framework for Education

- GEL offers a holistic account of thinking and learning, teaching, design of learning environments and technologies, and of formative and summative assessment practices.
- GEL is retained longer, comprehended better, and is more likely to be applied appropriately in novel contexts.
- GEL is more beneficial than many current educational frameworks because it focuses on how learners make meaning by connecting new ideas and symbolic representations to actions, perceptions, and prior experiences that are inherently meaningful.
- GEL spans a vast range of learning processes, from neural systems to community-based interactions, and includes conscious as well as unconscious learning processes.
- Learners experience greater engagement in GEL activities.

All too often, traditional educational experiences are ineffective in advancing students' content knowledge and in making formalisms meaningful. In addition, students quite often cannot demonstrate all that they know and can do. As a result, students can get by merely with rote recall and surface-level academic performance because their understanding is

DOI: 10.4324/9780429329098-12

weak, temporary, and shallow. It is incumbent upon us as a society to create educational experiences that are appropriate for how people actually learn, retain, and express knowledge. Students' learning environments, curricula, and educational technology need to be designed with meaningful learning of embodied learners in mind.

Students frequently ask why specific academic content is important, why they have to know it, and when they will really need to use it. In contrast, when formalisms and concepts are meaningfully learned, these concepts are better remembered, more thoughtfully applied, and more frequently used to support future learning and creative expression. As I have reviewed in the earlier chapters, grounded understanding can be achieved when gaining fluency with perceptual patterns and procedures, making explicit connections to one's common ground, linking to embodied experiences with action and metaphors for action and space, and participating in socially supported discourse practices. Achieving a grounded understanding helps students to see educational experiences as relevant, well-motivated, and meaningful.

While actual and simulated action are important for embodied learning, it is critical that readers appreciate that not *all* actions promote the desired forms of learning. Actions for learning must be intentionally chosen so that they are conceptually relevant. Similarly, the choices of spatial metaphors also must be made with care.

GEL also reveals ways that student learning and intellectual performance arises from the contributions of both unconscious and conscious processes. Educational experiences that recognize the individual and collective contributions of unconscious and conscious processes and design activities that support them will foster more fully integrated learning. These designed activities and experiences need to be created with recognition of the conditions in which unconscious and conscious processes are invoked and applied. Specifically, support for unconscious processes benefits from fluency, feedback, and opportunities to generalize their application to varied and related contexts. Conscious processing is enhanced with support for semantically congruent actions and metaphors, reducing cognitive load by means such as directing attention and cognitive offloading, situated memory retrieval of declarative knowledge and rules, and reflection. Collaborative learning contexts naturally foster integration of conscious and unconscious processes during the course of group participation.

Instructional practices that operate with GEL in mind can enhance students' educational experiences. The strategic use of gestures in instruction can effectively foster and maintain common ground as a basis for effective engagement and learning. Instructional gestures are effective at directing students' attention to what is important during curricular activities and for grounding ideas and symbolic formalisms to concrete and familiar experiences. Gestures can also invoke the kind of conceptual metaphors that are so important for grasping novel, abstract concepts in terms of concrete experiences such as spatial relations. As an overarching method, concreteness fading is a well-studied developmental progression that assists students in forming a grounded understanding of important disciplinary formalisms that can support future generalization and transfer of learning.

Assessment practices also benefit from an embodied perspective. Teachers can develop helpful formative assessment practices by attending to students' fluency with pattern recognition and procedures, and with students' production of gestures. Noticing these nonverbal forms of communication can help teachers to diagnose student progress, recognize emerging trouble spots, and identify readiness for future learning even when students cannot convey this verbally more accurately. Summative assessment practices can also improve when they include ways of documenting and evaluating students' verbal and nonverbal ways of knowing and distributed knowledge.

12.2 ON THE HORIZON: GROWTH AREAS FOR EDUCATION PRACTICES AND POLICIES

In order to fulfill the vision of an education system rooted in GEL, there are practices and policies that will need to be further refined before they can be widely adopted.

12.2.1 Teacher Education and Professional Learning

Teachers are the foundation of education. Education cannot substantially transform without changes being carried out by teachers. Furthermore, teachers' beliefs about learning and learners play a central role in guiding their instructional practices (Fang, 1996; Kagan, 1992; Thompson, 1992). For the principles and practices of GEL to make their way into classrooms, it is vital that teachers come to view their charge as educating *embodied* learners. This charge calls for significant changes in what teachers do in the classroom and how they themselves are educated.

To prepare teachers to implement GEL classrooms, teacher education programs need to cultivate practitioners who find value in the Grounded and Embodied Learning Thesis, and understand the central role of the body and embodied resources in thinking, learning, and assessment. For these programs, "cognition" becomes reframed as "grounded and embodied cognition" (Barsalou, 2008). This reframing explicitly incorporates the impact of action and perception during *online cognition*, when people are actively engaged in situated thinking. This reframing also explicitly acknowledges the power of sensorimotor simulations and grounding metaphors for *offline cognition*, the form of imaginative thinking that occurs when learners are removed from the original environment (Wilson, 2002).

Teachers' emerging knowledge of general and content-specific methods of instruction need to address effective use of gestures to direct learners' attention, make overt links among ideas, and connect ideas to formal representations. It is important that instructional gesture be regarded as an explicit instructional method in education. As an area of professional training, teacher educators have no reservations directing pre-service teachers how to talk. They do so because experience and research has shown that how teachers speak has enormous influence in what and how students learn. It is high time that teacher education programs acknowledge this same influence for instructional gestures.

Both newly minted teachers and old timers (a label I offer with great affection and admiration!) need to wield gestures as they would any tool of pedagogy. Gesture needs to be recognized as a highly versatile resource that teachers always have "on hand." When used with intention, gestures show themselves to be highly effective for fostering conceptual and procedural learning (Alibali & Nathan, 2012; Macedonia & von Kriegstein, 2012; Roth, 2001; Valenzeno, Alibali, & Klatzky, 2003), managing classroom discourse, and for responding to students' trouble spots as they arise. Classroom instructors need to learn to notice students' nonverbal behaviors as a way to contribute to teachers' formative assessment practices.

In terms of teacher talk, here too, much can be done to provide a more grounded and embodied experience to support meaningful learning. One area in particular is the thoughtful use of metaphor. Metaphors lurk everywhere in education speech, throughout all of the content areas. They are especially prevalent when discussing abstract ideas, and they do so in ways that can make these ideas more concrete and relate them to one's prior lived experiences, making the abstractions more meaningful. Metaphors can also extend one's understanding of a set of concepts to entirely new domains.

Teachers must also come to appreciate that embodied learning is often distributed. Few adults can perform all of their duties without instruments, tools, and colleagues. This is also true for learners. Schools do students little service by artificially isolating students from the social and environmental resources they need to think, learn, and create (Resnick, 1987). Often, these resources provide sources of cognitive offloading, which can enable successful reasoning. These resources may also *extend* cognition, integrating material resources that serve epistemic roles. Learners may, over time, internalize these epistemic functions, which can later be reinstated in the form of mental simulations that re-engage the original perceptual-motor processes in service of cognition. These are some of the powerful ways material resources fulfill a role as "things to think with" in both online and offline cognitive performance.

The use of cultural and scientific tools is also important for learners' development of appropriate discourse practices of communities of practice (John-Steiner & Mahn, 1996; Wertsch, 2009). Learners' first community of practice is often *school*, where there are many explicit and implicit norms for appropriate forms of participation. The awareness of learning as adopting new participatory practices also positions students to join other communities of processionals in the arts, humanities, science and technology, public service, and so on. Learning through community participation brings many of the elements listed above and throughout this book together into a more cohesive role. Communities of practice are living answers to students' penetrating questions of "Why do I need to know this?" and "When will I ever use this?"

Communities of practice are valuable for teachers as well. In my view, they should be the norm for teachers' professional environment. Teachers should feel supported to seek counsel when in crisis. It is best to do this within the context of a safe and supportive ongoing group of colleagues who already have discussed each teachers' goals and values. For it is in the context of these professional communities that teachers can rekindle their love of learning and teaching, come for advice, as well as reflect on their practice (Wineburg & Grossman, 1998).

12.2.2 GEL Perspective on Transfer of Learning

Transfer of learning is of great importance to education. As teachers are aware, formal education is premised on the notion of transfer of learning. Educators know they are not teaching and assessing everything that they think students need to know. They also understand that the world is rapidly changing and will present many new ideas and challenges for the next generation of citizens. The GEL framework makes two theoretical claims about the transfer of learning.

The first theoretical claim is that transfer is not solely ascribed to learners. Rather it is achieved by learners and their teachers in concert (Nathan & Alibali, in press). This follows from the observation that teachers—and this can also include peers, parents, and interactive technologies—are integral to learners' successful attempts to generalize previously learned associations and sensorimotor responses to new contexts. How transfer of learning is exhibited will be part of my discussion of assessment. For instruction, the important message is to recognize the central role the teacher plays in establishing and maintaining that sense of cohesion from one experience to another. Experiences designed to support transfer must support common ground by providing frequent—and often explicit—connections to students' prior learning and lived experiences. It falls to the teacher to skillfully fade away these supports as students (acting on their own and with peers) demonstrate autonomy in making these connections. This is why teachers and learners are both deemed integral to transfer of learning when viewed from within the GEL framework.

The second theoretical claim is that transfer of learning is the *default mode* for learners (Nathan & Alibali, in press), rather than a rarity. This is because the environment and each learner's internal body state are continually changing. As I have described earlier, people are predisposed to operate in a *predictive manner*. They are continually antici-pating, often unconsciously, what the current environment has to offer them and how they will need to respond. To function successfully, learners must generalize previously learned associations and sensorimotor responses to match one's current context (Nathan & Alibali, in press).

12.2.3 Expanding Assessment Practices

Knowledge from a GEL perspective includes ways of knowing that may be unconsciously expressed, expressed nonverbally, and distributed among a social network and array of cul-tural tools and discipline-based formalisms. Assessment practices need to reflect this in order to accurately document student knowledge.

In serving formative assessment, nonverbal behaviors offer teachers a rich, real-time source of diagnostic information about students' reasoning and readiness for intellectual development. Teachers can be trained to notice students' gestures and interpret them as a window into student thinking and development (Alibali, Flevares, & Goldin-Meadow, 1997). This is an important pedagogical skill that needs to be more widespread.

Summative assessments inform developmental decisions about student progress. Traditionally, assessments are designed to document verbalizable knowledge that is meant to be expressed in isolation from other students and most cognitive resources. To be valid indicators of embodied learning, summative assessments must instead be designed to evaluate students' achievements in situations that are comparable to how they think and learn. This includes documenting nonverbal ways of knowing and the distributed and extended nature of knowledge. Otherwise, they are not actually testing learners' true level of school-based learning, but of some other, more limited types of student performance.

Assessing transfer of learning is also vitally important for understanding the range of student achievement. Too often "successful" transfer is determined by experts applying external criteria. In contrast, as described earlier, transfer is recognized as a continual pro-cess mediated by a predictive architecture optimized to anticipate invariants and changes in one environment.

Transfer is exhibited when perceptions and actions that learners engaged in previous contexts are mapped to new contexts. This occurs only when learners experience cohe-sion between previous and current contexts and perceive them as "similar" (Lobato, 2003). Learners express that sense of cohesion across contexts through multimodal forms of behavior, including how they talk, act, and gesture. Students can exhibit the learning gains of *positive* near and far transfer for contexts that are perceived to share more or fewer contextual cues, respectively. *Negative* transfer can arise when contextual cues from the original setting cause learners to be less inclined to generate similarity relations than if the learner had never had the original experience.

In the GEL framework, learners can also demonstrate *false transfer* (Nathan & Alibali, in press), which occurs when contextual cues activate misleading modes of perceiving and acting than what the learner actually intends. Assessment methods that inhibit activation of body-based resources and restrict gesture production, as when typing and using a com-puter mouse, are a problem. These assessment practices, too, must be rethought in favor of methods that permit engagement of all one's embodied forms of reasoning and expression. Despite the potential costs and logistical demands, multimodal forms of responding, and assessments of distributed knowledge must become the gold standard because they will offer the most valid account of students' true thinking and learning.

12.2.4 Expanding Content: GEL for Humanities and Social Sciences

Embodied learning is important for effective social studies education (Sund et al., 2019). In assembling empirical evidence for this book, I became aware of the dearth of empirical research on embodied learning and teaching in the humanities and social sciences. This stood in contrast to the large body of work on language and reading, and for topics in mathematics, science, and engineering. As noted, I found some compelling works in areas of history education (reported in Chapter 10) focused on the comprehension and evaluation of historical documents and on the value of site-based learning. I was also excited to report on the role of computer simulation software for engaging students in modeling and discussions of the social impacts of historical events such as protests on policies and laws. In addition, I came across interesting work on the role of metaphors in civics education (Fischman & Haas, 2012). While providing a conceptual rather than empirical account, it also pointed toward the power of grounding to understand complex sociopolitical concepts.

Still, there was far less of this work than in the other major content areas, and the work spanned far fewer topics and grade levels. If this is an accurate account of the state of the literature, then it is one that deserves to be righted. Social studies and humanities are central to the human experience and to a well-rounded education. Students need to understand their lives and the changes going on around them with respect to history, geography, culture, philosophy, and the never-ending quest to understand such basic questions as, *Who are we?* and *What do we value?* I can think of nothing more central to the aims of this book than helping students to gain a grounded and embodied understanding of these important concepts in social studies and the humanities.

12.2.5 Spatial Reasoning in Curriculum Content

An embodied perspective on knowing and learning brings awareness of space to the fore. Thus, in researching this book, I was also struck, along with others, how little formal education is directed at cultivating spatial reasoning (Tversky, 2019; Uttal, et al., 2013). Spatial reasoning is often implicated as benefiting mathematics and science education (e.g., Gunderson et al., 2012; Stieff & Uttal, 2015). It is also central to the graphic and performing arts, such as graphic design, dance, and theater, along with many content areas within social studies and the humanities, such as geography and political science.

It seems that educators expect spatial thinking to spontaneously emerge from the various experiences students have in and out of school. It may be that education administrators and curriculum designers ascribe to an entity view of spatial reasoning—the notion that "you have it or you don't." This is a widely held view (Furnham, 2014) that sits in contrast to the incremental view—that a skill or body of knowledge can be cultivated with the appropriate investment of time and effort (Dweck, 2000). Empirically, it is known that training in spatial skills is highly effective, transfers broadly to novel spatial tasks, and can contribute to improvements in educational participation and performance (Uttal et al., 2013).

There is also a sense that, culturally, today's youth have far fewer experiences to develop spatial and construction skills than earlier generations (Eisenberg, 2005; Watson, 2002). Watson (2002) disparages the substitution of video games for construction kits, but the critique is not well constructed. Surely video games and other digital and material experiences, such as Makerspaces, offer much to the curious and driven craftsperson alike. Michael Eisenberg (2005), himself a virtuoso in cultivating construction experiences as a source of artistic expression, amusement, and mathematical reasoning, asks the community of educators and learning scientists to do more to understand the role of "The place of physical materials, 'real-world' play, and personalized scientific activity in children's lives" (p. 447).

Spatial systems for such tasks as orientation and visualization appear across cultures and throughout human development, as well as being shared with other species. These forms of reasoning and expression give rise to basic cultural artifacts as maps and graphic displays in books and art (Tversky, 2019). As several scholars have noted, spatial skills are part of emerging literacies in modern society (e.g., Rubel, Hall-Wieckert, & Lim, 2017; Taylor, 2017). Even so, the role of spatial reasoning in school learning is not well structured. This may be due, perhaps, to a longstanding bias that has privileged verbal forms of knowledge over imagistic ways of knowing. I strongly advocate rethinking this so that spatial reasoning earns a place among the basic skills for a well-rounded education. I expect there will be enormous pay-offs to individual development and societal progress.

12.2.6 Recommendations for Educational Leaders, Administrators, and Policy Makers

At the outset of this chapter, I talked about the central role of teachers to enact practices and principles of the GEL framework. Like many people, my tendency is to think of teachers as the sole sources of influence, and to overlook the important influences that principals, superintendents, and school board members have on changing education. I want now to explicitly enlist them in thinking about how educational spaces and experiences can be organized so GEL practices can thrive.

Principals, along with department chairs, are closely connected to the daily practices of classroom teachers. They establish school climate and criteria for professional conduct and accountability. These school leaders can have an enormous influence on teacher "buy in" of changing practices, including the practices I mentioned above. One overarching practice I have identified is encouraging teacher participation in sustained communities of practice. These are powerful systems for reflection, planning, and professional learning. They have the potential to positively influence all of the other facets of instruction and the classroom experience.

Assessment is another important area I have discussed throughout the book. It is of such central importance because it conveys professionally and publicly the kinds of knowledge educators in a community value. Here I want to expand the point by recognizing its influence on educational inclusion and democratization. All learners, but especially learners with diverse linguistic and cultural backgrounds, need to be able to express what they know and how they learn in both verbal and nonverbal ways. Privileging verbal forms of knowledge in the design of assessments reinforces certain well-entrenched inequities in education. Leadership that accepts broader assessment methods conveys to teachers that these forms of knowing are valued and can be used as a firm basis for students' cognitive development.

School leaders and administrators also can influence classroom instruction by acknowledging the role of embodied teaching practices to direct attention, make meaningful connections, and establish common ground with students. For example, learning to harness the power of perceptual fluency and procedural automaticity grounds many concepts and also frees up resources for other cognitive processes. While this is generally acknowledged as important in early reading and mathematics education, the potential benefits are far broader. Encouragement of the effective use of gestures during instruction and classroom management will contribute to student engagement and learning. Fostering sociodisciplinary norms helps students to develop the habits of mind that are so valuable for learning and problem solving. School leaders can direct resources so these new practices can be modeled and cultivated through professional development experiences. Leaders can signal their importance by making them explicit aspects of teacher evaluations and plans for professional growth.

School district specialists, superintendents, and school board members make curriculum choices. Policy makers, such as chief state school officers, members of state boards of education, and those serving on local governing boards serve an important role selecting curricula that engage students in active learning. Note that the *ways* students engage—the conceptual relevance of their movements and interactions—are crucial for contributing to the positive outcomes of GEL. I want these to be cautious selections and so I advise policy makers to watch out for the appeal of education fads. As approaches to embodied teaching and learning make their way through the popular press, policy makers and curriculum specialists need to be vigilant as informed consumers and adopters. They need to look for educational materials, practices, and principles that come from reputable sources. These are sources that vet their materials and draw on evidence-based practices.

If the education community has learned anything from expert blind spot research, it is that educational practitioners and curriculum specialists cannot simply look to their own learning experiences and intuitions to make decisions for students. These intuitions and experiences might serve as initial sources of inspiration that guide educators where to look for empirical and theoretical support. Where the research community is lagging behind practice—and it is *always* lagging—practitioners can look to action research approaches to tentatively test out methods. This is another place where their participation in professional communities of practice will chart a path toward crafting effective, well-tested, and thoughtfully implemented learning experiences for their students. It is also another way that sustained practitioner-researcher partnerships can advance both learning theory and educational practice.

12.3 EQUITY IN EDUCATION: A GEL PERSPECTIVE

12.3.1 Effects of Poverty and Oppression on Intellectual Development

The promise of the educational system to foster the intellectual and social development of all children cannot succeed without acknowledging and addressing the deleterious effects of systemic racism, poverty, and other institutionalized impediments to learning and academic engagement. In the United States, the greatest disparities are between White and Black Americans. The system-wide, intentional (if sometimes unconscious), and long-term oppression and disinvestment has institutionalized impoverished living and schooling conditions. This has significantly harmed and continues to harm the learning and academic performance of children of color.

One of the cornerstones of public education in the United States is the *Brown v. Board of Education of Topeka* (1954) decision by the US Supreme Court. The Court ruled unanimously that "separate educational facilities are inherently unequal." The ruling noted that state laws that established racially segregated schools were in violation of the Equal Protection Clause of the Fourteenth Amendment of the US Constitution. This landmark ruling was also significant in that the Justices relied on scientific research in challenging notions of "biological racism" and claims of the inherent intellectual inferiority or superiority of any genetically distinguishable group in reaching their decision.

Despite this significant court ruling, Black families in the twenty-first century experience, on average, less favorable housing, inferior academic experiences, and more limited career opportunities. These racial disparities perpetuate cycles of poverty, opportunity gaps, and achievement gaps that consistently fall along racial boundaries. Poverty disproportionately affects African American (39%) and Latinx (33%) children and adolescents, who experience poverty at more than twice the rate of non-Latino, White, and Asian children and adolescents (14%; Kids Count Data Center, Children in Poverty, 2014). There are fewer effective learning supports for Black and Latinx children living in poverty. They generally receive less nurturance from caregivers, are more likely to be exposed to unsafe and unstable living conditions, have greater food insecurities, more exposure to neurotoxicants in their environment, and encounter more incidents of violence (Boulton, 2015; Golden, 2016; Oulhote & Grandjean, 2016). Children living in poverty generally experience more sustained periods of chronic stress, which they obtain directly from their own experiences, as well as stresses that they absorb from family members (Luby, 2015).

Brain development and academic performance is negatively affected by living in poverty. Hair and colleagues (Hair, Hanson, Wolfe, & Pollak, 2015, 2016) examined MRI brain scans of 389 typically developing children from mothers who were all more highly educated than the general population. They examined children in families with incomes less than 1.5 times the federal poverty level. They found significantly lower gray matter volume of in brain areas associated with academic success, including the frontal lobe, which is responsible for emotion regulation, language processing and attention control; the temporal lobe, which is involved in memory and language processing; and the hippocampus, which is involved in memory and spatial reasoning. Hair and colleagues (2015) found that the greater the severity of poverty, the greater the reduction in gray matter.

My own city of Madison, Wisconsin exhibits some of the largest Black-White academic achievement gaps in the nation, even as it offers a variety of public enrichment resources and boasts of high academic achievement levels (Elbow, 2018). In order to educate all students, so each may reach their fullest potential, educational organizations must acknowledge and confront the existence and negative effects of systemic racism, poverty, and other forms of oppression.

These oppressive practices and policies can be meaningfully confronted by applying GEL principles. This is because of these oppressive views and behaviors are learned through embodied mechanisms. Negative stereotypes arise from pattern recognition processes that are bombarded with harmful portrayals of People of Color in the media, through ethnically and racially biased metaphors, and from racist and xenophobic discourse practices that continue undisrupted. The following sections briefly describe ways that negative stereotypes, implicit biases, and racist views and policies harm learners, and how these can be disrupted and replaced with practices that promote equity and socially just educational experiences.

12.3.2 Effects of Racist Stereotypes on Intellectual Performance

Racial stereotypes are a societal form of oppression that negatively influences scholastic and economic attainment in addition to the broad and deep effects of poverty. As an alarming example, high-achieving African American students experience substantially fewer academic resources, less rigorous curricula, and lower expectations than comparable White students (Azzam, 2008). African Americans with college degrees experience greater than twice the rate of unemployment than the population of college graduates as a whole (Jones & Schmitt, 2014). Claude Steele and colleagues have identified how culturally entrenched racial stereotypes are internalized by People of Color—these are forms of Type 3 processing directly influencing Type 1 and 2 processing —and how these adversely impact academic performance.

Stereotype threat, as it is called, is a situational threat that affects members of any group about whom a negative societal stereotype exists (Steele & Aronson, 1995). Where negative stereotypes apply, members of these groups are prone to the fear of being reduced to that stereotype. Experiencing this fear, often at an unconscious level, impairs cognition by interceding with competing thoughts on the very intellectual activities that demand the greatest cognitive resources.

Stereotype threat is a social as well as a psychological, phenomenon. Vulnerability comes not from internal doubts about one's own ability but rather from identification of stereotyped behavior with the domain (e.g., academic test performance) and the resulting concern the student experiences about being actively stereotyped with it (Steele & Aronson, 1995). It is impactful even among high-performing Black and White students, even those admitted to a highly selective academic institution (Steele, 1997).

In the original study (Steele & Aronson, 1995), which has since been replicated, Black and White Stanford University students took a test composed of some of the most diffi-cult items on the verbal GRE. While the Black students were equally capable as the White students on these test items, Black students significantly underperformed *when the test was framed as a measure of intellectual ability.* This is because that framing related the test to deep-seated and widely adopted societal stereotypes about the intellectual ability of Black individ-uals. It did not have this negative affect on White students, who do not share the stereotype. Black participants also significantly underperformed compared to equally qualified White participants when primed about their race just before taking the test.

Steele offers a number of ways to reduce stereotype threat. Notably, he argues that these remedies are contingent on whether students do or do not identify with the stereotype-threatening domain. For those who do identify and experience stereotype threat, there are effective ways mitigate its effects. One is to affirm that these students do, in fact, belong in these academic settings on the basis of their intellectual abilities. Another confirms that their perspectives are valued, which signals that such threats are not likely to be realized. Third is to ensure there is access to successful role models, which affirms that the threat is not insurmountable.

Regardless of whether students identify with the stereotype-threatening domain, there are several recommendations. For one, Steele's research showed that Black students avoided underperformance when the test was framed as *nondiagnostic* of their intellectual ability. Thus, test framing is an important consideration. Second, all students benefit from optimistic teacher-student relations that serve as a contradiction to the doubts cast by stereotypes. Third, giving students work that is challenging, while also providing sufficient time and resources (such as building on optimistic teacher-student relations) is also very effective. In contrast, presenting extra work as "remedial" reinforces these negative stereotypes, to students' detri-ment. Finally, affirming the incremental nature of intelligence and its expandability through intellectual investment is effective. Educators need to stress that all students are fundamen-tally able to learn and succeed on intellectually engaging tasks.

12.3.3 Addressing Implicit Bias

People's perceptions of racial differences are unsupported by current scientific literature. Nonetheless, people develop *implicit biases* that affect their judgments of certain social groups, largely based on skin color, which can operate outside of their awareness. Most people would be surprised to hear they operate with implicit biases in areas such as gender, social class, and race. Their conscious views can be quite at odds with their unconscious behaviors (Nathan, Tran, Atwood, Prevost, & Phelps, 2010). This is a consequence of *knowing-with*: Living in a society infused with certain institutionalized practices and norms of participation shapes people's behaviors in fundamental ways even though people may remain unaware of them (Kendi, 2019).

A common measure used to assess implicit race bias is the Black-White IAT (Implicit Association Test; Greenwald, McGhee, & Schwartz, 1998). Because of the unconscious nature of Type 1 processing, it must be measured by examining people's rapid associations. The IAT measures how strongly people hold associations between members of social groups, such as Black or White people, and evaluative terms, such as good or bad. People are thought to make a quicker response to items they deem closely related, even if unconsciously. A pro-White bias, for example, is revealed when the pattern of response times for an individual making selections over many trails favors White-good over Black-good. The IAT is hypothesized to reveal basic neural and affective processes relevant to implicit race bias (Cunningham, Raye, & Johnson, 2004) and discriminatory behavior.

Implicit bias is not inherently immoral. People surely *notice* differences in skin color, sex, body size, and it would be problematic for our survival and cognitive development if we did not. The societal issues arise not from classifying differences, but when people and organizations use these classifications to justify unfair or inequitable treatment that favors members of one social group or that penalizes members of another. Scholars such as Patricia Devine (1989) note that implicit biases do exist and perpetuate many of the negative effects described.

Some have learned these associations more strongly than others. This has consequences to how people act and change, as revealed in a study of the nature of prejudicial reactions (Devine, 1989). Devine found that high- and low-prejudice persons were equally aware of certain racial stereotypes. She also found that low-prejudice participants were more likely to use controlled Type 2 processing to inhibit some of these common cultural stereotyped responses that can follow from Type 1 processing. However, when Type 2 processing was interfered with, high- and low-prejudice participants make similar stereotypical evaluations. In an effort to reduce these unintended biased responses, Devine showed that those with low-prejudice biases were able to better inhibit the associations all participants had for stereotypes and to replace the race-based associations with more equitable thoughts.

Devine and her colleagues (2012) have shown that implicit biases can be reduced using some of the same ways got reducing undesirable habits, such as smoking and overeating (also see Oswald, Mitchell, Blanton, Jaccard, & Tetlock, 2013). In this "habit-breaking intervention" people confront their biases, develop situational awareness of when biased responses are most likely to happen, and learn to replace these with unbiased responses.

In one study, 90% of participants in the intervention, all non-Black, exhibited pro-White bias using the Black-White IAT prior to the training. Over the course of the 12-week intervention, those in the treatment group showed a significantly larger drop in pro-White implicit bias than those in the control group at four weeks and eight weeks after the training. Participants in the treatment group also showed greater concerns about discrimination and more awareness of their personal biases.

One inspiring approach is the role-play experiences created by Jane Elliott. Her original lesson in 1968 split her class of third-graders—all of whom were White, living an a nearly all-White community—according to eye color (Elliott, n.d.). Using a form of immersion education, blue-eyed students received privileges withheld from their brown-eyed classmates. In short order, those with blue eyes acted superior and highly discriminatory. Brown-eyed students showed remarkable losses in academic achievement and engagement in just one day (Bloom & Kennedy, 2005).

Still, a review of the most promising interventions for reducing implicit bias show them to be short-lived (Lai et al., 2014, 2016). This is very likely because these psychological interventions target Type 1 and Type 2 processing, but do little to address the sociocultural influences of Type 3 processing. The societal patterns that led to these biases in the first place were internalized over long periods of time. They have changed people's ways of knowing-with. Consequently, sustained changes to these implicit views requires individuals to make a considerable investment of time and effort.

12.3.4 Critically Relevant Pedagogy and Antiracist Education

Early forms of antiracism education based on limited interventions and appeals to multiculturalism, tolerance, and diversity are often perceived as falling short of eradicating systemic racist behaviors, policies, and social norms (Alemanji, 2017; Gillborn, 2007). In *How to Be an Antiracist*, Ibram X. Kendi (2019), a Guggenheim Fellow, contends that lasting change depends on people making daily, lifelong commitments with continued support. Otherwise the patterns experienced in society keep getting reinforced, and the gains that arise from Type 2 interventions will eventually be eroded by the continual influences of society and the media.

Critical Race Theory offers a systemic view. It "challenges the ways in which race and racial power are constructed and represented in American legal culture and, more generally, in American society as a whole" (Crenshaw et al., 1995, p. xiii).

Critical Race Theory is a broad and evolving framework built around several central tenets: Racism is "endemic in US society, deeply ingrained legally, culturally, and even psychologically" (Tate, 1997, p. 234). It challenges views from Liberalism of calls for neutrality, objectivity, color-blindness, and meritocracy as "camouflages." Instead, it elevates the experiential knowledge of People of Color and their use of stories and counterstories to report on and speak out against acts in both its overt and its tacit, institutional forms (Ladson-Billings, 1998). All of us need to hear members of oppressed groups tell *their* stories, not only accept the stories offered by those who have traditionally been in power. Critical Race Theory exposes that the legal gains for Black, Indigenous, and People of Color are driven by "interest convergence" (i.e., actual benefits to Whites as well as other groups; Bell, 1980) than achieving social justice for its own sake. Critical Race Theory shifts the discourse away from analyses of intent and focuses on the outcomes of actions and policies, since this is what actually affects the lives of those historically oppressed groups.

Several powerful approaches for instituting systemic change emerge from the perspective of Critical Race Theory. Gloria Ladson-Billings and William F. Tate, IV (1995) applied Critical Race Theory to education. One is generating effective approaches for educating Black, Indigenous, and People of Color that are empowering. Earlier, I reviewed an approach described by Tate (1995) that embedded mathematics learning within practices of epidemiology. Another falls under what Ladson-Billings (1995) labels *Critically Relevant Pedagogy*. As she described it:

> Instead of asking what was wrong with African American learners, I dared to ask what was right with these students and what happened in the classrooms of teachers who seemed to experience pedagogical success with them.
>
> (Ladson-Billings, 2014, p. 74)

These include legitimizing Black art forms such as spoken word and hip-hop as areas of university study, and recruiting these talented young People of Color just as campuses recruit student athletes. Many of these artists chose to pursue education and took these forms of expression into the classroom and offices of school leadership. Ladson-Billings (1995) notes that effective critically relevant pedagogical methods share several traits. They promote academic success, cultural competencies that celebrate their own cultures, and sociopolitical consciousness to analyze, and solve social problems. The interventions conducted by Tate, Ladson-Billings, and others show the importance of using common ground as a basis for effective education.

Another approach is changing the sociopolitical environment by introducing a critical lens on the construct of "whiteness" in the context of critical White studies (e.g., Gillborn, 2007; Delgado & Stefancic, 1997). One early precursor is described by Hacker (1992, p. 32) to draw White college students to the edges of their epistemic frame on racial equity. While these students generally argue that the Black American experience has improved, Hacker asks how much compensation these White college students would take to "trade places" and "become Black." White students feel justified in asking for as much as $50 million, or $1 million for each person for each year of the experiment. (Adjusting to 2020 dollars, this would be closer to $93 million per person.) As Hacker (1992) states, "The money would be used, as best it could, to buy protection from the discriminations and dangers White people know they would face once they were perceived to be black" (p. 32). Ladson-Billings (1998, p. 15) offers what this reveals, barely hidden from view: "Whites know they possess a property that People of Color do not and that to possess it confers, aspects of citizenship not available to others."

Systems of oppression take a huge toll on individual intellectual ability in both unconscious and conscious ways. Majority people also participate in these forms of oppression unconsciously as well as consciously (as Hacker's 1992 thought experiment shows). An education system charged with educating all of its students must confront these systems of oppression. In doing so, I advocate that practitioners and leaders draw on theories of embodied learning and teaching as a way to begin to change people's views and actions.

12.4 ON THE HORIZON: ACTION ITEMS FOR GEL RESEARCH AND DEVELOPMENT

12.4.1 Emotion in Learning and Education

Emotion is, of course, an embodied experience. It is also integral with cognitive processing and cultural participation (Matsumoto & Hwang, 2012; Niedenthal et al., 2005). One of the prevailing psychological models is that emotional experiences emerge from a combination of core affective states of pleasure and displeasure, along with cognitive judgments, and cultural norms (Barrett et al., 2007; Rolls, 2013). Yet research on the specific role that emotion plays in teaching and learning (as distinct from related topics like motivation and interest) is in short supply. This is an unfortunate circumstance, and I hope a temporary one. Here I wish to briefly highlight some important qualities of emotion that I expect to be relevant for future research efforts regarding embodied learning.

Emotional experiences can be reinstated through the kind of embodied simulation I have been discussing, even when the original stimulating event is past. This ability to simulate emotional states appears to be central to people's abilities to identify and respond to the emotions displayed by others (i.e., online emotional processing), as well as when emotions are invoked through language and reading, music, and pictures (i.e., offline emotional processing). For example, direct electrical (EMG) recordings showed that classifying words for their emotional content—a primarily cognitive task—spontaneously activates the reader's emotion-specific facial muscles (Niedenthal et al., 2009). A better understanding of the role emotion serves in grounding and meaning making has direct relevance for learning and instruction, as well as the design of embodied learning experiences.

Emotional processes are critical for judgment, decision making, and rationality (Damasio, 1994). 'Nature," Damasio (1994, p. 128) theorizes, "appears to have built the apparatus of rationality not just on top of the apparatus of biological regulation, but also from it and with it." Lakoff (2008, p. 13–14) concurs, calling for people to "understand that we are using real reason, shaped by our bodies and brains and interactions in the real world, reason incorporating emotion." A better appreciation of the relationship of emotion to processes such as judgment and decision making may mean that educational interventions targeting social and emotional learning may also show academic benefits in other forms of analytical reasoning.

Along with the role of emotion for cognition, there is value in understanding how people learn emotional responses. For example, children on the autism spectrum who show impaired emotional processing or struggle to understand others' social cues often do not benefit from direct instruction of emotion. Prompting these children with directed actions to mimic facial expressions and body movements through training and video game play does help them to identify and classify the emotional state of others (Deriso et al., 2012; Tanaka et al., 2010). This suggests interventions based on sensorimotor transduction may help to bring about conceptual learning of emotional states somewhat in the way this is observed in mathematical reasoning (Nathan & Walkington, 2017). There seems to be great promise for the future exploration of the role of emotion in GEL and for methods of GEL to support emotion learning.

12.4.2 Mindfulness and GEL

An embodied perspective on learning and instruction highlights ways that body-based responses can *inhibit* as well as improve educational effectiveness. Stress can have debilitating effects on intellectual performance by increasing anxiety, decreasing available attention, and contributing to emotional dysregulation. Furthermore, stressful events do not need to be immediately present to have impact. Sensorimotor simulations of stressful events produce comparable effects at the neural and behavioral levels (Lebois et al., 2015). Mindfulness training is a promising approach for reducing the negative effects of stress while also enhancing executive function and emotional regulation (Zelazo & Lyons, 2012). In this way, it brings together Type 1 and Type 2 processing.

Mindfulness interventions use body-based methods to reduce these stress responses. Mindfulness training typically directs one's awareness to the present moment, such as attending to the exhalation of one's breath (Kabat-Zinn, 2003). It adopts non-evaluative attention to one's thoughts and feelings, such as saying to oneself, "these are just my thoughts" and refocusing on one's breathing. For example, Mindfulness Based Stress Reduction (MBSR) training (Kabat-Zinn, 1982, 2003) has been successfully used in many clinical settings, including helping to alleviate chronic pain, anxiety, and depression (for reviews, see Baer, 2003; Grossman, Niemann, Schmidt, & Walach, 2004).

An emerging body of work reveals the promise of mindfulness-based practices among school-age students' academic performance (Burke, 2010). Benefits can include improving student-teacher relationships, reducing effects of ADHD, managing emotion regulation, and reducing stress (Frank, Jennings, & Greenberg, 2013). Mindfulness-based training for teachers also shows some promise for improving student-teacher relations and classroom management methods (Emerson et al., 2017). Efforts to scale-up mindfulness interventions for teachers are also showing success (Mihić, Oh, Greenberg, & Kranželić, 2020).

However, mindfulness practices that are observed in the United States and in many Western countries have been culturally appropriated from ancient Eastern practices. If they are helping people, should that matter? It *does* matter because these practices have been severed from their original sociocultural-historical contexts and placed in a completely foreign one, while the true teachers of these ancient practices are often excluded from the training. An example of some of the profound dissociation is described by Djikic (2014). As Westerners see it, mindfulness solves the problem of mindlessness, dysregulated behaviors, and poor decision making. From an Eastern, Buddhist, perspective, mindfulness addresses suffering, which is intrinsic to life.

This practice of cultural appropriation needs to be addressed by the education community. *Decolonization* (Tuck & Yang, 2012) as applied to mindfulness education offers an ethical path. It shifts to learning these practices from its true teachers, in their intended cultural and historic ways. Framing it in terms of Type 3 thinking, the fulness of the traditions will support a deeper form of grounding of meaning of the practices. Within this rich context, the influence on people's lives may be even greater. More broadly, the financial profits and acknowledgments of intellectual foundations would go to the proper originators.

12.4.3 Emerging Research Methods and Forms of Educational Technology

The philosophical underpinnings of GEL reach back decades, to the writings of Dewey, Gibson, Goffman, Merleau-Ponty and others. Yet the "embodied turn" in education has been dependent on recent technological advancements (e.g., Abrahamson & Lindgren, 2014; Lee, 2014). These advancements will continue to have a profound effect on the future of GEL research methods and the development of embodied learning technology.

Research Methods
Central to the "embodied turn" in education research has been the ability to record, replay, and analyze movement. Documentation of movement proceeded from written notes, to celluloid film, then videotape, digital video, touchpad tracing, digital accelerometers and gyroscopes, remote imaging sensors, haptics sensors, GPS/GIS, and whole-body motion capture. The field is now seeing early development of fully automated, and human-computer assisted speech, gesture, and movement analysis for individuals and groups (Javidi et al., 2020). This explosion of pre-processed data is feeding the emergence of multimodal learning analytics and education data mining to monitor, measure, and model complex patterns of embodied behavior (Blikstein & Worsley, 2016).

Beyond sound and movement, innovators are documenting other sensory modalities, such as touch and smell (McGee, 2020; Miyashita, 2020). These technological developments are likely to fuel new research methods and research questions to advance the exploration of the nature and influence of sensorimotor processes on learning, teaching, design, and assessment.

Educational Technology
Along with advancements in sensory devices came growth in the development of a host of embodied technologies. Many are already integrated in mobile devices such as smart phones and tablets to provide multifaceted information, including: 3D position, 3D motion, orientation, altitude, and proximity to one's hands or face, as well as tactile information for multitouch tracking and dynamic manipulation. For example, these capabilities are being used to develop grounded understanding of abstract mathematical symbol manipulation in arithmetic, fractions, algebra, and geometry (Hohenwater & Fuchs, 2004; Hulse et al., 2019; Sawrey et al., 2019; Swart et al., 2014), as well as for design in engineering, architecture, art, theater, and dance. Sensors found in consumer gaming consoles provide added functionality for tracking real-time single and multi-person motion capture that have been used

to support reasoning in mathematics and science (Abrahamson, 2009; Abrahamson et al., 2020; Johnson-Glenberg et al., 2014; Johnson-Glenberg & Megowan-Romanowicz, 2017; Lee, 2014; Walkington et al., 2019).

3D printing offers another area of growth in educational technology. Digital design tools provide teachers and learners new opportunities to create physical forms and devices that come from one's imagination (e.g., Eisenberg, 2002). The tangible products that result also provide new opportunities for youth to fabricate physical objects that convey their own social, cultural, and emotional affordances.

Highly immersive reality environments, such as those that support embedded phenomena and others for virtual reality (VR) describe another broad class that can support full-body movements and interaction with real and virtual objects and environments for science and engineering education (e.g., Dede, 2009; Johnson-Glenberg, 2018; Lindgren et al., 2016; Lindgren & Johnson-Glenberg, 2013). Physical anthropologists are recreating aspects of discovered settlements in order to provide immersive experiences that can reveal insights about ancient dwellings and cultural movements (Ma, Hall, & Leander, 2010). Project Odeuropa (n.d.; Brate, Groth, & van Erp, 2020) is recreating "smell experiences," an important component of memory and immersion that could enhance the educational experiences for history, archeology, chemistry, literature, theater, and many other fields.

Head mounted systems expand the portability of augmented reality (AR) systems that can overlay holographic images of manipulable objects in one's immediate environment (Dimmel et al., 2019). Recent AR developments also allow users to develop shared holographic images that can promote collaborative co-construction of 2D and 3D objects as well as rich multi-modal communication with one's collaborators (Walkington et al., 2020).

12.4.4 Authentic Practice Relies on Combining GEL Principles: Superposition

My experience in the National Mathematics center (Davenport, et al., 2020) taught me two important lessons about translating research-based learning to authentic practice. First, I learned that implementing evidence-based learning principles to novel curricula is far more complicated than is often implied in the research literature. Second, I learned that authentic educational practice involves *combining* principles of teaching and learning in novel ways that are seldom investigated by the research community. Planful instructional design inevitably relies on the *superposition* of learning principles that were initially formulated in isolation of one another in order to be responsive to the instruction and learning that actually takes place in natural contexts. I hope those lessons I have learned can prove helpful here. By deriving the learning principles that I have curated in Table 11.2 from both a general framework of grounded and embodied learning, and from investigations of their specific uses in classrooms, my intent is to articulate principles that will be compatible in practice. Some important through lines are worth highlighting.

One is the importance of grounding to achieve meaningful learning. Learning processes operating at different time scales ground novel formalisms and ideas in different ways, but all do so by connecting these new ideas and symbolic representations to one's lived experiences. Learners' perceptions and actions are inherently meaningful. Bringing novel ideas in line with these ways of knowing the world—whether through such processes as eye movements and motor programs, familiar spatial metaphors, or socially regulated participatory practices— provides a basis for making meaning and retaining what one learns. It also raises caution about expert blind spots of highly knowledgeable instructors whose ways of knowing-with and knowing-how differ from that of their students. For teachers, the adage "know thyself" should be tempered with the prescription to "know thy students." Combining principles with these considerations in mind will help to develop coherent educational experiences in practice.

A second through line is the interplay of unconscious, nonverbal ways of knowing, with conscious, verbal knowledge, and with socially distributed and enacted knowledge. Appreciation of the combined role of these various processes contributes to a rich picture of the nature of learning and learners that provides general guidelines for informing instruction and assessment. Learners will benefit when they are given license to articulate their intuitive ways of knowing. When these intuitions fall short, there is value in deconstructing the contexts in which inaccurate intuitions are activated for learners, and in clarifying the conditions under which they do and do not apply. Participation in the activities of communities of practice and collaborating in project-based learning experiences create excellent environments in which to elicit and then reflect on these processes and develop the self-awareness of how to direct their use most appropriately.

Combining principles of teaching and learning is certainly a matter that deserves greater attention from the education research community. Its success depends on developing strong partnerships with practitioners willing to engage in new practices, be observed, and offer critical advice about their place in classroom learning, instruction, and assessment.

12.4.5 GEL at the Organizational Scale

My focus in this book has been on exploring learning as it unfolds in the range from milliseconds in the biological realm through the conscious spectrum, and over months during sociocultural processes. I recognize that I have said relatively little about how even longer running processes of organizations learn and how they fit into this general framework. I see this as a pressing and promising area of future inquiry. Much about education is constrained and driven by very long-running processes that shape organizational structure, policies, and laws. The organizations involved include governmental institutions, such as local and state boards of education and the courts, as well as schools of education and other teacher education institutions that have enormous impact in how policies and practices are crafted and implemented.

My hope is that this is taken up by scholars looking to extend the GEL framework into these longer scales of time. I briefly offer several places I see this as a productive line of inquiry.

- One area is understanding how the educational community converges on professional standards for instructional practice, assessment, and teacher licensure. All human cultures educate their youth with respect to some set of expectations and have done so for millennia. An examination of how formal governmental regulations are grounded in these earlier cultural practices, and how they have developed in the modern era can offer insights into these organizational processes.
- Organizations have structure that is often hierarchical in nature. The system is rich with embodied metaphors of organizations as organisms, with the "heads" managing the "body." Organizations are also metaphorically conceptualized as a "culture" that develops its own language, rules of inclusion, and rituals. Closely related to this is the ways that people's beliefs, values, and practices come to align with the organizations they join. The products of organizations may be primarily in the form of reports and findings, yet they are treated as "objects" that are "conveyed" via social "conduits" to direct the "enactment" of policies and practices.

- Organizations learn and experience enduring changes in their behaviors. Understanding the nature of these learning processes from a GEL perspective may shed light on how and why some attempts at growth and change in education are more effective than others.
- One last direction explores the persistence of organizations even as people in the organization come and go. This persistence is reminiscent of how people maintain a sense of self, even as the cells of the body are completely replaced over time. Understanding what maintains this continuity as well as how organizations change in response to these dynamics can provide insights about the influence of the past on the future of education.

12.4.6 Farther Reaches of a GEL Timescale

My current focus on processes on the GEL timescale from milliseconds to years addresses a portion of the spectrum that spans ten orders of magnitude (that is, a one with ten zeroes). For me, it is an open question how far learning and knowing extend in either direction in time. Certainly it is possible to think about the nature of enduring cultural and political changes during the lifespan of nation-states that can span millennia, and of evolutionary processes of species that extend far longer. In proposing this framework, I invite people to consider ways of knowing that may apply broadly to environments, planets, and astronomical bodies and systems. In this vein, it would seem that the true upper bound is the age of the Universe. This would encompass the time since the Big Bang, the very first physical event scientists know about, which occurred some 10^{17} sec (between 12.5 and 13.82 billion years) ago (Riess et al., 2019).

At the other pole, one can imagine sub-cellular processes that may also exhibit properties of sentience, including perceiving, knowing, and learning. The *Resonance Theory of Consciousness* (Hunt & Schooler, 2019) builds on the understanding that a fundamental property of all matter is that it vibrates, and that these vibrations can change as they respond to and "sync up" with other vibrating entities. This form of spontaneous self-organization through synchrony is a critical part of the functioning of neuronal systems, physical systems, populations, and even systems composed entirely of radiation (Fries, 2005; Strogatz, 2004). The Resonance Theory of Consciousness proposes that *all matter* has at least *some* consciousness—a view called *panpsychism*—with larger entities, such as living things and social groups, exhibiting greater coherence in their synchronization. If sub-cellular and molecular vibrations are added to the GEL spectrum, the scale would extend down to phenomena that operate at 10^{-13} sec.

A spectrum that extends from molecular processes to encompass the known Universe brings the span of potential learning phenomena to 30 orders of magnitude. While quite speculative, it also puts in perspective the ten orders of magnitude of learning phenomena that are currently under investigation. The reader needs to remember, since this is a logarithmic scale, that the current GEL (grounded and embodied learning) framework is not *one-third* of this spectrum, but 10^{-20}, or *one ten-quintillionth*, the range of possible processes. That is, so far, the scientific exploration of learning is a truly miniscule portion of the potential span of physically realized phenomena. I personally find that humbling. I also consider this to be a striking invitation for further exploration. The stark relief of this comparison also begs the question raised by Tam Hunt (2018), "Why are some things conscious and others apparently not?" It is a question that is sure to puzzle scientists for many, many seconds.

12.5 CHALLENGES THAT LAY AHEAD

12.5.1 Reproducibility Crisis

Replication of empirical findings is a hallmark of a maturing field of scientific inquiry. In recent years, psychology has been hit by a "reproducibility crisis." There has been a slate of influential, peer-reviewed studies that employed rigorous research design methods and data analysis techniques that fail to show significant effects when scholars attempt to replicate them. Among them, several address embodied cognition. A partial list is shown in Table 12.1.

Social priming effects, such as finding that holding warm coffee makes people feel warmer towards others, have shown powerful effects of unconscious processes on one's actions and decisions. Although carefully reviewed and widely cited, several of these studies have failed to stand up to the high bar of being externally reproduced by scholars in other laboratories (Doyen et al., 2012). One of the canonical studies in this vein is the "elderly priming" study (Bargh, Chen, & Burrows, 1996). In this, participants surreptitiously primed to think about old age when they read certain words subsequently walked slower as they departed their psychology experiment.

Another phenomenon is the "power pose" (Carney, Cuddy, & Yap, 2010). This provided initial evidence that assuming body postures commonly seen by empowered people (e.g., leaning back in a chair with arms folded behind one's head with one's feet on a desk) leads to reliable changes in physiological and psychological measures associated with situational status and dominance. Others who sought to replicate it have failed to do so and have found that the effect will only hold in certain contexts. As such, it cannot now be seriously considered to be a basic body effect of its own (Cesario & McDonald, 2013). Since then, a concerted effort of 11 studies failed to replicate the original effects (Michigan State University, 2017). The poses may help people feel good, but it does not reliably produce the dominance effects originally theorized.

The Action-Sentence Compatibility Effect (Glenberg & Kaschak, 2002) is based on a set of studies that have long been regarded as important evidence for embodied cognition. The effect demonstrates ways that motor processing influences language processing. The original study, as well as numerous variants (e.g., Borreggine & Kaschak, 2006; Bub & Masson, 2010; Zwaan & Taylor, 2006) follow a common design. People read (or hear) sentences that describe actions toward or away from the reader. Participants judge whether each sentence they read was sensible by performing an action of their own (e.g., moving a joystick) either toward or away from the body. The effect has been observed when the actions described are concrete as well as abstract, as in these examples (with the actions underlined):

- Concrete: "Meghan <u>handed</u> you the book." or "You <u>handed</u> Meghan the book."
- Abstract: "Liz <u>told</u> you the story." or "You <u>told</u> Liz the story."

TABLE 12.1

A partial list of studies reporting benefits of embodied cognition that failed to replicate

Phenomenon	Representative citation
Social priming	Bargh, Chen, & Burrows (1996)
Power pose	Carney, Cuddy, & Yap (2010)
Action-Sentence Compatibility Effect (ACE)	Glenberg & Kaschak (2002)

The "effect" is that people are faster to make the sensibility judgment for sentences describing movements that are compatible to the response action toward or away from their body. When handing a book to another, using an away motion to respond occurs more rapidly, presumably because the "Yes it is sensible" response uses a compatible (away) motion of the joystick.

The effect has been observed across a number of studies, conducted in different labs by several different research teams and using a variety of different stimuli (e.g., Kaschak et al., 2018). Even so, a formal replication effort within the Open Science Framework OSF Reproducibility Project (Open Science Collaboration, 2015) failed to achieve replication. Morey and colleagues (2019; a team which notably included several investigators from the original studies) reported that "The results show that none of the 18 labs involved in the study observed a reliable [Action-Sentence Compatibility Effect], and that the meta-analytic estimate of the size of the [effect] was essentially zero" (p. 1).

There are smatterings of accounts about why these various effects in psychological research fail to replicate. For some, it may be that p-hacking and *HARKing* are significant factors in these false-positives. p-hacking is the practice of "shopping" for statistical methods that provide a favorable result (with a p-value under a widely accepted 5% threshold), but not reporting the outcomes of all the other failed tests (Simmons, Nelson, & Simonsohn, 2011). It is generally recognized that this is driven, in large part, by preferences for journals to publish significant findings (p-values less than 0.05), even though *non-significant* findings testing theoretically motivated hypotheses using appropriate research designs are equally important to advancing science. *HARKing* refers to "hypothesizing after the results are known" (Kerr, 1998). By generating theoretical accounts of the causal links of influences *after* the outcomes, *HARKing* amplifies low probability associations. This distorts the underlying probabilistic relationships between a theoretical outcome and the malleable factors thought to be causally responsible. Since the actual effect is on shaky grounds, the effects are less likely to be replicated.

HARKing and p-hacking do not seem to explain all of the documented replication failures. For example, the elderly priming study was not reproduced in its original form. However, the effect *was* obtained when the prime was cued *not* by the elderly references, but by the experimenters' expectations to show the effect (Doyen et al., 2012). It may be that investigators who are eager for their hypotheses to come true unconsciously signal experimental participants, who change their gate in response.

The reasons for the lack of replication for other studies that were driven by theory-based predictions and demonstrated in numerous other laboratories, such as the Action-Sentence Compatibility Effect, are still unclear. This has led to at least two important responses from the field, one methodological, and the other theoretical. As a methodological remedy, there is greater call for pre-registration of research studies with the specific hypotheses and methods publicly filed prior to data gathering. One advantage of pre-registration reported by the APA (Gonzales & Cunningham, 2015) is that "The result should be better studies that respond clearly to precisely formulated questions." Another benefit is that agreements by journals to publish the findings of studies with pre-registration on the basis of the merits of the questions and research methods, regardless of the outcome, should reduce the incidence of false-positives appearing in publication. Pre-registered studies, should, in principle, show much higher replication rates. It is probably still too soon to tell if this is the case, however.

The theoretical response may be a bit more troubling for the field, and for science in general. The *Decline Effect* is one that is well documented across many fields, including psychology, biology, and medical research. Over time, well-established findings are less pronounced. If it were due to the issues mentioned above, there would be a steep drop off. But there are many instances where the drop in the size of the effect is gradual. One such example is the "verbal overshadow" effect (Schooler & Engstler-Schooler, 1990), which replicates, but shows a roughly 30% decline across subsequent studies (Fallshore & Schooler, 1995). The *Decline Effect* may show it is simply that "the truth wears off" over time (Lehrer, 2010). This may all fit within a general recognition that extreme events show a regression toward the mean over time.

It may be the social psychology of doing psychological inquiry biases research even when scholars are keenly aware of such biases. In all, it is a reminder that scientists and consumers of science need to remain vigilant. There appears to be tremendous convergence of embodied effects, yet these must be culled from the noise of findings that may be spurious.

12.5.2 Disembodied Education: When Classrooms Goes Online, What Happens to GEL?

In 2020, in response to the global pandemic caused by COVID-19, nearly all public-school learning in the United States and worldwide moved online, at least temporarily, with many schools doing so long term. There should be no question that teaching and learning online is different than in-person schooling when there are such drastic changes in students' *learning conditions* (Jenkin, 1979; also see Marsh & Butler, 2013).

I was curious: What does GEL have to say about long-term remote learning and schooling during a pandemic? There is a rich research literature on distance education and long-term online learning, which has identified several common principles for success and some persistent challenges. I wanted to be able to identify what GEL could prescribe *beyond* these traditional recommendations.

Elias (2010, 2011) compiled the principles of effective online learning that follow the guidelines of Universal Instructional Design (UID). The focus understandably is on the equitable access to vital course information and offering flexibility in ways students can respond and fulfill course objectives. I list these briefly in Table 12.2. Alongside these recommendations for remote and distance learning from a traditional perspective, I provide additional recommendations that are derived from the GEL framework.

Each UID principle has a strong empirical base and a philosophy of inclusion and equitable participation of all learners. Yet many of these principles arise from traditional notions of learners and learning, of assessment, and of teachers as disembodied information processors. The additional GEL recommendations augment these important principles with sensitivity to the types of embodiment introduced in Table 4.3 (Chapter 4). Here, I highlight some of the most significant changes one can expect with remote, asynchronous, and online learning. *Anticipated body movement.* Online learning traditionally restricts the range and types of learners' movements, and consequently it is reasonable to expect it affords reduced learning. Whole-body movements are challenging when seated, communicating over a screen. Without explicitly planning for body-based forms of learning and communication, instructors will likely receive fewer visual cues of student engagement and ways of knowing than in a face-to-face classroom setting. Framing video signals to include learners' range of gestures and movements contributes to teachers' timely and useful formative assessment practices.
Gesture. When students are seated at a computer, with hands resting on a keyboard and mouse, their spontaneous production of gestures is restricted. Learners need to be freed from these restrictions to ensure the greatest learning and cognitive engagement.

Even when teachers are not visible to their students, most instructors will continue to gesture. However, they may do so less frequently and less intentionally when they know they are off-screen (e.g., during screen sharing of documents). For example, pre-service teachers in one study seldom used gestures to repair learners' trouble spots during videoconferences

TABLE 12.2
Traditional and GEL recommendations for remote learning

UID guidelines	Recommendations for traditional remote learning	Additional recommendations for GEL remote learning
Equitable use	• Accessible, online content • Provide translations	• Establish and maintain common ground with all learners • Support for nonverbal ways of knowing • Integrate conscious and unconscious processes
Flexible use	• Allow submissions in multiple formats • Accommodate a range of technical abilities and schedules	• Support for sensorimotor and place-based simulation • Place-based cognitive maps for learning and memory retrieval are less reliable
Simple and intuitive	• Simple interfaces • Minimize distractions • Options for offline	• Managing learner cognitive load, support cognitive offloading • Consistent mapping fosters greater procedural learning and perceptual fluency • Ground meaning of formalisms via verbal and visual linking, grounding metaphors
Perceptual information	• Provide captions, transcriptions, helpful descriptors	• Video frame includes gestures of teachers and students for multimodal communication • Plan for semantically congruent gestures to promote transduction
Tolerance for error	• Editable posts & redo options • Issue warnings in sound and text	• Rich situational feedback using interfaces and formative assessment encourages self-monitoring and self-directed error correction
Physical and technical effort	• Reduce physical & technical demands • Use assistive technology • Easy access to technical support	• Desirable difficulties increase learning and retention • Promote cognitive engagement, through action, participation, and social construction
Community of learners	• Support study groups	• Supports for distributed knowledge • Facilitate group participation through clear norms and mentoring • Internalization of social practices and epistemic properties of cultural and scientific tools
Instructional climate	• Frequent instructor–student contact and feedback	• Strategic use of gestures to direct attention, forge links to new ideas, and manage common ground • Establish and maintain social and sociodisciplinary norms • Guide learners through trajectories of concreteness fading • Plan awareness of one's expert blind spots
Assessment practices (added)		• Document multimodal, nonverbal, situated, and distributed ways of knowing • Video frame includes gestures and movement of students for formative assessment

(Holt, Tellier, & Guichon, 2015). To harness the communicative and pedagogical power of instructional gestures, such as their role in linking novel formalisms to their meaningful referents, teachers need to design their instructional environments with freedom of movement in mind. Teachers need to frame their video and utilize audio systems so they can freely gesture as a way to deliver multimodal communication and instructional gestures to their students. Standing is much better than sitting. Teachers should also use visual displays in their instructional setting to which they can point, trace, and perform simulated actions. *Simulation.* Simulation, model-based reasoning, spatial reasoning, metaphors, and action-cognition transduction all help learners to think, imagine, and to re-invoke prior experiences in service of reasoning about something else. For example, in one study, group cohesion was explicitly supported by speaking of the group of students in terms of a Ship metaphor (Simone et al., 2001). Supporting these forms of learning processes while online requires much greater intention than face-to-face classroom experiences. However, place-based learning and memory retrieval can be expected to be hampered when all learning is happening in the sample physical place as everything else in one's life. Elias (2011) notes that increased student access to mobile technologies enable students to bring the world into their learning environment, and also bring their learning environment into the world. Activities that encourage observing and retelling about phenomena to others can facilitate use of simulation and transduction processes in support of learning and help reduce some of the other limitations.

Materiality. Students in long-term online learning lose access to a rich, curated set of educational materials and their epistemic affordances. It is possible to recreate some of these things online, as with virtual instructional materials (Klahr, Triona, & Williams, 2007; Zacharia & Olympiou, 2011). Even when they are carefully matched, virtual and physical educational resources elicit different and complementary types of cognitive engagement. Puntambekar and colleagues (2020) found that middle school students (n = 115) who used virtual instructional materials for physics education focused their group discussions on scientific principles, such as analyzing the relationships between variables, making predictions, and interpreting science phenomena. Students who used physical materials instead, exhibited more discussion about experimental set-up, measurement, and calculation, all vital scientific practices for planning and executing their experiments. As educators recognize the importance of supporting both scientific reasoning and scientific and engineering practices (Crawford, 2009; NGSS, 2013; Rose, 2004), the role of material experiences must not get overlooked. Toward this end, it is also possible to repurpose objects from the home rather than narrow the range of curricular content used so it only deals with digital entities. The emergence of printable kits using paper and cardboard provide some relief. In the absence of these material experiences, students will face learning exclusively through secondary experiences (Laurillard, 2001/2013), which is not adequate for healthy cognitive development or technological advancement. Schools will need to develop ways for students to access quality educational and experiential materials.

12.5.3 Making Real Changes: Taking GEL to Scale

GEL presents a new paradigm for education, a radical rethinking about learning and learners, teaching and teachers, learning resources, physical environments, interactions, and assessments. In this sense, GEL calls for changes that run deep and are widespread. Yet, implementation of the principles derived from the GEL framework can start small. Change can start with individual teachers starting to notice how embodied learning and teaching are natural phenomena. Educational practitioners can start to make small changes to existing activities, such as prompting students to gestures, for example, and supporting learners in cognitive offloading and distributed knowledge. Teachers may begin to be more intentional in their use of spatial metaphors, tangible manipulatives, and ways they use their bodies to make connections and foster common ground for their students. Teachers may become more aware of how students' actions reveal qualities of their thinking, how students may indicate readiness to learn even before they can verbalize that development, and how the re-occurrences of situated motor behaviors from one context to another indicate successful transfer of learning.

Designers of curricula and learning technologies can start to think in terms of helping learners ground the meaning of formalisms and abstractions. Designers may consider complementing verbal channels with multimodal information, including images, movements, sounds, textures, and even smells. Activities can be designed to prompt learners to be more actively engaged, by incorporating conceptually relevant movement, constructing products that reify one's thinking, and supporting co-constructive collaboration with peers.

Embodied forms of assessment can supplement existing, verbal-heavy forms of testing with ways of exhibiting nonverbal intellectual processes. Some of these ways include using response times, perceptual pattern matching and procedural fluency in place of verbal responses. Testing methods can be used that avoid restricting students' body-based resources. Rubrics can be devised for evaluating individual and collaborative contributions to projects.

As these experiences unfold and accumulate, teachers, designers, specialists, administrators, and leaders need to talk with one another. By sharing goals, failures, and successes, the collective wisdom can grow, and the programs develop in ways that are responsive to the unique circumstances and values of each community. Through communication, communities of practice can form, and with them, routines, norms, and systems of representing and sharing products and methods.

Taking any educational program to scale, no matter how promising the underlying research, is a complex undertaking. There are many independent hurdles, including, but hardly limited to: the design of appealing and effective learning activities, curriculum materials and technological resources; practitioner learning; development of appropriate measures for documenting change and assessing learning; leadership support; changes in, or accommodations to organizational structures; and diffusion time for innovations and new practices to reach its user base. When radical changes to standard educational practices are called for, as they are for the GEL paradigm, there must also be considerable care given to cultivating practitioner-researcher-designer partnerships for creating new practices and innovations, securing funding for new classroom materials and teacher professional development, garnering leadership to gain support from school boards, parents, and the community at large, and political will from school, district, and state leaders to guide the process through it all, even in the face other, pressing needs.

12.5.4 Limitations of GEL: There is No Free Lunch

An important limitation to the GEL approach to education is that it is costly. It many ways it operates against the current factory model of education. This is evident in several of the signature practices advocated here, based on the research findings: learning that is engaged and connected to students' own common ground; instruction that is highly individualized to students' meaning making needs; assessment practices that document students' nonverbal and distributed learning practices; highly engaged, sustained community participation. All of these practices are time consuming and depend on the performance of highly skilled practitioners. I do not shy away from this limitation. I believe it to be a well-supported up-front cost that has enormous payoff down the line. By fostering meaningful learning through embodied principles of instruction and design, along with assessment practices matched to embodied ways of knowing, these initial investments will cultivate learners with a meaningful understanding of an ever-expanding set of content knowledge, and the skills to engage in any new topic as lifelong learners.

12.6 GEL: A PARADIGM FOR EDUCATION

I wrote this book because I saw a serious societal problem, and a way to solve it. The problem lies in a fundamental misrepresentation of learners and learning. Too often, learners are regarded as disembodied minds recording and computing their way through the world.

Learners, in my view, are something more than is represented by the traditional school experience. First and foremost, learners are embodied beings, who are contextually attuned to their surroundings, continually anticipating what their environment has to offer and how to best respond. It is true that new ideas, symbols, and theories can be formalized using technical language and symbols. However, to be *meaningful* to the embodied mind, these ideas and formalisms must be grounded in ways that learners already act, perceive, and imagine. To reason about them, the ideas have to exhibit form and movement. This is evident in the prevalence and semantic value the of spontaneous gestures and spatial metaphors that are naturally produced by learners as well as their instructors. Consequently, by virtue of inherent limitations in movement and simulated actions, humans may not be able to produce or understand all ideas. Such is the fundamental limit of the embodied mind.

Even within these limitations, there is an astoundingly vast and flexible set of processes for learning, reasoning, and creative thought. I have used time as an organizing structure to survey the broad set of intellectual phenomena that are so central to learning and education. Along the Grounded and Embodied Learning (GEL) timescale (Figures 3.5, 5.1, 7.1, 9.1), there are processes operating in bands that exhibit some common properties, yet operate in ways quite unlike the processes of neighboring bands. Type 1 processing, operating at the neural band, enacts thought via rapid, nonverbal processes outside of conscious awareness, yet has enormous influence on pattern recognition, intuition, judgment, and decision making, including complex social judgments. Type 2 processing at the slower, cognitive, and knowledge-based bands in the timescale, operates with conscious awareness while conducting sequential, verbalizable thought, and deliberative, rule-based analysis. Type 3 processing at the sociocultural bands, is immersed in norms-based, distributed group interactions that are often discourse based, and can be unconscious, but also hyper-conscious.

Once educators allow that students come to know and primarily understand the world as embodied learners, many standard practices seem inappropriate. Instruction is reframed as ways to support grounded meaning making and the adaptation of embodied ways of knowing and using ideas and formalisms as tools. There is recognition of a need for far more inclusive ways of assessing practical knowledge, that include ways of reasoning that are nonverbal, or emergent from complex social and material interactions. A GEL perspective leads to the unavoidable conclusion that education can and must be very different.

The movement for GEL is forming (e.g., EMIC, n.d.). There is growing awareness among educators and researchers of the effectiveness of embodied methods of teaching, learning, and assessment. As with any such paradigmatic shift, there is much that is not yet known. It will require considerable investments of funding for research, development, teacher education, and policy development for these powerful ideas to reach their potential. To succeed, this movement will need new partnerships with teachers, designers, scholars, and administrators. With the right resources, committed participants, community support, and evidence-based principles, we may soon see the proliferation of institutions and approaches with the capabilities that are truly fitting to educate the embodied mind.

REFERENCES

Abrahamson, D. (2009). Embodied design: Constructing means for constructing meaning. *Educational Studies of Mathematics, 70,* 27–47.

Abrahamson, D., & Lindgren, R. (2014). Embodiment and embodied design. In R. K. Sawyer (Ed.), *The Cambridge handbook of the learning sciences* (2nd ed.) (pp. 358–376). Cambridge University Press.

Abrahamson, D., Nathan, M. J., Williams-Pierce, C., Walkington, C., Ottmar, E. R., Soto, H., & Alibali, M. W. (2020). The future of embodied design for mathematics teaching and learning. In S. Ramanathan & I. A. C. Mok (Eds.). *Frontiers in education* [Special issue], 5(147). https://doi.org/10.3389/feduc.2020.00147

Alemanji, A. A. (Ed.). (2017). *Antiracism education in and out of schools*. Springer.

Alibali, M. W., Flevares, L. M., & Goldin-Meadow, S. (1997). Assessing knowledge conveyed in gesture: Do teachers have the upper hand? *Journal of Educational Psychology*, 89(1), 183.

Alibali, M. W., & Nathan, M. J. (2012). Embodiment in mathematics teaching and learning: Evidence from learners' and teachers' gestures. *Journal of the Learning Sciences*, 21(2), 247–286.

Azzam, A. M. (2008). Neglecting higher achievers. *Educational Leadership*, 66, 90–92. Retrieved from http://www.ascd.org/publications/educational-leadership.aspx

Baer, R. A. (2003). Mindfulness training as a clinical intervention: A conceptual and empirical review. *Clinical Psychology: Science and Practice*, 10(2), 125–143.

Bargh, J. A., Chen, M., & Burrows, L. (1996). Automaticity of social behavior: Direct effects of trait construct and stereotype activation on action. *Journal of Personality and Social Psychology*, 71(2), 230.

Barrett, L. F., Mesquita, B., Ochsner, K. N., & Gross, J. J. (2007). The experience of emotion. *Annual Review Psychology*, 58, 373–403.

Barsalou, L. W. (2008). Grounded cognition. *Annual Review of Psychology*, 59, 617–645.

Bell Jr, D. A. (1980). *Brown v. Board of Education* and the interest-convergence dilemma. *Harvard Law Review*, 93, 518–533.

Blikstein, P., & Worsley, M. (2016). Multimodal learning analytics and education data mining: Using computational technologies to measure complex learning tasks. *Journal of Learning Analytics*, 3(2), 220–238.

Bloom, S. G., & Kennedy, L. (2005). Lesson of a lifetime: Teacher Jane Elliott's unorthodox exercise to instruct her third graders in the consequences of racism still divides an Iowa town-and even her former students-nearly 40 years later. *Smithsonian*, 36(6), 82.

Borreggine, K. L., & Kaschak, M. P. (2006). The action–sentence compatibility effect: It's all in the timing. *Cognitive Science*, 30(6), 1097–1112.

Boulton, G. (2015). Growing up in severe poverty affects brain size, UW-Madison study shows. *Milwaukee Journal Sentinel*, Aug. 29.

Brate, R., Groth, P., & van Erp, M. (2020). Towards olfactory information extraction from text: A case study on detecting smell experiences in Novels. *arXiv preprint arXiv:2011.08903*.

Bub, D. N., & Masson, M. E. J. (2010). On the nature of hand-action representations evoked during written sentence comprehension. *Cognition, 116*, 394–408.

Burke, C. A. (2010). Mindfulness-based approaches with children and adolescents: A preliminary review of current research in an emergent field. *Journal of Child and Family Studies*, 19(2), 133–144.

Carney, D. R., Cuddy, A. J., & Yap, A. J. (2010). Power posing: Brief nonverbal displays affect neuroendocrine levels and risk tolerance. *Psychological science*, 21(10), 1363–1368.

Cesario, J., & McDonald, M. M. (2013). Bodies in context: Power poses as a computation of action possibility. *Social Cognition*, 31(2), 260–274.

Crawford, M. B. (2009). *Shop class as soulcraft: An inquiry into the value of work*. Penguin.

Crenshaw, K., Gotanda, N., Peller, G., & Thomas, K. (Eds.) (1995). *Critical race theory: The key writings that formed the movement*. Free Press.

Cunningham, W. A., Raye, C. L., & Johnson, M. K. (2004). Implicit and explicit evaluation: fMRI correlates of valence, emotional intensity, and control in the processing of attitudes. *Journal of Cognitive Neuroscience*, 16(10), 1717–1729.

Damasio, A. R. (1994). *Descartes' error*. Putnam.

Davenport, J. L., Kao, Y. S., Matlen, B. J., & Schneider, S. A. (2020). Cognition research in practice: engineering and evaluating a middle school math curriculum. *The Journal of Experimental Education*, 88(4), 516–535.

Dede, C. (2009). Immersive interfaces for engagement and learning. *Science*, 323(5910), 66–69.

Delgado, R., & Stefancic, J. (Eds.) (1997). *Critical White studies: Looking behind the mirror*. Temple University Press.

Deriso, D., Susskind, J., Tanaka, J., Winkielman, P., Herrington, J., Schultz, R., & Bartlett, M. (2012). Exploring the facial expression perception–production link using real-time automated facial expression recognition. In A. Fusiello, V. Murino, & R. Cucchiara (Eds.), *Computer vision—ECCV 2012 workshops and demonstrations* (Vol. 7584, pp. 270–279). Springer. doi:10.1007/978-3- 642-33868-7_27

Devine, P. G. (1989). Stereotypes and prejudice: Their automatic and controlled components. *Journal of Personality and Social Psychology*, 56(1), 5–18.

Devine, P. G., Forscher, P. S., Austin, A. J., & Cox, W. T. (2012). Long-term reduction in implicit race bias: A prejudice habit-breaking intervention. *Journal of Experimental Social Psychology*, 48(6), 1267–1278.

Dimmel, J., & Bock, C. (2019) Dynamic mathematical figures with immersive spatial displays: The case of Handwaver. In G. Aldon & J. Trgalová (Eds.), *Technology in mathematics teaching. Mathematics education in the digital era* (Vol. 13, pp. 99–122). Springer.

Djikic, M. (2014). Integrating Eastern and Western approaches. In A. Ie, C. T. Ngnoumen, & E. J. Langer (Eds.) *The Wiley Blackwell handbook of mindfulness* (pp. 139–148). Wiley-Blackwell.

Doyen, S., Klein, O., Pichon ,C.-L., & Cleeremans, A. (2012). Behavioral Priming: It's all in the mind, but whose mind? *PLoS ONE 7*(1): e29081. doi.org/10.1371/journal.pone.0029081

Dweck, C. S. (2000). *Self-theories: Their role in motivation, personality, and development.* Psychology Press.

Eisenberg, M. (2002). Output devices, computation, and the future of mathematical crafts. *International Journal of Computers for Mathematical Learning, 7*(1), 1–44.

Eisenberg, M. (2005). Constructing kids. *The Journal of the Learning Sciences, 14*(3), 443–447.

Elbow, S. (2018). Working on the achievement gap. *The Cap Times,* October 31. Retrieved from. https://madison.com/ct/news/local/education/working-on-the-achievement-gap/article_669f412d-d4fc-58b1-ae0c-1008b8979a2d.html

Elias, T. (2010). Universal instructional design principles for Moodle. *The International Review of Research in Open and Distributed Learning, 11*(2), 110–124.

Elias, T. (2011). Universal instructional design principles for mobile learning. *International Review of Research in Open and Distributed Learning, 12*(2), 143–156.

Elliott, J. (n.d.). Retrieved from https://janeelliott.com/

Emerson, L. M., Leyland, A., Hudson, K., Rowse, G., Hanley, P., & Hugh-Jones, S. (2017). Teaching mindfulness to teachers: A systematic review and narrative synthesis. *Mindfulness, 8*(5), 1136–1149.

EMIC (n. d.). Retrieved from https://embodiedmathematics.com

Fallshore, M., & Schooler, J. W. (1995). Verbal vulnerability of perceptual expertise. *Journal of Experimental Psychology: Learning, Memory, and Cognition, 21*(6), 1608.

Fang, Z. (1996). A review of research on teacher beliefs and practices. *Educational Research, 38*(1), 47–65.

Fischman, G. E., & Haas, E. (2012). Beyond idealized citizenship education: Embodied cognition, metaphors, and democracy. *Review of Research in Education, 36*(1), 169–196.

Frank, J. L., Jennings, P. A., & Greenberg, M. T. (2013). Mindfulness-based interventions in school settings: An introduction to the special issue. *Research in Human Development, 10*(3), 205–210.

Fries, P. (2005). A mechanism for cognitive dynamics: Neuronal communication through neuronal coherence. *Trends in Cognitive Sciences, 9*(10), 474–480.

Furnham, A. (2014). Increasing your intelligence: Entity and incremental beliefs about the multiple "intelligences." *Learning and Individual Differences, 32*, 163–167.

Gillborn, D. (2007). Critical race theory and education: Racism and anti-racism in educational theory and praxis. *Discourse: Studies in the cultural politics of Education, 27*(1), 11–32.

Glenberg, A. M., & Kaschak, M. P. (2002). Grounding language in action. *Psychonomic Bulletin & Review, 9*(3), 558–565.

Golden, A. L. (2016). Association between child poverty and academic achievement. *JAMA Pediatrics, 170*(2), 178–179.

Gonzales, J. E., & Cunningham, C. A. (2015). The promise of pre-registration in psychological research. *Psychological Science Agenda, 29*(8), 2014–2017.

Greenwald, A. G., McGhee, D. E., & Schwartz, J. L. (1998). Measuring individual differences in implicit cognition: The implicit association test. *Journal of Personality and Social Psychology, 74*(6), 1464.

Grossman, P., Niemann, L., Schmidt, S., & Walach, H. (2004). Mindfulness-based stress reduction and health benefits: A meta-analysis. *Journal of Psychosomatic Research, 57*(1), 35–43.

Gunderson, E. A., Ramirez, G., Beilock, S. L., & Levine, S. C. (2012). The relation between spatial skill and early number knowledge: The role of the linear number line. *Developmental Psychology, 48*(5), 1229.

Hacker, A. (1992). *Two nations: Black and White, separate, hostile, unequal.* Ballantine Books.

Hair, N. L., Hanson, J. L., Wolfe, B. L., & Pollak, S. D. (2015). Association of child poverty, brain development, and academic achievement. *JAMA Pediatrics, 169*(9), 822–829.

Hair, N. L., Hanson, J. L., Wolfe, B. L., & Pollak, S. D. (2016). Association between child poverty and academic achievement—in reply. *JAMA Pediatrics, 170*(2), 180–180.

Hohenwater, M., & Fuchs, K. (2004). *Combination of dynamic geometry, algebra and calculus in the software system GeoGebra.* University of Salzburg.

Holt, B., Tellier, M., & Guichon, N. (2015, September). The use of teaching gestures in an online multimodal environment: The case of incomprehension sequences. In G. Ferré & M. Tutton (Eds.), *Gesture and speech in interaction* (4th ed.). (pp. 149–154). University of Nantes.

Hulse, T., Daigle, M., Manzo, D., Braith, L., Harrison, A., & Ottmar, E. (2019). From here to there! Elementary: A game-based approach to developing number sense and early algebraic understanding. *Educational Technology Research and Development, 67*(2), 423–441.

Hunt, T. (2018). The hippies were right: It's all about vibrations, man! A new theory of consciousness. *Scientific American Observations,* December 5. Retrieved from https://blogs.scientificamerican.com/observations/the-hippies-were-right-its-all-about-vibrations-man/

Hunt, T., & Schooler, J. W. (2019). The easy part of the hard problem: A resonance theory of consciousness. *Frontiers in Human Neuroscience, 13*, 378.

Javidi, B., Pla, F., Sotoca, J. M., Shen, X., Latorre-Carmona, P., Martínez-Corral, M., ... & Krishnan, G. (2020). Fundamentals of automated human gesture recognition using 3D integral imaging: a tutorial. *Advances in Optics and Photonics*, *12*(4), 1237–1299.

Jenkins, J. J. (1979). Four points to remember: A tetrahedral model and memory experiments. In L. S. Cermak & I. M. Craik (Eds.), *Levels of processing in human memory* (pp. 429–446). Erlbaum.

John-Steiner, V., & Mahn, H. (1996). Sociocultural approaches to learning and development: A Vygotskian framework. *Educational Psychologist*, *31*(3–4), 191–206.

Johnson-Glenberg, M. C. (2018). Immersive VR and education: Embodied design principles that include gesture and hand controls. *Frontiers in Robotics and AI*, *5*, 81.

Johnson-Glenberg, M. C., Birchfield, D., Koziupa, T., & Tolentino, L. (2014). Collaborative embodied learning in mixed reality motion-capture environments: Two science studies. *Journal of Educational Psychology*, *106*(1), 86–104.

Johnson-Glenberg, M. C., & Megowan-Romanowicz, C. (2017). Embodied science and mixed reality: How gesture and motion capture affect physics education. *Cognitive Research: Principles and Implications*, *2*(1), 24.

Jones, J., & Schmitt, J. (2014). *A college degree is no guarantee* (No. 2014-08). Retrieved from http://cepr.net/publications/reports/a-college-degree-is-no-guarantee

Kabat-Zinn, J. (1982). An out-patient program in behavioral medicine for chronic pain patients based on the practice of mindfulness meditation: Theoretical considerations and preliminary results. *General Hospital Psychiatry*, *4*, 33–47.

Kabat-Zinn, J. (2003). Mindfulness-based interventions in context: past, present, and future. *Clinical Psychology: Science and Practice*, *10*(2), 144–156.

Kagan, D. M. (1992). Implication of research on teacher belief. *Educational Psychologist*, *27*(1), 65–90.

Kaschak, M., Zwaan, R. A., Glenberg, A., Morey, R. D., Ibanez, A., Gianelli, C., & Haaf, J. M. (2018). Action-sentence compatibility effect (ACE) pre-registered replication. Retrieved from osf. io/ynbwu

Kendi, I. X. (2019). *How to be an antiracist*. One World.

Kerr, N. L. (1998). HARKing: Hypothesizing after the results are known. *Personality and Social Psychology Review*, *2*(3), 196–217.

Kids Count Data Center, Children in Poverty (2014). Retrieved from https://datacenter.kidscount.org/data/tables/44-children-in-poverty-by-race-and-ethnicity#detailed/1/any/false/37,871,870,573,869,36,868,867,133,38/10,11,9,12,1,185,13/324,323 Accessed on Oct. 15, 2020.

Klahr, D., Triona, L. M., & Williams, C. (2007). Hands on what? The relative effectiveness of physical versus virtual materials in an engineering design project by middle school children. *Journal of Research in Science Teaching*, *44*(1), 183–203.

Ladson-Billings, G. (1995). Toward a theory of culturally relevant pedagogy. *American Educational Research Journal*, *32*(3), 465–491.

Ladson-Billings, G. (1998) Just what is critical race theory and what's it doing in a nice field like education? *International Journal of Qualitative Studies in Education*, *11*(1), 7–24,

Ladson-Billings, G. (2014). Culturally relevant pedagogy 2.0: aka the remix. *Harvard Educational Review*, *84*(1), 74–84.

Ladson-Billings, G., & Tate, W. F. (1995). Toward a critical race theory of education. *Teachers College Record*, *97*, 47–68.

Lai, C. K., Marini, M., Lehr, S. A., Cerruti, C., Shin, J. E. L., Joy-Gaba, J. A., ... & Frazier, R. S. (2014). Reducing implicit racial preferences: I. A comparative investigation of 17 interventions. *Journal of Experimental Psychology: General*, *143*(4), 1765.

Lai, C. K., Skinner, A. L., Cooley, E., Murrar, S., Brauer, M., Devos, T., ... & Simon, S. (2016). Reducing implicit racial preferences: II. Intervention effectiveness across time. *Journal of Experimental Psychology: General*, *145*(8), 1001.

Lakoff, G. (2008). *Women, fire, and dangerous things: What categories reveal about the mind*. University of Chicago Press.

Laurillard, D. (2001/2013). *Rethinking university teaching: A conversational framework for the effective use of learning technologies*. Routledge.

Lebois, L. A., Papies, E. K., Gopinath, K., Cabanban, R., Quigley, K. S., Krishnamurthy, V., ... & Barsalou, L. W. (2015). A shift in perspective: Decentering through mindful attention to imagined stressful events. *Neuropsychologia*, *75*, 505–524.

Lee, V. R. (Ed.). (2014). *Learning technologies and the body: Integration and implementation in formal and informal learning environments*. Routledge.

Lehrer, J. (2010). The truth wears off: Is there something wrong with the scientific method? *The New Yorker*. December 6. Retrieved from www.newyorker.com/magazine/2010/12/13/the-truth-wears-off

Lindgren, R., & Johnson-Glenberg, M. (2013). Emboldened by embodiment: Six precepts for research on embodied learning and mixed reality. *Educational Researcher*, *42*(8), 445–452.

Lindgren, R., Tscholl, M., Wang, S., & Johnson, E. (2016). Enhancing learning and engagement through embodied interaction within a mixed reality simulation. *Computers & Education*, *95*, 174–187.

Lobato, J. (2003). How design experiments can inform a rethinking of transfer and vice versa. *Educational Researcher*, *32*(1), 17–20.

Luby, J. L. (2015). Poverty's most insidious damage: The developing brain. *JAMA Pediatrics, 169*(9), 810–811.

Ma, J. Y., Hall, R., & Leander, K. M. (2010, June). Shifting between person, structure and settlement scales in anthropological field work. *Proceedings of the 9th International Conference of the Learning Sciences—Vol. 2* (pp. 158–159).

Macedonia, M., & von Kriegstein, K. (2012). Gestures enhance foreign language learning. *Biolinguistics, 6*(3–4), 393–416.

Marsh, E. J., & Butler, A. C. (2013). Memory in educational settings. In D. Reisberg (Ed.), *Oxford library of psychology. The Oxford handbook of cognitive psychology* (pp. 299–317). Oxford University Press. https://doi.org/10.1093/oxfordhb/9780195376746.013.0020

Matsumoto, D., & Hwang, H. S. (2012). Culture and emotion: The integration of biological and cultural contributions. *Journal of Cross-Cultural Psychology, 43*(1), 91–118.

McGee, H. (2020). *Nose dive: A field guide to the world of smells.* Penguin.

Michigan State University. (2017). Power poses' don't work, eleven new studies suggest. *ScienceDaily, 11,* September. Retrieved from www.sciencedaily.com/releases/2017/09/170911095932.htm

Mihić, J., Oh, Y., Greenberg, M., & Kranželić, V. (2020). Effectiveness of mindfulness-based social-emotional learning program CARE for teachers within Croatian context. *Mindfulness, 11*(9), 2206–2218.

Miyashita, H. (2020, October). Taste display that reproduces tastes measured by a taste sensor. *Proceedings of the 33rd Annual ACM Symposium on User Interface Software and Technology* (pp. 1085–1093). Association for Computing Machinery.

Morey, R. D., Kaschak, M. P., Díez-Álamo, A. M., Glenberg, A. M., Zwaan, R. A., Lakens, D., Ibáñez, A., García, A., Gianelli, C., Jones, J. L. & Madden, J. (2021). A pre-registered, multi-lab non-replication of the action-sentence compatibility effect (ACE). *Psychonomic Bulletin & Review.* hdl.handle.net/21.11116/0000-0008-3F7F-5

Nathan, M. J., & Alibali, M. W. (2021). An embodied theory of transfer of mathematical learning. In C. Hohensee and J. Lobato (Eds.), *Transfer of learning: Progressive perspectives for mathematics education and related fields* (pp. 27–58). Springer.

Nathan, M. J., Tran, N. A., Atwood, A. K., Prevost, A., & Phelps, L. A. (2010). Beliefs and expectations about engineering preparation exhibited by high school STEM teachers. *Journal of Engineering Education, 99*(4), 409–426.

Nathan, M. J., & Walkington, C. (2017). Grounded and embodied mathematical cognition: Promoting mathematical insight and proof using action and language. *Cognitive Research: Principles and Implications, 2*(1), 9.

NGSS Lead States. (2013). *Next generation science standards: For states, by states.* National Academies Press.

Niedenthal, P. M., Barsalou, L. W., Winkielman, P., Krauth-Gruber, S., & Ric F. (2005). Embodiment in attitudes, social perception, and emotion. *Personality and Social Psychology Review, 9,* 184–211.

Niedenthal, P. M., Winkielman, P., Mondillon, L., & Vermeulen, N. (2009). Embodiment of emotion concepts. *Journal of Personality and Social Psychology, 96*(6), 1120.

Odeuropa (n.d.). Retrieved from https://odeuropa.eu/

Open Science Collaboration. (2015). Estimating the reproducibility of psychological science. *Science, 349*(6251). doi.org/10.1126/science.aac4716

Oswald, F. L., Mitchell, G., Blanton, H., Jaccard, J., & Tetlock, P. E. (2013). Predicting ethnic and racial discrimination: A meta-analysis of IAT criterion studies. *Journal of Personality and Social Psychology, 105*(2), 171.

Oulhote, Y., & Grandjean, P. (2016). Association between child poverty and academic achievement. *JAMA Pediatrics, 170*(2), 179–180.

Puntambekar, S., Gnesdilow, D., Dornfeld Tissenbaum, C., Narayanan, N. H., & Rebello, N. S. (2020). Supporting middle school students' science talk: A comparison of physical and virtual labs. *Journal of Research in Science Teaching.* doi.org/10.1002/tea.21664

Resnick, L. B. (1987). The 1987 presidential address learning in school and out. *Educational Researcher, 16*(9), 13–54.

Riess, A. G., Casertano, S., Yuan, W., Macri, L. M., & Scolnic, D. (2019). Large Magellanic cloud cepheid standards provide a 1% foundation for the determination of the Hubble constant and stronger evidence for physics beyond ΛCDM. *The Astrophysical Journal, 876*(1), 85.

Rolls, E. T. (2013). What are emotional states, and why do we have them? *Emotion Review, 5*(3), 241–247.

Rose, M. (2004). *The mind at work: Valuing the intelligence of the American worker.* Viking.

Roth, W. M. (2001). Gestures: Their role in teaching and learning. *Review of Educational Research, 71*(3), 365–392.

Rubel, L. H., Hall-Wieckert, M., & Lim, V. Y. (2017). Making space for place: Mapping tools and practices to teach for spatial justice. *Journal of the Learning Sciences, 26*(4), 643–687.

Sawrey, K., Chan, J. Y.–C., Ottmar, E., & Hulse, T. (2019). Experiencing equivalence with graspable math: results from a middle-school study. In S. Otten, A. G. Candela, Z. de Araujo, C. Haines, & C. Munter (Eds.), *Against New Horizons*—Proceedings of the 41st Annual Conference of the North-American Chapter of the International Group for the Psychology of Mathematics Education (PME-NA) (pp. 1738–1743). University of Missouri.

Schooler, J. W., & Engstler-Schooler, T. Y. (1990). Verbal overshadowing of visual memories: Some things are better left unsaid. *Cognitive Psychology, 22*(1), 36–71.

Simmons, J. P., Nelson, L. D., & Simonsohn, U. (2011). False-positive psychology: Undisclosed flexibility in data collection and analysis allows presenting anything as significant. *Psychological Science, 22*(11), 1359–1366.

Simone, C. D., Lou, Y., & Schmid, R. F. (2001). Meaningful and interactive distance learning supported by the use of metaphor and synthesizing activities. *Journal of Distance Education, 16*(1), 85–101.

Steele, C. (1997). A threat in the air: How stereotypes shape intellectual identity and performance. *American Psychologist, 52*(6), 612–629.

Steele, C. M., & Aronson, J. (1995). Stereotype threat and the intellectual test performance of African Americans. *Journal of Personality and Social Psychology, 69*(5), 797.

Stieff, M., & Uttal, D. (2015). How much can spatial training improve STEM achievement? *Educational Psychology Review, 27*(4), 607–615.

Strogatz, S. (2004). *Sync: The emerging science of spontaneous order.* Penguin.

Sund, L., Quennerstedt, M., & Öhman, M. (2019). The embodied social studies classroom—Repositioning the body in the social sciences in school. *Cogent Education, 6*(1), 1569350. doi.org/10.1080/2331186X.2019.1569350

Swart, M. I., Friedman, B., Kornkasem, S., Hollenburg, S., Lowes, S., Black, J. B., ... & Nankin, F. (2014). Mobile movement mathematics: Exploring the gestures students make while explaining fractions. Presentation to the annual meeting of the American Educational Research Association. AERA.

Tanaka, J. W., Wolf, J. M., Klaiman, C., Koenig, K., Cockburn, J., Herlihy, L., ... Schultz, R. T. (2010). Using computerized games to teach face recognition skills to children with autism spectrum disorder: The Let's Face It! program. *Journal of Child Psychology and Psychiatry, and Allied Disciplines, 51*, 944–952. doi:10.1111/j.1469-7610.2010.02258.x

Tate, W. F. (1995). Returning to the root: A culturally relevant approach to mathematics pedagogy. *Theory into Practice, 34*(3), 166–173.

Tate IV, W. F. (1997). Critical race theory and education: History, theory, and implications. *Review of Research in Education, 22*(1), 195–247.

Taylor, K. H. (2017). Learning along lines: Locative literacies for reading and writing the city. *Journal of the Learning Sciences, 26*(4), 533–574.

Thompson, A. G. (1992). Teachers' beliefs and conceptions: A synthesis of the research. In D. A. Grouws (Ed.), *Handbook of research on mathematics teaching and learning* (pp. 127–146). Macmillan.

Tuck, E., & Yang, K. W. (2012). Decolonization is not a metaphor. *Decolonization: Indigeneity, Education & Society, 1*(1), 1–40.

Tversky, B. (2019). *Mind in motion: How action shapes thought.* Hachette UK.

Uttal, D. H., Meadow, N. G., Tipton, E., Hand, L. L., Alden, A. R., Warren, C., & Newcombe, N. S. (2013). The malleability of spatial skills: A meta-analysis of training studies. *Psychological Bulletin, 139*(2), 352.

Valenzeno, L., Alibali, M. W., & Klatzky, R. (2003). Teachers' gestures facilitate students' learning: A lesson in symmetry. *Contemporary Educational Psychology, 28*(2), 187–204.

Walkington, C., Gravell, J., Wang, M., & Nathan, M. J. (2020). Collaborative embodiment in geometric and spatial reasoning tasks using virtual reality. Paper submitted to the 2021 Annual Meeting of the International Society of the Learning Sciences. Bochum, Germany. ISLS.org.

Walkington, C., Woods, D., Nathan, M. J., Chelule, G., & Wang, M. (2019). Does restricting hand gestures impair mathematical reasoning? *Learning and Instruction, 64*, 101225. doi.org/10.1016/j.learninstruc.2019.101225

Watson, B. (2002). *The man who changed how boys and toys were made: The Life and Times of A. C. Gilbert, the Man Who Saved Christmas.* Viking.

Wertsch, J. V. (2009). *Voices of the mind: Sociocultural approach to mediated action.* Harvard University Press.

Wilson, M. (2002). Six views of embodied cognition. *Psychonomic Bulletin & Review, 9*(4), 625–636.

Wineburg, S., & Grossman, P. (1998). Creating a community of learners among high school teachers. *Phi Delta Kappan, 79*(5), 350.

Zacharia, Z. C., & Olympiou, G. (2011). Physical versus virtual manipulative experimentation in physics learning. *Learning and instruction, 21*(3), 317–331.

Zelazo, P. D., & Lyons, K. E. (2012). The potential benefits of mindfulness training in early childhood: A developmental social cognitive neuroscience perspective. *Child Development Perspectives, 6*(2), 154–160.

Zwaan, R. A., & Taylor, L. J. (2006). Seeing, acting, understanding: Motor resonance in language comprehension. *Journal of Experimental Psychology: General, 135*, 1–11.

Index